The Grammar, History and Derivation of the English Language, With Chapters on Parsing, Analysis of Sentences, and Prosody

THE

GRAMMAR, HISTORY, AND DERIVATION

OF THE

ENGLISH LANGUAGE

WITH CHAPTERS ON

PARSING, ANALYSIS OF SENTENCES, AND PROSODY

BY THE

Evan

REV. CANON DANIEL, M.A.

PRINCIPAL OF THE NATIONAL SOCIETY'S TRAINING COLLEGE, BATTERSEA
HON. CANON OF ROCHESTER CATHEDRAL

NEW AND REVISED EDITION

LONDON

NATIONAL SOCIETY'S DEPOSITORY

BROAD SANCTUARY, WESTMINSTER

1891

PRINTED BY
SPOTTISWOODE AND CO., NEW-STREET SQUARE
LONDON

PREFACE.

IT IS COMMONLY ASSUMED that Grammar is a purely verbal science, in which the student is mainly occupied in learning definitions, paradigms, and rules of syntax, and that it is, consequently, far inferior as an instrument of mental discipline to natural history and experimental science. The mode in which it has been too frequently taught gives some colour to this view; but, rightly taught, grammar is as much a *real* study as botany or chemistry. Words are *things*, as well as the symbols of things, and are subject to definite natural laws—to laws of growth and decay, to laws of inflexion and syntax, to laws affecting their signification. The study of these laws affords room for just the same sort of independent effort as the study of physical science. The facts of language are still where the grammarian originally found them, and the learner may, under proper direction, find them for himself, classify them for himself, and reason from them for himself. It is obvious, therefore, that grammar affords room for original observation, for generalization, for induction and deduction, and that if it were taught in this scientific spirit, its value as a formative study would be very high.

The distinguishing feature of this Grammar is set

forth in the opening paragraph. Starting with the
recognition of the fact that all the truths of which the
grammar of a language takes cognizance are to be found
in the language itself, the Author has everywhere invoked the co-operation of the student in the collection
and investigation of those truths. The exercises are,
for the most part, not mere echo-questions asking for
the matter of the chapters to which they are appended,
but questions based on specimens submitted for original
examination, just like the specimens put before a class
in Botany or Chemistry. These specimens have been
carefully collected during a period of teaching extending
over twenty years, and will be found to embrace most
of the difficulties which the language presents.

The Author has paid special attention to what are
generally called the 'exceptions' of accidence and construction, with a view to getting rid of them. The exceptions of grammar are not infractions of law, but instances
of laws that, in accordance with higher laws, are becoming, or have become, obsolete. It is of the highest
importance to the student to recognize this truth, and to
narrow, wherever he can, the area of knowledge that still
remains outside the domain of investigated law. Thus
only can knowledge be rendered scientific. Much has
been done of late years (notably by Dr. Morris) to explain the peculiarities of English accidence ; the Author
hopes that, by reference to the syntax of Old English,
he has himself done something to remove the anomalies
of English syntax.

The method of the Grammar is not exclusively inductive. Wherever it is possible the student is called upon to apply, in deductive exercises, the knowledge which he has acquired. Mr. Fitch, in one of the admirable lectures on Teaching delivered by him before the University of Cambridge, says, on the subject of text-books: ' One good test of a grammar or delectus, or of a manual of any kind, is this: Does it, as soon as it has helped the student to *know* something, instantly set him to *do* something which requires him to use that knowledge, and to show that he has really acquired it? *E.g.*, if it explains a new term, does it require the learner soon to use that term? If it states a rule, does it give him instantly occasion to put the rule in practice? If it points out a new logical or grammatical distinction, does it challenge him forthwith to find new instances and illustrations of that distinction?'[1] The Author trusts that the Grammar now submitted to teachers and students will not wholly fail to give satisfaction under the application of this test.

The history and derivation of the language are treated at greater length than in most school-books, but it is hoped that the importance of the subject will afford a sufficient justification for the course taken in this respect. In tracing the derivation of words the student will take care not to be deceived by mere coincidences of form and meaning. Dr. Donaldson used to say to his pupils, ' Whenever you come across an ingenious

---

[1] *Lectures on Teaching*, p. 84.

derivation, distrust it.' Every derivation ought to be supported, as far as possible, by historical evidence, by the known laws of phonetic change, and, in the case of words widely separated in form, by the intervening forms by which the root and the derivative are connected. The tracing of the changes of meaning which words undergo should be similarly conducted. The study of words in this rational way will not only lead the student to important conclusions in the science of language, but will bring him into contact with the sense-distinctions, the notions, the ideas, the thoughts, the feelings, the history, and the morality which are enshrined in words, and will prove a valuable discipline in the collection and investigation of evidence.

For the convenience of schools it is proposed to publish Parts I–IV. and Part V. separately : the former section under the title 'English Accidence, Parsing, Analysis, and Syntax ; ' the latter under the title ' The History and Derivation of the English Language.' These Parts will be complete in themselves, and independent one of the other.

The Author has had mainly in view the wants of young students, and more particularly of students in Training Colleges, the upper forms in Secondary and High Schools, and candidates for the University Local Examinations, for the Matriculation Examination of the London University, and for other public examinations. He desires to record his great obligations, in writing this Grammar, to the excellent grammars of Dr. Morris.

Dr. Adams, Dr. Abbott, and Mr. Mason, to Brachet's 'Historical French Grammar,' to the philological works of Archbishop Trench, and to the dictionaries of Mr. Wedgwood and Professor Skeat. The scholarly dictionary of Professor Skeat he has found invaluable. He has made a large use of the 'Anglo-Saxon' Gospels. Such Old English quotations as are not taken from Rask are drawn mainly from this source.

Teachers will render the Author a great service if they will kindly forward to him suggestions for the improvement of this Manual. He is well aware that a good text-book is the result of much elaboration; and, although he has had the advantage of long experience in teaching English, he is sure that he might derive much valuable help from the suggestions of teachers whose work has been of a somewhat different character from his own.

EVAN DANIEL.

St. John's College, Battersea :
  March 3, 1881.

NOTE TO SECOND EDITION.

The Author takes advantage of the issue of a Second Edition to thank reviewers and correspondents for many valuable suggestions. A considerable number of slight alterations have been made in the text, but none of such an extent as to prevent this edition from being used in class with the previous edition.

E. D.

January 6, 1883.

CONTRACTIONS.

Dan.	Danish	M.E.	Middle English
Du.	Dutch	N.	Norse
Fr.	French	O.E.	Old English
Ger.	German	O.H.G.	Old High German
Gk.	Greek	Sc.	Scotch
Icel.	Icelandic	Skt.	Sanskrit.
Lat.	Latin	Cog.	Cognate = of kindred origin

PART I.

ACCIDENCE.

SENTENCES.

1. ALL the facts with which a Grammar deals are to be found in the language to which the Grammar belongs; and it is in the language itself, not in books, that these facts are to be primarily sought. Grammarians do not impose rules on a language; they merely collect from the language rules already in existence, and set them forth in an orderly way.

2. If we take any paragraph of a book and examine it, we shall find that it is composed of a number of separate statements or utterances. These utterances are generally divided in print by a full stop, and are marked in speech by a falling of the voice when they come to an end. They are called **Sentences.**

In the following paragraph the sentences are marked off by vertical lines :—'Trade is stagnant. | The crops are drying up. | The sky is like brass. | The earth is like iron. | The peasants have commenced to eat the nauseous dogroot in lieu of bread.'

It is not always that sentences are so short as those in the foregoing paragraph. They may be enlarged in various ways, and extend to a considerable length.

3. A Sentence is a complete statement or utterance of a thought, e.g. *John walked home. Love thou thy parents. Did he wish to go ?*

A sentence that contains an assertion is called an **Assertive** Sentence, e.g. *He went to town;* one that contains a command or entreaty is called an **Imperative** Sen-

B

tence, e.g. *Be kind to the poor*; one that asks a question is called an **Interrogative** Sentence, e.g. *Were you there ?* one that expresses a wish is called an **Optative** Sentence (Lat. *opto*, I wish), e.g. *May we be happy !*

If we examine these sentences carefully, we shall find they each consist of two parts, viz. one relating primarily to some thing or person spoken of, or spoken to; the other, relating to what is said of, or to, that thing or person. The former part is called the **Subject** of the Sentence, the latter the **Predicate**.

(*a*) The Subject of an Assertive Sentence is the word or words denoting that about which the assertion is made; the Predicate is the assertion itself.

        (1) Gold is heavy.
        (2) To err is human.
        (3) He loves hunting.
        (4) That he is wrong is clear.

Subject	Predicate
(1) Gold	is heavy.
(2) To err	is human.
(3) He	loves hunting.
(4) That he is wrong	is clear.

(*b*) The Subject of an Imperative Sentence is the word denoting that to which the command or entreaty is given; the Predicate is the command or entreaty itself. The Subject of an Imperative Sentence is often not expressed.

        (1) Praise *ye* the Lord (Subj. expressed).
        (2) Go away (Subj. unexpressed).
        (3) Do *thou* likewise (Subj. expressed).

Subject	Predicate
(1) Ye	praise the Lord.
(2) ['Thou' or 'ye' (understood)]	go away.
(3) Thou	do likewise.

(c) The Subject of an Interrogative Sentence is the word denoting that concerning which the question is asked; the Predicate is that part of the sentence which relates to what is asked.

> (1) Lovest thou me ?
> (2) Did your father go to town ?

Subject	Predicate
(1) Thou	lovest me.
(2) Your father	did go to town.

(d) The Subject of an Optative Sentence is the word denoting that concerning which the wish is expressed; the Predicate is that part of the sentence which relates to the wish.

> (1) May he be prosperous !
> (2) Long live the king !

Subject	Predicate
(1) He	may be prosperous.
(2) The king	(may) live long.

Sometimes the order of the sentence is inverted; but whatever the order, the sentence must contain a Subject, expressed or understood, and a Predicate; e.g. *Him we sought in vain. Merrily goes the mill.*

Exercises.

Arrange in parallel columns as above the Subjects and Predicates of the following sentences :—

1. John ran to the bridge. 2. He was present at the inquest. 3. Oft on the dappled turf at ease I sit. 4. The stars of midnight shall be dear to her. 5. Low on his funeral couch he lies. 6. The praise of Bacchus then the sweet musician sang. 7. By fairy hands their knell is rung.

8.   Then shook the hills with thunder riven;
         Then rushed the steed to battle driven;
         And, louder than the bolts of heaven,
            Far flashed the red artillery.— *Campbell.*

9.   Her wing shall the eagle flap
                    O'er the false-hearted ;
                His warm blood the wolf shall lap
                    Ere life be parted.—*Scott.*

10.   Now fades the glimmering landscape on the sight,
        And all the air a solemn stillness holds.—*Gray.*

11. Come unto these yellow sands.—*Shakspere.*

12. That you have wronged me doth appear in this.—*Id.*

13. Haste thee, nymph.—*Milton.*

14. My days among the dead are past.—*Southey.*

PARTS OF SPEECH.

4. If we examine the separate words of which sentences are made up, we shall find that they discharge different functions, i.e. are used for different purposes. Let us consider the use of each word in the following sentences :—

The great black dog in the yard bit my little brother badly.

Two furious lions attacked the three horses, and speedily killed them.

He struck him angrily on the face, but did not hurt him.

The book was on the table, and the slate was under the chair.

Some of these words, as *dog, yard, brother, lions, horses, face, book, table, slate, chair,* are clearly names of things.

Some, as *bit, attacked, killed, struck, hurt,* tell us what things do.

Some, as *great, black, little, furious,* describe things.

Some, as *badly, speedily, angrily,* tell us how actions are done.

Some, as *the, my, a,* point out which things we refer to.

Some, as *two, three,* tell us how many things we are speaking of.

Some, as *them, he, him,* are not themselves the names of things, but are used instead of names.

Some, as *in, on, under,* point out certain relations between things.

Some, as *and, but,* join sentences.

5. Words that discharge the same function in a sentence are said to belong to the same part of speech.

To parse a word is, primarily, to say to which part of speech it belongs.

The number of parts of speech depends on the number of functions which words discharge in a sentence; but, as it is not worth while to notice every petty difference of function, and thereby multiply the number of parts of speech, most grammarians group words into eight parts of speech.

It does not matter whether we recognise seven, or eight, or nine, or ten parts of speech. What is of importance is—

    1. That we should have a sufficient number of parts of speech to enable us to classify *all* the words we use;

    2. That we should keep the parts of speech quite distinct;

    3. That we should not group together words having widely different functions, even though in some one respect they agree.

The names of the eight parts of speech which we shall recognise are—

The noun,	The adverb,
The pronoun,	The preposition,
The adjective,	The conjunction,
The verb,	The interjection.

6. Nouns are the names of things, i.e. of whatever we can think about; e.g. Here are *books, slates, pencils,* and *paper.*

Adjectives are words joined to nouns—

    1. **To describe things,** e.g. I have *good, old, red* wine.

    2. **To point out things,** e.g. Put *this* book on *that* table.

    3. **To express number or quantity,** e.g. Give me *some* bread and *two* or *three* apples.

Verbs are words which tell us, or help to tell us, what is done *by* **things** or *to* **things:**—The horse *neighs.* The horse *is beaten.*

Some verbs tell us what things ARE or BECOME:—The

horse *is* an animal. The horse *is* tired. The horse *grew* old and *became* useless.

Adverbs are words which tell us

1. **How, when, and where actions are done,** e.g. He behaves *well when* he stays *here.*

2. **The degree in which a thing or an action possesses a particular quality,** e.g. He is *very* happy and enjoys himself *exceedingly.*

Pronouns are words used instead of nouns, e.g. *You* and *I* saw *him.*

Prepositions are words that point out

1. **The relations between things,** e.g. The book *on* the table *by* the window; or

2. **The relation between actions or attributes and things,** e.g. The mouse ran *over* the chair, then *under* the table, then *behind* the clock, and at last got *into* a hole. The medicine is good *for* you.

Conjunctions are words which join words and sentences. John *and* James sang a duet. (Words.) He went to town *and* bought a net; *but* he forgot to bring my watch. (Sentences.)

Interjections are words of exclamation, e.g. *O,* come ye into the summer woods.

Alas ! the gratitude of man
Hath oftener left me mourning.—*Wordsworth.*

Exercises.

1. Describe the use of the words in italics in the following passage—

Hark ! to *the gentle* lullaby,
That *through* the *trees* is *creeping,*
Those sleepy trees that *nod their heads,*
Ere yet the *moon comes peeping,*
Like *a tender nurse,* to *see* if all
Her little ones *are sleeping.*—*C. Young.*

2. Name the parts of speech to which the words in italics in the following passages belong—

a. Not a *drum* was heard, not a *funeral note.*—*Wolfe.*

b. The *Assyrian came down* like a *wolf on* the *fold.*—*Byron.*

c.   *Alack !* there *lies* more peril in *thine eye*
     Than *twenty* of *their* swords.—*Shakspere.*

d. *His pity gave ere charity began.*—*Goldsmith.*

e.   And he was *kind*, and *loved* to sit
     In the *low hut or* garnished cottage,
     And praise *the* farmer's homely *wit*,
     And *share* the widow's homelier *pottage.*—*Praed.*

f.   *Alas*, for the *rarity*
     Of *Christian* charity.—*Hood.*

g. *O*, Mary, *go* and call the cattle *home*.—*Kingsley.*

h. *Ah, then* and there was *hurrying to* and *fro*.—*Byron.*

NOUNS.

7. Nouns are the names of things, and are so called from the Latin word *nomen* (French *nom*), a name.
Under the word 'things' we include—

1. Objects that we know by means of our senses, as *gold, horse, stone, London, Thomas.*

2. Qualities considered apart from the objects in which they are found, e.g. *truth, whiteness, beauty.*

3. Objects of whose existence we can form some conception, although we do not know them by means of our senses, e.g. *mind, spirit, God, conscience.*

4. Relations between things, as *cause, effect, purpose, resemblance, difference.*

5. Actions or states, as *walking, growing, existence, movement.*

'Things' are sometimes distinguished from 'persons' and 'places,' but in the definition given above the word 'thing' is used to denote *whatever we can think about.*

8. Nouns may be classified in various ways. Considered with reference to the *extent of their applicability* they are either Common or Proper.

A Common Noun is a name which may be applied to all the individuals of a class. It is common to them all, e.g. *man, river, port, city.*

A Proper Noun is a name which belongs to an individual as distinguished from one belonging to a class,

and is so called from the Latin *proprius,* one's own, e.g.
John, London, Broad Street, Prospect House.

Thus the name *man* is common to *all* men; the name *Thomas*
belongs to a *particular* man. A common noun distinguishes one
class from another class, as *men* from *birds*; a proper noun distinguishes one individual from another individual, as *Thomas* from
John, London from *Paris.*

Occasionally a proper noun is used to denote not a particular individual but one or more of a class, and in that
case it becomes common; e.g. we sometimes speak of a cruel
tyrant as ' a Nero.' In the following passage Macaulay used
proper nouns as common : ' To put the *Janes,* the *Souths,*
the *Sherlocks* into such a situation that they must either
starve or recant, . . . was a revenge too delicious to be
relinquished.' The historian does not mean by ' the Janes,
the Souths, and the Sherlocks ' persons bearing that name,
but persons occupying positions similar to those of the
divines mentioned.

When we speak of a family—as the Tudors, the Howards
—we use a name which is proper as regards the family
as a whole, though common as regards the members of the
family.

When we speak of ' The Queen,' meaning a particular
queen, as Queen Victoria, we convert a common into a
proper noun.

' I write to you,' said Bolingbroke to Prior, ' not as *The Minister*
to *The Secretary,* but as Harry to Mat.'

9. Considered with reference to *the mode in which things
exist,* the nouns denoting them are either Concrete or
Abstract.

A Concrete [1] Noun is the name of a thing which has a
real existence outside our own minds, e.g. *book, gold,
feather.*

An Abstract [2] Noun is the name of a quality considered
apart from the thing in which it is found, or of an action
considered apart from the doer of it, e.g. *whiteness, truth,
motion.* The only separate existence that the things denoted
by abstract nouns have, is a mental existence. So there can be

---

[1] From Lat. *concresco,* I grow together.
[2] From Lat. *abstraho,* I draw away from.

no action apart from the doer of it, though we may *think* of an action apart from the circumstances which attend its performance.

Abstract Nouns are formed from (*a*) adjectives, e.g. *goodness, redness, truth, justice*; (*b*) verbs, e.g. *speech, thrift* (from *thrive*), *shrift* (from *shrive*); (*c*) concrete nouns, e.g. *despotism, kingship, knavery*. The same noun may be concrete in one sense and abstract in another. Note the different uses in the following examples—

> *Truth* is opposed to falsehood (abstract).
> This *truth* is indisputable (concrete).
> Our ideas of *beauty* are derived from beautiful objects (abstract).
> She was one of the *beauties* of the court (concrete).

When an abstract noun is used in the plural, or restricted in its application by some adjective, as ' *a*,' ' *the*,' ' *his*,' &c., it is nearly always rendered thereby concrete; i.e. it no longer denotes an abstract quality, but some concrete object possessing the quality.

It will be observed that these modes of classifying nouns are independent one of the other. Hence, it would be wrong to say that nouns may be divided into Common, Proper, Concrete, and Abstract, as if the four classes were co-ordinate and based on one principle of classification. We ought to say that they may be divided into either common and proper, or into concrete and abstract. A noun may be at the same time common and concrete, e.g. man, stone; or proper and concrete, e.g. London, Thomas.

The following table represents the various classes of nouns included under the heads Common and Proper :—

Common. 1. Names of concrete objects, e.g. gold, tree.
            2. Names of qualities, e.g. truth.
            3. Immaterial objects, e.g. spirit, mind.
            4. Relations, e.g. cause, effect.
            5. Actions or states, e.g. motion, life.

            Common becoming Proper, e.g. the Queen.

Proper.   1. Names of persons, places, &c., John, London.
            2. Proper becoming Common, e.g. a Nero, some Cromwell.
            3. Proper in one respect, and Common in another, e.g. the English, the Tories.

Exercises.

1. Point out the nouns in the following passage—

Rats !
They fought the dogs and killed the cats,
    And bit the babies in the cradles,
And ate the cheeses out of the vats,
    And licked the soup from the cook's own ladles,

Split open the kegs of salted sprats,
Made nests inside men's Sunday hats,
And even spoiled the women's chats
    By drowning their speaking
    With shrieking and squeaking
In fifty different sharps and flats.—*Browning.*

2. Arrange in two columns the common and proper nouns in the following passages—

a. My name is Norval; on the Grampian hills
My father feeds his flocks.—*Home.*

b. Be England what she will,
With all her faults she is my country still.—*Churchill.*

c. Some mute, inglorious Milton here may rest,
    Some Cromwell guiltless of his country's blood.—*Gray.*

d. But Knowledge to their eyes her ample page,
    Rich with the spoils of time, did ne'er unroll ;
Chill Penury repressed their noble rage
    And froze the genial current of their soul.—*Id.*

e. England is not now what it was under the Edwards and the Henries.

f. That man is little to be pitied whose patriotism would not gain force upon the plain of Marathon, or whose piety would not grow warmer among the ruins of Iona.—*Johnson.*

g. What can ennoble sots, or slaves, or cowards?
Alas ! not all the blood of all the Howards.—*Pope.*

h. There have been many Diogenes and as many Timons, though but few of that name.

i. Aldeborontiphoscophornio !
Where left you Chrononhotonthologos ?—*Carey.*

k. Cæsar crossed the Rubicon and marched to Rome.

l. The Bacons were related to the Cecils.

m. In Xanadu did Kubla Khan
A stately pleasure-dome decree,
Where Alph, the sacred river, ran.—*Coleridge.*

n. While stands the Coliseum
Rome shall stand.—*Byron.*

o. I've stood upon Achilles' tomb,
  And heard Troy doubted; men will doubt of Rome.—*Byron.*

p. The Emperor met the Queen at Boulogne.

q. The English are not a military people.

Give instances from the foregoing passages of (*a*) proper nouns becoming common; (*b*) common nouns becoming proper.

3. Arrange in two columns the concrete and abstract nouns in the following passages—

a. Words are the daughters of earth, and deeds are the sons of heaven.—*Indian saying.*

b. Confidence is a plant of slow growth in an aged bosom.
  E. of Chatham.

c. Praise undeserved is scandal in disguise.—*Pope.*

d. A little learning is a dangerous thing;
  Drink deep or taste not the Pierian spring:
  There shallow draughts intoxicate the brain,
  And drinking largely sobers us again.—*Id.*

e. Forgive us all our sins, negligences, and ignorances.
  Liturgy.

f. The evil that men do lives after them:
  The good is oft interred with their bones.—*Shakspere.*

g. So farewell hope, and with hope farewell fear,
  Farewell remorse; all good to me is lost:
  Evil! be Thou my good.—*Milton.*

h. My hopes are gone; my worst fears are realized; my goods are seized.

THE INFLEXION OF NOUNS.

10. Nouns undergo various changes of form in order to express changes of meaning. Thus *lion* is changed into *lions* to express a change of number, into *lion's* to express possession, and into *lioness* to express a she-lion. These changes are called **inflexions** from the Latin *flecto*, I bend; the word that is *inflected* being regarded as bent from its simple form.

GENDER OF NOUNS.

11. Nouns that are the names of males are said to be of the **Masculine Gender**, e.g. sailor, master, lord, Harry. The names of females are said to be of the **Feminine Gender**, e.g. wife, girl, queen, Harriet. The names of things that have no sex are said to be of the **Neuter Gender** (Lat. *neuter*, neither), e.g. book, London.

The word Gender means kind or class, and comes from the Latin *genus*, a sort or kind. Thus Shakspere writes, 'Supply it with one *gender* of herbs or distract it with many' (*Othello*). In some languages the gender of nouns is, for the most part, independent of sex, and depends on the terminations of the nouns. Thus in Latin, *mensa*, a table, is feminine; *oculus*, an eye, is masculine. So in Old English, *tunge*, a tongue, was feminine; *dæg*, a day, was masculine. In modern English both *tongue* and *day* are neuter. Gender should not be confounded with sex. Gender is a distinction between *words*, sex a distinction between *things*.

Gender is not strictly an inflexion, except in those cases in which the gender is expressed by the termination, e.g. giant, giantess; testator, testatrix.

Nouns that admit of being applied without inflexion to things of *either sex*, as *friend, parent, dove, cousin, bird,* are said to be of the **Common Gender.**[1]

12. When impersonal things are personified, i.e. when they are spoken to, or spoken of, as if they were living persons, we often attribute to them sex; and the nouns which name them are then said to be of the masculine or feminine gender, according as masculine or feminine qualities are attributed to them. Thus we often speak of the Sun, Death, Time, as masculine; of Nature, Virtue, Religion, Law, as feminine.

The gender of nouns denoting sexless things is, of course, arbitrary. In O.E. *sun* is feminine, *moon* is masculine; in modern English the genders of these words are reversed. We, thinking mainly of the beauty and gentle motion of the moon, make *moon* feminine. Our forefathers, when they made 'moon' masculine, probably thought of the moon as 'the measurer, the ruler of days and weeks and seasons, the regulator of the tides, the lord of their festivals, and the herald of their public assemblies' (Max Müller). The sailor invariably speaks of his ship as feminine; in a similar way the engine-driver speaks of his engine; both giving expression, in this way, to a certain admiration and fondness for the things with which they are, respectively, so closely associated.

'It is curious to observe that country labourers give the feminine appellations to those things only which are more closely identified with themselves, and by the qualities and condition of which their own efforts and character as workmen are affected. The mower calls his scythe a *she*; the ploughman calls his plough a *she*; but a prong, or a shovel, or a barrow, which passes promiscuously from

---

[1] Some nouns that were formerly of the common gender are now restricted to one sex. E.g. girl, hoyden, niece, shrew, courtesan, termagant, witch, wench, man.

hand to hand, and which is appropriated to no particular labourer, is called a *he*.'—Cobbett.

Many of our old English writers make the gender of English nouns correspond to the gender of the equivalent nouns in Latin and Greek.

13. The differences of gender are indicated in three ways in English, viz.—

(1) By different words:

bachelor (Low Lat. *baccalarius*, a cowherd, from *bacca*, a Low Lat. form of *vacca*, a cow)

maid *or* spinster

boar (O.E. *bár*)

sow (O.E. *sugu*)

boy (cp. Ger. *bube*)

girl (dim. of Low Ger. *gör*, a little child)

brother (O.E. *bróthor*)

sister (O.E. *sweóstor*)

buck (O.E. *bucca*, he-goat)

doe (O.E. *dá*)

bull (Icelandic *boli*)

cow (O.E. *cú*)

bullock (dim. of bull) *or* steer

heifer (O.E. *heahfor*, from *heah*, high, and *fear*, ox; = full-grown ox *or* cow)

cock

hen (fem. of O.E. *hana*, cock)

colt *or* foal (O.E. *fola*)

filly (dim. of *foal*)

dog *or* hound

bitch (O.E. *bicce*. Cp. Ger. *betze*)

drake (= king of the ducks)

duck (= diver)

drone (O.E. *drán*, from the noise it makes)

bee (also used as of the common gender. Originally fem.)

earl (O.E. *eorl*, a warrior)

countess (fem. of count)

father (the feeder)

mother (root *ma*, to produce); dam (Lat. *domina*)

gaffer (from *grandfather*)

gammer (from *grandmother*)

gander (O.E. *gandra*. The *d* is not a part of the root. See note on *goose*)

goose (originally contained an *n*. Cp. Ger. *gans* = goose; gannet, the Solan goose, O.E. *ganota* = wild goose)

hart (O.E. *heort* = the horned one) *or* stag (Icelandic *steggr*, a gander. The name is given to many male animals)

roe (O.E. *rá*) *or* hind (O.N. *hind*, a female deer)

horse (O.E. *hors*) *or* stallion (O.F. *estalon*)

mare (O.E. *mere*, a mare: *mearh*, a horse, was mas.)

husband (O.E. *hus*, house; *bonda*, proprietor)

wife (O.E. *wíf* = woman. Cp. fish-wife, goodwife [goody], house-wife [huzzy]. Also Ger. *weib* = woman)

king (O.E. *cyn-ing*, son of the tribe. Cp. kin, kind)

queen (from root *gan*, to produce Cp. O.E. *cwén-fugel* = hen-bird)

lord (O.E. *hláford*, from *hláf*, loaf; *weard*, keeper)

lady (O.E. *hlǽfdige*, from *hláf*, loaf, and *dæger*, kneader) man (originally com. gen.; cp. Ger. *mensch*)

woman (= wife-man)

monk (Gk. *monachos*, solitary) *or* friar (Lat. *frater*, brother)

nun (Low Lat. *nonna*, mother; old fem. *mynchyn*)

nephew (O.E. *nefa*. Cp. Ger. *neffe*; Lat. *nepos* = grandson. Cp. 1 Tim. v. 4, where 'nephews' = 'grandchildren')

niece (Lat. *neptis*, granddaughter)

papa (root *pa*, to nourish. Cp. *father*, Lat. *pater*)

mama (same root as mother. Cp. Lat. *mamma*, breast)

ram *or* wether

ewe (O.E. *eowu*)

sir (Lat. *senior*, elder)

madam (Lat. *mea*, my; *domina*, lady)

sire (see 'sir')

dame (Lat. *domina*, lady)

sloven (cognate with *slop, slobber, slabber*)

slut (cp. slattern)

son (Sanscrit *su*, to beget)

daughter (= milker. Cp. Gk. *thugatēr* and O.E. *dug*, a teat)

uncle (Lat. *avunculus*, dim. of *avus*, grandfather)

aunt (Lat. *amita*, a father's sister. Cp. *ant*, from O.E. *æmete*)

wizard (O.F. *guisc-art*, a very wise man; Icelandic, *viskr*, wise)

witch (O.E. *wicce*, fem.; *wicca*, mas.)

In modern English 'servant' is of the common gender. In Bible English it is masculine, the feminine being 'maid,' e.g. 'nor his servant, nor his maid' (Ex. xx. 17, P. Book version. Cp. Ps. cxxiii. 2).

(2) **By distinctive terminations**, mostly derived either directly or indirectly from Latin, e.g.—

-trix, as testator, testatrix; executor, executrix.

-ess (Norman French *-esse*, Latin *-issa*), as actor, actress; master, mistress; emperor, empress; duke, duchess; lad, lass (Welsh *llawd*, a lad; fem. *llodes*, a girl). It will be observed that some of these words undergo other modifications, besides taking the affix.

-ice, as improvisatore, improvisatrice (Italian).

-ine, as hero, heroine (Greek); landgrave, landgravine; margrave, margravine (German).

-en, the only instance of this termination in modern English is *vixen*, the feminine of *fox*. Comp. the German feminine termination *-in*, e.g. Freund, a male friend, Freundin, a female friend. So Fuchs, Fuchsin.

In Old English we find several distinctive gender terminations. Thus, all nouns ending in *a* were masculine; most nouns ending in *e* were feminine; e.g. *wuduwa*, a widower; *wuduwe*, a widow. The old feminine suffix *-stere* still survives in *spinster*, though a spinster no longer means, as it did once, a female spinner. In many other words this suffix survives, but is no longer distinctively feminine, e.g. punster, rhymester, huckster (originally a female hawker). It also survives in many proper names, as Bagster (contracted into Baxter) from baker; Brewster, from brewer; Webster,[1] from webber, i.e. a weaver; Kempster, a comber; Whitster, a bleacher. By degrees –ster ceased to be a distinctively feminine termination, and it became necessary to add the termination –ess. Hence such words as song–str–ess; seam–str–ess.[2]

(3) **By using nouns or pronouns, having gender, as prefixes or affixes**, as he-goat, she-goat; man-child, female-child; he-bear, she-bear; man-servant, maid-servant; cock-sparrow, hen-sparrow. *Woman*=wife-man.

As a rule feminine nouns are formed from the masculine. The following are exceptions : *gander* from *gans*, the old form of *goose; bridegroom* from *bride* and *guma*=man; *drake* (=duck-king) from *önd*, a duck (Norse) and *rake*=king (comp. rick in bishop-rick); *widower* from widow.

Exercises.

1. Place in parallel columns the masculine and feminine nouns in the following passages, and state what considerations probably determined the gender in each case—

a.   But Knowledge to their eyes her ample page
     Rich with the spoils of time did ne'er unroll.— *Gray.*

b.   When Music, heavenly maid, was young,
     While yet in early Greece she sung. — *Collins.*

c.   And Hope enchanted smiled and waved her golden hair.—*Id.*

d.   Next Anger rushed, his eyes on fire.—*Id.*

e.   The meek-eyed Morn appears, mother of dews.—*Thomson.*

f.   Knowledge is proud that he has learnt so much,
     Wisdom is humble that he knows no more.— *Cowper.*

g.   Mont Blanc is the monarch of mountains ·
     We crowned him long ago.—*Byron.*

h.   The river glideth at his own sweet will.— *Wordsworth.*

i.   Overhead the moon sits arbitress.—*Milton.*

k.   Late, late yestreen I saw the new moone
     Wi' the auld moon in her arme.—'*Sir Patrick Spens.*'

l.   Earth, with her thousand voices, praises God.— *Coleridge.*

---

[1] 'Need gars (i.e. makes) naked men rin and *websters* spin.'
                                        Scotch Proverb.
[2] In O.E. *seamere* means a tailor.

2. What are the feminine nouns corresponding to : prince, steer, ram, viscount, ogre, sorcerer, colt, buck, boar, abbot, marquis, stepson, pea-cock, gaffer, landlord, Jew, gentle-man, foster-father, czar, earl, sloven, black-cock ?

3. Give the gender of the following words : heifer, hart, witness, friend, tree, fairy, sylph, naiad, squirrel, pony, author, murderer, cousin, aunt, child, landlord, tenant, proprietress, nag, filly, tigress.

NUMBER.

14. Number is that inflexion which nouns undergo to indicate whether they stand for one object or for more than one. That form which is used to denote *one* thing is said to be of the singular number, or, more briefly, singular, e.g. *man, ox, tree, calf*. That form which is used to denote *more than one thing* is said to be of the plural number, or plural, e.g. *men, oxen, trees, calves*.

15. The plurals of English nouns are formed in the following ways—

(1) **By adding es or s to the singular,** e.g. brush, brushes; book, books.

In O.E. many nouns formed their plurals in *as*, which was subsequently modified into *es*. As *s* was a common plural termination in Norman French also, the termination *es* came to be gradually applied to large numbers of words which originally formed their plurals in other ways.

We still retain the termination *es* in the case of nouns ending in the singular in a sibilant, i.e. a hissing sound (*s, x, z, sh,* soft *ch*), e.g. gases, kisses, boxes, topazes, fishes, churches. We also use it to form the plurals of some nouns ending in **o**, as potatoes, heroes. The following nouns in **o** form their plurals by adding s only, bravo, zero, solo, tyro, folio, quarto.

Nouns ending in **y**, preceded by a vowel, form their plurals by the addition of *s*, as keys, boys, days. If the *y* be preceded by a consonantal sound, *s* is added, and the *y* is changed into *ie*, e.g. ruby, rubies; lady, ladies. In M.E. the singular ended in *ie*, so that the plural in *ies* was then regular. *Soliloquy* has for its plural *soliloquies*, the *u* before the *y* forming part of the consonantal sound *cw*.

Many nouns of native origin ending in **f** or **fe** form their plurals in **ves**, e.g. calf, calves; leaf, leaves; knife, knives.

Some nouns in *f*, of Norman-French origin, as chief, brief, relief; and some of native origin, as puff, ruff, stuff, roof, cliff, dwarf, strife, and fife, form their plurals in *s*.

F at the end of O.E. words had probably the sound of *v*, a sound which it still retains in *of* and in the Lancashire pronunciation of *if*. Comp. strife, strive; wife, wive; calf, calve; half, halve; shelf, shelve.

Dwarf did not originally terminate in *f*, but in *h* or *g*, its old forms being *dweorh* and *dweorg*, and the final letter being gutturalized. Comp. *genoh*, the old form of *enough*, pronounced *enuff*.

(2) **By adding en to the singular,** as ox, oxen. In *brethren* and *children* we have double plurals, the old plurals being *brothra* or *brothru* and *cildru*. The termination *en* would appear to have been added when the old plural endings in *ra* and *ru* had become obsolete. In northern English the plurals *brether* and *childer* are still heard. *Chicken* (O.E. cycen from cock) was used in M.E. both as a singular and plural, but the original form of the plural was *cycenu*. Comp.—

> Children and chicken
> Will always be picking.—*Old Proverb.*

Bracken is probably a plural of *brake* (a fern so called from its broken appearance); *kine*, the plural of cow, is a double plural, the old plural being *cÿ*. (The Scotch still use *kye* as a plural.) *Swine* is probably connected with *sow*, but is not the plural of it. In O.E. it is used as a singular as well as a plural.

In our early writers we find *treen* (trees), *fone* (foes), *eyne* and *een* (eyes), *been* (bees), *pesen* (peas), *toon* (toes), *fleen* (flees). In the Bible we find *hosen* (Dan. iii. 21).

In provincial English may still be heard ' *eye-breen* ' (eyebrows), *housen*, ' *shoon* and *hone* ' (shoes and stockings).

(3) **By changing the vowel sound, without adding any new ending,** e.g. man, men (O.E. *man, menn*); woman, women (O.E. *wíf-man, wíf-menn*); foot, feet (O.E. *fót, fét*); mouse, mice (O.E. *mús, mýs*).

The addition of a syllable in O.E. was nearly always accompanied by a modification of the vowel sound in the root-word. In the foregoing words the change of vowel indicates that a syllable has been lost. The O. Saxon plural of *foot* was *fóti*.

The plurals of nouns directly borrowed from other lan-

C

guages usually follow the laws of inflexion of those languages; e.g.—

1. Latin singulars in *a* form their plurals in *æ*, as *formula, formulæ, minutia* (not used), *minutiæ*.

2. Latin singulars in *us*, for the most part, form their plurals in *i*, as *radius, radii ; tumulus, tumuli ; genius, genii. Genus, genera,* and *hiatus, hiatus,* follow other laws.

3. Latin singulars in *um* and Greek singulars in *on* form their plurals in *a*, as—

addendum	addenda	maximum	maxima
animalculum	animalcula	memorandum	memoranda
arcanum	arcana	phenomenon	phenomena (Gk.)
automaton	automata (Gk.)	prolegomenon	prolegomena
corrigendum	corrigenda	(not used)	(Gk.)
criterion	criteria (Gk.)	·sanatorium	sanatoria
desideratum	desiderata	spectrum	spectra
minimum	minima	stratum	strata

4. Latin singulars in *es* and Greek in *is* form their plurals in *es*, as—

analysis	analyses (Gk.)	parenthesis	parentheses(Gk.)
axis	axes (Gk.)	series	series
basis	bases (Gk.)	species	species
ellipsis	ellipses (Gk.)	superficies	superficies

5. Latin singulars in *ix* or *cx* form their plurals in *ices*, as—

appendix	appendices	radix	radices
calix	calices	vortex	vortices

6. The following are peculiar—

Greek: iris, irides; miasma, miasmata; chrysalis, chrysalides.

Italian: bandit (Jeremy Taylor, 'bandito'), banditti ;[1] dilettante, dilettanti ; libretto, libretti ; virtuoso, virtuosi.

French: beau, beaux ; monsieur, messieurs ; madame, mesdames.

Hebrew: cherub, cherubim; seraph, seraphim.

Some foreign nouns have adopted an English plural without wholly losing their own. Thus we have vortexes and vortices ; indexes and indices ; formulas and formulæ. Occasionally we take advantage of these double forms to express two different shades of meaning, e.g.—

---

[1] 'Bandit' is from the Italian 'bandito,' a person placed under the ban of the law. The regular plural in *-s* is common, more especially after numerals. 'Banditti' is generally used in a collective sense, e.g. 'The country was infested with banditti.'

formulæ = general mathematical and scientific expressions.
formulas = prescribed forms of words.

indexes = the lists of contents of books.
indices = the letters or figures in Algebra, which show
the powers to which quantities are to be
raised.

geniuses = people of genius.
genii   = certain imaginary beings who often figure in
Oriental stories.

The tendency of the language is to make all foreign nouns
conform to the general law for forming the plural. We
retain the original plurals in certain stereotyped forms of
expression, but employ the new in ordinary conversation.

16. Some native nouns have two plurals, e.g.—

brothers, used of brothers by blood.
brethren, used of members of the same community.

cloths, kinds of cloth.
clothes, articles of apparel.

dies, instruments for stamping.
dice, small cubes used in games of chance.

pennies, separate coins, e.g. I have seven new pennies.
pence, money valued in pennies, e.g. I have seven pence.

peas (not a native word), used of peas considered separately.
pease, used of peas considered collectively, as a vegetable
product. The *s* is part of the root, the Latin singular
being *pisum*. Cp. Welsh *pys*.

17. Some nouns have only one form for singular and
plural, e.g. deer, sheep, grouse, swine, salmon, cod, trout,
mackerel. Some are used as collective nouns, as fish, cannon, carp, but form regular plurals when applied indivi-
dually, as fishes, cannons, carps. Cp. 'full of great *fishes*'
(John xxi. 11) with 'Bring of the *fish* which ye have now
caught' (v. 10).

The names of measures, numbers, weights, &c., when
preceded by a numeral, are frequently not inflected for the
plural, as five *yoke* of oxen, a hundred *head* of cattle, four
pair, six *brace*, seven *stone*, five *hundred*, three *score*, six
gross, five *fathom*, two *foot*, ten *year*.

The same rule holds in German. Comp. sechs *Fuss*; zwei *Paar*; drei *Dutzend*; sieben *Stück*; vier *Pfund*; ein Regiment von tausend *Mann*. See Becker's German Grammar, p. 127.

Abstract nouns are invariably singular. When they are used in the plural, they are converted into concrete nouns. See § 9.

'It is of the Lord's *mercies* that we are not consumed, because His *compassions* fail not.'—Lam. iii. 22.

Names of materials are ordinarily singular, e.g. wheat, gold, silver, timber, clay; but the plural form may be used to denote various kinds of the material spoken of, e.g. sugars, silks, wines.

18. Some nouns are used in the plural, but not in the singular, e.g. bellows, pincers, pliers, tweezers, scissors, shears, snuffers, spectacles, tongs, trousers (all of which denote things composed of *two parts*), annals, archives, assets, aborigines, amends, dregs, entrails, hustings, lees, matins (in the sense of morning prayers), measles, mumps, molasses, nuptials, espousals, oats, odds, obsequies, premises, staggers, shambles, thanks, tidings, trappings, vespers, victuals, vitals, wages. 'All which nature, or art, or habit has made plural, have no singular.' (Cobbett.)

Amends is a plu. formed from the Fr. *amende*; with *bellows* cp. Mœso-Gothic *balgs*, plu. *balgeis*, a wine-skin; *breeches* and *breeks* are double plurals, *breek* being the O.E. plural of *bróc* = breeches, and formed like *feet*, pl. of *foot*; *hustings* is a meaningless plural of the Icelandic *hústhing*, from *hús*, house, and *thing*, a council; *gallows* is the plu. of O.E. *galga*, a gibbet; *mean*, Fr. *moyen*, is still used as a singular (as a mathematical term); *measel* was used as a singular in M.E.; *odds* is from Icel. *oddi*, a triangle, a point of land. Cp. *oddamathr*, the third or *odd* man who gives the casting vote.

Politics, *ethics*, *optics*, *logics*, *physics*, *mechanics*, are plural in form, to correspond with the equivalent Greek plurals, but are commonly regarded as singular. In Greek the science itself was denoted by a feminine singular, a treatise upon it by a neuter plural.

19. *News*, *pox* (pocks), and *pains* are really plurals, but are generally used as singulars. *Alms*, *riches*, *summons*, and *eaves* are really singular.

Alms is from the O.E. ælmesse, which is from the Greek eleëmo-sunē. *Riches* is from the Norman-French *richesse*. Comp. largesse, noblesse, &c. *Eaves* is from the O.E. singular, *efese*, which had the same meaning as our modern word *eaves*, but primarily meant a margin, edge. Comp. O.E. *efesian*, to trim. *Summons* is said to be from the Latin *summoneas*. Similarly *capias, habeas corpus, scire facias*, and other writs are called from the opening Latin words. Some derive 'summons' from O.F. *semonce* (Lat. *submonitio*), a warning.

20. Compound nouns usually attach the sign of the plural to the leading word in the compound, e.g. courts-martial, fathers-in-law, hangers-on, knights-errant. Occasionally the compound is treated as one word and the sign of the plural is affixed to the end, e.g. lord-chancellors, spoonfuls, lady-friends. In men-servants and women-servants each element of the compound takes a plural form.

'The earth brought forth by *handfuls*,' Gen. xli. 47. In Matt. xiv. 20, and the parallel passages, 'twelve baskets full,' the word 'full' is emphatic and not part of the compound *basketful*. The Greek is δώδεκα κοφίνους πλήρεις. See Mark vi. 43, Rev. Ver.

21. Collective nouns differ from ordinary plurals in denoting a number of objects without being inflected. Comp. *books* with *mob*. To make *book* plural we add *s* to it. *Mob* may have a plural meaning in its uninflected form.

Collective nouns may be used either in the singular or plural number. We have *mobs* as well as *mob*, *armies* as well as *army*. When the plural is used the singular collective is regarded as denoting a single unit.

An uninflected collective noun may be regarded as singular or plural, according as the idea of singularity or plurality is uppermost in our minds. *When the unity of the multitude is uppermost*, we use the noun as a singular; when *the multitude of the units is uppermost*, we use the noun as a plural. Comp.

> The mob *are* greatly excited.
> The mob *was* speedily dispersed.

Exercises.

1. State the number of the nouns in the following passages—

a. Hills rise on hills and Alps on Alps arise.—*Pope.*

b. Try to make amends.

c. Let a gallows be made of fifty cubits high.—*Bible.*

d. We had to encounter fearful odds.

e. The wages of sin is death.—*Bible.*

f. A fair day's wage for a fair day's work.

g. Who'll buy my herring ?—*Scotch Ballad.*

h. A tanner will last you nine year.—*Shakspere.*

i. I lost all my valuables.

2. Give the plurals of hoof, wolf, valley, staff, hero, Dutchman, German, Mussulman, domino, index, radius, erratum, parenthesis, nebula.

3. Give instances of nouns that have (*a*) no singular, (*b*) a seemingly plural form with a singular meaning.

4. Some nouns have the same form for singular and plural. Give instances.

5. Give instances of Collective Nouns.

6. Correct or justify the following :

a. Evil *were* the *news* he heard.

b. Ill *news rides* fast, while good *news baits.*

c. How oft the *means* to do ill-deeds *makes* ill-deeds done !

d. The *odds are* against us.

e. Mathematics are useful.

f. Behold the *people is* one, and they have all one language.

g. The *clergy were* in favour of the measure.

h. 'The *Pleasures* of Memory' *was* written by Rogers.

i. By *this means* shall we sound what skill she hath.

k. The *College* of Cardinals *have* elected a new Pope.

l. The *army was* defeated.

m. Full *fathom five* thy father lies.

n. Surely the *people is* grass.

o. The *people are* dissatisfied.

p. Why *do* the *people* imagine a vain thing?

q. It was six *foot* long.

r. The *odds* against him *is* very considerable.

7. Give instances of nouns that have two plurals. Discriminate between the meanings of the two.

CASE.

22. **Case** (from Lat. *cado,* I fall) is an **inflexion** of nouns and pronouns, for showing the relation which they bear to other words. Thus in the sentence 'John has

James's hat,' the addition of the termination '*s* shows that the 'hat' belongs to James. The term '*case*' is also employed to denote certain grammatical relations of nouns and pronouns, even though those nouns and pronouns have *no distinct forms* to express those relations.

The learner will be assisted in understanding the distinctions of case by analysing a simple sentence.

In the sentence 'John gave a book to James,' 'John' tells us who it is of whom the assertion is made, and is called the 'Subject' of the sentence. It is said to be in the **Nominative Case.**

The word 'gave' tells us what is said about the 'Subject,' and forms what is called the 'Predicate' of the sentence.

The words 'a book to James' tells us *what* was given and *to whom* it was given, and are called the *Completion of the Predicate.*

After a transitive verb the word denoting the immediate object of the action is called the *Direct Object,* and is said to be in the **Objective Case**; the word which denotes an object indirectly affected by the action is called the *Indirect Object,* and is also said to be in the Objective Case. In the sentence given above, 'book,' denoting the thing actually given, is the Direct Object; 'James,' denoting the person to whom the book was given, is the Indirect Object; both 'book' and 'James' are in the Objective Case.

23. The **Nominative Case** is that form of a Noun or Pronoun which is used to express the Subject of the Sentence, e.g. *Henry* laughed; *I* sang; *you* wept; *he* smiled.

The term would appear to have been applied originally to that form of the noun which indicated merely the *name* (nomen) of a thing.

When a noun stands for a person or thing spoken to, it is sometimes called the **Nominative of Address.** In Latin many nouns take a distinct form, called the **Vocative Case,** when so used, from Lat. *voco,* I call. In English the Vocative form is the same as the Nominative, e.g.—

> *John* did it (Nom.)
> *John,* do not do it (Voc.)

Sometimes we find in a sentence a noun or pronoun qualified by a participle, but having no connection, either as subject or object, with the finite verb in the predicate. Such a noun or pronoun is usually called the **Nominative Absolute** (Lat. *ab*, from ; *solutus*, loosened), because it is, as it were, *loosed* from the main sentence—

> The *coach* having gone, I was obliged to walk on foot.
> *This* being done, we went for a walk.
> On we marched, our *companions* following slowly behind.

The function of the Absolute clause is to express *time, cause, condition*, or *accompanying circumstance*, and is, strictly speaking, adverbial. In O.E. the dative case was used in absolute clauses. Dr. Abbott prefers to call the Nominative Absolute the Subject Absolute.

24. The **Possessive Case** is that form of a Noun or Pronoun which is used to show that the thing denoted is the possessor of something ; e.g. *John's* book ; the *boy's* clothes. The Possessive Case is the only noun-case in modern English which has a distinctive termination.

It is usually formed by adding *s* with an apostrophe before it ('*s*) to the Nominative ; e.g. John's, men's.

If the Nominative singular or Nominative plural end in a sibilant, the Possessive Case is indicated by the mere addition of the apostrophe, e.g. the *boys'* clothes : the *girls'* bonnets ; *Moses'* rod ; for *conscience'* sake ; for *righteousness'* sake ; *Felix'* room ; *Phœbus'* fire ; *Lycurgus'* laws. Milton writes ' for *intermission* sake.' The modern tendency is to use *s*, as well as the apostrophe, after Proper Nouns ending in a sibilant. Thus we say ' St. James's Church,' ' Chambers's Journal,' ' Bass's Ale.'

In O.E. the Possessive Case was expressed in the singular by the termination *es*, which was pronounced as a separate syllable. The apostrophe (from Greek *apo*, away, and *strophe*, a turning) stands for the omitted vowel. Even in Shakspere the vowel is occasionally sounded, e.g.—

> ' To show his teeth as white as whalës bone.'

The use of the apostrophe is comparatively modern, and is somewhat inconsistently restricted to the possessive case, as there has been a similar elision of the vowel in the *plural* of many nouns in which the apostrophe is not used ; e.g. the plural ' smiths ' is a contraction of ' smith*as*,' the plural ' days ' of ' dag*as*.' In the ' Spectator ' we find the apostrophe used in writing plurals, e.g. ' Purcell's opera's,' ' the making of grotto's,' but the practice has been abandoned except in forming the plurals of particles and of letters used as nouns ; e.g. ' There are too many who's in the sentence,' ' Dot your i's and cross your t's.'

It was absurdly supposed by some of the old grammarians that the ending of the possessive case was a corruption of the pronoun *his.* Unfortunately for this theory, *his* is itself the possessive case of *he* or *hit* (it), and the *s* in it would still have to be accounted for. Moreover, the theory would clearly not account for the possessive case of feminine and plural nouns. 'Jane's child' could not be 'Jane his child;' nor could 'the men's swords' be 'the men his swords.'

In accordance with the theory we find in the Prayer Book 'Jesus Christ *His* sake;' and in the Bible (Ed. 1611), 'Asa *his* heart,' 1 Kings xv. 14; 'Mordecai *his* matters,' Esth. iii. 4; 'By Naomi *her* instruction Ruth lieth at Boaz *his* feet,' heading to Ruth iii.

In the case of a compound noun the apostrophe is always appended to the last noun, e.g. 'the Lord Chancellor's wig,' 'the Lord Admiral's ship;' the two nouns being regarded as forming only one compound noun. When two nouns are in apposition, i.e. when one is used to define the other more closely, we generally place the sign of the possessive case after each, e.g. 'Smith's, the bookseller's.'

In modern English the possessive case is chiefly used with reference to living things, e.g. John's hand, the bird's wing, the horse's tail. In speaking of inanimate things we generally employ the preposition *of* instead of the usual case-ending. Thus we say 'the weight of the stone,' not 'the stone's weight.'

25. The **Objective Case** is that form which a noun or pronoun takes when it is the Direct or Indirect Object in a sentence. (See § 22.) In English grammar nouns are said to be in the Objective Case, even when they have no distinct *form* to express it, if they stand in an *objective relation* to the other words of the sentence.

The word [1] used to express the Direct Object is sometimes called the Accusative Case. The origin of this term, which is borrowed from Latin Grammar, is not clear. Dr. Abbott conjectures that 'possibly the Romans regarded the

---

[1] In consequence of the loss of distinctive forms for the Objective Case of nouns, we are now compelled to depend very much upon *position* to indicate the objective relation. In Latin the words, *pater filium amat* (the father loves the son), would convey the same meaning, in whatever order the words were arranged, the form of *pater* showing that it is the Subject of the sentence, the form of *filium* showing that it is the Direct Object of the sentence. But in the corresponding English sentence, 'The father loves the son,' we are left to infer that 'son' is the Direct Object from its position *after* the verb. We could not alter the order of the words without producing ambiguity. Cp. 'The father the son loves,' 'The son the father loves.'

object as being in front of the agent, like an *accused* person confronted with the prosecutor.'

The Indirect Object is sometimes called the Dative Case (i.e. the Giving Case, from Lat. do, datum, *I give*, being mainly used after verbs of *giving*).

Some O.E. nouns had a form distinct from the Nom. for the Dir. Obj.; still more had a distinct form for the Ind. Obj. Thus the acc. of *steorra*, a star, was *steorran*; of *wylen*, a female slave, was *wylne*; of *gifu*, a gift, was *gife* or *gifu*. The dat. of *leáf*, a leaf, was *leáfe*; of *smith*, a smith, was *smithe*. In modern English the Object, whether Direct or Indirect, takes, if a noun, the same form as the nominative. Compare—

> The *boy* cried (Nom.).
> I heard the *boy* (Direct Obj.).
> I gave it to the *boy* (Indirect Obj.).

English pronouns have distinct forms for the Nominative and Objective Cases, but not for the Direct and Indirect Objects. Compare—

> *I* saw James (Nom.).
> James saw *me* (Direct Obj.).
> He gave it to *me* (Indirect Obj.).

In order to determine whether a noun is in the Nominative or Objective Case we have to consider the construction of the sentence. If the noun be the Subject of the sentence, no matter whether the verb that follows be in the Active or Passive Voice, it is said to be in the Nominative Case. It is a mistake to say that the Nominative Case is used to denote the doer of the action. In the sentence 'John was beaten,' 'John' is in the Nominative Case; John was not the beater; he was beaten.

26. The **Direct Object** is governed by a *transitive verb*. To find it out in a sentence, put *whom* or *what* before the verb, and the answer will reveal it. Thus, in the sentences 'I struck John,' 'He praised the book,' the answers to the questions 'Whom did I strike?' 'What did he praise?' viz. *John* and *book*, are the Direct Objects.

27. The **Indirect Object** usually follows the preposition *to* or *for*, expressed or understood, e.g. 'Give the book to *William*;' 'Give *William* the book;' 'This book is for *you*;' 'Tell *me* a story;' 'He wrote *me* a letter.'

As a rule the Subject of a sentence precedes the verb, but in interrogative, imperative, and rhetorical constructions it frequently follows it, e.g.—

O wherefore come *ye* forth ?—*Macaulay*.
Be *thou* faithful.—*Bible*.
' Where,' said *he*, ' are you going ? '
Still is the toiling *hand* of Care.— *Gray*.
Great is *Diana* of the Ephesians.—*Bible*.
Few and short were the *prayers* we said.— *Wolfe*.

After the introductory adverb '*there*' the Subject nearly always follows the verb—

There was no *room*.

In interrogative and rhetorical constructions the Objective Case often precedes the verb or preposition which governs it.

Jesus I know, and *Paul* I know.—*Bible*.
Whom did you see ?
Whom did you give it to ?

In what are called adjective clauses (see § 127) the Objective Case *always* precedes the *verb*, but may precede or follow the *preposition*.

This is the book *which* you sought.
This is the book *in which* I was reading.
This is the book *which* we were reading *in*.

Grammarians sometimes distinguish other objects ; but, clearly, no other objects can be co-ordinate with the Direct and Indirect Object. Every object must of necessity be either Direct or Indirect. Under the head of Direct Objects should also be included—

1. *The Reflexive Object*, an Object referring to the same person or thing as the Subject of the sentence, e.g.—

I injured *myself*.
Turn *thee*, O Lord.—*Bible*.
He who hath bent *him* o'er the dead.—*Byron*.

2. *The Cognate Object* (from Lat. *co*, together ; *gnatus*, born), an Object akin in meaning with the verb, which is generally intransitive, e.g.—

I have fought a good *fight*.—*Bible*.
He slept a refreshing *sleep*.
He ran a *race*.

Under the head of Indirect Objects should also be included—

1. *The Factitive Object*, a secondary object used with a Direct Object, or with the Subject of a verb in the Passive Voice, after verbs of *making, creating, appointing, thinking, believing, supposing,* &c. It is so called because *make* (Lat. *facio*) is a type of the class of verbs which are used in this construction—

We made John (Dir. Obj.) our *leader* (Fac. Obj.).
The king created him a *peer* (Fac. Obj.).
We thought the gardener (Dir. Obj.) a capable *man* (Fac. Obj.).

The verb ' to be ' is sometimes used to connect the Direct Object with the Factitive Object.

2. The Adverbial Object, an object used to express *time, space, weight, price, age,* &c.—

He walked two *hours* every *day* last *week* (Time).
He never stirred an *inch* (Space).
It weighed five *pounds* (Weight).
It was worth *sixpence* (Value).
He was six *years* old (Age).

The government of these objects is sometimes explained by supplying a preposition before them, but no preposition was used before them in O.E., and no preposition is needed to explain their government now. The relations of *time, space,* &c., were expressed in O.E. by various oblique cases that were not governed by verb or preposition, but were simply demanded by the idiom of the language. Cp. the 'accusative of time and space,' the 'ablative of measure, time, and place,' &c., in Latin.

Nouns and pronouns attached to other nouns or pronouns, and denoting the same person or thing, are said to be in **apposition** (Lat. *ad*, near ; *pono*, I place) with the word which they limit.

Did you know Turner, the *painter ?* (Dir. Obj. in apposition with ' Turner ').
He called at Smith's, the *grocer's* (Poss. in apposition with ' Smith's ').
Jones, the *head-boy*, got the prize (Nom. in apposition with ' Jones ').
I gave it to John, the *waiter* (Ind. Obj. in apposition with ' John ').

Nouns are also used in apposition after **copulative verbs** (Lat. *copula*, a link), as *be, become, grow* (intrans.), *turn* (intrans.), *turn out* (intrans.), *prove* (intrans.), *continue* (intrans.), *remain.*

He was a *sailor.*
He became a *merchant.*
He continued a *soldier.*
He proved a bad *fellow.*

28. In O.E. there were five cases, the Nominative, Possessive, Dative, Accusative, and Ablative. No English noun possessed a distinctive form for each case. The Nominative and Accusative of some nouns were alike ; the Dative and Ablative of other nouns were alike. Most of the old case-endings were lost in the three centuries which followed the Norman conquest. The declensions of two old nouns are subjoined by way of illustration—

Singular.

Nom.	smith	steorr-a (a star)
Poss.	smith-es	steorr-an
Dat.	smith-e	steorr-an
Acc.	smith	steorr-an
Abl.	smith-e	steorr-an

Plural.

Nom.	smith-as	steorr-an
Poss.	smith-a	steorr-ena
Dat.	smith-um	steorr-um
Acc.	smith-as	steorr-an
Abl.	smith-um	steorr-um

It will be observed that all the case-endings of ' steorra ' have disappeared, and that the possessive singular and the nominative and accusative plural, the only surviving case-endings of ' smith,' are contracted.

Lady-day (i.e. our Lady's day), lady-bird (our Lady's bird), Sunday (O.E. Sunnan-dæg, i.e. Sun's day), Monday (O.E. Mónan-dæg, i.e. Moon's day), Friday (O.E. Frige-dæg, i.e. Friga's day), contain old possessives. The poss. of *hlǽfdige* was *hlǽfdigan*; of *sunne, sunnan*; of *móna, mónan*. The *s* in Tuesday (Tiwes dæg), in Wednesday (Wodnes dæg), and in Thursday (Thunores dæg = the thunderer's day), is a remnant of the old possessive. So is it in *daisy* (day's eye), *monkshood, bridesmaid,* and in many names of places, as *Wansborough* (Woden's borough). In *huntsman, bondsman, oarsman,* &c., the *s* appears to be euphonic. In Witenagemote (the meeting of the wise men), the termination *-ena* of the genitive plural is preserved. With *Lady-day* (properly Lady day) contrast *Lord's day.*

Exercises.

1. Pick out the Nominative Case in each of the following passages—

I saw John. John saw me. We heard the men talking. The book is on the table. We have had enough of action. Where is John's book? My son John is at school. Mary, go and call the cattle home. The butcher weighed the meat. The meat weighed six pounds. John is now a man, six foot high.

a. There was no leaf upon the forest bare.

b. Round the cape of a sudden came the sea.—*Browning.*

c. Uneasy lies the head that wears a crown.—*Shakspere.*

d.   Thy joys no glittering female meets,
         No hive hast thou of hoarded sweets —*Grey.*

c.   The love where Death hath set his seal
       Nor age can chill, nor rival steal,
       Nor falsehood disavow.—*Byron.*

2. Pick out the nouns in the Objective Case—

a.   Now fades the glimmering landscape on the sight,
       And all the air a solemn stillness holds,
       Save where the beetle wheels his droning flight,
       And drowsy tinklings lull the distant folds.—*Gray.*

b.   His death, which happen'd in his berth,
       At forty odd befel;
       They went and told the sexton, and
       The sexton tolled the bell.—*Hood.*

c. Me this unchartered freedom tires.—*Wordsworth.*

d.   And when the sun begins to fling
       His flaring beams, me, goddess, bring
       To archèd walks of twilight groves,
       And shadows brown that Sylvan loves.—*Milton.*

e.   Behold where Dryden's less presumptuous car
       Wide o'er the fields of glory bear
       Two coursers of ethereal race
With necks in thunder clothed, and long-resounding pace.
                         Gray.

3. Distinguish between the Direct and Indirect Object in the following passages—

a. Tell John a story.

b. Grant your brother his request.

c. Heaven send the prince a better companion !—*Shakspere.*

d. Heaven send the companion a better prince !—*Id.*

e. Saddle me the ass.—*Bible.*

f. Villain, I say, knock me at this gate.—*Shakspere.*

g.   Give sorrow words; the grief that does not speak
       Whispers the o'er-fraught heart and bids it break.—*Id.*

4. State the case of each of the nouns in the following passages—

a.   Society, Friendship, and Love,
       Divinely bestowed upon man,
       O, had I the wings of a dove,
       How soon would I taste you again !—*Cowper.*

b. I wish our friends joy.

c.   There's a pang in all rejoicing,
       A joy in the heart of pain,
And the Wind that saddens, the Sea that gladdens,
       Are singing the self-same strain.—*B. Taylor.*

d. Were England united, we might defy the world.

e. Here rests his head upon the lap of earth.—*Gray*.

f. Cromwell, I charge thee, fling away ambition.—*Shakspere*.

g.   Where go the poet's lines?
      Answer, ye evening tapers;
    Ye, auburn locks, ye, golden curls,
      Speak from your folded papers.—*Holmes*.

h. That is the lord-high-admiral's ship.

i.   Like driftwood spars, which meet and pass
      Upon the boundless ocean plain,
    So on the sea of life, alas!
      Man meets man—meets and quits again.—*M. Arnold*.

k. Order gave each thing view.—*Shakspere*.

l. Out of this nettle, danger, we pluck this flower, safety.—*Id*.

5. Give instances of (*a*) the Factitive Object; (*b*) the Cognate Object; (*c*) the Adverbial Object.

6. What is meant by the Nominative Absolute? Give instances.

PARSING OF NOUNS.

29. The complete parsing of a noun should show

1. The part of speech to which it belongs;
2. Its inflexions in the sentence in which it occurs;
3. Its syntactical relations with other words in the sentence.

Case, with the exception of the Poss., is not, strictly speaking, an *inflexion* of modern English nouns, but is included with the inflexions in the subjoined scheme for convenience.

SPECIMEN.

And more true *joy Marcellus* exiled feels
Than *Cæsar* with a *senate* at his *heels*.

Word	Class	Inflexions	Syntactical Relations
joy	Noun, common	sing., neut., obj.	gov. by 'feels'
Marcellus	Noun, proper	sing., masc., nom.	subj. to 'feels'
Cæsar	Noun, proper	sing., masc., nom.	subj. to 'feels' understood
senate	Noun, common	sing., neut., obj.	gov. by 'with
heels	Noun, common	plur., neut., obj.	gov. by 'at'

Parse the nouns in the following passages—

a. Worth makes the man, and want of it the fellow.—*Pope.*

b. Let bygones be bygones.

c. Hypocrisy is the homage which vice pays to virtue.
Rochefoucauld.

d.   And raw in fields the rude militia swarms;
Mouths without hands; maintained at vast expense,
In peace a charge, in war a weak defence;
Stout once a month they march, a blustering band,
And ever, but in times of need, at hand.—*Dryden.*

e. As cold waters to a thirsty soul, so is good news from a far country. —*Bible.*

f. The Kembles were remarkable actors.

g.   Nobles and heralds, by your leave,
Here lies what once was Matthew Prior;
The son of Adam and of Eve,
Can Bourbon or Nassau claim higher?—*Prior.*

h. I think there be six Richmonds in the field.—*Shakspere.*

i.   Perhaps it may turn out a sang,
Perhaps turn out a sermon.—*Burns.*

k. For my voice, I have lost it with hollaing and singing of anthems.—*Shakspere.*

l. O, monstrous! but one halfpenny-worth of bread to this intolerable deal of sack!—*Id.*

m. Seeing is believing.

n. Diamond me no diamonds! prize me no prizes!—*Tennyson.*

o. Who ever knew truth put to the worse in a free and open encounter?—*Milton.*

p. He laughed a hearty laugh.

q. The being of God is a kind of law to His working.—*Hooker.*

r. Dreaming dreams no mortal ever dared to dream before.
Poe.

s. Ethics is the science of morals.

t. They sought Him among their kinsfolk and acquaintance.
Bible.

u. Virtue itself turns vice, being misapplied.—*Shakspere.*

v. There is much virtue in your ' If.'—*Id.*

w.   E'en while I speak the transient Now is past,
And death more near this sentence than the last.

x. I did not know the ins and outs of the place.

y. She moves a goddess, and she looks a queen.—*Pope's Homer.*

ADJECTIVES.

30. Adjectives are words joined to nouns—

1. To *describe* things, e.g. I have *good, old, red* wine.
2. To *point* out things, e.g. Put *this* wine on *that* table.
3. To express *number,* or *quantity,* or *order* in a series, e.g. Put *two* glasses and *some* wine on the *second* table.

In other words, adjectives are used to *qualify* or *limit* nouns. Some writers confine the term adjective to words that *qualify* the noun, i.e. to the first class enumerated above; but the name adjective (Lat. *adjectivus* = admitting of being added to something) is equally applicable to words that merely *limit* the noun, i.e. merely restrict its application.

31. Adjectives of Quality are used to describe a thing, and are said to qualify the noun that denotes the thing, e.g. The *old* tree is still standing. When forming part of the predicate the adjective may qualify a pronoun, e.g. He is *old*.

Beginners should be careful to distinguish between Concrete Nouns and Adjectives having the same form, e.g.—

White dazzles my eyes (Concrete Noun).
The *white* chalk dazzles my eyes (Adj.).

They should also be careful not to speak of adjectives as denoting the qualities of *nouns*. Adjectives denote the qualities of the *things* designated by nouns.

Some writers are very fond of using adjectives as Abstract Nouns. Thus they speak of 'the Beautiful,' 'the True,' 'the Sublime,' and so forth.

Adjectives are also often used in the place of Concrete Nouns, e.g. The rich (i.e. rich persons) should not forget the poor (i.e. poor persons).

32. When an adjective, standing either before or after a noun, forms with it a kind of compound name, it is said to qualify the noun **attributively,** e.g.—

A *blue* sky. The *white* rose. A *happy* day.
At length a *universal* hubbub *wild.—Milton.*
Or flocks or herds or *human* face *divine.— Id.*
Full many a gem of *purest* ray *serene.—Gray*

D

As a rule adjectives used attributively *precede* the noun
which they qualify, but, as may be seen from the previous
examples, they may also follow it.

33. When an adjective is used without a following noun
to form part of the predicate of a sentence, it is said to
qualify its noun or pronoun **predicatively,** e.g.—

> The way was *long,* the wind was *cold,*
> The minstrel was *infirm* and *old.—Scott.*

> *Happy* the man, and *happy* he alone,
> He who can call to-day his own.—*Dryden.*

Adjectives used predicatively usually follow the word
which they qualify, but may precede it.

Adjectives are often used predicatively after (*a*) verbs of seeming, (*b*) verbs relating to posture, (*c*) verbs denoting continuance :—

> *a.* He seemed *happy.*
> *b.* He stood *silent.*
> *c.* He remained *rich.*   (See SYNTAX.)

Note the difference between ' He looked *cold* ' and ' He looked
coldly.'

34. An adjective is sometimes used to supplement verbs
of making and thinking, as *make, create, render, think, believe, call, deem, suppose, consider.*

> He made us *happy.*
> We thought him *clever.*
> He was rendered *miserable.*

The adjective in this construction is said to qualify the
word to which it is attached **factitively** (from Lat. *facio,* I
make). Dr. Abbott would regard such combinations as
' made-happy' and ' thought-clever' as compound verbs.

Some adjectives can be used predicatively but not attributively, e.g. *alone, well, afraid, unwell, aware, athirst.*

The learner should carefully distinguish between adjectives and
adverbs that are alike in form. Cp. ' a *long* pole ' with ' he lived
long ;' ' a *fast* runner ' with ' he ran *fast.*' These adverbs formerly
ended in -*e,* but the *e* has been dropped, and now they can be recognised only by considering their function.

35. Adjectives of Quantity express number and quantity, and are said to *limit* the nouns to which they are joined.
They include—

I. Definite Numerals—

    a. **Cardinal,** e.g. one, two, three, four, dozen, &c. Cardinal numerals are so called from the Lat. *cardo,* a hinge, because they are the most important, the others being for the most part formed from them. Thus, *three* gives *third ; four, fourth ;* &c.

    One. O.E. *an.* Cognate with Lat. *unus* and Germ. *ein.* The indefinite article *an,* of which *a* is a contraction, retains the original form of *one,* but, except in a few instances, has lost the force of a numeral. Comp.—

    ' Two *a* penny,' i.e. two for one penny.
    ' All of *a* size,' i.e. of one size.
    ' They are both of *a* tale,' i.e. they tell one story.—*Shakspere.*
    ' Two of *a trade* can never agree.'
    ' A' things hae *an* end (i.e. one end), an a pudding has twa.'
                         Scotch proverb.

    ' *Ae* ha'f o' the warld kens na how the ither ha'f lives.'—*Id.*

    Two. O.E. *twá,* fem. and neut. of the masculine form *trégen.* Whence our word *twain.* Cp. *twin, between.*
    Three. O.E. *thrý,* masc.; *threó,* fem. and neut.
    Four. O.E. *feower.*
    Fire. O.E. *fíf ;* originally contained an *n.* Cp. Ger. *fünf,* Lat. *quinque,* Gr. *pente.*
    Six. O.E. *sex.* Cp. Lat. *sex,* Ger. *sechs.*
    Seven. O.E. *seofon.* Cp. Lat. *septem,* Ger. *sieben.*
    Eight. O.E. *eahta.* Cp. Lat. *octo,* Ger. *acht,* Fr. *huit,* Welsh *wyth* (pronounced *ooith*).
    Nine. O.E. *nigon.* Cp. Lat. *novem,* Ger. *neun.*
    Ten. O.E. *týn.* Cp. Goth. *taihun,* Ger. *zehn.* Ten has lost the guttural sound represented by the *h* in Gothic and German; but the lost sound reappears in twenty (O.E. *twentig*), i.e. two-ten.
    Eleven. O.E. *endleofan. End* = one, *leofan* = leave. Cp. Goth. *a'nlif.* Some suppose leofan represents some old root meaning ten. If this view be correct, *eleven* would correspond to the Lat. *undecim.*
    Twelve. O.E. *twelf. Twe* = two, *lf* = leofan. Cp. Goth. *tralif.* See *Eleven.*
    Dozen. Fr. *douzaine.* From *douze,* twelve. Lat. *duodecim.*
    Thirteen. The suffix *-teen* = ten.
    Twenty. See *Ten.*
    Score. O.E. *scéran,* to cut. Accounts were formerly kept by cutting notches in a stick called a *tally,* from the French *tailler,* to cut. Twenty was probably the number of notches which it was found convenient to cut on a single stick. Cp. ' Whereas before our forefathers had no other books but the *score* and the tally, thou hast caused printing to be used.'—*Hen. VI, Pt. II.*

Hundred. O.E. *hund.* Hund was originally prefixed to numerals from 70 to 120, e.g. *hund-seofontig*, seventy; *hund-eahtatig*, eighty; *hund-enlufontig*, a hundred and ten; *hund-twelftig*, a hundred and twenty. It would appear to have been a contraction of the Gothic *taihun*, ten; if so, the forms given above would mean ten times seven, ten times eight, &c. Wedgwood says that the termination *raed* in Old Swedish means a reckoning up to ten.

Thousand. O.E. *thúsend.* O.H.G. *zenstunt* (=probably *ten hundred*).

Million. Lat. *mille*, a thousand.

    b. **Fractional**, e.g. half, quarter, third, &c.

    c. **Multiplicatives.** These are formed in two ways, viz. (1) by the English suffix *-fold*, as an-fald (=one-fold, now obsolete), two-fold, &c.; and (2) out of Latin elements, e.g. simple (from *sim*=one, cp. *semel*, once, and *plico*, I fold); duplex, duple or double; triple, treble; quadruple; quintuple; &c.

    d. **Both.** O.E. *bá*, fem. and neut. of *bégen.* Later forms are *bátwá*, *bútú*=both, the two.

    e. **None** and **No.** Negative forms of *an* and *a* (one), e.g. 'none occasion' (now becoming obsolete), 'no hope.' Cp. mine and my.

When used without a following noun the Cardinal and Fractional Numerals should be parsed as Numeral Pronouns or Nouns. 'What! all my pretty *ones*' (*Shakspere*). 'They came in *twos* and *threes*.' 'A *half* is sometimes more than the *whole*.' 'Two *thirds* of the people were English.'

When used with Adjectives, Adverbs, and Prepositions, both definite and indefinite numerals may be employed adverbially; as 'half timidly,' 'half bold and half shy,' 'threefold greater abundance.'

       The slow wise smile that round about
         His dusty forehead drily curled,
       Seemed *half*-within and *half*-without,
         And full of dealings with the world.—*Tennyson.*

2. Indefinite Numerals.

    Any, all, few, little, less, least, enough, enow, many, much, more, most, several, divers, certain, whole, some.

Any. O.E. *ǽnig.* From *án*, one. E.g. 'any word,' 'any man.'

All. O.E. *eal.* The genitive plural of this word, *ealra*, survived in the form of *alder* as late as the 16th century. Shakspere writes alderliefest, i.e. dearest of all. For 'liefest' cp. 'I had as *lief.*' Ger. *lieb*, dear.

Few. O.E. *feáw* : e.g. 'few men.'

Little, less, least. 'Much cry and little wool.' Note the difference between the qualitative adjective little, the adjective of quantity, and the numeral pronoun. Cp.—

> *Little* boats should keep near the shore (Adj.).
> A *little* leaven leaveneth the whole lump (Num.).
> Here a *little* and there a *little* (Num. Pron.).
> A *little* more than a *little* is much too much (Num. Pron.).

Enough. O.E. *genoh.* *Enow* probably represents the old plural. Cp. 'meat *enough* and men *enow.*' Dr. Johnson says that 'enow' is the only plural form of an adjective surviving in English.

Many, much, more, most. O.E. *manig.*

Several. Lat. *separare*, to sever. E.g. 'several persons.' The primary meaning survives in the expression, 'a *several* house.'

Certain. Lat. *cerno*, I separate. Note the difference between the uses of this word in the following sentences: 'I am *certain* (=sure) he was here;' '*certain* men of our company.' In the former it is an adjective of quality, in the latter a demonstrative adjective.

Divers, from same source as *diverse*. It is used both with a singular and a plural noun; e.g.—

> A *divers* posture.—*Bacon.*

> *Divers* gentlemen.—*Shakspere.*

Whole. O.E. *hál*, healthy, entire. E.g. 'the *whole* number,' 'the *whole* city.'

Some. O.E. *sum.* E.g. 'I have *some* money.' In 'some eight or nine years ago,' *some* has the force of *about*.

All these indefinite numerals may be used pronominally, e.g.—

> *Any* of them will do.
> *All* is lost except honour.
> *Many* are called but *few* are chosen.—*Bible.*
> There's *little* to earn and *many* to keep.—*Kingsley*
> The *least* of them would suffice.
> *Enough* is as good as a feast.
> *Several* of them were good.
> *Divers* of them came from far.—*Bible.*
> For before that *certain* came from James.—*Ib.*
> I preserved the *whole* of it.

36. Demonstrative Adjectives are such as are used to point out, with greater or less precision, the things of which we are speaking, and include—

1. The so called definite article [1] 'the' (O.E. se, seó, thæt). The old definite article was inflected for gender, number, and case. The definite article is used—

a. To point out some particular thing referred to; e.g. it was said of a great statesman that he was never in want of *a* word; of his rival that he was never in want of *the* word; viz. the word which precisely expressed his meaning.

b. To point out that we are speaking of a whole species or class, e.g. '*the* lion,' '*the* ocean,' '*the* good,' 'there is but one step from *the* sublime to *the* ridiculous.'

In such constructions as the following, *the* represents thí, the old ablative of the article, e.g. '*the* more *the* merrier,' i.e. by how many more by so many merrier; '*the* rather.'

2. **Pronominal Adjectives,** i.e. words which may be used for a noun or to limit a noun. In virtue of the former power they are called pronominal; in virtue of the latter, adjective, e.g. *these* books, *each* day, *either* book, *any* boy, *my* tea, *some* food. These will be dealt with more fully hereafter. They may be classified as follows—

a. Demonstrative, this, these, that, those, such, same.
b. Distributive, each, every, either, neither.
c. Indefinite, other, some.
d. Possessive, my, thy, his, her, &c.
e. Interrogative, which, what.
f. Ordinal Numerals.

1. *Definite,* as first, second.
2. *Indefinite,* as next, previous, last, former, latter, every other, alternate.

---

[1] *Article,* Lat. *articulus,* a little joint. 'A name (*a*) correctly given by the Greeks to their "article" because it served as a joint uniting several words together; (*b*) then loosely used by the Latins (as was natural, seeing they had no "article") of any short word, whether verb, conjunction, or pronoun; (*c*) foolishly introduced into English, and once used to denote "the" and "a"'—Dr. Abbott, *How to Parse.*

It will be observed that when these words are followed by a noun they do not stand *for* that noun, but merely limit it. They are, therefore, clearly not *pronouns* in such constructions.

Exercises.

Classify the adjectives in the following passages—

a. When bad men combine, the good must associate; else they will fall, one by one, an unpitied sacrifice, in a contemptible struggle.
Burke.

b. Sweet day! so cool, so calm, so bright.—*Herbert.*

c.   For who, to dumb forgetfulness a prey,
    This pleasing anxious being e'er resigned,
    Left the warm precincts of the cheerful day,
    Nor cast one longing, lingering look behind ?—*Gray.*

d. My sentence is for open war.—*Milton.*

e. There's but a shirt and a half in all my company; and the half-shirt is but two napkins, tacked together and thrown over the shoulders like a herald's coat without sleeves.—*Shakspere.*

f. Three misbegotten knaves in Kendal green.—*Id.*

g. There be four of us here have ta'en a thousand pound this day morning. . . . I am a rogue if I were not at half-sword with a dozen of them two hours together. I have scaped by miracle. I am eight times thrust through the doublet; four through the hose.
Id.

h.   There were his young barbarians all at play,
    There was their Dacian mother—he, their sire,
    Butchered to make a Roman holiday.—*Byron.*

i.   Fresh as the first beam glittering on a sail,
    That brings our friends up from the underworld,
    Sad as the last which reddens over one
    That sinks with all we love below the verge;
    So sad, so fresh, the days that are no more.—*Tennyson.*

k. One sun by day—by night ten thousand shine.

l.   *Friend.*

Master Caperwit, before you read, pray tell me,
Have your verses any adjectives ?

Master Caperwit.

Adjectives ! would you have a poem without
Adjectives ? they are the flower, the grace of all our language
A well-chosen epithet doth give new soul
To fainting poesy, and makes every verse
A bride ! With adjectives we bait our lines
When we do fish for gentlewomen's loves.

And with their sweetness catch the nibbling ear
Of amorous ladies; with the music of
These ravishing nouns we charm the silken tribe,
And make the gallant melt with apprehension
Of the rare word.   I will maintain it against
A bundle of grammarians, in poetry
The substantive itself cannot subsist
Without its adjective.

Friend.

But, for all that,
Those words would sound more full, methinks, that are not
So larded; and, if I might counsel you,
You should compose a sonnet clean without them.
A row of stately substantives would march
Like Switzers, and bear all the field before them;
Carry their weight; show fair, like deeds enrolled;
Not writs that are first made and after filled.
Thence first came up the title of blank verse;—
You know, sir, what blank signifies?— where the sense,
First framed, is tied with adjectives like points,
And could not hold together without wedges:
Hang it, 'tis pedantic, vulgar poetry.
Let children, when they versify, stick here
And there these peddling words for want of matter.
Poets write masculine numbers.—*Shirley.*

COMPARISON OF ADJECTIVES.

37. Various objects may possess the same quality in different degrees.   Thus they may be all white, but one may be whiter than another, and one may be the whitest of them all.   To mark these different degrees the adjective which denotes the quality is inflected.

38. The simple form of the adjective is said to be of the **Positive Degree**, e.g. 'a *bright* day,' 'a *large* tree.'

That form of the adjective which is used to show that something possesses the quality denoted by the adjective in a higher or lower degree than something else, is said to be of the **Comparative Degree**, e.g. 'This tree is *larger* than that,' 'Choose the *less* evil.'

Some adjectives denoting qualities that do not admit of comparison are not compared.

Such are adjectives denoting—

a. Material, as golden, wooden.

b. Figure, as square, triangular.

c. Time, as monthly, annual.

d. Place, as European, insular.

e. Other qualities which exist only in the highest degree, e.g. extreme, top, bottom, perfect, eternal, perpetual, everlasting.

In some cases, however, these adjectives are no longer strictly used in their literal sense, and in such cases are often compared. Thus we have 'extremest,' 'more perfect,' &c.

That form of the adjective which is used to show that a thing possesses the quality denoted by the adjective in the highest or lowest degree, is said to be of the **Superlative Degree** (Lat. *super*, above; *latus*, carried), e.g. 'This is the *largest* tree,' 'Choose the *least* evil.'

39. Formation of the Comparative Degree.

1. By the addition of *-r* or *-er*, e.g. 'a wiser man,' 'a fairer scene.' If the positive degree end in *y*, the *y* is changed into *i* before the termination *-er*, e.g. holy, holier. If it end in a consonant preceded by a short vowel, the consonant is doubled, e.g. red, redder.

2. By placing the words *more* or *less* before the positive form; e.g. more extraordinary, less distinguishable.

As a rule the only adjectives that form their comparative degree with the help of 'more' are words of two or more syllables.

Some adjectives have the comparative form, but do not take *than* after them. They include—

1. Certain English adjectives, some of which would appear to be formed from prepositions, e.g. hinder, latter, nether, inner, utter, outer, &c.

2. Certain Latin adjectives which have been adopted in their comparative form, e.g. exterior, interior, junior, senior, major, minor.

40. Formation of the Superlative.

1. By the addition of *-st* or *-est* to the positive degree, e.g. 'the *wisest* man,' 'the *fairest* scene.'

2. By the suffix *-most*, e.g. 'the foremost,' 'the inmost,' 'the utmost.' This suffix is supposed to be compounded of two elements. In O.E. there were two superlative endings, viz. *-ema* and *-est* or *-ost*. The following are specimens of the former—

O.E.	O.E.
innema (*inmost*)	forma (*foremost*)
útema (*outmost*)	æftema (*aftermost*)
nithema (*nethermost*)	ufema (*uppermost*)
hindema (*hindmost*)	midema (*midmost*)

Compare the Latin superlatives extre*mus*, in*fimus*, supre*mus*, opt*umus* (old Latin), post*umus*.

It seems probable that the termination -*st* was added when the force of the old termination was lost. We find in O.E., in addition to the above, such forms as *innemest, ytemest, nithemest*, &c.

3. By placing the words *most* or *least* before the positive degree; e.g. most musical, most melancholy, least worthy.

Extreme and *supreme* are Latin superlatives, but are often used in English as of the positive degree.

41. Irregular Comparisons—

1. *By change of vowel*, as in old, elder, eldest.
2. *By contraction*, as in late, latter, last.
3. *By taking one degree from one root and another from another*, as good, better, best.
4. *By forming the comparative and superlative from adverbs or prepositions*, e.g. neath, nether, nethermost.

Late, latter (later), **last** (latest). The duplicate forms in the comparative and superlative degree have now distinct significations.

Old, elder (older), **eldest** (oldest). The distinctions between our use of 'older' and 'elder,' and of 'oldest' and 'eldest,' are very nice. Dean Alford says : ' We cannot say " Methuselah was the *eldest* man that ever lived ;" we must say, "the *oldest* man that ever lived." Again, it would hardly be natural to say "his father's oldest born," if we were speaking of the firstborn. If we were to say of a father, " He was succeeded by his oldest son," we should convey the impression that that son was not the *eldest*, but the oldest surviving after the loss of the eldest. And these examples seem to bring us to a kind of insight into the idiomatic difference. " Eldest " implies not only more years, but also priority of right [Qy. in *time*]; nay, it might sometimes even be independent of actual duration of life. A firstborn who died an infant was yet the *eldest* son. If all mankind were assembled, Methuselah would be the oldest, but Adam would be the eldest of men.'—*Queen's English*, p. 140. It may be added that we do not apply 'elder' and 'eldest' to things or places. We should not say of one of two cities that it was the *elder* of the two.

Nigh, nigher, nighest (next).
Near, nearer, nearest.

The positive form in O.E. was *neah*, so that our present positive form *near* is really a comparative, and *nearer* a double comparative. Cp.—

To kirke the *narre* (nearer)
From God the *farre* (farther).—*Old Proverb.*

The superlative *next* is contracted from *nighest*, the *gh* having been gutturalized. So 'highest' was contracted into *hext*. Cp.—

When bale is *hext*, boot is *next.—Old Proverb.*

i.e. when trouble is at its highest, then the remedy is nearest.

Rathe, rather, rathest. Of these forms *rathe* survives only in poetry; *rather* has ceased to be used as an adjective, and is now used as an adverb, but still in the sense of *sooner*; and *rathest* is obsolete; e.g.—

Twin buds too *rathe* to bear
The winter's unkind air.—*Coleridge.*

The men of *rathe* and riper years.—*Tennyson.*

Rathe-ripe fruit (i.e. early fruit).—*Suffolk dialect.*

His *rathere* wyf (i.e. his former wife).—*Robert of Gloster.*

Good, better (O.E. betera), **best** (betest). The root of *better* is O.E. *bót*, boot, remedy, compensation. Cp. O.E. *bet* (adv.), better; *bétan*, to make better. *Bet* is said to be still used in the sense of *good* in Herefordshire.

Bad, Evil, Ill—worse, worst. The origin of the positive form is obscure. *Bad* does not occur in O.E. *Worse* and *worst* are formed from O.E. *weor*, bad. The -*se* of the comparative = -*re*.

Much, Many—more, most. O.E. *micel, mára, mæst.* The root is *mag*-, great. *Micel* is a diminutive of *much*. *More* is now used both as an adjective and adverb. In O.E. *mára* was the comparative of the adjective, and *má* of the adverb.[1]

Little, less, least. O.E. *lytel, lœssa, lœsest, lœst.* The root is *lite.* Cp.—

Moche and lite (i.e. great and little).—*Chaucer.*

Little is a diminutive of *lite*. *Less* and *least* are from a root *las*, meaning *infirm*; they are, probably, cognate with *loose*, and with the suffix -*less*.

Far, farther, farthest. O.E. *feor, fyrra, fyrrest.* The *th* in *farther* has been inserted from a false analogy with the adverb *further*, which is the comparative of *forth*. The old comparative of *far* was *fyrra*, which subsequently was modified into *farre* and *farrer*. In the West of England people still speak of the 'narrer side' and the 'farrer side.' See quotation under 'Near.'

After, a comparative of *af* = *of*. Cp. *after*-math, *after*-thought.

First, a superlative of *fore*. The old superlative was *forma*, which appears in former and foremost.

---

[1] Cp. 'Gyf thar *mare* byth, thæt byth of yfele' (If there be more, that is of evil), Matt. v. 37. 'And hig thæs *the má* betweox him wundredon' (And they wondered at this the more among themselves), Mark vi. 51.

Hinder, comp. of *hind*.   Cp, 'the *hind* wheels.'
Inner, comp. of *in*.   Cp. 'the *Inner* Temple.'
Utter, comp. of *out*.   Cp. 'the *utter* bar.'
Nether, comp. of *neath*.   Cp. *beneath*, *nether*-stocks, *Netherlands*, *nether* lip.
Over, comp. of O.E. *ufan* = above.   Cp. '*Over* Leigh.'
Upper, comp. of *up*.

PARSING OF ADJECTIVES.

The *first* person I met said that he had seen *my two youngest* brothers.

Word	Class	Inflexions	Syntactical Relations	
first	Ord. Num.	Super. of *fore*	limiting	'person'
my	Poss. Adj.	1st per. sing.	,,	'brothers'
two	Card. Num.		,,	'brothers'
youngest	Qual. Adj.	Super. deg.	,,	'brothers'

Exercises.

Parse the adjectives in the following passages—

a. O, welcome pure-eyed Faith, white-handed Hope,
     Thou hovering angel, girt with golden wings.—*Milton.*

b. Is not old wine wholesomest, old pippins toothsomest, old wood burns brightest, old linen washes whitest? Old soldiers, sweetheart, are surest, and old lovers are soundest.— *Webster.*

c.   If parts allure thee, think how Bacon shined,
         The wisest, brightest, meanest of mankind.—*Pope.*

d. Small service is true service while it lasts.— *Wordsworth.*

e. The more we are the merrier.

f. Of two evils choose the less.

g. Bring the rathe primrose that forsaken dies.—*Milton.*

h. More matter with less art.—*Shakspere.* ·

i. The next day they came to Bath.

k. The ripest fruit first falls.—*Shakspere.*

l. That was the most unkindest cut of all.—*Id.*

m.   Sweet bird, that shunn'st the noise of folly,
         Most musical, most melancholy.—*Milton.*

n. And Caleb gave her the upper springs and the nether springs.
                                                        Bible.

o. And He will cause to come down for you the rain, the former rain and the latter rain in the first month.—*Ib.*

PRONOUNS.

42. Pronouns are words used instead of nouns or the equivalents of nouns. They differ from nouns in not being names; they resemble nouns in referring to persons or things. E.g. 'John told *me* that *he* would call for *us* before *we* went to see *them*.'

Pronouns enable us to avoid a tedious repetition of nouns, but they do much more than this. 'I,' for instance, not only stands for my name, but identifies me as the speaker. 'Thou' not only stands for the name of the person addressed, but points him out. 'He' not only stands for the name of the person spoken of, but also identifies him with some person previously referred to.

When pronouns are used to define or limit nouns, they clearly cease to be pronouns. In the sentence 'John brought *this* book,' 'this' does not stand *for* the noun 'book,' and is not a pronoun, but a demonstrative adjective. Such adjectives are called sometimes adjective pronouns and sometimes pronominal adjectives, but the learner should distinctly understand that, though they are pronominal in origin, they are not pronominal in function, and that it is function alone which determines the part of speech to which a word belongs.

As pronouns may be used instead of the equivalents of nouns, it follows that they may be used instead of—

1. An adjective used as a noun, e.g. 'The *good* are happy, but *they* are not always successful.'
2. A numeral, e.g. 'The first *three* won prizes, and *they* richly deserved them.'
3. A verbal noun, e.g. 'He was fond of *fishing*, and *it* agreed with his health.'
4. A gerundial infinitive, e.g. '*It* is pardonable *to err.*'
5. A noun sentence, e.g. 'That two and two are four is indisputable, and no one will deny *it*.'

Pronouns are divided into: 1. Personal, 2. Demonstrative, 3. Possessive, 4. Emphatic, 5. Reflexive, 6. Relative, 7. Interrogative, 8. Distributive, 9. Reciprocal, 10. Quantitative, 11. Numeral, 12. Indefinite.

Exercises.

1. Point out the pronouns in the following passages—
2. I come to bury Cæsar, not to praise him.—*Shakspere.*

b.
>All the world's a stage,
>And all the men and women merely players;
>They have their exits and their entrances;
>And one man in his time plays many parts,
>His acts being seven ages.—*Shakspere.*

c. I myself saw him.

d. They loved each other warmly.

e. Some one said that I gave each of them something.

f. Which of the three did he give to the boy who hurt himself?

2. What do the pronouns in the following passages stand for?—

a.
>For of all sad words of tongue or pen,
>The saddest are these: 'It might have been.'—*Whittier.*

b.
>That I have ta'en away this old man's daughter
>It is most true; true, I have married her.—*Shakspere.*

c.
>How sharper than a serpent's tooth it is
>To have a thankless child.—*Id.*

d. To be or not to be: that is the question.—*Id.*

e. That he is mad, 'tis true.—*Id.*

f.
>He that lacks time to mourn, lacks time to mend.
>Eternity mourns that. 'Tis an ill cure
>For life's worst ills, to have no time to feel them.—*Taylor.*

PERSONAL PRONOUNS.

43. Personal Pronouns are used to denote

1. The person speaking (the First Person);
2. The person spoken to (the Second Person);
3. The person spoken of (the Third Person).

There is one important difference between pronouns of the first and second person and pronouns of the third: the former have no inflexion for gender, there being no necessity to indicate the sex of the person speaking and the person spoken to; the latter, however, are inflected for gender, and, in this respect, resemble the demonstratives. Some grammarians classify personal pronouns of the third person with the demonstratives.

44.   INFLEXION OF PERSONAL PRONOUNS.

Case	First Person		Second Person		Third Person	
	Sing.	Plur.	Sing.	Plur.	Sing.	Plur.
Nom.	I	We	Thou	Ye *or* you	He She It	They
Poss.	My	Our	Thy	Your	His Her Its	Their
Obj.	Me	Us	Thee	You	Him Her It	Them

I originally ended in *c* or *ch*, of which traces long survived in provincial English. Comp. ''*Ch*'ill pick your teeth, Zir.' [A speech put into the mouth of Edgar, who has assumed the character of a Somersetshire peasant, in 'King Lear.'] ''*Ch* was bore at Taunton Dean; where should I be bore else?' (*Somersetshire proverb*.) Cp. Lat. *ego*, Ger. *ich*.

My (O.E. *mín*), **thy** (O.E. *thín*), **our** (O.E. *úre*), and **your** (O.E. *eower*) are not now used as personal pronouns but as demonstrative adjectives, i.e. they cannot stand by themselves, but require to be followed by the noun which they limit. They were, however, originally used as personal pronouns. They should be carefully distinguished from the corresponding possessive pronouns, *mine, thine, ours, yours*, which not only can be used without a following noun, but can themselves be used in the Nominative or Objective case, e.g. '*Mine* is *thine*;' 'You take *mine*, and I will take *yours*.'

Before a vowel and the aspirate the older forms *mine* and *thine* are still used in poetry in preference to *my* and *thy*. Comp. *an* and *a*; *none* and *no*. The learner should be careful to observe that *mine* is not formed from *my*, but *my* from *mine*.

Me (O.E. *mé*) is used both as a Direct Object, e.g. 'He struck *me*,' and as an Indirect Object, e.g. 'He gave *me* the book.' It is as an Indirect Object that it is used with the impersonal verbs, e.g. *Methinks* [i.e. it seems to me, from O.E. *thincan*, to seem, not from *thencan*, to think], and after certain interjections, e.g. 'Woe is *me*.'

We (O.E. *we*). Comp. Ger. *wir*.

Us (O.E. *us*). Used both as a Direct and Indirect Object, e.g. 'He trusted *us*' (Dir.); 'He gave *us* some food' (Ind.).

Thou (O.E. *thú*). This pronoun is now rarely used except in poetical and elevated language. Its old use will be best illustrated by the following passage from Fuller: 'We maintain that *thou* from superiors to inferiors is proper as a sign of command; from equals to equals is passable as a note of familiarity; but from inferiors to superiors, if proceeding from ignorance, hath a smack of clownishness; if from affectation, a tone of contempt.' Comp.—

If thou *thou'st*[1] him some thrice, it shall not be amiss.
Shakspere.

All that Lord Cobham did was at *thy* instigation, *thou* viper! for I *thou* thee, *thou* traitor.—(*Lord Coke*, addressing Raleigh.)

Prithee don't *thee and thou* me; I believe I am as good a man as yourself.—*Miller of Mansfield.*

You began to be substituted for *thou* in the 13th century.

Thee (O.E. *thé*) is used both as a Direct and Indirect Object, e.g. 'I love *thee*;' 'I gave *thee* my word.'

Ye (O.E. *ge*, probably pronounced *ye*—comp. y-clept, i.e. ge-clept, called) was exclusively used formerly as the Nominative Case, but

---

[1] Comp. the use of the French verb *tutoyer*, i.e. to use *tu* and *toi* in speaking to a person.

is now so used only in elevated language, having been superseded by the objective form *you*, e.g. 'I know *you* not whence *ye* are' (*Bible*); '*Ye* have not chosen me, but I have chosen *you*' (*Ib.*) Shakspere, however, occasionally reverses the pronouns, e.g. 'I do beseech *ye*, if *you* bear me hard.' By Milton's time the two pronouns had become hopelessly confused.

> I call *ye* and declare *ye* now, returned
> Successful beyond hope to lead *ye* forth.—*Milton.*

You (O.E. *eow*) is now used—

    1. As a nominative plural of courtesy, e.g. 'How are *you*, sir?'
    2. As a real Nominative plural, e.g. '*You* were there, boys.'
    3. As a Direct Obj., e.g. 'I know *you*.'
    4. As an Indirect Obj., e.g. 'I give *you* my word.'

He (O.E. *he*) is often corrupted in Middle English and in modern provincial into *a*, e.g. 'Quoth *a*,' i.e. quoth he.

> And then my husband—God be with his soul!
> '*A* was a merry man—took up the child.—*Shakspere.*

> And I thowt *a* said what *a* owt to 'a said an I comed awääy.
>   *Tennyson.*

Him (O.E. *him*) was originally the Dative of 'he.' For the dative suffix -m compare who-m, whil-om, seld-om. The old Accusative was *hine*, which had entirely disappeared even as early as the 14th century. Cp. Ger. *ihm* (Dat.), *ihn* (Acc.).

His (O.E. *hise*) is a true possessive formed from he. Comp. Devonshire 'bees.' It may be used either adjectivally or pronominally, e.g. 'This is *his* book;' '*His* is better than yours.'

She (O.E. *seó*, the feminine definite article). The old feminine personal pronoun was *heo*, which survives as *hoo* in the Lancashire dialect. Comp.

> Eawr Marget declares, had *hoo* clooas to put on,
> *Hoo*'d goo up to Lunnon an' talk to th' greet mon,
> An' if things were na awtered when there *hoo* had been,
> *Hoo*'s fully resolved t' sew up meawth an' eend;
>   *Hoo*'s neawt to say again t' king,
>   But *hoo* loikes a fair thing,
> An' *hoo* says *hoo* can tell when *hoo*'s hurt.—*Mrs. Gaskell.*

Her in modern English represents—

    1. The O.E. *hire* (Poss.), e.g. I have *her* book.
    2. The O.E. *hire* (Dat.), e.g. I gave *her* a book.
    3. The O.E. *hi* (Acc.), e.g. I saw *her*.

It (O.E. *hit*). The suffix -t was a neuter suffix. Comp. tha*t*, wha*t*.

Its (O.E. *his*) is a comparatively modern word. It does not occur once in the Authorized Version of the Bible (1611); though in some modern editions it has crept into Lev. xxv. 5, where the true reading is 'it.' See below. Comp.

> 'If the salt have lost *his* savour.'
> 'The fruit-tree yielding fruit after *his* kind.'

'Its' occurs once in Shakspere's 'Measure for Measure,' i. 2, and frequently in 'The Winter's Tale.' Bacon never uses the word. Milton uses it twice at least, e.g. 'The mind is *its* own place.' By Dryden's time (1631–1700) the word had become thoroughly naturalized. Commenting on the following line in Ben Jonson's 'Catiline,' 'Though heaven should speak with all *his* wrath at once,' he says, '*Heaven* is ill syntax with *his*.'

In Middle English, and still in the English of the north-western counties, we find *it* used as a possessive, e.g.—

> The hedge-sparrow fed the cuckoo so long,
> That it's had *it* head bit off by *it* young.—*King Lear.*

Go to *it* grandame, child . . . *it* grandame will give it a plum.
>
> *K. John.*

Even now we write it-self, not its-self. See Trench's 'English Past and Present,' and Craik's 'Julius Cæsar.'

They (O.E. *thá*), **Their** (O.E. *thára*), **Them** (O.E. *thám*) were respectively the Nom., Poss., and Dat. plurals of the old definite article. The plurals of the old third personal pronoun were: Nom. *hí*, Poss. *hira*, Dat. *him*, Acc. *hí*.

PARSING OF PERSONAL PRONOUNS.

45. '*He* and *I* saw *you* pointing at *us*.'

Word	Class	Inflexions	Syntactical Relations
he	Pron., personal	3rd per., sing., nom.	subj. to 'saw'
I	„ „	1st per., sing., nom.	„
you	„ „	2nd per., plu., obj.	gov. by 'saw'
us	„ „	1st per., plu., obj.	gov. by 'at'

Exercises.

1. Parse the personal pronouns in the following passages—

a. O pardon me, thou bleeding piece of earth,
That I am meek and gentle with these butchers.—*Shakspere.*

b. O thou invisible spirit of wine, if thou hast no name to be known by, let us call thee devil.—*Id.*

E

c. The ox knoweth his owner, and the ass his master's crib.
Bible.

d. They are like the deaf adder that stoppeth her ear.—*Ib.*

e. In their death they were not divided.—*Ib.*

f. His nose was as sharp as a pen, and 'a babbled of green fields.
Shakspere.

g. That my hand may be restored me again.—*Bible.*

h. Lend not unto him that is mightier than thyself; for if thou lend him, count it but lost.—*Ib.*

i. I told him to give it you.

2. Give examples in which 'him,' 'her,' 'us,' 'them,' and 'you' are used: *a.* As Direct Objects ; *b.* As Indirect Objects.

EMPHATIC PRONOUNS.

46. The Emphatic Pronouns are compounded of some part of the personal pronouns and the word *self* (O.E. silf), e.g. myself, thyself, himself, ourselves, yourselves, themselves. They are generally used in apposition, but may be used independently, e.g. ' He *himself* promised to do it ;' ' We *ourselves* are to blame.'

Himself hasted to go out.—*Bible.*

We should expect, following the analogy of myself, thyself, &c., that in the third person we should find his-self and their-selves ; but *himself* and *themselves* are used both as Nominatives and Objectives.

47. The Emphatic Pronouns are similar in form to the Compound Reflexive Pronouns ; they should not, however, be confounded with them. Compare the use of *se* (Reflexive) and *ipse* (Emphatic) in Latin.

The Possessive Case of the Emphatic Pronouns is formed with the help of *own* (past part. of owe), e.g. my own, thy own, &c.

Self was originally an adjective, meaning *same*, its plural being *sylfe.* In process of time it came to be used substantively, and then formed its plural in -*res.* Shakspere used it as a noun, e.g. 'my single self.' Cp. 'one's self,' 'a man's self.'

It is thought by some that *my, thy,* &c., in the compounds *myself, thyself,* &c., are corruptions of the datives me and *thee.* Certain it is that in O.E. we find such combinations as *ic me silf* = I myself, *thù the silf* = thou thyself, &c. The Irish, who have retained many archaic forms that were taken over to their country by Strongbow and his successors, invariably say *me*-self. Comp. moi-même, toi-même, &c., in French.

REFLEXIVE PRONOUNS.

48. Reflexive Pronouns are used, with certain verbs, to show that the action denoted by the verb is, as it were, reflected or bent back upon the agent, e.g. 'He washed *himself.*' They are either **simple**, as me, thee, him, &c.:

> I gat *me* to my Lord right humbly.—*Bible.*
> I'll lay *me* down and dee.—*Scotch Ballad.*
> He sat *him* down at a pillar's base.—*Byron.*

or **compound**, as myself, thyself, &c., e.g.—

> You wronged *yourself* to write in such a case.—*Shakspere.*
> Thou shalt love thy neighbour as *thyself.*—*Bible.*

RECIPROCAL PRONOUNS.

49. Reciprocal Pronouns denote a mutual relationship or reciprocity of action, e.g. 'They are related to *each other*,' 'They love *each other*,' 'Little children, love *one another*.'
Each other is used with regard to two things;
One another with regard to more than two: e.g.—

> John and James love each other.
> We should all love one another.

If these compound forms be decomposed, it will be found that *each* and *one* are in apposition with the subject, and that *other* and *another* are objectives. Thus the foregoing examples mean respectively,

> John and James love, each [loving] the other.
> We should all love, one [loving] another.

Prepositions are used before the compound form, but govern only the second element in it, viz. *other* and *another*: e.g. 'They ran after one another' = 'they ran one after another.'

POSSESSIVE PRONOUNS.

50. Possessive Pronouns differ from possessive cases[1] of the personal pronouns in form and construction. The latter can only be used with some following noun; the possessive pronouns can be used alone and have cases of their own.

[1] These cases are clearly adjectival, being never used alone. We cannot say 'This is *my*' or 'This is *thy*.'

E 2

Compare '*my* hat,' '*your* horse,' with 'this is *mine*, that is *yours*.' The Possessive Pronouns are *mine, thine, his, hers, ours, yours, theirs*. It should be observed that the possessive pronouns discharge a double function: they stand for the name of the possessor and of the thing possessed. Hence they have a twofold 'person.' So far as they stand for *persons*, they are of the same grammatical person as the pronouns from which they are formed. So far as they stand for *things*, they are invariably of the third person. In the sentence 'mine is good,' mine is etymologically of the first person, syntactically, as is clear from the verb, of the third.

Ours, yours, theirs, and *hers* are double possessives, the r being part of the old plural possessive suffix, and the *s* being part of the singular possessive suffix. They are not found in O.E.

DEMONSTRATIVE PRONOUNS.

51. Demonstratives are used to point out the things to which they refer. When used with a noun following, they should be called **Demonstrative Adjectives**, e.g. '*This* book belongs to *that* shelf;' when used independently, they should be called **Demonstrative Pronouns**, e.g. '*This* is mine; *that* is yours.'

The demonstrative pronouns are *this, that, such, same, the* before comparatives in such constructions as 'the taller the better,' *yon, yonder.*

This (O.E. mas. *thes*, fem. *theôs*, neu. *this*) and its plural **these** (O.E. *thás*) refer to objects near the speaker, or to the latter of two things mentioned, e.g. 'This tree (one near the speaker) is larger than *that*.'

> Some place their bliss in action, some in ease;
> *Those* call it pleasure, and contentment *these.—Pope.*

> Self-love, the spring of motion, acts the soul;
> Reason's comparing balance rules the whole;
> Man, but for *that*, no action could attend;
> And, but for *this*, were active to no end.—*Id.*

That (O.E. *that*) and its plural **those** (O.E. *thás*) refer to objects at some distance from the speaker, or to the former of two things mentioned. See the quotations under 'This.' Hence *this* and *these* may be called the **Proximate Demonstratives**; *that* and *those* the **Remote Demonstratives**.

Such (O.E. *swilc*) is a compound of *swá*=so and *líc*=like.

Comp. *thilk*=the like. It may be called the **Demonstrative of Comparison**, e.g.—

> *Such* as go down to the sea.—*Bible.*
>
> Let me have men about me that are fat;
> Sleek-headed men and *such* as sleep o' nights.—*Shaksperc.*
>
> *Such* were the notes thy once loved poet sung.—*Pope*

When followed by a noun, *such* is a *demonstrative adjective*. Before a singular noun it is often followed by *a* : e.g.

> In *such* a night as this.—*Shakspere.*

The ordinary correlative of the demonstrative adjective 'such,' is 'as,' but occasionally 'such' is employed, e.g.—

> *Such* mistress, *such* Nan,
> *Such* master, *such* man.—*Tusser.*

Same (M.E. *same*) is usually preceded by one of the demonstratives, *the, this, that, self,* and followed by its correlative *as.* It may be used pronominally or adjectively, e.g.—

> He is the *same* as he ever was (Pro.).
>
> That *same* day in the following year, and on the self-*same* hour, the mysterious stranger appeared again (Adj.).

Self was formerly used as a demonstrative adjective, e.g.—

> Shoot another arrow that *self* way.—*Shakspere.*
>
> At that *self* moment enters Palamon.—*Dryden.*

Same and *self* may be called **Demonstratives of Identity**.

The before comparatives is the O.E. *thý,* the ablative of the so-called definite article, and = *by that,* e.g. ' *The* more *the* merrier,' i.e. ' *By that* more, *by that* merrier.'

> I fruitless mourn to him that cannot hear,
> And weep *the more* because I weep in vain.—*Gray.*

Yon, yond, yonder (O.E. *geond,* adv., comp. *beyond*) are used as pronouns in provincial, but not in standard English.

> *Yon* flowery arbours, *yonder* valleys green.—*Milton.*

Comp. Ger. *jener*=that. The *d* is probably no part of the original word, but has been added to strengthen the word. Comp. spend, lend, sound, &c., in all of which the *d* has been added to the root. Notice also the tendency of the illiterate to say *drownd* for *drown,* and *gownd* for *gown.*

In the following passages *yon* and *yonder* are adverbs—

> Him that *yon* soars on golden wing.—*Milton.*
>
> I and the lad will go *yonder.*—*Bible.*

PARSING OF EMPHATIC, REFLEXIVE, RECIPROCAL, POSSESSIVE, AND DEMONSTRATIVE PRONOUNS.

52. (*a*) 'We *ourselves* saw them talking to *each other*, and pluming *themselves* on their success.'

(*b*) '*These* are *mine*. What have you done with *yours ?*'

Word	Class	Inflexions	Syntactical Relations
ourselves	Pron., emph.	1st, plu., nom.	in apposition with 'we'
each ⎱ other ⎰	Pron., recipr.		
each	Pron., distrib.	3rd, sing., obj.	in appos. with 'them'
other	,, ,,	3rd, sing., obj.	gov. by 'to'
themselves	Pron., reflex.	3rd, plu., obj.	gov. by 'pluming'
these	Pron., dem., prox.	3rd, plu., nom.	subj. to 'are'
mine	Pron., poss.	1st,[1] sing., nom.	after verb 'to be'
yours	,, ,,	2nd,[1] plu., obj.	gov. by 'with'

Exercises.

1. Parse the pronouns belonging to the foregoing classes in the following passages—

   a.   This can unlock the gates of Joy,
           Of Horror that and thrilling fears.— *Gray.*

   b. Yonder is a book of mine.

   c. Theirs but to do and die.—*Tennyson.*

   d. Virtue is its own reward.

   e. I do repent me.

   f. Mark ye how close she veils her round.—*Keble.*

   g. Little children, love one another.—*Bible.*

   h. And Elisha said, Take bow and arrows. And he took unto him bow and arrows.—*Ib.*

   i. Why should that name be sounded more than yours ?
                                 Shakspere.

2. Distinguish between the possessive case of the personal pronouns and possessive pronouns, and illustrate your answer by examples.

3. Distinguish between Emphatic, Reflexive, and Reciprocal Pronouns.

---

[1] See § 50, p. 52. Syntactically considered, these Pronouns are of the 3rd person.

RELATIVE PRONOUNS.

53. **Relative Pronouns** stand for some noun, or noun-equivalent, previously expressed, and, at the same time, connect adjective clauses with principal sentences. (See p. 142.)

The boy *that* threw the stone is here.

Here *that* stands for the noun *boy,* and at the same time connects the adjective clause '*that threw the stone*' with the principal sentence '*the boy is here.*'

The noun, or noun-equivalent, for which the relative stands, is called the **Antecedent.** The antecedent may be—

1. A *noun,* e.g. 'This *man,* who was once rich, is now poor.'

2. A *pronoun,* e.g. '*I,* who speak to you, am he.'

3. A *gerundial infinitive,* e.g. '*To err,* which is a weakness incidental to humanity, is pardonable.'

4. A *noun clause,* e.g. '*That he should in every case be consulted,* which is what he demands, is unreasonable.'

The names **relative** and **antecedent** are not happily chosen; for all pronouns *relate* to some noun or noun equivalent, and the so-called *antecedent* sometimes *follows* the relative, e.g.—

To *whom* little is forgiven, the *same* loveth little.—*Bible.*

A preferable name to antecedent would be *correlative.*

The antecedent is frequently omitted, e.g.—

How shall I curse ∧ *whom* God hath not cursed ?—*Bible.*

Who steals my purse ∧ steals trash.—*Shakspere.*

The relative is also frequently omitted, e.g.—

The man ∧ I saw was tall.

There is a willow ∧ grows askant the brook.—*Shakspere.*

Men must reap the things ∧ they sow.—*Shelley.*

Let all the ends ∧ thou aim'st at be thy country's, Thy God's, and truth's.—*Shakspere.*

54. The Relative Pronouns are *that, who, which, what, whoso, whoever, whatever, whichever, whosoever, whichsoever, whatsoever, as, but.*

That (O.E. *thæt*) was originally the neuter singular demonstrative, but is now used without regard to gender or number, e.g. 'The *boy that* did it is here,' 'The little *girl that* was lost is found,' 'The *flowers that* were gathered are on the table.'

That differs from *who* and *which* in two respects—

1. It cannot be used as a relative *after* a preposition.

2. It is exclusively used when the adjective clause that it introduces is logically part of the subject or object on which it depends, e.g. 'The house that I built is for sale.' We could not say 'The house, which I built,' without ambiguity, for the adjective clause introduced by 'which' does not limit the subject, but is, as it were, thrown in parenthetically. This nice distinction is often disregarded even by good writers. 'That' may be called the *defining relative*. (See Bain's *English Grammar*, p. 23.) Dr. Abbott says: '*Who* introduces a new fact about the Antecedent : *that* completes the Antecedent. This is the general rule, subject to a few exceptions arising from the desire of euphony.' (*How to Parse*, p. 307.)

That is often used in our old writers without an antecedent, e.g. 'Take *that* thine is, and go thy way.' (*Bible*.) 'We speak *that* we do know and testify *that* we have seen.' (*Ib.*)

'That' and 'what,' when used without correlatives, are sometimes called *Compound Relatives*, and parsed as equivalent to 'that which.' It is one thing, however, to treat them as equivalent to 'that which,' and another to parse 'that which' instead of them. If the correlative be not supplied, the double function of the compound relative should be pointed out. The Compound Relative may be equivalent to—

1. Two Nominatives : This is *what* he was.

2. Two Objectives : I have *what* I want.

3. Nom. and Obj. : This is *what* I want.

4. Obj. and Nom. : I know *what* he is.

Who (O.E. *hwá*) was originally an Interrogative Pronoun, and was not used as a relative before the 16th century. Ben Jonson (1574–1637) recognises only one relative, 'which.' 'Whose' and 'whom' came into use as relatives much earlier. E.g. 'I beseech thee for my son Onesimus, *whom* I have begotten in my bonds; *which* in time past was to thee unprofitable.' (*Bible*, 1611.) 'Who,' however, is of common occurrence as a relative in the Bible, e.g. 'God, *who* at sundry times,' &c.; 'and deliver them, *who* through fear,' &c.

'Who' is declined as follows—

	Sing. and Plu.
Nom.	Who
Poss.	Whose
Obj.	Whom

Whose (O.E. *hwæs*) is used of all genders, but there is a noticeable tendency to substitute 'of which' for it, when we speak of inanimate objects.

Whom (O.E. *hwám*) was originally a dative. It is now used both as a Direct and Indirect Objective, e.g. 'This is the man *whom* I saw,'

'This is the man *to whom* I gave it.' 'Whose' and 'whom,' like 'who,' were originally interrogatives. The old accusative was *hwone*. Compare the substitution of *him* for *hine*. (See § 44.)

Which (O.E. *hwilc*) is compounded of *hwá* = who and *lic* = like. Comp. *such* from swá-lic, *thilk* (provincial) from the-lic. *Which* was originally an interrogative and used of any gender and both numbers. It is now restricted to the neuter gender.

Which is sometimes preceded by *the*, e.g.—

> 'Twas a foolish quest,
> *The which* to gain and keep he sacrificed the rest.

Comp. Fr. le-quel, la-quelle, &c.

It is declined as follows—

	Sing. and Plu.
Nom.	Which
Poss.	Whose
Obj.	Which

Which is sometimes used adjectively, e.g.—

> *Which* thing I hate.—*Bible.*

What (O.E. *hwæt*) is the neuter of *who* (O.E. *hwá*), and was originally an interrogative. In modern English it is never preceded by a correlative, but is sometimes followed by one, e.g.—

> This is ∧ what it was.
> I have ∧ what I want.
> *What* he hath won, *that* hath he fortified.—*Shakspere.*
> *What* thou wouldst highly, *that* wouldst thou holily.—*Id.*

'What' should be treated as a simple relative, whenever its correlative is expressed. The combination 'that what' sounds harsh to modern ears, but it is common enough in our early writers. See remarks on *That.*

> *That what* we have we prize not to the worth.—*Shakspere.*

'What' is sometimes used adjectively, e.g.—

> Two such I saw, *what* time the laboured ox
> In his loose traces from the furrow came.—*Milton.*

'What' is here equivalent to 'at *that* (time) *at which.*'

It is also used adjectively in exclamatory sentences with the force of *how great*, e.g.—

> O, *what* a fall was there !—*Shakspere.*
> O, *what* a falling off was there !—*Id.*
> *What* a piece of work is a man !—*Id.*

What . . what is sometimes used adverbially in the sense of *partly*, e.g.—

> *What* with one thing and *what* with another I am nearly driven wild.

Ben Jonson calls it, in this construction, an 'adverb of partition.'

What is declined as follows—

	Sing. and Plu.
Nom.	What
Poss.	Whose
Obj.	What

Whosoever follows the inflexion of *who*; poss. *whose*-soever, obj. *whom*soever. *Whoso, whoever, whatever, whichever, whosoever, which-soever, whatsoever*, are generally used without any expressed correlative, e.g.—

> Whosoever shall eat this bread and drink this cup of the Lord unworthily, [he] shall be guilty, &c.—*Bible.*

These compounds may be called **Indefinite Relatives.**

As (O.E. *alswá* = all so) is used as a relative after *such, same* (cp. Lat. *idem, qui*), *so much, as many, as much, that,* &c.

> Such *as* sleep o' nights.—*Shakspere.*
> Tears such *as* angels weep.—*Milton.*
>   Art thou afeard
> To be the same in thine own act and valour
> *As* thou art in desire ?—*Shakspere.*
> That gentleness *as* I was wont to have.—*Id.*
>   These hard conditions *as* this time
> Is like to lay upon us.—*Id.*
> I have as much *as* I want.
> You can have as many *as* you like.

With this construction compare also the use of the correlative pronouns, tantus, quantus ; talis, qualis ; tot, quot, in Latin.

But is frequently used after negative prepositions with the force of a relative and an adverb of negation, e.g.—

> There breathes not clansman of thy line
> *But* would have given his life for thine.—*Scott.*

i.e. *who* would *not* have given, &c.

Cp. Lat. quin = qui non.

INTERROGATIVE PRONOUNS.

55. Interrogative Pronouns are used in asking questions, e.g. *who, which, what, whether, whoever, whichever, whatever.* Of these *which* and *what* may be used adjectively, e.g. ' Which book do you want ?' ' What voice was that ?'

Whether (O.E. *hwá*, and suffix *-ther*[1]) means *which of the two*, e.g.
Whether of them twain did the will of his father ?—*Bible.*

---

[1] The suffix *-ther* appears in various forms in most of the Indo-Germanic languages. It carries with it the idea of duality, or of

DISTRIBUTIVE PRONOUNS.

56. The Distributive Pronouns are *each, every, either, neither.*

Each (O.E. *ælc* = *á*, ever, or *eall*, all, and *lic*, like).

Every (O.E. *ever-ælc* = ever-each) is used pronominally in early English, e.g. 'Every of your wishes' (*Shakspere*), but is now used only as an adjective. 'Each' and 'every' are both singular, but 'each' refers to individuals considered separately, 'every' to individuals considered collectively.

Either (O.E. *æg-hwá* = whoever + the dual suffix *-ther*) means literally *whoever of the two*, e.g. 'Which of the two will you have? *Either.*'

Either is sometimes incorrectly used in the sense of *both*, e.g. 'on either side.'

Neither (O.E. *náther*) is the negative form of *either*. It is properly used as a singular, e.g. 'Neither of the two *was* satisfactory,' but is sometimes used as a plural, e.g. 'Neither *are* correct.' The justification of the latter use is to be found in the fact that by excluding each of two things we exclude both.

INDEFINITE PRONOUNS.

57. Indefinite Pronouns are so called because they do not indicate specifically the individuals to which they refer. They are *any, certain, divers, whit, aught, naught, other, somebody, one, any one, anything, anybody, something, some one, somewhat, nothing, no one, nobody.*

Any (O.E. *ænig*) is formed from *án* = one. Cp. *ullus* from *unus*. *Any* may refer either to number or to quantity, e.g.—

>   Have you *any* of the apples?
>   Have you *any* of the flour?

When followed by a noun *any* is used adjectively.

Certain, e.g.—

>   There came from the ruler of the synagogue's house *certain* which said.—Mark v. 35.

Divers (Lat. *diversus*, different; O.F. *divers*)—

>   But when *divers* were hardened.—Acts xix. 9.

Whit (O.E. *wiht*, a creature, a thing) occurs most frequently with 'a' before it, e.g. 'not a whit,' but it is also used without 'a,' e.g.—

>   Our youth and wildness shall no *whit* appear.—*Shakspere.*

---

one thing considered in relation to another, e.g. other, father, mother, brother, sister, either, neither. Lat. uter = whether; alter = the other of two; neuter = neither, &c.

Aught (O.E. *áht* = a whit, anything).

Naught (O.E. *n-áht* = no whit, nothing). Bearing in mind the derivation, the spelling *aught* and *naught* seems preferable to *ought* and *nought*.

Other (O.E. *other* = one of two). The *o* probably represents *one*, *-ther* is the dual suffix. (See footnote, § 55.)

Some (O.E. *sum* = certain) is used either of number or quantity. With numerals *some* has the force of *about*, e.g. '*some* four or five,' and should be parsed as an adverb.

One is said to be a corruption of the French *on*, which is itself a corruption of the Latin *homo*. But we find *mon* = man[1] used in the same sense in Robert of Gloster, and *man* is used in the same sense in German. Cp.—

> Ici *on* parle français.
> Hier spricht *man* Deutsch.
> *One* can do what *one* likes with *one's* own.

In spite of the analogy of French and German, it is difficult to believe that *one* is a corruption of *mon* or *on*. It seems more probable that the indefinite pronoun grew out of the numeral *one*.

One is also used indefinitely in other combinations, and sometimes even qualified by an adjective, e.g.—

> What, all my little *ones*?—*Shakspere*.
> The great *ones* eat up the little *ones*.—*Id*.
> I am not *one* to beg and pray.

None (O.E. *nán* = *ne án* = not one). The adjective form is *no*, e.g.—

> Have you *no* bread? I have *none*.
>
> High stations tumult, but not bliss, create :
> *None* think the great unhappy but the great.

Body is sometimes used pronominally, e.g.—

> Gin a *bodie* meet a *bodie*.
> The foolish *body* hath said, &c.

Something and **Somewhat** are also used adverbially, e.g.—

> He is *somewhat* clever.
> He is *something* better.

It will be observed that these compound indefinite pronouns are all formed in the same way—

> Any, any-one, any-body, any-thing, any-whit.
> Some, some-one, some-body, some-thing, some-what.
> No, no-one, no-body, no-thing, no-whit.

Of these, *somewhat* is, perhaps, a corruption of somewhit.

---

[1] *Man* is apparently used in the same indefinite way in Zech. xiii. 5 : 'For *man* taught me to keep cattle from my youth.' So again in Mark viii. 4 : 'From whence can a *man* satisfy these men' &c., where the Greek is δυνήσεταί τις,

PARSING OF RELATIVE, INTERROGATIVE, DISTRIBUTIVE, AND INDEFINITE PRONOUNS.

58. ' *Who* are those *whom* I see, *each* holding a flower in her hand? *Some* are old and *others* young. Tell me *what* they seek.'

Word	Class	Inflexions	Syntactical Relations
who	Pro., interr.	3rd, plu., nom.	subj. to 'are '
whom	Pro., rel.	,, obj.	gov. by 'see '
each	Pro., distrib.	3rd, sing., obj.	in appos. with 'whom '
some	Pro., indef.	3rd, plu., nom.	subj. to 'are '
others	,, ,,	,, ,,	,,
what	Pro., rel.	3rd, sing., obj.	gov. by 'seek '

Exercises.

1. Parse the pronouns belonging to the foregoing classes in the following passages—

a. If any one say anything to you.—*Bible.*

b. Whoso sheddeth man's blood, by man shall his blood be shed.
Ib.

c. There is no one but knows how noble he is.

d. Whoever is first shall get the prize.

e. He is the same as ever he was.

f. I will take such as you have.

g. What man dare I dare.—*Shakspere.*

h. What's in a name?—*Id.*

i. What is one man's poison is another man's meat.

k. One that feared God.—*Bible.*

l.   Each in his narrow cell for ever laid,
        The rude forefathers of the hamlet sleep.—*Gray.*

m. A woman's nay doth stand for naught.—*Shakspere.*

n.   Nothing of him that doth fade
        But doth suffer a sea-change
        Into something rich and strange.—*Id.*

o. Nothing extenuate, nor set down aught in malice.—*Id.*

p.   He nothing common did, or mean,
        Upon that memorable scene.—*Marvell.*

q.   There's naught in this life sweet,
       If men were wise to see't,
         But only melancholy.—*Fletcher.*

r.   For aught that ever I could read,
       Could ever hear by tale or history,
       The course of true love never did run smooth.
                       Shakspere.

s. What men daily do, not knowing what they do !—*Id.*

t. When you have nothing to say, say it.

u. What he hath won, that hath he fortified.

v. None of these things moved him.

2. Give instances in which *what, some, each, other, either,* are used adjectively.

3. Give instances in which *something, somewhat, nothing, aught,* are used adverbially.

THE VERB.

59. A verb (Lat. *verbum,* a word) **is the part of speech by means of which we make assertions.** It was so called as being pre-eminently *the* word in a sentence.

Verbs are used to express (1) what a thing *does,* as 'the tree *grows*;' (2) what is *done* to a thing, as 'the tree is *felled*;' (3) in conjunction with a noun or adjective, to express what a thing *is, becomes,* or *seems* to be, as 'He *is* a sailor; She *became* queen; They *seemed* happy.'

60. Verbs are divided into Transitive and Intransitive.

A **transitive verb** (from *transire,* to go across) denotes an action which, as it were, passes over from the doer of it to the object of it, e.g. 'he *broke* his knife,' 'he *praised* my dog.'

An **intransitive verb** is one which denotes a state or action terminating in the agent, e.g. ' he *sleeps*,' we *live*.'

The following are examples of verbs commonly intransitive used transitively—

     He *walked* to Dover (intrans.). He *walked* the horse (trans.).
     The bird *flew* (intrans.). He *flew* his kite (trans.).
     He *ran* to me (intrans.). He *ran* the needle into his hand (trans.).

It will be observed that the transitive forms in the foregoing examples are all causative, i.e. they denote some action which is the cause of another. Thus 'walked' (trans.) = made to walk; 'flew' (trans.) = made to fly; 'ran' (trans.) = made to run.

In a few instances we have distinct causative forms of the verb—

	Causative
drink	drench (as in 'drenching a horse')
rise	raise
lie	lay
sit	set
fall	fell

The following are examples of verbs ordinarily transitive used intransitively—

> The earth *opened* and swallowed them up.
> The door *shut* before I could enter.
> I could not *refrain* from speaking.

Other such verbs are *extend, rest, keep, remove, intrude, obtrude, melt, move, swing, reform.*

Some grammarians explain this construction by assuming that there is an ellipsis of the Reflexive Object after the verb, as if when we say 'the table *moves*,' we mean that 'the table moves *itself.*' This view is supported by the analogy of languages in which the Reflexive Object is actually expressed in such constructions.

The following verbs, most of which relate to the senses, are as often used transitively as intransitively: *smell, feel, taste, weigh, measure*, e.g.—

Trans.	Intrans.
He *smells* the rose.	The rose *smells* sweet.
He *feels* the water.	The water *feels* cold.
He *weighs* the meat.	The meat *weighs* six pounds.
He *measures* the table.	The table *measures* five feet by four.

Intransitive verbs, when followed by a preposition (which in such constructions may be looked on as a separable prefix), are often used transitively, e.g.—

> He *laughed* at me. I was *laughed* at = I was *derided.*
> He *spoke* to me. I was *spoken* to = I was *addressed.*

Intransitive verbs compounded with prepositions are often thereby rendered transitive. Cp. *come* and *overcome*; *lie* and *overlie*; *speak* and *bespeak.*

Some intransitive verbs are **Copulative** (Lat. *copula*, a link), i.e. they are used to connect a noun, pronoun, or adjective with the subject or object of a sentence. Such are *be, become, grow, continue, remain.*

> He *is* a mason.
> I knew him *to be* an honest man.

He *became* a great poet.
I wished him *to remain* a sailor.
He *grew* a stalwart man.

These verbs take the same case after them as they have before them.

Verbs are inflected for Voice, Mood, Tense, Number, and Person.

Exercises.

1. Distinguish between Transitive and Intransitive Verbs.

2. Give instances of—

a. Verbs ordinarily intransitive used transitively.

b. Verbs ordinarily transitive used in the Active Voice without any expressed Object.

3. What is a Causative Verb?   Give instances.

4. Classify the verbs in the following passages—

a. They make a solitude and call it peace.

b.   She walks the waters like a thing of life,
       And seems to dare the elements to strife.—*Byron.*

c. Know ye the land where the cypress and myrtle
    Are emblems of deeds that are done in their clime;
    Where the rage of the vulture, the love of the turtle
    Now melt into sorrow, now madden to crime?—*Id.*

d. The cakes ate short and crisp.

e. It stirs, it rises, it crawls.

f. Whilst the smith talked the iron cooled.

g. O my offence is rank, it smells to heaven.—*Shakspere.*

h. The heaven's breath smells wooingly here.—*Id.*

i. It tastes of the cask.

k. The valiant never taste of death but once.—*Shakspere.*

l. He swam the Eske river.—*Scott.*

m. He returned the letter.

n. He returned home.

o. As he was felling the tree he fell down.

p. He rose up to raise the window.

q. Having laid down his hat, he lay on the sofa.

r. He proved a thorough knave.

s. He proved the accuracy of his method.

t. She seemed happy.

u. We read three hours a day.

v. He slept night and day.

w. He remained a soldier.

x. He continued a carpenter several years.

VOICE.

61. Voice is that form which transitive verbs assume to show whether the subject of the sentence denotes the *doer* or the *object* of the action.[1]   The form which is used in the former case is called the **Active Voice**, in the latter case the **Passive Voice.**   Compare the following—

Active.	Passive.
He *wrote* a book.	The book *was written* by him.
He *loves* me.	I *am loved* by him.
He *will hurt* me.	I *shall be hurt* by him.
The cat *killed* the bird.	The bird *was killed* by the cat.

62. An Intransitive Verb, inasmuch as it denotes an action terminating in the doer, can have no Direct Object, and is therefore incapable of being used in the Passive Voice. When used with a following preposition, an intransitive verb may, as we have seen, be used transitively; and the verb thus compounded may be used in the Passive Voice.   Thus, though we cannot say ' he *was laughed*,' or ' he *was spoken*,' we can say ' he *was laughed at*,' and ' he *was spoken to*.' In these cases the real verb is the verb *plus* the preposition.

63. In converting an Active into a Passive construction we may make either the Direct or the Indirect Object of the active verb the Subject of the passive verb.

I taught him music.	*Music* was taught him by me.
	He was taught music by me.
You gave him an apple.	An *apple* was given him by you.
	He was given an apple by you.
I promised him a new coat.	A new *coat* was promised him by me.
	He was promised a new coat by me.
You showed him the way.	*He* was shown the way by you.
	The *way* was shown him by you.

---

[1] Note the language used.   The real object of the *action* should not be confounded with the grammatical Object of the *Sentence.* In the sentence ' The table was struck,' the real *object* of the action was the table, but the *name* of that object is the grammatical *Subject* of the sentence.

F

In some languages the Passive Voice is expressed by inflexion, but all our passive forms are compounded of some
part of the verb *be*, and the perfect participle of the verb,
e.g. *I am│beaten—I was│beaten—I shall be│beaten—I have
been│beaten—I had been│beaten—I shall have been│beaten.*

The beginner should carefully discriminate between transitive
verbs in the Passive Voice and the perfect tenses of certain intransitive verbs of motion, which are also compounded of the verb 'to be'
and the perfect participle. E.g. *go, come, rise, fall, arrive, depart,
ascend, descend, pass, escape, return, enter,* &c.

Cp. 'He *is beaten*' (Pass.) with 'He *is gone*' (Act.); 'He *is
raised*' (Pass.) with 'He *is risen*' (Act.).

Exercises.

1. What do you mean by the Passive Voice?

2. Classify the voices of the verbs in the following passages—

a. He is going, but he is not gone.

b. The letter was returned to me.

c. As soon as he was returned he called on me.

d. The book was given him by me.

e. The sun is risen.

f. The kings of the earth are gathered and gone by together.
Bible.

g. I am escaped with the skin of my teeth.—*Ib.*

h. My way of life is fallen into the sear.—*Shakspere.*

i. I have been studying.

k. His days were passed in business.

l. [He] is passed from death unto life.—*Bible.*

m. Some are born great, some achieve greatness, and some have
greatness thrust upon them.—*Shakspere.*

n. When I said I would die a bachelor, I did not think I should
live till I were married.—*Id.*

o. Thou hast ascended up on high.—*Bible.*

p. For David is not ascended into the heavens.—*Ib.*

q.   That which we call a rose
By any other name would smell as sweet.—*Shakspere.*

3. Convert the following Active constructions into Passive
ones—

a. I taught him the art of fencing.

b. He showed me the way to do it.

c. I gave him a book on the subject.

d. The cat killed the mouse.

e. I shall finish my task by noon.

f. He had shot the deer.

MOOD.

64. Mood (from the Lat. *modus*, manner) is that inflexion which a verb undergoes to show the *mode* or manner in which the action or state denoted by the verb is presented to the mind.

65. The Indicative Mood (Lat. *indico*, I point out) is that form which is used in making unconditional assertions, in asking questions, and in making even conditional statements, if the condition be considered as really existent, e.g. I *bought* a book. *Did* he *go*? If he *is* honest, as I am sure he is, he will get on.[1]

66. The Imperative Mood (Lat. *impero*, I command) is that form which is used to express a command or entreaty, e.g. 'Come here;' 'Give me some drink, Titinius' (Shakspere). We cannot give a command to ourselves, but we may associate others with ourselves in some entreaty or invitation. Hence, though we have no imperative *singular* of the first person, we have an imperative *plural* of that person, e.g.—

Part we in friendship from your land.—*Scott.*

Now *tread* we a measure, said young Lochinvar.—*Scott.*

Go we to the king.—*Shakspere.*

Praise we the Lord.

> *Publish* we this peace
> To all our subjects.—*Shakspere.*

Break we our watch up.—*Id.*

Although, from the nature of the case, the Imperative Mood is most commonly of the second person, indirect commands or entreaties may be expressed by an imperative of the third person, e.g.—

Thy will *be done.*—*Bible.*

The Lord *make* His face to shine upon thee.—*Ib.*

The Lord *be* with you.—*Prayer Book.*

Cursed be he that first cries 'Hold! enough!'—*Shakspere.*

---

[1] Note the difference between this construction and the following: 'If he *be* honest, and about that I have my doubts, he will pay the money he owes.'

Unto which He *vouchsafe* to bring us.—*Prayer Book.*

Be Kent unmannerly when Lear is mad.—*Shakspere.*

In modern English it is customary to use a periphrastic expression instead of the imperative of the first and third persons. Thus we say 'Let us pray,' not 'Pray we;' 'Let him go,' not 'go he.' Such periphrases are really compounded of the imperative of 'let,' governing the pronoun as a Direct Object and the gerundial infinitive (see below) as an Indirect Object.

67. The Subjunctive Mood (Lat. *subjungo*, I subjoin) is that form of the verb which is used to express supposition, doubt, or uncertainty,[1] e.g. 'If I *were* he, I would not go.' It is so called because the verb expressing the uncertainty is generally employed in the dependent or *subjoined* clause. The subjunctive is generally introduced by one of the following words: *if, lest, except, so, that, though, unless, till, however, whoever.*

If. If it *were* so, it is a grievous fault.—*Shakspere.*

Lest. Love not sleep, lest thou *come* to poverty.—*Bible.*

Except. I will not let thee go except thou *bless* me.—*Ib.*

So. And so thou *lean* on thy fair Father, Christ.—*Tennyson.*

That. Speak to my brother that he *divide* the inheritance with me.—*Bible.*

Though. Though He *slay* me, yet will I trust in Him.—*Ib.*

Unless. I had fainted unless I *had believed.*—*Ib.*

Till. Till civil-suited morn *appear.*—*Milton.*

However. Howe'er the world *go.*—*Shakspere.*

Whoever. Whoever he *be*, he has not acted nobly.

---

[1] Latham gives the following rule for determining the cases in which the Subjunctive should be employed. 'Insert immediately after the conjunction one of the two following phrases: (1) *as is the case*; (2) *as may or may not be the case.* By ascertaining which of these two supplements expresses the meaning of the speaker, we ascertain the mood of the verb which follows. When the first formula is the one required, there is no element of doubt, and the verb should be in the indicative mood. *If (as is the case) he is gone, I must follow him.* When the second formula is the one required, there is an element of doubt, and the verb should be in the subjunctive mood. If (*as may or may not be the case*) he be gone, I must follow him.'—*Hist. of Eng. Lang.,* p. 646. The tendency of modern English is to get rid of the subjunctive.

It must not be supposed that the conjunctions enumerated above are always followed by the Subjunctive. Some of them are often used with the Indicative, e.g. 'If two and two *are* four.' Here there is no uncertainty, and the subjunctive would have been improperly used.

Not unfrequently we find the subjunctive used without any introductory particle, e.g.—

> *Had* I a sword in my hand, I would slay him.
>
> *Were* I not Alexander, I would be Diogenes.
>
> *Be* it scroll, or *be* it book,
> Into it, knight, thou must not look.—*Scott.*

68. The **Infinitive Mood** (Lat. *infinitus*, unbounded) is that form of the verb which denotes an action or state without any reference to an agent, e.g. ' *To err* is human.' Here *to err* is equivalent to *erring* or *error*. The Infinitive has no number or person, and might be regarded in some respects as an Abstract Noun.

In O.E. the infinitive was treated as a noun. It ended in -*an* or -*en* in the Nominative and Accusative Case, and in -*anne* or -*enne* in the Dative Case. In the former cases it was used without the preposition ' to '; in the Dative it was preceded by ' to,'[1] e.g.—

Nom. and Acc.	*etan*, to eat.
Dat.	*tó etanne*, to eat.

The **Dative of the infinitive** is called by some grammarians the **gerundial infinitive** from its resemblance in function to the Latin gerund. By others it is called the **supine**, because in some of its functions it resembles the Latin supines.

When both the simple infinitive and the gerundial infinitive had lost their distinctive terminations, they came to be confounded, and it was at this period that the preposition ' to,' which, as we have seen, properly belongs to the dative or gerundial infinitive, came to be attached to the simple infinitive, even in the Nominative and Accusative Case.

[1] Even before the Conquest the distinction was not invariably observed, as is clear from the following passage : 'Ne wene ge thæt ic come sybbe on eorthan *to sendanne* : ne com ic sybbe *to sendanne* ac an sweord. Ic com sothlice mann *asyndrian* ongean hys fæder,' &c. Matt. x. 35. [Think ye not that I come peace on earth to send : I come not peace to send but a sword. I come, indeed, a man [to] sunder against his father, &c.] Here, after the same verb ' come,' the infinitive is used with and without ' to,'

The following passages from the 'Anglo-Saxon' Gospels will serve to illustrate the difference between the simple infinitive and the gerundial infinitive—

a. Hu mæg theş his flæsc us *syllan* (simple infinitive) *to etanne* (gerundial infinitive)?—John vi. 52. [How may this (man) his flesh us give to eat?] ⠀⠀

b. Me gebyrath *to wyrcanne* (gerundial infinitive) thæs weorc the me sende, tha hwyle the hyt dæg ys : nyht cymth, thonne nan man *wyrcan* (simple infinitive) ne mæg.—John ix. 4. [Me it behoveth to work the work of him which sent me : the night cometh when no man may work.]

c. And he hig asende godspel *to bodigenne* ; and he him anweald sealde untrumnessa *to hælanne,* and deofel-seocnessa út *to adrifanne.* —Mark iii. 14, 15. [And he them sent the gospel to preach ; and he them power gave sicknesses to heal, and devil-sicknesses out to drive.]

d. Hig næfdon hlaf *to etanne.*—Mark iii. 20. [They had-not bread to eat.] ⠀⠀

e. Gif hwá earan hæbbe *to gehyranne.*—Mark iv. 23. [If any one ears have to hear.] ⠀⠀

f. Eart thú the *to cumenne* eart? oththe we othres sceolon *abidan* (simple infinitive)?—Matt. xi. 3. [Art thou he which to come art ? or should we wait for another ?]

g. Tha næron alyfede *to etanne.*—Luke vi. 4. [Which they were not allowed to eat.]

h. And eal seo mænigeo sohte hine *to æthrinanne.*—Luke vi. 19. [And all the multitude sought him to touch.]

The Simple Infinitive is used after auxiliaries, e.g. I may *go* ; he should *go* ; he might *go.*

The Gerundial Infinitive may be used—

1. As a noun, e.g.—

> *To go* is impossible (Subj.)
> *To reign* is worth ambition (Subj.)
> He wished *to reign* (Dir. Obj.)
> We wished him *to go* (Indir. Obj.)

2. To qualify a noun, e.g.—

> We have bread *to eat*, and water *to drink*, and clothing *to put on.*

3. To express purpose after a verb of going or coming (cp. the Latin supine in *-um*), e.g.—

> A sower went out *to sow* his seed.
> I am come *to tell* you.

4. To limit an adjective (cp. the Latin supine in -*u*), e.g.—

Marvellous *to relate.*
Wonderful *to say.*
Quick *to forgive.*

The gerundial infinitive is also often used parenthetically, e.g. 'He soon left, and (*to tell* you the truth) I was not sorry when he went.'

After *bid, dare, make, feel, see, hear, let,* the simple infinitive is used. Most of these verbs governed the simple infinitive in O.E. (See p. 198.)

Exercises.

1. What is meant by mood?

2. Define indicative mood, subjunctive mood, infinitive mood.

3. Give instances of imperatives of the first and third person.

4. Give a list of the words which are commonly followed by the Subjunctive Mood.

5. When is the indicative used after 'if'?

6. Name the mood of the verbs in the following passages:—

a.
    So silently we seemed to speak,
    So slowly moved about,
    As we had lent her half our powers
    To eke her living out.—*Hood.*

b.
    If 'twere done when 'tis done, then 'twere well
    It were done quickly.—*Shakspere.*

c. Weep no more, lady.

d.
    She doeth little kindnesses,
    Which most leave undone, or despise.—*Lowell.*

e. To be or not to be: that is the question.—*Shakspere.*

f. It is cruelty to beat a cripple with his own crutches.—*Fuller.*

g. Be swift to hear, slow to speak.—*Bible.*

h. There is a time to weep, and a time to laugh.—*Ib.*

i. He must go.

k. Returning were as tedious as go o'er.—*Shakspere.*

l. If my aunt were a man, she would be my uncle.

m. The Lord judge between thee and me.—*Bible.*

n. Be it so.

o. The apparel oft proclaims the man.—*Shakspere.*

p.
    The ages roll
    Forward; and forward with them, draw my soul
    Into time's infinite sea,

And to be glad or sad I care no more :
But to have done, and to have been, before
I cease to do and be.—*Lord Lytton.*

q.　　　　　　If such there be, where'er
Beneath the sun he fare [i.e. go]
He cannot fare amiss.—*Id.*

r.　　　　　　It were all one
That I should love a bright particular star
And hope to wed it.—*Shakspere.*

s.　　　If all the year were playing holidays,
To sport would be as tedious as to work.—*Id.*

t. I do not give you to posterity as a pattern to imitate, but an example to deter.—*Junius.*

u. [He had not] the heart to conceive, the understanding to direct, or the hand to execute.—*Id.*

7. In what respects does the simple infinitive differ from the gerundial infinitive?

PARTICIPLES AND VERBAL NOUNS.

69. A participle (Lat. *participo*, I take part) is a word which partakes of the nature of a verb and of an adjective, e.g. a *living* creature, a *defeated* general.

There are only two simple participles in English, the Imperfect Active and the Perfect Passive. The former ends in *-ing* (O.E. -ende), e.g. 'the *rolling* waves,' 'the *heaving* tide.' The latter generally ends in *-en* or *-ed*, e.g. 'a *spoken* word,' 'a *slighted* suitor,' and sometimes is identical in form with the Infinitive, e.g. 'a *cut* rose,' 'a plant *put* in the ground.'

In O.E. many participles had a distinctive prefix, viz. *ge*, which survives in a disguised form in *yclept* (=ge-clept, from clepian, to call).

With the help of the verbs 'have' and 'be' we may, in the case of transitive verbs, have six participial forms.

	Active	Passive
Imperfect .	Writing	Being written
Perfect . . .	Having written	Written Having been written
Perfect Progressive	Having been writing	

70. Simple participles can be used either attributively or predicatively, e.g. 'A *rolling* stone,' 'A river *gleaming* in the sun,' 'A *defeated* general,' '*Defeated* again and again, he at last beat a retreat.' The compound participles are used only predicatively, e.g.—

Having lived in the East, he was familiar with oriental customs.
Having been writing all the morning, he was fatigued.
His money *being exhausted*, he returned home.
The tree, *having been felled*, was cut up and carted away.

Many adjectives are compounded of participles and prefixes, e.g. *unforgiven, unpremeditated, ill-shaped, well-born, misbegotten.* These should not be treated as participles, there being no such verbs as unforgive, unpremeditate, &c.

In O.E. the perfect participle of a transitive verb was inflected, and agreed with the noun which it governed, e.g. 'He hæfth man *geweorhtne*' (he hath man created). Here 'geweorhtne' is the Accusative Case of 'geweorht.' It will readily be understood how such an expression as 'I have my hands washed' might be changed into 'I have washed my hands.'

71. The student should carefully distinguish between the imperfect participle, which always qualifies a noun, either attributively or predicatively, and the **Verbal Noun**, which also ends in modern English in -*ing* (O.E. -ung). Comp. 'A *running* sore' (Part.) with 'In *running* along' (Verbal Noun). The Verbal Noun denotes action or state. It may be used as the Subject or Object of a sentence, and may itself govern an objective case, e.g.—

Seeing is *believing*.
He loves *hunting* the hare.
He was fond of *hunting*.
In *hunting* the deer he was injured.

In such expressions as 'a hunting whip,' 'a fishing rod,' the verbal noun forms part of a compound noun, the parts of which ought properly to be joined by a hyphen. 'A glittering stream' means a stream that glitters; but 'a hunting whip' does not mean a whip that *hunts*; it means a whip *for hunting*.

In Shakspere and the Bible we find such forms as 'a dying,' 'a preparing,' 'a brewing.' The *a* in these expressions is a corruption of *on* or *in*, and governs the verbal noun which follows. In modern English this preposition has been dropped. Johnson wrote 'My "Lives" are reprinting,' i.e. are *in reprinting*. In still more modern phrase we say 'are being reprinted,'

Exercises.

1. What is a participle?

2. Distinguish between simple and compound participles.

3. Classify the participles of
      (*a*) A transitive verb.
      (*b*) An intransitive verb.

4. Classify the participles and verbal nouns in the following passages :—

  a. Forty and six years was this temple in building.—*Bible*.

  b.   All friendship is feigning ;
           All loving is mere folly.—*Shakspere*.

  c. The rolling stone gathers no moss.

  d. Gothic architecture is frozen music.

  e.   ' Finis,' an error or a lie, my friend ;
           Of writing foolish books there is no end.

  f. I go a fishing.—*Bible*.

  g.   It is the bright day brings forth the adder
           And that craves wary walking.—*Shakspere*.

  h.   Doubtless the pleasure is as great
           Of being cheated as to cheat.—*Butler*.

  i. I see men as trees walking.—*Bible*.

  k. I saw her threading beads.

  l.   Call you that backing of your friends ?
           A plague upon such backing !—*Shakspere*.

  m.   Life is as tedious as a twice-told tale,
           Vexing the dull ear of a drowsy man.—*Id*.

  n.   I preached as never sure to preach again,
           And as a dying man to dying men.—*Baxter*.

  o. But O ! for the touch of a vanished hand.—*Tennyson*.

  p. Having defeated the Gauls, he returned to Rome.

  q.   There is a pleasure sure
    In being mad which none but madmen know.—*Dryden*.

  r. There is some ill a-brewing towards my rest.—*Shakspere*.

  s. Beloved by his friends, and detested by his foes, he died at the height of his fame.

  t. Having been writing all the morning, I was somewhat tired.

  u.   Let the galled jade wince,
      Our withers are unwrung.—*Shakspere*.

  v. Borrowing dulls the edge of husbandry.—*Id*.

w.   It is a tale
Told by an idiot, full of sound and fury,
Signifying nothing.—*Shakspere.*

x. For you and I are past our dancing days.—*Id.*

TENSE.

72. Tense (Lat. *tempus*, time) is that form which a verb assumes to indicate (1) the *time* of the action or state denoted by the verb, and (2) the *completeness or incompleteness* of the action or state.

As Time is divisible into Past, Present, and Future, and every action may be considered as perfect or imperfect in each of these three divisions, we get a sixfold classification of the tenses, viz.—

		Active		Passive
Present	Imperfect	I love	I am loving	I am loved
	Perfect	I have loved	I have been loving	I have been loved
Past	Imperfect	I loved	I was loving	I was loved
	Perfect	I had loved	I had been loving	I had been loved
Future	Imperfect	I shall love	I shall be loving	I shall be loved
	Perfect	I shall have loved	I shall have been loving	I shall have been loved

It will be observed :

1. That the only simple tenses, i.e. the only tenses formed by inflexion, are the *Present Imperfect* and the *Past Imperfect Active.*

2. That the perfect and future tenses, the progressive forms active, and the whole of the passive voice are compound, the perfect tenses consisting of the verb 'have'[1] and the perfect participle, the future consisting

[1] Verbs of 'going' and 'coming,' 'rising' and 'falling,' form their perfect tenses with 'be' as well as 'have,' but with a slight change of meaning. Compare 'He *is* gone' with 'He *has* gone.' The perfect formed by means of 'be' is used to denote the state of the subject, the perfect formed by means of 'have' to denote the completeness of the action.

of 'shall' or 'will' and the infinitive, the progressive forms consisting of the verb 'be' and the imperfect participle, and the passive voice of the verb 'be' and the perfect participle.

3. That the distinction of Perfect and Imperfect is independent of *time*, and relates to the completeness or incompleteness of the action or state as conceived in the mind. We can think of an action or state as completed in the past, present, or future. Compare :

> I *had written* the letter before you arrived (Past Perf.).
> I *have written* the letter and despatched it (Pres. Perf.).
> I *shall have written* the letter before you arrive (Fut. Perf.).

In the progressive forms the distinction of Perfect and Imperfect does not relate to the action or state denoted by the principal verb, but to the state of the subject of the verb as indicated by the auxiliaries. Thus :

> I have been writing = I have been engaged in writing.
> I had been writing = I had been engaged in writing, and so on.

73. The **Present Imperfect Tense** is employed (1) to describe something going on now, e.g. 'He loves me;' (2) to describe something that goes on regularly, e.g. 'He goes to school;' (3) instead of the future, e.g. 'He leaves for Paris to-morrow;'[1] (4) instead of the past tense, as when we describe some past occurrence as though it were happening under our eyes, e.g. 'Towards noon Elector Thuriot *gains* admittance; *finds* De Launay indisposed for surrender; nay, disposed for blowing up the place rather. Thuriot *mounts* with him to the battlements : heaps of paving-stones, old iron, and missiles *lie* piled,' &c. (Carlyle's 'French Revolution').

The **Present Perfect Tense** is used to denote that an action or state is completed at this present time, e.g. 'I *have done* the deed,' 'He *is gone*.'

The **Past Imperfect Tense** is used to denote that an action or state was going on at some past time, e.g.—

> I *lived* at Paris = I used to live at Paris.
> I *was reading* while he *was playing*.

---

[1] Here the notion of futurity is expressed not by the verb alone, but by the adverb and verb together.

The **Past Perfect Tense** denotes an action or state that was completed before some other past action or state, e.g.—

> I *had written* my letter before you commenced yours.
> He *was gone* before we arrived.

The **Future Imperfect Tense** denotes an action or state that will occur or be going on at some future time, e.g.—

> I *shall go* to Paris.
> I *shall be going* to Paris.
> He *will be* happy.

In O.E. there was no distinct future tense, the present being generally used as a future.[1] The auxiliaries 'shall' and 'will' were originally principal verbs, '*shall*' meaning to be under an obligation, and '*will*' meaning to will. 'Shall' is now used exclusively as an auxiliary, but still carries with it a sense of obligation in the second and third persons, e.g.—

> Thou shalt not steal.
> He shall do it.

'Will' is still occasionally used as a principal verb, e.g. 'He does what he *will*;' 'whosoever *will* be saved' (Quicunque vult salvus esse); 'The lusts of your father ye *will* do' (θέλετε ποιεῖν)—John viii. 44; 'Be it unto thee even as thou *wilt*' (θέλεις)—Matt. xv. 28; 'I *will* (θέλω) that thou give me,' &c.—Mark iv. 25. The auxiliary 'will' is used to express determination in the first person, but mere futurity in the second and third. These distinctions will be remembered by means of the following doggrel rhymes :—

> In the first person simply *shall* foretells,
> In *will* a threat or else a promise dwells ;
> *Shall* in the second and the third does threat,
> *Will* simply then foretells the future feat.

It follows that we cannot use either 'shall' or 'will' to form the future tense in all three persons. The proper future tense runs as follows :—

> I   shall write
> Thou wilt write
> He   will write.

---

[1] We occasionally, however, find the compound future as in modern English, e.g. 'Ge nyton on hwylcere tíde eower Hlaford *cuman wyle*' [Ye know not at what hour your Lord will come]— Matt. xxiv. 42 ; 'The mannes Sunu *wyle cuman*' [The Son of man will come]—Matt. xxiv. 44.

In interrogation, however, we use 'shall' in the second person, for 'will' would then appeal too strongly to the determination of the person addressed. Comp.

> *Shall* you go ?
> *Will* you go after what I have said ?

There is another peculiarity connected with the use of 'shall' which ought to be noticed. *Shall* is used to express absolute certainty on the part of the speaker. Hence it is used in the predictions of Holy Writ, and in the statement of the necessary truths of geometry, e.g.—

> Heaven and earth *shall pass* away.—*Bible.*
> The two sides *shall be* equal

The **Future Perfect Tense** denotes an action or state which will be completed before some other future action or state, e.g.—

> We *shall have departed* before you will arrive.

In colloquial English we often use the Future Imperfect for the Future Perfect, as we use the Present Imperfect for the Future Imperfect :—

> We shall go before you arrive =
> We shall have gone before you will arrive.

NUMBER.

74. The **Number** of a Verb is that form which it assumes to indicate whether its Subject is singular or plural, e.g. 'I am,' 'we are;' 'thou art,' 'ye are;' 'he is,' 'they are;' 'I was,' 'we were,' &c. Many of our distinctive plural forms are now lost. Thus we say, 'I write,' 'we write,' 'I wrote,' 'we wrote,' making no difference in form between the singular and plural.

It is customary for sovereigns, editors, and preachers to use the plural of the first person when speaking of themselves in their respective official capacities, e.g.—

> *Rich. We* are amazed ; and thus long have *we* stood
> To watch the fearful bending of thy knee,
> Because *we* thought *ourself* thy lawful king ·
> And if *we* be, how dare thy joints forget
> To pay their awful duty to *our* presence ?
> *Shakspere,* Rich. II., iii. 3.

> Given under *our* hand and seal.

PERSON.

75. The **Person** of a verb is that form which it assumes to indicate whether its subject is the person speaking (the *first* person), or the person spoken to (the *second* person), or the person or thing spoken of (the *third* person), e.g. I *am* (1st pers.); thou *art* (2nd pers.); he *is* (3rd pers.).

The person-endings of verbs were originally pronouns which, instead of being placed *before* the verb, as our present subject pronouns are, were placed after it.

The ending of the first person singular was originally -*m*, of which the only trace surviving in English is found in a-*m*. Cp. Lat. su*m* (I am), ame*m* (I may love), Greek ei*mi* (I am). This *m* was undoubtedly connected with the *m* in our existing pronouns of the first person, me, my, mine.

The ending of the second person singular is now -*st*, but was originally -*t*, e.g., thou hast, thou writest, thou lovedst, &c. This termination, which has been lost altogether by the subjunctive, is probably a degraded form of a pronoun of the second person. Cp. the *th* in *thou*, the *t* in the Latin pronoun *tu*, and the *s* in the Greek pronoun *su*. Traces of the original ending are to be found in art, wilt, and shalt.

The ending of the third person singular is -*th*, of which -*s* is a softened form, e.g., 'He praye*th* best who love*th* best,' 'He love*s* me.' It represents a pronoun of the third person. Compare the *th* in *th*at and *th*is.

In O.E. the indicative present plural ended in **-th** in all three persons; the plurals of the past indicative and the subjunctive tenses ended in **-on**. In M.E. the termination **-en** was used in the plural of all the tenses, e.g.—

> But whanne the bischopis and mynystris hadd*en* seen hym thei crie*den* and seid*en*, Crucifie, crucifie hym.—John xix. 6, *Wiclif's Version.*

> Ye wit*en* not whanne the tyme is.—Mark xiii. 33.

Ben Jonson says: 'The persons plural keep the terminations of the first person singular. In former times, till about the reign of Henry VIII., they were wont to be formed by adding -en: thus,—

> loven, sayen, complainen.

But now (whatsoever is the cause) it hath quite grown out of use, and that other so generally prevailed, that I dare not to presume to set this afoot again: albeit (to tell you my opinion) I am persuaded that the lack hereof, well considered, will be found a blemish to our tongue. For considering *time* and *person* be, as it were, the right and left hand of a *verb*, what can the maiming bring else, but a laming to the whole body?'

Exercises.

1. What is meant by the Perfect Tenses?

2. Classify the tenses.

3. Show that this classification is applicable to the progressive or continuous forms of the verb.

4. Name the tenses of the verbs in the following passages :—

   a.   There rolls the deep where grew the tree.
           O Earth, what changes hast thou seen !—*Tennyson.*

   b. He was speaking as I entered.

   c. Shall you go to see him ?

   d. The gale had sighed itself to rest.

   e. I will listen to your song.

   f. Will you permit me to go ?

   g. Shall you go yourself ?

   h. He had learnt his lesson before he went to school.

   i. He leaves school next Christmas.

   k. We had been strolling on the moor when we met him.

   l. He was come now to the gate.

   m. If thou wilt, thou canst make me clean.—*Bible.*

   n.   Men are we, and must grieve when even the shade
           Of that which once was great is passed away.— *Wordsworth.*

   o. We shall have been waiting there an hour before the coach comes in.

   p. Ye shall see my face no more.

   q. He is working in the garden.

   r.   Five times outlawed had he been
           By England's king and Scotia's queen.

5. What is meant by Number and Person in the case of verbs ?

6. What parts of the verb have distinctive personal endings in modern English ?

7. What was the origin of these endings ?

CONJUGATION.

76. To conjugate a verb is to arrange in order its various forms according to their mood, tense, person, and number.

Verbs are classified for this purpose according to the way in which they form their past tense. Verbs that form their past tense by a change of the radical vowel are called **Strong Verbs**, e.g.—

Pres.	Past.	Perf. Part.
write	wrote	written
fall	fell	fallen
draw	drew	drawn

The perfect participle of these verbs formerly ended in **-en**. In some cases this ending is altered into *-ne*, as in *done, gone*; in others it is dropped altogether.

Verbs that form their past tense by the addition of *-d, -t,* or *-ed* to the present are called **Weak Verbs**. The perfect participle of these verbs ends in *-d* or *-t*, e.g.—

Pres.	Past.	Pref. Part.
love	loved	loved
build	built	built
gird	girt	girt

One of the most ancient modes of forming the past tense was by reduplication, the intention of the reduplication being apparently to give the impression that the action was *thoroughly* done. In Latin and Greek, reduplicated perfects are of common occurrence, but in English the only surviving examples of them are *did*, the past tense of *do*, and *hight* (originally hêht) the past tense of *hâtan*, to be called. A contraction of the reduplicated perfect probably led to a modification of the root-vowel. It is in this way that such perfects as *fēci* in Latin are explained. The original perfect would appear to have been some such form as *fefici*, which would first contract into *fe-ici*, and then into *fēci*. Coalescence of the root-vowel and the augment-vowel will not explain the vowel change in *do, did*, for here the consonant that once separated the two vowels has been retained. What happened in this case was clearly this, the root-vowel was dropped altogether and the augment-vowel was retained.

The *-d* of the past tense of weak verbs represents the O.E. *-de*, which is a contraction of *dede* or *dyde*, the reduplicated past of *do*, so that I *loved* = I *love-did*; thou *lovedst* = thou *love-didst*.

As the past tense of weak verbs is formed by the addition of a suffix, which is itself the past of a strong verb, the strong verbs are to be regarded as the more ancient. All our primitive or root verbs belong to the strong class; all our derivative and borrowed verbs belong to the weak.[1] The weak verbs are sometimes called regular, because they all form their past tense in the same way; but the name is objectionable, because it implies that the strong verbs are irregular, whereas they also follow laws, though the laws are not so obvious.

---

[1] Ben Jonson speaks of the class of weak verbs as 'the common inn to lodge every stranger and foreign guest.'

77. COMPLETE CONJUGATION OF A TRANSITIVE VERB.

ACTIVE VOICE.

Indicative Mood.

PRESENT IMPERFECT.

Simple Form.

1. I love / We love
2. Thou lovest / Ye love
3. He loveth *or* loves / They love

Progressive Form.

1. I am loving / We are loving
2. Thou art loving / Ye are loving
3. He is loving / They are loving

PAST IMPERFECT.

Simple Form.

1. I loved / We loved
2. Thou lovedst / Ye loved
3. He loved / They loved

Progressive Form.

1. I was loving / We were loving
2. Thou wast loving / Ye were loving
3. He was loving / They were loving

FUTURE IMPERFECT.

Simple Form.

1. I shall love / We shall love
2. Thou wilt love / Ye will love
3. He will love / They will love

Progressive Form.

1. I shall be loving / We shall be loving
2. Thou wilt be loving / Ye will be loving
3. He will be loving / They will be loving

Imperfect Tenses

PRESENT PERFECT.

Simple Form.

1. I have loved   We have loved
2. Thou hast loved   Ye have loved
3. He has loved   They have loved

Progressive Form.

1. I have been loving   We have been loving
2. Thou hast been loving   Ye have been loving
3. He has been loving   They have been loving

PAST PERFECT.

Simple Form.

1. I had loved   We had loved
2. Thou hadst loved   Ye had loved
3. He had loved   They had loved

Progressive Form.

1. I had been loving   We had been loving
2. Thou hadst been loving   Ye had been loving
3. He had been loving   They had been loving

FUTURE PERFECT.

Simple Form.

1. I shall have loved   We shall have loved
2. Thou wilt have loved   Ye will have loved
3. He will have loved   They will have loved

Progressive Form.

1. I shall have been loving   We shall have been loving
2. Thou wilt have been loving   Ye will have been loving
3. He will have been loving   They will have been loving

(*Perfect Tenses*)

Imperative Mood.

PRESENT IMPERFECT.

2. Love (thou); Love (ye).

PRESENT PERFECT.

(Wanting in this verb.[1])

---

[1] A few verbs allow of a Present Perfect Imperative. Thus we say, 'Begone,' 'Have done.'

G 2

Subjunctive Mood.

PRESENT IMPERFECT.

Simple.

1. If I love   If we love
2. If thou love   If ye love
3. If he love   If they love

Progressive.

1. If I be loving   If we be loving
2. If thou be loving   If ye be loving
3. If he be loving   If they be loving

PAST IMPERFECT.

Simple.

1. If I loved   If we loved
2. If thou lovedst   If ye loved
3. If he loved   If they loved

Progressive.

1. If I were loving   If we were loving
2. If thou wert loving   If ye were loving
3. If he were loving   If they were loving

FUTURE IMPERFECT.

Simple.

1. If I should love   If we should love
2. If thou shouldst love   If you should love
3. If he should love   If they should love

Progressive.

1. If I should be loving   If we should be loving
2. If thou shouldst be loving   If ye should be loving
3. If he should be loving   If they should be loving

Imperfect Tenses

PRESENT PERFECT.

Simple.

1. If I have loved   If we have loved
2. If thou have loved   If ye have loved
3. If he have loved   If they have loved

Progressive Form.

1. If I have been loving   If we have been loving
2. If thou have been loving   If ye have been loving
3. If he have been loving   If they have been loving

PAST PERFECT.

Simple.

1. If I had loved   If we had loved
2. If thou hadst loved   If ye had loved
3. If he had loved   If they had loved

Progressive.

1. If I had been loving   If we had been loving
2. If thou hadst been loving   If ye had been loving
3. If he had been loving   If they had been loving

FUTURE PERFECT.

Simple.

1. If I should have loved   If we should have loved
2. If thou shouldst have loved   If ye should have loved
3. If he should have loved   If they should have loved

Progressive.

1. If I should have been lov- If we should have been loving
   ing
2. If thou shouldst have been If ye should have been loving
   loving
3. If he should have been lov- If they should have been loving
   ing

(margin: Perfect Tenses)

Infinitive Mood.

	Simple.	*Progressive.*
Imperfect	love	be loving
Perfect	have loved	have been loving
Gerundial Infinitive Imperf.	to love	to be loving
Gerundial Infinitive Perfect	to have loved	to have been loving

Participles

	Simple.	*Progressive.*
Imperfect	loving	
Perfect	having loved	having been loving

Verbal Noun.

Loving

PASSIVE VOICE.

Indicative Mood.

PRESENT IMPERFECT.

1. I am loved [1]	We are loved
2. Thou art loved	Ye are loved
3. He is loved	They are loved

PAST IMPERFECT.

1. I was loved	We were loved
2. Thou wast loved	Ye were loved
3. He was loved	They were loved

FUTURE IMPERFECT.

1. I shall be loved	We shall be loved
2. Thou wilt be loved	Ye will be loved
3. He will be loved	They will be loved

Imperfect Tenses

PRESENT PERFECT.

1. I have been loved	We have been loved
2. Thou hast been loved	Ye have been loved
3. He has been loved	They have been loved

PAST PERFECT.

1. I had been loved	We had been loved
2. Thou hadst been loved	Ye had been loved
3. He had been loved	They had been loved

FUTURE PERFECT.

1. I shall have been loved	We shall have been loved
2. Thou wilt have been loved	Ye will have been loved
3. He will have been loved	They will have been loved

Perfect Tenses

Imperative Mood.

PRES.   2. Be (thou) loved ; Be (ye) loved.

---

[1] The Progressive Form is rarely used in the Passive Voice. Such forms as 'I am being loved,' 'I was being loved,' 'I shall be being loved,' are very awkward, and it is questionable whether they are English at all.

Subjunctive Mood.

PRESENT IMPERFECT.

<table>
<tr><td>1. If I be loved</td><td>If we be loved</td></tr>
<tr><td>2. If thou be loved</td><td>If ye be loved</td></tr>
<tr><td>3. If he be loved</td><td>If they be loved</td></tr>
</table>

PAST IMPERFECT.

<table>
<tr><td>1. If I were loved</td><td>If we were loved</td></tr>
<tr><td>2. If thou wert loved</td><td>If ye were loved</td></tr>
<tr><td>3. If he were loved</td><td>If they were loved</td></tr>
</table>

FUTURE IMPERFECT.

<table>
<tr><td>1. If I should be loved</td><td>If we should be loved</td></tr>
<tr><td>2. If thou shouldst be loved</td><td>If ye should be loved</td></tr>
<tr><td>3. If he should be loved</td><td>If they should be loved</td></tr>
</table>

Imperfect Tenses

PRESENT PERFECT.

<table>
<tr><td>1. If I have been loved</td><td>If we have been loved</td></tr>
<tr><td>2. If thou have been loved</td><td>If ye have been loved</td></tr>
<tr><td>3. If he have been loved</td><td>If they have been loved</td></tr>
</table>

PAST PERFECT.

<table>
<tr><td>1. If I had been loved</td><td>If we had been loved</td></tr>
<tr><td>2. If thou hadst been loved</td><td>If ye had been loved</td></tr>
<tr><td>3. If he had been loved</td><td>If they had been loved</td></tr>
</table>

FUTURE PERFECT.

<table>
<tr><td>1. If I should have been loved</td><td>If we should have been loved</td></tr>
<tr><td>2. If thou shouldst have been loved</td><td>If ye should have been loved</td></tr>
<tr><td>3. If he should have been loved</td><td>If they should have been loved</td></tr>
</table>

Perfect Tenses

Infinitive Mood.

Imperfect	be loved
Perfect	have been loved
Gerundial Infinitive Imperfect	to be loved
Gerundial Infinitive Perfect	to have been loved

Participles.

Imperfect, being loved.
Perfect, having been loved

STRONG VERBS.

78. The strong verbs may be classified as follows—

I. *Verbs which modify the root-vowel to form the past imperfect tense, and form the perfect participle in -en or -n.*

Present Imperfect	Past Imperfect	Perfect Participle	Present Imperfect	Past Imperfect	Perfect Participle
arise	arose	arisen	hide	hid	hidden
bear (to carry)	bare or bore	borne	hold	held	holden or held
bear (to give birth to)	bore	born	lie	lay	lien or lain
			ride	rode	ridden
			rise	rose	risen
beget	begat	begotten	see	saw	seen
bid	bade or bad	bidden	seethe	sod	sodden or sod
bite	bit	bitten			
blow (to bloom)	blew	blown	shake	shook	shaken
			shear	shore	shorn
blow (of wind)	blew	blown	shrink	shrank	shrunken or shrunk
break	broke or brake	broken	shrive	shrove	shriven
			sink	sank	sunken or sunk
chide	chid	chidden			
choose	chose	chosen	slay	slew	slain
cleave	clave or clove	cloven or cleft	smite	smote	smitten
			speak	spoke or spake	spoken
draw	drew	drawn			
drink	drank	drunken or drunk	steal	stole	stolen
			stride	strode	stridden
drive	drave or drove	driven	strike	struck or strake	stricken or struck
eat	ate or eat	eaten	strive	strove	striven
fall	fell	fallen	swear	swore or sware	sworn
fly	flew	flown			
forbid	forbade	forbidden	take	took	taken
forget	forgot	forgotten	tear	tore or tare	torn
forgive	forgave	forgiven	thrive	throve	thriven
forsake	forsook	forsaken	throw	threw	thrown
freeze	froze	frozen	tread	trod	trodden
get	got	gotten or got	wear	wore	worn
			weave	wove	woven or wove
give	gave	given			
grow	grew	grown	write	wrote	written

II. *Verbs which modify the root-vowel to form the past imperfect, and drop the ending -en in the perfect participle.*

abide	abode	abode	shoot	shot	shot
awake	awoke	awoke *or* awaked	sing	sang	sung
			sit	sat	sat
begin	began	begun	slide	slid	slid
behold	beheld	beheld	sling	slung	slung
bind	bound	bound	slink	slunk	slunk
climb	clomb *or* climbed	climbed	spin	span	spun
			spring	sprang	sprung
cling	clung	clung	spit	spat	spit
come	came	come	stand	stood	stood
dig	dug	dug *or* digged	stave	stove	stove
			stick	stuck	stuck
find	found	found	sting	stung	stung
fling	flung	flung	stink	stank *or* stunk	stunk
fight	fought	fought			
grind	ground	ground	string	strung	strung
hang (*of things*)	hung	hung	swim	swam	swum
			swing	swung	swung
meet	met	met	wake	woke	waked
ring	rang	rung	win	won	won
run	ran	run	wind	wound	wound
shine	shone	shone	wring	wrung	wrung

III. *Verbs which at present are alike in the present imperfect and past imperfect, and drop the participial ending -en.*

bid (*offer*)	bid	bid	shed	shed	shed
burst	burst	burst	shut	shut	shut
cut	cut	cut	slit	slit	slit

WEAK VERBS.

The weak verbs may be classified as follows—

I. *Verbs which form their past imperfect tense and their perfect participle in -ed or -d, e.g.—*

love	loved	loved

II. *Verbs which contract -ed into -t without vowel-change.*

bend	bent	bent	lend	lent	lent
blend	blent	blent	rend	rent	rent
build	built	built	send	sent	sent
gild	gilt	gilt	spend	spent	spent
gird	girt	girt	wend	went	

III. *Verbs that form their past tense in -ed, -d, or -t, and, as a consequence of the syllable originally added to form the past tense, modify the root-vowel.*

bereave	bereft	bereft	light	lit	lit
beseech	besought	besought	lose	lost	lost
bleed	bled	bled	mean	meant	meant
breed	bred	bred	meet	met	met
buy	bought	bought	read	read	read
catch	caught	caught	say	said	said
cleave	cleft	cleft	seek	sought	sought
clothe	clad	clad	sell	sold	sold
deal	dealt	dealt	shoe	shod	shod
dream	dreamt	dreamt	sleep	slept	slept
feed	fed	fed	speed	sped	sped
feel	felt	felt	sweep	swept	swept
hide	hid	hid	teach	taught	taught
keep	kept	kept	tell	told	told
kneel	knelt	knelt	think	thought	thought
lead	led	led	weep	wept	wept
leap	leapt	leapt	work	wrought	wrought
leave	left	left			

IV. *Verbs which have the same form for the present and past imperfect tense and for the perfect participle, the -d or -t having been merged in the -d or -t of the uninflected verb ;* as cast, cost, cut, hit, hurt, knit, let, put, rid, shed, shred, shut, slit, spit, split, spread, sweat, thrust.

Some verbs follow the weak conjugation in the past imperfect and the strong in the perfect participle, e.g.—

lade	laded	laden	show	showed	shown
mow	mowed	mown	sow	sowed	sown
rive	rived	riven	strew	strewed	strewed *or*
saw	sawed	sawn			strewn
sew	sewed	sewn	wax	waxed	waxen

The following verbs, now weak, were originally strong—

ache	ached (ok)	ached (oke)
blind	blinded (blent)	blinded (y-blent)
carve	carved (carf)	carved (carven)
climb	climbed (clomb)	climbed (clomben)
clothe	clothed (clad)	clothed (y-clad)
crow	crowed (crew)	crowed (crown)
delve	delved (delf)	delved (delven)

dread	dreaded (drad)	dreaded (a-drad)
drown	drowned (dreint)	drowned (a-drent)
fare	fared (fore)	fared (y-fare)
fill	filled (fulle)	filled (y-fuld)
fold	folded (fald)	folded (folden)
fret	fretted (frat)	fretted (fretten)
fetch	fetched (fet)	fetched (fought)
gnaw	gnawed (gnew)	gnawed (gnawn)
grave	graved (grove)	graved (graven)
hang	hanged *or* hung (heng)	hanged *or* hung (y-honge)
heat	heated (het)	heated *or* heat (i-het)
heave	heaved (hove *or* heft)	heaven (hoven)
help	helped (help)	helped (holpen)
hew	hewed (hew)	hewed (hewn)
knit	knitted (knot)	knitted (knit)
laugh	laughed (lough)	laughed (i-lowe)
melt	melted (molt)	melted (molten)
pitch	pitched (pight)	pitched (y-pight)
reach	reached (raught)	reached (i-raught)
seethe	seethed (sod)	seethed (sodden)
sew	sewed (seu)	sewed (sewn)
shape	shaped (shope)	shaped (shapen)
shear	sheared (shore)	sheared (shorn)
sleep	sleeped *or* slept (slep)	sleeped *or* slept
snow	snowed (snewed)	snowed
starve	starved (starf)	starved
spend	spended (sped)	spended (y-sped)
squeeze	squeezed (squoze)	squeezed (squozen)
stretch	stretched (straught)	stretched (straighten)
sweat	sweated (swot)	sweated (sweaten)
swell	swelled (swol)	swelled (swollen)
walk	walked (walk)	walked
weep	weeped *or* wept (wep)	weeped *or* wept
yield	yielded (yald)	yielded (yolden)

The following verbs are now strong, but were formerly weak—

betide	betid	betid		spit	spat *or* spit	spat
dig	dug	dug			*or* spet	
hide	hid	hidden		wear	wore	worn
stick	stuck	stuck				

The participles *lorn* and *forlorn* are formed from the obsolete verb *leósan*, to lose, perf. part. loren. Comp. *froren* = frozen, from *freosan*, to freeze. *Tight, distraught*, and *straight*, are respectively the perfect participles of *tie, distract*, and *stretch*, but are now used only as adjectives. Many old participles are preserved in compound adjective forms, e.g. *uncouth* = unknown, from *cuth*, perf. part. of *cunnan*, to know; *ill-gotten; misbegotten; unkempt*, from *comb; unborn*, from *bear; unbidden*, from *bid; unthrift*, from *thrive; bed-ridden* is a corruption of O.E. *bed- rida* (*rida*, a rider, knight).

Exercises.

1. Classify the verbs as strong or weak in the following passages—

a. We forded the river and clomb the high hill.—*Byron.*

b.   And yet he glanced not up, nor waved his hand,
Nor bad farewell, but sadly rode away.—*Tennyson.*

c. And all this throve until I wedded thee.—*Id.*

d.   And all his kith and kin
Clave to him.—*Id.*

e.   When Adam dalve [delved] and Eve span,
Who was then the gentleman?

f. And Jacob abode with Laban.—*Bible.*

g.   Ice-chained in its headlong tract
Have I seen a cataract,
All throughout a wintry noon,
Hanging in the silent moon ;
All throughout a sun-bright even,
Like the sapphire gate of heaven ;
Spray and wave, and drippings frore,
For a hundred feet and more
Caught in air there to remain
Bound in winter's crystal chain.—*I. Williams.*

h. It snewed in his hous of mete and drynk.—*Chaucer.*

i.   A clerk ther was of Oxenford also,
That unto logik hadde long igo.—*Id.*

k.   And when he rood men might his bridel heare
Gyngle in a whistlying wynd so clere.—*Id.*

l. Ful semely aftur hire mete she raught.—*Id.*

m. And thereon heng a broch of gold ful schene.—*Id.*

2. Give the past imperfect tense and perfect participle of the following verbs : stick, grind, wink, ring, forbear, wring, swear, seethe, sting, smite, weave.

3. Give instances of (*a*) verbs formerly weak now strong, (*b*) formerly strong now weak. Account where you can for the changes.

4. Classify the strong verbs, as far as you can, according to their vowel changes.

THE PARSING OF FINITE VERBS.

79. In parsing finite verbs we should state—

1. Whether the verb be transitive or intransitive.[1]
2. The voice, if passive.
3. The mood, tense, number, and person.
4. The syntactical relations in which the verb stands to its subject.

The compound tenses should be parsed as though they were simple.

> The autumn *is* old,
>   The sere leaves *are flying*;
> He *hath gathered* up gold,
> And now he *is dying*:
>   Old Age, *begin* sighing.

Word	Class	Inflexions	Syntactical Relations
is	Verb, intrans., copulative	indic. ; pres. imperf. tense; 3rd per.; sing.	agreeing with its subj. ' autumn '
are flying	Verb, intrans.	indic.; pres. imperf. prog.; 3rd per.; plu.	agreeing with its subj. ' leaves '
hath gathered	Verb, trans.	indic.; pres. pf. tense ; 3rd per.; sing.	agreeing with its subject ' he '
is dying	Verb, intrans.	indic.; pres. imperf. prog.; 3rd per.; sing.	agreeing with its subj. ' he '
begin	Verb, trans.	imper.; pres. imperf. tense; 2nd per.; sing.	agreeing with its subj. ' thou,' unders'ood

[1] Copulative verbs like 'be,' 'become,' 'continue,' 'remain' are intransitive, but should be further described as copulative.

Exercises.

Parse the finite verbs in the following passages—

a.   I wandered lonely as a cloud
             That floats on high o'er vales and hills,
             When all at once I saw a crowd,
             A host of golden daffodils.—*Wordsworth.*

b.   My heart aches, and a drowsy numbness pains
             My sense, as though of hemlock I had drunk,
             Or emptied some dull opiate to the drains.—*Keats.*

c.   We look before and after,
             And pine for what is not :
         Our sincerest laughter
         With some pain is fraught ;
Our sweetest songs are those that tell of saddest thought.
                                     Shelley.

d.   Howe'er it be, it seems to me
         'Tis only noble to be good.—*Tennyson.*

e. Be thou familiar, but by no means vulgar.—*Shakspere.*

f. Now see I by thine eyes that this is done.—*Tennyson.*

g.   If pride were his, 'twas not their vulgar pride
         Who in their base contempt the great deride ;
         But, if that spirit in his soul had place,
         It was the jealous pride that shuns disgrace.

h. Cursed be the social lies that warp us from the living truth.
                                     Tennyson.

i. I have been abused.

k. I shall have been here ten years at Christmas.

l. As it were with shame she blushes.—*Tennyson.*

m.   I could lie down like a tired child,
             And weep away the life of care
             Which I have borne and yet must bear.—*Shelley.*

n. I had fainted unless I had believed to see the goodness of the
Lord in the land of the living.—*Bible.*

o.   Speak ! though this soft warm heart, once free to hold
         A thousand tender pleasures, thine and mine,
         Be left more desolate, more dreary cold,
         Than a forsaken bird's nest filled with snow
         'Mid its own bush of leafless eglantine—
         Speak ! that my torturing doubts their end may know.
                                     Wordsworth.

PARSING OF INFINITIVES, PARTICIPLES, AND VERBAL SUBSTANTIVES.

80. In parsing the infinitive state—

1. Whether the verb be transitive or intransitive.
2. Active or passive; perfect or imperfect.
3. Its syntactical relations: whether Subject, Direct Object, or Indirect Object; whether governed by another verb, or used to qualify a noun or adjective, &c.

N.B.—Infinitives have **no number or person.**

In parsing participles state—

1. Whether formed from transitive or intransitive verbs.
2. Active or passive; imperfect or perfect.
3. Syntactical relations, whether qualifying attributively or predicatively.

EXAMPLE.

'*Having completed* my drawing, I went *to see* my brother *felling* his oaks; but a shower came on and compelled me *to turn* back. I returned thoroughly *exhausted*, and was glad to amuse myself with *turning* over the pages of a novel.'

Word	Class	Inflexions	Syntactical Relations
having completed	Verb, trans.	Perf. participle	qualifying 'I' predicatively
to see	„ „	Gerund. infin. imperf.	gov. by 'went'
felling	„ „	Imperf. participle	qualifying 'brother' predicatively
to turn	Verb, intrans.	Gerund. infin. imperf.	ind. obj., gov. by 'compelled'
exhausted	Verb, trans.	Participle imp., passive voice	qualifying 'I' predicatively
turning	Noun, verbal	3rd person, sing.	obj. case, gov. by 'with'; governing, in virtue of its verbal force, 'pages'

Exercises.

Parse the infinitives and participles in the following passages :—

a.   Thus done the tales, to bed they creep,
       By whispering winds soon lulled asleep.—*Milton.*

b.   Hence, vain deluding joys,
       The brood of folly without father bred !—*Id.*

c.   The shrivelled wing,
     Scathed by what seemed a star,
   And proved, alas, no star, but withering fire,
   Is worthier than the wingless worm's desire
   For nothing fair or far.—*Lord Lytton.*

d. To spend too much time in studies is sloth.—*Bacon.*

e. There's little to earn and many to keep.—*Kingsley.*

f.   Here, under leave of Brutus and the rest . . .
       Come I to speak in Cæsar's funeral.—*Shakspere.*

g.   Bid me to live, and I will live
         Thy Protestant to be;
       Or bid me love, and I will give
         A loving heart to thee.—*Herrick.*

h. Bid him go and tell his sister to come.

i. O, pardon me, thou bleeding piece of earth.—*Shakspere.*

j. Passion, I see, is catching.—*Id.*

k Having been defeated once, he did not seek another engagement.

l. To seek philosophy in Scripture is to seek the dead among the living.

m. We shall often talk of this in days to come.

n.   My story being done,
   She gave me for my pains a world of sighs.—*Shakspere.*

o. Teaching is the best way of learning.

p. I told him to ask his friend to come.

q. He was commanded to depart.

r. Our greatest glory is not in never falling, but in rising every time we fall.—*Confucius.*

s. A man lives by believing something, not by debating and arguing about many things.—*Carlyle.*

ANOMALOUS VERBS.

81. Some verbs are complete in their tenses, but deviate in some respects from the conjugation of both strong and

weak verbs. Others, as 'must' and 'ought,' are defective in certain moods and tenses. Both classes may be called **Anomalous**; the latter is commonly called **Defective**.

BE.

(Principal Verb and Auxiliary.)

82. The verb *be* is compounded of parts of four distinct verbs. Comp. *am, are, be, was.*

Indicative Mood.

PRESENT IMPERFECT.

1. I am   We are
2. Thou art   Ye are
3. He is   They are

PAST IMPERFECT.

1. I was   We were
2. Thou wast   Ye were
3. He was   They were

Subjunctive.

PRESENT IMPERFECT.

1. If I be   If we be
2. If thou be   If ye be
3. If he be   If they be

PAST IMPERFECT.

1. If I were   If we were
2. If thou wert   If ye were
3. If he were   If they were

Imperative.

2. Be thou   Be ye

Infinitive.

Simple Infin. Imperfect   Be   Perf. Have been.
Gerundial Infin. Imperfect   To be   Perf. To have been.

Participles.

Imperfect   Being
Perfect   Having been

The compound tenses are regular.

Am (O.E. com). The *-m* is a trace of an old pronoun of the first person. Cp. *me*, Lat. *sum*, &c.

H

We had formerly another form of the present tense, viz.

I be	We be
Thou beest	Ye be
He be	They be

It still survives in provincial English, and traces of it may be found in the A. V. of the Bible, e.g.—

> The Philistines *be* upon thee.
> We *be* twelve brethren, sons of one father.

Art (O.E. eart). The *-t* represents an old pronoun of the second person. Comp. Ger. *du bist* = thou art ; wil*t*, shal*t*.

Is has lost its old pronominal suffix *-th*. Comp. Ger. *er ist* = he is ; Lat. *est*, &c.

Are (Scandinavian *aron*). The O.E. plural was *sind* or *sindon*. *Are* never occurs in O.E. It was introduced by the Danes.

Was (O.E. wǽs), the past tense of *wesan*, to be. Comp. Ger. *gewesen* = been.

Wast. The old form was *wǽre*. *Wert*, which is sometimes used as a past tense, was evidently formed from *wǽre*.

Were (O.E. wǽron).

In O.E. negative forms of the verb 'be' are of common occurrence, e.g. nam = am not.

83. The verb *be* is used :

1. *As a principal verb* in the sense of *to exist*, e.g.—

God *was*, and *is*, and ever *will be*.
Before Abraham *was* I *am*.—*Bible*.

2. *As a principal verb* to express either *absolute identity* or *the relation of a thing to its class*, e.g.—

Two and two *are* four.
John *is* a soldier.
Soldiers *are* men.
Men *are* bipeds.

The verb discharges this function when used with an adjective to form the predicate :

He *is* good =
He belongs to the class of things called good.

3. *As the auxiliary of the Passive Voice*, e.g.—

He *is* beaten.

4. *As the auxiliary of the perfect tenses of verbs of going and coming*, &c., e.g.—

He *is* gone.
We *are* come.

5. *As a mood auxiliary, having the force of obligation or intention,* e.g.—

He *is* to be shot to-morrow.

84. HAVE.

(Principal Verb and Auxiliary.)

Only two tenses of this verb are irregular.

Indicative Mood.

PRESENT IMPERFECT.

1. I have	We have
2. Thou hast	Ye have
3. He has	They have

PAST IMPERFECT.

1. I had	We had
2. Thou hadst	Ye had
3. He had	They had

Hast = havest
Has = haves
Had = haved

85. The verb *have* is used—

1. *As a transitive verb* in the sense of *to possess,* e.g.—

He *has* a book.

2. *As the tense auxiliary of the perfect tenses,* e.g.—

He *has* struck the target.

3. *As a mood auxiliary of obligation,* e.g.—

He *has* to learn his lesson before he can play.

In this construction some may prefer to regard *has* as a transitive verb governing the gerundial infinitive which follows.

In O.E. negative forms, such as *nave* = have not, *nast* = hast not, *nath* = hath not, &c., are of common occurrence.

86. OWE.[1]

Indicative.

PRESENT IMPERFECT TENSE.

1. I owe.	We owe.
2. Thou owest	Ye owe
3. He owes	They owe

---

[1] *Owe* is now conjugated regularly when it means *to be in debt.*

PAST IMPERFECT TENSE.

(Used as an auxiliary with both past and present meaning.)

1. I ought	We ought
2. Thou oughtest	Ye ought
3. He ought	They ought

Owe is from the O.E. *ágan*, to own, possess. Hence the secondary meanings, 'to have as a duty,' 'to owe.' The verb *own* is another form of *ágan*. The adjective *own* is the perfect participle of *ágan*.
Owe is often used in the sense of *possess* in Shakspere, e.g.—

> I am not worthy of the wealth I *owe*.
> > *All's Well that Ends Well*, ii. 5.

> Be pleased then
> To pay that duty which you truly *owe*
> To him who *owes* it.—*K. John*, ii. 1.

Ought is properly a past tense, but is sometimes used as a present, to express the sense of being under a moral obligation, e.g.—

> He *ought* to have done it (Past).
> He *ought* to do it (Present).

In M.E. we find *ought* used in the sense of the Lat. *debeo*, e.g.—

> He *oughte* to him 10,000 talents.—*Wiclif*, Matt. xviii. 24.

> One of his felowes which *ought* him an hundred pence.—Tyndale's *N. T.* A.D. 1534.

> [He said] you *ought* him a thousand pound.—*Shakspere*, Hen. IV. Part I., iii. 3.

87.   WIT.

Indicative.

PRESENT IMPERFECT TENSE.

1. I wot	We wot
2. Thou wot *or* wottest	Ye wot
3. He wot *or* wotteth	They wot

PAST IMPERFECT TENSE.

1. I wist	We wist
2. Thou wist	Ye wist
3. He wist	They wist

Ger. Inf.	To wit
Imp. Part.	Witting
Perf. Part.	Wist

Wot is from O.E. *witan*, to know. Comp. 'to wit,' 'wittingly,' 'unwittingly': e.g.—

> I *wot* not who hath done this thing.—Gen. xxi. 26.

> My master *wotteth* not what is with me.—Gen. xxxix. 8.

Wot ye not that such a man as I can certainly divine ?— Gen. xliv. 15.

Wist ye not that I must be about my Father's business ?— Luke ii. 49.

The *s* in *wist* was probably inserted to connect the *t* of the root with the *te* of the past tense, and then superseded the first *t*. Comp. mu*st*.

The form ' I wis,' which often appears in the Elizabethan poets, is a corruption of *ywis* = truly, certainly. Comp. Ger. gewiss. There is no verb *wiss* in the language, though commentators have invented one to explain a form which they did not understand. Comp.—

For in her mind no thought there is,
But how she may be true, *I wis.*—*Surrey.*

Ywis, it is not half way to her heart.
Taming of the Shrew, i. 1.

There be fools alive, *I wis*,
Silvered o'er ; and so was this.—*Merchant of Venice*, ii. 8.

Macaulay has imitated this archaism in ' Horatius : '

I wis, in all the senate
There was no heart so bold, &c.

88. DARE.

(Intransitive = Lat. audeo.)

Indicative.

PRESENT IMPERFECT TENSE.

1. I dare	We dare
2. Thou darest	Ye dare
3. He dares (dare)	They dare

PAST IMPERFECT TENSE.

1. I durst	We durst
2. Thou durst	Ye durst
3. He durst	They durst

Subjunctive.

PRESENT IMPERFECT TENSE.

1. I dare	We dare
2. Thou dare	Ye dare
3. He dare	They dare

PAST IMPERFECT TENSE.

1. I durst	We durst
2. Thou durst	Ye durst
3. He durst	They durst

The intransitive verb *dare* should be carefully distinguished from the transitive verb *dare* (*provoco*), which belongs to the weak conjugation, and further differs from the intransitive verb in taking the preposition 'to' before the gerundial infinitive. In Shakspere the intransitive verb 'dare' sometimes takes the infinitive with 'to' after it, e.g. 'I *durst*, my lord, to *wager* she is honest.' (Othello, iv. 2.) Cp.

> (Intrans.) I dare *do* all that may become a man :
> Who dares *do* more is none.—*Shakspere.*

> (Trans.) I dare thee but *to breathe* upon my love.—*Id.*

Dare is properly the past tense of the verb *durran*, but is now used as a present.

Durst is the proper past of the intransitive verb *dare*. In modern English it is often superseded by 'dared.' It is sometimes, but incorrectly, used as a present tense.

The *st* in *durst* is obviously not the *st* of the second person, for it occurs in the first and third person also. The *s* is part of the root ; the *t* is part of the past ending. In Greek we find θαρρεῖν and θαρσεῖν (tharrhein and tharsein)=to dare.

DEFECTIVE VERBS.

89. Verbs that have not the full complement of moods and tenses are called defective. Most of the auxiliary verbs are defective ; so are some principal verbs, e.g.—

Quoth (past imperfect tense) from O.E. *cwéthan*, to say. Cp. *bequeath*, to say how one's property is to be disposed of after death. Dr. Adams thinks that *quote* is from the same source, but Wedgwood derives it from Lat. *quot*, how many, and explains it ' to cite or note with chapter and verse.'

Wont (perfect participle) from O.E. *wunian*, to dwell ; hence to continue, to be used or accustomed to. Cp. Ger. *wohnen*, to dwell ; O.E. *wune*, a habit, custom ; e.g.—

> And as He was *wont*, He taught them again.—Mark x. 1.

Worth (imperative) from O.E. *weorthan*, to become, to happen. Cp. Ger. *werden*, to become. Cp.—

> Woe *worth* the chase, woe *worth* the day
> That cost thy life, my gallant grey !—*Scott.*

Here *worth* = betide, and ' chase ' and ' day ' are dative cases.

Hight (past imperfect tense, passive voice ; also perfect participle) from O.E. *hátan* = to be called, e.g.—

> An ancient fabric raised t' inform the sight
> There stood of yore, and Barbican it *hight* (= was called).
> *Dryden.*

> This grisly beast, which Lion *hight* by name.
> *Mids. Night's Dream*, v. 1.

The **Impersonal** Verbs are all defective, e.g.—

Methinks = it seems to me. From O.E. *thincan*, to seem, a different verb from *thencan*, to think. In M.E. we find 'it thinketh me ;' 'it thought them,' &c.

Meseems. From O.E. *seman*, to seem, appear.

Melisteth. From O.E. *lystan* = to will, please. By the sixteenth century both 'seem' and 'list' were beginning to be used as personal verbs, e.g.—

> What *seemeth* you best I will do.—2 Sam. xviii. 4.

> For when it *seemed* him good.—Lat. Rem. p. 30.

> If he had *listed*, he might have stood on the water.
>
> Latimer, *Serm*. p. 205.

But Shakspere writes 'me *seemeth* good,' *Rich. II.* ii. 2.

AUXILIARY VERBS.

90. Certain verbs are used with other verbs to express various relations of voice, mood, and tense, and are hence called **auxiliary** or **helping verbs**, the verbs with which they are used being called, by way of distinction, **principal verbs.** All of these verbs were originally capable of being used independently, and some of them—as *have, be, will, let*—can be so used now ; but the others—as *may, can, shall, must*—are no longer capable of standing alone. The Auxiliary Verbs may be classified as follows—

1. **Voice Auxiliary,** *Be.* 'In O.E. *weorthan* and *wesan* were used with the passive participle to form the passive voice.' (Morris.) The voice auxiliary may be parsed with the principal verb, as forming one compound expression, or separately. The former seems preferable.

2. **Tense Auxiliaries,** e.g. *have, be, shall, will.*

Have is used to form the *perfect tenses.*

Be is also used to form the *perfect tenses of intransitive verbs of going and coming,* &c.

Shall and *will* are used to form the *future tenses*, but cease to be tense auxiliaries when they express other relations than that of time. Thus 'shall' is a tense auxiliary in the first person, but not in the second, except in interrogative sentences, and so on. The tense auxiliaries, like the voice auxiliary, may be parsed either with the principal verb or separately.

3. **Mood Auxiliaries** are used to express various relations of mood, and more particularly as signs of the subjunctive and imperative ; e.g. I will ask that he *may go* ; though he *should go* ; *let* him *10* = go he.

Let is used (1) as *a principal verb* in the sense of *allow*, e.g. he *let* me go; (2) *as a sign of the imperative* in the first and third persons, e.g. *let* us go, *let* him go.

In parsing, mood auxiliaries may be treated either separately or with the principal verbs which they govern.

91.   SHALL.

Indicative Mood.

PRESENT IMPERFECT TENSE.

1. I shall	We shall
2. Thou shalt	Ye shall
3. He shall	They shall

PAST IMPERFECT TENSE.

(With both present and past meaning.)

1. I should	We should
2. Thou shouldst	Ye should
3. He should	They should

Subjunctive Mood.

PAST IMPERFECT TENSE.

1. If I should	If we should
2. If thou shouldest *or* shouldst	If ye should
3. If he should	If they should

Shall has no imperative, no infinitive, and no participles.

The original infinitive was *sculan* = to owe, out of which meaning grew the sense of obligation or necessity which appears in some of the forms of shall.[1]

In the first person of the present indicative *shall* is a tense auxiliary, expressing time and nothing more; in the second and third it expresses either *determination* on the part of the speaker or some *obligation* that the person addressed or spoken of is under.

---

[1] Cp. 'Hú micel *scealt* thú?' [How much owest thou?]—Luke xvi. 5. 'Be ure & he *sceal* swelten' [By our law he ought to die].—John xix. 7. 'For by the faithe I *shal* to God.'—Chaucer. The obligatory sense comes out strongly in the past imperfect tense, e.g. 'You *should* be attentive.' Grimm says, 'Skal, debeo, implies a form *skila*; *skila* must have meant "I kill or wound;" *skal*, "I have killed or wounded, and I am therefore liable to pay the were-geld" [penalty].' Quoted by Dr. Adams, who points out that in German *schuld* means both debt and guilt.

92.
WILL.
Indicative Mood.

PRESENT IMPERFECT TENSE.

1. I will   We will
2. Thou wilt   Ye will
3. He will   They will

PAST IMPERFECT TENSE.

(With both present and past meaning.)

1. I would   We would
2. Thou wouldest *or* wouldst   Ye would
3. He would   They would

Subjunctive Mood.

PAST IMPERFECT TENSE.

1. If I would   If we would
2. If thou wouldest *or* wouldst   If ye would
3. If he would   If they would

In O.E. there were two verbs *willan*, to will, and *wilnian*, to desire. The former was conjugated ic wille, thu wilt, he wile, we willath, &c.; past ic wolde. The latter was regular, and had for its past tense ic wilnode. Owing to the similarity of meaning the forms of the two verbs were often confounded.

In the first person *will* retains its sense of exercising the will; in the second and third it expresses simple futurity unless it be emphasized, and then it recovers its original meaning, e.g.—

He *will* go, although I have asked him to stop.

In the following passages *will* is the principal verb—

If thou *wilt* ($\theta\acute{\epsilon}\lambda\eta\varsigma$) thou canst make me clean. And Jesus put forth His hand, and touched him, saying, I *will* ($\theta\acute{\epsilon}\lambda\omega$), be thou clean.—Matt. viii. 3.

For it is common with princes, saith Tacitus, to *will* contradictories.—*Bacon.*

For the good that I *would* ($\theta\acute{\epsilon}\lambda\omega$), I do not; but the evil which I *would* ($\theta\acute{\epsilon}\lambda\omega$) not, that I do.—Rom. vii. 19.

To *will* is present with me.—Rom. viii. 18.

I *will* ($\theta\acute{\epsilon}\lambda\omega$) not send them away fasting.—Matt. xv. 32.

Dean Alford would render 'I am not willing to.' See also Matt. xx. 14, 'I *will* give unto this last,' &c., where the Dean would render 'It is my will to give.'

93.   MAY.

Indicative Mood.

PRESENT IMPERFECT TENSE.

1. I may	We may
2. Thou mayest	Ye may
3. He may	They may

PAST IMPERFECT TENSE.

(With both present and past meaning.)

1. I might	We might
2. Thou mightest *or* mightst	Ye might
3. He might	They might

Subjunctive Mood.

Tenses same as those of the Indicative.

May has no imperative, no infinitive, and no participles. The *y* is a softened form of *g*, the old infinitive being *mágan*.[1] Cp. *day* from *dæg*. The old second person singular of the present tense was *thú meaht*. *Mayest* is a comparatively modern form.

In optative sentences *may* expresses a desire, but the original force of the verb is not wholly lost. '*May* you be happy' probably meant originally, ' I desire that nothing may prevent you from being happy.'

May is now often used in subjunctive constructions where formerly the simple subjunctive was used, e.g.—

That we *show* forth Thy praise.—*Prayer Book.*

Mow, p. *mought*, is a cognate form of *may* which survives in provincial English.

94.   CAN.

Indicative Mood.

PRESENT IMPERFECT TENSE.

1. I can	We can
2. Thou canst	Ye can
3. He can	They can

PAST IMPERFECT TENSE.

(With both present and past meaning.)

1. I could	We could
2. Thou couldst	Ye could
3. He could	They could

---

[1] The root = to be able, to increase, to grow. Cp. '*Might* and *main*,' 'A *main* strong man' (provincial).

Subjunctive Mood.

PRESENT IMPERFECT TENSE.

1. If I can   If we can
2. If thou canst If ye can
3. If he can   If they can

PAST IMPERFECT TENSE.

1. If I could   If we could
2. If thou couldst If ye could
3. If he could   If they could

Can is from the O.E. *cunnan*, to know, to be able, e.g.—

Ne *cann* ic eow [I know you not].—Matt. xxv. 12.

He seede *canst* thou Greek?—*Wiclif's Bible.*

I lerne song, I *can* but small gramere.—*Chaucer.*

In evil, the best condition is not to will, the second not to *can.*—*Bacon's Essays,* xi.

Cp. 'to *con* a lesson,' '*uncouth*'=unknown, '*cunning*'=as an adj. *knowing*, as a subst. *knowledge*. With regard to the connection in meaning between *can*, to know, and *can*, to be able, cp. Bacon's saying, '*Knowledge* is *power.*'

Can was originally a past tense.[1] Hence, like other past tenses, it has no personal endings for the first and third persons.

Could represents the O.E. past tense, *cuthe.* The *l* has been inserted in it from following the false analogy of *would* and *should*, in which the *l* forms part of the root.

95.   DO.

(Auxiliary.)

Indicative Mood.

PRESENT IMPERFECT TENSE.

1. I do   We do
2. Thou dost Ye do
3. He does   They do

---

[1] Latham says with regard to certain apparent present tenses in English: 'In English there are at least nine of these words—(1) dare and durst, (2) own=admit, (3) can, (4) shall, (5) may, (6) mean and mind, (7) wot, (8) ought, (9) must. Of these none present any serious difficulties when we look at them simply in respect to their meaning: . . . dare=I have made up my mind; own=I have got possession of; mind=I have re-collected my ideas; and wot=I have informed myself. *Can* originally equalled, I have learned; *shall*, I have been obliged, I should; *may*, I have got the power; *must*, I have been constrained.'

PAST IMPERFECT TENSE.

1. I did	We did
2. Thou didst	Ye did
3. He did	They did

Imperative.   Do (thou); do (ye).

The Subjunctive Mood runs, I do, Thou do, He do, &c.

Do is used in four different ways in English—

    1. *As a principal verb,* in the sense of *facio,* e.g.—

        I *do* you to wit = I make you to understand.

O.E. *dón,* to do, make, cause, to put.

    2. In the sense of Lat. *valere,* to be well, e.g.—

        How do you *do*?

        This will never *do*.

        Lord, if he sleep, he shall *do* well.—*Bible.*

This *do* comes from the O.E. *dugan,* to avail, to profit, to be good for. Cp. *doughty,* as in ' doughty deeds,' ' a doughty warrior.'

    3. *As an emphatic auxiliary,* e.g.—

        I *do* hope that he will come.

    4. *As an interrogative auxiliary,* e.g.—

        Does he draw ?

Here there is no emphasis on the auxiliary. We use ' does' simply to avoid the abruptness of ' Draws he ?'

96.   MUST.

Indicative Mood.

PRESENT AND PAST IMPERFECT TENSE.

1. I must	We must
2. Thou must	Ye must
3. He must	They must

Must was the past tense of the O.E. verb mótan, to be able, to be obliged, but is now used both as a past and present tense. Compare 'He must have done it,' where it is past, with ' Must I do it ?' where it is present. The old present ran, 1. mót, 2. móst, 3. mót, 1, 2, 3, plu. móton; the past being, 1. móste, 2. móstest, 3. móste, 1, 2, 3, plur. móston

The *s* in *must* was probably inserted to connect the *t* of the root with the final *-te* of the past tense. The first *t* then became blended with the *s*. Comp. the insertion of the *s* in *wist*.

PARSING OF AUXILIARIES.

97. The parsing of an auxiliary ought to show—

1. What kind of auxiliary it is.
2. Mood, tense, number, and person.
3. Agreement with subject.

An auxiliary may be parsed with the principal verb, but it is better to parse mood auxiliaries by themselves, and treat the principal verbs as infinitives governed by them.

Tense and voice auxiliaries should be parsed with the principal verbs.

EXAMPLES.

1. 'I *can* not say what he *may* have done, but I know what he *could* do.'

2. 'If he *could* do it, he *should* have done it.'

Word	Class	Inflexions	Syntactical Relations
1. Can	mood auxiliary	indic.; pres. impf.; 1st per.; sing.	agreeing with its nom. 'I.'
may	,, ,,	indic.; pres. impf.; 3rd per.; sing.	agreeing with its nom. 'he.'
could	,, ,,	indic.; past impf.; 3rd per.; sing.	agreeing with its nom. 'he.'
2. Could	,, ,,	subj.; past impf.; 3rd per.; sing.	agreeing with its nom. 'he.'
should	,, ,,	indic.; past impf.; 3rd per.; sing.	agreeing with its nom. 'he.'

Exercises.

Parse the auxiliary verbs in the following passages—

a. Oh, could I fly, I'd fly with thee.—*Logan.*
b. Thou shalt not steal.
c. He shall go, whether he likes it or not.
d. The line A B shall coincide with the line B C.
e. He may go at twelve if he can finish his work.
f.　　Why then should I seek further store
　　　And still make love anew?
　　　When change itself can give no more,
　　　'Tis easy to be true.—*Sedley.*

g.   Can storied urn or animated bust
          Back to its mansion call the fleeting breath ?—*Gray.*

h.   What must the king do now ?   Must he submit ?
          The king shall do it.—*Shakspere.*

i. If he should come, I would ask him to stop with us.

k. Then some one said, ' We will return no more.'—*Tennyson.*

l. Shall you visit her ?

m. Will you visit her ?

n. May I ask whether you would like to see him ?

o. He ought to have been ashamed of himself.

p. He ought to go.

q.   I could a tale unfold, whose lightest word
          Would harrow up thy soul.—*Shakspere.*

r. 'Twere good you let him know.—*Id.*

s.   While feeble expletives their aid do join,
          And ten low words creep into one dull line.—*Pope.*

t. How do you do ?

u. He might have been living at this moment, had he taken ordinary care of himself.

ADVERBS.

98. Adverbs (from *ad*, to, and *verbum*, a word) are words used with verbs, adjectives, other adverbs, and prepositions, to qualify or limit their application as regards *manner, time, place, degree, cause, effect,* &c.

1. *With verbs,* e.g. ' He wrote *rapidly*' (manner); ' He lived *here* (place) *formerly*' (time). Under the verb may be included the verbal noun, and certain nouns having a verbal force but not the form of verbal nouns, e.g. ' He lost time through wandering *about*;' 'His residence *here* was of brief duration.'

2. *With adjectives,* e.g. ' He was *very* tall' (degree); ' It was *exquisitely* beautiful' (manner); '*Nearly* three hundred people set out' (extent).

3. *With adverbs,* e.g. ' He wrote *very* rapidly' (degree); ' He drew *marvellously* well ' (manner).

4. *With prepositions,* e.g. ' It was *partly* on and *partly* off the table' (extent).

5. Adverbs are also often used to qualify an assertion, e.g. '*Perhaps* he was not there. He will *undoubtedly* come.'

It is sometimes said that adverbs may limit nouns and pronouns, and the examples urged in support of the assertion are such as the following: ' Only John was there,' ' Only I am left.' But in these sentences ' only' is not an adverb. It has an adverbial form, but it discharges the function of an adjective, being equivalent to *alone*.

In O.E. *án* (=one) was used in most places where we now use *only*. Cp. the use of *unus* in Latin : ' Ego *unus* supersum ' (I *only* survive). (See Dr. Abbott's *How to Parse*, p. 37.) In the following passages *only* is equivalent to *alone* (Lat. *solus*). 'Him *only* shalt thou serve,' Matt. iv. 10 (αὐτῷ μόνῳ). 'Who can forgive sins but God *only* ? ' Mark ii. 7 (εἰ μὴ εἷς, ὁ Θεός). 'The *only* true God,' John xvii. 3 (τὸν μόνον). *Even* sometimes seems to limit a noun, e.g. ' *Even* Homer sometimes nods.' Dr. Abbott explains this as 'a short way of saying "Even (so wakeful a poet as) Homer," so that, in reality, "even" modifies an implied adjective.'

99. Adverbs may be classified either according to their function or according to their meaning. As regards their function they may be divided into Qualificative and Limitative.

Qualificative Adverbs express some quality, e.g. ' She sang *sweetly* ;' ' He was *wonderfully* clever.'

Limitative Adverbs express some relation of time, place, degree, e.g. 'He wrote *yesterday* ;' 'She was *here* ;' 'He is *very* good.'

Adverbs that discharge the function of conjunctions as well as of adverbs are called **conjunctive adverbs** or **adverbial conjunctions,** e.g. 'He wrote the book *while* he was here.' Here 'while' connects the adverbial clause ' while he was here' with the principal sentence ' He wrote the book.' In the sentence 'This is the house *where* he lived,' the adverb 'where' connects the adjective clause with the principal sentence. Here 'where '=in which.

The conjunctive adverb discharges a similar function to that discharged by the conjunctive or relative pronoun. The relative pronoun connects an adjective clause with the principal sentence ; the conjunctive adverb connects either an adverbial or adjective clause with it. Comp.—

I bought the book *when* I was in town. (Adv. Clause.)
This is the place *where* he died. (Adj. Clause.)

And as the relative pronoun has always a correlative or antecedent, expressed or understood, so has the conjunctive adverb. Thus in the first example 'then ' is to be understood in the principal sentence, 'I bought the book [then] when I was in town.' This correlative is rarely expressed except for emphasis, e.g. 'When he says so, *then*, and not till then, will I believe it.'

> *When* priests are more in word than matter;
> *When* brewers mar their malt with water;
>
> *Then* shall the realm of Albion
> Come to great confusion.—*Lear*, iii. 2.

The conjunctive adverbs betray in their form their close relation to the relative pronoun. They are *where, when, whence, whither, why* (e.g. 'This is the reason *why* he did it'), *whereat, whereby, wherefore, whereupon, wherewith, wheresoever, as* (e.g. 'He talked *as* he was walking;' 'This is as good *as* that is'), *than.*

100. Adverbs may also be classified according to their meaning as follows :—

1. **Adverbs of Place,**[1] e.g. *here, there, where, above, below, yonder, before, after, without, in, out, up, down, backwards, forwards, anywhere, nowhere, elsewhere, somewhere, anywhither, nowhither, somewhither, homewards, schoolwards,* &c.

Many of these may be further grouped under the heads Demonstrative and Interrogative Adverbs of Place, e.g.

Interrogative	Demonstrative	
Where?	Here	There
Whence?	Hence	Thence
Whither?	Hither	Thither
Whereby?	Hereby	Thereby
Wherein?	Herein	Therein
Whereto?	Hereto	Thereto
Wherefrom?	Herefrom	Therefrom
&c.	&c.	&c.

2. **Adverbs of Time,** e.g. *when, now, then, after, before, whenever, any time, some time, to-day, to-morrow,*

---

[1] Many words are prepositions as well as adverbs of place. When such words limit the verb by themselves, they are adverbs; when they govern a case and are part of a clause which limits the adverb, they are prepositions. In the following sentences, 'Come *up*,' 'come *in*,' 'Charge, Chester, charge; *on*, Stanley, *on*' (Scott), 'up,' 'in,' and 'on' are adverbs: in the following they are prepositions:—'The cat climbed *up* the tree;' 'He laid it *in* the box;' 'It stood *on* the table.'

yesterday, formerly, presently, hereafter, by-and-by, immediately, early, late, lately.

3. **Numeral Adverbs.** These may be subdivided into—

    a. *Ordinal* adverbs, e.g. (Definite) *firstly, secondly, thirdly,* (Indefinite) *alternately, finally.*

    b. *Distributive* adverbs, e.g. *singly, two ly two, by threes, by companies,* &c. Comp. the Latin adverbs in *-atim,* e.g. verbatim (word by word), literatim (letter by letter), turmatim (troop by troop).

    c. *Adverbs of Repetition,* e.g. (Definite) *once, twice, thrice, four times,* (Indefinite) *often, frequently, occasionally, constantly, intermittently.*

4. **Adverbs of Degree,** e.g. *very, exceedingly, nearly, slightly, wholly, partly, scarcely, quite, little, less, least, much, more, most.*

5. **Adverbs of Cause and Effect,** e.g. *therefore, wherefore, because, consequently, why.*

6. **Adverbs of Affirmation and Negation,** e.g. *yes, yea, no, nay, indeed, assuredly, certainly.*

7. **Adverbs of Manner,** e.g. *rapidly, slowly, wisely, badly, well, stealthily, gradually, so, thus, somehow, anyhow, better, worse, anywise, lengthwise.*

Most of the adverbs of manner are formed from adjectives by the addition of the suffix *-ly* (líc = like). Adverbs so formed should be distinguished from adjectives having the same termination, e.g. manly, womanly, motherly. In the following passage the same word occurs both as adjective and adverb:—' To convince all that are *ungodly* (adj.) among them of all their *ungodly* (adj.) deeds which they have *ungodly* (for ungodlily, adv.) committed.' (Jude i. 15.)

101. Adverbs are formed—

1. **From Nouns.** Thus from the old *Dative* plural in *-um* we have whil*om* and seld*om* ; from the *Genitive* in *-es* we have need*s* (= of necessity), now-a-days, always, betimes, eftsoons, unawares, once (= on*es*), twice (= twi*es*), &c. From the *Accusative* we have alway (O.E. eal*ne* weg).

In O.E. we find several adverbial compounds containing the element *-mǽlum* (the Dative plural of *mǽl,* time, a portion), e.g. sticce-mǽlum = piece-meal. Shakspere has 'limb-meal' = limb by limb, 'inch-meal' = inch by inch. When the inflexional ending was dropped, prepositions were in most cases used before the noun. Thus, instead of 'sóthes,' we now say 'of a truth;' instead of 'nihtes,' we say 'by night,' or 'of a night;' instead of 'ágnes thances,' we say 'of his own free-will.'

We have also a large class of adverbs compounded of a noun and preposition. Thus from a [1] = in, on, we have abed, aboard, asleep, aloft (= on loft, up in the air, O.E. loft, the air), afoot, ahead, adrift, afloat, astern, aback, aground, ajar (= on the jar, i.e. on the turn, from O.E. ceorran, to turn). Similarly are formed forsooth, besides (= by sides), betimes, perchance, perhaps.

A considerable class of adverbs was formerly compounded of nouns and the suffix -long or -ling, e.g. headlong, sidelong, darkling ('So out went the candle, and we were left darkling '—K. Lear), nose-lings = on the nose, nose-forward. (See an interesting paper on these compounds by Dr. Morris, 'Phil. Proceedings.')

Another class of adverbs is formed from nouns and pronouns by the addition of -wise (= ways), e.g. length-wise, end-wise, any-wise, other-wise, &c.

Uncompounded nouns used adverbially were originally oblique cases. Thus nouns of time how long were formerly put in the accusative, e.g. 'Why stand ye here all the day (ealne dæg) idle ? ' Nouns of time when were put sometimes in the ablative, e.g. 'I will come another time' (othre sithe); and sometimes in the Dative, e.g. 'He came the second day' (on othrum dæge). Nouns denoting measure, value, weight, age, &c., were put in the genitive, e.g. 'He was two ells high' (twegra elna heáh); 'It was worth sixpence' (sex peninga wyrthe). Nouns used with the comparative of adjectives to express measure were put in the ablative, e.g. 'The body was a span (sponne) longer than the coffin.' (See Rask, pp. 120–21.)

2. From Adjectives. In O.E. adverbs derived from adjectives were distinguished by the ending -e. Thus from the adjectives riht (right), wid (wide), lang (long), were formed the adverbs rihte, wide, lange. By degrees this e was dropped, and then the adverb and adjective became identical in form, e.g. fast, hard, right (as in 'right reverend'), far, ill, late, early, loud, high.

In modern English, adverbs are formed from adjectives by the addition of -ly (O.E. -lice, an adverbial termination formed from the adjective termination -lic, in accordance with the foregoing law), e.g. truly, merrily. Even adverbs of Romance origin take the termination -ly, e.g. soberly, poorly, humanly.

3. From Pronouns. Thus, connected with who, we have where, whence, whither, when, how, and why (O.E. hwí); connected with thou and the, and that, we have there, then, thence, thither, thus, the (before comparatives); connected with he we have here, hence, hither. A similar connection between the adverbs of time and place

---

[1] These O.E. compounds are to be distinguished from French compounds of à (= ad, to), such as apart (= à part).

and pronominal stems is observable in other languages. Comp. Lat, *hic* = this, *hic* = here, *huc* = hither.

The (O.E. thý) before comparatives is the ablative or instrumental case of the definite article. Compare never*the*less, i.e. never *by this* less.

How (O.E. hú) and *why* (O.E. hwí) are ablative forms of *who* (O.E. hwá).

Not (O.E. nóht, also náht) is a contraction of the pronoun *naught* (from *ne*, no, and *áht* = a wiht, a thing). Comp 'not a whit,' a phrase which contains the element 'whit' twice over.

Nothing, something, somewhat, naught, aught, are all used adverbially, e.g. 'He was *somewhat* injured.'

> He will hold thee, when his passion shall have spent its novel force,
> *Something* better than his dog, a little dearer than his horse.
> *Tennyson.*

In these cases we may of course regard the words *somewhat, something,* &c., as pronouns governed by the preposition 'by' understood.

In virtue of their pronominal character adverbs of time and place are sometimes preceded by prepositions and used as if they were nouns, e.g. 'from then,' 'till now,' 'since then,' 'since when,' 'from above,' 'from beneath,' &c.

4. **From Prepositions,** e.g. *to* and *fro, fore* and *aft, by* and *by, be-sides* (= by-sides), *be-fore, be-hind, be-neath, be-times,* &c., *forth* (from *fore*, before), *forth-with, for-ward, in, within, underneath, on, onwards, off, adown* (O.E. *of dúne*, from the hill), *thoroughly, too, up, upwards, over, out, without.*

5. **From Numerals,** e.g. *once, twice, thrice.* In addition to our simple adverbs we have a large number of adverbial phrases, e.g. *on high, at last, at least, at best, of yore, of old,* &c.; we have also many compound forms, e.g. *may-be, may-hap, howbeit, albeit, howsoever, wheresoever.*

6. **From other Adverbs,** e.g. nearly, mostly, firstly, lastly.

COMPARISON OF ADVERBS.

102. Some adverbs, as adverbs of manner, duration, space, and degree, admit of comparison, e.g. 'John wrote *more rapidly* than James, but Henry wrote *most rapidly* of all;' 'Mary came *sooner* than Jane, but Harriet came *soonest.*'

In O.E. the endings of the comparative and superlative degree were respectively *-or* and *-ost.* These have now been corrupted into *-er* and *-est.* In Modern English, adverbs are most commonly compared by the help of *more* and *most.* The chief exceptions are those adverbs, like hard, fast, slow, early, &c., that are compared like the cognate adjectives.

The following are instances of irregular comparison.

Positive	Comparative	Superlative
ill *or* badly	worse	worst
much	more	most
nigh *or* near	nearer	nearest *or* next
forth	further	furthest
well	better	best
little	less	least

PARSING OF THE ADVERB.

103. In parsing an adverb we should state—

1. The part of speech to which it belongs.
2. The class and sub-class to which it belongs.
3. Its degree of comparison.
4. Its syntactical relations.

Adverbs of manner are said to *qualify*; adverbs of time and place are said to *limit*. Some grammarians use the wider word 'modify' to cover both qualification and limitation.

EXAMPLES.

a. ' *Then* he *quickly* made up his mind to stay *there no longer.*'

b. ' He fell *where* he was shot, and *soon after* died.'

Word	Class	Inflexions	Syntactical Relations
a. Then	Adverb of time (demonstrative)	. . .	limiting 'made up'
quickly	Adverb of manner	positive degree	qualifying 'made up'
there	Adverb of place (demonstrative)	. . .	limiting 'stay'
no	Adverb of negation	. . .	limiting 'longer'
longer	Adverb of time (duration)	comp. degree	limiting 'stay'
b. Where	Adverb conjunctive (place)	. . .	limiting 'was shot,' correlative to 'there' understood
soon	Adverb of time (duration)	. . .	limiting 'after'
after	Adverb of time (order)	. . .	limiting 'died'

Exercises.

1. Classify adverbs.

2. How may adverbs be classified according to their derivation? Give instances.

3. Parse the adverbs in the following passages—

a.   Oh 'darkly, deeply, beautifully blue,'
       As some one somewhere sings about the sky.—*Byron.*

b.   They never taste who always drink,
       They always talk who never think.—*Prior.*

c.   To die is landing on some silent shore,
       Where billows never break nor tempests roar;
       Ere well we feel the friendly stroke 'tis o'er.—*Garth.*

d. When I said I would die a bachelor, I did not think I should live till I were married.—*Much Ado about Nothing.*

e. Full fathom five thy father lies.—*Tempest.*

f. Love me little, love me long.—*Marlowe.*

g.   I am not now in fortune's power;
       He that is down can fall no lower.—*Butler.*

h.   He knew what's what, and that's as high
       As metaphysic wit can fly.—*Id.*

i.   O yet we trust that somehow good
       Will be the final goal of ill.—*Tennyson.*

k.   To every man upon this earth
       Death cometh soon or late.—*Macaulay.*

l.   Right against the eastern gate
       Where the sun begins his state.—*Milton.*

m. I am yours truly.

n. I am entirely of your opinion.

o. Is she not passing fair?—*Two Gentlemen of Verona,* iv. 4.

p. They shall go in and out and find pasture.—*John* x. 9.

q. How sweet the moonlight sleeps upon this bank.—*M. of V.*

r. He goes to and fro, twice a day, every other week.

s. Honour pricks me on. Yea, but how if honour prick me off when I come on? how then? Can honour set to a leg? No.—*Henry IV. Part I.* v. 1.

PREPOSITIONS.

104. Prepositions (from *præ*, before, and *positus*, placed) are so called because they are generally [1] placed *before* a noun

[1] The preposition is often placed at the end of adjective clauses and interrogative sentences, e.g.—
    This is the book that you were talking *of*.
    Whom were you talking *to*?

or pronoun. They express some relation between a thing,
or an action or an attribute, and some other thing, e.g.—

> The book *on* the table is yours.
> I wrote *on* the table.
> Hallam is good *on* constitutional history.

The preposition was originally prefixed to the verb, which it
limited adverbially; it then came to be used independently; finally
it was used with nouns and pronouns.

105. Prepositions may be classified according to the
relations which they denote, as of time, place, reason, purpose, cause, &c., or according to their form, as into Simple
and Compound.

The **Simple Prepositions** are *at, by* (O.E. be, bi=about),
for, from, in, of, off (O.E. of=from, comp. Lat. *ab*), *out*
(O.E. ût, comp. utter), *on, through* (O.E. thurh: comp. *thyrel*,
a hole, drill; nostril=nose-thyrel, nose-hole), *till, to, up,
with.*

The **Compound Prepositions** may be subdivided into—

a. **Those formed from comparatives,** e.g. *after* (from
af=of=from), *over* (from *of*), *under* (from *in*).

b. **Those formed from other prepositions,** e.g. *abaft,
about* (from a=on+be+out), *afore, before, behind, beneath, but* (from be and out),[1] *into, throughout, underneath, until, unto, within, without,* &c.

c. **Those formed from nouns and adjectives,** e.g.
aboard (=on board), *across* (=on the cross), *adown*
(=off the down=from the hill), *among* (=in the multitude, from O.E. gemang, an assembly), *abreast, against*
(=on the opposite, O.E. gean=opposite), *along* (O.E. andlang), *amid* (=in the mid), *anent* (O.E. ongean, opposite; the *g* was probably sounded like *y*), *around* (=on
the round), *aslant* (=on the slant), *astride* (=on the
stride), *athwart* (O.E. thweort, cross, oblique), *below,
beside, between* (=by the *two*, comp. twain, twin, &c.),
betwixt, since (M.E. sithens, from O.E. sith=late), *ere*
(O.E. ǽr=early), *inside, outside.*

d. **Those formed from verbs,** e.g. *except, notwith-*

---

[1] Comp. the Duke of Sutherland's motto, 'Touch not the cat *but*
(i.e. without) the glove.'

standing, concerning, during, respecting, touching, saving, save.

These may still be regarded as participles. Thus 'There was no one there save [1] John '= There was no one there, John being saved or excepted. 'Notwithstanding my expostulation, he went home'= My expostulation notwithstanding, he went home. ' During the fortnight he was very ill '= The fortnight during (i.e. enduring, lasting) he was very ill. 'Saving your reverence, there was no one there '= I, saving your reverence, may say that no one, &c.

106. In addition to prepositions expressed by a single word we have a considerable number of prepositional phrases, e.g. *abreast of, ahead of, in spite of, in place of, instead of, in lieu of, in behalf of, by dint of, for the sake of.* These prepositional phrases may be parsed as such or resolved into their constituent parts.

When we come to inquire into the meaning of the prepositions, we find that they were almost invariably used to express first space, then time, then other relations. Comp.

> John stood *by* James (place).
> I shall be there *by* six (time).
> It was done *by* James (cause).

PARSING OF PREPOSITIONS.

107. In parsing a preposition it is enough to state—

1. The part of speech to which it belongs.
2. The syntactical relations between it and the rest of the sentence.

EXAMPLE.

' The doctor whom you heard me speak *of* came *with* me *to* town.'

Word	Part of Speech	Syntactical Relations
of	Preposition	governing 'whom'
with	,,	governing 'me'
to	,,	governing 'town'

[1] ' Save' is used participally in the following passages, in which, it will be observed, it does not govern the following word :—' There was no stranger in the house *save we* two' (i.e. we two *being saved*) (1 Kings iii. 18); 'When all slept sound *save she* ' (i.e. she *being saved*) (Rogers, *Italy*, 108).

Exercises.

1. Classify prepositions with regard to their origin.

2. Trace the various meanings of 'of' and 'to.'

3. Parse the prepositions in the following passages—

a. Under which king, Bezonian ? speak or die.—*Shakspere.*

b. He hath eaten me out of house and home.—*Id.*

c. A plague of sighing and grief! it blows a man up like a bladder.—*Id.*

d. What is the opinion of Pythagoras concerning wildfowl ?—*Id.*

e.　　　Why should a man, whose blood is warm within,
　　　　Sit like his grandsire cut in alabaster ?—*Id.*

f. An essay concerning all things and certain others.

g. We have houses to live in, and beds to lie on, and fires to warm ourselves at.

h.　　　A fellow in a market town
　　　　Most musical, cried razors up and down.—*Wolcott.*

i.　　　But war's a game which, were their subjects wise,
　　　　Kings would not play at.—*Cowper.*

k.　　　Along the cool sequestered vale of life
　　　　They kept the noiseless tenor of their way.—*Gray.*

l. What is it you object to ?

m.　　　I hear a lion in the lobby roar ;
　　　　Say, Mr. Speaker, shall we shut the door
　　　　And keep him there, or shall we let him in
　　　　To try if we can turn him out again ?—*Bramston.*

n. A prophet is not without honour, save in his own country.
　　　　　　　　　　　　　　　　　　　　　　Bible.

o. Notwithstanding our entreaties, he crossed the river.

p. The schoolmaster is abroad, and I trust to him, armed with his primer, against the soldier in full military array.—*Brougham.*

q. From out waste places comes a cry.—*Tennyson.*

r. All this coil is long of you.—*Shakspere.*

CONJUNCTIONS.

108. **Conjunctions** (from *con*, together, and *jungo*, I join) are so called because they join words, phrases, and sentences together, e.g.—

　　　John *and* I sang a duet (words).
　　　He was unwilling either to sing *or* play (phrases).
　　　Careless their merits *or* their faults to scan (phrases).
　　　John sang *and* I played (sentences).

It is sometimes asserted that conjunctions never join mere words. This is clearly a mistake. The sentence, 'John and James are there,' may be resolved into 'John is there and James is there,' but it is impossible to decompose the following sentences in this way :—

> He and his wife are a happy pair.
> I sat between my brother and sister.
> Three and four are seven.

Some grammarians regard the conjunction in the last sentence as a preposition having the force of *with*, but prepositions govern the objective case, and we cannot say 'John and *me* sang a duet.'

Relative pronouns and certain adverbs of time and place are conjunctive, i.e. they unite a dependent clause to the main sentence. They differ from simple conjunctions in being an integral part of the dependent clause. Comp.

> This is the book *which* I bought.
> This is the place *where* he fell.
> Here is the place, *and* here he fell.

109. Conjunctions may be classified according to the *nature of the sentences or clauses joined together*, as Co-ordinative or Subordinative, or according to their own *signification*.

Co-ordinative conjunctions couple co-ordinate sentences and clauses, e.g. *and, both, but, either, or, neither, nor.*

Subordinative conjunctions couple dependent or subordinate clauses with the principal sentence, e.g. *that, if, lest, though, although, unless, except, because, since* (when it introduces a reason). All the conjunctive adverbs are, so far as they are conjunctions, of this class.

110. Conjunctions may also be classified according to their meaning as **Copulative**, *and, both*; **Adversative**, *but, yet, still*; **Disjunctive**,[1] *either . . . or, neither . . . nor, whether . . . or*; **Causal**, *because*; **Illative**, *since, for*; **Conditional**, *if, unless, except*; **Concessive**, *though, although.*

---

[1] It has been objected to this name that the compound term Disjunctive Conjunction is paradoxical. What is meant by it is that the Disjunctive Conjunction is conjunctive as regards the sentences joined, but disjunctive as regards the sense. It disjoins either the subjects or predicates of the sentences joined together, e.g. 'Either John or James (one of the two, but not both) did it.' 'John either wrote or read' (did one of these two things, but not both). The term 'disjunctive' is borrowed from logic, in which science it is applied to propositions such as the foregoing.

In addition to the simple conjunctions we have many conjunctive phrases, e.g. *on the other hand, since that,*[1] *after that, before that, in order that, lest that,* &c. In parsing, these phrases may be dealt with as wholes or decomposed.

Conjunctions that go in pairs, like *either . . . or, neither . . . nor, though . . . yet, both . . . and,* are called **Correlative** conjunctions.

111. Conjunctions are, for the most part, degraded forms of other parts of speech, especially of verbs, nouns, pronouns, adverbs, and prepositions.

And is cognate with the O.E. prefix *and-*, which appears in *a*long (O.E. andlang) and *a*nswer (O.E. andswarian), and had the force of *over against*. **And** or **an**, in the sense of *if*, is the Icel. *enda*, if. As this sense grew obsolete, *if* was added to *and* or *an*. See Matt. xxiv. 48.

Both (O.E. bá, the neuter dual).

Either, or (O.E. other), **neither, nor**, are all of pronominal origin.

If (O.E. gif) was formerly supposed to be the imperative of the verb 'give.' Cognate forms are Icel. *ef*, Dutch *of, if*, O.Sax. *ef, of, if*, O.H.G. *iba*, condition; dat. *ibu*, on condition, if.

Yet (O.E. get, gyt) is derived by some from 'get.'

Lest. 'Not for *least*, as often erroneously said, but due to *less*. It arose from the A.S. equivalent expression *thý læs the*, as in the following sentence: "Nelle we thás race na leng teón, *thý læs the* hit eów æthryt thynce "= we will not prolong this story further, lest it seem to you tedious. (Sweet's "A. S. Reader," p. 94, l. 211.) Here *thý læs the* literally =*for the reason less that*, where *thý* (= for the reason) is the instrumental case of the definite article ; *læs* = less ; and *the* (=that) is the indeclinable relative. At a later period *thý* was dropped, *læs* became *les*, and *læs the*, coalescing, became one word, *lesthe*, easily corrupted into *leste*, and lastly to *lest*, for ease of pronunciation.' (Skeat's 'Etymological Dictionary.')

Because = by cause.

Except = O.E. out-take.

PARSING OF CONJUNCTIONS.

112. In parsing conjunctions, state

1. Class and sub-class.
2. Sentences or clauses joined.

[1] In M.E. *that* is often redundantly used after other conjunctions, e.g. '*Before that* certain came from James, he did eat with the Gentiles,' Gal. ii. 12. Most of these conjunctions are of the temporal class (adverbial conjunctions of time), e.g. *since, after, before.*

EXAMPLE.

'*If* John *and* James go to town, I hope *that* they will buy me a Shakspere.'

Word	Class	Syntactical Relations
if	Conjunction (conditional), subordinative	connecting the conditional clause 'If John and James,' &c., with the principal sentence 'I hope,' &c.
and	Conjunction (copulative), co-ordinative	connecting 'John' and 'James,' or 'If John [go to town]' with '[if] James go to town'
that	Conjunction, subordinative	connecting the noun clause 'that they,' &c., with the principal sentence 'I hope'

Exercises.

1. What is meant by

    a. A subordinative conjunction?
    b. A co-ordinative conjunction?

2. Classify conjunctions according to their meaning.

3. Parse the conjunctions in the following passages :—

a. God made the country, and man made the town.—*Cowper.*

b. He thought as a sage, though he felt as a man.—*Beattie.*

c. O, could I flow like thee, and make thy stream
My great example, as it is my theme!
Though deep yet clear, though gentle yet not dull;
Strong without rage, without o'erflowing full.—*Denham.*

d.   Poets are sultans, if they had their will;
For every author would his brother kill.

e. Between you and me, his conduct has not been satisfactory.

f. My two brothers and our two cousins played a delightful quartet.

g. If I will that he tarry till I come, what is that to thee?—*Bible.*

h. I had fainted unless I had believed.—*Ib.*

i. Ye shall not go hence, except your youngest brother come hither.—*Ib.*

k. Though He slay me, yet will I trust in Him.—*Ib.*

l.   Stone walls do not a prison make,
Nor iron bars a cage.—*Lovelace.*

m. If I were you, I would go.

n. Because I love you, I will let you know.

o. We are commanded to forgive our enemies, but we are nowhere commanded to forgive our friends.

p. I will send it, provided you promise that you will return it to me.

q.
>Delay no longer, speak your wish,
>Seeing I must go to-day.—*Tennyson.*

4. Certain words are used sometimes as adverbs, sometimes as prepositions, and sometimes as conjunctions. Illustrate this remark from the following passages :—

a. There was no one there except me.

b. Except ye repent, ye shall all likewise perish.

c.
>For what are men better than sheep or goats
>That nourish a blind life within the brain,
>If, knowing God, they lift not hands of prayer
>Both for themselves, and those who call them friend ?
>>*Tennyson.*

d. He has been ill since yesterday.

e. Since he does not improve, I think you had better send for the doctor.

f. This is for you.

g. He cannot be poor, for he gives money to every good cause.

h. The tree is living yet.

i. He is generous, yet he is never prodigal.

INTERJECTIONS.

113. Interjections (from *inter*, between, and *jacio*, I throw) are used to express the emotions of the mind or the feelings of the body, and are so called because they are thrown into the constructions in which they occur, without, as a rule, standing in any syntactical relation to them.

>But she is in her grave—and oh
>The difference to me !— *Wordsworth.*

114. Many interjections were originally involuntary ejaculations. Such are *O, oh, ah, fie, pshaw, pooh, heigh ho.*

O is used with the vocative, and as an exclamation of pleasure.

Oh expresses some emotion, as of pain.

Ah is more restricted than *oh* to *mental* pain. It also expresses astonishment.

Fie expresses condemnation. 'Fie upon thee ! '

Pshaw expresses contempt for something stated.

Pooh also expresses contempt. It 'seems connected with the French exclamation of physical disgust: *Pouah, quelle infection !* ' (Earle's 'Phil. of the Eng. Tongue,' p. 196).

Heigh ho expresses a somewhat sentimental weariness.

Some interjections are corrupted forms of other parts of speech.

Lo is erroneously supposed to be connected with *loc*, the old imperative of the verb *look*, and the use of the word has supported the derivation suggested by its form.

Neither shall they say, *Lo* here ! or *Lo* there !—Luke xvii. 21. It is only another form of the O.E. *lá*, which was used both as an emotional interjection and in the vocative construction. *Law*, *la*, and *lawks* may be corruptions of *la* or euphuistic corruptions of *Lord*. In O.E. we find also *Eala* = O, e.g. ' Eala thu wif, mycel is thin geleáfa ' [O woman, great is thy faith]—Matt. xv. 28.

Hail! is the O.E. *hǽl*, whole, sound. Comp. 'Hǽl wæs thu, Judæa Cyning' [Hail, King of the Jews; lit. Hale be thou, king &c.]—Matt. xxvii. 30.

So **All hail!**—

Did they not sometime cry ' All hail ! ' to me ?—*Shakspere*.

Wo (O.E. *wá*) should be distinguished from the noun *woe* (O.E. *woh* = wickedness, misery). ' Wo, wo, wo (orig. *oväi*), to the inhabiters of the earth ! '—Rev. viii. 19.

Alas and **Alack** are probably from Fr. *hélas* (Lat. *lassus*, weary). The prefix *a* represents the French interjection *hé*.

Hear, hear, is now an interjection of approval.

Some interjections are disguised oaths, e.g.—

Zounds, i.e. God's wounds; **'sdeath**, i.e. God's death, &c.

Some are contracted devotional utterances, e.g.—

Marry, i.e. Mary.

Some are expressions of courtesy, e.g.—

Gramercy, i.e. *Grand-merci* = great thanks.
Good-bye, i.e. God be wi' you.
Adieu, i.e. I commend you to God (*à Dieu*).
Farewell, i.e. May you fare well.
Welcome, i.e. You are well or opportunely come.

115. Many of our O.E. interjections have undergone great corruption.

Thus, the O.E. *wá-lá-wá*, which is compounded of *wá* and *lá* (see above), was first corrupted into *well-a-way*, and subsequently into *well-a-day*. So *alack-a-day* (whence lackadaisical) has been corrupted into 'lauk-a-daisy.' In this word the element *lauk* has probably been confounded with 'Lord.' Comp. the euphuistic 'lauk-a-mercy.'

Fudge is said to have originated in a Captain Fudge, who was notorious for his lies. (See D'Israeli's 'Curiosities of Lit.' vol. iii.) It is much more probable that it is a word of onomatopoetic origin. A great many interjections expressive of contempt or disgust begin with *pu* or *fu*, 'representing the sound made by blowing through the barely opened lips, and hence expressing the rejection of anything nasty.' (Wedgwood.) Garnett derives 'fudge' from Welsh *fug*, deception.

Several interjections have come to us from the Holy Scriptures, e.g. **Hallelujah, Alleluia** (= Praise ye the Lord), **Hosanna** (= Save now), **Amen** (= So be it).

Some interjections are followed by the Objective Case, e.g. '*Ah me !*' '*Oh me !*' Occasionally they are followed by the Nominative—

Ah ! wretched *we*, poets of earth.—*Cowley.*

PART II.

ANALYSIS OF SENTENCES.

THE SUBJECT.

116. Every sentence, as we have seen, consists of two parts, viz. the Subject and the Predicate. The precise function of the Subject varies with the sentence (see § 3); but, in general terms, the Subject may be defined as the word or words standing for that about which we speak. The precise function of the Predicate will also vary with the sentence; in general terms it may be defined as that which is said about the Subject.

The Subject must be a noun or its equivalent :—

1. **Noun.** *John* is here. Where is *John*? Long live the *king*!

2. **Pronoun.** *He* is here. Where is *he*? May *he* be happy!

3. **Adjective.** The *good* are happy.

4. **Gerundial Infinitive.** *To err* is human.

5. **Verbal Noun.** *Fishing* is my favourite sport.

6. **A word, phrase, or sentence quoted.** ' " *Forward* " was our watchword' (word); ' " Good night, sir," was heard from a hundred mouths' (phrase); ' " England expects every man to do his duty," was the signal given at Trafalgar ' (sentence).

7. **A noun clause.** ' *That he should be disappointed* is not surprising.'

In Imperative sentences the subject is often not expressed, e.g. 'Go home,' i.e. Go *thou*, or go *ye*, home. The noun denoting the person addressed is never the Subject of the sentence, e.g. 'John, may *you* be happy.' Here 'John' is the vocative, and 'you' is the Subject of the sentence.

Exercises.

Point out the Subject in the following sentences, and state, in each case, what part of speech it is:—

a. I am reading. *b.* John was there. *c.* Where is Harry? *d.* Go away. *e.* The elephant sometimes sleeps standing. *f.* Art is long. *g.* Life hath quicksands. *h.* Trust no future. *i.* This is the place. *k.* Ring out, wild bells. *l.* There is no death.

m. Drinking is the soldier's pleasure.—*Dryden.*

n. Skating is a delightful pastime.

o. To rise early is healthful.

p. Riding is a pleasant exercise.

q. To draw well requires time.

r. 'Up guards and at 'em,' were the words used.

s. Your 'if' is the only peacemaker.—*Shakspere.*

t. Then they praised him soft and low.—*Tennyson.*

u. Each foeman drew his battle blade.—*Campbell.*

v. How he came by his large fortune was not known.

w. That you have wronged me doth appear in this.—*Shakspere.*

x. Not a drum was heard.—*Wolfe.*

y. Whence he came did not appear.

z. The great ones devour the little ones.

ENLARGEMENT OF THE SUBJECT.

117. As the Subject of a sentence must always be a noun or its equivalent, it may be enlarged by whatever words, phrases, or clauses qualify or define a noun. Thus it may be enlarged by—

1. One or more **adjectives** :

> *Honest* men avoided him.
> *Faithful, industrious, and energetic,* he soon got on.
> *This large, old, red* book is mine.

2. **Words in apposition** :

> Dr. Dee, *the astrologer,* lived in the sixteenth century.
> Friendship, *the great bond of society,* was rare.
> *It* is our duty to forgive our enemies.

In this last example the true Subject is 'To forgive our enemies,' as we may see by inverting the sentence, 'To forgive our enemies is our duty.'

3. Participles or participial phrases :

His father, *having failed*, left the country.
Sobbing and weeping, she sank back in her chair.
Loved by his friends, and respected even by his enemies, he died at a ripe old age.

4. A prepositional phrase :

The fear *of man* was a snare to him.
A man *of position* was wanted.

5. A noun in the possessive case or a possessive adjective:

Harry's hat flew off.
My uncle is coming.
My father's brother-in-law was there.

6. The gerundial infinitive :

Bread *to eat* was not to be had.
The life *to come* will reveal many mysteries.
A house *to let* faced us.

118. These various modes of enlargement may be combined, e.g.—

William *the Conqueror, Harold's old enemy, a man of great ambition and capable of great achievements, having carefully prepared for the enterprise and attracted adventurers from all parts of Europe to share in it,* crossed the Channel, *resolved on the conquest of England.*

Here the simple sentence is 'William crossed the Channel.' The separate enlargements may be exhibited as follows :—

1. 'the Conqueror.' Noun in apposition.

2. 'Harold's old enemy.' Noun in apposition.

3. 'a man of great ambition and capable of great achievements.' Noun in apposition.

4. 'having carefully prepared for the enterprise.' Participial phrase.
'and [having] attracted adventurers from all parts of Europe.' Participial phrase.

5. 'resolved On the conquest of England.' Participial phrase.

It will be observed that nouns and verbs, *wherever*

K

they occur in a sentence, may be enlarged by words that qualify or limit; and that transitive verbs, *wherever they occur*, may govern an objective case.

Exercises.

1. Point out the enlargements of the subject in the following passages, stating in each case how the enlargement is formed :—

a. Open rebuke is better than secret love.—*Bible.*

b. Three wives sat up in the lighthouse tower.—*Kingsley.*

c. A threefold cord is not quickly broken.—*Bible.*

d. Having kissed his mother and said good-bye, Tom set off.

e. My uncle Thomas, the colonel of the 71st, is coming to-morrow.

f. She lived unknown.

g. The glory of war attracted him.

h. Now laughing, and now weeping, she pressed him again and again to her breast.

i. Smith, the bookseller, has retired from business.

k. A sudden thought strikes me.

l. Mine be a cot beside the hill.—*S. Rogers.*

m. There is another and a better world.

n. The royal navy of England hath ever been its greatest defence.

o. Winter lingering chills the lap of May.—*Gray.*

p. Ill fares the land, to hastening ills a prey.—*Goldsmith.*

q. Years following years steal something every day.—*Pope.*

r. Having obtained his share of the property, he emigrated to America.

s. Crushed, disappointed, and heartbroken, he withdrew into private life.

t   A falcon, towering in her pride of place,
        Was by a mousing owl hawked at.—*Shakspere.*

u. His mother's last words, disregarded at the time, often came back to his mind.

v. Born in a provincial town, the son of humble parents, educated in a third-rate grammar school, without the patronage of the great and without having recourse to any unworthy means, he fought his way to the highest distinctions.

2. Enlarge the subjects in the following sentences : (i) by adjectives, (ii) by participial phrases, (iii) by appositional phrases :—

a. The rose is dead. *b.* The house is for sale. *c.* Servants are not to be had. *d.* Apples are cheap. *c.* Rome is now a third-rate city. *f.* Henry V. defeated the French. *g.* The thief escaped. *h.* Why do you complain? *i.* He left England. *k.* She was never contented. *l.* He did not arrive in time. *m.* Paul went to Athens. *n.* Thomas has opened a new shop. *o.* Hannibal defeated the Romans. *p.* The ship sank beneath the waves. *q.* Westminster Abbey was commenced by Edward the Confessor. *r.* Shakspere and Milton are the glory of English literature.

THE PREDICATE.

119. The Predicate may consist of one or more words, but must contain some finite part of a verb, i.e. some part having number and person.[1]

The simple Predicate may be—

1. A single verb :—

> Time *flies.*
> John *departed.*
> The house *was built.*
> He *should have been pleased.*
> They *might be listening.*

It will be observed from these examples that the verb may be intransitive or transitive. If transitive, it must be in the Passive Voice. A transitive verb in the Active Voice can never *alone* form the predicate.

2. A copulative verb and a noun, pronoun, or adjective. Under the head of 'copulative' may be mentioned (*a*) the verb 'to be,' (*b*) verbs of becoming, e.g. *become, turn out, prove, grow* (intrans.)—

> *a.* John *is a sailor.*
> He *is happy.*
> They *are persons* of some property.

> *b.* He *became an author.*
> They *turned out utterly worthless.*
> He *proved a trustworthy servant.*
> She *grew strong and healthy.*

The verb 'to be,' if it denote *existence*, may be used by itself to form a predicate, e.g.—

> God *is.*
> There *are* savages in Africa.

The adverb 'there' in the last example is simply introductory, having wholly lost its ordinary force as a demonstrative adverb. If

---

[1] The infinitive and participles have no number and person, and can never alone form the predicate of a sentence.

we wish to define the *place* of existence we are obliged to use a
second adverb, e.g.—

> There are savages *there*.
> There are shops *here*.

Exercises.

1. Point out the predicates in the following sentences—*a.* The
sky is clear. *b.* The wind rises. *c.* John got up. *d.* The postman,
having delivered his letters, returned. *e.* Where were you? *f.* Your
father's uncle was a sailor. *g.* I am a poor old man. *h.* He grew a
great giant. *i.* The rain ceased. *k.* They can all swim. *l.* How
pleasant it is! *m.* There were a great many flowers in the lanes.
n. He was soundly thrashed. *o.* How did your horse turn out?
p. Babylon is fallen. *q.* Silent he stood and firm. *r.* The scheme
will answer. *s.* The whole of his fortune was dissipated. *t.* The
desert shall rejoice. *u.* Was she happy and contented? *v.* He was
a writer of no little ability. *w.* He could not have been so foolish.
x. The poetry of earth is never dead. *y.* A thing of beauty is a joy
for ever.

2. Collect from the foregoing examples instances in which the
predicate is composed of (*a*) a verb alone, (*b*) a copulative verb
and a noun or adjective.

COMPLETION OF THE PREDICATE.

120. Transitive verbs in the Active Voice cannot, by
themselves, form a complete predicate. If a person were
to say ' John built,' or ' John gave,' we should want to know
what John built or gave. The word or words completing
the assertion is called the completion of the Predicate. Thus
in the sentences, ' John built *a house*,' ' John gave *a book*,'
' a house' and ' a book' would be called the Completion of
the Predicate. The word governed by the transitive verb
is called the **Direct Object**.

Transitive verbs used intransitively do not require any object to
complete the assertion, e.g. 'The table *moves*,' ' This flower *smells*
sweet,' ' The cakes *ate* sharp and crisp,' ' The sentence *reads* odd.'

121. The Direct Object may be a noun or its equivalent :—

1. **Noun** : I saw *John*.

2. **Pronoun** : They met *us*.

3. **Adjective used as a noun** : We praise *the diligent*.

4. **Gerundial infinitive** : He loves *to sing*.

5. **Verbal noun** : He loves *reading*.

6. **A noun clause** : I heard *that he was there*.

7. **A phrase or sentence**: He said '*Off with their heads!*'
'*What is your opinion?*' said he.

It may be enlarged in the same way as the subject.

1. I saw John, *your brother* (by a noun in apposition).

2. I saw *your brother's* house (by a possessive case).

3. I saw *your younger* brother (by adjectives).

4. I saw John *sitting on the stile* (by a participial phrase. See § 123.)

5. I saw the brother *of your friend* (by a prepositional phrase).

6. We had books *to read* (by a gerundial infinitive).

122. Some verbs require two objects to complete the nse of the predicate, e.g. verbs of *giving, promising,* &c. 'e cannot *give* without giving *something* to *somebody*. We nnot promise without promising *something* to *somebody*. ı the sentence 'We gave the book to John,' 'book' is the irect Object, denoting the *thing* actually given, John is the ırson *to whom* the book is given. Nouns occupying a milar position to 'John' in this sentence are called **Indirect** bjects.

The Indirect Object may occur after—

1. Verbs of *giving, promising, refusing, telling,* &c.—
I presented the picture *to Mary*.
He promised the book *to me*.
She refused *him* his request.
He told a story *to the children*.

The Indirect Object used with these verbs is sometimes called ıe **Dative Object**. It may, or may not, be preceded by a pre-ısition.

2. Verbs of *making, creating, appointing, wishing, thinking,* &c.—
We made him *king*.
They elected him *mayor*.

The Indirect Object in these constructions is sometimes called ıe **Factitive Object** (from facio, *I make*), the verb 'make' being type of the class. It may or may not be preceded by the verb ʒo be.' The Factitive Object, when used after the Active Voice, is called by Dr. Abbott the Objective Supplement; when used after the Passive Voice, the Subjective Supplement.

3. Verbs of *guilt, innocence,* &c.—

He accused him *of treason.*
He acquitted him *of the charge.*

4. *Intransitive verbs,* e.g.—

I live *for you.*
He laughed *at me.*

Some writers would, in such constructions, couple the preposition with the verb, and regard the two as forming a compound verb, governing a Direct Object; but there is no necessity for this.

123. The Indirect Object may be—

1. **A Noun** : I gave the book *to John.*

2. **A Pronoun** : I promised *him* a present.

3. **A Gerundial Infinitive** : I ordered him *to follow.*

After 'bid,' 'dare,' 'make,' 'let,' and verbs relating to the *senses,* the preposition 'to' is often omitted : I bade him *go*; I saw him *die.*

4. **A Participle or Participial Phrase** : I heard him *talking in the hall.*

A Participial Phrase may, in such constructions, be regarded as an enlargement of the Direct Object.

5. **An Adjective used factitively** : We made him *happy.*

We may, of course, look upon the adjective in this construction as part of an infinitive phrase.

The Indirect Object may be enlarged in the same way as the Direct Object, and, when a part of the verb, may be enlarged by an adverb or its equivalent :—

I heard him sing *exquisitely.*
They saw her struggling *in the water.*

Exercises.

1. Point out the Direct and Indirect Objects in the following passages, and state in each case what the Objects consist of :—

a. I gave her a book.

b. We appointed him our leader.

c. I will give you my consent.

d. Tell me a story.

e. I forced him to come.

f. We could hear the sea roaring.

g. We gave the bread to a poor old man sitting by the wayside.

h. He was made a colonel of volunteers.

i. He was suspected of untruthfulness.

k. We pronounced him innocent.

l. To whom did you give it?

m. He praised him for his self-denial.

n. Bid me discourse.

o. Give me an ounce of civet, good apothecary.

p. Wipe your hands perfectly dry.

2. State how the Objects are enlarged in the following sentences :—

a. I have a fine old house.

b. He gave it to my dear brother.

c. We made the ablest man in our body our leader.

d. I considered the eldest of her children very clever.

e. He taught me to speak French.

f. We could see them trying to swim against the current.

g. I left him reading in the library.

THE EXTENSION OF THE PREDICATE

124. The Predicate of a Sentence may be extended by an adverb or its equivalent.

1. *By one or more adverbs* : Time flies *swiftly and imperceptibly.*

2. *By an adverbial phrase* : He spoke *in a pompous way.*

3. *By an adverbial clause* : He was reading *when we entered.*

4. *By an infinitive phrase* : He did it *to please us.*

5. *By an absolute participial phrase : The clock having struck six,* we set out.

These extensions of the Predicate may be classified under the heads of Time, Place, Magnitude, Weight, Price, &c

1. Extensions of Time.

a. Time when.—He is writing *now*. *When* did he arrive? He died *the day before yesterday*. *The clock having struck ten*, we went to bed.

b. Time how long.—He lived *long*. I stayed there *several years*. He has been staying at Rome *for the winter*.

c. Time how often.—He wrote *frequently*. They visited us *every year*. We saw him *every other day*.

2. Extensions of Place.

a. Rest in a place.—He lives *here*. They reside *next door to us*. We remained *in the country*.

b. Motion towards a place.—Come *hither*. They came *to us*. We went *to the pantomime*. Go *home*. Go *thy way*.

c. Motion from a place.—They came *hence*. He arrived *from York*. *Whence* did you get it?

3. Extensions of Magnitude.

It was *a foot* long. He ran *three miles*. It measured *four acres*. It extended *for miles around*. He was *a head* taller.

4. Extensions of Weight and Price.

a. Weight.—It weighed *four pounds*. He was *twenty pounds* lighter.

b. Price.—It was worth *sixpence*. It cost me *six pounds*.

5. Extensions of Manner.

a. Manner (proper).—She sang *exquisitely*. He wrote *with great rapidity*.

b. Degree.—I was *exceedingly* glad. They were *very nearly* upset.

c. Circumstance.—He came *with his friends*. They remained *with their father's consent*.

6. Extensions of Cause and Effect.

a. Cause.—They obeyed *from fear*. He went astray *through going into bad company*. He was taught *by me*.

b. Instrument.—He made a boat *with a knife*.

c. Material.—It was made *of gold*.

d. Form.—He constructed it *of a circular shape*.

e. Purpose.—He worked hard *to get the prize*. We built a house *to live in*. A law was passed *to put down mendicancy*.

f. Effect.—He laboured *in vain*. They petitioned the Crown *without success*.

It should be observed that these adjuncts may be used to qualify or limit a verb in any part of a sentence :—

To write *well* requires careful study. (Subject.)
I love to drive *rapidly*. (Obj.)

Exercises.

1. Point out the adverbial extensions of the Predicate in the following sentences, and classify them under the foregoing heads :—

a. The bird sings very sweetly.

b. He stayed in Rome three years.

c. How cleverly he talks !

d. She died in the year 1840.

e. He was going to Canterbury.

f. How far did he go ?

g. He caught cold from not changing his damp clothes.

h. A trumpet is made for playing on.

i. He swam three miles on a cold day.

k. In a few moments after the ship sank.

l.   I stood in Venice, on the Bridge of Sighs.—*Byron.*

m.   On the ear
Drops the light drip of the suspended oar.—*Id.*

n.   He sinks into thy depths with bubbling groan,
Without a grave, unknelled, uncoffined, and unknown.—*Id.*

o.   So sinks the day-star in the ocean-bed.—*Milton.*

p.   I could lie down like a tired child.—*Shelley.*

q.   A thing of beauty is a joy for ever.—*Keats.*

r.   Then felt I like some watcher of the skies.—*Id.*

s.   Twelve years ago I was a boy,
A happy boy, at Drury's.—*Hood.*

t.   To every man upon this earth
Death cometh soon or late.—*Macaulay.*

u.   We watched her breathing through the night.—*Hood.*

v. They go from strength to strength.—*Bible.*

w. Man is born unto trouble.—*Ib.*

x. Man doth not live by bread alone.—*Ib.*

y. There the weary be at rest.—*Ib.*

z. I have been a stranger in a strange land.

2. Give instances of adverbial extensions (*a*) of the Subject, (*b*) of the Direct Object, (*c*) of the Indirect Object,

3. How would you classify the absolute clauses in the following examples ?—

a. The wind being favourable, we set sail.

b. The object being a good one, we shall support it.

c. He out of the way, we should have no difficulty.

d. The sun having risen, we proceeded on our journey.

4. Classify adverbial extensions.

ANALYSIS OF SIMPLE SENTENCES.

125. In analysing simple sentences, the learner will do well to note the following hints :—

1. Seek out first the Subject of the sentence, remembering that the Subject in Imperative sentences is often not expressed. If the Subject be a noun or pronoun, it must be in the Nominative Case.

2. Seek out next the Predicate, remembering that it must be a finite verb, i.e. a verb having number and person, not a participle or infinitive.

3. If the verb be transitive and in the Active Voice, seek out the Direct Object, and, if there be one, the Indirect Object. The former will generally be found by placing whom ? or what ? after the verb ; the latter by placing *to* whom ? or *to* what ? after the verb.

4. Next seek for any enlargements there may be of the Subject and Predicate.

5. Remember that as copulative verbs can never alone form a Predicate, the nouns or adjectives which they connect with the subject will form part of the Predicate :—

He *is a carpenter* (Pred.)

They *are happy* (Pred.)

6. Do not confound the noun or pronoun in an absolute clause with the Subject of the sentence :—

The coach having gone, *we* returned (Subj.)

7. Do not confound the Direct Object followed by a Gerundial Infinitive with the Subject and Predicate :—

I saw *him* (Dir. Obj.) *die* (Ind. Obj.)

8. The simple negative should be taken with the Predicate.

9. The introductory particle 'there' is ranked with the Adverbial extensions.

10. Treat Interrogative sentences as though they were Assertive.

11. Interrogative Pronouns may be either Subjects or Objects:—

> *Who* is going to town? (Subj.)
> *Whom* did you see? (Obj.)

12. Interrogative Adverbs should be ranked with the Adverbial extensions.

13. In dealing with such imperative constructions as 'Let us go,' treat 'let' as an Imperative of the second person, 'us' as Direct Object, 'go' as Indirect Object.

14. Conjunctions, Interjections, and Vocatives are not integral parts of a sentence, and should be treated separately. This remark is not intended to apply to Adverbial Conjunctions, which, in virtue of their adverbial function, form integral parts of the sentences in which they occur.

15. Remember that a transitive verb may have an Object in any part of the sentence, but that an Objective Case is not necessarily the Object *of a sentence*:—

> To save *money* in such circumstances is not easy (in the Subject).
>
> I tried to catch *some fish* (here one Direct Object depends on another).
>
> I asked him to catch *some fish* (here a Direct Object depends on an Indirect Object).

Unless it be in a detailed analysis, take no separate notice of any Direct Object, except *the Direct Object which forms the completion of the Predicate*.

Examples.

1. Imperial Cæsar, dead and turned to clay,
   Might stop a hole to keep the wind away.—*Shakspere.*

2. There is a special Providence in the fall of a sparrow.—*Id.*

3. The sun himself looks feeble through the morning mist.—
   G. Eliot.

4. A suppressed resolve will betray itself in the eyes.—*Id.*

5. Why did you not give him some temporary aid?

6. Let us make the most capable man among us our leader.

7. The war being now over, and the troops having been ordered home, George determined to settle down in some quiet part of his native country.

Subject	Predicate	Completion of Predicate	Extension of Predicate
1. Imperial Cæsar, dead and turned to clay,	might stop	a hole (Dir. Obj.)	to keep the wind away (purpose)
2. A special Providence	is		there (introductory); in the fall of a sparrow (place)
3. The sun himself	looks feeble		through the morning mist (place)
4. A suppressed resolve	will betray	itself (Dir. Obj.)	in the eyes (place)
5. You	did not give	some temporary aid (Dir. Obj.) him (Ind. Obj.)	why (reason)
6. [You]	let	us (Dir. Obj.) make the most capable man among us our leader (Ind. (Obj.)	
7. George	determined	to settle down in some quiet part of his native country (Ind. Obj.)	the wars being now over, and the troops having been ordered home (time and circumstances)

Exercises.

Analyse, in the same way as the foregoing—

a.   The world is too much with us; late and soon,
       Getting and spending, we lay waste our powers.

Wordsworth.

b. We are sometimes required to lay our natural, lawful affec-
tions on the altar—*G. Eliot.*

c. It is better sometimes not to follow great reformers of abuses
beyond the threshold of their own homes.—*Id.*

d.
Little Ellie sits alone
Mid the rushes of a meadow,
By a stream-side on the grass.—*Mrs. Browning.*

e.
Week in, week out, from morn till night,
You can hear his bellows roar.—*Longfellow.*

f.
Toiling,—rejoicing,—sorrowing,
Onward through life he goes ;
Each morning sees some task begin,
Each evening sees its close.—*Id.*

g.
Stern o'er each bosom reason holds her state,
With daring aims, irregularly great ;
Pride in their port, defiance in their eye,
I see the lords of human-kind go by.—*Goldsmith.*

h. In a mind charged with an eager purpose and an unsatisfied
vindictiveness, there is no room for new feelings.—*G. Eliot.*

i. The reward of one duty is the power to fulfil another.

k.
All silently the little moon
Drops down behind the sky.—*Longfellow.*

l.
He nothing human alien deems
Unto himself.—*Lord Lytton.*

m.
He tore out a reed, the great god Pan,
From the deep cool bed of the river.—*Mrs. Browning.*

CLAUSES AND COMPLEX SENTENCES.

126. A Clause is a limb of a sentence containing a subject and predicate of its own, but incapable of standing
alone. Some writers speak of such clauses as sentences,
but, if we define a sentence as a *complete* utterance of
thought, it is clear that a dependent clause cannot be con-
sistently called a sentence.

A sentence containing one or more clauses is called
complex, as distinguished from a simple sentence, which
contains only one subject and one predicate. The main
sentence is called, relatively to dependent clauses, the **principal sentence.**

127. Clauses are classified according to their functions
as (1) Noun, (2) Adjective, and (3) Adverbial.

I. **A Noun Clause** is one which, with reference to the whole sentence, discharges the function of a noun. It may be—

1. *The Subject* :

> *That he was there* is not to be denied.
> *Why he came* did not appear.
> *How he arrived* was not told me.
> *Where he was born* cannot now be ascertained.

2. *An enlargement of a Noun* :

> The fact, *that he deserted his colours,* was suppressed.

3. *A part of the Predicate* :

> My motive was *that I might help him.*
> The alleged reason was *that nature abhors a vacuum.*

4. *The Direct Object* :

> I heard *that he was there.*
> You saw *why he avoided me.*
> Do you know *where he is?*

Noun clauses are often introduced by the subordinative conjunction 'that,' and by interrogative pronouns and adverbs, as 'what,' 'who,' 'which,' 'where,' 'how.' Sometimes 'that' is suppressed—

> I knew ∧ he was here.

II. **Adjective Clauses** are so called because they qualify or limit some noun or pronoun in the same way as simple adjectives. They may, clearly, occur wherever a noun occurs. Thus they may be attached—

a. To the Subject : The man *that stole the gun* is caught.

b. To the Direct Object : I saw the man *that stole the gun.*

c. To the Indirect Object : I gave the reward to the man *that apprehended the thief.*

Adjective sentences may be introduced by *a relative pronoun,* or by *an adverb of place or time,* as 'where,' 'when,' 'wherein,' 'why,' 'wherethrough,' 'wherefore,' or by a preposition followed by a relative pronoun :—

> The book *that I bought* is on the table.
> The reason *why he came* was obvious.
> The place *where they live* is near my home.
> The house *in which this event happened* is taken down.
> This is the way *in which the knot is untied.*

Very frequently the introductory word is omitted :—

> The book ∧ I bought is on the table.
> The reason ∧ he came was obvious.

III. **Adverbial Clauses** are so called because they qualify or limit a verb. They may occur wherever a verb may occur. Thus they may be attached to—

a. The Subject : To write, *when we are not disposed to write,* is irksome.

b. The Predicate : I write *when I can.*

c. The Direct Object : He loves to write *after we have gone to bed.*

d. The Indirect Object : I requested him to write *as often as he could.*

e. A Participial Phrase : Having written my letter *before he arrived*, I was able to send it off at once.

Adverbial Clauses may be classified in the same way as simple adverbs. See § 99.

ANALYSIS OF COMPLEX SENTENCES.

128. In analysing complex sentences observe the following rules :—

1. Break up the complex sentence into (*a*) the simple sentence, (*b*) the dependent clauses.

2. Remember that, as the dependent clauses discharge the function of simple parts of speech, they may form an integral part of the principal sentence, and will, therefore, figure twice over in the analysis.

3. Under the head 'Sentences and Clauses' write out the sentences or clauses in the order of prose. If they are long, give the first words and the last, marking the omission by asterisks.

4. Each finite verb must belong to a separate sentence or clause.

5. Do not be misled by the part of speech which introduces a clause. An adverb may introduce a noun clause, an adjective clause, or an adverbial clause—

> *Where he got to* did not appear (Noun).
> The place *where he resides* is on a hill (Adj.).
> I was standing *where you are standing now* (Adv.).

A relative pronoun may introduce a noun clause or an adjective clause—

> *Who he was* I could not find out (Noun).
> The man, *who was a carpenter*, is apprehended (Adj.).

6. Remember that clauses are classified according to the *function* they discharge. Ask yourself, therefore, in each case what is the function which the clause you are treating discharges. Does the clause stand for a noun ? Does it define a noun ? Does it qualify or limit a verb ?

7. The relative pronoun *what* presents some difficulty on account of its entering into both the main sentence and the adjective clause. It may be dealt with in one of two ways: (1) we may supply the antecedent 'that' and treat 'what' as a simple relative, or (2) we may repeat the pronoun in both the principal sentence and the adjective clause, and treat it as a compound relative.

8. Similarly the indefinite relatives 'whoever,' 'whosoever,' 'whatsoever,' &c., may form part of the principal sentence and of the adjective sentence, and may be treated in the same way as *what*.

> *Whosoever* is found in this plantation will be punished.
> He can have *whatever* he wants.

EXAMPLES.

1. High on the shore sat the great god Pan,
   While turbidly flowed the river.—*Mrs. Browning.*

2. Then felt I like some watcher of the skies
   When a new planet swims into his ken.—*Keats.*

3. Elizabeth clearly discerned the advantages which were to be derived from a close connection between the monarchy and the priesthood.—*Macaulay.*

4. While he was speaking, I perceived that the audience, who had at first strongly opposed him, were gradually coming round to his opinions.

5. To work when others are idle will enable you to idle when others are at work.

6. I told him that I remembered the words he said to me at my departure.

Sentence or Clause	Kind of Sentence or Clause	Subject	Predicate	Completion of Predicate	Extension of Predicate
1. (a) The great god Pan sat high on the shore	Principal to (b)	the great god Pan	sat		high on the shore (place) while turbidly flowed the river (time)
(b) while the river flowed turbidly	Adverbial to (a)	the river	flowed		while (time) turbidly (manner)
2. (a) Then I felt like some watcher of the skies	Principal to (b)	I	felt		then (time) like some watcher of the skies [feels] (comparison)
(b) when a new planet swims into his ken	Adverbial to [feels]	a new planet	swims		when (time) into his ken (place)

3. (a) Elizabeth clearly discerned the advantages	Principal to (b)	Elizabeth	discerned	the advantages (Dir. Obj.)	clearly (manner)
(b) which were . . . priesthood	Adjective to (a)	which	were to be derived		from a close connection between the monarchy and the priesthood (condition)
4. (a) I perceived that the audience . . . opinions	Principal to (b) and (c)	I	perceived	that the audience were coming slowly round to his opinions (Dir. Obj.)	
(b) that the audience . . . opinions	Noun to (a)	the audience	were coming		round to his opinions (direction) slowly (manner)
(c) while he was speaking	Adverbial to (a)	he	was speaking		while (time)
5. (a) To work will enable you to be idle	Principal to (b) and (c)	to work	will enable	you (Dir. Obj.), to be idle (Ind. Obj.)	
(b) when others are idle	Adverbial to 'to work' in (a)	others	are idle		when (time)
(c) when others are at work	Adverbial to 'to be idle' in (a)	others	are at work		when (time)

Exercises.

Analyse the following sentences, showing the nature and function
of the subordinate clauses—

a.
      My spirit flew in feathers then
        That is so heavy now,
      And summer pools could hardly cool
        The fever of my brow.—*Hood.*

b. A failure establishes only this, that our determination to
succeed was not strong enough.

c. A man knows just as much as he taught himself—no more.

d.
      'Tis sweet, as year by year we lose
      Friends out of sight, in faith to muse
      How grows in Paradise our store.—*Keble.*

e.
          My way of life
Is fallen into the sere and yellow leaf ;
And that which should accompany old age,
As honour, love, obedience, troops of friends,
I must not look to have ; but, in their stead,
Curses, not loud but deep, mouth-honour, breath,
Which the poor heart would fain deny, and dare not.
                       Shakspere.

f.
    Now is the winter of our discontent
    Made glorious summer by this sun of York,
    And all the clouds that lowered upon our house
    In the deep bosom of the ocean buried.—*Id.*

g. Having visited the house where my grandfather was born, we
went round the town, whilst my father called upon his lawyer.

h.
    But I saw a glowworm near,
    Who replied, What wailing wight
    Calls the watchman of the night ?
    I am set to light the ground
    While the beetle goes his round.

i.
    And, friends, dear friends, when it shall be
    That this low breath is gone from me,
    And round my bier ye come to weep,
    Let one most loving of you all
    Say, ' Not a tear must o'er her fall !
    He giveth his belovèd sleep.'—*Mrs. Browning.*

k.
    I saw a vision in my sleep
    That gave my spirit strength to sweep
      Adown the gulf of time :
    I saw the last of human mould
    That shall creation's dawn behold,
      As Adam saw her prime.—*Campbell.*

l. Just so we have heard a baby, mounted on the shoulders of its father, cry out, 'How much taller I am than papa!'—*Macaulay.*

m. Men who are eagerly pressing forward in pursuit of truth are grateful to every one who has cleared an inch of the way for them.—*Id.*

n. The reason why the seven stars are no more than seven is a pretty reason.—*Shakspere.*

o. I know not why he should be so angry.

p. Where he was born, who brought him up, how he lived, and whither he went after he was lost sight of, we are not told.

q. Whether it is worth while going through so much to learn so little, as the charity-school boy said when he got to the end of the alphabet, I can't say.—*Dickens.*

r.   The wind had no more strength than this,
       That leisurely it blew,
   To make one leaf the next to kiss
       That closely by it grew.—*Drayton.*

COMPOUND SENTENCES.

129. A compound sentence is one which consists of two or more co-ordinate sentences linked together by a conjunction, e.g—

I went to town, | and | I bought a watch.

The relation between the various members of a compound sentence may be—

1. *Copulative*, as when one sentence is simply added on to another, e.g.—

Their cities were burnt to the ground, and they themselves were carried into captivity.

The conjunctions most frequently used to express the copulative relation are *and, also, moreover, nor* (=and not), *furthermore.*

Very frequently we drop the conjunction altogether, and separate the co-ordinate sentences by commas or semicolons, e.g.—

He was a tall, spare man; his brother was short and corpulent.

The first condition of human goodness is something to love; the second something to reverence.—*G. Eliot.*

2. *Adversative*, as when one sentence is opposed to another co-ordinate with it, e.g.—

> He could write, | but | he could not draw.

The chief adversative conjunctions are *but, yet, still, however, nevertheless, on the other hand, notwithstanding*.

3. *Disjunctive*, as when two assertions are presented as alternatives, e.g.—

> He either had no share in it, or else he told a lie.

The chief disjunctive conjunctions are *or, otherwise, else*.

4. *Causative*, as when one sentence expresses the consequence of something stated in the other, e.g.—

> A thaw had set in on the previous evening; the ice was, consequently, unfit for skating on.

The chief conjunctions used to express the causative relation between co-ordinate sentences are *therefore, consequently, hence, accordingly*.

5. *Illative*, as when one sentence expresses an inference drawn from a sentence co-ordinate with it, e.g.—

> Like poles of magnets repel; therefore these poles will repel.

The chief illative conjunctions are *therefore, consequently, hence, whence, wherefore, accordingly, for, since, inasmuch as*.

CONTRACTION OF COMPOUND SENTENCES.

130. Sometimes we find two or more subjects having the same predicate, e.g.—

> *Thomas* and *Henry* went to the cricket-match;

sometimes one subject with two or more predicates, e.g.—

> He *ran, wrestled,* and *boxed* better than any other man in the university;

sometimes one predicate with two objects, e.g.—

> He knew *French* and *German*;

sometimes two predicates with one common object, e.g.—

He *loved* and *honoured* his parents.

It is not necessary to resolve these contracted sentences into their component parts if the fact of their contraction be noticed.

ANALYSIS OF COMPOUND SENTENCES.

131. In analysing compound sentences observe the following rules—

Add to the tables previously used a column for the insertion of connecting words. Such a column is rarely needed in dealing with complex sentences, because the connecting word is generally an integral part of the dependent clause.

2. Distinguish between subordinate clauses and co-ordinate sentences.

3. Wherever there is a contracted subject, predicate, or object, treat it as simple, and place against it the word ' Contracted.'

4. Parenthetical sentences are independent of the constructions in which they occur, and should be dealt with separately.

5. Be chary of interpolating words. If they are really necessary insert them in brackets like the following [ ].

EXAMPLES.

1.   Our deeds shall travel with us from afar,
       And what we have been makes us what we are.
G. Eliot.

2.   Be good, sweet maid, and let who will be clever,
       Do noble things, not dream them all day long;
       And so make life, death, and that vast forever,
            One grand, sweet song.—*Kingsley.*

3. Because half-a-dozen grasshoppers under a fern make the field ring with their importunate chink, while thousands of great cattle, reposing beneath the shadow of the British oak, chew the cud and are silent, pray do not imagine that those who make the noise are the only inhabitants of the field—that, of course, they are many in number—or that, after all, they are other than the little, shrivelled, meagre, hopping—though loud and troublesome—insects of the hour.—*Burke.*

Sentences and Clauses	Kind of Sentence or Clause	Connecting Word	Subject	Predicate	Completion of Predicate	Extension of Predicate
1. (a) Our deeds . . . afar	Co-ordinate with (b)		Our deeds	shall travel		with us (circumstance) from afar (place)
(b) [that] what we have been makes us [that] what we are	Co-ordinate with (a)		[that] what we have been	makes	us (Dir. Obj.) what we are (Ind. Obj.)	
(c) what we have been	Adjective to (b)	and	we	have been what		
(d) what we are	,, ,,		we	are what		
2. (a) Be good, sweet maid	Co-ordinate with (b) (d)		[thou]	be good		
(b) let [them] be clever	Co-ordinate with (a)	and	[you]	let	[them] (Dir. Obj.) be clever(Ind.Obj.)	
(c) who will [be clever]	Adjective to (b)		who	will = wish	be clever(Ind.Obj.)	
(d) Do [thou] noble things	Co-ordinate with (a) and (b)		[thou]	do	noble things (Dir. Obj.)	
(e) [do] not dream them all day long	Co-ordinate with (a), (b), and (d)		[thou]	[do] not dream	them (Dir. Obj.)	all day long (time)
(f) And so make life . . . one grand, sweet song	Co-ordinate with (a), (b) (d) (e)	and	[thou]	make	life, death, and that vast forever(Dir. Obj.), one grand sweet song (Fac. Obj.)	

		Connective	Subject	Predicate	Object	Adverbial
3. (a) Pray	Principal (parenthetical)		[I]	pray	[you] (Dir. Obj.)	
(b) do not imagine that &c...hour	Principal to (c), (e), and (f)		[you]	do not imagine	that those &c.... hour (Dir. Obj.)	
(c) that those are the only inhabitants of the field	Noun clause to (b)	that	those	are the only inhabitants of the field		
(d) who make the noise	Adjective to (e)		who	make	the noise (Dir. Obj.)	
(e) that, of course, they are many in number	Noun clause to (b)	that	they	are many in number		of course (effect)
(f) or that, after all, they are ...the hour	" "	or that	they	are other than the little... hour		after all (time)
(g) because half-a-dozen...chink	Adverbial of reason to (b)	because	half-a-dozen grass-hoppers under a fern	make	the field (Dir. Obj.) ring (Ind. Obj.)	with their importunate chink (instrument)
(h) while thousands... and are silent	Adverbial of time to (g), contracted		thousands of great cattle repos-ing &c.	1, chew 2, are silent	the cud (Dir. Obj.)	

Exercises.

Analyse—

1.   She sat beneath the birchen tree,
             Her elbow resting on her knee;
             She had withdrawn the fatal shaft,
             And gazed on it, and feebly laughed.
             The knight to stanch the life-stream tried :
             ' Stranger, it is in vain ! ' she cried.
             ' This hour of death has given me more
             Of reason's power than years before;
             For as these ebbing veins decay
             My frenzied visions fade away.'—*Scott.*

2. There is no despair so absolute as that which comes with the first moments of our first great sorrow, when we have not yet known what it is to have suffered and be healed, to have despaired and to have recovered hope.—*G. Eliot.*

3.   I will not feed on doing great tasks ill,
             Nor dull the world's sense with mediocrity.—*Id.*

4. The one enemy we have in this universe is stupidity, darkness of mind, of which darkness again there are many sources, every sin a source, and probably self-conceit the chief source.—*Carlyle.*

5.   Music when soft voices die
             Vibrates in the memory;
             Odours, when sweet violets sicken,
             Live within the sense they quicken.—*Shelley.*

6.   Why should we faint and fear to live alone,
             Since all alone, so Heaven has willed, we die,
        Nor even the tenderest heart, and next our own,
             Knows half the reasons why we smile and sigh ?—*Keble.*

7. Great men are the fire-pillars in this dark pilgrimage of mankind; they stand as heavenly signs, ever-living witnesses of what has been, prophetic tokens of what may still be, the revealed embodied possibilities of human nature.—*Carlyle.*

8.   Knowledge is now no more a fountain sealed;
             Drink deep until the habits of the slave,
             The sins of emptiness, gossip and spite
             And slander die.   Better not be at all
             Than not be noble.—*Tennyson.*

9.   If it were done when 'tis done, then 'twere well
             It were done quickly: if the assassination
             Could trammel up the consequence, and catch
             With his surcease success; that but this blow
             Might be the be-all and the end-all here,
             But here, upon this bank and shoal of time,
             We'ld jump the life to come.—*Shakspere.*

10.   Who knows whither the clouds have fled?
        In the unscarred heaven they leave no wake;
    And the eyes forget the tears they have shed,
        The heart forgets its sorrow and ache;
    The soul partakes the season's youth,
        And the sulphurous rifts of passion and woe
    Lie deep 'neath a silence pure and smooth,
        Like burnt-out craters healed with snow.—*Lowell.*

PUNCTUATION.

132. The object of punctuation is to break up written composition into sentences, and to render to the mind of the reader, through his eyes, the same kind of assistance which the modulation of the voice renders through the ear. It follows that in punctuating a passage we must be mainly guided by its analysis. The only other consideration which we need take into account is the necessity for stops. It is not every clause as shown by a rigid analysis that is 'stopped off.' Stops are used only where they are necessary to make the writer's meaning clear.

133. The stops used in English punctuation are :—
    The comma (,) (Gk. komma, *a part cut off*).
    The semicolon (;) (Gk. kōlon, *a member*).
    The colon (:).
    The full stop or period (.) (Gk. peri, *around*; hodos, *a way*).
    The note of admiration (!).
    The note of interrogation (?).
    The parenthesis ( ) (Gk. para, *beside*; en, *in*; thesis, *a placing*).

The Comma.

134. The Comma is used

(1) To separate short co-ordinate sentences :—

He could not write to me yesterday, *but* he proposes to write to me to-day.

If, however, the co-ordinate sentences are of considerable length, it is better to separate them by a semicolon :

Love has a way of cheating itself, like a child who plays at hide-and-seek; it is pleased with assurances that it all the while disbelieves.—*G. Eliot.*

(2) To separate noun, adjective, and adverbial clauses from the rest of the sentence of which it forms part :—

(*a*) *That he should have accomplished so remarkable a feat in fourteen days,* is simply incredible (Noun Clause).

(*b*) A diffident man likes the idea of doing something remarkable, *which will create belief in him without any immediate display of brilliancy* (Adjective Clause).— *G. Eliot.*

(*c*) *While the book was in the press,* the prophecy was falsified (Adverbial Clause).

When the outer disguise of obvious affectation was removed, you were still as far as ever from seeing the real man (Adverbial Clause).

His voice, *even when it sank to a whisper,* was heard to the remotest benches (Adverbial Clause).

If the clause be short, the comma may be omitted :—

(*a*) I said *that he was gone* (Noun Clause).

(*b*) The man *that did it* is apprehended (Adjective Clause).

(*c*) Nero fiddled while Rome was burning (Adverbial Clause).

(3) To separate a noun in apposition from the word on which it is dependent.

Raphael, *the greatest of painters,* died young.

If the two nouns are closely connected, the comma may be omitted :—

The river Jordan flows into the Dead Sea.
Paul the Apostle preached at Athens.

(4) To separate the 'Nominative of Address' (Vocative), the 'Nominative Absolute,' and adverbial and participial clauses from the principal sentence :—

My dear friends, make yourselves at home.

The morning being fine (Nom. Abs.), *and there being every prospect of our having a good view* (Nom. Abs.), we set out, *at about seven o'clock* (Adv. Clause), to ascend the mountain.

The king, *having obtained fresh supplies of money* (Participial Clause), postponed the calling of Parliament.

(5) To separate quoted words from the words which introduce them :—

'Ignorance,' *says Ajax,* 'is a painless evil ;' so, *I should think,* is dirt, considering the merry faces that go along with it.— *G. Eliot.*

(6) **To separate a series of co-ordinate subjects or predicates** :—

Many an irritating fault, many an unlovely oddity, has come of a hard sorrow, which has crushed and maimed the nature just when it was expanding into plenteous beauty (Co-ordinate Subjects).— *G. Eliot.*

If all the redhaired people in Europe *had,* during centuries, *been outraged and oppressed, banished from this place, imprisoned in that, deprived of their money, deprived of their teeth, convicted of the most improbable crimes on the feeblest evidence, dragged at horses' tails, hanged, tortured, burned alive,* if, when manners became milder, *they had still been subject to debasing restrictions, and exposed to vulgar insults, locked up in particular streets in some countries, pelted and ducked by the rabble in others, excluded everywhere from magistracies and honours,* what would be the patriotism of gentlemen with red hair ? (Co-ordinate Predicates).—*Macaulay.*

(7) **To separate connective and affirmative adverbs** from the sentence in which they occur :—

> *Again,* it can be shown that rents have steadily risen.
> He would, *most assuredly,* deny it.
> I, *indeed,* scarcely ever call upon him now.

(8) **To indicate the omission of a word** :—

Histories make men wise ; poets, witty ; the mathematics, subtle ; natural philosophy, deep ; moral, grave ; logic and rhetoric, able to contend.—*Bacon.*

(9) **To separate a series of adjectives or adverbs** qualifying the same word :—

> He was shrewd, cautious, cunning, and selfish.
> He led a godly, righteous, and sober life.
> He wrote accurately, forcibly, and readily.

The Semicolon.

135. The semicolon is used **to separate co-ordinate sentences, consisting of two or more members**—

They bow the knee and spit upon her ; they cry, 'Hail !' and smite her on the cheek ; they put a sceptre in her hand, but it is a fragile reed ; they crown her, but it is with thorns ; they cover with purple the wounds which their own hands have inflicted on her ; and inscribe magnificent titles over the cross on which they have fixed her to perish in ignominy and pain.—*Macaulay,* Review of Southey's 'Colloquies of Society.'

The Colon.

136. The colon is used to separate parts of a paragraph that are not united by any connective word, and yet are grammatically independent—

> The fiery soul abhorred in Catiline,
> In Decius charms, in Curtius is divine :
> The same ambition can destroy or save,
> And makes a patriot as it makes a knave.—*Pope.*

> The lights begin to twinkle from the rocks :
> The long day wanes : the slow moon climbs : the deep
> Moans round with many voices.—*Tennyson.*

The Period or Full Stop.

137. The period is used to separate sentences that are independent one of another in meaning—

Italian ships covered every sea. Italian factories rose on every shore. The tables of Italian money-changers were set in every city. Manufactories flourished. Banks were established.—*Macaulay.*

It is also used after abbreviations, as e.g. ; i.e. ; A.D.—

> Consult the statute ; *quart.* I think, it is,
> *Edwardi sext.* or *prim.* et *quint. Eliz.*

The Note of Interrogation.

138. A note of interrogation is used after a **direct question**—

> ‘Where are you going ? ’ said I.

Indirect questions do not take a note of interrogation after them—

> I asked him why he objected.

When a series of questions are united in a compound sentence, the questions are separated by commas, semicolons, or colons, and the note of interrogation is placed after the last only.

The Note of Exclamation, etc.

139. The note of exclamation is used—

1. After interjections and exclamatory sentences—

But hush ! hark ! a deep sound strikes like a rising knell.—*Byron.*

2. After invocations—

> Yet, Italy ! through every other land
> Thy wrongs should ring, and shall, from side to side;
> Mother of Arts !—*Byron.*

The **Parenthesis** ( ) separates one sentence from another, between the parts of which it is introduced.

> And if at the same time he ridicules (as is often done) the absurdity of a claim to infallibility, &c.—*Whately.*

Brackets [ ] are generally used to separate interpolated words from the passage in which they occur.

The **Dash** is used to mark some hesitation of mind or difficulty of utterance—

> Arm ! arm ! it is—it is—the cannon's opening roar.—*Byron.*

Careless writers often use the dash as a substitute for other stops. Sterne's writings are full of dashes.

The **hyphen** (from Gk. *hypo, hyp* before an aspirate, under; and *hen,* one) is used when it is necessary to separate the syllables of a word, or to unite two or more words into one compound word, as walk-ing ; bed-ridden ; the never-to-be-forgotten.

The hyphen is generally used in compounds of recent formation, that have not been completely welded into one, or in compounds in which we wish to preserve the separate significance of the component parts. Thus we do not divide ' blackbird ' or ' blacksmith,' but we put a hyphen between the parts of words like head-waiter, play-hours, man-cook, high-church, non-existent, ultra-radical, sea-serpent, fire-engine, swift-moving, lack-lustre.

The **Apostrophe** (') is used to mark the elision of a letter : as lov'd, tho', don't. It is rarely used in prose, except in recording conversations. Cobbett says the apostrophe ' ought to be called the mark not of *elision,* but of laziness and vulgarity.'

The **Guillemets** (" ") are used to separate a quotation from the passage in which it occurs. A quotation within a quotation is usually marked off by single inverted commas (' ')—

> " But one in a certain place testified saying, ' What is man, that thou art mindful of him ? ' "

The **Caret** (Lat. *careo*, I am wanting) (∧), is used to indicate that a word which had been omitted is inserted above. Cobbett calls it 'the blunder-mark.'

The **Diæresis** (Gk. *di*, apart; *haireō*, I take away) (¨), is placed over the second of two vowels, when it is intended that both should be sounded separately, as 'coöperative,' aërial.

Asterisks (***) are used to mark the omission of words, as when only the beginning and end of a passage are quoted.

The **Paragraph** (¶) is used to mark the beginning of a new subject.

The **Section** (§) (Lat. *seco*, I cut) marks the smaller divisions of a book : as, see Book ii. § 8.

The **Cedilla** (Italian zediglia=*little z*) is used to show that *c* has a soft sound before *a, o,* and *u,* in words borrowed from the French ; as façade, Alençon.

PART III.

SYNTAX.

AGREEMENT, GOVERNMENT, QUALIFICATION, AND LIMITATION.

140. Syntax (from Gk. *syn*=with, and *taxis*=arrangement) is that part of grammar that deals with the relations subsisting between the words in a sentence, and with the laws regulating the forms and positions that words assume in order to express these relations.

Syntactical relations may be grouped under four heads, Agreement, Government, Qualification, and Limitation.

141. Agreement is that law of language which requires that one word should assume the *same* gender, number, and case, or the same number and person as another.

I. **The Verb** agrees with its subject in number and person, *I am*; *thou art*; *they are.* If the subject consists of several words of different persons, the verb agrees with the first in preference to the second, and with the second in preference to the third, e.g. 'You and I *were* there.' 'He and you *were* there.' As we have the same form for the plural of all three persons, this rule scarcely needs to be mentioned ; but in parsing, the learner might be perplexed in determining the person of the verb in such constructions.

II. **The Relative Pronoun** agrees with its antecedent, or correlative, in number and person, e.g. '*He who* slanders me is my enemy ;' 'The *books that* were there are gone.' Here 'who' agrees with 'he,' and 'that' with 'books.'

The relative pronoun formerly agreed with its antecedent in gender, but we have no distinctive forms for masculine and feminine now. We can distinguish between rational beings and irrational, not between male and female.

The man *who* (qui).   The animal *which* (quod).
The woman *who* (quæ).

III. The Demonstrative Adjectives, 'this' and 'that,' with their plurals 'these' and 'those,' agree in number with the nouns which they limit.   Comp.

I have *this book*.   I have *these books*.

IV. Words **in apposition** agree in case with the words to which they are attached, e.g.

I, John Smith, do hereby declare, &c.
We saw *Mr. Brown, the publisher*.

There were formerly other instances of agreement in English. Thus adjectives once agreed with the nouns which they qualified in gender, number, and case, just as in Latin.

142. Government is that law which requires a word to assume a certain form or position, to express the relation in which it stands to some other word, e.g.—

I. Transitive Verbs and Prepositions govern the objective case, e.g.—

He *struck me*.   James *struck John*.
John gave the *book* to *James*.

In the first of these examples we express the relation of the verb to its object by using a particular form of the pronoun called its Objective Case. This form allows us to arrange the words of the sentence in any order without loss of clearness. ' *Me* he struck' would be as clear as 'He struck *me*.' In the second and third examples, as we have no longer a distinct form for the objective case of nouns, we are obliged to indicate the objective relation of *John* in Ex. 2, and *James* in Ex. 3, by *position*. We usually place the Objective Case *after* a verb or preposition. 'James John struck' would clearly be ambiguous.

In O.E. certain verbs governed the Dative, e.g. fyligan = to follow, beódan = to bid, andswarian = to answer; others governed the possessive, e.g. wilnian = to desire, wundrian = to wonder at, fandian = to tempt, &c.

II. One Verb governs another in the Infinitive Mood, e.g.

I *may go* (Simple Infinitive).
He *wished to go* (Gerundial Infinitive).

III. Certain adjectives govern the Objective Case, e.g.

He was *like* his *father*.   He was *near me*.

In O.E. certain adjectives denoting *likeness* governed the Dative Case, adjectives denoting *measure, value, weight, age, excess, want, guilt, innocence,* &c., governed the Possessive Case. In modern English the relation between the adjective and the noun, in these cases, is, for the most part, expressed by means of prepositions. Even 'like' and 'near' are often followed by 'to,' e.g.

But no more *like my father* than I *to Hercules.—Hamlet.*

Come *nearer to me.*

But it is a mistake to look upon the shorter form as a contraction of the longer. The preposition only crept in when the Dative inflexion was lost.

143. Qualification is that relation which subsists between a qualitative word and the word to which it is joined. Thus the qualitative adjective qualifies its noun, e.g. 'A *good boy*,' and the qualitative adverb qualifies its verb, e.g. 'He *wrote rapidly*.'

144. Limitation is that relation which subsists between a word and some other word, whose application it restricts.

I. **Quantitative** and **demonstrative adjectives** limit their noun, e.g.

I have *four* apples.
He has *my* book.
I will take *that* flower.

II. **A noun in apposition** limits the word to which it is attached, e.g.

Smith, *the carpenter*, was there.

III. **Nouns in the possessive case and possessive adjectives** limit the nouns which follow them, e.g.

John's horse is in the stable.
My groom was there.

IV. **Adverbs** of time, place, and degree, limit the words with which they are used, e.g.

We live *there*.
He is dead *now*.
It is occasionally *very* bad.

V. The **Gerundial Infinitive** limits the noun or adjective to which it is attached: A house *to let*; bread *to eat*; good *to drink*.

M

Questions.

1. What does Syntax relate to ?

2. Name the chief syntactical relations.

3. Define each.

4. Give instances (*a*) of Agreement, (*b*) of Government, in the following examples—

a. Wisdom sits with children round her knees.—*Wordsworth*.

b. If an idiot were to tell you the same story every day for a year, you would end by believing him.—*Burke*.

c. They calculate their depth by their darkness, and fancy they are profound because they feel that they are perplexed.—*Curran*.

d. 　　　　　　Thou shalt not lack
The flower that's like thy face, pale primrose ; nor
The azured harebell like thy veins ; no, nor
The leaf of eglantine, whom not to slander,
Outsweetened not thy breath.—*Shakspere*.

e. 　　　Who ne'er his bread in sorrow ate,
　　　　Who ne'er the mournful midnight hours,
　　　Weeping upon his bed has sate,
　　　　He knows you not, ye heavenly powers.—*Goethe*.

f. 　　　O, many a shaft at random sent,
　　　　Finds mark the archer never meant.—*Scott*.

g. 　　By the apostle Paul, shadows to-night
　　Have struck more terror to the soul of Richard
　　Than can the substance of ten thousand soldiers.

Richard III.

5. Give instances from the foregoing examples of (*a*) Qualification and (*b*) Limitation.

THE NOMINATIVE CASE.

145. The subject of a sentence, if a noun or pronoun, is said to be in the Nominative Case, though it is only the pronouns that have, in modern English, forms for the Nominative distinct from the Objective forms—

Napoleon crossed the Alps.
He saw him.

The Nominative is also used to form part of the Predicate, after :

(1) **Copulative verbs**, e.g. *be, become, turn out, prove*—

John is a *sailor*.
He became a *sailor*.
He turned out a good-for-nothing *fellow*.
He proved a useful *servant*.

(2) **Verbs denoting continuance,** e.g. *remain, continue—*

He remained a *Liberal.*

(3) **Verbs of naming—**

He was named *John.*[1]

(4) **Verbs of seeming—**

He seemed an honest *man.*
He appeared a *servant.*
He looked a *rascal.*

146. Ellipsis of the Nominative.—The Nominative is often omitted in imperative constructions—

Come, dear children, come away down.—*M. Arnold.*

The true nominative to 'come' is 'ye' understood. 'Children' is the Vocative, or Nominative of Address, as it is sometimes called.

The Nominative is often omitted in Optative sentences and familiar Assertive sentences—

Would [i.e. I would] he were here.
Thank [i.e. I thank] you.

The subject of impersonal verbs is often omitted, e.g.—

Methinks [i.e. it seems to me].
If you please [i.e. if it please you].

The Nominative is sometimes omitted before the Relative Pronoun—

Who steals my purse steals trash.—*Shakspere.*

147. The Nominative in Apposition.—The Nominative is sometimes followed by a noun or pronoun in apposition with it—

The witch, *she* held the hair in her hand.—*Kirke White.*

His breath *it* was lightning, his voice *it* was storm.—*Scott.*

---

[1] Comp. 'He byth *Johannes* genem med' [He is named John] Luke i. 60. 'Simonem, se wæs genemmed *Petrus*' [Simon, which was named Peter]. Matt. iv. 18. Verbs of *naming* were sometimes followed by the Nominative, even when used in the Active Voice. Rask gives the following examples :—'Thá wæs sum consul (thæt we *heretoha* hátath)' [There was a certain consul (whom we call heretoga)]; 'Forthý hit man hæt *Wislemutha*' [They therefore call it the mouth of the Vistula]. But the rule was not fixed. In Luke i. 59, we find the accusative after the Active Voice: 'And nemdon hyne hys fæder naman *Zachariam.*'

Sometimes the noun itself is repeated for rhetorical effect—

> Tears, idle *tears*, I know not what they mean,
> *Tears* from the depth of some divine despair,
> Rise in the heart and gather to the eyes.—*Tennyson.*

A pronoun is often used in apposition with an infinitive phrase or noun clause, e.g.—

> *It* is human to err.
> *It* is well known that he wrote the book.

Dr. Abbott calls 'it' in these constructions the Preparatory Subject. The true subjects in the foregoing examples are 'to err' and 'that he wrote the book.'

A noun is sometimes used in apposition with the whole predicate of a previous sentence—

> He showed me over the house, an *attention* which I much appreciated.

148. The 'Nominative' Absolute.—Occasionally a subject is found qualified by a participle used predicatively, but without any finite verb. Such a subject, being independent of the principal sentence, is generally called the Nominative Absolute, though a more accurate name for it would be the **Subject Absolute.**

> The *wind* being favourable, we set sail.

The syntactical function of the Absolute construction is to mark the *time, reason, cause, conditions, or some accompanying circumstances* of the action denoted by the finite verb in the principal sentence. Hence it is essentially adverbial. Dr. Abbott calls it the **Adverbial Subject.**

> The *clock* having struck six, we set out (Time).
> *Fever* having broken out, we left the town (Reason).
> The *doors* not fitting, the rooms were, of course, draughty (Cause).
> The *terms* being reasonable, I will take the house (Condition).
> Away he went, *I* vainly endeavouring to keep up with him (Accompanying Circumstance).

The learner should take care not to confound the Subject Absolute with a nominative which is qualified predicatively by a participle, and at the same time the subject of the sentence. Comp.

> *Cæsar*, having been defeated, returned to Rome

with

> *Cæsar* having been defeated, *his troops* returned to Gaul.

In the former sentence 'Cæsar' is not the Subject Absolute, but the Nominative to 'returned;' in the latter 'Cæsar' is the Subject Absolute, 'troops' being the Nominative to 'returned.'

The participle qualifying the Subject Absolute is often omitted—

> *He* ∧ away, we should have no opposition.
> *Dinner* ∧ over, we adjourned to the play-room.

In Latin the Subject Absolute is expressed by means of the Ablative Case; in Greek, for the most part, by the Genitive; in O.E. by the Dative.[1]

Exercises.

Parse the nominatives in the following passages—

a.   Then I shall be no more;
And Adam wedded to another Eve,
Shall live with her enjoying; I extinct.—*Milton.*

b.   The pass was steep and rugged,
    The wolves they howled and whined;
But he ran like a whirlwind up the pass,
    And he left the wolves behind.—*Macaulay.*

c.   Far above it, on the steep,
    Ruined stands the old château,
Nothing but the donjon keep
    Left for shelter or for show.—*Longfellow.*

d. If he had continued a soldier, he would have risen to a position of authority.

e. Next Anger rushed, his eyes on fire.—*Collins.*

f. It is a glorious thing to die for one's country.

---

[1] The following are examples from O.E.—'Upasprungen*re* sun*nan*,' the sun having risen; 'He hí up-a-hóf, hyre hand*a* gegripen*re*,' he lifted her up, her hand having been grasped; 'Tha cwæth he, to-somne geclyped*um* his leorning cnyht*um*,' then quoth he, his disciples being called together (Mark viii. 1).

g.   That I have ta'en away this old man's daughter
It is most true.—*Shakspere.*

h.   My story being done,
She gave me for my pains a world of sighs.—*Id.*

i. He was appointed commander.

k.   Here lay Duncan,
His silver skin laced with his golden blood.—*Shakspere.*

l. Silver and gold have I none, but such as I have give I thee.
    Bible.

m. Teeth hadst thou in thy head when thou wert born.
    Shakspere.

n. Deborah, a prophetess, the wife of Lapidoth, she judged Israel at that time.

o.   Life, I know not what thou art,
But know that thou and I must part;
And when, or how, or where we met,
I own to me's a secret yet.—*Mrs. Barbauld.*

p.   There are who ask not if thine eye
Be on them.—*Wordsworth.*

THE POSSESSIVE CASE.

149. The Possessive Case appears to have at first denoted origin,[1] and this sense it still retains in many constructions. The learner should distinguish between the subjective and the objective use of the possessive case. '*His* praise' may mean either—

(1) The praise which he bestows, e.g. I valued his praise;

or—

(2) The praise which is bestowed on him, e.g. The people were loud in his praise.

The Possessive in the former example would be called by some grammarians the **Subjective Genitive**, inasmuch as it denotes the *subject* of the action; the possessive in the latter example they would call the **Objective Genitive**, because it denotes the *object* of the action.

150. The possessive relation is now expressed, by means

[1] Hence the name *Genitive* is sometimes applied to this case (Lat. *genitivus*, relating to birth or generation, from *gigno, genui, genitum,* I beget).

of a preposition governing the objective case, in many cases in which it was formerly expressed by inflexion, e.g.—

The house of my father = My father's house.

In some instances we use both the apostrophe and the preposition, e.g., 'This is a work *of Cicero's.'* Here 'of' must be regarded as governing 'works' understood.

In some instances we find 'of' with its dependent noun, where we might expect a noun in apposition, e.g.: The city of London; the river of Jordan. It has been proposed to call this construction the *Appositive Genitive* (Rushton's 'Rules and Cautions,' p. 83).

Thus there are four ways in which the possessive relation may be expressed in English.

1. By inflexion, e.g. 'John's gun.'

2. By the preposition 'of,' e.g. 'The hope of England.'

3. By a combination of methods 1 and 2, e.g. 'A play of Shakspere's.'

4. By apposition, e.g. 'The borough of Cardiff.'

In O.E. the possessive was used to denote—

(1) *Time when*, e.g. *thæs dæges*, on that day. Some trace of this is preserved in such expressions as—

Let me have men about me, that are fat;
Sleek-headed men and such as sleep o' *nights.—Shakspere.*

He comes *of a Monday.*

(2) *Measure, weight, age, value, &c.*, e.g.—

Twe*gra* elna heah, two ells high.
Six penni*ga* wyrthe, sixpence worth.
Wí*tes* scyldig, deserving of punishment.
Ánes geáres lamb, a yearling lamb; literally, a lamb of year.
Threóra míla brád, three miles broad.

Hence probably arose such expressions as the following, which Dr. Angus somewhat inconsiderately pronounces erroneous :—

' Let a gallows be made *of* fifty cubits *high* ' (Esther v. 14). 'An heifer *of* three years *old* ' (Is. xv. 15). The genitive is dependent on the adjectives ' high,' ' old.' In modern English we sometimes drop the adjective in these constructions, and sometimes the sign of the genitive. Thus we say, 'A child of three years,' or 'A child three years old,' but neither of these constructions is intelligible except in the light of the old one that it has superseded.

(3) *The matter of which a certain measure is stated*, e.g.—

> Hund sestra el*es*, a hundred measures of oil.
> Fíf pund wætr*es*, five pounds of water

In O.E. many verbs governed the possessive case, e.g. *wilnian, lystan,* to desire, *wundrian,* to wonder at, *fandian,* to tempt, *thurfan,* to need, *fægnian,* to be glad of, *onbyrgan,* to taste of. (See Rask, p. 124.)

This law of O.E. syntax probably accounts for the modern pro-vincialisms 'taste *of* it,' ' smell *of* it,' &c., which are very common in the eastern counties.

The prepositions 'of,' 'to,' 'with' = against, sometimes govern the genitive in O.E., e.g.—

> Of gerad*ra* word*a* ic misfó, I lack fitting words.
> Tó æfenn*es*, In the evening.
> He éfste with thæ*s* her*es*, He hastened against the army.

When two or more possessives are in apposition, we usually put the sign of the possessive after the second only.

> For thy servant David's sake.—*Bible.*

Occasionally the possessive stands alone, the noun limited being understood, e.g.—

> Have you seen St. Peter's?

Sometimes the possessive is used to limit the verbal noun, e.g.—

> By *his* own showing he is wrong.

Exercises.

1. Give instances (*a*) of the Subjective Genitive, (*b*) of the Objective Genitive.

2. Explain the construction of the following phrases :—

    a. It weighed three *pounds.*

    b. It was three *feet* long.

    c. He comes *of a Monday.*

    d. Three yards *of cloth.*

3. Give instances of compound words in which the case-ending of the possessive is preserved.

THE OBJECTIVE CASE.

151. The Objective Case of modern English is that form of the noun or pronoun which is used after a transitive verb in the Active Voice or after a preposition ; e.g.—

He loved *me* (Dir. Obj.).
He gave it to *me* (Ind. Obj.).

152. The Accusative Case or Direct Object. The direct object of a transitive verb may be a noun or the equivalent of a noun.

(*a*) We saw the *sea* (Noun).

(*b*) I heard *him* (Pronoun).

(*c*) We saw the *dancing* (Verbal Noun).

(*d*) I love *to read* (Gerundial Infinitive).

(*e*) I heard *that he was here* (Noun Clause).

The verbal noun and the gerundial infinitive may themselves have direct objects :—

He loved *hunting* the *hare*.
I love *to read German*.

153. Cognate Object. Intransitive verbs are sometimes used transitively with an object of cognate or kindred meaning. Such an object may be regarded as direct in form, though adverbial in function.

a. Let me die the *death* of the righteous.—*Bible.*

b. I have fought a good *fight.*—*Id.*

c. He ran a *race.*

d. Dreaming *dreams* no mortal ever dreamed before.—*Poe.*

e. He snored the *snore* of the weary.—*G. H. Lewes.*

In (*a*) 'the death of the righteous'=righteously; in (*b*) 'a good fight'=well; in (*c*) 'a race' tells us the circumstances of the running; in (*d*) 'dreams no mortal,' &c., tells us the character of the dreaming'; in (*e*) 'the snore,' &c., describes the 'snoring.'

154. Double Accusatives. The verb 'teach,' like the Latin 'doceo,' may govern two accusatives, one of the person, another of the thing—

I taught *him French.*

Comp. 'Quis *musicam* docuit *Epaminondam*?' (Who taught Epaminondas music?) This anomaly is to be accounted for by the fact that teaching involves a twofold process. We teach not only the *subject*, but we teach *the pupil through the subject*.

When the mind is fixed mainly on the subject taught and not on the pupil, the word denoting the pupil may be regarded as an indirect object, governed by 'to' expressed or understood, but there is no trace of this 'to' in our early writers. It does not occur once in the A.V. of the Bible. The usage of O.E. is settled by the following passage—

> And he ongan *hig* fela læran.—Mark vi. 34.

[And he began to teach them many things]. *Hig* is the Accusative form ; the Dative would be *Him* or *Heom*.

155. Factitive ¹ Accusative. Verbs of *making, appointing, creating*, in the Active Voice, govern two accusatives, one of the person and another of the result of the action denoted by the verb—

> We made him *king*.
> They created him a *peer*.
> We appointed him our *treasurer*.

Verbs of *thinking, considering, supposing, believing*, &c. follow the same construction—

> We thought him an able *man*.
> We considered him a trustworthy *person*.

Dr. Abbott would call the second object the **Objective Supplement of the verb**. Similarly, he would call the retained object after a passive verb the **Subjective Supplement**—

> We made him *king* (Obj. Supplement).
> He was made *king* (Subj. Supplement).

156. The Dative or Indirect Object denotes an object more or less remotely affected by an action, or by an attribute—

> He gave the apple to *John*.
> The book will be useful to *you*.

It must not be supposed that the preposition always precedes the Dative Object. In O.E. both verbs and adjectives governed the Dative Case without the intervention of a preposition.

¹ From *facio*, I make, the verb 'make' being a typical representative of the class.

The Dative is most frequently used after (*a*) verbs of *giving* (whence its name), *promising, showing, telling,* &c.; as 'I gave it *him*,' 'He promised *me* a book,' 'Show *him* the way,' 'Tell *him* a story;' (*b*) impersonal verbs, as *think* (=seem), *seem, list*: as '*methinks*,' '*meseems*'—

> *Her* seemed she scarce had been a day
> One of God's choristers.—*D. G. Rossetti.*

(*c*) adjectives of *similarity, dissimilarity, proximity,* &c. : as 'He is near *you*,' 'She is like *him*,' 'They are unlike each other;' (*d*) certain interjections, as *woe! ah! well!*

> Woe is *me.—Psalms.*
> Well is *thee.—Ib.*

157. The Dative of the personal pronouns is sometimes used familiarly, to indicate that the person denoted by the pronoun is specially *interested* in some action performed in his behalf—

> He plucked *me* ope his doublet.—*Shakspere.*
> Rob *me* the exchequer.—*Id.*
> Knock *me* this gate, and rap *me* well.—*Id.*
> Your tanner will last *you* nine year.—*Id.*

This Dative is called in Latin the Dativus Ethicus, because the matter spoken of is regarded with interest (Gr. ĕthos) by the person concerned.

158. In O.E. the Dative was used in Absolute Constructions. This Dative Absolute occurs once or twice in Milton, but has now entirely disappeared—

> *Him* destroyed . . .
> For whom all this was made, all this will soon
> Follow.—*Milton.*

Many verbs formerly governed the Dative Case, which now govern the Accusative, e.g. *fyligan,* to follow; *beódan,* to bid; *andswarian,* to answer; *gelýfan,* to believe; *hýrsumian,* to obey.

The following prepositions governed the Dative, *bé,* about; *bý,* by; *of; fram,* from; *æt,* at; *tó; ǽr,* before; *feor,* for; *gehende,* near; *behconan,* on this side; *behindan,* behind; *beæftan,* after; *benorthan,* to the north of; *betweox,* betwixt; *bufan,* above; *bútan,* without; *on-ufan,* above; *tó-eácan,* besides; *neah,* near; *intó; æfter; unfeor,* near; *tóweard,* toward; *begeondan,* beyond; *with northan,* to the north of; *betrynan,* between; *beneothan,* beneath; *binnan,* within; *on-innan,* inside; *tó-emnes,* along.

159. The Adverbial Object is so called, because it discharges the function of an adverb in limiting the predicate as regards *time, place, measure,* &c.—

a. Time when: He died last *week*.

b. Time how long: He lived forty *years*.

c. Time how often: He came to see us every other *day*.

d. Place: He went *home*. Go thy *way*.

e. Weight, measure, space, age, &c. :

> It weighed six *pounds*.
> It measured four *feet* by two.
> He ran three *miles*.
> The army of the Canaanites, nine hundred *chariots* strong, covered the plain of Esdraelon.—*Milman*.
>
> He is a *trifle* better.
> In everything that relates to science I was a whole *encyclopædia* behind the rest of the world.—*C. Lamb*.
>
> If the English were in a paradise of spontaneous productions, they would continue to dig and plough, though they were never a *peach* nor a *pine-apple* the better for it.
> *S. Smith.*
>
> He was six *years* old.
> It blew a *hurricane*.
> The waves rose *mountains* high.

160. The following idiomatic constructions contain Adverbial Objects of a somewhat different character—

> Bind him *hand* and *foot*.—*Bible*.
> They turned him out, *neck* and *crop*.
> Destroy it, *root* and *branch*.
> They fell upon it, *tooth* and *nail*.
> Out with him, *bag* and *baggage*.

In O.E. the Adverbial Object was expressed in various ways—

a. Nouns of time answering to the question *how long* were put in the accusative—

> Hwí stande ge her *ealne dæg* ídele ?
> (Why stand ye here all the day idle?)

b. Nouns answering the question *when* were put in the ablative, sometimes in the dative governed by a preposition, sometimes in the genitive—

> Ablative: *Othre sithe*, another time.
> Dative: On *thǽre tíde*, at that time.
> Genitive: *Thǽs dages*, on that day.

c. Nouns denoting *measure, value, weight, age,* and the like, were put in the genitive. (See examples, § 150.)

d. The ablative was used to limit the comparative of adjectives—

> Se líchama wæs *sponne* lengra thære thryh. (The body was a *span* longer than the coffin.)

Many of these adverbial constructions are often explained by supplying prepositions to govern the objective case. It should be remembered, however, that these prepositions have not dropped out of the construction, but have been stuck in. The syntactical function of the adverbial object was indicated, not by a preposition, but by inflexion.

Questions.

1. What do you mean by a Direct Object?

2. Give instances of the Cognate Object.

3. After what verbs does the Factitive Object occur?

4. Parse the objectives in the following passages—

a. Give sorrow words.—*Shakspere.*

b. I yielded and unlocked her all my heart.—*Milton.*

c. I gat me to my Lord right humbly.—*Bible.*

d. He lived a life of infamy, and died a death of shame.

e.   An hour they sat in council ;
       At length the mayor broke silence :
       For a guilder I'd my ermine gown sell ;
       I wish I were a mile hence.—*R. Browning.*

f. What were you looking at?

g. Teach me, O Lord, the way of Thy statutes.—*Bible.*

h. But no more like my father than I to Hercules.—*Shakspere.*

i.   Earthly power doth then show likest God's
       When mercy seasons justice.—*Id.*

k. I thought him a gentleman.

l. I was asked a question, and was found fault with because I could not answer it.

m. He wrote two hours a day.

n.   Soprano, basso, even the contra-alto,
       Wished him five fathoms under the Rialto.—*Byron.*

o.   Whose flag has braved a thousand years
       The battle and the breeze.—*Campbell.*

p. He was a head and shoulders taller than his countrymen.

q.   She shuddered and paused like a frighted steed,
       Then leaped her cable's length.—*Longfellow.*

r.   Renowned Spenser lie a thought more nigh
To learned Chaucer.—*Basse.*

s. And if his name be George I'll call him Peter.—*Shakspere.*

t.   But flies an eagle flight, bold, and forth on,
Leaving no track behind.—*Id.*

u. Let her paint an inch thick, to this favour she must come.—*Id.*

v. And he said unto his sons, Saddle me the ass. So they saddled him the ass.—*Bible.*

w. He was nothing the better for his voyage.

x. The salmon measured twenty inches round, and weighed forty pounds.

y. Whip me such honest knaves.—*Shakspere.*

z. Why, he drinks you, with facility, your Dane dead drunk.—*Id.*

5. What do you mean by the Adverbial Object ? Give instances of your own of its various uses.

6. Explain the following constructions—

a. I wish you all sorts of prosperity with *a little more taste.*
                                              Gil Blas.

b. For evil news rides *post*, while good news baits.—*Milton.*

c. It may well wait a *century* for a reader, as God has waited six thousand *years* for an observer.—*Brewster.*

d. My Lord St. Alban said that Nature did never put her precious jewels into a garret four *stories* high.—*Bacon.*

e. O thou invisible spirit of wine, if thou hast no name to be known by, let us call thee *devil.*—*Shakspere.*

f. Ay, every *inch* a king.—*Id.*

g. I was promised the *post.*

h. For riches certainly make *themselves* wings.—*Bible.*

i. He will laugh *thee to scorn.*—*Id.*

k. The hope of truth grows stronger *day by day.*—*Lowell.*

l. Like some tall *palm* the mystic fabric sprung.—*Heber.*

m.   Near the *lake* where drooped the willow
Long *time* ago.—*G. P. Morris.*

n.   His locked, lettered, braw brass collar
Showed him the *gentleman* and *scholar.*—*Burns.*

o.   In men this blunder you will find :
All think their little set *mankind.*

ADJECTIVES.

161. It is sometimes said that English adjectives have the same gender, number, and case as the nouns they qualify, but this is no longer true; they have wholly lost their inflexions for gender and case, and it is only '*this*' and '*that*,' with their plurals '*these*' and '*those*,' that agree in number with their nouns—

> *This* is the boy.
> *These* are the boys.

Shakspere sometimes uses the plural demonstrative with collective nouns, but the example is not to be followed—

> *These* kind of knaves I know.—*Lear*, ii. 2.

Adjectives used as nouns sometimes take a plural form, e.g. 'edibles,' 'opposites,' 'goods,' 'equals,' 'coevals,' 'contemporaries,' 'annuals,' 'weeklies,' &c. In the Athanasian Creed we find 'incomprehensibles' and 'eternals.'

162. Adjectives are used to qualify or limit nouns or their equivalents. The qualification may be attributive, predicative, or factitive.

When the adjective forms part, as it were, of a compound noun, it is said to qualify it or limit it **attributively**, e.g.—

> The *little* girl has the *blue* dress.
> The *seven* children were there.

Occasionally we find the adjective used to qualify pronouns attributively, e.g. 'Poor *me* !'

When the adjective follows a copulative verb, it qualifies or limits the subject **predicatively**—

> They are *happy*.
> To err is *human*, to forgive *divine*.
> He became *rich*.
> He remained *single*.
> He continued *poor*.
> He grew *wealthy*.
> We are *seven*.
> That he holds these views is *notorious*.

Verbs relating to the senses are often similarly followed

by adjectives that qualify their noun or pronoun predicatively—

>He looked *angry*.   It felt *cold*.   It tasted *hot*.

When the adjective follows verbs of *making, thinking, considering*, &c., it is said to qualify its noun or pronoun **factitively**—

>We made him *happy*.
>We thought him *strange*.
>He was considered *clever*.

163. Adjectives are often used both as abstract and as concrete nouns, and when so used should be parsed accordingly.

Abstract Nouns.

>The *sublime* and the *ridiculous* are often so nearly related that it is difficult to class them separately.   One step above the *sublime* makes the *ridiculous*, and one step above the *ridiculous* makes the *sublime* again.—*Paine.*

Concrete Nouns :

>Formed by thy converse happily to steer
>From *grave* to *gay*, from *lively* to *severe.*—*Pope.*

>Then happy *low*, lie down.—*Shakspere.*

164. The adjective form is often used adverbially—

>*Slow* rises worth by poverty depressed.—*Dr. Johnson.*

>Drink *deep*, or taste not the Pierian spring.—*Pope.*

In adverbial phrases the word qualified by the adjective is often not expressed; as, ' at large,' ' from the least to the greatest,' ' in short,' ' in general,' ' in particular.'

165. When the participle of a transitive verb is used adjectively, it loses its power of governing a noun :—

>He was very *sparing* of his speech.

166. Position of Adjectives.—The adjective may be used before or after its noun—

>He sinks into thy depths with *bubbling* groan
>Without a grave, *unknelled, uncoffined*, and *unknown*.
>>>>>>*Byron.*

Occasionally in archaic English we find one adjective precede, and another follow, the same noun—

>And he was a *good* man and a *just.*—*Luke* xxiii. 50.

>A *great* door and *effectual* is opened unto me.—1 *Cor.* xvi. 9.

The question is sometimes raised whether we should say 'the two first' or 'the first two.' Both expressions are correct if used in their proper places. 'The two first' compares the two at the head of a series with *all the rest*; 'the first two,' with *other twos*.

167. Certain adjectives can be used only predicatively, e.g., *ware, aware, afraid,* &c. *Ware* (O.E. wær) was formerly used attributively as well as predicatively. Now we use *wary* instead of *ware* in attributive constructions—

> They were *ware* of it.—*Acts* xiv. 6.
> Of whom be thou *ware.*—*2 Tim.* iv. 15.

Abroad, asleep, awake, and many other similarly formed words, are not adjectives but adverbs. The *a* has the force of *on*—

> An ambassador lies *abroad* for the good of his country.
> *Sir H. Wotton.*

Adjectives that have words dependent on them are never used attributively, and may precede or follow their nouns—

> *Reckless* of criticism, the premier followed the dictates of conscience.
> He was a man *full* of learning.

168. Comparison of Adjectives.—The comparative form should never be used when more than two objects or classes of objects are compared, nor the superlative when only two are compared. In archaic English double comparatives and double superlatives are sometimes employed for emphasis [1]—

> He shall find
> Th' unkindest beast *more kinder* than mankind.
> *Shakspere.*
> This was the *most unkindest* cut of all.—*Id.*

'Lesser' has established itself in the language.

The superlative form is sometimes used to indicate that the quality denoted by the adjective is possessed in a pre-eminent degree. In such constructions it is called the **Superlative of Pre-eminence,** e.g. 'He was the *truest* of friends, and the *kindest* of parents.'

---

[1] Ben Jonson says: 'This is a certain kind of English Atticism, or eloquent phrase of speech, imitating the manner of the most ancientest and finest Grecians, who, for more emphasis and vehemencies' sake, used so to speak.'

N

169. Government of Adjectives.—In O.E. the comparative without 'than' was followed by the ablative; the superlative was followed by the genitive.[1] Traces of the ablative have been already pointed out under the head 'Adverbial Object.' The only traces of the genitive are *alder*best (= best of all), *alder*-liefest (= dearest of all), which are found as late as the sixteenth century.

Some writers use the objective case after the comparative even when *than* is expressed. Thus Milton writes—

> Satan, than *whom* none higher sat.

But this construction is ungrammatical, and contrary to the usage of O.E. Comp. 'Fortham Fæder ys mare thonne *ic*,' [Because the Father is greater than I], John xiv. 28.

'Than' is a conjunction, and, like other conjunctions, takes the same case after it as before it. Historically considered, 'than' is a secondary form of 'then.' 'This is better *than* that' = this is better, then that is better [i.e. is next in order of superiority].

170. The only adjectives that now govern cases are (*a*) *like* and *near*, and (*b*) adjectives of *measure, worth*, &c. (See § 142.) 'Like' and 'near' are sometimes followed by 'to,' and hence some writers assume that even when the preposition is not expressed, the dative is governed by it; but in O.E. the dative was immediately governed by the adjective, e.g. *eow* gelíc [like you, dat.]—John ix. 55.

> Some said he is *like him.*—*Bible.*
> So we grew together
> *Like to* a double *cherry*, seeming parted.—*Shakspere.*
> And homeless *near* a thousand *homes* I stood,
> And *near* a thousand *tables* pined and wanted food.
> *Wordsworth.*
> *Nearer*, my God, *to thee.*—*Adams.*

171. Pronominal Adjectives.—Some of these are often incorrectly used.

Each and *every* take singular verbs and singular pronouns after them. (See § 188.)

---

[1] Rask gives the following examples: 'Se líchama wæs sponne lengra *thære thryh*' [The body was a span longer than the coffin]. 'Gif he (se anweald) becymth tó thám *eallra* wyrrestan men, and tó thám the his *eallra* unweorthost bith' [If it (the power) falls to the worst man of all, and to him who is of all the most unworthy of it]. P. 121.

Either and *neither* refer to one of two things. ' Either '
is incorrectly used for ' each ' in the following quotations—

> They crucified two others with Him, on either side one,
> and Jesus in the midst.—*Bible.*

> On either side of the river was the tree of life.—*Ib.*

Other, in accordance with its original meaning, refers to
the second of two. *Another* is used when more than two
objects are spoken of.

172. The Articles.—The indefinite article is used in
speaking of *any* individual of a species, the definite article
in speaking of *some particular* individual. ' *A* Greek slave '
means any slave of the Greek nation; '*the* Greek slave '
means some particular Greek slave who has been previously
referred to; ' The Greek Slave ' (with a capital S) the famous
statue so called. Comp. '*the* Duke,' '*the* Queen,' '*the* right
man in *the* right place.'

In O.E. there was no indefinite article, *an* having invariably the
sense of *one.* 'Where an indefinite signification was required no
article was prefixed, and the sentence followed the Latin construction. "Theodric wǽs Christen," Theodoricus fuit Christianus,
Theodoric was a Christian, as we should now express it.' (*Harrison.*)
Comp. ' Man wǽs fram God asend ' [A man was from God sent],
John i. 6.

The indefinite article, in accordance with its original
meaning, is generally used with a singular noun, but may be
used after the adjective 'many' and before numerals—

> (*a*) Full many *a* flower is born to blush unseen.—*Gray.*

> (*b*) *A* thousand spurs are striking deep.—*Macaulay.*

> (*c*) About *an* eight days after these sayings.—*Bible.*

In the first of these sentences *a* fixes the attention on the
isolated flower, while ' *many* ' asserts the frequency of the
occurrence. Omit the article, and the picture of the individual flower is lost in the general statement. In (*b*) 'thousand' may be regarded as a collective adjective; so 'eight
days ' in (*c*) may be regarded as meaning ' a period of eight
days.' Comp. ' *a* few books,' ' *a* great many people,' ' *a* vast
host.'

Position of the Indefinite Article.—When a noun is preceded by an adjective and an indefinite article, the latter is
usually placed before the adjective; but after *such, many,*

N 2

what, and adjectives preceded by *so*, the article is placed immediately before the noun—

> *A* rich, well-born, and benevolent gentleman.
> Such *a* sight.
> What *a* day !
> So great *a* reputation.

When several nouns, denoting *different* objects, are mentioned, the article should be placed before each—

> *A* mason and *a* carpenter were there.

When the nouns denote the same object, the article is not repeated—

> *A* plumber and glazier was there.

The following is inaccurate—

> A feeble senate and enervated people.—*Gibbon.*

When a noun is preceded by a string of adjectives, the article is usually placed before the first only, but, for the sake of emphasis, may be repeated before each—

> *A* noisy, pompous, and over-dressed person strutted up and
>   down.
> It was *a* cruel, *a* disgraceful, *a* dishonourable thing to do.

The indefinite article is sometimes used *before an adjective after a noun*—

> He was *a* learned man and *a* cunning.—*Bulwer.*

The indefinite article before a proper noun makes it common, e.g. ' a Newton,' ' a Shakspere.'

173. The Definite Article was originally a demonstrative, and retains somewhat of its original force.

' **The** ' is used before adjectives to denote—

> (*a*) A class, as ' the good,' ' the rich.'
> (*b*) An abstract idea, e.g. ' the true,' ' the beautiful.'

The is often used before a singular noun to denote the whole species, e.g. ' *The* laurel is an evergreen.' Note the difference between this use of ' the ' and the following use of it : ' *The* laurel that you see was brought from Japan.' In both constructions ' the ' is demonstrative ; in the former it points out the species, in the latter the individual tree, which is further defined by the adjective clause.

The, like *a,* is used before a proper noun to denote a

person resembling some well-known character designated by the noun.

He was *the* Crichton of the university.

The placed before a common noun often converts it into a proper noun—

The Queen visited *the* university.

The is sometimes used, as in French, for the possessive adjective in cases where no ambiguity would be occasioned by its employment—

He was shot in *the* shoulder.
He had an affection of *the* heart.

The is used before the names of rivers, mountains, seas, oceans—'the Danube,' 'the Alps,' 'the Adriatic.' It is used before one name of a town—'*the* Hague.'

The before comparatives is the ablative of the demonstrative, and is used adverbially—

The more they think, *the* less they say.

The use of *the* before the relative is now nearly obsolete—

Where there was a garden, into *the* which he entered.
John xviii. 1.

Verbal nouns formed from transitive verbs, if preceded by *the*, should be followed by *of*—

In *the* writing *of* this book.

It would be incorrect to say, 'In the writing this book,' though we might say, 'In writing *this* book.'

Questions.

1. Give instances of the various ways in which an adjective may qualify a noun.

2. What is meant by saying that an adjective qualifies its noun factitively ?

3. Give instances of adjectives that cannot be used attributively.

4. In O.E. some adjectives governed the Dative Case, some the genitive. Give instances. What traces of this government survive ?

5. Parse the adjectives in the following examples—

a.　　　Richer by far is the heart's adoration,
　　　　Dearer to God are the prayers of the poor.—*Heber*.

b. I found him sad and left him happy.

c. Better fifty years of Europe than a cycle of Cathay.—*Tennyson.*

6. Explain the syntactical relations of the italicized adjectives in the following—

a.   Jewels five-words *long*
          That on the stretched forefinger of all time
          Sparkle for ever.—*Tennyson.*

b.   A man's best things are *nearest* him,
          Lie *close* about his feet.—*Lord Houghton.*

c.   And earthly power doth then show *likest* God's
          When mercy seasons justice.—*Shakspere.*

d.   Why should we faint and fear to live alone,
          Since all alone, so Heaven has willed, we die,
          Nor even the tenderest heart and *next* our own,
          Knows half the reasons why we smile and sigh?—*Keble.*

e. I awoke one morning and found myself *famous.*—*Byron.*

f. We made them *happy.*

g. He was three years *older* than I.

h. Wine that maketh *glad* the heart of man.—*Bible.*

i. He fashioneth their hearts *alike.*—*Ib.*

7. What is the difference between the definite and the indefinite article?

8. State the function of the articles in the following passages:—

a. It is not good that the man should be alone; I will make him an help-meet.—*Bible.*

b. Which in time past were not a people, but are now the people of God.—*Ib.*

c.   And dar'st thou then
          To beard the lion in his den,
          The Douglas in his hall?—*Scott.*

d.   From liberty each nobler science sprung,
          A Bacon brightened, and a Spenser sung.—*Savage.*

e. The Niobe of nations, there she stands.—*Byron.*

f. When he was taken down, the head was severed from the body.

g. He lives at the Hall.

h.   When the good, and the bad, and the worst, and the best,
          Have gone to their eternal rest.—*Poe.*

9. Examine the following passages, and correct them where necessary—

a. In every parallelogram any of the parallelograms about the diameter, together with the two complements, is called a gnomon.

b. For as the lightning that lighteneth out of the one part under heaven, shineth unto the other part under heaven.

c. He had no reason for the valuing the book.

d. We sent a letter to Mr. Brown, the chairman and the treasurer of the society.

10. Parse the articles in the following—

The more you stroke a cat, the higher he raises his back.

11. Examine the syntactical accuracy of the following passages :—

a. He laid his hand upon 'the Ocean's mane,'
And played familiar with his hoary locks.—*Pollock.*

b. But on and up where Nature's heart
Beats strong amid the hills.—*Lord Houghton.*

c. Our worser thoughts Heaven mend.—*Shakspere.*

d. It is observable that each one of the letters bear date after his banishment.—*Bentley.*

e. The green trees whispered low and mild.—*Longfellow.*

f. Silent he stood and firm.

g. Is she as tall as me ?—*Shakspere.*

PRONOUNS.

174. Pronouns agree in gender, number, and person with the nouns for which they stand.

The following are exceptions to this rule—

a. It is often used in apposition with masculine and feminine nouns, e.g. : *It* is a boy. *It* is a girl.

b. It is used of things possessing sex when the sex is not known, or is immaterial to the purpose of the speaker, e.g. : ' A child is impressionable ; *it* needs to be guarded from evil influences.'

c. It may be used in apposition with a plural noun, e.g. : ' *It* is they.'

d. It is sometimes used redundantly—

Not lording *it* over God's heritage.

Whether the charmer sinner *it* or saint *it*,
If folly grow romantic I must paint it.—*Pope.*

175. A noun of multitude may be represented by a plural pronoun if we wish to call attention to the separate individuals of whom the multitude is composed—

This people's heart is waxed gross, and *their* eyes they have closed.—Matt. xiii. 15.

176. The same rule should be observed in the employment of pronouns after 'or' 'and 'nor' as in the employment of verbs.   If the antecedent be singular, the pronoun should be singular.   Hence the following is wrong :—

When do we ever find a well-educated Englishman or Frenchman embarrassed by an ignorance of the grammar of *their* respective languages ?—*S. Smith.*   [His.]

This rule is frequently broken when disjunctive antecedents are of different genders, the speaker seeking to avoid the incongruity of using a pronoun differing in gender from one of the antecedents by employing a plural pronoun having no gender : ' If a man or woman lose *their* good name, *they* will not easily recover it.'

177. Personal Pronouns are often incorrectly used in elliptical constructions.   If the ellipse be filled up the relation of the pronoun will be at once seen.   The following passages are ungrammatical—

He first said that he was good as *me*, then that he was better than *me*.   [As *I* . . . than *I*.]

> And though by Heaven's severe decree
> She suffers hourly more than *me*.—*Swift*.   [More than *I*.]

It is not fit for such as *us*, to sit with the rulers of the land.—*Scott*.   [For such as *we*.]

Sorrow not as *them* that have no hope.—1 Thess. iv. 13.   [As *they*.]

178. Personal pronouns are often incorrectly used with the verb 'to be,' which takes the same case after it as before it, e.g.—

Whom do men say that *I* am ?—*Bible*.

But if there is one character more base, more infamous, more shocking than another, it is *him* who, &c.—*S. Smith.*

179. In O.E. 'ye' is the nominative, and 'you' the accusative form, e.g.: 'I know *you* not, whence *ye* are' (Bible).   This distinction is no longer observed.   'Ye' is now used ' in the two extremes of *solemnity* and *familiarity*; whilst " you " is more properly confined to ordinary narrative and familiar occasions' (Harrison).   'Thou' is used like ' ye' in solemn, contemptuous, and familiar speech,

The antecedent to a relative pronoun may be a noun or its equivalent. Adjectives and the possessive case of nouns or pronouns should not be used as antecedents. Hence the following is wrong—

Homer is remarkably *concise, which* renders him lively and agreeable.—*Blair.*

The plural of respect and the singular should not be used in the same passage. The following is objectionable :—

I will send upon *you* famine and evil beasts, and they shall bereave *thee.*—Ezek. v. 17.

It is worth noting that in spoken English the Personal Pronouns, when unemphatic, are sounded as though they were mere enclitics[1] of the verb. Thus we pronounce 'Give me thy hand' as though it were written 'Giveme thy hand.' This law is specially observable in the use of the Indirect Object, e.g.—

And he said Saddle me the ass, and they saddled him.

If 'me' and 'him' be emphasized, the meaning is ludicrously altered.

180. The Relative Pronoun must agree with its antecedent in number and person.

The following is wrong—

> Thou great first cause, least understood,
> *Who* all my sense *confined,*
> To know but this that Thou art good,
> And that myself am blind.—*Pope.*

The relative pronoun is sometimes said to agree in gender with its antecedent, but the agreement is not strictly one of gender. We cannot say 'The house who,' but neither do we say 'The bull who.' 'Who' is used of male or female *rational* creatures; 'which' of male or female *irrational* creatures, and inanimate objects. 'Whose,' however, is often used of both irrational and sexless things.

> He spoke of love, such love as spirits feel,
> In worlds *whose* course is equable and pure.—*Wordsworth.*

The modern tendency is to use 'of which' instead of 'whose' in these constructions.

---

[1] Enclitics (from Gk. en, *upon*, klinō, *I lean*) are particles which unite so closely with the preceding word as to throw their accent on it.

181. That, the neuter of the demonstrative, and **the,** indeclinable, were originally our only relative pronouns. **Who, which,** and **what** were interrogatives.

That is often used without an expressed antecedent. (See § 54.)

In O.E. the demonstratives *se, seó, that,* were used as demonstratives in the principal sentence, and as relatives (but, probably, originally as demonstratives) in the adjective clause also.

The indeclinable demonstrative *the* was often used instead of the declinable demonstrative in the second clause, the declinable form being unnecessary, e.g. 'Sý geblessod *se the* com on Drihtnes naman' (Be blessed he who comes in the Lord's name). In consequence of this use of *the* in the adjective clause, *the* came to be used more and more as a relative pronoun. Sometimes we find it used both as demonstrative and relative, e.g. '*The the* on me belýfth' [*He who* believeth in me].

That was often used without an antecedent in O.E.: 'We cythath *that* we gesawon' [We testify *that* we saw]—John iii. 11; 'Ic wrat *that* ic wrat' [I wrote *that* I wrote]—John xix. 21.

This use of *that* probably grew out of the union of *that* and *the* into *thætte,* a form which often occurs in O.E. with the force of *that which.* In like manner, *se-the* (= he who) is compounded into one word.

What is similarly used without an antecedent. (See § 54.) As an interrogative it may be used directly or indirectly.

> *What* is the matter ?
> He asked *what* I wanted.

What, like *that,* was sometimes used without an antecedent, even in O.E.: 'Se theowa nat *hwæt* se hláford deth' [The servant knoweth not *what* the lord doeth]—John xv. 15.

182. *Whoso, whosoever, whatsoever, whichever,* and *whichsoever* are generally used without correlatives.

In O.E. these indefinite or universal relatives were formed by placing *swá* (= so) before and after the pronoun. The explanation of this construction will be best understood by an example : 'Biddath swá hwæt swá ge wyllon' [Lit. Ask so, what so ye will—i.e. Ask whatsoever ye will]—John xv. 7. *Swá,* as a demonstrative adverb, was treated like the demonstrative pronoun.

Occasionally the correlative is used with the indefinite relative, but never immediately before it :—

'*Whosoever* will, let *him* take the water of life freely.'— Rev. xxii. 17

But is used, after negative clauses, with the force of a relative pronoun and a negative. (See § 54.)

As is used as a relative after *such, same, so much, so great,* &c. :—

> Art thou afeard
> To be the *same* in thine own act and valour
> *As* thou art in desire ?—*Shakspere.*

I have as much *as* you have (Obj.).
He is such *as* he always was (Nom.).
Take as much *as* you want (Obj.).

183. *Pronominal adverbs,* as *when, where, whence, how, why, whereas, wherein, whereby,* &c., are used like the relative pronouns, after nouns of time, place, manner, cause, effect, &c., and are sometimes governed by prepositions.

In O.E. these adverbs are used only interrogatively, the conjunctive adverbs corresponding to them being respectively *then, there, thence,* &c. The use of the conjunctive adverbs in *wh-* appears to have come in with the use of the relative pronoun *who.*

> The hour *when* he appeared was six.
> The place *where* we met him was close by.
> The source *whence* it comes is well known.
> The question *how* it is to be done is solved.
> The reason *why* he asked was obvious.

184. Ellipse of the Antecedent. The antecedent is often omitted before the relative. (See § 53.)

> There are ⋀ who ask not if thine eye
> Be on them.—*Wordsworth.*

> I dare do all that may become a man ;
> ⋀ Who dares do more is none.—*Shakspere.*

> A servant with this clause
> Makes drudgery divine ;
> ⋀ Who sweeps a room as for thy laws
> Makes that and the action fine.—*G. Herbert.*

> ⋀ Whom the gods love die young.

185. Ellipse of the Relative. In O.E. and in modern familiar language the relative is often omitted. (See § 53.)

> For there was no man ⋀ knew from whence he came.
> *Tennyson.*

Here is the book ⋀ I told you of.

186. Redundant use of 'that.' In O.E. 'that' is often used redundantly after certain conjunctive words. It probably had a demonstrative force, and limited the words which followed it.

Which that—

> Wot ye not where there stont a litel town,
> *Which that* icleped is Bop-up-and-down ?—*Chaucer.*

When that—

> *When that* the poor have cried Cæsar hath wept.
> *Shakspere.*

Similarly we find **who that, if that, after that, save that, since that, but that, if that, now that, lest that, in respect that, before that,** &c. In all these constructions 'that' is now a subordinative conjunction.   In passages like the following, the word ' that ' should not be emphasized : ' For before *that* certain came from James he did eat with the Gentiles ' (Gal. ii. 12).   The least stress upon it produces the impression that it is a pronoun governed by 'before,' whereas ' before that ' is a conjunctive adverb connecting the adverbial clause ' certain came from James ' with the principal sentence ' he did eat with the Gentiles.'

187. Possessive Pronouns may be used as the Subject or the Object (Direct or Indirect) of a sentence :—

> *Mine* is better than yours (Subj.).
> You have *mine* (Dir. Obj.).
> You gave my boy a book, and I gave *yours* one (Ind. Obj.).
> I made it *mine* (Fact. Obj.).

The Possessive Pronouns should be carefully distinguished from *my, thy,* &c., the possessive cases of the personal pronouns, which are used only adjectively.

The longer forms, mine, thine, &c., were formerly used adjectively as well as substantively : compare ' Si *thin* nam gehálgod' [Be thy name hallowed] with 'Hér thú hæfst thæt thín is' [Here thou hast that thine is].

188. Distributive Pronouns.—*Either* and *neither* should never be used of more than two objects.   Hence such sentences as the following are wrong:—' Neither of the three was suitable;' ' Either of the three will do.'   In the former, ' not one ' should have been used instead of ' neither ;' in the latter, ' any one ' instead of ' either.'

The other, in accordance with its original meaning, is applied, like the Latin *alter,* to the *second* of two objects—

> Two women shall be grinding at the mill, the *one* shall be taken and the *other* left.—*Bible.*

The following is inaccurate:—'The house of Baal was full from one end to another' (2 Kings x.). [Read 'the other.' The house could not have more than two ends.]

Another is used indefinitely, like the Latin *alius*, of more than two objects. Hence the following is wrong—

> We saw them hanging by myriads one to *the other*.

Each and *every* are both distributive, and refer to one of many, but 'each' gives prominence to the separate individuals of which the whole is composed, 'every' to the whole viewed in its totality. 'Each' implies that every one is included, 'every' that none is excluded—

> I expect *every one* [no one being excluded] to do his duty. *Each* [separate one] had his place appointed, *each* his course.—*Milton*.

The following is inaccurate—

> And they were judged every man according to their works.

None, though literally meaning *not one*, and therefore singular, usually takes a plural verb—

> None of the officers were taken.

189. Reciprocal Pronouns.—*Each other* is used in speaking of two persons; *one another* of more than two.

> Righteousness and peace have kissed *each other*.—*Bible*.
> The four artists hated *one another* cordially.

The following sentence is inaccurate—

> He belonged to a Mutual Admiration Society, the members of which spent their time in lauding *each other*.

190. Qualification of Pronouns.—Pronouns may be qualified by adjectives predicatively, but not attributively. Yet Shakspere writes—

> The fair, the chaste, and unexpressive *she*.

So Crashaw—

> Whoe'er she be,
> That not *impossible* she,
> That shall command my heart and me.

Questions.

1. Justify or correct the following—

a. If every one swept before their own doors, the street would be clean.

b. If two circles touch one another internally.

c. Let you and I endeavour to improve the inclosure of the Cave.
Southey.

d. Which none may hear but she and thou.—*Coleridge.*

e. If an ox gore a man or a woman so that they die.—*Bible.*

f. He was fonder of nothing than of wit and raillery; but he is far from being happy in it.—*Blair.*

g. This seven years did not Talbot see my son.—*Shakspere.*

h. Who say ye that I am?—*Bible.*

i. Whom do men say that I am?—*Ib.*

k. Some men are too ignorant to be humble, without which there can be no docility and no progress.—*Berkeley.*

l.   O Thou my voice inspire,
    Who touch'd Isaiah's hallowed lips with fire.—*Pope.*

m. The ingenious nation who have done so much for modern literature, possess in an eminent degree the talent of narrative.
Blair.

n.   Him I accuse
    The city ports by this hath entered.—*Shakspere.*

o. None of the enemy were taken.

p. Each of the sexes should keep within its particular bounds, and content themselves to exult within their respective districts.
Addison.

q. Neither of the three will do.

r.   The nations not so blest as thee
    Must in their turn to tyrants fall.—*Thomson.*

s. It was thought to be him.

t. None but the brave deserve the fair.—*Dryden.*

u. It cannot be him.

v. I have not wept this forty years.—*Dryden.*

2. Give instances of your own of the ellipsis (*a*) of the relative pronoun, (*b*) of its antecedent.

3. State the rules for the use of *who, which,* and *that.*

VERBS.

191. Verbs agree with their nominatives in number and person. When a verb has two or more singular subjects joined by a copulative conjunction, the verb is plural—

> John and James *are* here.
> To conceive and to carry out *are* two different things.

If, however, two nouns represent one thing, or two things that are closely related, they are regarded as forming a compound noun, and the verb is singular—

> Bread and butter *was* to be had in plenty.
> Brandy and water *was* his favourite beverage.
> To read and write *was* once an honourable distinction.
> *Hazlitt.*
> When distress and anguish *cometh* upon you.—*Bible.*
> But even their mind and conscience *is* defied.—*Ib.*

192. Collective nouns take a singular or plural verb, according as the idea of singularity or plurality is uppermost in the mind of the speaker—

> The multitude *was* swayed like one man.
> The multitude *are* on our side.
> Behold, the people *is* one, and *they* have all one language.
> *Bible.*

When two or more singular nouns connected by *and* are preceded by *each* or *every*, the verb is singular—

> Each boy and girl *is* to have a prize.
> Every man and every woman *contributes* something.

193. When two singular nouns are connected by 'as well as,' or by a preposition, the verb is singular—

> Humanity, as well as expediency, *demands* it.
> John, together with James, *does* not outweigh Henry.

194. Two singular nouns connected by *or* or *nor* take a verb in the singular—

> Either John or James *was* there.
> Neither John nor James *was* there.

Sometimes we find a plural verb after *neither . . . nor*, the negative disjunctives having a certain copulative force 'Either' and 'or' are *alternative*; 'neither' and 'nor' imply that the predicate is applicable to *both* the subjects.

The rule which determines the number of the verb would appear to be as follows: if the speaker's intention is to give prominence to the exclusion of *both*, use the plural; if to give prominence to the exclusion of *each separately*, use the singular.

195. When a verb comes between its two subjects, it agrees with the first—

> The earth *is* the Lord's and the fulness thereof.—*Bible.*

When several subjects follow the verb, the verb usually agrees with the first—

> Ah then and there *was* hurrying to and fro,
> And gathering tears and tremblings of distress,
> And cheeks all pale, which but an hour ago
> Blushed at the praise of their own loveliness.—*Byron.*

> Thine *is* the kingdom, and the power and the glory.—*Bible.*

196. When several subjects of different numbers are connected by *or* or *nor*, the verb generally agrees with the last mentioned; but it is better to repeat the verb after each subject.

> The king, or rather his advisers, *were* opposed to that course.

197. The verb *to be* is made to agree with the nominative that follows it, when that nominative is the subject uppermost in the mind of the speaker—

> The wages of sin *is death.*
> His pavilion *were* dark *waters* and thick *clouds* of the sky.
> > *Bible.*

Compare with these examples the following, in which the true subject is coincident with the nominative before the verb—

> His wages *are* his only means of subsistence.
> His remarks *were* the subject of much comment.
> Our supporters *are* but a handful.

198. As the relative pronoun agrees with its antecedent in number and person, the verb in an adjective clause will also agree with the antecedent in these respects. Hence the following is wrong—

> This is one of the finest poems that *was* ever written.

199. When a relative pronoun has two antecedents, one a pronoun, and the other a noun in apposition with it, the verb agrees with the antecedent on which greatest stress is laid. Comp.—

> It is I, who *bid* you go.
> It is I, your master, who *bids* you go.

In the first of these examples stress is laid on the ' I,' and on the obligations arising out of the personality of the speaker ; in the second, the stress is laid on ' master,' and the obligations arising out of the relations between a servant and his master.

When the pronoun *it* precedes the verb, and another pronoun follows it, the verb agrees with the appositional subject, *it*—

> It *is* we. It *is* ye. It *is* they.
> In O.E. the verb agreed with the true subject : ' Ic hyt com ' [I it am]—Matt. xiv. 27. Comp. Mark vi. 50 ; John vi. 20. ' Ic sæde cow thæt ic hit com ' [I said to you that I it am]—John xviii. 8.

200. When two or more subjects, having a common predicate, are of different persons, the verb agrees with the first in preference to the second, and with the second in preference to the third ; the explanation being that a subject of the first person and one of the second are equivalent to a plural pronoun of the first person, and that a subject of the second person and one of the third are equivalent to a plural pronoun of the second person—

> You and I [i.e. we] are.
> You and he [i.e. you two] are.

Attraction, however, often leads to a violation of this rule, the verb being made to agree with the last mentioned subject, no matter what its person. Thus we often have—

> Neither you nor he *is* right.
> Either I or he *is* wrong.

It would be better to avoid these harsh constructions by giving each subject its own predicate.

> Neither are you right, nor is he right.
> Either he is wrong or I am wrong.

201. Government by Verbs.—All transitive verbs in the Active Voice govern a Direct Object.

> I *love* him.
> He *admires* Milton.

o

'Teach' governs two Direct Objects—

> I taught *him French.*

Verbs of *giving, promising,* &c., govern a Direct Object of the thing, and a Dative Object of the person—

> I gave him (Dative) an apple (Dir. Obj.)

Either of these Objects may be converted into the Subject of the verb in a passive construction—

> *He* was given an apple.
> An *apple* was given him.

Dr. Abbott would call the remaining Object the **Retained Object.** (See § 63.)

Verbs of *making, believing, thinking,* &c., govern a Direct Object and a Factitive Object—

> I made him (Dir. Obj.) steward (Fact. Obj.)

The Factitive Object is in the Nom. case in passive constructions—

> He was made *steward.*

202. Many intransitive verbs are followed by a Dative Object. This object is no longer governed directly by a verb, but by an intermediate preposition. The only instances in which an intransitive verb governs an Indirect Object, are those supplied by the impersonal verbs, ' *meseems,*' ' *methinks,*' &c.

The verb ' *to be,*' and other copulative verbs, as ' *become,*' ' *grow,*' ' *remain,*' ' *continue,*' take the same case after them as before them. In these constructions, the case after the verb is determined, not by any government of the verb, but by apposition with the word before the verb—

> He (Nom.) is a sailor (Nom.)
> I wished him (Obj.) to be a sailor (Obj.)
> He became a *fop* (Nom.)
> He grew a lusty *youth* (Nom.)
> He remained a *soldier* (Nom.)
> He continued a *servant* (Nom.)

203. The Indicative Mood is used (1) predicatively to make an assertion, (2) interrogatively to ask a question, (3) hypothetically in speaking of facts—

> 1. He was there.
> 2. Was he there?

3. If it *is* the duty of a child to obey his parents, it is your duty to obey yours.

4. If satire *charms*, strike faults, but spare the man.—*Young.*

204. The Imperative Mood may be used in the first person plural, the second person or the third person—

> Break *we* our watch up.—*Shakspere.*
> That *be* far from thee.—*Bible.*
> Sleep *dwell* upon thine eyes.

> Bone and Skin, two millers thin,
>   Would starve us all, or near it,
> But *be* it *known* to Skin and Bone
>   That Flesh and Blood can't bear it.
>   *Byrom,* On Two Monopolists.

In the first and third person, a compound form is often used which is capable of being resolved into an imperative of the second person and an infinitive. We can say 'Let us go,' as well as 'Go we,' 'Let him go,' as well as 'Go they.' 'Let' has here lost its original force of 'allow,' and is used as a mere sign of the imperative. Comp. 'Release his hands and *let* him go,' with 'Let us pray.' 'Let him go'='Allow him to go;' 'let us pray' is a periphrastic imperative (=oremus). In parsing, these compound imperatives of the first and third person had better be broken up, as shown above.

In O.E. the verbal conjunction *uton, utcn,* was used with the infinitive to express purpose or desire: '*Uton* gán and sweltan mid him' [Let us go and die with him]—John xi. 16. '*Utan* wircan mannan' [Let us make man].

205. The Subjunctive Mood is used to express—

1. Uncertainty in the mind of the speaker—

If he *were* present, he ought to know.

2. Contingency of the fact—

If he *be* present to-morrow, give him this note.

3. Analogy—

[He saw] a certain vessel descending unto him, as it *had been* a great sheet.—Acts x. 11.

'As it *were.*'

o 2

4. Consequence—

Get on your night-gown, lest occasion *call* us,
And *show* us to be watchers.—*Shakspere.*

Pray for thy servants unto the Lord thy God, that we *die*
not.—*Bible.*

5. A wish—

O that I *were* there!
I would that I *were* dead.—*Tennyson.*
I would my daughter *were* dead at my foot, and the jewels
in her ear! would she *were hearsed* at my foot, and the
ducats in her coffin!—*Shakspere.*

206. The Subjunctive Mood is always dependent upon
some antecedent clause, expressed or understood, to which it
is *subjoined*, whence its name. This antecedent clause in
hypothetical constructions is called the *Protăsis*, or Condition; the clause containing the consequence is called the
Apodŏsis, or Consequence.

The condition is often introduced by one of the following words: *if, lest, unless, except, though, that, however,* &c.
(See § 67.) Sometimes the conjunction is suppressed—

Would I describe a preacher such as Paul,
Were he on earth, would hear, approve, and own,
Paul should himself direct me.—*Cowper.*

Had I but *served* my God with half the zeal
I served my king, He would not in mine age
Have left me naked to mine enemies.—*Shakspere.*

Did I *tell* this, who would believe me?—*Id.*

The tendency of modern English is to get rid of the subjunctive, but there are certain idiomatic constructions in
which it occurs, like 'as it were,' for which it would be
difficult to find equivalents, e.g.—

Harrison contends that the subjunctive mood should never be
used except when the fact referred to has not taken place. He says:
'There can be no contingency of a *fact* apart from futurity.'
This is perfectly true, but there may be uncertainty in the mind
of the speaker with regard to the past or the present—

If it *were* so, it was a grievous fault.—*Shakspere.*
If thou *love* me, practise an answer.—*Id.*

In O.E. the subjunctive was used (1) in principal sentences to
express a wish or command; (2) in dependent sentences (*a*) in
indirect narrative; (*b*) after verbs of thinking and desiring; (*c*) to
express purpose; (*d*) to state what is proper; (*e*) to express result;

(*f*) to express hypothetical comparison ; (*g*) in conditional clauses ; (*h*) in concessive clauses after *theah* (though), and in many other cases. See Sweet's Grammatical Introduction to his 'Anglo-Saxon Reader,' pp. xcvii–xcix.

207. The principal clause upon which the subjunctive clause is dependent may be in the indicative, imperative, or subjunctive—

> Even so our eyes wait upon the Lord our God (Indic.), until He *have* mercy upon us.—*Bible.*
> If it *be* thou, bid me come (Imper.).
> If it were done when 'tis done (Subj.), then '*twere* well (Subj.)
> It *were done* quickly.—*Shakspere.*

Compound forms often take the place of the simple subjunctive. Comp.—

> With whom, if he *come* shortly, I will see you.—*Bible.*
> If he *should come*, I should be glad to see him.

The simple subjunctive forms of ' have' and 'be' are of very common occurrence—

> I *had* fainted [i.e. should have fainted] unless I had believed to see the goodness of the Lord.—*Bible.*
> A good razor never hurts or scratches, neither would good wit *were* men [if men would be] as tractable as their chins.—*Hare.*

208. The **Simple Infinitive** is used with the auxiliaries *may, do, can, must, shall,* and *will.* It is also used after the following principal verbs : *dare* (intrans.), *let, bid, see, hear, feel, need, will, gin* (=begin).

May—
> Men *may come* and men *may go.*—*Tennyson.*

Can—
> Unless above himself he *can*
> *Erect* himself, how poor a thing is man !—*Daniel.*

Do—
> While feeble expletives their aid *do join.*—*Pope.*

Must—
> For men *must work* and women must weep.—*Kingsley.*

Shall—
> *Shall* I, wasting in despair,
> *Die*, because a woman's fair ?—*Wither.*

Will—
> I *will make* a Star-Chamber matter of it.—*Shakspere.*

Dare—
> For without Thee I *dare* not *die.—Keble.*

Let—
> *Let* those *love* now who never loved before,
> *Let* those who always loved now love the more.—*Parnell.*

Bid—
> *Bid* me *discourse,* I will enchant thine ear.—*Shakspere.*

See—
> A spirit hath not flesh and bones as ye *see* me *have.—Bible.*
> Thou shalt not *see* thy brother's ox *fall* by the way.—*Ib.*

Hear—
> I *hear* thee *speak* of the better land.—*Mrs. Hemans.*
> We *heard* him *say,* I will destroy this temple.—*Bible*

Feel—
> No man e'er *felt* the halter *draw*
> With good opinion of the law.—*Trumbull.*

Need—
> What *need* we fear who knows it ?—*Shakspere.*

Will [1] = wish—
> Whosoever *will* be *saved* (Quicunque *vult* salvus esse).
> *Athanasian Creed.*

Gin [2]—
> Of a wright I will you tell
> That some time in this land *gan dwell.*
> *The Wright's Chaste Wife.*

In O.E. the simple infinitive is commonly used after *may, can, shall, will, let, syllan* (to give), *onginnan,* to begin, *verbs of perception and commanding,* and the verbal conjunction *uton* or *utan* (= let us)—

> Hwá *mæg* synna *forgifan* ? [Who may sins forgive ?]
> Mark ii. 7.

> Nú *cunne* ge *to-cnáwan* heofenes hiw ? [Now can ye discern the heaven's hue ?]—Matt. xvi. 3.

> *Sceal* ic *hón* eowerne cyning ? [Shall I crucify your king ?]
> John xix. 15.

> Thám the *wylle* æt thé *borgian.* [To him who will of thee borrow.]—Matt. v. 42.
> And he the út-gangende, *ongan bodian.* [And he then out-going, gan preach.]—Mark i. 45.

---

[1] *Willing* is followed by *to*—
> *Willing to wound,* and yet afraid to strike.—*Pope.*
[2] *Gin* sometimes takes *to* after it—
> The glowworm shows the matin to be near,
> And *gins to pale* his ineffectual fire.
Begin always takes *to* after it.

Syle mé *drincan.* [Give me to drink.]—John iv. 7.
And hig *sprecan* ne *lét.* [And them to speak he let not.]
Mark i. 34.
Ne mæg se Sunu nán thing dón, buton thæt he *gesyth* his
Fæder *dón.* [The Son may do no thing except that
He seeth his Father do.]—John v. 19.
Hét thá bære *settan.* [He ordered the bier to be set down.]
Uton gán. [Let us go.]—John xi. 16.

In very early times the distinction between the Simple Infinitive
and the Gerundial Infinitive was sometimes disregarded, as is clear
from the following passage :—

Hwæther ys ethre *tó secganne* (Ger. Inf.) tó thám laman,
Thé synd thine synne forgyfene : hwæther thé *cwéthan*
(Simple Infin.). [Whether is easier to say to the lame,
To thee are thy sins forgiven; or to say to thee, &c.]—
Mark ii. 9.

209. In later M.E. we find many other verbs followed
by the infinitive without the preposition 'to,' e.g. *ought,
intend, endure, seem, constrain, forbid, vouchsafe,* &c. :—

You *ought* not *walk* upon a labouring day.—*Shakspere.*
Your betters have *endured* me *say* my mind.—*Id.*
How long within this wood *intend* you stay ?—*Id.*

On the other hand we often find the preposition 'to' used
before the infinitive where we omit it :—

I *durst,* my lord, *to wager* she is honest.—*Shakspere.*

He *maketh* both the deaf *to hear,* and the dumb *to speak.*—*Bible.*

Still losing when I *saw* myself *to win.*—*Shakspere.*

Let and Do in certain technical phrases take the Gerundial Infinitive :—

I *do* you *to wit.*
I *let* you *to know* by these presents.

210. The Gerundial Infinitive was originally the Dative
of the Infinitive, and was used—

1. To express *purpose* : 'Út eóde se sædere his sæd *tó sáwenne.*'
[Out went the sower his seed to sow.]—Matt. xiii. 3.

2. *To limit or qualify nouns and adjectives.* 'Hig næfdon *hláf tó
etanne.*' [They had not *bread to eat.*]—Mark iii. 20.
'Gif hwá *eáran* hæbbe *tó gehyranne.*' [If any man ears have to
hear.]—Mark iv. 23.

3. *As the subject or object of a sentence* : 'Eow ys geseald *tó
witanne* Godes ríces gerýnu.' [To you is given *to know* the mysteries of God's kingdom.]—Mark iv. 11.

4. *To express necessity or duty in a passive sense.* 'He is *tó lufi-genne*' [He is worthy to be loved. Literally, He is to love]. This use survives in such idioms as 'He is to blame.' Dr. Johnson thought that 'blame' in this construction was the noun 'blame.' It is the Active Gerundial Infinitive with a passive signification. In O.E. there was no Passive inflexion. The Active verb is used to express the Passive as well as the Active idea, e.g. 'Is eác *tó witanne*' [It is besides to be known], 'Hyne hét his hláford *gesyllan*' [Him his lord commanded *to be sold*]. Expressions like 'A house to let' [i.e. to be let], 'What is there to see?' [i.e. to be seen], 'Bread to eat' [i.e. to be eaten], 'Hard to bear' [i.e. to be borne], are to be explained in the same way.

5. *In apposition.* '*Hit* is sceamu *tó tellanne*' [It is shame to tell].

6. *To express some future obligation* : 'Thone calic the ic *tó drincenne* hæbbe' [the cup that I to drink have].

211. The Gerundial Infinitive is still used in all these ways :—

(1) I am going *to speak* (Purpose).

(2) The world *to come*[1] (Limits Noun).
Apt *to teach* (Limits Adj.).

(3) *To err* is human (Subj.).
He loved *to hunt* (Dir. Obj.).
I told him *to hunt* (Indir. Obj.).

(4) I am *to speak* [Necessity].
It has *to be done* [Necessity].
The Lord's name is *to be praised* [Duty].

(5) It is idle *to talk* of that now [Apposition].

The primary idea involved in 'to,' the sign of the Gerundial Infinitive, is that of *direction towards some object*. This explains most of the foregoing constructions. In 'I am going to speak,' speaking is the object to which my going is directed. In 'John is apt to teach,' teaching is the object in the direction of which the aptitude of John *is shown*.

As some act of the will or understanding must precede most of our actions, verbs denoting such acts frequently precede the Gerundial Infinitive, e.g. *mean, intend, will, wish, desire, resolve, purpose, refuse, promise, agree.*

As again the actions of other persons are often dependent on our own actions, verbs of causation are frequently followed

[1] The Gerundial Infinitive is here equivalent to the Latin future participle in *-rus*. This use of the Gerundial Infinitive explains a passage in 'In Memoriam,' which has perplexed many readers: 'And Love the indifference to be,' xxvi.

by the Gerundial Infinitive, e.g. *compel, force, order, command, make, teach, request, urge, exhort,* &c.

212. Have is used both with the Simple and the Gerundial Infinitive :—

> It is heaven upon earth to *have* a man's mind *move* (Ind. Obj.) in charity, *rest* in Providence, and *turn* upon the poles of truth.—*Bacon.*
> I *have to make* (Dir. Obj.) a speech.

213. The Gerundial Infinitive is sometimes governed by *for* : 'What went ye out *for* to see ?' (Bible). It is often found after 'how' as part of the subject or object of a sentence :—

> *How* not *to do* it seemed the object of their exertions.
> I know both *how to be abased*, and I know *how to abound.*—*Bible.*

Also after 'what.'

> I do not know *what to do.*

214. The Gerundial Infinitive is often used parenthetically to state a purpose, or to limit an assertion :—

> Indeed, *to speak feelingly of him*, he is the card or calendar of gentry.—*Shakspere.*
> During the century and a half that followed, there is, *to speak strictly*, no English history.—*Macaulay.*

215. The Simple Infinitive is sometimes used where we should expect the Gerundial Infinitive :—

> And art thou, dearest, changed so much
> As *meet* my eye, yet mock my touch ?—*Byron.*

> Better *be* with the dead
> Whom we to gain our peace have sent to peace,
> Than on the torture of the mind to lie
> In restless ecstasy.—*Shakspere.*

> As good almost *kill* a man as *kill* a good book.—*Milton.*

216. When two or more infinitives are connected by conjunctions, the preposition 'to' is not usually repeated before each :—

> To sigh, yet feel no pain,
>   To weep, yet scarce know why ;
> To sport an hour with Beauty's chain,
>   Then throw it idly by.—*Moore.*

217. Participles, in virtue of their adjective force,

qualify their nouns attributively or predicatively, and, in virtue of their verb force, may govern a case. Originally they agreed with their nouns in gender, number, and case.

> Now fades the *glimmering* landscape on the sight (Attrib. Qual.).—*Gray.*
> Then shook the hills with thunder *riven* (Pred.).—*Campbell.*
> Then marked they, *dashing* broad and far (Pred.),
> The *broken* billows of the war (Attrib.),
> And *plumèd* crests of chieftains brave (Attrib.),
> *Floating* (Pred.) like foam upon the wave.—*Scott.*
> I saw him *reading* his book. (Qualifying 'him' predica-tively and governing 'book').

218. The imperfect participle in *-ing* (O.E. -ande, -ende) should be carefully distinguished from the verbal noun in *-ing* (O.E. -ung) :—

> *Seeing* is *believing* (Verbal Nouns).
> *Toiling, rejoicing, sorrowing,*
> Onward through life he goes (Imp. Participles).

The verbal noun closely resembles in some of its functions the Gerundial Infinitive. Thus, instead of saying '*Seeing* is *believing*,' we might say *To see* is *to believe.* Indeed some grammarians recognize an infinitive in *-ing.* Again, 'I saw him *standing*' is nearly equivalent to 'I saw him *stand.*' In O.E. the imperfect participle was used in this construc-tion. 'Tha se Hælend geseah . . . thone leorning cnyhte *standende*' [When the Saviour saw . . . the disciple stand-ing, &c.]—John xix. 26.

219. In the perfect tenses of transitive verbs, the perfect participles originally agreed with the Object. Thus, 'Until they had slain him' would have been in O.E. 'Until they had him slain' [Oth thæt hic hine of-slægenne hæfdon]. The verb *hæfdon* (had) governs *hine* (him), and *of-slægenne* (slain) is the accusative singular participle qualifying 'hine' (him). At a later period the participle was left uninflected. The perfect participles of intransitive verbs came, by a false analogy, to be used like the perfect participles of transitive verbs.

220. After the verb *to be* the perfect participle originally agreed with the subject. Comp.—

> Hé wǽs cumen [He was come].
> Hé wǽron cumene [They were come].

The imperfect participle was formerly inflected and agreed with the noun which it qualified—

> Nyste nán thæra *sittendra* (Gen. Plu.) tó whám he thæt
> sæde. [None of those sitting there knew to whom he
> said that.]—John xiv. 28.

Now that our participles have ceased to agree with their nouns, it is better to regard them as parts of the compound verbal forms into which they enter.

221. Participles do not admit of comparison unless their verb force is merged in their adjective force; and then, of course, they are participles in form only—

> It is not till our *more pressing* [i.e. urgent] wants are suffi-
> ciently supplied, that we can attend to the calls of
> curiosity.—*Goldsmith.*
> Your *most devoted* servant.

222. The Imperfect Participle is often used after intransitive verbs like *continue, begin,* &c.—

> They continued *asking* him.—John viii. 7.

As these verbs are also used transitively, the learner might be tempted to regard the imperfect participle as a verbal noun, governed by the finite verb (see Dr. Angus, p. 315), but the usage in O.E. was the same as it is now—

> Tha hig thurwunedon hine *acsiende* (Nom.) [When they
> continued asking him.]—John viii. 7.

223. The participle is largely used in absolute constructions—

> These nine in buckram that I told thee of, their points
> *being broken*, began to give me ground.—*Shakspere.*

The participle is sometimes omitted in such constructions—

> In gallant trim the gilded vessel goes;
> Youth on the prow, and pleasure at the helm.—*Gray.*

Not unfrequently the noun or pronoun on which the participle depends is omitted—

> But, *granting* now we shall agree,
> What is it you expect from me?—*Butler.*
> God that made the world and all things therein, *seeing* that
> He is Lord of heaven and earth, dwelleth not in tem-
> ples made with hands.—Acts xvii. 24.

It is highly probable that many of our prepositions, as *regarding, concerning, saving, respecting, touching, according, notwithstanding,* were originally participles—

> During the day = the day during.
> Notwithstanding your opposition = your opposition notwithstanding.
> Saving your presence = we saving your presence, or your presence saved, &c.

Questions.

1. Give instances of verbs that govern two objects.

2. Explain 'methinks,' 'her seemed,' 'him listeth.'

3. The following verbs may be used transitively or intransitively, *continue, become, grow, turn.* Give examples. State in each example the case of the noun following the verb.

4. State the uses of (*a*) the Indicative Mood, (*b*) the Subjunctive.

5. After certain verbs the preposition 'to' is suppressed before the Gerundial Infinitive. Give a list of them.

6. The Active Gerundial Infinitive has sometimes a passive sense. Give instances.

7. Explain the use of the perfect participle in the formation of the perfect tenses of the Active Voice.

8. Discuss the following sentences; state whether you consider any of them incorrect; and, if so, why.

a. It was thought to be him.

b. The river has overflown its banks.

c. Let us make a covenant, I and thou.

d. None but the brave deserves the fair.

e. Whether I am right or not, you are certainly wrong.

f. Whom say ye that I am?

g. I am a man that have travelled and seen many nations.—*Steele.*

h. Impossible, it can't be me.—*Swift.*

i. If you were here, you would find three or four in the parlour after dinner, whom you would say pass their time very agreeably.

Locke.

k. It is they who do the mischief.

l. He was a man whom you would have thought would have been above falsehood.

9. Justify or correct the following—

a. It is me.

b. Either you or I are wrong.

c. More curates are what we want.

d. The ransom of a man's life are his riches.—*Bible.*

e. There is a way which seemeth right unto a man, but the end thereof are the ways of death.—*Ib.*

f. A special feature of the Reformatory Exhibition were the workshops.

g. The mechanism of clocks and watches were wholly unknown.

h. The consequences of this disastrous policy remains to be considered.

i. No people ever was more rudely assailed by the sword of conquest than this country.

| *k.* The sun has rose and gone to bed
Just as if Partridge were not dead.—*Swift.*

l. Words interwove with sighs found out their way.—*Milton.*

m. A second deluge learning thus o'errun,
And the monks finished what the Goths begun.—*Pope.*

n. I will scarce think you have swam in a gondola.—*Shakspere.*

o. I have formerly talked with you about a military dictionary.
Johnson.

p. Friend to my life, which did not you prolong,
The world had wanted many an idle song.

q. If thou bring thy gift to the altar, and there rememberest that thy brother hath aught against thee.—*Bible.*

r. I intended to have written to you.

s. A laggard in love and a dastard in war
Was to wed the fair Ellen of young Lochinvar.—*Scott.*

t. Great pains was taken.

u. The general with his troops were taken prisoners.

v. Nor heaven nor earth have been at peace to-night.—*Shakspere.*

w. He or I is in the wrong.

x. There was racing and chasing on Cannobie Lea.—*Scott.*

y. Now abideth faith, hope, and charity.—*Bible.*

z. Godliness with contentment is great gain.—*Ib.*

10. State the function of the Gerundial Infinitive in the following passages—

a. Ring in the Christ that is to be.—*Tennyson.*

b.   So many worlds, so much to do,
So little done, such things to be.—*Id.*

c. 'Tis sweet to hear the watch-dog's honest bark
Bay deep-mouthed welcome as we draw near home.—*Byron.*

d.   To live in hearts we leave behind
        Is not to die.— *Campbell.*

e.   Minds that have nothing to confer
        Find little to perceive.— *Wordsworth.*

f.   A maid whom there were none to praise
        And very few to love.—*Id.*

g.   For fools rush in where angels fear to tread.—*Pope.*

h.   Vice is a monster of so frightful mien
        As to be hated needs but to be seen.—*Pope.*

i. I never could believe that Providence had sent a few men into the world ready booted and spurred to ride, and millions ready saddled and bridled to be ridden.—*Rumbold,* 1685.

k.   What shall I do to be for ever known,
        And make the age to come my own ?—*Cowley.*

l.   O ! it is excellent
     To have a giant's strength ; but it is tyranny
     To use it like a giant.—*Shakspere.*

m. Of two evils the less is always to be chosen.

n. He is to be executed to-morrow.

o.   Teach him how to live,
   And, oh ! still harder lesson, how to die.—*Porteus.*

ADVERBS.

224. Adverbs qualify or limit other adverbs, verbs, adjectives, and prepositions. Some adverbs have also a conjunctive force. The distinction between the adjective and the adverb is not always easy to draw. In the sentences 'He is awake,' 'He is ill,' it is difficult, at first, to say whether 'ill' and 'awake' are adverbs or adjectives. 'Ill' is not used in this sense attributively, nor is 'awake' used attributively. We cannot say 'an ill person' or 'an awake child.' In spite of this, 'ill' and 'awake' seem to have more in common with adjectives than with adverbs. Cp. He is *sick*, He is *sleepy.* 'Ill' is a Norse doublet of 'evil;' 'awake' is a shortened form of 'awaked.'

Adverbs sometimes limit a whole sentence or even an unexpressed verb—

     Unfortunately for him, he was never taught a trade.
     Happily, I had some money in my pocket.

Here we may assume an ellipse of 'it *happened,*' or 'it *fell out.*'

225. Adverbs are occasionally used as adjectives—

> The *then* king.—*Shakspere*.
> Use a little wine for ... thine *often* infirmities.—*Bible*.

Adjectives are often erroneously used for adverbs—

> They fall *successive* and *successive* rise.—*Pope*.

226. Position of the Adverb.—The adverb is usually placed *before* adjectives and other adverbs, *after* verbs, and *between* the auxiliary and the perfect participle; but its position is often varied for rhetorical effect—

> *Then*, and not till *then*, he replied.
> *Meanwhile*, his audience had slipped away.

When an adverb is used with several other words, to more than one of which it might belong, it should be placed as close as possible to the word which it qualifies.

The following passages are ungrammatical from a disregard of this rule—

> Her bosom to the view was *only* bare.—*Dryden*.

The poet meant 'Her bosom only.'

> Thales was *not only* famous for his knowledge of nature, but also for his moral wisdom.

Here 'not only' should be placed after 'famous.'

> The safety-matches will *only* ignite upon the box.

Here 'only' should be placed after 'ignite.'

As a rule, it is safest to place 'only' before the word or words which it limits.

227. Double and (in O.E.) **Treble Negatives** strengthen the negation; in Modern English they destroy each other, and are equivalent to an affirmative—

> Ne geseáh næfre nán man God (No man [n]ever saw [not] God).
> He *never* yet *no* vilanie *ne* sayde
> In all his life unto *no* manere wight.—*Chaucer*.
> The man that hath no music in himself,
> *Nor* is *not* moved with concord of sweet sounds,
> Is fit for treasons.—*Shakspere*.
> Thou *never* didst them wrong, *nor no* man wrong.

228. No is often incorrectly used for *not* in disjunctive constructions—

> Whether he be the man or *no* I cannot say.

'No' can be used as an adverb only in answer to a question. The ellipse in the foregoing sentence is [or whether he be *not*].

229. Ever and **Never** should be distinguished. 'Ever' is used, (1) as an adverb of time, equivalent to 'always;' (2) as an adverb of degree, to indicate that the adjective which it limits is to be taken in its widest possible extent.

> Be it *ever* so humble, there is no place like home.

Here, 'ever so' = howsoever.

Never is used (1) as an adverb of time, (2) as a strong adverb of negation—

> He answered him to *never* a word.

In the following passages *never* is used for *ever*—

> Charm he *never* so wisely.—*Bible*.
>
> The Lord is king, be the people *never* so impatient.—*Ib*.
>
> Though *ne'er* so rich, we scorn the elf
> Whose only praise is sordid pelf.

On the other hand *ever* is used for *never* in the following—

> We seldom or *ever* see those forsaken who trust in God.
>   *Atterbury*.

230. Adverbs in -ly and Adjectives in -ly.—In consequence of the harsh effect of repeating the -ly sound, we often, in the case of adjectives ending in *-ly*, use the adjectival for the adverbial form—

> Which they have *ungodly* committed.—*Jude* 15.
> May truly and *godly* serve thee.

We have in the Bible 'wilily' and 'holily.' So Shakspere writes—

>   What thou wouldst highly
> That wouldst thou *holily*.

Such forms may generally be avoided by some periphrasis. Instead of saying 'It was masterly done,' or 'It was masterlily done,' we can say, 'It was done in a masterly way.' (See Harrison, p. 344.)

231. After Verbs relating to the Senses the adjective occupies the position commonly occupied by the adverb, but should not be confounded with it. Writers are sometimes tempted to use the adverb instead of the adjective in this construction, e.g.—

> This construction sounds *harshly.—Murray.*
> This sentence reads *oddly.*

What we really mean in these sentences is, ' This construction is harsh when read aloud ; ' ' This sentence seems odd when read.'

232. Demonstrative Adverbs are capable of expressing, without the aid of prepositions, relations of time and space, e.g. hence = from this place ; henceforth = from this time forward, &c.

> Come *hither, hither,* my little page.— *Byron.*
> Haste *hither,* Eve.—*Milton.*
> I *thither* went.—*Id.*

Many of our best writers, however, use prepositions with these adverbs—

> Those empty orbs *from whence* he tore his eyes.—*Pope.*

Questions.

1. Point out the functions of the adverbs in the following passages—

a. Hence with denial vain and coy excuse.—*Milton.*

b.
> Life went a-maying
> With Nature, Hope, and Poesy
> When I was young !
> When I was young ?   Ah woful when !
> Ah ! for the change 'twixt Now and Then !—*Coleridge.*

c.
> Hard by a cottage-chimney smokes
> From betwixt two aged oaks.—*Milton.*

d.
> Our then dictator,
> Whom with all praise I point at, saw him fight.—*Shakspere.*

e. In choosing wrong I lose your company.

f. He must needs go through Samaria.— *Bible.*

g. Thereby hangs a tale.—*Shakspere.*

2. Justify or correct the following sentences—

a. The moon shines bright.

b. Thou hast done right, but we have done wickedly. —*Bible.*

c. Breathe soft ye winds, ye waters gently flow

P

d. How sweet the moonlight sleeps upon this bank.—*Shakspere.*

e. I feel queerly.

f. He looks sad.

g. A quarter's notice is required previous to the removal of a pupil.

h. Burke's terrible account of that merciless code reads moderate by comparison with this summary of Papal Bulls.—*Times.*

i. Paul was long speaking.

k. I hope shortly to see you.

l. The machine is in thoroughly working order.[1]

3. Discuss the accuracy of the following passages—

a. This England never did, nor never shall,
   Lie at the proud foot of a conqueror.—*Shakspere.*

b. For thoughts are only criminal, when they are first chosen, and then voluntarily continued.—*Johnson.*

c. Think only of the past, as its remembrance give you pleasure.

d. [The pestilence] could be only imputed to the just indignation of the gods.

e. By greatness I do not only mean the bulk of any single object, but the largeness of the whole view.—*Addison.*

f. This thoroughfare is only to be used by persons having business at this house.

g. 'Whether love be natural or no,' replied my friend gravely, 'it contributes to the happiness of every society into which it is introduced.'—*Goldsmith.'*

h. His face was easily taken, both in painting and sculpture, and scarce any one, though never so indifferently skilled in their art, failed to hit it.—*Welwood's 'Memoirs.'*

i. I never was, nor never will be false.—*Shakspere.*

k. The sellers of the newest patterns at present give extreme good bargains.—*Goldsmith.*

l. For sinners also lend to sinners to receive as much again.

m. No one had exhibited the structure of the human kidneys; Vesalius having only examined them in dogs.—*Hallam.*

n. Ill news rides fast.

o. One species of bread, of coarse quality, was only allowed to be baked.—*Alison.*

p. It smelled disagreeably.

---

[1] Some of these examples are taken from Dean Alford's 'Queen's English.'

q. Alas ! said I, he has paid dear, very dear, for his whistle.
Franklin.

r. They established the kingdom of Jerusalem, which subsisted near two hundred years.—*Robertson.*

s. Such a violation of right came with a peculiar bad grace from France.—*Alison.*

t. This tragedy is alike distinguished for the lofty imagination it displays and for the tumultuous vehemence of the action.—*Hazlitt.*

u. Xenophon's sword was first drawn for a Persian prince, and last for a Spartan king.—*McCullagh.*

v. A masterly mind was equally wanting in the cabinet and in the field.—*Southey.*

w. The object of Bible Societies is so simple that all Protestants, at least, concur in their support.—*Channing.*

x. From thence will He fetch thee.—*Bible.*

y. But vigour and resolution are not alone capable of achieving success, though they are generally necessary towards it.—*Alison.*

z. The American Indian exhibits a degree of sagacity which almost appears miraculous.—*Id.*

PREPOSITIONS.

233. Prepositions are used to point out the relations between things, or between actions or attributes and things. In Modern English they are regarded as all governing the same case; but in O.E. they governed different cases, and some prepositions, according to the sense in which they were used, governed two or three cases—

Thus *geond* (beyond), *ymb* (about), *thurh* (through), &c., governed the Acc.; *be* (about), &c., the Dat.; *andlang* (along), the Genitive; *for* (for), *beforan* (before), &c., the Acc. and Dat.; *mid* (with), the Acc., Dat., and Abl.; *with*, the Acc., Dat., and Genitive.

As a rule, prepositions denoting direction *towards* a place governed the Acc., and prepositions denoting *rest or motion in* a place governed the Dat.

234. Prepositions govern nouns or their equivalents. They usually come between the words which they logically connect, but in rhetorical constructions and in adjective sentences they are often separated from the words dependent on them—

In the golden lightening
Of the setting sun,
O'er which clouds are brightening,
Thou dost float and run. --*Shelley.*

He is an author whom I am very fond *of*.

Of here connects 'fond' and 'whom.'

As the relative pronoun 'that' never takes a preposition before it, the preposition governing it is often thrown to the end of the adjective clause—

> The house *that* we live *in* is not our own.
>
> Those nine in buckram *that* I told thee *of.—Shakspere.*

The preposition should never be widely separated from its dependent words. The following are objectionable—

He betrothed himself oftener to the devil in one day than Mecænas did in a week to his wife, *that* he was married a thousand times *to.—Butler's Remains.*

These more sterling *qualities* of strict moral conduct, regular religious habits, temperate and prudent behaviour, sober industrious life—qualities which are generally required of public men, even if more superficial accomplishments should be dispensed with—he had absolutely nothing *of.—Brougham.*

A common consequence of this separation of the preposition from its dependent word is the disregard of the fact that the preposition governs the objective case. The following passages are incorrect from this cause—

> *Who* are you speaking *of?* (whom).
>
> *Who* servest thou *under?* (whom).—*Shakspere.*
>
> We are still much at a loss *who* civil power belongs *to* (whom).—*Locke.*

235. Sometimes several prepositions are used with but one object. Such constructions (especially when they involve a suspension of the sense) are intolerably harsh. The following is objectionable on this ground—

> To suppose the zodiac and the planets to be efficient *of,* and antecedent *to,* themselves, &c.—*Bentley.*

It is better to avoid these constructions by repeating the noun, or by using the noun after one preposition and a pronoun after the other.

> Though virtue borrows no assistance *from,* yet it may often be accompanied *by,* the advantages of fortune.—*Blair.*

This sentence might be corrected by inserting 'advantages of fortune' after 'from,' and 'them' after 'by.'

236. The dependent case is often omitted in adjective clauses—

> Shall there be a God to swear *by* [i.e. by whom to swear] and none to pray to [i.e. to whom to pray]?—*Hooker.*

In such constructions the preposition is thrown to the end of the adjective clause—

> For I must use the freedom ʌ I was born *with*.
>
> *Massinger.*

In the passive forms of verbs compounded with prepositions the preposition is used after the verb—

> I was laughed *at*.
> He was communicated *with*.
> A considerable bill was run *up*.
> He was run *through*.
> The ship was run *down*.

237. Certain verbs, nouns, and adjectives take with them special prepositions—

Absolve *from*.
Abhorrence *of*.
Accord *with* (Intrans.).
  „ *to* (Trans.).
Acquit *of*.
Accuse *of*.
Affinity *to* or *between*.
Adapted *to* or *for*.
Agree *with* (persons).
  „ *to* (proposals).
Attend *to* (something said).
  „ *upon* (a person).
Bestow *upon*.
Boast *of*.
Call *on*.
Change *for*.
Confer *on* (Trans.).
  „ *with* (Intrans.).
Confide *in* (Intrans.).
  „ *to* (Trans.).
Conform *to*.
Comply *with*.
Consonant *with*.
Convenient *to* or *for*.
Conversant *with*.
Correspond *with* (persons).
  „ *to* (things).
Dependent *on* or *upon*.
Derogatory *to*.

Derogate *from*.
Differ *from* (not *with*).
Different *from* (not *to*).
Disappointed *of* (what we do not get).
  „ *in* (what we do get).
Dissent *from*.
Exception *to*.
Free *from*.
Glad *of* or *at*.
Independent *of*.
Insist *upon*.
Involve *in*.
Lay hold *on*.
Martyr *for* (a cause).
  „ *to* (a disease).
Need *of*.
Prevail *upon*.
Profit *by*.
Recreant *to*.
Reconcile *to* (person).
  „ *with* (statement).
Resolve *on*.
Take hold *of*.
Taste (noun) *of*.
  „ *for*.
Think *of*.
  „ *on* (obsolete).
Thirst *for*, *after*.

The following are objectionable—

> The Italian universities were forced to send for their professors *from* Spain and France.—*Hallam.*

The abhorrence of the vast majority of the people *to* its
provisions.—*Alison.*

Such were the difficulties *with* which the question was involved.—*Id.*

The prefix compounded with the verb often determines
the preposition which should follow the verb, e.g. *sym*pathise
with ; *in*volve *in,* &c.

238. Prepositions should be used in strict accordance
with their sense.

'*In* implies a state of being; *into,* an act. We pour water
into the pail; when there it is *in* the pail.'—*Harrison.*

On implies a state of rest; *upon* formerly implied motion
to, but is now frequently confounded with *on.*

'*With* denotes concomitancy or assistance; *by* the proximate cause; as, "The soldiers entered the breach *with*
loaded muskets; their leader fell mortally wounded *by*
a musket ball." '—*Harrison.*

Between properly refers to only two things; *among* to any
number more than two. 'It was divided *between* two.'
'It was divided *among* twenty.'

239. Double Prepositions are sometimes used to indicate
some twofold relation of place—

'We drew it *from under* the table,' i.e. We drew it *from*
a place that was *under* the table, or We drew it from its
place *under* the table. So 'over against the church' =
over the way, *against* or opposite to the church.

These double prepositions should not be confounded with
the common combination of an adverb with a preposition,
e.g. *away from, out from, up to, down from,* &c.

Take thy beak *from out* my heart, and take thy form *from
off* my door.—*Poe.*

240. Prepositions are often used to govern pronominal
adverbs—

The waters which came down *from above.*—*Bible.*

241. Prepositions are often used with adjectives to form
adverbial phrases, e.g. *at large, on high, in short, in brief,*
&c.

Withal is properly an adverb, but is sometimes used as a
preposition at the end of a sentence—

I'll tell you *who* time ambles *withal, who* time trots *withal,
who* time galops *withal,* and *who* he stands still *withal.*
Shakspere.

Questions.

1. What are the syntactical functions of prepositions?

2. In what respects do the O.E. prepositions differ from the modern?

3. Give instances of double prepositions?

4. Correct or justify the following—

a. Two more guns were sent for from Waterford.—*Macaulay.*

b. The accounts they gave of the favourable reception of their writings with the public.—*Franklin.*

c. This was surely too slender a thread to trust a business of that weight to.—*Bentley.*

d. Yet to their general's voice they soon obeyed.—*Milton.*

e. The only animal we saw for some time was an opossum, which the native discovered in a tree, and climbed up for.—*Landor.*

f. After killing his wife and children, he laid them upon a pile which he had erected for that purpose, and then setting fire to the whole, rushed and expired in the midst of the flames.—*Goldsmith.*

g. He was killed with kindness.

h. Michael Angelo planned a totally different façade to the existing one.—*Taylor* ('Convent Life in Italy').

i. It is to this last new feature of the Game Laws to which we intend to confine our notice.—*S. Smith.*

k. You have bestowed your favours to the most deserving.—*Swift.*

l. If poesy can prevail upon prose.—*Addison.*

m. I do likewise dissent with the ' Examiner.'—*Id.*

n. The wisest princes need not think it any diminution to their greatness, or derogative to their sufficiency, to rely upon counsel.
Bacon.

o. The cat jumped on to the chair.

p. He saw several rusty guns lying upon the bottom.

q. He was a contemporary with Addison.

r.   Thou art a girl, as much brighter than her,
    As he is a poet sublimer than me.—*Prior.*

s. Meanwhile the losses sustained by the partisan warfare in his rear, and the frightful progress of famine and disease, rendered it indispensable for the French army to move.—*Alison.*

t. The conversations of men of letters are of a different complexion with the talk of men of the world.—*I. D'Israeli.*

u. From whence comes he?

v. Your opinion is very different to mine.

w. I beg to differ with you.

x. They cannot be absolved of their responsibilities.

5. Give instances of words used both as adverbs and prepositions.

6. Parse the words italicized in the following passages—

a. And now go *to*; I will tell you what I will do *to* my vineyard; I will take away the hedge *thereof*, and it shall be eaten up; and break *down* the wall thereof, and it shall be trodden *down.—Isaiah* v. 5.

    b.   *Up* the airy mountain,
                Down the rushy glen.—*Allingham.*

c. They have patched *up* their ruptured friendship.

d. The Lord shall preserve thy going *out* and thy coming *in* from this time forth, and even *for* evermore.—*Bible.*

e. The ship stood *off* the shore.

f. The house was broken *into.*

g. That was not thought *of.*

h. *Off* with his head.—*Shakspere.*

CONJUNCTIONS.

242. Conjunctions connect words, clauses, and sentences. It is sometimes urged that the so-called conjunctions which connect words are really prepositions, that, e.g. in the sentence 'John and Jane sang a duet,' *and* has the force of *with*; but, however this may be, we cannot say 'John and *me* sang a duet;' in other words, *and* does not govern the objective case, and is therefore deficient in the most distinctive mark of a preposition.

That frequently introduces noun clauses. When the noun clause is the object of the sentence, the conjunction connects the noun clause with the principal sentence—

    I said *that* I was willing.

    That all men would be cowards if they dare,
    Some men, we know, have courage to declare.—*Crabbe.*

When the noun clause is the subject of the sentence, the conjunctive power of *that* is not so obvious—

    That I know not what I want is the cause of my complaint.
                                  Johnson.

Not unfrequently a conjunction is employed to link what is said with some previous remark, or to anticipate some unexpressed objection—

> *But*, you will say, what is the good of all this?

> Lord, *and* what shall this man do ?—*Bible.*

243. Conjunctions generally connect the same cases of nouns and pronouns, and the same moods and tenses of verbs; but, strictly speaking, they have no power of government.

> I engaged *him* as a *tutor* (Obj.).
> *He* was engaged as a *tutor* (Nom.).
> He *watched* and *wept*, he *prayed* and *felt* for all.

> *Goldsmith.*

The following sentences are wrong—

> Leave Nell and *I* to toil and work.—*Dickens.*

> He and me are going to the opera.

The objection to coupling different moods and tenses arises from the see-saw effect it produces—

> She came, sees, conquers, and departs.

> The arena swims around him—he *is gone !*
> Ere *ceased* the inhuman shout.—*Byron.*

Certain conjunctions are generally followed by the subjunctive. (See § 67.)

> In O.E. *thæt* (that), *theáh* (though), *swylce* (as if), *thý læs the* (lest), *tó thon thæt* (to the end that), *gif* (if), *hwæther* (whether), *sam . . . sam* (whether . . . or), *butan* (in the sense of *unless*), are generally followed by the subjunctive.

244. Some adjectives, adverbs, and conjunctions require special conjunctions.

The comparative of adjectives and adverbs is followed by *than*—

> I have *more than* I want.
> He wrote *more rapidly than* his sister.

Than also follows *other*, *otherwise*, and *else*—

> It is nothing *else than* robbery.
> There is no *other* book *than* this to be had.
> If it be *otherwise than* I stated, &c.

When *other* and *else* are used in the sense of *in addition to*, they are followed by *besides* or *but*—

> I have *other* strings to my bow *besides* this.
> We have nothing *else but* that.

245. *Such, as, so, &c., take as after them—*

> Would I describe a preacher *such as* Paul.—*Cowper.*
>
> Getting on his legs *as* well *as* he could.—*Dickens.*
>
> Everything is *so* contrived *as* to aggrandize Achilles.
> > *Blair.*
>
> The affections are not *so* easily wounded *as* the passions.
> > *Dickens.*

The following is objectionable—

> The higher-waged workmen are considered as securing
> little, if any more, and perhaps, not so much, comfort
> to their families, than the other families.
> > *R. Chambers.*

Such and *so* sometimes take *that* after them—

> *Such* is the emptiness of human enjoyment *that* we are
> always impatient of the present.—*Johnson.*
>
> He spoke *so* loud *that* I was nearly stunned.

246. *Though* requires *yet ; whether or ; either or ;
neither nor ; both and ; nor nor ; or or—*

> *Though* deep *yet* clear ; *though* gentle *yet* not dull.
> > *Denham.*
>
> *Whether* it be I *or* they.—*Bible.*
>
> *Either* go *or* stop.
>
> He *neither* consented *nor* refused.
>
> I am debtor *both* to the wise *and* unwise.—*Bible.*
>
> *Or* by the lazy Scheldt *or* wandering Po.—*Goldsmith.*
>
> I whom *nor* wealth *nor* avarice move.—*Walsh.*

Or is sometimes used to connect *two different things* and
sometimes to connect *two different names of the same thing.*
This frequently leads to ambiguity : *e.g.* ‘A verbal noun or
participial substantive’ leaves it uncertain whether we
use ‘verbal noun’ and ‘participial substantive’ to denote
two *different* things or as equivalent names of the *same*
thing. The ambiguity may be removed by using ‘ either ’
before the first thing mentioned, if different things are
referred to.

247. Adjectives, adverbs, and conjunctions having different correlatives should not be used in the same construction. The following are objectionable—

The application of gravel and sand effect as much, if not more improvement in consolidating and decomposing the mass, than either lime or dung.

Jackson's 'Agriculture.'

248. When singular nouns are joined by a copulative conjunction, they take a verb in the plural; when joined by a disjunctive conjunction, they take a verb in the singular. The following is wrong—

Nor light nor darkness bring his pains relief.—*Johnson.*

249. The subordinative conjunction *that* is often omitted—

Are you sure ∧ he is gone?
But Brutus says ∧ he was ambitious.—*Shakspere.*

Exercises.

1. Illustrate by examples the various functions of Conjunctions.

2. Correct or justify the following—

a. Thou hast been wiser all the while than me.—*Southey.*

b. Than whom none higher sat.

c. Give unto Thy servants that peace which the world cannot give, that both our hearts may be set to obey Thy commandments, and also, &c.

d. A man may see a metaphor or an allegory in a picture, as well as read them in a description.—*Addison.*

e. This is none other but the voice of God.—*Bible.*

f. It must indeed be confessed that a lampoon or a satire do not carry in them robbery or murder.—*Spectator.*

g. He was neither an object of derision to his enemies or of melancholy to his friends.—*Junius.*

h. Yet no sooner does the morning dawn, and daylight enter his room, but this strange enchantment vanishes.—*Hervey.*

i.   Which neither listlessness nor mad endeavour,
        Nor man, nor boy,
        Nor all that is at enmity with joy,
        Can utterly abolish or destroy.— *Wordsworth.*

k. He is stronger than me.

l. Did he not tell thee his faults, and entreated thee to forgive him?

m. If he understands the subject and attend to it, he can scarcely fail of success.

n.   Nor lute, nor lyre his feeble powers attend,
Nor sweeter music of a virtuous friend.

o. Female blandishments never either absorbed his mind nor clouded his judgment.—*Alison.*

p. Scarcely had Richard taken up the cross than his admirers afforded a very notable specimen of the mischievous inequality of chivalrous ethics.—*Mackintosh.*

q. He likes you better than me.

r. You are a much greater loser than me.—*Swift.*

3. Give a list of Conjunctions that are commonly followed by the Subjunctive.

INTERJECTIONS.

250. Interjections, as a rule, have no syntactical relation with the constructions in which they occur—

Alas! I have nor hope nor health.—*Shelley.*

In such constructions as *Oh me! Ah me!* the 'me' may be regarded as an objective case (*the Dative of Disadvantage*) governed by some preposition understood. Comp. 'Woe is me,' i.e. 'Woe is to me.'

Interjections often occur in other elliptical constructions—

O well is thee.—Ps. cxxviii. 2 [i.e. O well it is for thee].

Oh! for a lodge in some vast wilderness.—*Cowper* [i.e. O, how I long for, &c.].

O that they were wise.—*Bible* [i.e. O how I wish that, &c.].

O well for the fisherman's boy,
That he shouts with his sisters at play!—*Tennyson.*

Sometimes the objective is used without the interjection which usually precedes it—

Me miserable!—*Milton.*

Interjections such as *farewell, adieu, welcome, good-bye,* &c., are elliptical forms of speech rather than interjections.

PART IV.

PROSODY.

————

251. Prosody is that part of grammar which deals with the laws of verse. The chief respect in which verse differs from prose is in its regular succession of accented and unaccented syllables. This regularity of accent is called **Rhythm.** Prose passages are often rhythmical, but the writer of prose is under no necessity to observe any regularity of accent. The versifier, on the other hand, though he may occasionally deviate from the measured rhythm of his verse, is bound to observe certain definite laws in the accentuation of his lines.

The following passage from 'The Old Curiosity Shop' might, with the insertion of a word here and there, be arranged in metrical lines—

'And nów the béll—the béll she hád so óften heárd by níght and dáy, and lístened tó with sólemn pleásure, álmost ás a líving voíce—rung íts remórseless tóll, for hér, so yoúng, so beaútiful, so goód. Decrépit áge, and vígorous lífe, and bloóming yoúth, and hélpless ínfancý, poured fórth—on crútches, ín the príde of stréngth and heálth,' &c. (Ch. lxxii.)

The other ornaments of verse are *rhyme* and *alliteration,* neither of which, however, is essential.

252. Rhyme, or, as the word would be more correctly spelled, **Rime,** consists in a certain similarity of sound in the final syllable or syllables of two or more words. Three things are essential to a perfect rhyme—

1. Identity in the vowel sounds and, if the words end in a consonant, in the consonants also, e.g. *try* and *cry*; *sight* and *light*. Identity of letters is not enough. The identity must be one of sound. '*Lose*' and '*close*,' '*heath*' and '*death*,' are not rhymes.

2. Difference in the consonants preceding the vowel, e.g. '*way*' and '*lay*;' '*hour*' and '*power*.'

3. Similarity of accent, e.g. '*sing*' and '*fling*.' '*Flinging*' and '*sing*' would not be good rhymes.

Words like '*oar*' and '*ore*,' '*eye*' and '*I*,' are called *assonances*. Though tolerated in French verse, they are not generally considered allowable in English. The following is an instance from Tennyson—

> He saddens, all the magic *light*
> Dies off at once from bower and hall,
> And all the place is dark, and all
> The chambers emptied of *delight*.

Rhymes of one syllable are called **single**, e.g. '*band*,' '*hand*.' **Double rhymes** extend over two syllables, e.g. '*crying*' and '*trying*;' '*sharing*' and '*caring*.' **Triple** rhymes extend over three syllables, e.g. '*scrutiny*' and '*mutiny*;' '*dutiful*' and '*beautiful*.' It will be observed from these examples that the first syllables of Double or Triple Rhymes conform to the laws of single Rhymes, and that the second and third syllables are identical.

Humorous writers sometimes make a rhyme extend over two or even three words, and sometimes divide a word in half to produce a rhyme, e.g.—

> An hour they sat in *council*,
> At length the Mayor broke *silence*:
> For a guilder I'd my ermine *gown sell*,
> I wish I were a *mile hence.*—*Browning.*

> Sun, moon, and thou, vain world, adieu,
> That kings and priests are plotting in ;
> Here doomed to starve on water gru-
> el, never shall I see the U-
> niversity of Gottingen,
> niversity of Gottingen.— *Gifford.*

The rhymes may occur at the end or in the middle of the rhyming lines, e.g.—

> Ho trumpets, sound a war-note!
> Ho, lictors, clear the *way*!
> The knights will *ride*, in all their *pride*,
> Along the streets *to-day*.—*Macaulay*.

253. Alliteration consists in the frequent recurrence of the same initial letter. In O.E. poetry it was the chief ornament of verse and was regulated by definite laws, the leading one of which is thus stated by Marsh—

'In each couplet three emphatic words (or, by poetic license, accented *syllables*), two in the first line, and one in the second, must commence with the same consonant, or with vowels; in which latter case the initial letters might be, and generally were, different. The position of the alliterated words in the first line was arbitrary, and varied according to the convenience of the poet, but the alliteration in the second line should fall on the first emphatic word.'—(*Eng. Lang.* 390.)

This kind of verse continued to be used as late as the fourteenth century. A specimen is subjoined from 'Piers Ploughman'—

> *P*ilgrims and *p*almers
> *P*lighten hem togider
> For to *s*eeken *S*aint Jame
> And *s*aintes at Rome.

In the hands of a skilful writer alliteration is very effective, but, when indulged in to excess, is offensive and ludicrous. Shakspere ridicules its abuse in more passages than one. Thus he makes Kent in 'King Lear' say with burlesque grandiloquence—

> *S*ir, in good *s*ooth, in *s*incere verity,
> Under the allowance of your great aspéct,
> Whose in*f*luence, like the *w*reath of *r*adiant *f*ire
> On *f*lickering *P*hœbus' *f*ront ...

Still more alliterative is Bottom's speech—

> Whereat, with *b*lade, with *b*loody *b*lameful *b*lade,
> He *b*ravely *b*roached his *b*oiling *b*loody *b*reast.

The following specimens show that alliteration may produce a pleasing effect when managed with skill—

> The *m*ighty *m*aster *s*miled to see
> That love was in the next degree;

'Twas but a kindred *s*ound to *m*ove,
For pity *m*elts the *m*ind to love.
*S*oftly *s*weet, in Lydian *m*easures
*S*oon he *s*oothed his *s*oul to pleasures.—*Dryden.*

Our *s*incerest laughter
With some pain is fraught ;
Our *s*weetest songs are those that tell of *s*addest thought.
Shelley.

254. Metre is a rhythmical arrangement of words measured off in lines of equal or varying length.

A foot is the unit of metre. It consists of a group of two or three syllables, one of which is accented. See KINDS OF FEET.

A verse is a cycle of feet, forming a line of poetry.

A couplet is composed of two consecutive lines, rhyming together ; a **triplet** is composed of three such lines.

KINDS OF FEET.

255. Feet may be divided into dissyllabic and trisyllabic. A dissyllabic foot, if accented on the second syllable, is called an **Iambus**,[1] if on the first syllable a **Trochee.**[2] If we represent an accented syllable by *a* and an unaccented syllable by *x*, an

Iambus would be represented by *x a*, e.g. *divíne*; a
Trochee   „   „   *a x*, e.g. *háppy.*

In classical poetry another kind of dissyllabic foot is recognized, viz. the **Spondee**, which consists of two long syllables.

Trisyllabic feet may be divided into—

The **Anapæst**[3] (*x x a*), having the accent on the third syllable, as *serenáde.*

The **Dactyl**[4] (*a x x*), having the accent on the first syllable, as *mérrily.*

---

[1] From Gk. *iaptein*, to throw, because used in satirical poetry.
[2] From Gk. *trochaios*, tripping, and that from *trechō*, I run, because of its sprightly movement.
[3] *Anapæst*, from Gk. *ana*, back, and *paistos* (*paio*, I strike), struck ; an anapæst being a dactyl reversed.
[4] *Dactyl*, from Gr. *daktylos*, a finger, so called because, like a finger, it consists of one long and two short joints.

The **Amphibrach** [1] (*x a x*), having the accent on the middle syllable, as *beliéving*.

These various kinds of feet are all illustrated in the following lines of Coleridge, but the terms, *long* and *short*, which he employs, are to be understood as meaning respectively *accented* and *unaccented*, rather than long and short in the sense which would be attached to those terms in classical metres.

> Tróchee | tríps from | lóng to | shórt,
> From lóng | to lóng | in sól | emn sórt
> Slow spon | dee stalks ; | strong foot ! | yet | íll able
> Éver to | cóme up with | dáctyl tri | sýllable. |
> Iám | bics márch | from shórt | to lóng ; |
> With a leáp | and a boúnd | the swift án | apæsts thróng ; |
> One sýlla | ble lóng with | one shórt at | each síde |
> Amphíbrach | ys hástes with | a státely | stride. |

256. Verses are classified according to the kind of *foot* and the number of feet occurring in them. Thus we have Iambic, Trochaic, Anapæstic, Dactylic, and Amphibrachic verse. A verse of one foot we call **Monometer**; one of two feet **Dimeter**; one of three feet **Trimeter**; one of four feet **Tetrameter**; one of five feet **Pentameter**; one of six feet **Hexameter**.

DISSYLLABIC VERSE.

Iambic Measures.

(*a*) Iambic lines of one foot (**Monometer**) are of rare occurrence.

(*b*) *Iambic Dimeter.*

> With ráv | ished eárs |
> The món | arch heárs, |
> Assúmes | the gód, |
> Afféots | to nód. | —*Dryden.*

(*c*) *Iambic Trimeter.*

> His swórd | was ín | its sheáth |
> His fin | gers héld | the pén |
> When Kém | penfélt | went dówn |
> With twíce | four hún | dred mén. —*Cowper.*

---

[1] *Amphibrach*, from Gk. *amphi*, on both sides, and *brachys*, short, so called because it consists of a short syllable on each side of a long one.

Q

(d) Iambic Tetrameter.

A perfect woman, nobly planned
To warn, to comfort and command ;
And yet a spirit still and bright
With something of an angel-light.—*Wordsworth.*

This is the measure in which Scott's poems are, for the most part, written. To relieve its monotony he frequently introduced triplets and lines of irregular length.

(e) Iambic Pentameter.

'Tis hard to say, if greater want of skill
Appear in writing or in judging ill ;
But of the two, less dangerous is the offence
To tire our patience than mislead our sense.—*Pope.*

This is what is commonly called **Heroic Measure.** It was much used by Chaucer, Dryden, and the poets of the last century, and is well fitted for satire, didactic poems, and narrative. Pope brought it to great perfection, but rendered it somewhat monotonous by not sufficiently varying the cæsura or pause in the course of the line, and by too frequently closing his sentences at the end of a line. More recent poets have introduced great variety into the structure of Heroic verse.

Unrhymed pentameters are what is ordinarily called **Blank verse.** See § 263.

(f) Iambic Hexameter.

Upon the midlands now the industrious muse doth fall ;
That shire which we the heart of England well may call,
As she herself extends (the midst which is decreed)
Betwixt St. Michael's Mount and Berwick bordering Tweed
Brave Warwick, that abroad so long advanced her Bear,
By her illustrious Earls renowned everywhere.—*Drayton.*

This measure is sometimes called **Alexandrine,** from an old French poem written in it, celebrating Alexander the Great. Alexandrine verses are rarely used, except to relieve the monotony of pentameters. Pope ridicules the too frequent employment of it for this purpose—

A needless Alexandrine ends the song,
Which like | a wound | ed snake | drags its | slow length | along. |

The Alexandrine gives a noble close to the Spenserian stanza—

> How oft do they their silver bowers leave
> To come to succour us that succour want !
> How oft do they with golden pinions cleave
> The flitting skies like flying pursuivant,
> Against foul fiends to aid us militant !
> They for us fight, they watch and duly ward,
> And their bright squadrons round about us plant ;
> And all for love and nothing for reward :
> O, why|should Heaven|ly God|to men|have such|regard ?|
> *Spenser.*

(g) *Iambic Heptameter.*

> Now glory to the Lord of hosts, from whom all glories are !
> And glory to our Sovereign Liege, King Henry of Navarre !
> *Macaulay*

This measure is sometimes written in lines of four and three feet alternately, the latter being the only rhyming lines.

Such an arrangement of this verse is usually adopted in our hymn-books and in ballads.

It is hence called **Service** or **Ballad Metre.**

Mixed Metre.—For the sake of variety poets often vary the length of their lines and the arrangement of the rhymes—

> No mate, no comrade Lucy knew ; (Tetrameter)
> She dwelt on a wide moor, (Trimeter)
> The sweetest thing that ever grew
> Beside a human door.—*Wordsworth.*

> She took me to her elfin grot,
> And there she wept and sighed full sore,
> And then I shut her wild, wild eyes
> With kisses four.—*Keats.*

Hypermeter.—The examples that have been given thus far have been symmetrical, i.e. the lines have contained an exact number of feet ; but occasionally we find lines with one or two syllables in excess of the normal number. Such lines are called **hypermetric.**

> Day after day, day after day,
> We stuck, nor breath nor motion (Hypermetric),
> As idle as a painted ship
> Upon a painted o₁cean (Hypermetric).—*Coleridge.*

Q 2

257.   **Trochaic Measures.**

(a) Trochaic Dimeter.

Rích the|treásure, '.
Swéet the|pleásure.—*Dryden.*

(b) Trochaic Trimeter.

Whén the|lámp is|sháttered,
Whén the|cloúd is|scáttered.

(c) Trochaic Tetrameter.

With a full but soft emotion,
Like the swell of Summer's ocean.—*Byron.*

Then with deep sonorous clangor
Calmly answering their sweet anger
When the wrangling bells had ended,
Slowly struck the clock eleven,
And, from out the silent heaven,
Silence on the town descended.—*Longfellow.*

(d) Trochaic Pentameter.

Narrowing in to where they sat assembled,
Low voluptuous music winding trembled.—*Tennyson.*

(e) Trochaic Hexameter.

Holy! Holy! Holy! all the saints adore Thee.—*Heber.*

(f) Trochaic Heptameter.

Hollow is the oak beside the sunny waters drooping.
                              Lord Lytton.

Hypermetric lines are very common in the trochaic
measure. Indeed, if it were not for such lines, single rhymes
would be impossible in trochaic verse.

> Shall I, | wasting | in de|spair,|
> Die be|cause a | woman's | fair?|—*G. Wither.*

In the | market-|place of | Bruges | stands the | belfry | old and |
    brown ; |
Thrice con|sumed and | thrice re|builded,| still it | watches | o'er the |
    town. |—*Longfellow.*

TRISYLLABIC VERSE.

258.   **Anapæstic Measures.**

Anapæstic Monometer.

As ye sweép
Through the deép.—*Campbell*

Anapæstic Dimeter.

In my ráge | shall be seén |
The revénge | of a queén. | —*Addison.*

Anapæstic Trimeter.

I am món | arch of áll | I survéy. | —*Cowper.*

Anapæstic Tetrameter.

In the dówn | hill of life | when I find | I'm declín | ing
May my lót | no less fór | tunate bé |
Than a snug | elbow-chair | can afford | for reclin | ing,
And a cot | that o'erlooks | the wide sea ! | —*Collins.*

Anapæstic lines are frequently varied by the introduction
of other kinds of feet, and by hypermetrical feet.

'Tis the last | rose of sum | mer
Left bloom | ing alone ; |
All her love | ly compan | ions
Are fa | ded and gone. | —*Moore.*

259.   **Dactylic Measures.**

Dactylic Monometer.

Mérrily,
Cheérily.

Dactylic Dimeter.

Toúch her not | scórnfully ;
Thínk of her | moúrnfully,
Géntly, and | húmanly,
Nót of the | staíns of her—
Áll that re | maíns of her
Nów, is pure | wómanly.—*Hood.*

Dactylic Trimeter.

Mérrily, | mérrily, | sháll I live | nów |
Únder the | blóssom that | hángs on the | boúgh. |
                                Shakspere.

Bríghtest and | bést of the | sóns of the | mórning, |
Dáwn on our | dárkness and | lénd us thine | aíd ; |
Stár of the | eást, the ho | rízon a | dórning, |
Guíde where our | ínfant Re | deémer is | laíd. | —*Heber.*

260.   **Amphibrach Measures.**

Amphibrachic Dimeter.

But vaínly | thou wárrest ; |
For this is | alóne in |
Thy pówer to | decláre, |
That ín the | dim fórest |
Thou heárd'st a | low moáning.— *Coleridge.*

Amphibrachic Trimeter.

The flésh was | a picture | for painters | to stúdy, |
The fát was | so white and | the leán was | so rúddy. |
Goldsmith.

Oh, húsh thee, | my bábie, | thy síre was | a knight, |
Thy móther | a lády | both lóvely | and bríght : |
The wóods, and | the gléns, and | the tówers which | we seé, |
They áll arc | belónging, | dear bábie, | to theé.—*Scott.*

If we read the first two syllables of an amphibrachic line as an iambus, the remainder of the line may be considered as anapæstic, e.g.—

There cáme | to the beách | a poor éx | ile of É | rin,
The déw | on his thín | robe was heá | vy and chíll.
Campbell.

Similarly, if we read the first two syllables of a dactylic line as a trochee, the remainder of the line may be considered as amphibrachic, e.g.—

Bríghtest | and bést of | the sóns of | the mórning. |

MIXED VERSE.

261. A great deal of modern poetry is written in irregular feet, to the great relief of the reader, who soon tires of symmetrical verses, 'half up and half down.'

Thére be | nóne of | Beaúty's | daúghters |
   With a má | gic like theé : |
Ánd like | músic | ón the | wáters |
   Is thý | sweet voicc | to mé. |
Whén, as | if its | soúnd were | caúsing |
The chárm | èd ó | cean's paús | ing,
The wáves | lie still | and gleám | ing,
And the lúlled | winds seem | dreáming.—*Byron.*

The blés | sed dá | mozél | leaned oút |
   From the góld | bár of | heáven ; |
Her eýes | were deép | er thán | the dépth |
   Of wá | ters stilled | at é | ven ; |
She hád | three lí | lies ín | her háir, |
   And the stárs | in her hánd | were séven. | —*Rossetti.*

Coleridge's 'Christabel' and Byron's 'Siege of Corinth' are written in lines composed of mixed feet, but having invariably the same number of strong accents.

In the yeár | since Jé | sus díed | for mén, |
Eighteen | húndred | ycars and | tén, |
Wé were | a gál | lant cóm | paný, |
Riding | o'er lánd | and sáil | ing o'er seá. |

262. Various attempts have been made to naturalize the classical metres in English, but none of them have been eminently successful. The following are specimens—

Hexameters.

Strongly it | bears us a|long in | swelling and | limitless | billows;
Nothing be|fore and | nothing be|hind but the | sky and the | ocean. |
Homeric Hexameter, translated from Schiller by Coleridge.

Hexameters and Pentameters.

In the hex|ameter | rises the | fountain's | silvery | column ; |
In the pent|ameter | aye | falling in | melody | back. |
Coleridge, Ovidian Elegiac.

Woulds't thou|know thy|self ?   Ob|serve what thy|neighbours
are |doing, |
Woulds't thou thy|neighbours|know?| Look through the|depths
of thy | heart. |

' "The hexameter verse," says Nash, an Elizabethan writer, "I grant to be a gentleman of an ancient house (so is many an English beggar), yet this clime of ours he cannot thrive in ; he goes twitching and hopping in our language like a man running upon quagmires, retaining no part of that stately smooth gait which he vaunts himself with among the Greek and Latin." '—Quoted in D'Israeli's *Curiosities of Literature*, ii. p. 30.

Sapphics.

Sapphics are so called from the famous Greek poetess, Sappho of Lesbos.

Cold was the | night wind, | drifting | fast the | snow fell, |
Wide were the | downs and | shelter|less and | naked, |
When a poor | wanderer | struggled | on her | journey, |
Weary and | waysore.—*Southey.*

Needy | knife-grind|er, whither | are you | going ? |
Rough is | the road, | your wheel is | out of | order ; |
Bleak blows the | blast—your | hat has | got a | hole in't, |
So have your | breeches. |—*Canning.*

Alcaics.

Alcaics were called after Alcæus of Lesbos. The scheme of them is somewhat complex.

O might|y mouth'd | in|ventor of | harmonies, |
O skill'd | to sing | of Time or E|ternity, |
God-gift|ed or|gan voice | of Eng|land, |
Milton, a | name to re|sound for | ages. |—*Tennyson.*

BLANK VERSE.

263. All unrhymed verse may be called *blank*, but the term Blank Verse is generally restricted to unrhymed lines of five iambic feet, such as are usually employed by Shakspere in his plays, and by Milton in his great epics. Blank Verse is the noblest of all our measures, and admits of the widest variety of handling.

The chief licenses which it allows of are the following—

1. A trochee or anapæst may be substituted for an iambus in almost any part of the line, but rarely occurs in the second or fifth foot.

Oút of|my weák|ness ánd|my mé|lanchó|ly.—*Hamlet.*

Tweáks me|by the nóse?|gives me|the líe|in the
    throát.|—*Ib.*

Shakspere often begins a line with a trochee, when the previous line ends with an unaccented syllable—

—all my smooth body.
Thús was|I,sleep|ing, by|a bro|ther's hand.|—*Hamlet.*

2. An unaccented syllable, or even two such syllables, may be added to the last foot.

Which the poor heart would fain deny and dare|not.
Macbeth.

3. Shakspere often writes lines of one, two, three, and even six feet, but rarely lines of four feet. When short lines come in succession, they are generally to be scanned as though forming one continuous line.

—and smear
The sleep|y grooms|with blood.|
Mac. I'll go|no more.|—*Macbeth.*

4. When a full stop or colon occurs in the course of a line, Shakspere frequently begins the last hemistich as though it were a new line. Thus, if the first hemistich ends with an unaccented syllable, he often begins the second with another unaccented syllable; if it ends with an accented syllable, he often begins the second with another accented syllable.

And makes|as health|ful mu|sic. It ís|not mad|ness.
Hamlet.
Brief let|me be:|—Sleép|ing|within|mine or|chard.|
Ib.

In scanning Shakspere's blank verse it is sometimes necessary to glide over a short syllable.

> Of thinking too precisely on | the event. | —*Hamlet*.

> Which are too intrinse to unloose.—*King Lear*.

Sometimes a monosyllable is pronounced as a dissyllable.

> Nor rain, | wind, thun | der, fi | re are | my daugh | ters.
> >*King Lear.*

> What do *you* think,
> You, the | great toe | of this | assem | bl-y ? | —*Coriolanus.*

> The raven himself is hoarse
> That croaks | the fa | tal ent | r-ance | of Dun | can.
> >*Macbeth.*

> The parts | and gra | ces of | the wrest | l-er. |
> >*As You Like It.*

> Which is | as bad | as die | with tick | l-ing. |
> >*Much Ado about Nothing.*

> Fearing | to strength | en that | impa | ti-ence. |
> >*Julius Cæsar.*

> And there | receive | her ap | proba | ti-on. |
> >*Measure for Measure.*

> My mor | tifi | ed spi | rit. Now bid | me run. |
> >*Julius Cæsar.*

> But for | your pri | vate sat | isfac | ti-on. | —*Ib.*

> That ban | ishèd— | that one | word ban | ish-ed. |
> >*Romeo and Juliet.*

> And last | ing in | her sad | remem | br-ance. |
> >*Twelfth Night.*

> O, how | this spring | of love | resem | bl-eth. |
> >*Two Gentlemen of Verona.*

> But Bru | tus says | he was | ambi | ti-ous. | —*Julius Cæsar.*

In reading, these short syllables should be only faintly sounded.

The accent is often shifted in Shakspere, e.g.—

> That sweet aspéct of princes and their ruin.
> >*Henry VIII.*

> Why thy canónized bones, hearsèd in death.—*Hamlet.*

> That thou, dead corse, again in cómplete steel.—*Ib.*

STANZAS.

264. A **Stanza** is a regularly recurring group of verses.
Of such groups there are endless varieties. The best known
are the following:

Gay's Stanza.

'T was when the seas were roaring
　With hollow blasts of wind,
A damsel lay deploring,
　All on a rock reclined.

Elegiac Octosyllabics.

A love-song I had somewhere read,
　An echo from a measured strain,
Beat time to nothing in my head
　From some odd corner of the brain.
It haunted me the morning long
　With weary sameness in the rhymes,
The phantom of a silent song
　That went and came a thousand times.
Tennyson, ' Miller's Daughter.'

Ballad or Service Stanza. See § 256.

Elegiacs.

The boast of heraldry, the pomp of power,
And all that beauty, all that wealth e'er gave,
Await alike th' inevitable hour:—
The paths of glory lead but to the grave.—*Gray.*

Rhymes Royal.

It chaunced me on day beside the shore
Of silver-streaming Thamesis to bee,
Nigh where the goodly Verlame stood of yore,
Of which there now remains no memorie,
Nor any little moniment to see,
By which the traveller that fares that way,
This once was she, may warned be to say.
Spenser, ' Ruines of Time.'

Spenserian Stanza. See § 256. This stanza consists of
nine lines, the first eight being Iambic Pentameters, and the
last line an Alexandrine. The rhyming lines are the 1st and
3rd; the 2nd, 4th, 5th, and 7th; and the 6th, 8th, and 9th.
This is the stanza in which Spenser's ' Faërie Queen' and
Byron's ' Childe Harold' are written.

Ottava Rima consists of eight heroic lines, the first six
rhyming alternately, the last two in succession.

'T was in the season when sad Philomel
   Weeps with her sister, who remembers and
Deplores the ancient woes which both befel,
   And makes the nymphs enamoured, to the hand
Of Phaeton by Phœbus loved so well
   His car (but tempered by his sire's command)
Was given, and on the horizon's verge just now
Appeared, so that Tithonus scratched his brow.
      Byron, Translation of ' Morgante Maggiore.'

Terza Rima consists of heroics with three rhymes at intervals.

Many are poets who have never penn'd
   Their inspiration, and perchance the best:
   They felt, and loved, and died, but would not lend
Their thoughts to meaner beings; they compressed
   The god within them, and rejoined the stars
   Unlaurelled upon earth, but far more blessed
Than those who are degraded by the jars
   Of passion, and their frailties linked to fame,
   Conquerors of high renown and full of scars.
Many are poets, but without the name,
   For what is poesy but to create
   From overflowing good or ill; and aim
At an external life beyond our fate,
   And be the new Prometheus of new men
   Bestowing fire from heaven and then, too late,
Finding the pleasure given repaid with pain,
   And vultures to the heart of the bestower,
   Who having lavished his high gift in vain,
Lies chained to his lone rock by the sea shore.
      Byron, ' Prophecy of Dante.'

The Sonnet is a short poem of fourteen iambic pentameters. It was one of the earliest forms of Italian verse, and was brought to a high state of perfection by Dante and Petrarch. The Italian sonnet is divided into two parts: the **Octave**, consisting of two quatrains and possessing only two rhymes; and the **Sestette**, consisting of two terzettes or groups of three lines, and possessing two and sometimes three rhymes. The order of the rhymes rarely varies in the octave; in the sestette there is greater variety. English sonnets are often written on the Italian model, but many so-called sonnets have little in common with the Italian sonnet beyond the fact that they are poems fourteen lines long. Wordsworth's sonnet written on Westminster Bridge is of the genuine Italian type. His sonnet on the Sonnet is not so strictly constructed, the couplet in which it ends being of rare occurrence in Italian.

Octave

Scorn not the sonnet; critic, you have frowned
Mindless of its just honours : with this key
Shakspere unlocked his heart; the melody
Of this small lute gave ease to Petrarch's wound ;
A thousand times this pipe did Tasso sound ;
Camoëns soothed with it an exile's grief ;
The sonnet glittered a gay myrtle leaf
Amid the cypress with which Dante crowned

Sestette

His visionary brow ; a glowworm lamp,
It cheered mild Spenser, called from Faëry-land
To struggle through dark ways; and when a damp
Fell round the path of Milton, in his hand
The thing became a trumpet, whence he blew
Soul-animating strains—alas, too few !— *Wordsworth.*

PART V.

—+—

THE HISTORY OF THE ENGLISH LANGUAGE.

265. When we carefully examine a number of languages, we find that, in spite of external differences, many of them closely resemble one another in their vocabularies, inflexions, and syntax. Such resemblances could not be accidental, and point to some relationship, more or less close, between the peoples speaking the languages. The history of mankind, so far as it is known, enables us to test these conclusions. Thus the most cursory examination of English and German would lead us to infer that the English and German people were closely related, and the history of the English people informs us precisely what the degree of relationship was.

266. By extending our examination over the languages of Europe and Asia we are led to the conclusion that most of the languages of Europe and some of the most important languages of Asia are descended from some common tongue. It has been further inferred that this tongue (to which the name Aryan[1] has been given) was spoken by a people living to the north-west of Hindostan. The languages derived from the Aryan are called Indo-Germanic.

[1] 'Ârya is a Sanskrit word, and in the later Sanskrit it means *noble, of a good family.* It was, however, originally a national name. . . . The etymological signification of Arya seems to be "one who ploughs or tills."'—Max Müller, *Lectures on the Science of Language,* i. 266–8. Comp. Lat. *arare,* Engl. *ear* = to plough.

By carefully collecting the words which the Indo-Germanic languages have in common—words, therefore, which the Indo-Germanic peoples must have possessed before their dispersion—we may form some conception of the state of civilization which the Aryans had attained to before they were scattered. Arguing in this way it has been inferred by philologists that the Aryans were an agricultural and nomadic people. 'They knew the arts of ploughing, of making roads, of building ships, of weaving and sewing, of erecting houses ; they had counted at least as far as one hundred. They had domesticated the most important animals, the cow, the horse, the sheep, the dog ; they were acquainted with the most useful metals, and armed with iron hatchets, whether for peaceful or warlike purposes. They had recognised the bonds of blood and the bonds of marriage; they followed their leaders and kings, and the distinction between right and wrong was fixed by laws and customs. They were impressed with the idea of a Divine Being, and they invoked it by different names.' (Max Müller, *Lect. on the Science of Lang.* i. 265.)

The following words will serve to show the close resemblance which subsists between English and Sanskrit.

Sanskrit	English	Sanskrit	English
pitri	father	dvau	two
mâta	mother	tri	three
bhrâtri	brother	sastha	sixth
svasâr	sister	saptan	seven
sûnu	son	navan	nine
duhitri	daughter	yuga	yoke
na	no	mûsha	mouse
upa	up	udra	water
upari	over	nâman	name
abhi	by	sadas	seat
sîd-âmi	I sit	gâ	go
sa-sâd-a	I sat	dhâ	do
bhu	be	asti	is

267. The first Aryan people who left their Asiatic home for Europe would appear to have been the **Kelts.** They were gradually pressed forward by succeeding waves of immigration, and their descendants are now to be found almost exclusively on the fringe of the Atlantic—in the Highlands, in Ireland, in Wales, in the Isle of Man, and in Brittany.

The **Kelts** were followed by the **Italic** tribes who settled in Italy, and the **Hellenic** tribes who settled in Greece. Then came the **Teutons** who settled in Germany and Scandinavia, the **Slavonians** who settled in Russia, Poland, and

Bohemia, and the **Lithuanians** who settled on the southern shores of the Baltic.

The only peoples in Europe not of Aryan extraction are the Jews, the Finns, the Lapps, the Esths of Esthonia, the Magyars of Hungary, the Turks, and the Basques in the north of Spain.

268. The following table shows the relation of the leading Indo-Germanic languages—

I. Indic or Hindû .
1. Sanskrit (dead).
2. Hindû, Hindustanî, Bengalî, Mahratti.
3. Cingalese.
4. Romany (the basis of the Gipsy dialects).

II. Iranic (from *Iran*, the great table-land of Persia)
1. Zend (dead).
2. Modern Persian.

III. Keltic . . .
1. Erse or Irish.
2. Gaelic.
3. Welsh.
4. Manx.
5. Brézonec or Armorican (spoken in Brittany).
6. Cornish (dead).

IV. Italic . . .
1. Latin, Oscan, Umbrian, and other old Italian dialects.
2. Romance dialects which have sprung from (1)—
   a. Italian.
   b. French.
   c. Spanish.
   d. Portuguese.
   e. Roumansch (spoken in the Grisons, a canton of Switzerland).
   f. Wallachian.

V. Hellenic or Greek .
1. Ancient Greek, with its various dialects, as Attic, Ionic, Doric, &c.
2. Modern Greek or Romaic.

VI. Teutonic

1. Low German or Low Dutch, with its dialects—
   a. Mœso - Gothic, formerly spoken in Dacia (dead).
   b. Continental Saxon (dead).
   c. English.
   d. Dutch.
   e. Frisian, spoken in Friesland (Holland).
   f. Flemish.
2. Scandinavian with its dialects—
   a. Icelandic.
   b. Danish.
   c. Norwegian.
   d. Swedish.
3. High German or High Dutch, the name given to modern German.

VII. Windic

1. Lettic—
   a. Old Lettic (dead).
   b. Modern Lettish, spoken in Lithuania.
2. Slavonic—
   a. Russian.
   b. Polish.
   c. Bohemian or Czech.
   d. Bulgarian.
   e. Illyrian.

269. It will be seen from the foregoing table that English is a Low German language, and that it is closely related to the Scandinavian languages and to modern German. It was introduced into this country in the course of the latter half of the sixth century and the former half of the seventh by various Low German tribes, of whom the best known are the Angles, the Saxons, and the Jutes. The Angles are supposed to have come from the neighbourhood of the district still called Angeln in the Duchy of Schleswig. They settled in the east, north-east, and central part of England; the Jutes or Frisians, who came from Jutland, settled in Kent and the Isle of Wight; the Saxons, who came from the north of Germany, settled in the south of England, where they have left traces of their occupation in the names Essex, Sussex, Wessex. Whatever their original differences of descent, the settlers soon called themselves English and their new home England. To the native Kelts whom they found in possession of the country they were all Saxons.

270. In spite of the large number of words that have been introduced into our language from foreign sources, it still remains, both in its vocabulary and its grammar, essentially Teutonic. If we examine an English dictionary, indeed, we find somewhat less than one-third of the words that it contains to be of Teutonic origin, but there is a wide difference between a language as represented by a dictionary and the same language as spoken or written. The dictionary includes every word in the language, common or uncommon; but the English we speak and write is mainly composed of a small number of words that occur over and over again. Estimating the proportions of the various elements of the language by the frequency of their occurrence, it has been found that about thirty-two out of every forty words as they stand in our classic authors are of purely Teutonic origin. In the following extracts the only words not of Teutonic origin are printed in italics:—

And they made ready the *present* against *Joseph* came at *noon*; for they heard they should eat bread there. And when *Joseph* came home, they brought him the *present* which was in their hand into the house, and bowed themselves to the earth. And he asked them of their welfare and said, Is your father well, the old man of whom ye spake? Is he yet alive? And they answered, Thy *servant* our father is in good health, he is yet alive. And they bowed down their heads and made *obeisance*. And he lift up his eyes, and saw his brother *Benjamin*, his mother's son, and said, Is this your younger brother, of whom ye spake unto me? And he said, God be *gracious* unto thee, my son.—Gen. xliii. 25–29.

[9 foreign words out of a total of 128.]

Of *genius*, that *power* which *constitutes* a *poet*; that *quality*, without which *judgment* is cold and knowledge is *inert*; that *energy* which *collects*, *combines*, *amplifies* and *animates*; the *superiority* must, with some *hesitation*, be *allowed* to Dryden. It is not to be *inferred* that of this *poetical vigour* Pope had only a little, because Dryden had more; for every other writer since Milton must give *place* to Pope; and even of Dryden it must be said, that if he has brighter *paragraphs*, he has not better *poems*.—*Dr. Johnson.*

[20 foreign words out of a total of 87.]

Then fare thee well, mine own true love,
The world hath now for us
No greater *grief*, no *pain* above
The *pain* of *parting* thus.— *T. Moore.*

[4 foreign words out of a total of 25.]

S

The following statistics are given by Professor Marsh :—

	Saxon words in every 40
Chaucer (2 tales)	37
New Testament (13 chapters). . .	37
Sir T. More (7 folio pages) . . .	34
Shakspere (3 acts)	36
Milton's ' L'Allegro '	36
,,　　' Paradise Lost ' . . .	32
Pope's ' Essay on Man '	32
Macaulay's ' Essay on Bacon '. . .	30
Ruskin's ' Painters '.	29
Tennyson's ' In Memoriam ' . . .	36

It is instructive to look at this matter from another point of view. Sharon Turner says : ' In three pages of Alfred's " Orosius " I found 78 words which have become obsolete out of 548, or about $\frac{1}{7}$. In three pages of his " Boetius " I found 143 obsolete out of 666, or about $\frac{1}{5}$. In three pages of his " Bede " I found 230 obsolete out of 969, or about $\frac{1}{4}$.' It has been calculated that about $\frac{1}{5}$ of the old English language has become obsolete.

THE PURELY ENGLISH ELEMENT IN MODERN ENGLISH.

271. English, as introduced into this country, was highly inflected, and consisted exclusively of Teutonic elements. The words in our language that are of purely Teutonic origin may be ascertained by a careful examination of Old English literature, and by a comparison of English with the languages of those peoples with whom we have been historically connected ; but, once they are classified, they may also be recognised, for the most part, by (a) their length, (b) their grammatical function, (c) the laws of inflexion to which they are subject, (d) their spelling, (e) their component parts, and (f) their meaning.

a. **Length.**—Most of our monosyllabic words are of purely Teutonic origin : *ear, eye, book, skull,* &c. We have about 250 monosyllabic words of Greek or Latin origin, e.g. *ace, age, aid, aim, air, aisle, alms, arch, ark, aunt,* &c. Both of these classes owe their shortness mainly to the contractions consequent upon long and frequent use. Most of our monosyllables of classical origin have undergone contraction in passing through French.

b. **Grammatical Function.**—Nearly all our numerals, conjunctions, prepositions, and all our pronouns and demonstrative adjectives are Teutonic: *one, two ; and, but ; of, by ; I, thou, he ; a, the, this,* &c.

c. **Inflexions.**—Nearly all the words which undergo vowel changes are Teutonic :—

(*a*) Nouns, as *mouse, foot, brother.*

(*b*) Strong verbs, as *come, fall, swim,* &c.

(*c*) Defective verbs, as *must, ought.*

(*d*) Adjectives compared irregularly, as, *good, bad, old, little, much, many.*

(*e*) Nouns forming their plural in *-en* and *-ves,* as *ox, wife, loaf.*

d. **Spelling.**—Certain combinations of letters are characteristic of Teutonic words : **wh-** (O. E. hw-), as in *who, what, which, why,* &c. ; **kn-** (O.E. cn-), as in *know, knight,* &c. ; **sh-** (O.E. sc-), as in *ship, shape,* &c. ; **th-,** as *thou, this, thin, thick,* &c. ; **gl-,** as *glad, glee, glow,* &c. ; **gn-,** as *gnaw, gnat* ; the terminations -**ough** (O. E. -oh), as *rough, enough,* &c.

e. **Component Parts.**—Most words with O.E. prefixes and suffixes are Teutonic, as *un*-true, *be*-lieve, *en*-trust, &c., king-*dom,* friend-*ship,* lamb-*kin.* Occasionally we find an English prefix with a Romance root, as *un*-governable, and occasionally an English root with a Romance suffix, as starv-*ation,* flirt-*ation.* Sometimes, too, we find a Romance root with both prefix and suffix English, as *un*pleasant*ness.*

f. **Meaning.**—As might be expected, the names of common natural objects, especially such as are indigenous, of such artificial objects and occupations as belong to a primitive stage of civilization, of family relationships, of the various parts of the body, of common actions, emotions, and mental processes, of common attributes, of simple relations, &c., are mostly Teutonic :

(*a*) **Natural Objects :—**

1. Animal kingdom : *ox, cow, horse, mare, beetle, bee, fly, cock, boar, deer, fish, mole, bird, crane, frog, fowl, goose, hawk, sparrow, feather, wing, hair, nail, &c.*

2. Vegetable kingdom : *oak, apple, leek, cowslip, daisy, hawthorn, groundsel, flax, oakum.*

3. Mineral kingdom : *stone, clay, water, gold, silver, iron.*

4. Physical phenomena : *rain, hail, sleet, snow, spring, summer, winter, day, night.*

(*b*) **Artificial Objects.**

1. Domestic : *house, hearth, bed, seat, besom, board, bucket, cot, &c.*

2. Agricultural : *farm, wagon, acre, barley, wheat, chaff, calf, rick, orchard, sheep, &c.*

3. Simple arts, manufactures, and commerce : *smith, cheap, cloth, weave, buy, sell, hammer, nail, smith, anvil, &c.*

(*c*) **Relationships** : *father, mother, sister, brother, widow, widower, child, bride, husband, wife.*

(*d*) **Parts of the body** : *head, chin, eye, ear, hair, leg, hand, toe, bone, skin, ankle, belly, &c.*

(*e*) **Emotions and simple mental processes** : *love, hate, fear, like, dread, think, believe, dream, &c.*

(*f*) **Common actions** : *sit, stand, walk, run, eat, creep, crawl, lie, rise, step, yawn, gape, wink, fly, &c.*

(*g*) **Attributes** : *good, bad, black, red, green, yellow, brown, white, grey, hot, cold, fair, foul, hard, soft, &c.*

272. If we analyse our language on another principle, and divide words that admit of the division into *generic* and *specific*, we shall find that the specific are, for the most part, of English, and the generic of classical origin; classification and the abstraction which precedes it being processes that are characteristic of advanced stages of civilization.

Generic :—
Colour, motion, sound, crime.

Specific :—
White, red, black, grey, &c. (colour).
Walking, running, &c. (motion).
Singing, laughing, &c. (sound).
Theft, murder,-robbery, &c. (crime).

Hence it is that words of English origin are much more forcible, poetical, and picturesque than words of classical origin. They call up to the mind not philosophical abstractions, but sensuous images. On the other hand, for the purposes of classification and philosophy the purely English part of our language is deficient. It would not be easy to find English equivalents for such words as 'impenetrability,' 'incomprehensibility,' 'relation,' &c. 'We particularize and define things in Anglo-Saxon; we generalize and define abstractions in words of classic origin.' (Dr. Angus.)

273. The following extract[1] is from a poem called 'The Beowulf,' which is supposed to have been brought over by the English from the continent, but was not reduced to writing until the tenth century. It had probably by this time been considerably modernized.

Cwædon thæt he wære	[They] said that he was
wyrold-cyninga	of the kings of the world
manna mildusta	of men mildest
and mon-thwærust,	and gentlest,
leodu lithost	to his people the most gracious
and leof-geornost	and for glory the most eager.

274. In order that the learner may compare Old and Modern English the more closely, a passage of the Old English Gospels with an interlinear translation is subjoined.

Thys Godspel gebyrath to ealra halgena mæssan.
This Gospel befits to of-all saints [the] mass.

Sothlice[2] tha se Hælend geseah tha mæniw he
Truly when the Healer saw the many [multitude], he

astah[3] on thone múnt: and tha he sæt tha genealæhton his
ascended into the mount: and when he sat then near-drew his

leorning-cnihtas to him: and he ontynde[4] his muth
learning-knights [disciples] to him: and he opened his mouth

and lærde[5] hig, and cwæth: Eadige synd tha gastlican
and taught them, and quoth: Blessed are the ghostly [spiritu-

---

[1] Quoted by Professor Meiklejohn (*Book of the English Language*).

[2] *Sothlice.* From *sóth*, truth. Comp. forsooth, soothsayer, in sooth.

[3] *Astah.* From *astigan*, to mount. Comp. stirrup [O.E. stíg-ráp, a mounting rope].

[4] *Ontynde.* From *ontynan*, to open.

[5] *Lærde.* From *læran*, to teach. Comp. Ger. *lehren*, to teach.

thearfan[1]; fortham heora[2] ys heofena[3] ríce.[4]
ally]   poor;   because theirs is of-the-heavens the-kingdom.

Eadige synd[5] tha the nu wepath[6]; fortham the hi beoth[7]
Blessed are those who now weep; because that they be

gefrefrode. Eadige synd tha líthan; fortham the hig eorthan ágan.
comforted. Blessed are the meek; because that they earth own.

Eadige synd tha the rihtwisnesse hingriath and thyrstath;
Blessed are those who rightcousness hunger [after] and thirst

fortham the hig beoth[8] gefyllede. Eadige synd tha
[after]; because that they be filled. Blessed are the

mild-heortan; fortham the hig mild-heort-nysse begytath.
mild-hearted; because that they mild-hearted-ness get [obtain].

Eadige synd tha clǽn-heortan; fortham the hig God geseoth.
Blessed are the clean-hearted; because that they God see.

Eadige synd tha gesibsuman[9]; fortham the hig beoth Godes
Blessed are the peace-loving; because that they be God's

bearn genemnde. Eadige synd tha the ehtnysse tholiath[10] for
bairns named. Blessed are those who persecution suffer for

rihtwisnysse; fortham the heora ys heofenan ríce.
righteousness; because that theirs is of-the-heavens the-kingdom.

Eadige synd ge thonne hig wyriath eow, and ehtath eow, and
Blessed are ye when they curse you, and persecute you, and

secgath ælc yfel ongean eow leogende, for me. Geblissiath[11]
say each evil against you lying, for me. Rejoice

and gefægniath[12]; fortham the eower mèd ys mycel on
and be-fain; because that your meed is much [great] in

---

[1] *Thearfan.* From *thearfa*, poor, destitute. Cp. Ger. *dürftig*.

[2] *Heora.* Gen. plu. of *he, heó, hit*; he, she, it.

[3] *Heofena.* Gen. plu. of *heofon*, heaven.

[4] *Ríce.* Comp. -*ric* in bishopric.

[5] *Synd.* Pres. indic. 1st per. plu. 'Are' came in with the Danes.

[6] *Wepath.* Pres. indic. 3rd per. plu.

[7] *Beoth gefrefrode.* Present used for future. There is no genuine future in O.E.

[8] See previous note.

[9] *Gesibsuman.* From *sib*, peace; *gesibsum*, peace-loving. *Sib* also = relation. Comp. *gossip*, i.e. godsib, related in God, the old name given to a sponsor in baptism.

[10] *Tholiath.* Indic. pres. 3rd per. plu. From *tholian*, to suffer (Sc. *thole*).

[11] *Geblissiath.* Comp. O.E. *blis*, bliss, joy.

[12] *Gefægniath.* Comp. *fain* = glad. 'Fair words make fools fain.'

heofenum: swa hig · ehton tha witegan,[1] the beforan eow
heaven: so they persecuted the prophets, which before you
wæron. Ge synd eorthan sealt; gif thæt sealt awyrth
were. Ye are of-the-earth [the] salt; if the salt exist-not
on tham the hit gesylt bith, hit ne mæg syththan[2] to
in that [with] which it salted is, it not is-good after for
nahte, buton thæt hit sy út-aworpen,[3] and sy fram
naught, but that it may-be out-cast, and may-be by
mannum fortreden. Ge synd middan-geardes leoht. Ne mæg seo
men, trodden. Ye are mid-earth's light. Not may the
ceaster[4] beon behyd, the byth uppan múnt aset. Ne
city be hid which is upon [a] mount set. Neither
hig ne ælath heora leoht-fæt[5] and hit under cyfe settath,
they not light their lamp and it under [a] bushel set,
ac ofer candel-stæf; thæt hit onlihte · eallum tham[6]
but upon [a] candle-staff; that it [may] light to-all those
the on tham huse synd. Swa onlihte eower leoht beforan
which in the house are. So shine your light before
mannum, thæt hig geseon eowre gódan weorc, and wuldrian
men, that they may-see your good works, and glorify
eowerne[7] Fæder the on heofenum ys.
your Father which in [the] heavens is.—Matt. v. (ed. Thorpe.)

THE KELTIC ELEMENT IN MODERN ENGLISH.

275. The relations of the Keltic group of languages may
be seen from the subjoined table :—

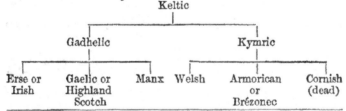

	Keltic		
Gadhelic		Kymric	
Erse or Irish	Gaelic or Highland Scotch	Manx	Welsh	Armorican or Brézonec	Cornish (dead)

[1] *Witegan.* Acc. plu. of *witéga,* a prophet, a declarer of judgment. [O.E. *wite,* affliction, punishment, a fine.]
[2] *Syththan.* Comp. *since* (M.E. sithence).
[3] *Aworpen.* From *worpian,* to cast, throw.
[4] *Ceaster.* From the Latin *castra,* a camp. Comp. Chester, Lancaster, &c. [5] *Fæt,* a vessel. Comp. *vat.*
[6] *Eallum tham.* Dat. plu. of *eall,* and the definite article, *se, seó, thæt.*
[7] *Eowerne.* Acc. sing. of *eower,* the poss. case of *ge* (ye).

The language spoken by the Ancient Britons is now represented by Welsh. We might have expected that, when the English came over to this country, their language would be largely enriched by the language of the conquered Britons, if not absorbed by it; but, as a matter of fact, very few Keltic words were admitted into English in early times. The Britons would appear to have been, for the most part, either slaughtered or driven before their victorious foes. It has been conjectured that the English occasionally married British wives and employed British women as servants, most of the Keltic words introduced into English being connected with the kitchen and menial occupations, e.g. *crock, clout, cradle, darn, mop.*

The Keltic element in Modern English includes:—

1. Geographical names given by the Britons themselves.

Rivers: *Aron* (the name of fourteen rivers in Great Britain), *Exe* (of which Axe, Esk, Usk, and Ux, all meaning water, are various forms), *Ouse, Thames, Dee, Don,* &c.

Mountains and hills: *Penmaenmawr, Mendip, Malvern, Chiltern,* &c.

Counties: *Glamorgan, Kent* (cant = a corner, comp. 'cantle:' 'Cut me a huge cantle out,' *Hen. IV.*), *Cornwall,* &c.

Islands: *Arran, Bute, Mull, Man,* &c.

Towns: *Penzance, Penrith, Cardiff, Caerleon, Carlisle, Caernarvon,* &c.

2. Keltic components of geographical names.

Aber (mouth of a river): *Abergavenny, Aberdeen,* &c.

Ard (high): *Ardnamurchan, Lizard,* the high fort

Auchin (field): *Auchinleck*

Bal (a village): *Balmoral*

Ben (mountain): *Ben Nevis, Ben Macdui.* The Welsh form is *Pen,* e.g. *Pen-y-gant*

Blair (a clearing): *Blair Athol*

Brae (rough ground): *Braemar*

Caer (fort): *Caermarthen, Carlisle*

Cairn (a heap of stones): *Cairngorm*

Combe (Welsh, cwm, pronounced coom, a valley): *Ilfracombe, Crwmbrân, Crwmyoy,* &c.

Craig, Carrick, Crick (a craggy hill): *Craigputtock, Carrickfergus, Crickhowell*

Dun (hill): *Dumbarton*

Inch[1] or Ennis (island): *Inchcape*

Inver (another form of Aber = a mouth of a river): *Inverary*

---

[1] Scott uses *inch* as a common noun:—

'The blackening wave is edged with white,
To *inch* and rock the sea-mews fly.'

Kill (cell, chapel): *Kilgerran*
Lin (a pool): *Linton,* *indale*
Llan (a sacred enclosure): *Llan-
daff, Lampeter, Launceston*
(Church of St. Stephen)

Strath (broad valley): *Strath-
more*
Tre (town): *Oswestry* (town of
St. Oswald)

3. Words derived directly from the Welsh.

4. Words derived through Norman French from the Keltic language spoken in France.

It is not always easy to separate classes (3) and (4), the evidence supplied by O. E. literature being too limited to be decisive on the subject. The following[1] is a list of words from both sources:—

Balderdash (baldorddus, *prating*)
Barrow (berfa, *a mound*)
Basket (basgawd)
Bill (bwyell, *hatchet*)
Bogie, bug-bear (bwg, *hobgoblin*)
Bran (bràn, *skin of wheat*)
Cabin (cab, caban, *hut*)
Carol (carawl, *love-song*)
Chine (cefn, *back*)
Clout (clwt, *patch*)
Coble (ceubal, *boat*)
Cock in *cock*boat (cwch, *boat*)
Cocker (cockru, *to indulge*)
Cower (cwrian, *to squat*)
Crimp (crim, *crimp, ridge*)
Crisp (crisb, *crisp*)
Crockery (crochan, *pot*)
Crook (crog, *hook*)
Crowd (crwth, *fiddle*)
Cudgel (cog, *truncheon*; cogel, *short staff*)
Cuts = lots (cwtws, *lots*)
Dainty (dantaeth, *choice morsel*)
Darn (darn, *patch*)
Dock (tociaw, *to cut short*)
Filly (filawg, *a young mare*)?
Flaw (fflaw, *splinter*)
Fleam (fflaim, *cattle-lancet*)
Flummery (llymry, *jelly made with oatmeal*). For the *fl* cp. Fluellen for Llewellyn.

Frieze (ffris, *nap of cloth*)
Fudge (fug, *deception*)
Funnel (ffynel, *chimney*)
Garter (gardas, from gar, *shank,* tas, *tie*)
Glen (glyn, *valley*)
Goal (gwyal, *mark*)
Goblin (coblyn, *a sprite*)
Gown (gwn)
Griddle (greidell, *iron baking-plate*)
Gruel (grual)
Grumble (grymialu, *to murmur,*)
Gyve (gefyn, *fetter*)
Harlot (herlawd, *youth*; herlodes, *hoyden*)
Hawk (hochi, *to expectorate*)
Hem (hem)
Hitch (hecian, *to halt*)
Hog (hwch, *swine*)
Hoyden (hoeden, *flirt*)
Kex (cecys, *hemlock*)
Kick (cic, *foot*; ciciaw, *to kick*)
Kiln (cyl, cylyn)
Knell (cnul, *passing bell*)
Knob (cnap, *button*; cnwb, *knob*)
Knock (cnoc, *rap*)
Knoll (cnòl, *hillock*)
Lad (llawd, *youth*)
Lass (llodes, *girl*)
Lath (llath)

---

[1] Selected from the list given in Garnett's *Philological Essays.*

Lukewarm (lug, *partial*). This derivation is doubtful. Cp. O.E. *wlæc*, tepid

Mattock (matog)

Mesh (masg, *stitch in netting*)

Mop (mop)

Muggy (mwygl, *sultry*)

Nudge (nugiaw, *to shake*)

Pail (paeol, *pail* or *pot*)

Pan (pan, *cup* or *bowl*)

Paunch (paneg, penygen, *entrails*)

Peck (peg, peged, *a measure*)

Pellet (peled, *a little ball*)

Piggin (picyn, *a small hooped vessel*)

Pimple (pwmp, *round mass*; pwmpl, *knob*)

Pitch (piciaw, *to throw*)

Pottage (potes, *a cooked mess*)

Rail (rhail, *fence*)

Rasher (rhasg, *slice*)

Rim (rhim, *raised edge* or *border*)

Rug (rhuwch, *rough garment*)

Size (syth, *glue*)

Smooth (esmwyth, *even, soft*)

Soak (soegi, *to steep*)

Solder (sawduriaw, *to join, cement*)

Stook (ystwc, *shock of corn*)

Tackle (tacl, *instrument, tool*)

Tall (tal, *lofty*)

Tarry (tariaw, *to loiter*)

Task (tasg, *a job*)

Tassel (tasel, *fringe, tuft*)

Ted = *to spread hay* (teddu, *to spread*)

Tenter (deintur, *frame for stretching cloth*)

Tinker (tincerdd, literally *tail-trade, lowest craft*)

Toss (tosiaw, *to throw*)

Trace (tres, *chain* or *strap for drawing*)

Trip (tripiaw, *to stumble*)

Vassal (gwas, *youth, servant*)

Wain (gwain, *carriage*)

Wall (gwall, *rampart*)

Want (chwant, *desire*)

Wed (gweddu, *to yoke, marry*)

Welt (gwald, *hem, border*)

Wicket, Fr. guichet (guiced, *little door*)

Many Keltic words formerly existing in the language have become obsolete or survive only in provincial dialects : *cam* (crooked); *imp* (to engraft) ; *kern* (a light-armed Keltic soldier); *crowd*, a fiddle ; *bug*, a ghost (comp. *bug-bear*); *cuts* in the phrase ' to draw cuts,' i.e. lots. Others survive only in provincial dialects : *kephyll*, a horse (Craven dialect); *cocker*, to fondle (Lanc.); *flasket*, a basket (Lanc. and Devon.).

5. Words derived from various Keltic sources in modern times—

bard	clan	kilt	pony	shillelagh
bog	claymore	pibroch	reel	slogan
brogue	fillibeg	plaid	shamrock	whiskey

276. The Scandinavian Element in Modern English.— The name Scandinavian is applied somewhat loosely to Denmark, Norway, and Sweden. From the close of the eighth to the close of the tenth century, people from these countries—commonly known as Danes, Northmen, Norsemen, and Normans—made descents upon various parts of the coasts of England, Scotland, Ireland, and France, and ultimately a Danish dynasty obtained possession of the English throne. Their first appearance in this country is thus recorded in the 'A. S. Chronicle' under the year A.D. 787 : 'This year took King Beorhtric King Offa's daughter to wife. And in his days came first three ships of Northmen from Hæretha (?) land. And then the reeve thereto rode, and them would drive to the king's town, because he wist not what they were; and him they there slew. These were the first ships of Danish men that the land of the English people sought.' In 867 the Danish invasions were resumed with greater vigour, and in 878 Alfred concluded a treaty with Guthorm, the Danish leader, by which he ceded to the Danes all the country lying along the eastern coast from the Thames to the Forth, together with a large part of the midlands. 'The boundary ran along the Thames to the mouth of the Lea, then by Bedford and the river Ouse to the old Roman road called Watling Street.' (Freeman.) The territory occupied by the Danes was thenceforward known as the Danelagh. In 1013 Sweyn, King of Denmark, successfully invaded England, and added it to his dominions. His descendants retained possession of the English throne until A.D. 1042.

277. As the Danes were, like the English, a Teutonic people, it is not always easy to distinguish between words of English and of Scandinavian origin. The Scandinavian element in modern English includes—

1. **Geographical names** (chiefly in the East and North of England and round the coast)—

Ark, a *temple* or *altar* : *Arkholme, Grimsargh.*
Beck, a *brook* : *Holbeck, Beckford, Wansbeck* (Woden's beck).
By, a *town* : *Grimsby* (Grim's town), *Whitby* (White town), *Tenby* (Dane's town).

There are in England over 600 towns with names ending in -*by*. Of these 200 are in Lincolnshire and 150 in Yorkshire. Only one is found south of the Thames.

Dal, a *valley* : *Scarsdale.*
Ey or ea, *island* (comp. Faroe = Sheep Islands; Stromsoe = Stream island) : *Orkney, Sheppey, Selsey* (Seals' island).
Fell, a *rock-hill* (comp. Norsk *fjeld*, Dovrefjeld) : *Scawfell, Snafell, Cross Fell, Goat Fell.*

Force, *waterfall* (comp. Norsk foss, as in Vöring Foss, Mörk Foss): *Scale Force, Low Force.*

Ford, forth, firth, an *inlet of the sea* (comp. Norsk fiord): *Firth of Forth, Seaforth, Milford.*

Garth, *enclosure* (comp. Norsk gaard): *Applegarth, Fishguard.*

Gate, *way*: *Sandgate.*

Gill, a *ravine*, a small gravelly stream: *Eskgill, Ormesgill.*

Holm, an *island* (comp. Bornholm in the Baltic): *Langholm, Steep Holm* (Bristol Channel).

Kirk, *church*: *Kirkby, Ormskirk, Kirkcudbright* (= St. Cuthbert's church).

There are altogether forty-one towns in England having names that begin with *kirk-*. Of these seventeen are in Yorkshire and seven in Lincolnshire.

Ness, a *headland*: *Dungeness, Sheerness.*

Scar, scarth, a *steep rock*: *Scarborough, Scarsdale, Gate Scarth.*

Skip, a *ship*: *Skipwith, Skipsea, Skipton.*

Suther, sutter, sodor, *south*: *Sutherland, Sutterby, Sodor.*

Tarn, a *mountain lake*: *Loughrigg-Tarn, Flat-Tarn.*

Thing, ting, ding, a *place of meeting*: *Thingwall, Tingwall, Dingwall.* Cp. *husting* (hús-thing).

Thorpe, thorp, throp, drop, a *village*: *Bishopsthorpe, Burnham-thorpe, Milnthrop, Staindrop.*

Toft, a *small field*: *Lowestoft.*

Wig, wick, wich, a *small creek* or *bay*: *Wigtoft, Greenwich, Norwich, Sandwich, Ipswich, Wick, Berwick.*

With, *wood*: *Langwith.*

2. Names of Persons.—The termination *-son* is Danish: *Anderson, Swainson.*

3. Words in common use—

are	bustle	daze	flimsy	ling	same
bait	cake	die	fro	loft	scold
blunt	call	din	gait	lubber	sky
boil	carouse	doze	gust	lurk	slant
bole	cast	droop	husting	muck	slush
box (blow)	chime	drub	ill	odd	sly
bray	curl	dwell	irk	pudding	ugly
braze	dairy	earl	kid	rap	whim
buckle-to	dash	fellow	kindle	root	weak

The following Scandinavian words are either obsolete or used only in provincial dialects:

at, *to*, as a sign of the gerundial infinitive	gar, to *make*
	greet, *cry*
boun, *ready*	lowe, *flame*
busk, *prepare*	neif, a *fist*
flit, to *change houses*	shaw, a *small wood*

The phonetic decay of O.E. in the tenth century is doubtless to be mainly ascribed to the Danish invasions.

THE LATIN ELEMENT IN MODERN ENGLISH.

278. The Romans occupied Britain for about four hundred years. The Latin introduced by the Romans themselves has been called *Latin of the First Period*. The Latin brought in through intercourse with the Church of Rome between the coming over of St. Augustine and the Norman Conquest is called *Latin of the Second Period*. The Latin that came to us through the Normans in the corrupt form of Norman French is called *Latin of the Third Period*. The Latin that has been introduced by scholars since the revival of learning (latter part of the fifteenth century) is called *Latin of the Fourth Period*.

I. LATIN OF THE FIRST PERIOD, A.D. 43–410.

279. .The words of Latin origin that have survived from this period are connected with the military stations and the great Roman roads. They are only six in number—

Castra, a camp : *Lancaster, Castor, Caistor, Chester, Bicester, Gloucester, Exeter* (Ex-cester).
Colonia, a colony : *Lincoln*.
Fossa, a trench : *Fossway, Fossbury, Fossdyke*.
Portus, a harbour : *Porchester, Portsmouth*.
Strata, a paved way : *Strutton, Stradbrook, Ystrad* (common in Wales), *Stretton, Streatham, Street*.
Vallum, a rampart : *Wallbury* (Essex), *Wall Hill* (Hereford-shire), both old Roman forts.

II. LATIN OF THE SECOND PERIOD, A.D. 596–1066.

280. The close connection between the Church of England and the Church of Rome, consequent upon the mission of St. Augustine, the translation into English of Latin books, and the growing commerce of England with southern Europe, led to the introduction of a large number of words of classical origin. These consisted mainly of

(a) Ecclesiastical terms—

altar (altare)
ark (arca), a chest
candle (candela)
chalice (calix), a cup,
  O.E. calc
chapter (caput)
cloister (claustrum),
  a shut place. Lat.
  claudo, I shut. O.E.
  clustor

cowl (cucullus)
creed (credo)
cross (crux)
disciple (discipulus)
feast (festus)
font (fons)
mass (missa), O.E.
  mæsse
offer (offero)
pagan (paganus)

pall (pallium), a cloak
porch (porticus)
preach (prædicare).
  O.E. predician
sacrament (sacra-
  mentum)
saint (sanctus). O.E.
  sanct

The following are of Greek origin, but came to us first
in Latin forms.

alms (eleemosyna)
anchorite (anchorita),
  a hermit
apostle (apostolus).
  O.E. postol
bishop (episcopus),
  an overseer. O.E.
  biscop
canon (canon)
clerk (clericus), a
  person chosen by
  lot (kleros)

deacon (diaconus), a
  servant
heretic (hæreticus).
  Haireo, I choose
hymn (hymnus)
martyr (martyr), a
  witness
minster (monasteri-
  um). O.E. mynster
monk (monachus).
  O.E. munce

priest (presbyterus).
  O.E. preost
psalm (psalma)
psalter (psalterium)
stole (stola), a robe
synod (synodus), a
  coming together

(b) Names of foreign animals, trees, plants, &c.—

agate (gagates).
  Originally Gk.
anise (anisum). Orig.
  Gk.
beet (beta)
box (buxus)
camel (camelus).
  Orig. Gk.
cedar (cedrus)
cherry (cerasus)
crystal (crystallum).
  Orig. Gk.
cucumber (cucumis)
elephant (elephas).
  O.E. olfend
elm (ulmus)
fig (ficus)

hellebore (hellebo-
  rus). Orig. Gk.
laurel (laurus)
lettuce (lactuca)
lily (lilium)
lion (leo)
mallow (malva)
marble (marmor)
millet (milium)
mule (mulus)
oyster (ostrea)
palm (palma)
pard (pardus). Orig.
  Gk.
peach (persicum)
peacock (pavo)
pear (pirum)

pearl (perla)
pease (pisum)
pepper (piper)
phœnix (phœnix).
  Orig. Gk.
pine (pinus)
pumice (pumex)
rue (ruta)
sponge (spongia).
  Orig. Gk.
sycamore (sycamo-
  rus). Orig. Gk.
tiger (tigris)
trout (tructa)
turtle (turtur)
vulture (vultur)

(c) Miscellaneous words—

acid (acidus), sharp
anchor (ancora)
axle (axis)
belt (balteus)
bench (bancus)
bile (bilis)
butter (butyrum
castle (castellum)
chancellor (cancella-rius)
cheese (caseus)
chest (cista)
circle (circulus)
city (civitas)
cook (coquus)
coulter (culter)
crest (crista)
crisp (crispus)
crown (corona)
cymbal (cymbalum) Orig. Gk.
ell (ulna)

empire (imperium)
epistle (epistola). Orig. Gk.
fever (febris)
fork (furca)
gem (gemma)
giant (gigas). Orig. Gk.
grade (gradus)
inch (uncia)
metre (metrum). Orig. Gk.
mile (mille)
mint (moneta)
mortar (mortarium)
muscle (musculus)
nurse (nutrix)
ounce (uncia)
palace (palatium)
philosopher (philo-sophus). Orig. Gk.
plant (planta)

plaster (plastrum). Orig. Gk.
plume (pluma)
pound (pondus)
prove (probo)
provost (præpositus)
purple (purpur)
rheum (rheuma). Orig. Gk.
rule (regula)
sack (saccus)
school (schola). Orig. Gk.
senate (senatus)
spade (spatha)
table (tabula)
temple (templum)
theatre (theatrum). Orig. Gk.
title (titulus)
tunic (tunica)
verse (versus)

III. LATIN ELEMENT OF THE THIRD PERIOD, A.D. 1066–1480.

281. The Normans who invaded England in 1066 had previously invaded France (A.D. 876), and had settled in that part of the country that we now call Normandy. They soon gave up their own language in France and adopted French, a language containing various Teutonic and Keltic elements, but consisting mainly of debased Latin. When they established themselves in England they brought with them their new language. French would appear to have been the language commonly used by our English kings right down to the end of the fourteenth century. Professor Craik says that 'it is not known that, with the exception of Richard II., any of them ever did or could speak English.' The influence of the court, however, was trivial by the side of that exerted by the large body of Normans who came over with the Conqueror, and by the constant stream of communication that was kept up with France so long as we retained our continental possessions. 'A very great number of Normans, all speaking French, were brought over and settled

in the kingdom.   There were the military forces, by which
the conquest was achieved and maintained, both those in
command and the private soldiers ; there was a vast body of
churchmen spread over the land, and occupying eventually
every ecclesiastical office in it, from the primacy down to
that of the humblest parish or chapel priest, besides half
filling, probably, all the monastic establishments ; there were
all the officers of state and inferior civil functionaries down
to nearly the lowest grade ; finally, there were, with few
exceptions, all the landholders, great and small, throughout the kingdom.   The members of all these classes and
their families must have been at first entirely ignorant of
English, and they and their descendants would naturally
continue for a longer or shorter time to use only the language
of their ancestors.'[1]

French soon came to be exclusively used in the pleadings
in the higher law-courts.   All the new laws were promulgated in Latin until 1272, when they began to be drawn up
sometimes in Latin but more frequently in French.   After
1487 they were promulgated in English.

Thus, for some hundreds of years, French was spoken by
the most influential classes of the country—by the Court,
by the landowners, by the clergy, by the lawyers, and by
their attendants.   It ought not to surprise us, therefore,
that during this period large numbers of French words found
their way into the language.   But though we borrowed
largely from the French in our vocabulary, we did not borrow
from it at all in our grammar.   Our laws of inflexion and
syntax did, indeed, during this period undergo great changes,
but it was not through the substitution of the laws of French
grammar for those of our own.   English remained English,
and by degrees was adopted by the Normans themselves.

282.   The loss of our French possessions in the reign of
King John must have greatly contributed to naturalize the
Anglo-Normans in England, and to weaken their hold of the
French language.   Craik dates the decline of the French
language in England to the strong anti-French feeling en-
gendered by the French wars of Edward III.   Certain it is
that the decline went on at a very rapid rate from the
middle of the fourteenth century.   Higden, writing towards

[1] *Outlines of the Hist. of the Eng. Lang.,* p. 46.

the close of the century, informs us that in 1349 boys were no longer required to learn their Latin through French.[1] In 1362 English was substituted for French and Latin in our courts of law.

It should be noted that Latin words coming to us through French have, for the most part, undergone very considerable contraction.

They consist of—

(a) **Terms connected with Feudalism, War, and the Chase—**

aid	buckler	fealty	leash	relief	trumpet
armour	captain	forest	mail	scutage	truncheon
arms	chivalry	guardian	march	scutcheon	vassal
array	couple	harness	mew	sport	venison
assault	covert	herald	palfrey	squirrel	vizor
banner	dower	homage	peer	standard	war
battle	esquire	joust	quarry	tallage	ward
brace	falcon	lance	reclaim	tenant	warden

---

[1] 'This apayringe (*disparaging*) of the birthe tonge is bycause of tweye thinges: oon is for children in scole, agenes the usage and maner of all other naciouns beth (*are*) compelled for to leve her (*their*) own langage, and for to construewe her (*their*) lessouns and her (thingis) a Frensche, and haveth siththe (*since*) that the Normans come first into England. Also gentil mennes children beth ytaught for to speke Frensche from the tyme that thei beth (*are*) rokked in her (*their*) cradel, and kunneth (*can*) speke and playe with a childes brooche. And uplondish (*upstart*) wol likne hemself to gentil men, and fondeth with gret bisynesse for to speke Frensche, for to be the more ytold of. This maner was myche yused to-fore the first moreyn (*murrain*, the Great Plague of 1348), and is siththe (*since*) some del ychaungide. For John Cornwaile, a maistre of grammer, chaungide the lore (*teaching*) in grammer scole, and construction of Frensch into Englisch, and Richard Pencricke lerned that maner [of] teching of him, and other men of Pencricke. So that now, the yere of our lord a thousand three hundred four score and fyve, of the secunde King Rychard after the Conquest nyne, in alle the gramer scoles of Englond children leveth (*leave*) Frensch, and construeth and lerneth an (*in*) Englisch, and haveth therby avauntage in oon side and desavauntage in another. Her (*their*) avauntage is, that thei lerneth her (*their*) gramer in lesse tyme than children were wont to do. Desavauntage is, that now children of gramer scole kunneth (*knoweth*) no more Frensch than can her lifte heele (*their left heel*). And that is harm for hem (*them*) and (*if*) thei schul passe the see and travaile in strange londes, and in many other places [cases?] also. Also gentil men haveth now much ylefte for to teche her (*their*) children Frensch.'- From Trevisa's Translation of Higden's *Polychronicon*, i. 59.

T

(b) Legal terms—

advocate	case	estate	larceny	plaintiff	statute
annoy	chancellor	fee	mulct	plea	suit
approver	contract	felony	nuisance	prison	summons
arrest	court	judge	paramount	puisne	surety
assize	damage	justice	parliament	sentence	trespass
attorney	dowry				

(c) Titles—

baron	constable	duke	lieutenant	mayor	usher
chancellor	count	equerry	marquis	prince	viscount

(d) Terms connected with the Church—

baptism	charity	homily	piety	religion	sermon
Bible	devotion	idolatry	pilgrim	sacrifice	tonsure
ceremony	friar	penance	relic		

(e) Terms connected with Domestic Life, Cooking, Dress, &c.—

attire	broil	curtain	lace	pork	sturgeon
beef	chair	dress	mutton	salmon	veal
boil	chamber	furniture	pantry	sausage	veil
boot	costume	garment	parlour		

(f) Terms connected with the Family—

aunt	consort	cousin	parent	spouse	uncle

Over and above the terms belonging to these classes, large numbers of French words must have been introduced by the numerous imitators and translators of French books, by foreign craftsmen who settled in England, by traders with the continent, by scientific men, and by soldiers who had returned from the French wars.

IV. LATIN ELEMENT OF THE FOURTH PERIOD. FROM A.D. 1480.

283. The revival of learning, the invention of printing, the great religious and political controversies of the sixteenth and seventeenth centuries, the study of science and philosophy, and the almost exclusive study of classical literature in our grammar schools and universities, have all contributed in various ways to swell the Latin element in the English language during the last 400 years. The Latin words of this period are mainly taken from the Latin direct, and are readily recognised by the little alteration that they have undergone, as compared with Latin words that have come to us through the French. In some instances the same word has come to us in both ways. In such cases we have almost invariably given the derivatives slightly different meanings. Comp.—

Latin	English Derivative coming direct	English Derivative coming through French
ratio	ratio *and* ration	reason
potio	potion	poison
lectio	lection	lesson
traditio	tradition	treason
securus	secure	sure
benedictio	benediction	benison
oratio	oration	orison
persequor	persecute	pursue
balsamum	balsam	balm
pœnitentia	penitence	penance
superficies	superficies	surface
legalis	legal	loyal

CHANGES IN LATIN WORDS.

284. The most important specific changes which Latin words undergo in passing through French are the following.

1. Loss of letters in the beginning of words (*Aphœresis*)—

adamas	diamant	diamond
hemikrania (ἡμικρανία)	migraine	megrim = a pain affecting one side of the head
oryza	riz	rice

2. Loss of letters in the body of words (*Syncope*). The *accented* or *tonic* vowel, as it is called, in the Latin word always remains unchanged. The *unaccented* or atonic vowel, if short, whether occurring immediately before or after the tonic vowel, disappears. When two consonants occur together in the Latin word, the first usually disappears in the derivative, e.g. captivus, chétif; when a consonant occurs between two vowels, it usually disappears in the derivative, e.g. crudelis, cruel.

(*a*) *Syncope of vowels*—

computare	compter	count	positura	posture	posture
oraculum	oracle	oracle	tabula	table	table

(b) Syncope of consonants—.

alligare	allier	ally		invidere	envier	envy
antiphona	antienne	anthem		mutare	muer	mew (to
crudelis	cruel	cruel				moult)
denegare	dénier	deny		obedire	obéir	obey
desiderare	désirer	desire		plicare	plier	ply
dotare	douer	dower		precari	prier	pray
duplicare	doubler	double		regalis	royal	royal
frigere	frire	fry		rotundus	rond	round
implicare	employer	employ		vivenda	viande	viand

3. Loss of the final syllable (*Apocope*)—

aim (æstimare)	inch (uncia)	rest (restare)
aunt (amita)	join (jungere)	round (rotundus)
beast (bestia)	joy (gaudium)	rule (regula)
blame (blasphemia)	lace (laqueus)	safe (salvus)
chafe (calefacere)	male (masculus)	scan (scandere)
chain (catena)	mix (miscere)	scent (sentire)
count (computare)	pain (pœna)	seal (sigillum)
cue (cauda)	paint (pingere)	sound (sonus)
cull (colligere)	pay (pacare)	space (spatium)
dame (domina)	plait (plectere)	spice (species)
dress (dirigere)	point (punctum)	spoil (spolium)
face (facies)	poor (pauper)	strain (stringere)
feign (fingere)	porch (porticus)	sue (sequor)
fig (ficus)	praise (pretiare)	sure (securus)
found (fundere)	preach (prædicare)	test (testis)
frail (fragilis)	price (pretium)	treat (tractare)
fry (frigere)	prove (probare)	veal (vitulus)
glaive (gladius)	quiet (quietus)	vice (vitium)
gout (gutta)	ray (radius)	view (videre)
heir (hæres)		

4. Change of vowels—

ă	acer	aigre	eager	ĕ	lacĕrta	lézard	lizard
	grătum	gré	mau*gre*		mĕrcan-	marchand	merchant
ĭ	mănus	main	main-tain		tem		
	măcer	maigre	meagre		fĕrus	fier	fierce
	căput	chef	chief	ī	dīluvium	déluge	deluge
	săl	sel	salt-*cel*lar	ĭ	pĭrum	poire	pear
			(salière)		intrare	entrer	enter
ē	rēgalis	royal	royal		insigne	enseigne	ensign
	vēna	veine	vein		crīsta	crête	crest
	frēnum	frein	*re*frain		lingua	langue	language
	vēlum	voile	veil		bĭlancem	balance	balance
	prevalēre	prévaloir	prevail		silvaticus	sauvage	savage
	retinej	retenir	retain	ŏ	hŏra	heure	hour

ŏ	prŏbare	prouver	prove	gŭber-nare	gouverner	govern
	cŏrium	cuir	{ cuirass / currier	gutta	goutte	gout
	cŏpula	couple	couple	abund-are	abonder	abound
	fŏlium	feuille	foil			
	post	puis	pu-ny (puis né)	turris	tour	tower
				musca	mousse	moss
ŭ	cŭbare	couver	covey	œ cælum	ciel	ceiling

5. Syllabic changes.—*a*. The double consonant ct be-comes it after a vowel—

conductum	conduit	conduit	fructus	fruit	fruit
factus	fait	feat	lactuca	laitue	lettuce
tractare	traiter	treat	biscoctus	biscuit	biscuit
punctum	point	point			

b. *Al* is often softened into *au*, and *el* into *eau*—

salvus	sauf	safe	galbinus	jaune	*jaun*dice
saltus	saut	somer*sault*	bellus	beau	*beau*tiful

c. *Ol* and *ul* are often softened into *ou*—

pulverem	poudre	powder	culter	coutre	coulter
collocare	coucher	couch			

6. Change of consonants.

Interchange of b, p, f, v (labials).

capulum	câble	cable	ebur	ivoire	ivory
curvare	courber	curb	bos, bovis	bœuf	beef
deliberare	délivrer	deliver	ripa	rive	ar*riv*e
gubernare	gouverner	govern	paravere-dus	palefroi	palfrey
recipere	recevoir	receive			
cooperire	couvrir	cover	caballus	cheval	*cheva*lier
febris	fièvre	fever			{ van
fiber	bièvre	beaver	ab ante	avant	*vaunt*-courier
sapor	saveur	savour			
brevis	bref	brief	probare	prouver	prove
pauper	pauvre	poor			

Interchange of p, b, and v, with g soft.

This takes place when *b* is followed by *ia, io, ea,* or *ea*. The *i* was sounded like *j*, and ultimately passed into *g*.

pipionem	pigeon	pigeon	rabies	rage	rage
cambiare	changer	change	lumbus	longe	loin
abbreviare	abréger	abridge	diluvium	déluge	deluge
cavea	cage	cage	salvia	sauge	sage

Interchange of c hard with g.

locare	loger	lodge	crassus	gros	gross
acer	aigre	eager	sugere	sucer	suck
		(sharp)	aquila	aigle	eagle
macer	maigre	meagre	cupelletum	gobelet	goblet

Change of c into ch.

cantare	chanter	chant	castus	chaste	chaste
carmen	charme	charm	camera	chambre	chamber
caput	chef	chief			

Interchange of c soft, s, and t.

racemus	raisin	raisin	gratia	grâce	grace
ratio	raison	reason	satio	saison	season
factio	façon	fashion	placere	plaisir	pleasure

Interchange of d, soft g, and j.

jungere	joindre	join	gaudere	jouir	en*joy*
judex	juge	judge	gemellus	jumeau	{ gimmal
diurnalis	journal	journal			{ gimbals
stadium	étage	stage			

Interchange of l, m, n, r (liquids).

lazulus	azur	azure	scandalum	esclandre	slander
turtur	tourtre	turtle	cartula	chartre	charter
peregrinus	pélerin	pilgrim	capitulum	chapitre	chapter
cophinus	coffre	coffer	ordinem	ordre	order
mappa	nappe	napkin	pampinus	pampre	pamper
computare	conter	count (vb.)			

Interchange of x, s, and z.

exire	issu	issue	exagium	essai	essay
textus	tissu	tissue	duodecim	douze	dozen
oryza	riz	rice			

7. Insertion of letters :

At the beginning of a word (*Prosthesis*).

(1) *Vowels.*—The Gauls and other Keltic peoples appear to have had great difficulty in pronouncing initial *s* followed by *c, m, p,* or *t,* and to have been led, in consequence, to prefix an *e* to these combinations to render them easier of pronunciation.

status	état	estate
stabilire	établir	establish
specialis	O.F. especial	especial
scutum	écu (escu)	escutcheon (O.F. escusson); esquire (O.F. escuyer)
spondere	épouser	espouse
scala	escalade	escalade
spatula	espalier	espalier, epaulet

(2) *Consonants.*

altus	haut	hautboy, hauteur
ascia	hache	hatchet

b. In the middle of the word (*Epenthesis*)—

n laterna	lanterne	lantern
pictorem	peintre	painter
b numerare	nombrer	number
simulare	sembler	seem, re-semble
assimulare (Low Lat. to bring together, from *simul*)	assembler	assemble
tremulare	trembler	tremble
humilis	humble	humble
camera	chambre	chamber
d cinerem	cendre	cinder
tenerem	tendre	tender
genus	gendre	gender
pulverem	poudre	powder
ponere	poindre	com-*pound*
r perdricem	perdrix	partridge

c. At the end of a word (*Epithesis*)—

sine	sans	sans	certe	certes	certes

Many of the Latin words introduced into the language in the sixteenth and seventeenth centuries, such as *mansuetude, eluctate, ludibundness, stultiloquy, sanguinolency,* &c., were subsequently rejected as either needless or awkward. Words are still constantly formed from Latin roots for literary and scientific purposes, but the tendency of modern writers is to employ, wherever it is possible, words of purely English origin.

SPANISH AND PORTUGUESE ELEMENTS IN ENGLISH.

285. The vast dominions of Spain during the sixteenth century made its language very widely known. An examination of the words in the following list will show that they were introduced mainly from the Spanish settlements in the New World.

Spanish.

alligator (el lagarto, *the lizard*)

armada (armada, *an armed fleet*. Fem. of armado, p.p. of armar, *to arm*). Armadillo (the little armed one) is a dim. from the same source

barricade (barrica, *a barrel*)

battledore (batador, *a flat piece of wood with a handle for beating wet linen in washing*)

bravado (bravada, *ostentation*)

cannibal (an eater of flesh. From the Cannibals or Caribs, the original inhabitants of the West Indies)

caparison (caparazon, the carcase of a fowl, *the cover of a saddle*)

caracole (caracol, *a turn of a horse*)

carbonado (to score a piece of meat for cooking. Ultimately from Lat. carbo, *a burning coal*)

castanet (castaña, *a chestnut*. From the noise made by chestnuts when roasting)

chocolate (Mexican chocolatl, so called from the *cacao*-tree)

cigar (cigarro; originally a kind of tobacco grown in Cuba)

cochineal (cochinilla, *a wood-louse*. 'When the Spaniards came to America they transferred the name to the animal producing the scarlet dye, which somewhat resembles a wood-louse in shape.'—*Wedgwood*)

cork (corcho. Lat. cortex, *bark*).

creole (criar, *to create*)

desperado, one *despaired* of

dismay (desmayar, *to faint*)

duenna. (Ultimately from Lat. domina, *lady*)

El dorado (*the golden land*. A name given by the Spaniards to an imaginary city *of fabulous wealth* in the New World)

embargo (embargar, *to impede*)

embarrass (embarazar, *to hinder*)

filibuster (filibote, *a fast-sailing vessel*. A corruption of the English *fly-boat*)

filigree (filigrana. 'A kind of work in which the entire texture or *grain* of the material is made up of twisted gold or silver wire, from *filo*, wire, and *grano* = grain.'—*Wedgwood*)

flotilla (dim. of flota, *a fleet*)

grandee (grande, *great*)

grenade (granada, *pomegranate*. Lat. granum, *grain*). 'Grenadier' is from the same source

indigo (indico; literally *Indian*, most of the indigo of commerce coming from India)

jennet (ginete, *a nag*. Originally a horse-soldier. From 'Arab Zenáta, a tribe of Barbary celebrated for its cavalry.'—*Skeat*)

matador (the person who contends with the bull in bull-fights. From *matar*, to slay)

mosquito (mosca, *fly*. Lat. musca)

mulatto (mulato, offspring of white and black parents. Cp. *mule*)

negro (Lat. niger, black)

octoroon

pamphlet (papelete, *a written newspaper*). Skeat favours the derivation from Lat. *Pampila*, a female historian of the first century, who wrote numerous epitomes

olio (ola, a dish of different kinds of vegetables and meat. Lat. olla, *a pot*)

peccadillo (dim. of pecado, *a sin*)

picaroon (picaro, *a knave*)

port (Oporto)

punctilio (Lat. punctum, *point*)

quadroon (Lat. quatuor, *four*). The offspring of a white and a mulatto. Hence *quarter-blooded*

renegade = 'runagate' (Bible); an apostate

savannah (sabana, *a sheet*)

sherry (Xeres)

tornado (tornada, *a return*)

vanilla (vayna, *a knife-case*)

Portuguese.

albatross (alcatraz, *a sea-fowl*)

ayah

caste (casta, *race*. This from casta, *pure*, with reference to purity of blood)

cobra

cocoa-nut. 'Called coco by the Portuguese in India on account of the monkey-like face at the base of the nut, from *coco* a bug-bear, an ugly mask to frighten children.'—*Wedgwood*.

commodore (commendadôr, *a commander*)

fetish (feitiço, *sorcery, charm*)

marmalade (marmelada, from marmelo, *a quince*)

moidore (moeda d'ouro, *money of gold*)

palanquin (palanque, *a pole*)

palaver (palavra, *a word*)

tank (tanque, *a tank, pool*. Lat. stagnum)

yam

ITALIAN ELEMENT IN ENGLISH.

286. The introduction of Italian words in English is mainly to be referred to the following causes:—

a. The study of Italian literature, a literature which takes historical precedence of all the literatures of modern Europe. Italy had produced Dante, Petrarch, and Boccaccio long before any other European country could boast of any writer of distinction. From the time of Chaucer down to the time of Milton the literature of Italy exercised a powerful influence on that of England.

b. The study of Italian architecture and of the fine arts, as music, painting, and sculpture, in all of which Italy has long enjoyed the pre-eminence.

c. The importation of Italian manufactures.

alarm (all' arme, *to arms*)

alert (all' erta, ultimately from erectus, *raised up*)

alto

ambassador (ultimately from Gothic andbahts, servant)

ambuscade (bosco, *bush*)

bagatelle (bagatella, *a trifle*)

balcony (balco, *an out-jutting corner of a house*)

baldacchino. See § 291

ball (ballare, *to dance*)

ballad (ballare, *to dance*)

balloon (augmentative from balla, *ball*. Cp. saloon from sala)

balustrade (balaustro, *a small pillar*; so called from its resemblance to the flower of the wild pomegranate tree, *balausto*)

bandit (under a ban)

bankrupt (banco, a money-changer's bench; rotto, Lat. ruptus, *broken*. When a banker failed his bench at the public bourse was broken)

banquet (dim. of banco, *bench*)

biretta

bosky (see Ambuscade)

bravado

bravo

brigade (brigata, *a company*)

brigantino, brigand (briga, *strife*)

brocade = embroidered

broccoli (plur. of broccolo, *a sprout*)

bronze

buffoon (buffare, *to jest*)

burlesque (burlare, *to make a jest of*)

bust (busto, *a bust, stays, boddice*)

cadence (cadenza)

caitiff (cattivo, *captive*; hence *wretched*)

cameo

cannon (cannone, *a large pipe*. Lat. canna, *a reed*)

canteen (cantina, *wine-vault*)

canto (cantare, *to sing*)

caprice (capra, *goat*. 'A movement of the mind as unaccountable as the springs and bounds of a goat.'—*Trench.*)

captain (capitano, *head-man*. Lat. caput, *head*)

caricature (an overloaded representation of anything; caricare, *to load*)

carnival (carnovale. Mid. Lat. carnis levamen, *solace of the flesh*)

cartoon (cartone. Aug. of carta, *paper*)

cascade (cascata, from cascare, *to fall*)

casemate (casa, *house*; matto, *foolish*, '*dummy*.' 'Hence the sense is dummy-chamber, or dark chamber.'—*Skeat*)

casino (casino, *summer-house*; dim. of casa, *house*)

catafalque

cavalcade (cavallo, *horse*)

charlatan (ciarlare, *to chatter*)

citadel (citadella. Dim. of citta, *city*)

colonnade

companion (compagno, originally *a messmate*. From Lat. panis, *bread*)

comrade (camerata. Properly *a bed fellow*. Lat. camera, *a chamber*)

concert (ultimately from Lat. consero, *to weave together*)

contralto

conversazione

cornice (Gk. korōnis, *wreath*. Lat. corona, *crown*)

corridor (correre, *to run*)

cupola (dim. of Low Lat. cupa, *cup*)

curvet (curvare, *to bow*)

dilettante (dilettare, *to delight*)

ditto (detto, *said, aforesaid*)

doge (doge, *captain*. Lat. dux)

domino (Lat. dominus. 'Originally a dress worn by a master.' —*Skeat*)

extravaganza

fiasco

folio, port-folio (foglio, *a leaf of paper*)

fresco (a painting executed on wet or *fresh* plaster)

gabion (aug. of *gabbia*, cage. Lat. cavea)

gala, galloon, gallant (gala, *ornament*)

garnet (granato, *pomegranate*. The garnet is so called from the resemblance which it bears in colour to the pomegranate)

gazette (gazzetta, *chit-chat, gossip*)

generalissimo

gondola (dim. of gonda)

granite (granito, so called from the small grains of which it is composed)

grate (grata, *grate, gridiron*. Lat. crates, *hurdle*)

grotto (grotta, *a cave*)

guitar (Lat. cithara)

gulf (golfo. Gk. kolpos, *bosom*)

harlequin

imbroglio. Cp. Fr. brouiller

improvisatore (Lat. improvisus, not foreseen)

incognito (= unknown)

influenza

intaglio (tagliare, *to cut*)

inveigle (invogliare, *to make one willing*)

lagoon (lagone, *pool*. Lat. lacus)

lava (lavare, *to wash*)

lazaretto. See § 290

lute-string (a sort of silk; lustrino, *a shining silk*. Lat. lustrare, *to shine*)

macaroni (macare, *to bruise, crush*)

Madonna = my Lady

madrigal, properly a pastoral song; (mandria, *fold, herd*)

malaria (mal' aria, *bad air*)

manifesto

martello, an alarm tower (martello. From Lat. martulus, *a little hammer*, by which the alarm-bell was struck)

masquerade

mezzotinto = half - tinted (Lat. medius, *middle*; tinctus, *painted*)

motett (dim. of motto)

motto (motto, *a word*)

moustache (mostazzo, *snout, face*)

niche (nicchio, *a recess for a statue*)

nuncio (Lat. nuntius, *messenger*)

palette (dim. of *pala*, spade)

pantaloon. See § 290

parapet, a wall breast-high (parare, *to ward*; petto, *breast*; Lat. pectus)

pedant. Qy. Gk. paideuein, *to instruct*

piano-forte

piazza (Lat. platea, *a broad street*)

pigeon (pigione. From pipiare, *to peep*)

pistol. See § 291

policy (of insurance)

porcupine (porco spinoso, *the spiny pig*)

portico

proviso

quarto

regatta (a Venetian boat-race)

rocket (rochetto, *a bobbin to wind silk on*)

ruffian (ruffiano, *a swaggerer*)

scaramouch

serenade (evening-music. Sereno, *fair*. Used of the weather)

sketch (schizzare, *to squirt, sketch*)

soar (sorare, *to hover like a hawk*)

sonnet (sonare, *to sound*)

soprano, sovran (*uppermost*. Lat. supra)

stanza (stare, *to stand*)

stiletto (a pocket-dagger; Lat. stylus, *a pointed instrument to write with*)

stucco

studio

tenor

terrace (terrazza, *coarse earth, a walk*)

terra - cotta. Literally *baked - earth*

tirade

torso (orig. *the stump of a cabbage*)

trombone (aug. of tromba, *trumpet*)

umbrella

vedette (vedere, *to see*)

vermicelli. Literally small worms; Lat. vermiculus, dim.

of vermis, *a worm*

vermilion (vermiglio. *scarlet*, from the worm, Lat. vermis, of the gall-nut from which the scarlet dye was obtained)

vertu (Lat. virtus, *manliness*)

virtuoso

vista

volcano (Lat. Vulcanus, *the god of fire*.

zany. 'The name of John in some parts of Lombardy, but commonly taken for a silly John or foolish clown in a play.'—*Wedgwood*.

DUTCH ELEMENT IN ENGLISH.

287. The large commercial intercourse, and the close political relations, between England and Holland during the seventeenth century led to the introduction of many trading and nautical terms, the Dutch being during this period the carriers of Europe and extensive importers of colonial produce.

block. Cp. W. *ploc*

boom (boom, *a tree, pole*. Cp. beam)

boor (boer, *peasant*)

bow-sprit. Spriet, *a piece of cleft wood*

hoy (huy, *a small vessel*)

lubber (lobbes, *a booby*)

luff (loeven, *to keep close to the wind*)

reef, vb. (Rieve, *a rake, comb*)

Schiedam

schooner

skates (N. skaten, *narrow at the end*)

skipper (schipper, *a sailer*)

sloop (sloepe, *a shallop, a light vessel*)

smack

smuggle (schmuggeln).

spoor

stiver, a Dutch coin of the value of about a penny

taffrail (tafereel, from tafel, *a table*)

wear (a ship)

yacht (jaghten, *to chase*)

GERMAN.

288. From German we have derived very few words, the obvious reason being that its base is identical with the base of our own language. Moreover, Germany was late in the field of literature, art and science. We have imitated German originals in a few compound terms, such as folk-lore, hand-book, stand-point, &c., but we are averse to those many-syllabled compounds in which Germans delight.

cobalt (kobalt. 'A nickname given by the miners, because it was poisonous and troublesome to them; it is merely another form of G. *kobold*, a demon, goblin.'—*Skeat*)

feldspar (G. feldspath = field-spar)

hornblend (blenden, *to dazzle*)

landgrave (landgraf. From land and graf, *count*. Cp. O.E. gerefa, governor, as in sheriff = shire-reeve, port-reeve. The fem. landgravine seems to have come through the Dutch, land-gravin. The Ger. form is land-gräfin)

lansquenet (landsknecht, *foot-soldier*)

loafer (laufen, *to run*; cp. gassenlaufer, *a street-idler*)

margrave (markgraf. From mark, *a march, border*, and graf, *count*)

meerschaum (meer, *sea*; schaum, *foam*)

morganatic ('M H.G. morgen-gabe, morning-gift, a term used to denote the present which, according to old usage, the husband used to make to his wife on the morning after the marriage-night.'—*Skeat*. Low Lat. *morganatica*)

nickel (nickel, said to be an abbreviation of kupfer-nickel, copper of *Nick* or *Nicholas*; 'a name given in derision because it was thought to be a base ore of copper.'—Mahn's *Webster*)

plunder ('Brought back from Germany about the beginning of our Civil War by the soldiers who had served under Gustavus Adolphus and his captains.'—*Trench*)

quartz (quarze or querze)

zinc (First called zinctum.)

MISCELLANEOUS ELEMENTS IN ENGLISH.

289. Arabic. Most of the words from this source are connected with astronomy and the other branches of science, for which we are mainly indebted to the Moors of Spain.

admiral	attar	cipher	giraffe	monsoon	sirocco
alchemy	azimuth	civet	harem	mosque	sofa
alcohol	azure	coffee	hazard	mufti	sultan
alcove	bazaar	cotton	jar	nabob	syrup
alembic	caliph	crimson	koran	nadir	talisman
algebra	candy	damask	lemon	naphtha	tambourine
almanac	camphor	dragoman	lime	opium	tariff
amber	carat	elixir	lute	ottoman	vizier
arrack	caravan	emir	magazine	salaam	zenith
arsenal	carob-tree	fakir	mattress	sherbet	zero
artichoke	chemise	felucca	minaret	shrub	
assassin	chemistry	gazelle	mohair	simoom	

Persian.

bashaw	emerald	kaffir	paradise	sash	simoom
check	hookah	lac	pasha	scimitar	taffeta
checkmate	howdah	lilac	pawn &	sepoy	tiffin (Ang-
chess	jackal	musk	rook(chess)	shawl	lo-Indian)
dervish	jasmine	orange	saraband	sherbet	turban

Hindu.

banian	cowrie	loot	palanquin	rupee	toddy
bungalow	curry	mulliga-	pariah	shampoo	
calico	dimity	tawny	punch	sugar	
chintz	durbar	muslin	pundit	suttee	
coolie	jungle	pagoda	rajah	thug	

Chinese.

bohea	hyson	junk	pekoe	soy
congou	joss-stick	nankeen	satin	tea

Malay.

amuck	caddy	gamboge	mango	rattan	upas
bamboo	caoutchouc	gong	orang-	rum	
bantam	cockatoo	gutta percha	outang	sago	

Turkish.

bey	chibouk	fez	kiosk	seraglio	yashmak
caftan	chouse	janizary	odalisque	tulip	yataghan

Hebrew.

abbey	cabal	hallelujah	leviathan	rabbi	seraph
abbot	cherub	hosanna	manna	Sabaoth	shibboleth
amen	ephod	Jehovah	Paschal	sabbath	
Behemoth	Gehenna	jubilee	Pharisee	Sadducees	

Polynesian.

boomerang	kangaroo	taboo	tattoo

American.

buccaneer	hammock	lama	opossum	squaw	wigwam
calumet	hominy	mahogany	pampas	tobacco	
condor	jaguar	maize	pemmican	tomahawk	
guano	jalap	mocassin	potato	tomato	

Russian.

czar	drosky	knout	morse	ukase

Hungarian. Hussar, uhlan.

Tartar. Caviare, steppe, mammoth.

African Dialects. Assegai, gorilla, kraal, zebra, canary.

290. Words derived from names of persons and things, real and fictitious.

Amazon, the name of a warlike nation of women in Scythia. From Gk. a, *without*; mazos, *breast*. They were said to cut off their right breast in order to use the bow with greater freedom.

Ammonite, a fossil shell, so called from its resemblance to the horns ascribed to Jupiter Ammon, who was represented as a man with ram's horns.

Argosy, from the ship Argo.

Assassin, a fanatical Syrian sect of the thirteenth century, who, under the influence of *haschisch*, an intoxicating drink made from hemp, assassinated many of the leading Crusaders.

Atlas, from the demi-god, who was said to bear the world on his shoulders, and whose figure is often represented on the covers of atlases.

August (the month), from Augustus Cæsar.

Bacchanalian, from Bacchus.

Bluchers, from Marshal Blücher.

Boycott (verb), from Captain Boycott, an Irish land agent, who was cut off by the Land League in 1880 from all communication with the people among whom he lived.

Brougham, from Lord Brougham.

Buhl, from Boule, a famous French worker in ebony.

Burke (verb), from Burke, a famous murderer.

Camellia, so called by Linnæus in honour of Kamel, a Moravian Jesuit, who wrote a history of the plants of the island of Luzon.

Chauvinism, from Chauvin, the chief character in Scribe's 'Soldat Laboureur,' who is possessed by a blind idolatry for Napoleon.

Chimera, from Chimæra, a fabulous monster, half goat, half lion.

Cicerone, from Cicero.

Colt (a revolving pistol), from the inventor.

Cravat, from the Croats or Crabats, from whom the fashion of wearing the cravat was derived.

Dædal, from Dædalus, a mythological personage famous for his skill and ingenuity.

Daguerreotype, from Daguerre, the inventor.

Dahlia, from Dahl, a Swede, who introduced the dahlia into Europe.

Della Cruscan, from the celebrated academy at Naples, called Della Crusca (= of the Sieve) because it undertook to purify the Italian language. Applied in England to a cluster of poetasters who lived towards the close of the last century, and were notorious for their bad taste and mutual admiration.

Deringer (a pistol), from the inventor.

Dolomites, called after Dolomieu, a French geologist.

Doyly, called from the maker.

Draconian, from Dracon, the Athenian legislator, who affixed the penalty of death to almost every crime.

Dunce, a disciple of Duns Scotus, a great schoolman, who died A.D. 1308. The name was used opprobriously by the Thomists, the disciples of Thomas Aquinas, who were the great opponents of the Scotists.

Epicure, from Epicurus, a Greek philosopher who taught that pleasure was the highest good.

Euphuistic (Gk. euphuēs, of good figure), from 'Euphues, or the Anatomy of Wit,' and 'Euphues and his England,' two books written by Lyly, a wit of the reign of Queen Elizabeth. They were characterised by great affectation and pedantry.

Faun, fauna, from Faunus, a rural deity.

Filbert, called after St. Philibert, a Burgundian saint, whose anniversary, August 22 (old style), falls just in the nutting season.—*Skeat*.

Flora, from Flora, the goddess of flowers.

Fribble, from a feeble-minded character so called in Garrick's farce, 'Miss in her Teens.' The verb is of earlier date.

Fuchsia, from Fuchs, a German botanist.

Galvanism, from Galvani, an Italian.

Garibaldi, a red shirt, called after the great Italian patriot.

Gladstone, a bag, called from the statesman of that name.

Gordian, from Gordius, the Phrygian king, that tied the knot which Alexander the Great cut through.

Gorgonise, possessing the power of Medusa, one of the Gorgons, who turned into stone any one she looked at.

Grimalkin, from gray Malkin.   Malkin is a dim. of Moll (Mary).

Grog, so called after Admiral Vernon, who wore *grogram* breeches, and was familiarly called 'Old Grog.' About 1745 he ordered his sailors to dilute their rum with water.—*Skeat*.

Guillotine, from the name of the inventor, Dr. Guillotin.

Hansom, from the inventor.

Hector (verb), from Hector, the bravest of the Trojan chiefs. 'There is a certain amount of big talk about him.'—*Trench*.

Herculean, from Hercules.

Hermetic, from Hermes.

Hipocras, a wine said to be mixed according to the directions of Hippocrates.

Jacobin, so called from the hall of the Jacobin Friars where the Jacobins used to meet.

Jacobite, an adherent of James II. (Jacobus).

January, from the god Janus, who presided over the beginning of everything.

Jeremiad, a tale of woe; from Jeremiah, the author of the 'Lamentations.'

Jesuit, one of the Order of Jesus.

Jovial, born under the influence of Jupiter or Jove, 'the joyfullest star, and of the happiest augury of all.'—*Trench*.

July, from *Julius* Cæsar, after whom the month was called.

June, from Junius, the name of a Roman clan.

Kit-Kat. 'A portrait of about 28 by 36 in. in size is thus called, because it was the size adopted by Sir Godfrey Kneller (died 1723) for painting portraits of the Kit-Kat Club.'—*Skeat*. The club was so called from dining at the house of Christopher Kat, a pastry-cook.

Knickerbockers, from Diedrich Knickerbocker, the imaginary author of Washington Irving's 'History of New York.'

Lazaretto and *lazar*-house, from Lazarus.

Lynch, from an American of the name, who was famous for taking the law into his own hands.

Macadamize, from Macadam, who first proposed the mode of paving roads which goes by his name.

Mackintosh, from the inventor.

Magnolia, from Magnol, a French botanist.

March, the month of Mars, the god of war.

Mariolatry, the worship of the Virgin Mary (Gk. latreia = service). *Marigold* comes from *Mary* and *gold*.

Martial, born under the influence of Mars, the god of war.

Martin, a nickname of a bird of the swallow kind. See *Parrot*.

Martinet, a severe disciplinarian, called after an officer of that name who organized the French infantry under Louis XIV.

Maudlin, from Magdalene, who is generally represented in pictures with tearful eyes.

Mausoleum, from the famous monument erected in memory of Mausolus, king of Caria.

May, the month of Maia, 'the increaser.' Root, *mag-*.

Mentor, from Mentor, the instructor of Telemachus.

Mercurial, born under the influence of Mercury.

Merry Andrew, a name given originally to Andrew Borde (1500-1549), an itinerant physician.

Mesmerism, from Mesmer, a German physician of the last century.

Morris and *morris*-dance, from Spanish Moro, a Moor.

Negus, from Colonel Negus, who first mixed the beverage called after him.

Nicotine, from Nicot, 'who first introduced the tobacco-plant to the notice of Europe.'—*Trench*.

Orrery, from Lord Orrery, for whom the first orrery was constructed.

Pæan = the healing, a name given to Apollo. Subsequently transferred to a song dedicated to Apollo, then to the war-song sung before battle. *Peony* is from the same source.

Palladium, from Gk. Palladion, the famous statue of Pallas, on which the safety of Troy was believed to depend.

U

Pandar, from Pandarus.

Panic, from Pan, the god of flocks and shepherds. He was fabled to appear suddenly to travellers, to their great terror. Hence any sudden fright was ascribed to Pan, and called a Panic fear.

Parrot, Parakeet (Fr. perroquet), from Perrot, the diminutive of Pierre, Peter, 'from the habit of giving men's names to animals with which we are specially familiar, as Magpie (for Margery-pie, Fr. Margot), Jackdaw, Jack-ass, Robin-redbreast, Cuddy (for Cuthbert) for the donkey and hedge-sparrow. When parrot passed into English, it was not recognised as a proper name, and was again humanized by the addition of the familiar Poll; Poll-parrot.'— *Wedgwood*.

Pasquinade, from Pasquin, a Roman cobbler of the fifteenth century, famous for his sarcastic speeches. After his death his name was transferred to a torso which was dug up near his shop. Epigrams and satirical verses on public characters are still attached to this torso, and are hence called pasquils or pasquinades.

Petrel, a dim. of Peter, the allusion being to the apostle's walking on the water.

Phaeton, from Phaethon.

Philippic, from the discourses delivered by Demosthenes against Philip of Macedon.

Pickwick, a cigar, from a character of Dickens. Abusive words are said to be used in a 'Pickwickian' sense, when they are not intended to convey their literal meaning. See Pickwick, ch. I.

Pinchbeck, called after the inventor, Christopher Pinchbeck, in the eighteenth century.

Plutonic, igneous, from Pluto, the god of the infernal world.

Protean, from Proteus, who was said to constantly assume some new shape whenever any one wished to catch hold of him to learn from him the secrets of futurity.

Punch is a corruption of Punchinello, which is itself a corruption of Pulcinello, the name of a droll character in Neapolitan comedy. The beverage called Punch is named from Hindi *panch*, five, the reference being to the five ingredients: viz. brandy or whiskey, water, lemon-juice, spice, and sugar.

Quassia, from a negro sorcerer of Surinam of this name, who discovered the properties of quassia. Quassy is a common negro name.

Quixotic, from Don Quixote.

Rodomontade, from Rodomont, a famous Moorish hero in Boiardo's 'Orlando Inamorato' and Ariosto's 'Orlando Furioso.' He is represented as performing incredible prodigies of valour.

Samphire, 'Herbe de *Saint Pierre*' (St. Peter).

Sarcenet, Saracen's silk.

Saturnine, born under the influence of the god Saturn. Hence stern, severe.

Silhouette, a portrait cut out in black paper, from M. de Silhouette, a French minister, who made himself very unpopular by cutting down useless expenses.

Simony, from Simon Magus.

Spencer, from Earl Spencer.

Stentorian, from Stentor, whom Homer describes as shouting as loud as fifty other men.

Syringa, a shrub, from the stems of which pipe-stems are made From Syrinx, a nymph who was changed into a reed.

Talbotype, from Talbot, the inventor.

Tantalize, from Tantalus, who was fabled to be condemned to suffer eternal thirst, and at the same time to be placed in the midst of water, which receded from him whenever he tried to drink of it.

Tawdry, from St. Etheldreda.   Comp. Tooley from St. Olave, Trowel from St. Rule, Tanton from St. Anton, Torrey from St. Oragh, Toll from St. Aldate, &c.   (See Stanley's 'Canterbury Cathedral,' note p. 236.)   The name *tawdry* is said to have been first applied to the cheap finery sold at St. Audry's Fair.   Another explanation is given by Wedgwood.   St. Audry died of a swelling in her throat, which she considered as a judgment upon her for having been vain of her necklace in her youth.   Hence the name came to be applied to a necklace.

Thrasonical, from Thraso, a swaggerer in one of Terence's plays.

Tontine, from its inventor, Tonti, an Italian.

Valentine, from St. Valentine.

Vernicle, from St. Veronica, who, according to the legend, gave a napkin to the Saviour to wipe His face when He was on the way to Calvary, and received it back with the imprint of His face on it.

Volcano and *Vulcanite*, from Vulcanus, the god of fire.

Voltaic, from Volta, an Italian.

Wellingtons, from the Duke of Wellington.

291. Words derived from names of places, real and imaginary.

Academy, from Academia, the gymnasium where Plato taught.

Agate, from Achates, a river of Sicily

Arabesque, Arabian-like in design.

Arras, from Arras.

Artesian, from Artois, where the wells so called were first used.

Attic, from Gk. Attikos, Athenian.   The Athenian edifices were believed to have been built with a low top story.

Baldacchino, from Baldacco, the medieval form of Babylon.

Bantam, from Bantam in Java.

Bayonet, from Bayonne.

Bedlam, from Bethlehem.

Bergamot, from Bergamo, in Lombardy.

Bezant, a coin, from Byzantium.

Bilbo, a rapier, and *Bilboes*, bars of iron used on board of ships to fasten the feet of prisoners; from Bilbao in Spain.

Bohemian, leading a wild sort of gypsy life.   In France the gypsies are called Bohémiens.

Brobdingnagian, from Brobdingnag, an imaginary country, peopled by a gigantic race, in 'Gulliver's Travels.'

Buncombe, from Buncombe, in North Carolina. The phrase 'speaking for Buncombe' originated in the course of a debate in Congress on the Missouri question. The House was anxious to come to a vote, but a member insisted on speaking, on the ground that he was bound 'to make a speech for Buncombe.'

Calico, from Calicut.

Cambric, from Cambray.

Canary (both bird and wine), from the Canary Islands.

Candy-tuft, from the Island of Candy.

Canter, the pace ascribed to the Canterbury pilgrims.

Carronade, a short piece of ordnance. From Carron in Scotland, where it was first made.

Caryatides, from the women of Caryæ, in Laconia.

Cashmere, cassimere, kersey, kerseymere, from Cashmere.

Chalcedony, from Chalcedon.

Cherry, from Cerasos, in Pontus.

China, from the country.

Copper and *cypress* (the tree), from Cyprus.

Cordwainer, from Cordova, once famous for its leather.

Currants, from Corinth.

Damson, Dame's Violet (viola damascena), and *damascene*, from Damascus.

Delf, from Delft in Holland.

Diaper, from Ypres in the Netherlands.

Dittany, Gk. diktamnos, so called from Mount Dicte, in Crete, where it grew abundantly.

Dollar, from G. thaler, 'an abbreviation of Joachimsthaler, a coin so called because first coined from silver obtained from mines in Joachimsthal (i.e. Joachim's dale), in Bohemia, about A.D. 1518.'—*Skeat*.

Elysian, from Elysium, described by Homer as a happy land whither favoured heroes pass without dying.

Ermine, 'the spoil of the Armenian rat.'—*Trench*.

Faience, from Faenza in Italy.

Florin, a coin of Florence. 'Florins were coined by Edward III. in 1337, and named after the coins of Florence.'—*Skeat*.

Fustian, 'from Fostal, a suburb of Cairo.'—*Trench*.

Galloway, a small species of horse, first bred in Galloway.

Gamboge, from Cambodia.

Gasconade, boasting, a vice to which the Gascons are said to have been much addicted.

Gingham, from Guingamp, in Brittany, where it is made.

Guernsey, after the island so called.

Guinea, 'originally coined (in 1663) of gold brought from the Guinea coast.'—*Trench*.

Gypsy, a corruption of Egyptian. The gypsies, who are really of Indian origin, were supposed to come from Egypt.

Hessians, boots so called because worn by the Hessian soldiers.

Hock, from Hochheim in Germany, whence the wine comes.

Hollyhock, from M.E. *holi*, holy, and *hoc*, a mallow. 'The holly-hock was doubtless so called from being brought from the Holy Land, where it is indigenous.'—*Wedgwood*.

Indigo, from India.

Italics, so called from having been invented by Aldo Manuzio, an Italian (A.D. 1447–1515). Originally called *Aldines*.

Jalap, from Jalapa or Xalapa, in Mexico.

Jane, from Genoa.

Japan, from the country.

Jersey, from the island so called. 'Jersey' was the name formerly given to the finest wool.

Jet (Lat. gagates), from the Gages, a river in Lycia where jet is found.

Laconic, short and pithy, like the speech of the Laconians

Landau, from Landau in Bavaria.

Liliputian, from Liliput, a country peopled by a very small race, in 'Gulliver's Travels.'

Lockram, a sort of unbleached linen made at Loc-renan, in Brittany.

Lumber. 'The lumber-room was originally the Lombard-room, or room where the Lombard banker and broker stowed away his pledges.'—*Trench*.

Mæander, from the River Mæander, in Asia Minor.

Magnesia and *magnet*, from Magnesia, in Thessaly.

Majolica, from Majorca.

Malmsey and *Malvoisie*, from Malvasia, in the Morea.

Mantua, a lady's gown, from Mantua in Italy. The It. for gown is *manto*. This may have been corrupted into mantua, from an impression that the *manto* derived its name from Mantua.

Milliner, a dealer in wares from Milan. The word originally denoted a dealer in all sorts of Milan goods.

Morocco, *Morris*, and *morel*, from Morocco, in North Africa.

Muslin, from Mosul.

Nankeen, from Nankin, in China.

Palace and *Palatine*, from Mons Palatinus in Rome, on which stood the Palatium or residence of the emperors. The hill was called from Pales, a pastoral goddess.

Paramatta, a fabric named from Paramatta in New South Wales.

Parchment, from Pergamum, where it was first made.

Peach, from Persia. Lat. persicus, a peach-tree.

Pheasant, from the Phasis, a river of Colchis.

Pistol, from Pistoja (Pistola), near Florence. The Spanish crowns were jocularly called *pistoles* from their reduction in size.

Port, from Oporto.

Quince (Fr. *cognasse*, It. *cotogno*), from Cydon, a town of Crete.

Rhubarb (Rha barbarum), from the Rha or Volga, from the banks of which it was first obtained.

Sardonic, 'from a herb growing in Sardiria, which, if eaten, caused great laughing, but ended in death.' *Wedgwood*.

Savoy, from the country so called.

Shalloon, from Chalons.

Shallot. Lat. allium ascalonicum. Fr. eschalotte, from Ascalon.

Sherry, from Xeres.

Solecism, from Soloe, a city in Cilicia, the people of which spoke a very bad Greek.

Spaniel, fron Spain.

Stoic, from Stoa Pœcile, a portico at Athens, where Zeno, the philosopher, the founder of the Stoic school, taught.

Swede, a Swedish turnip.

Tarantula, from Tarentum : a species of spider, whose bite was believed to be incurable except by ceaseless dancing.

Tobacco is said to derive its name from Tabaco, a province of Yucatan. But this is doubtful. 'Las Casas says that in the first voyage of Columbus the Spaniards saw in Cuba many persons smoking dry herbs or leaves in tubes called *tabacos*.'—*Webster*.

Utopian, from Utopia, the name given by Sir Thomas More to an imaginary island enjoying the most perfect system of laws.

Worsted, from a village of the same name near Norwich.

ONOMATOPOETIC [1] OR IMITATIVE WORDS.

292. Without entering into the question of the extent to which words may be referred to a mimetic origin, there can be no doubt that large numbers of words, particularly the names of animals and of sounds, are to be ascribed to this source. Wedgwood says : 'We still for the most part recognise the imitative intent of such words as the clucking of hens, cackling or gaggling of geese, gobbling of a turkey-cock, quacking of ducks or frogs, cawking or quawking of rooks, croaking of frogs or ravens, cooing or crooing of doves, hooting of owls, bumping [booming] of bitterns, chirping of sparrows or crickets, twittering of swallows, chattering of pies or monkeys, neighing or whinnying of horses, purring or mewing of cats, yelping, howling, barking, snarling of dogs, grunting or squealing of hogs, bellowing of bulls, lowing of oxen, bleating of sheep, baaing or maaing of lambs.'—*Pref. to Dict.* He gives the following list of words denoting sounds—

'Bump, thump, plump, thwack, whack, smack, crack, clack, clap, flap, flop, pop, snap, rap, tap, pat, clash, crash, smash, swash, splash,

---

[1] From Gk. onoma, *a name*, and poiein, *to make*.

lash, dash, craunch, crunch, douse, souse, whizz, fizz, hiss, whirr, hum, boom, whine, din, ring, bang, twang, clang, clank, clink, chink, jingle, tingle, tinkle, creak, squeak, squeal, squall, rattle, clatter, chatter, patter, mutter, murmur, gargle, gurgle, guggle, sputter, splutter, paddle, dabble, bubble, blubber, rumble.'

To these might be added *thud*, *ping* (the sound of a rifle-bullet passing through the air), and many others. Our poets use words of this class with admirable effect—

> I heard the ripple *washing* in the reeds,
> And the wild water *lapping* on the crag.
> > Tennyson (*Morte d'Arthur*).

> The lime—a summer home of *murmurous* wings.
> > Id. (*Gardener's Daughter*).

> The ice was here, the ice was there,
> The ice was all around :
> It *cracked* and *growled*, and *roared* and *howled*,
> Like noises in a swound.—*Coleridge* (*Ancient Mariner*).

> A sailor's wife had chestnuts in her lap,
> And *mounched*, and *mounched*, and *mounched*.
> > Shakspere (*Macbeth*).

Examine Southey's *How the Water comes down at Lodore.*

293. Reduplicated Words—

click-clack. Of imitative origin

ding-dong. Of imitative origin

dingle-dangle. Dan. dangle, *to dangle*

gew-gaw. O.E. give-gove, from *gifan*, to give. Jamieson says that in N. Britain a *Jew's harp* is called a *gew-gaw*

helter-skelter

higgledy-piggledy

hob-nob, hab-nab, from *habban*, to have, and *nabban*, to have not. Cp. nill = will not, nis = is not, &c. 'Hob-nob is his word ; give't or take't' (*Twelfth Night*, iii. 4)

hocus-pocus. Dog-Latin used by jugglers. The derivation usually assigned, from 'Hoc est corpus,' is groundless

hodge-podge, a corruption of *hotch-pot*. Fr. hoche-pot, Du.

hutspot ; 'hodge-podge, beef or mutton cut into small pieces' (*Sewel*, quoted by Skeat). O.D. hutsen, to shake

hugger - mugger, secretly and hurriedly. 'Clandestinare, to hide or conceal by stealth, or in hugger-mugger.'—*Florio*

hum-drum. Of imitative origin

hurly-burly. Fr. hurler, to howl. Corrupted into *hullabaloo*

mingle-mangle

namby-pamby

nick - nack, or knick - knack. Knack was used formerly in the sense of trifle, toy.

pell-mell. O.F. pesle-mesle, confusedly. Fr. mesler (mêler), to mix

riff-raff. O.E. *rif and raf*. *To raff* formerly meant to scrape or rake together. Hence riff-

raff = refuse, scum. See Wedgwood
see-saw
shilly-shally. Qy. Shill-I, Shall-
I?
skimble-skamble

slip-slop
tag-rag
tittle-tattle
topsy-turvy
zig-zag

PERIODS OF THE ENGLISH LANGUAGE.

294. A language lives, grows, and decays, just as a nation or individual does. The life of the English language has been divided in a variety of ways; but, for all practical purposes, it is sufficient to recognise three leading divisions—

1. **Old English** (A.D. 450–1066), sometimes called Anglo-Saxon. The distinguishing features of the language during this period were the following—

a. The language was unmixed, i.e. it contained no foreign elements.

b. It was highly inflexional. **Nouns, Pronouns,** and **Adjectives** had five cases; the gender of nouns was indicated by the termination; the personal pronouns had dual forms; **Adjectives** had a *definite* declension used when the adjective was preceded by a demonstrative adjective, by a possessive pronoun, or by a genitive case, and an *indefinite* form used in all other constructions; in both declensions they had distinct forms for gender; **Verbs** had a greater variety of forms than at present to mark differences of person and mood, but had no proper future tense; the gerundial infinitive was distinguished from the simple infinitive not only by 'to' before it, but by the termination *-ne*; the **Participles** agreed with nouns in gender, number, and case, the passive participle agreeing with the direct object after 'have;' the imperfect participle ended in *-ende*; many of the perfect participles took the prefix *ge-*.

c. The **Syntax** differed from modern English in many important respects. Some verbs governed the accusative, some the dative; oblique cases were used, often without any verbs or prepositions to govern them, to express certain shades of meaning; large numbers of adjectives governed cases; prepositions governed a variety of cases; the completer apparatus of inflexions allowed of a wider variety in the order of words; in some cases there was a fixed order different from ours; thus the negative *ne* always stands before its verb.

2. **Middle English** (1066–1480) which may be subdivided into

Early Middle English (1066–1250),
Late Middle English (1250–1480).

Early Middle English.—Even before the Conquest English gave clear signs of losing its elaborate system of inflexions, but after 1066 the phonetic decay proceeded with great rapidity. The language ceased to be used by the educated classes, and was only to a slight extent used for literary purposes. The Normans who learned it were probably indifferent to nice grammatical distinctions, and would naturally give a preference for those forms and laws of the language which most nearly corresponded to their own.

The chief differences between Old English and Early Middle English are the following : (1) the substitution of *-e* for the other vowel endings, *-a*, *-o*, and *-u*; (2) the definite articles *the, theo, thæt*, take the place of *se, seó, thæt*; (3) the dative plural in *um* disappears ; (4) adjectives begin to lose their distinctive case- and gender-endings; (5) the gerundial infinitive occasionally loses its final *-ne*, and the simple infinitive its final *-n*; (6) the imperfect participle ends in *-inde*; (7) auxiliaries are more widely used.

Dr. Morris has pointed out that in the Midland dialects still greater changes had taken place; *-es* is now the ordinary sign both of the nom. plural and of the gen. singular and plural; the passive participles have dropped the prefix ; the plural of the present indicative ends in *-en* instead of *-th*; *aren* (are) has taken the place of *beoth*.

Late Middle English.—(1) Most of the remaining inflexions of nouns and adjectives are confounded, and eventually disappear ; (2) the genitive in *-es* gains ground ; (3) dual pronouns disappear ; (4) a final *e* is used to mark the plural of adjectives ; (5) the termination of the gerundial infinitive is often reduced still further to - : (6) the imperfect participle in *-ing* appears; (7) many strong verbs are

converted into weak ones; (8) the imperative plural ends in
-*eth*; (9) final *e* is still used to distinguish adverbs from
cognate adjectives.

295. 3. Modern English (1480 to present time).

Since the invention of printing the language has not
undergone any considerable changes in its grammar, but it
has been greatly enriched in its vocabulary. During the
sixteenth and seventeenth centuries the syntax was in a very
unsettled condition. It may be considered to have been
fixed by the middle of the last century. With an increased
knowledge of Early English, there has been a noticeable
tendency to revive old words.

EARLY ENGLISH DIALECTS.

296. Dr. Morris, who has made a special study of the
subject, says that in the fourteenth century there were three
leading English dialects—

1. **The Southern,** spoken south of the Thames.

2. **The Midland,** spoken between the Thames and the
Humber.

3. **The Northern,** spoken between the Humber and the
Firth of Forth.

They may be distinguished by the forms of the plural of
the present indicative; in the Southern this part of the
verb ended in -eth, in the Midland in -**en**; in the Northern
in -**es**.

WORDS CURIOUSLY CORRUPTED IN SPELLING.

297. Many words owe their present form to false theories
with regard to their derivation; others to endeavours made
to give them a familiar or native look; others to economy
of effort in pronunciation and in representation.

adder, O.E. nadder. Cp. umpire from numpire (non-par),
orange for norange (Per.
náranj), ouch for nouch (O.F.
nouche, a buckle), apron for
napron. The dropping of the
n is probably owing to the
prefixing of *an* and *mine*

andiron, O.F. andier, a fire dog.
No connexion with *iron*

artichoke, from It. articiocco,
Sp. alcachofa, Ar. ardischauki,

earth-thorn. Introduced into Europe by the Moors

azure, Low Lat. lazur. 'The initial *l* seems to have been mistaken for the definite article, as if the word were l'azur; we see the opposite change in *lierre*, ivy, a corruption of l'hierre from the Lat. hedera, ivy' (Skeat). Cp. lapis lazuli. Arabic, lájward, lapis lazuli

baldmoney or *bawdmoney*, a plant formerly called *valde bona* (very good)

belfry, M.E. *berfray*, O.F. *berfroit*, M.H.G. *berefrit*, watchtower. With 'berc' cp. O.E. beorgan, to protect. No connexion with 'bell'

brimstone = burn-stone, from *brennen*, to burn. Cp. *brindled*

bustard, O.F. *oustarde*, Lat. *avis tarda*, slow bird.

butcher, O.F. bocher, a slaughterer of goats. See Wedgwood. From O.F. *boc*, a goat; not from *bouche*, mouth

butler = bottler

buxom, O.E. bocsam, pliable

caltrop, from Lat. calx, *heel*, and M.L. trappa, a snare. A name first given to the caltrop used to impede cavalry, and then to the prickly heads of the plant caltrop

carfax, a place where four ways meet. O.F. carrefourqs. Lat. *quatuor*, four; *furca*, a fork

carouse, Ger. *gar aus, right out*. Used of drinking a bumper. Carousal appears to be from a different source. It. *garosello*, a festival, tournament. Cp. Fr. *carrousel*, a tilting match

cartridge, Fr. *cartouche*

caterpillar = hairy-cat. O.F. chate, she-cat; *pelouse*, from Lat. *pilosus*, hairy. Cp. woolly-bear

causey and *causeway*, from Fr. chaussée, Low Lat. *calceata via*, Lat. calx, lime

celandine, swallow-wort. Gk. chelidonion, from chelidōn, a swallow

chance-medley, Fr. chaude mêlée = hot fray. *Chaud*, warm; *mêler*, to mix. No connexion with *chance*

cheat, from *escheat*

clove, Lat. *clavus*, nail. From its resemblance to a nail

constable, from *comes stabuli*, count of the stable

coster-monger. Costard-monger (= apple-seller)

counterpane, Low Lat. *culcita puncta*. Lat. *culcitra*, quilt; *puncta*, pricked, stitched. No connection with *counter* or *pane*

cray-fish, crawfish, from O.F. escrivisse. Cp. Ger. *Krebs*, a crayfish, crab. No connexion with *fish*

curmudgeon = corn-mudgin = corn-hoarding. 'Mutching' is still used in the west of England in the sense of to hide, to play truant

currants, from Corinth

curtle-axe, from *cutlass*. Fr. *coutelas*. No connexion with *axe*

cushion, Fr. *coussin*

custard, orig. *crustade*

cuttle-fish, O.E. cudele

daffodil, daffadowndilly, Gk. asphodelos

demijohn, corruption of *damagan*, the name given in Egypt and the Levant to a large glass bottle

dirge, from dirige (= direct), the first word in the antiphon, Ps. v. 8, sung in the office for the dead

dropsy, Lat. *hydrops*, from Gk. *hydōr*, water

easel, from Du. ezel, a little ass

or Ger. *esel.* Cp. clothes-*horse*
and Fr. *chevalet,* an easel

elecampane, Lat. enula cam-
pana

ember-days, O.E. ymb-rene.
That from *ymb,* about ; *rene,*
circuit. Not from *quatuor
tempora*

frontispiece, Low Lat. fronti-
spicium, from *specio,* I see.
No connexion with *piece*

fumitory, Lat. fumus terræ,
earth-smoke, from the belief
that it was produced from
vapours rising from the earth

furbelow, Fr. *falbala,* a flounce.
No connexion with *fur* or *below*

gilly-flower, O.F. giroflée, Lat.
caryophyllum, Gk. karyophyl-
lon, *nut-leaf.* No connexion
with *flower*

ginger, Lat. zingiber, Gk. zig-
giberis

grocer, O.F. grossier, a whole-
sale dealer, a dealer *en gros*

gudgeon, Lat. gobius, Fr. goujon
as though from gobio

hamper, Low Lat. *hanaperium,*
a large vessel for keeping
cups in. Low Lat. *hanapus,*
a drinking cup

hatchment, corruption of *achieve-
ment*

hore-hound, M.E. hore-hune, O.E.
hune = hore-hound. No connexion with *hound*

humble-pie, from *umbles,* the
entrails of a deer

hussif, a roll of flannel, with a
pin-cushion attached. Icel.
húsi, a case

hussy = housewife

icicle = ice-gicel. The termination is not to be confounded
with the dim. ending -icle.
Gicel itself = a small piece of
ice, and is therefore redundant

jerked-beef. A corruption of
charqui, the South American
name f᷎ ᷎ it

Jerusalem artichoke, It. girasole,
sunflower ; Lat. *gyrus* (Gk.
gyros), a circle, *sol,* sun. The
artichoke is a kind of sunflower. No connexion with
Jerusalem

Job's tears, a corruption of
Juno's tears (Gk. Heras da-
kruon)

lanthorn, Lat. lanterna. No
connexion with *horn*

liquorice, Gk. glykyrrhiza =
sweet root. From *glykys,*
sweet ; *rhiza,* root

luke-warm, O.E. *wlæc,* tepid

mandrake, Gk. mandragoras

nonce, in ' for the nonce ' = for
the once, for the one occasion.
M.E. *for then ones.* The *n*
belongs to the article, and
represents the *m* of the dat.
of the article, viz. *tham.* Cp.
newt from an ewt ; nuncle,
from mine uncle ; nickname
for eke-name ; nugget or nin-
got for ingot

nuncheon, M.E. *none schenche,*
noon-drink. *None* = noon,
from Lat. *nona,* the ninth
hour. *Schenchen,* to pour out.
Luncheon is a variant.

nutmeg = musk-nut, M.E. note-
muge, O.F. muge, musk, Lat.
muscus

ostrich, Lat. avis struthio =
ostrich bird ; Gk. strouthion,
ostrich

pax-wax, a sinew in the neck.
Called also *fix-fax, paxy-
waxy, pack-wax, fax-wax.*
From O.E. fax-wax = hair-
growth. ' Presumably because
the hair grows down to the
back of the neck and there
ceases.'—*Skeat. Fax* is the
O.E. feax, hair. Cp. Fair-fax
= fair hair. *Wax* is the O.E.
weaxan, to grow. See Way's
interesting note in the
' Promptorium Parvulorum '

pea-cock, Lat. pavo

pea-jacket, Du. pij, a rough woollen coat. 'Jacket' is redundant. No connexion with *pea*

peal of bells, Fr. *appel*, a call with drum or trumpet

pellitory, a wild flower growing on walls. Lat. parietaria, from *paries*, a wall

penthouse, O.E. pentice, Lat. appendicium. No connexion with *house*

periwinkle (the plant), Lat. *pervinca*

periwinkle (shell-fish), O.E. pinewincla, a winkle eaten with a pin (*Bosworth*)

pick-axe, O.F. pikois. No connexion with *axe*

porpoise, Lat. *porcus*, pig; *piscis*, fish

posthumous, Lat. *postumus*, last. No connexion with *humus*, the ground

privet, from *primprint*, a reduplicated form of *prim*, the original name, with dim. termination

quandary, Icel. *vandræthi*, difficulty, M.E. *wandreth*, evil plight. 'The use of *qu* for *w* is not confined to this word.' —*Skeat*

quinsy, O.F. *squinancie*, Gk.

kynagchē, dog-throttling; *kyōn*, dog; *agchein*, to choke

sexton, Fr. *sacristain*, sacristan

somersault, Fr. *soubresault*, Lat. *supra*, above, *salio*, I leap

squirrel, Fr. écureuil, Gk. skiouros = bushy-tail. From Gk. *skia*, shade, and *oura*, tail

steward, O.E. stige-weard, a servant who looked after the cattle, the domestic offices, &c. O.E. *stige*, a sty. Cp. O.N. stivarde; also *stia*, sheephouse

sweet alison, a species of *alyssum*. Not a lady's name.

tansy, Fr. *tanasie*, Gk. *athanasia*, immortality

treacle, L. theriaca, Gk. thēriakē, viper's flesh : theriōn, a name often given to the viper. Originally, an antidote to the viper's bite

truffle, from Lat. terræ tuber. It. tartuffola

verdigris, Fr. verd-de-grise. Lat *viride æris*, green of brass. No connexion with *grease*

walrus = whale - horse. O.E. *hwæl*, whale ; hors, horse.

wassail, O.E. wǽs hál = be whole

windlass. 'Formerly windes, as in Du. (from *as*, axis) an axle for winding.'— *Wedgwood*

yawn, O.E. geanian

ENGLISH SOUNDS AND LETTERS.

298. Our present English alphabet,[1] which is a modification of the Roman, consists of twenty-six letters, three of which, viz. *c*, *q*, *x*, are redundant. The O.E. alphabet had no *j*, *q*, *v*, or *z*, but it had two letters which have since been lost, viz. ð (*eth*), which was merely a crossed *d* to represent

---

[1] Alphabet. From alpha beta, the names of the first two letters of the Greek alphabet. The earliest letters were probably pictures of objects whose names began with a certain sound. Such pictures would necessarily soon be simplified and used as mere conventional

the flat *th* in *then*, and þ (*thorn*) which represented the sharp *th* in *thin*. *j*, which is another form of *i*, was introduced in the seventeenth century. *q, v,* and *z* were introduced in the Middle English Period. Ben Jonson says of *q* : '*q* is a letter which we might well, very well, spare in our alphabet, if we would but use the serviceable *k* as he should be, and restore him to the right reputation he had with our forefathers. [This is a mistake ; see below.] For the English Saxons knew not this halting *q*, with her waiting-woman *u* after her, till custome, under the excuse of expressing enfranchised [naturalized] words with us, intreated her with our language in quality, quantity, &c., and hath now given her the best of *k*'s possessions.' *v* is another form of *u*. *w* is literally a double *u* ; in O.E. it was represented by the runic character þ (*wen*). *k* was of very rare occurrence ; only twenty-three words beginning with *k* are given in Bosworth's 'Anglo-Saxon Dictionary.'

The actual number of sounds in English is forty-six. To compensate for the insufficiency of our alphabet, some letters represent more than one sound, and some sounds are represented by a combination of letters. Various other artifices are employed for the same purpose, such as using a final *e* to indicate that the previous vowel is long, and doubling a consonant to indicate that the previous vowel is short.

299. Letters are divided into vowels and consonants.

A **vowel** is a sound which can be produced without the assistance of any other, as *a, e, i, o, u.*

A **consonant** (from Lat. *con*, together ; and *sonans*, sounding) is a sound which cannot be produced without the aid of a vowel.

The letter *a* represents four simple sounds, as in *pate, pall, part, pat.*

e represents three simple sounds, as in *mete, met, pert.*

i represents one simple sound, as in *bit.*

o represents three simple sounds, as in *note, not, or.*

u represents three simple sounds, as in *prude, pull, pun.*

These sounds are represented in a wide variety of other ways—

1. The *a* in *pate* is represented by *ai* in *pail, ay* in *pay, eigh* in *weigh, ea* in *great, au* in *gauge, ao* in *gaol, ey* in *they.*

2. The *a* in *pall* is represented by *au* in *laud*, *aw* in *flaw*, *oa* in *broad*, *awe* in *awe*, *ou* in *ought*, *o* in *for*, *ough* in *thought*.

3. The *a* in *part* is represented by *au* in *launch*, *ua* in *guard*, *ea* in *heart*, *ah* in *ah*, *er* in *clerk*, *Derby*, *Berkshire*, *Berkeley*.

4. The *a* in *pat* is represented by *ua* in *guarantee* and by *ai* in *plaid*.

5. The *a* in *Mary* is represented by *ai* in *chair*, *ei* in *heir*, *e* in *there*.

6. The *e* in *mete* is represented by *ee* in *meet*, *ea* in *meat*, *eo* in *people*, *ei* in *receive*, *ie* in *believe*, *fiend*, *ey* in *key*, *ay* in *quay*, *i* in *marine*, *ae* in *aether*, *oe* in *phoenix*.

7. The *e* in *met* is represented by *a* in *any*, *ai* in *said*, *ay* in *says*, *u* in *bury*, *ea* in *bread*, *eo* in *leopard*, *Leonard*, *Geoffrey*, *ei* in *heifer*, *ie* in *friend*, *ue* in *guest*.

8. The *e* in *pert* is represented by *u* in *murder*, *ea* in *earth*, *er* in *berth*, *ir* in *birth*, *yr* in *myrrh*, *oe* in *does*.

9. The *i* in *bit*[1] is represented by *y* in *cymbal*, *u* in *busy*, *o* in *women*, *ei* in *forfeit*, *ie* in *sieve*, *ui* in *guilt*, *ee* in *breeches*, *ia* in *carriage*.

10. The *o* in *note* is represented by *oa* in *goat*, *oe* in *toe*, *eo* in *yeoman*, *ow* in *sow*, *ew* in *sew*, *au* in *hautboy*, *eau* in *beau*, *oo* in *door*, *ow* in *owe*, *ough* in *though*.

11. The *o* in *not* is represented by *a* in *what*.

12. The *o* in *or* is also represented by the *a* in *pall*; see above.

13. The *u* in *prude* is represented by *o* in *prove*, *oe* in *shoe*, *œu* in *manœuvre*, *w* in *win*, *oo* in *rood*, *ue* in *true*, *ui* in *fruit*, *ou* in *through*.

14. The *u* in *pull* is represented by *oo* in *good*, *o* in *wolf*, *ou* in *could*.

15. The *u* in *pun* is represented by *o* in *love*, *oo* in *blood*, *ou* in *rough*; see above, *e* in *pert*.

300. Two vowels sounded together without a break between them are called a diphthong (Gk. *di*, two, *phthoggos*, a sound). There are in English four diphthongs, which are variously represented in spelling:

1. *I* as in *mine*, consisting of the *a* in *ah* and the *e* in *mete*, and represented by *y* in *thy*, *ie* in *die*, *ei* in *height*, *ye* in *dye*, *ai* in *aisle*, *ey* in *eye*, *uy* in *buy*, *ui* in *guise*.

2. *Oi* as in *noise*, consisting of the *a* in *pall* and the *i* in *sit*, and represented by *oy* in *joy*, and *uoy* in *buoy*.

3. *Eu* as in *feud*, consisting of *i* in *hit* and the *u* in *rude*, and re-

[1] Long *i* is a diphthong; see § 300.

presented by *u* in *tube*, *eu* in *feud*, *ew* in *few*, *ue* in *sue*, *ui* in *suit*, *ew* in *ewe*, *ieu* in *lieu*, *eau* in *beauty*, *iew* in *view*, *ou* in *youth*.

4. *Ou* as in *noun*, consisting of the *a* in *cat* and the *u* in *rude*, and represented by *ow* in *how*.

It will be observed that some diphthongs are represented by single letters, and on the other hand some single sounds are represented by two or more letters.

The letters *w* and *y* are sometimes called *semi-vowels*, because, although commonly ranked with the consonants, they have somewhat of the power of vowels; but in some combinations they are pure vowels, e.g., *w* represents *oo* in *wine*; *y* represents long *i* in *deny*, *tyrant*; short *i* in *city* and *tyranny*; *e* in *mete* in *you*. Ben Jonson says of *w* that 'though it have the seat of a consonant with us, the power is always *vowelish*, even when it leads the *vowel* in any syllable.' So he says of *y*: '*Y* is also mere [i.e. purely] vowelish in our tongue, and hath only the power of an *i*, even where it obtains the seat of a consonant.'

301. Consonants are sometimes divided into liquids, sibilants, and mutes.

The **liquids** are *l*, *m*, *n*, *r*, and are so called because their sound when produced *flows on*.

The **sibilants** (Lat. *sibilare*, to hiss) are *s*, *x*, *z*, *j*, soft *c*, soft *g*, and soft *ch*, and are so called because of their *hissing* sound.

The **mutes** are so called because, when sounded after a vowel, they stop the passage of the breath. They are classified, according to the organs by which they are produced, as follows:—

Labials (Lat. *labium*, lip), *p*, *b*, *f*, *v*.

Dentals (Lat. *dens*, tooth), *t*, *d*, *th* as in *thin*, and *th* as in *then*.

Gutturals (Lat. *guttur*, throat), *g*, *k*, hard *c* as in *cat*, and *ch* as in *loch*.

In O.E. final *h* was guttural.

The mutes are further distinguished as sharps and flats.

Sharps or hard sounds, as *p*, *f*, *t*, *th* in *thin*, *k* in *kick*, *ch* in *loch*.

Flats or soft sounds, as *b*, *v*, *d*, *th* in *thine*, *g* in *get*.

Ng is called a **nasal** sound from passing through the nose (Lat. *nasus*, nose).

H is called **the aspirate** (from Lat. *aspiro*, I breathe upon), as though it were the only aspirate, but *f*, *th* (both sharp and flat), *t*, *sh*, *ch* (in *church*), *z* (in *azure*), and *j* (in *jest*) are all spirants. Ben Jonson says of *h* : 'Whether it be a letter or no, hath been much examined by the ancients. . . . But be it a letter or spirit (i.e. breath) we have great use of it in our tongue, both before and after *vowels*. And though I dare not say she is (as I have heard one call her) the *queen-mother of consonants* ; yet she is the life and quickening of *c, g, p, s, t, w* ; as also *r* when derived from the aspirate Greek ῥ, as cheat, ghost, alphabet, shape, that, what, rhapsody.' In modern English *h* is never used before a consonant, but in O.E. it is frequently found before *l*, as *hlid*, lid; before *n*, as *hnesc*, nesh; before *r*, as in *hræfen*, raven; before *w*, as in *hwíl*, while. In *who* (O.E. hwa) the *w* sound has been suppressed ; in *what, which, whether*, and other words, the *h* is sometimes suppressed. In Ben Jonson's time the *h* was sounded in these words. He represents *what, which, wheel, whether*, as sounded '*hou-at, hou-ich, hou-eel, hou-ether.*' (See Engl. Gram. on letter *w*.)

Redundant letters.

C soft might be represented by *s*, *c hard* by *k*.
Q might be represented by *k*.
X might be represented by *ks* or *qs*.

302. Table of Mute Consonant Sounds.

MUTES.

	Sharp		Flat	
		Aspirated		Aspirated
Labials	*p*	*f = ph*	*b*	*v*
Dentals	*t*	*th* (in *thick*)	*d*	*th* (in *thou*)
Gutturals	*k*	*ch* (in *loch*)	*g* (in *bag*)	*gh* (in *laugh*)
Sibilants	*s* (in *sit*)	*sh* (in *ship*) *tch* (in *chest*)	*z* (in *zest*) *s* (in *dogs*)	*zh* (in *azure*) *dzh* (in *judge*)

A perfect alphabet would contain a separate character for each sound, and no sound would be represented by more

v

than one letter. The English alphabet is defective in the following respects :—

1. It has only twenty-six letters (of which four are redundant) to represent forty-six sounds.

2. Only eight letters have unvarying sounds.

3. The same symbol represents a variety of sounds.

4. The same sound is represented in a variety of ways. The thirteen vowel sounds are represented in 104 different ways. Long *o* is represented in thirteen different ways, long *i* in seven.

INTERCHANGE AND MODIFICATION OF SOUNDS.

303. The chief causes that produce modifications in the sounds of words are the following—

1. **Economy of effort,** tending to make words easier of pronunciation. This leads to

a. The **assimilation** of letters that cannot be easily sounded together; thus *godsib* becomes *gossip*; *dipped, dipt*; *adfirm, affirm*; *ad-rogate, arrogate*; *synpathy, sympathy*.

b. The **dissimilation** of letters that cannot be easily pronounced in close succession; e.g. the Lat. *populalis* becomes *popularis*; the Lat. *cœluleus, cœruleus*.

c. The **omission of sounds,** as in *hláford*, lord; *brægen*, brain; *paralysis*, palsy; *crudelis*, cruel; *geréfa*, reeve.

An omission at the beginning of a word is called **aphæresis** (Gk. *ap*, away; *haireo*, I take), e.g. ooze (O.E. *wos*), enough (O.E. *genoh*), tansy (Gk. *athanasia*); in the middle **syncope** (Gk. *syn*, with; *kopto*, I cut), e.g. head (O.E. heá*f*od), hail (O.E. ha*g*ol), lark, laverock; at the end **apocope** (Gk. *apo*, away; *kopto*, I cut), e.g. eft (O.E. efe*t*e), oakum (O.E. acum*b*a).

d. The **insertion of sounds,** to facilitate the utterance of other sounds, as the *b* in *slumber* (O.E. slummerian); the *d* in *gender* (Fr. genre); the *t* in *tyrant* (Gk.

tyrannos); the *n* in *messenger* (messager), *passenger* (passager), and *porringer* (porridger).

The addition of a letter to the beginning of a word is called **prosthesis** (Gk. *pros*, towards; *thĕsis*, aplacing), e.g. *n*ickname (ekename), *h*aughty (Lat. altus), *n*once (once); in the middle, **epenthesis** (Gk. *epi*, upon; *en*, in), e.g. post*h*umous (Lat. postumus); at the end **epithesis** (Gk. *epi*, upon), e.g. wit*ch* (O.E. wicca), wret*ch* (O.E. wrecca), soun*d*, compoun*d*, thum*b*, lim*b*.

2. **The difficulty experienced by different peoples in producing particular sounds.** Thus the Keltic peoples could not pronounce combinations like *sp* and *st* without placing a vowel before them. Hence the Latin *sperare* becomes in French espérer; *status* became *estat* (état). The Normans could not sound our *w*, and substituted for it *gu*. Comp. *guard* and *ward*; *guarantee* and *warranty*; *guichet* and *wicket*. Modern Italian turns the Latin *fl* into *fi* (comp. Lat. *flos*, It. *fiore*), *gl* into *ghi* (comp. Lat. *glans*, It. *ghianda*), and *pl* into *pi* (comp. Lat. *planus*, It. *piano*).

Difficulty of pronunciation often leads to a transposition of letters (**metathesis**). Comp. O.E. *acsian* with *ask*; *gaers* with *grass*; *nosethirls* with *nostrils*; *tucs* with *tusk*; *waps* with *wasp*. This tendency is very noticeable in children.

The changes which the sounds of a language undergo follow, with considerable regularity, certain definite lines—

1. The root-vowel is nearly always modified in words of English origin when a syllable is added. Thus, the O.S. plural of fót (*foot*) was fóti, the present plural is *feet*. Even in words of Romance origin we observe a similar tendency. Comp. nātion with nătional.

2. There is a noticeable tendency in all languages to assimilate the short vowels that precede and follow a liquid; m*i*rabilia (Lat.), maraviglia (It.); b*i*lancia (Lat.), b*a*lance.

3. Accented syllables tend to become long, unaccented short: orátio (Lat.), oraíson (Fr.), órison (Eng.). Unaccented syllables are very liable to disappear altogether, especially at the end of a word.

4. Consonants produced by the same organ are liable to be interchanged.

x 2

Labials: p, b, f, v. Comp. e*p*iscopus (Lat.), *b*ishop; godsi*b*, gossi*p*; *p*lat (Fr.), *f*lat; co*b*web, co*p*web (O.E. atter-cop, spider); provost, præpositus (Lat.); se*v*en, sie*b*en (Ger.); o*v*er, o*b*er (Ger.); tur*b*a (Lat.), troo*p*; ca*b*allus (Low Lat.), chi*v*alry; star*v*e, ster*b*en (Ger.); *f*at (O.E.), *v*at; cna*p*a (O.E.), kna*v*e.

P is often inserted between *m* and *t*, as in em*p*ty (emtig), sem*p*ster (seámestre); **b** after *m*, as in num*b*er (Lat. nume-rus), hum*b*le (Lat. humilis); **f** has disappeared from many words, as in hawk (O.E. hafoc).

Dentals: t, th (in thick), **d, th** (in then). Lat*t*a (O.E.), la*th*; *th*eil (Ger.), *d*eal; bur*th*en, bur*d*en; fa*d*er (O.E.), fa*th*er; *d*orp, *th*orpe; *th*al (Ger.), *d*ale; lacer*t*a (Lat.), lizar*d*; coul*d*, cu*th*e (O.E.); char*t*a (Lat.), car*d*; fi*dd*le, fi*th*ele (O.E.); par*t*ridge, per*d*rix (Fr.).

D and **t** often creep into words after *n*, as in len*d* (O.E. lǽnan), riban*d* (Fr. ruban), pheasan*t* (O.F. phaisan), tyran*t*.

Gutturals: h, k, ch (in loch), **g** (in bag). *H*ortus (Lat.), *ch*ortos (Gk.); macer (Lat.), mai*g*re (Fr.); draco (Lat.), dra*g*on; cithara (Lat.), *g*uitar; cornu (Lat.), *h*orn; octo (Lat.), ei*gh*t (O.E. ea*h*tā); dau*gh*ter, toc*h*ter (Ger.); *h*ester-nus (Lat.), *y*esterday (O.E gyrstan-dæg); rectus (Lat.), ri*gh*t; *k*ist (Sc.), *ch*est.

G, when initial, often disappears or turns into *y* or *e*, as in if (O.E. *g*if), enough (O.E. *g*enoh), yclept (*g*e-clept); in the body and at the end of words it often turns into *w* or *ow*, as in fowl (O.E. fu*g*ol), maw (O.E. ma*g*a), sorrow (O.E. sor*g*). Under French influence initial *g* has become *w*, as in wafer (O.F. *g*auffre).

H final has become *gh* in many words, as in nigh (O.E. nea*h*), thigh (O.E. theo*h*).

Liquids: l, m, n, r. Turtu*r* (Lat.), turt*l*e; purpu*r*a (Lat.), purp*l*e; pe*r*egri*n*us (Lat.), pi*l*grim; ma*r*mor (Lat.), ma*r*b*l*e; co*m*es (Lat.), cou*n*t; ra*n*ço*n* (Fr.), ra*n*so*m*; ga*rn*i-so*n* (Fr.), ga*rr*ison. The liquids are very liable to become assimilated to consonants with which they are connected. Comp the changes undergone by the prefixes *in, com,* &c.

L has dropped out of such (O.E. swilc), each (O.E. ælc), and as (O.E. ealswa). It has crept into could, participle (participium), and principle (principium).

M has been changed into *n* in ransom (redemptionem), noun (nomen), count, sb. (comitem), count, vb. (computare).

N has been dropped in umpire, auger, adder, apron, orange; it has been added in *n*ewt and *n*once.

R has crept into hoarse (O.E. hás), and groom (O.E. guma).

Sibilants: s, z, sh. Dizzy (O.E. dysig), radish (Lat. radix), a*s*k (O.E. ac*s*ian), fish (O.E. fi*s*c, pl. fi*s*cas and fi*x*as), nur*s*e (Lat. nutri*x*).

Sc initial in O.E. has become *sh*, as in *sh*ip (O.E. scyp), sheep (O.E. scéap).

S has dropped out of hautboy (Fr. hautbois), puny (Fr. puisné), and pea (Lat. pisum). It has crept into island, splash, smelt, demesne, aisle.

Cs and **cks** are sometimes converted into *x*, as in bu*x*om (O.E. bocsam), co*x*comb (cockscomb), po*x* (pocks).

5. Combinations of consonants nearly always lead to assimilation, or to suppression of one of the two; e.g. god*s*ib, go*ss*ip; blet*s*ian (O.E.), ble*ss*. If a sharp and a flat consonant come together, either the sharp is made flat or the flat made sharp; e.g. whip*p*ed (whip*t*), slip*p*ed (sli*pt*), wi*v*es (pr. wi*vz*), brea*th*es (pr. brea*thz*).

ACCENT.

304. The accent on words is liable to undergo great changes, which contribute to bring about other changes. To notice the latter effect first:

1. *Unaccented syllables are liable to disappear.* Thus O.E. *eage* becomes *eye*; O.E. *gerefa*, *reeve*; Lat. *historia*, *story*; O.E. *eln-boga*, *elbow*; Lat. *terminus*, *term*, &c.

2. *Unaccented syllables are liable to blend.* Thus *example* becomes *sample*; O.F. *escuier* becomes *squire*, &c.

This law often puts us on the track of discovering the original form and the relations of a word. When we find two consonants blended together like *kn*, we may pretty safely infer that they represent an old syllable, and that a short unaccented vowel has dropped out from between them. We should not at first sight connect *knee* with *genu*. But if we insert a short vowel between the *k* and *n* the connexion becomes obvious.

In O.E. the accent was invariably placed on the root syllable. In classical words that have come to us through the French the accent is often placed on the last syllable. Most of these words are derived from originals, the penultimate syllables of which were long and accented. Hence, when the final unaccented syllables dropped off, the accented penultimate syllable became the final and accented syllable of the derivative; e.g. *canal, antique, baptize, august, robust, morose*, &c.

The shifting of accent is owing to

1. Contractions, themselves often owing to the disappearance of unaccented syllables;

2. The influence of native accent upon foreign, and *vice versâ*;

3. The license of poets;

4. Convenience in differentiating words similarly spelt. Compare

áccent (sb.) and accént (vb.)		mínute (sb.) and minúte (adj.)	
cómpact (sb.) „ compáct (adj.)		súbject (sb.) „ subjéct (vb.)	
éxpert (sb.) „ expért (adj.)		súpine (sb.) „ supíne (adj.)	

GRIMM'S LAW.

305. If we compare the various languages of the Indo-Germanic family, we find that the words of which they are composed have a certain family likeness. Thus the Sanskrit *bhratri* clearly corresponds to the Greek *phrater*, the Latin *frater*, the Gothic *brôthar*, the Old High German *pruoder*, the modern German *bruder*, and the English *brother*.

If we proceed a step further and arrange a number of these corresponding words in three groups, viz. the **Classical** (including Sanskrit, Greek, Latin, &c.), **Low German** (including English, Dutch, &c.), and **High German** (including Old High German, Middle High German, and Modern High German), we shall find certain sounds in one of these groups correspond regularly to certain sounds in the other, so that, if we know a word in one group, we can predict with tolerable certainty what will be the form of the corresponding words in the other groups.

The law which regulates these correspondences was first discovered by a Danish philologist, named Rask, but was more fully elaborated by Grimm, the great German philologist, after whom it is now called. Grimm found—

1. That an **Aspirate** in the Classical languages is represented by a corresponding **Flat** (or **soft**) sound in Low German, and a **Sharp** (or **hard**) sound in High German, e.g.—

	Classical	*Low German*	*High German*
Labials	Lat. frater	Eng. brother	O.H.G. prucder
Dentals	Gk. thugatĕr	„ daughter	„ tohtar
Gutturals	„ chthes	O.E. gyrsta = yester	„ kïstar

2. That a **Flat** (or **soft**) mute in the Classical languages is represented by a corresponding **Sharp** (or **hard**) sound in Low German, and an **Aspirate** sound in High German—

Labials	Lat. labor	Eng. slip	Ger. schleifen
Dentals	„ duo	„ two	„ zwei
Gutturals	„ ego	O.E. ic	„ ich

3. That a **Sharp** (or **hard**) consonant in the Classical languages is represented by an **Aspirate** in Low German, and by a **Flat** (or **soft**) sound in High German—

Labials	Lat. pater	Eng. father	Ger. vater
Dentals	„ tu	„ thou	„ du
Gutturals	„ caput	„ head (O.E. heafod)	„ haupt

'If it be remembered that *soft* = *flat* and *hard* = *sharp*, the whole of Grimm's law can be remembered by the mnemonic word **ASH**, with its varying forms **SHA** or **HAS**, according to the sound which is to come first.' (Dr. Morris, *Hist. Eng. Gram.* p. 48.) The mnemonic for the first law will be **ASH**, for the second **SHA**, and for the third **HAS**.

CHANGES OF MEANING IN WORDS.

306. Words, through a variety of causes, undergo, in process of time, great changes of meaning as well as of form. Thus

1. Words having a *specific* meaning come to be used *generically*, and *vice versâ*. Compare the various meanings of *sycophant* (lit. fig-show-er), *spice* (originally species), *meat* (originally any food, as in green-meat, meat-offering, sweet-meat), *idiot* (Gk. idiōtēs, a private person), *miser* (wretched), *disaster, influence, religious, kind, painful, worship, blackguard, duke, bark, comprehend.*

2. Words once of the *common gender* come to be restricted to *a particular sex*, e.g. *girl, shrew, coquet, harlot, wench, slut, termagant, hag, hoyden, jade.* (See note, p. 12.) Archbishop Trench gallantly remarks on these words that they 'must, in their present exclusive appropriation to the female sex, be regarded as evidences of men's rudeness, and not of women's deserts.' ('Eng. Past and Present,' p. 285.)

3. Words shift their meaning with an alteration in the *things* they denote. This is the source of one of the most common fallacies by which men are deceived. Because things that have come down to us from the past have borne the same name continuously, we are tempted to think of them as one and the same in different ages, whereas there may be little or nothing in common between them except the name. This is well illustrated by the names of churches, sects, and parties.

4. Words shift their meaning through *the association of ideas.* Compare the different meanings of *generous* (well-born), *knave* (boy), *villain* (a resident on a *villa* or country estate), *servile, boorish, urbane, polite, heathen, pagan, churlish, gossip, cheat, demure, prude.*

5. *Abstract* terms are used for *Concrete*, and *Concrete* for *Abstract*. Compare the various senses of *youth, beauty, age, faith, reason, subject, object.*

6. Words are abused *to soften the offensiveness, or cover the wickedness, of the things they denote.* Such words we call euphemisms. Compare the meanings of *ordinary, plain, love-child, annexation, simple, innocent,* and the slang names

for vice and crime, as of theft, drunkenness, &c. This tendency is often coupled with an endeavour to diguise the form of the word. When we cannot invent or discover a fine word to cover what is wrong, we alter the form of some existing word. This accounts for the great changes which oaths and imprecations undergo. Compare 'odds boddikins,' 'by'r lakin,' 'divel,' 'zounds,' 'sdeath,' 'marry,' &c.

7. Words come to be applied metaphorically, e.g. *flower, body, head, spur, stimulus, grasp, taste, post.*

8. One part of speech is made to do duty for another. Thus nouns are used as verbs and adverbs, participles as prepositions, adjectives as adverbs, &c. Cp. the different senses of *home, house, coal, fire, ship, lodge, point, shape, except, save, right, will, soft.*

9. Economy of effort leads to the employment of words for phrases and even for sentences.

WORD-BUILDING AND DERIVATION.

307. When we examine words carefully, we find that some of them are closely allied in form and meaning. The original element which is common to them all, and from which they all seem to be derived, is called their root. On further examination we find that the meaning of the root is modified in various ways. Thus by means of certain syllables (**prefixes**) placed at the beginning of the root, we add the ideas of negation, opposition, deterioration, direction; by means of certain syllables (called **suffixes**) placed at the end of the root, we convert one part of speech into another; by joining one word to another we make new words (called **compounds**). Compounds are distinguished from the corresponding uncompounded phrases by (1) their accent, (2) their meaning. We say 'a black bird,' putting the accent on 'bird,' but we say 'a blackbird,' putting the accent on 'black.' With regard to meaning, the effect of composition in this example is to convert a phrase of generic, into one of specific, meaning. 'A black bird' means any black bird; 'a blackbird' a specific sort of black birds. New compounds are generally connected by a hyphen. Old compounds frequently modify the vowel of the first element.

Compound Nouns.

1. *Noun and Noun*: housetop, churchyard, manslayer, evensong. The two elements are sometimes united by the sign of the possessive, e.g. monkshood, Wednesday (Woden's day).

In many cases one or both of the elements have become obsolete or ceased to be significant:—

Bridal = bride-ale.
Daisy = day's eye.
Garlick = gar-leek = spear-leek (O. E. gár, spear).
Goshawk = goose-hawk.
Grunsel = ground-sill.
Huzzy = house-wife.
Icicle = is-gicel (lump of ice).
Lapwing = lepe-wing (from its mode of flight).
Orchard = ort-yard (wort or herb garden).
Tadpole = toad-head ('bullhead,' provincial English). 'Pole' has no connexion with *pool*. Cp. the provincial name pol-wiggle. Also poll-tax, catch-pole.

2. *Noun and Adjective* : freeman, quicksilver, underhand, court-martial, twilight (=two light), midnight, midriff (=mid bowel). (Compounds in which the adjective follows the noun are, for the most part, of French origin.)

3. *Noun and Verb* : cutpurse, pick-pocket, skinflint, spendthrift, godsend, stopgap, stopcock, turnkey, windfall, windhover.

4. *Noun and Preposition or Adverb* : bypath, byword, offshoot, foretaste, afterthought.

5. *Verb and Adverb* : castaway, runaway, drawback, outgoings, outlay, welcome, offset, down-sitting, uprising, income, farewell.

Compound Adjectives.

1. *Noun and Adjective* : pea-green, snow-white, praise-worthy, brand-new, shame-fast (wrongly written shame-faced), wilful. Many of these compounds take the termination -ed; e.g. long-haired, crop-eared, tender-hearted, pigeon-breasted, hare-lipped, eagle-eyed, lion-hearted, dog-eared. In O.E. we find such compounds as mild-heorte (mild-hearted), án-eage (one-eyed). Cp. barefoot.

2. *Noun and Participle* : heart-rending, heart-broken, storm-tossed, sea-girt, earth-born, match-making.

3. *Verb and Adverb* : well-bred, high-born, underdone, over-done.

Compound Verbs.

1. *Noun and Verb* : browbeat, backbite, henpeck.

2. *Verb and Adverb* : outdo, overdo, understand, doff (=do off), don (=do on), dout (=do out), dup (=do up).

3. *Verb and Adjective* : whitewash, fulfil (=fill full).

Compound Adverbs.

1. *Noun and Noun* : lengthways, endways.

2. *Noun and Adjective* : head-foremost, breast-high, meanwhile, sometimes, always, to-night, otherwise.

3. *Preposition and Noun* : above-board, outside.

4. *Adverb and Preposition* : hereafter, therein, whereupon.

PREFIXES.

308. Of English Origin.

I. Inseparable.

a (O. E. on); abed, aboard, asleep, anon (in one), athwart (on the cross), aloft (in the lift = sky), a-brewing (in the brewing).

a (O. E. of = from); adown (= from the down), akin.

a (O. E. ge); among, alike, aware.

an (O. E. and = against); answer, along.

at (O. E. æt); atone, ado (= at do, to do), twit (= ætwitan, to twit).

be (O. E. be = by); used (*a*) to make intransitive verbs transitive : bethink, bemoan, bespeak; (*b*) to intensify the meaning of verbs: beseech (= beseek), besmear, bedaub, bedraggle; (*c*) to make transitive verbs out of adjectives or nouns: benumb, befriend, betroth; (*d*) with nouns: behest (O. E. hæs, command), behoof, bequest.

In '*believe*' the prefix be- has taken the place of ge- (O. E. *gelyfan*). We cannot suppose that the *ge-* has been turned into *be-*. Probably the *ge-* was dropped, as in many other words, and the *be-* was added at a later period. So *begin* takes the place of *onginnan*, and *benray* of *on-wreon*.

e (O.E. ge); enough (O.E. genoh).

em (O. E. ymb = about); ember (O. E. ymb-rene, circuit), umstroke (circumference). This prefix has been completely displaced, except in the one word Ember, by the Latin prefix. In Bosworth's Dictionary there are two columns of words beginning with it.

for (O.E. for) = through, thoroughly, out-and-out; as forgive. It often adds the idea of deterioration (comp. the German ver-) : forbid, fordo (to destroy), forswear, forlorn, forget.

fore = before ; forebode, forecast, forefather, forenoon.

gain (O.E. gegn) = against ; gain-say, gain-stay.

h-, determinate with respect to the person speaking ; here, hence. hither, he. *s-* has a similar force ; e.g. so, such.

i or y (ge, participial prefix. Used also in other parts of speech. See Rask, § 276) ; yclept, i-wis (gewis), wrongly written I wis ; hand*i*work, hand*i*craft.

mis (O.E. mis-), wrong : mislike (nearly displaced by *dislike*), mistake, mislead, mistrust, misdeed.

n- (O.E. ne, not); none (from án, one), never, nilly, in nilly-willy, nob in hob-*nob*.

nether (O.E. down); nethermost, nether-stocks.

sand (O.E. sam)=half; sand-blind. Cp. samwis=half-wise; sam-cucu=half-alive, half-quick; or, as we should say, half dead.

th-, determinate with reference to the person spoken to; this, that, there, thence, thither, thou, they, the.

to (O.E. to)=to. This prefix often has the force of the Ger. *zer*, e.g. to-break, Judges ix. 53. Cp. *to-weorpan*, to overthrow; *to-wendan*, to subvert. To=this in to-day. 'In the dialect of the western counties "this year" is commonly expressed by "to year." In Scotland and Ireland "the day," "the night," "the year," are the ordinary expressions; "it 'll no rain the day," &c.'—*Dean Alford.*

un (O.E. un, on)=(1) not; unclean, unkind, unrighteous. (2) =back; untie, undo, unlock, unfold. (3)=on; unto, until. The form *on-* for *un-* may often be heard in provincial English.

wan (O.E. wan)=lacking; wanhope (=despair), wanton (lacking in breeding, from *teón*, to lead).

wh (O.E. hw-), interrogative; who, which, what, where, whence, whither, why.

with (O.E. wither)=against, back; withstand, withdraw, withhold.

2. Separable.

after; afternoon, after-math (from *mow*), afterward.

all; almighty, alone, almost, also, as (=alswa), although.

forth; forthcome, forward.

fro=from (O.E. fram); froward. Cp. toward.

ill; ill-deed, ill-luck, ill-health.

in; income, inlay, inborn, inbred, into.

mid; midmost, midsummer.

of=from; offspring, offal (off-fall), offshoot.

on; onset, onward, onslaught.

out, ut; outcast, outlet, utter, uttermost

over=(1) over (O.E. ofer); overflow, over-wise, over-near, overmuch. (2) upper (O.E. ufera=higher); over-hand, overcoat; common in names of places.

through, thorough; throughout, thoroughfare

twi=two; twilight, twin.

under; underlet, undergrowth, underbred, underhand.

up; upbear, upbraid (upgebredan, to cry out on ; cp. bray), up-right, upstart.

wel, well; welcome, well-born, welfare.

309. Prefixes of Latin Origin.

These come to us either directly from the Latin, or through the modern Romance languages. In the latter case they generally undergo considerable modification.

a, ab, abs (Fr. a, av), *away from*; abate, avert, abuse, abound, abstract, abstain, avaunt (= ab ante). In advance (Fr. avancer) and advantage (Fr. avantage) the *d* has no proper place.

ad (Fr. a), *to*, changes into **ac, af, ag, al, an, ap, ar, as, at**, to assimilate with the initial consonant of the root; advise, abate, accord, afford, aggrieve, allude, annex, announce, appear, arrive, assimilate, attain. Disguised : abbreviate, abridge. Before *v* the *d* sometimes disappears, e.g. avow, avenge. Later forms : adieu, adroit, alarm, alert, apart.

amb-, am-, *round*; amputate, ambition, ambiguous.

ante (Fr. an), *before*; antedate, antediluvian, ancestor (ante cessor), ancient.

bis, bi, *twice*; bisect, biscuit (= twice baked).

circum, circu, *round*; circumference, circulate, circuitous.

com, *with*, becomes **col, con, cor**, according to the following consonant, **co** if the root begin with a vowel; compound, constant, collocate, corrupt, coæval, co-exist. In counsel and countenance, *con* is changed into *coun*. In count (computare), cost (constare), custom (consuetudinem), cull (colligere), costive (constipatus), cousin (consanguineus), count (comes), kerchief, curfew, the prefix has undergone further changes.

contra, contro (Fr. contre), *against*; often takes the form of counter in English; contradict, controvert, contredanse, contrast, contraband (Goth. *band*, prohibition), control (counterroll, check-book), counterfeit, counterpane. This prefix is converted into a root in *encounter*.

de (Fr. dé, de), *down from*; describe, descend, devise, demure (O.F. de murs = de bons murs, of good manners), denouement (Lat. nodus, a knot). Disguised : distill.

demi (Fr. demi, Lat. dimidium), *half*; demi-quaver, demi-god.

dis (Fr. des, de), *in two, apart*; hence negation, opposition. **Dis** becomes dif, di, according to the following root; dissimilar, differ, deluge (diluvium, Fr. déluge), digest, dilate, descant, spend. Hybrids : distrust, disbelieve, distaste.

ex, e (Fr. es, e), *out of, from*, becomes **ef** before **f**: extol, effect, educe, especial, essay, escape, cheat (or escheat, from ex and cedere). In amend (emendo), astonish (étonner), sample (example), issue (exire), it is disguised. In *execute* the *x* of the prefix has blended with the *s* of the root (sequor).

extra, *beyond*; extraordinary, extravagant, stranger (extraneus).

in (Fr. **em, en,** Ital. **im**), *in, into, on*, changes into **il, im, in, ir**; infer, incur, illusion, improve, innate, irradiate, encourage, embrace, embroil. Hybrids: embody, endear, entrust. Disguised: ambush (Ital. imboscarsi = to get into a wood), anoint (in-unctus).

in, *not*; innocent, infant (not speaking), incurable, improper, illegal, irregular, incapacitate, enemy (Lat. inimicus).

inter, intro (Fr. **entre**), *between, within*; intercede, international, interpret, introduce, enterprise, entertain, entrails.

male (Fr. **mau**), *ill*; malediction, maugre.

mis (Fr. **més,** from Lat. minus), *less*; hence used in a bad sense; mischief, mischance. Not to be confounded with the Teutonic prefix *mis-*.

ne, *no*; **non,** *not*; neglect, negotiate, nonsense, nonchalance, nonexistent. Disguised in umpire (= non par, uneven).

ob, *against*, changes into **oc, of, op,** &c.; obtain, obdurate, occur, offend, oppose, ostensible, omit.

pene, *almost*; peninsula, penultimate.

per (Fr. **par**), *through*, changes into **pel**; pertain, permit, pellucid. Disguised: pardon (perdonare), pilgrim (peregrinus), pursue (persequor), pursuivant, parson. Hybrid: perhaps.

post, *after*; postpone. Disguised: puny (Fr. **puis né** = post natus, after-born).

præ, pre (Fr. **pré**), *before*; prevent, predict. Disguised: provost (= præpositus), preach (prædicare), provender (præbeo, to furnish), prison, apprise, comprise, &c. (all from præhendo).

præter, *beyond, past*; preternatural, preterite.

pro (Fr. **pour**), *for, forth, before*, changes into **pol, por, pur**; pronoun, proceed, pollute, portrait, purloin, purvey, purchase. Disguised: proxy (procurator), prune (Fr. provigner), prudent.

re, red (Fr. **re**), *back, again*; redound, receive, recreant. Disguised in rally (religare), ransom (redemptio), runagate (renegado). Hybrids: relay, reset, recall.

retro, *backwards*: retrograde. Disguised: rear, arrears, rearward.

se, sed (Fr. **se**), *apart*; secede, sedition, sure, sober (se ebrius).

semi, *half*; semiquaver, semicircle.

sesqui, *one half more*: sesquipedalian.

sub (Fr. **sou**), *under*, changes into **suc, suf, sug, sum, sup, sur,**

sus; subtract, succour, suffer, suggest, summons, surrender, suspend, supplant. Disguised: sojourn (séjourner), sudden (subitaneus), sombre (Lat. sub umbrâ).

subter, *beneath*; subterfuge.

super (Fr. sur), *over*; supernatural, supercilious, superscription, surface, surfeit, surname, surtout (over-all), soprano, sovereign.

trans, tra (Fr. tré), *beyond*; translate, tradition, travesty, trespass. Disguised: treason (traditio), traitor (traditor), trance (transitus), trestle.

ultra, *beyond*; ultramontane, ultra-Tory, outrage (O.F. oultrage).

vice (Fr. vis), *instead of*; viceroy, viscount.

310. Greek Prefixes.

When *p, k,* or *t* comes before an aspirated vowel, it is changed into the corresponding aspirate, e.g., *epi* before *hemera* gives *ephemeral*; *meta*, before *hodos* gives *method*.

an, a (ἀν, ἀ), *not*; anomaly, anonymous, apteryx, atheist.

amphi (ἀμφί), *on both sides, round*; amphibious, amphitheatre.

ana (ἀνά), *up, again, back*; anaphora, analyse, aneurism.

anti (ἀντί), *against, opposite to*; antithesis, antitype, antipodes, antarctic, antidote.

apo, ap (ἀπό), *away from*; apostrophe, apology, aphelion.

arch, archi, arche (ἀρχή), *chief*; architect, archimandrite, archangel, archetype, arch-heresy.

auto, auth (αὐτός) *self*; autograph, automaton, authentic, autonomy, autotype, autopsy.

cata, cat (κατά), *down*; cataclysm, catacomb, catalogue, catapult, catechism, category, cathartic, cathedral, catholic, catoptrics.

dia (διά), *through*; diagnosis, diagonal, diabolic, diapason. Disguised: devil (Lat. diabolus, Gr. diabolos), deacon.

di, dis (δίς), *twice*; dilemma, diphthong, dissyllable, diploma.

dys (δυς), *ill, bad, hard*; like our *un*- and *mis*- dysentery, dyspepsia.

ec, ex (ἐκ, ἐξ), *out of*; eccentric, ecclesiastic, ecstasy, exorcise, exarch, exegesis, exodus, exoteric, exotic, eclogue, ellipse.

en, el, em (ἐν), *in*; encaustic, encyclical, encomium, ellipse, emporium, empiric, empyrean, emphasis.

epi, ep (ἐπί), *upon*; epitaph, epiphany, epoch, epact, ephemeral.

eu (εὖ), *well*; euphemism, eulogy. Disguised: evangelist.

hemi (ἡμί), *half*; hemisphere, hemistich.

hyper (ὑπέρ), *above, beyond*; hyperbole, hypercritical, hyperborean.

hypo, hyp (ὑπό), *under*; hypochondria, hypocrite, hyphen.

meta, met (μετά), *after*, implies change; metaphor, method, methylene.

mono, mon (μόνος), *alone*; monograph, monogram, monody, monk, monad.

pan (πᾶν), *all*; pantheist, panacea, panorama.

para, par, pari (παρά), *by the side of*; paradigm, parallel, parallax, paroxysm, palsy, parhelion, parish; *not* paraffine (Lat. parum).

peri (περί), *round*; periphery, perigee, period, peristaltic.

pro (πρό), *before, forth*; prologue, problem, proboscis, prophet.

pros (πρός), *towards*; prosody, proselyte, prosthesis.

syn, sym, sy, sys, syl (σύν), *with*; synagogue, sympathy, syllogism, system, systole, syzygy.

NATIVE SUFFIXES.

311. Noun Suffixes.

-ard, -art (augmentative); braggart, drunkard, dotard, blinkard, laggard, dastard, dullard. Bastard is Welsh.

-craft (O.E. cræft = skill, art, strength); as in priestcraft, woodcraft, witchcraft, leechcraft.

-d (participial suffix); deed (from do), seed (from sow).

-dom (O.E. dóm = doom. From deman, to judge. Comp. deem, dempster. Ger. -thum): power, authority, office, state; as in kingdom, Christendom, halidom (= holiness), thraldom, wisdom, heathendom, freedom. In O.E. we find bisceopdóm, (= bishopdom), abbotdóm. Modern forms: beadledom, rascaldom, scoundreldom.

-en. Diminutive: maiden, chicken, kitten. Feminine termination (Ger. -in): vixen (from fox), mynchen (nun, from munuc, monk).

-er (O.E. -a), agent; comer (O.E. cuma), slayer (O.E. slaga).
   (O.E. -er) instrumental; finger (= fanger, taker). Disguised: stair (*stigan*, to mount).
   (O.E. -ere) denoting a male agent; player, sower, writer, fuller. Disguised: beggar, sailor.

-hood (O.E. hád = person, state, quality. Comp. Ger. -heit); as in manhood, wifehood, priesthood, childhood, brotherhood, knighthood, sisterhood, neighbourhood, hardihood, likelihood. Likelihood has been corrupted probably by following the analogy of livelihood, from lif-lode = course of life. -head in Godhead is another form of this suffix.

-ing (diminutive); farthing, tithing, Riding.
   (Patronymics): Bildeging, son of Baldæg; Wódening, son of Woden; Browning, Harding. Names of places in -ingham.

-ling (diminutive: comp. Ger. -lein, diminutive); darling, gosling, duckling, underling, nestling, twinkling, starveling, fatling, firstling, hireling.

-kin (dim: comp. Ger. -chen); pipkin (from *pipe*), lambkin, lakin (= ladykin), firkin (from *four*), manikin, bodkin, gherkin.
(Patronymics): Hawkins (Hal), Perkins (Peter), Watkins (Walter), Simpkins (Simon), Dawkins (David).

-kind (O-E. cýn), as in mankind, womankind.

-le (O.E. -el), instrument or agent; beadle (from beodan, to bid), steeple (from stepan, to raise), awl, settle, skittle (from sceotan, to shoot).

-lock, -ledge (O.E. lác, gift, play) used to form abstract nouns: as in wedlock, knowledge. In O.E. we find reáflác (= rapine), wiflác (= wedlock), scinlác (= apparition), feohtlác (= battle).

-lock, -lic (O.E. leac, = leek): garlic (spear-leek, from gar = spear), hemlock, charlock, houseleek, harlock.

-ness. Abstract: darkness, goodness, wildness, wilderness, witness.

-nd (from ending of imperfect participle); friend, fiend, errand.

-ock (O.E. -uca). Diminutive and patronymic: hillock, bullock, ruddock (red-breast), Maddock, and Maddox (from Matthew), Pollock (from Paul).

-om -m; barm, doom (deem), seam (sew), bloom (blow), blossom, bosom.

-red (red, counsel); hatred, kindred, Ethelred (= noble in counsel), Mildred (= mild in counsel), sib-rede (relationship).

-ric (O.E. rice, rule, sway, dominion. Comp. Ger. -reich); bishopric. In O.E. we find kingric and abbotric.

-ry (O.E. ru) = place; as in brewery, heronry, piggery, rookery; fishery; *collective*, yeomanry; *abstract*, knavery.

-rel. Diminutive; cockerel, wastrel (a spendthrift, ne'er-do-weel), mongrel.

-ship, -skip, -scape (O.E. scipe = form, state, from scapan, to shape. Comp. Ger. -schaft); friendship, worship (O.E. weorth-scipe), landscape, also landskip, fellowship, ownership, workmanship, ladyship, lordship.

-stead (O.E. stéde, place); home-stead, bed-stead; names of places in -stead.

-ster (O.E. estre), a female agent; webster, tapster, brewster, baxter. This suffix denotes an agent simply, without regard to sex, in punster, deemster (deempster), maltster, songster, huckster. Modern forms: youngster, oldster, roadster.

-th (abstract), -t (from ending of pass. part.); uncouth (= un-known), wealth, height (Milton writes higth), length, dearth, ruth, spilth, stealth, strength, troth, truth, width, after-math (*moweth*), mirth (merry), earth (from *ear*, to plough), sloth (from *slow*), berth (from *bear*), shrift (from *shrive*), drift (from *drive*), gift, rift, theft, weft, flight, drought (from *dry*), draft and draught (from *draw*).

-ther, -der, -ter (agent, or instrument, with accompanying idea of duality); father, mother, sister, brother, daughter; (mere agency) water (wet), winter (wind), rudder (row), bladder (blow), laughter (laugh), murder, feather.

-tree (O. E. treow); roof-tree, axle-tree, rood-tree, gallows-tree.

-wright (O. E. wyrhta = workman); ship-wright, wain-wright (= wagon-maker), wheel-wright.

-ward = keeper; woodward, hayward, bearward, steward.

-y (O. E. ig); body, honey.

-y, -ie (diminutive); lady, doggie, Charlie, lassie.

312. Adjective Suffixes.

, ed, -d (participial); cold, loud, ragged, wretched, long-eared, new-fangled (fangan, to take; taken up with new things).

-en (material of which a thing is made); wooden, golden, silvern, cedarn, flaxen, linen (from *lin*, flax), oaken, hempen.

-en (participial); bounden, molten, drunken, forlorn, shorn, torn.

-ern (denoting the region of the globe); southern, eastern, northern, western.

-er; clever, sliper (= slippery).

-fast (O. E. fæst = firm); steadfast, rootfast, soothfast, shame-fast (wrongly written shamefaced).

-fold (O. E. feald. Comp. Lat. -plex, from plico); twofold, manifold. *Simple* has taken the place of anfeald (onefold).

-ful (O. E. ful = full); sinful, wilful, needful.

-ish, -ch (O. E. -isc, partaking of the nature of); boorish, childish, heathenish, churlish, uppish, outlandish, waspish, peevish, whitish, greenish, goodish. Patrial adjectives: English, Welsh (Wylisc), Irish. Modern: young-mannish.

-le (O. E. -el); little (lyte), mickle, tickle (superseded by *ticklish*), brittle (*bryttan*, to break), idle, stickle (Devonshire = steep).

-m; warm, grim.

-less (O. E. leás, loose, destitute of); sinless, fearless, toothless.

-like -ly (O. E. líc = like); warlike, wifelike, childlike; manly, womanly, bodily, godly, ghastly (ghostlike).

-ow (O. E. -u and -wa) ; narrow, fallow, callow.

-right (O. E. riht) ; upright, downright.

-some (O. E. -sum, Ger. -sam. Not connected with the pronoun *some*) ; longsome, winsome, lissom (lithe), buxom (*bugan*, to bend), gladsome, wholesome.

-teen, ten ; thirteen, fourteen.

-eth (O. E. -othe), ordinal ; fifth, tenth, fifteenth.

-ty (O. E. -tig, Ger. -zig), tens in numeration ; twenty, thirty.

-wise, ways ; righteous (rightwis).

-ward, direction ; homeward, seaward, landward, heavenward, awkward (wrong-way-ward), froward, toward.

-y (O. E. -e) ; worthy, smithy ; (O. E. -ig), guilty, dizzy (dysig = foolish), wealthy, healthy, mighty, any, many, dreary ; (O. E. -iht denotes *material*) hairy, stony.

313. Adverbial Suffixes.

-ere (place where) ; here, there, where.

-es, -se, -ce, -s (genitive) ; unawares, sometimes, besides, else, hence, thence, needs, eftsoons.

-ly (O. E. lice) ; wilfully, only, badly, purely.

-ling, -long (direction) ; darkling, grove-ling, sidelong.

-meal (O. E. mælum, dat. pl. of *mæl*, time, portion) ; piecemeal, limb-meal, flock-meal = troop-wise (Chaucer), stound-meal (Chaucer) = hour by hour. In O.E. we have styccemǽlum = stitch-meal ; sceáfmǽlum = sheaf-wise.

-om (dative termination) ; whilom, seldom.

-ther (direction towards) ; hither, thither.

-ward, -wards (direction) ; homeward, homewards, hitherward, inwards.

-wise, -way, ways ; anywise, nowise, otherwise, straightway, always.

314. Verb Suffixes.

-el (frequentative) ; dabble, dwindle (O. E. dwinan, to fade), dibble (dip), dazzle (daze), grapple (grap, grab, gripe), sparkle, startle, mingle, struggle (stray), swaddle (swathe), dribble (drop), nestle, niggle, nibble (neb = bill), waddle (wade), gabble (gab, comp. gabber and jabber), gaffle (gaf = hook), curdle, hurtle (hurt), hustle.

-er (frequentative) ; patter (pat), clatter, chatter, sputter (spit), batter (beat), glimmer (gleam), simmer, stagger (stay), flitter, flutter (flit), stutter (M.E. stut), stammer, wander (wand), welter.

After adjectives -er is causative ; linger (long), lower, hinder.

-en (causative); lengthen, soften, sweeten, fatten, brighten, lighten.

-en, -on (sign of the infinitive preserved); gladden (gladian), hearken (heorcnian), reckon (O. E. recan).

-k (frequentative) ; hark (hear), talk (tell), stalk (steal).

-se (O. E. -sian) (causative); cleanse, rinse (Ger. rein = pure).

Verbs are often formed from nouns by some change (*a*) of the radical vowel, (*b*) of the final consonant, (*c*) or of both.

(*a*) breed (brood), feed (food).

(*b*) graze (grass), glaze (glass), halve (half), calve (calf).

(*c*) breathe (breath), bathe (bath).

Causative verbs are formed in some instances by a modification of the root-vowel of the corresponding intransitive forms. Comp. drink and drench, rise and raise, lie and lay, sit and set, fall and fell. In O.E. we had *yrnan*, to run, and *ærnan*, to let run ; *byran*, to burn (intrans., ardeo), and *bærnan*, to burn (trans., uro); *sincan* (intrans.), *sencan* (trans.); *weallan*, to boil (intrans.), *wyllan*, to boil (trans.), &c. The common causative ending in O.E. was -ian.

SUFFIXES OF LATIN ORIGIN.

315. Noun Suffixes.

-age (Lat. -aticum) forms abstract nouns; age, savage (silvaticum), voyage (viaticum), personage, marriage, homage, salvage. Hybrids : mileage, tonnage, poundage, shrinkage, bondage.

-an, -ain (Lat. -anus), *connected with* ; publican. Disguised : chaplain, captain, certain, humane, mundane, sexton (sacristan). Modern forms: antiquarian, civilian, courtesan, artisan, partisan.

-al, -el (Lat. -alis, *possessing the qualities of*); cardinal, animal, canal, channel, hospital, hostel, hotel, spital, jewel (Mid. Lat. jocale, from *gaudium*).

-ant, -ent (Lat. -antem, entem), *denotes an agent*; assistant, merchant, agent, student, miscreant, recreant. Giant is from Gk. gigantos, gen. of gigas.

-ance, -ancy, -ence, -ency (Lat. -antia, -entia), forms abstract nouns from the present participle; distance, constancy, consistence, consistency. Disguised: chance (cadentia).

-and, -end (Lat. -andus, -endus), forms nouns from the gerundive; legend (something to be read), deodand (to be given to God), prebend, provender (a portion to be provided).

-ary (Lat. -arium) denotes the place where anything is kept;

laundry (lavo, I wash), vestry, sacristy, granary, aviary, seminary, salt-cellar (salière), saucer (for holding sauce), larder (a place for keeping bacon, Fr. lard), pantry (panis, bread). Modern: vinery, chapelry. Hybrids: Jewry, nunnery (Ital. nonna).

Hybrids in **-ery, -ry**, denoting *condition*, a *collection*; thievery, knavery, cookery, slavery, rookery, piggery.

-ary, -er (Lat. -arius), denotes *a person engaged in some trade*; statuary, secretary. Disguised in chancellor (cancellarius), farrier, vicar, archer, butcher, carpenter, mariner, butler (=bottler), officer, engineer (ingeniator), usher (ostiarius), brigadier, premier.

-ate (Lat. -atus, ending of pass. part.; Fr. -é, -ée), *agent*; advocate, curate, legate, legatee, trustee, ally, covey. Consulate and primate are differently formed.

-ce (Lat. -cium); edifice, benefice, sacrifice.

-el (Lat. -ela); quarrel, cautel, candle, tutelage.

-el (Lat. -allus, -ellus, -illus, -ulus), *diminutive*; chancel (cancelli), title, chapel, mettle, people, castle, pommel, veal (vitulus), libel, seal (sigillum). Disguised: roll (rotula). Hybrids: cockerel, dotterel, pickerel.

-en (Lat. -enus, -ena, -enum), alien. Disguised in vermin, venom, chain (catena).

-ern (Lat. -erna); lantern, cavern, cistern, tavern.

-et, -ot, -ette, -let (diminutive); pocket, cygnet, fillet, coquette, paroquette, flageolet, coronet, owlet, circlet, cutlet (costa, rib), casket, corset, cruet, pullet, ballot, chariot, tartlet.

-ess (late Lat. -issa), *female agent*; empress, governess, sorceress. Hybrids: murderess, sempstress.

-ice, -ise (Lat. -itia, Fr. -isc, -ice, -esse); service, merchandise, justice, malice, largesse, riches.

-ice, -ish (Lat. -icem, acc. of words in -*x*); pumice, radish. Disguised: judge (judex), race (radix).

-icle, -ucle (Lat. -iculus, -uculus, -ellus, -ulus), diminutive; particle, versicle, article, fable (fabula), stable, people, table, miracle, pinnacle (penna, wing), peril (periculum), tabernacle (from taberna), reticule, riddle. Disguised: rule (regula), carbuncle (a little coal, carbo), ferule, damsel (dominicella = little lady), parcel (a little part), morsel (a little bite, from mordeo), model (modus), muscle (musculus), corpuscle (corpusculum), uncle (from avunculus), vessel (from vas).

-iff (Lat. -ivus), adjectival: caitiff, plaintiff, bailiff.

-ine, -in (Lat. -inus), adjectival; divine, cousin (consanguineus).

-in (Lat. -inem, acc. termination); virgin, origin, margin

-ion, -tion, -sion, -son, -som, -cion (Lat. -ionem, acc. termination),
denotes primarily the *action*; action, potion, lection, position,
vacation, poison (potio), season (satio), venison (venatio),
liaison (ligatio), lesson (lectio), ransom (redemptio), benison
(benedictio), malison (maledictio), foison (abundance, from
fusio).

-m, -me; charm (carmen), crime. Disguised: noun (nomen), renown, leaven, volume, régime.

-ment (Lat. -mentum); instrument, vestment, document, impediment, moment (a moving force), monument, ornament.
Modern forms: parliament, enchantment, nourishment, garment. Hybrids: acknowledgment, fulfilment, atonement.

-mony (Lat. -monium); ceremony, testimony, matrimony, sancti-
mony, acrimony.

-on (Lat. -o); falcon, carbon, mansion, pigeon (Lat. pipio).

-oon (Fr. -on; Ital. -one), *augmentative*; balloon, dragoon, har-
poon, saloon, buffoon, poltroon, cartoon. Disguised in trombone.

-our, -or (Lat. -orem, acc.; Fr. -eur), *abstract*; labour, savour,
ardour, clamour, amour. Modern: behaviour, grandeur.

-or, -our, -er (Lat. -torem, acc.; Fr. -teur), *agent*; actor, auditor,
victor, monitor, saviour, governor, emperor, compiler (com-
pilator), founder (fundator), juror (jurator), emperor (impe-
rator), preacher (prædicator), juggler (joculator), author
(auctor).

-ory, -ger, -or, -our, -er (Lat. -orium, -oria), *place*; refectory, repertory, auditory, dormitory, lavatory, oratory, dormer, manger
(manducatorium), parlour (parlatorium).

-t (Lat. -tus, p. part.); act, usufruct, fruit, fact, feat, joint, rent
(reddere, to give back), point, debt, suit, comfit (=confect),
conceit (concept), counterfeit.

-ter (Lat. -ter); master (magister, from magis), minister (from
minus).

-tery (Lat. -terium), *employment, condition*; ministry, mastery.

-trix (Lat. -trix), *feminine agent*; executrix, testatrix, improvisatrice.

-ter, -tre (Lat. -trum); cloister, theatre, spectre.

-tude (Lat. -tudinem, acc.), latitude, longitude, altitude, beatitude, fortitude, custom (consuetudinem).

-ty (Lat. -tatem, acc.), *abstract*; charity, bounty (bonitas), vanity,
cruelty, poverty (paupertas), fealty (fidelitas).

-ure (Lat. -ura) denotes *action*; juncture (joining), aperture,
ointure, measure (mensura), picture. Modern: verdure,
jointure, enclosure, caricature.

-y (Lat. -ia); family, copy, victory, story.

-y (Lat. -icus); enemy.

-y (Lat. -ium); joy (gaudium), study, augury, remedy.

-y (Lat. -atus); ally, deputy.

-y (Lat. -ies); progeny.

316. Adjective Suffixes.

-aceous (-aceus), *material*; farinaceous, argillaceous.

-acious (-acem, acc.), *propensity*; tenacious, veracious, loquacious, voracious.

-al (Lat. -alis), *belonging to*; legal, loyal, regal, royal, equal.

-an, -ane, -ain (-anus), *belonging to*; urban, urbane, human, humane, certain. Disguised in dean (decanus), piano, courtesan.

-ant, -ent (-antem, -entem, acc. of pres. part.); distant, trenchant, current, accident.

-ar (Lat. -aris), *belonging to*; secular, regular, singular. Disguised: premier.

-ary, -arian, -arious (Lat. -arius), *belonging to*; contrary, necessary, agrarian, gregarious.

-atic (Lat. -aticus); lunatic, fanatic (from fanum), aquatic.

-ate (Lat. -atus, pass. part. and adjectival); determinate, desolate, private.

-ble (Lat. -abilis, -ebilis, -ibilis), *denotes the possibility of something being done*; movable, amiable, soluble, feeble (Lat. flebilis. Cp. foible). Hybrid: eatable, drinkable.

-ble, -ple (Lat. -plex), *fold*; double, duple, triple, treble.

-esque (Lat. -iscus, Fr. -esque); picturesque, burlesque, grotesque. Disguised: morris (Moresco), a Moorish dance.

-fic (Lat. -ficus); terrific.

-ic (Lat. -icus), *belonging to*; civic, classic, barbaric. Disguised in indigo (= Indicus).

-id (Lat. -idus), *possessing the quality expressed by the verb*; frigid, morbid, acid, tepid.

-il, -ile (Lat. -ilis), passive; docile, mobile, fragile, civil. Disguised: subtle, gentle, frail (fragilis).

-ine (Lat. -inus), *belonging to*; divine, crystalline, lacustrine, canine.

-ive (Lat. -ivus), *inclined to*; pensive, active, native, captive. Disguised: resty (restive), massy (massive). Hybrid: talkative.

-lent (Lat. -lentus), *fulness*; opulent, corpulent, fraudulent, violent (vis).

-ory (Lat. -orius); illusory, amatory, admonitory.

-ose, -ous (Lat. -osus), *fulness*; verbose, grandiose, glorious, curious, envious.

-ous (Lat. -us); assiduous, ingenuous, omnivorous. Hybrids: wondrous, timeous, boisterous. Righteous is O.E. rihtwis.

-se (Lat. -sus), *participial*; tense, intense.

-te, -t (Lat. -tus), *adjectival*; chaste (castus), fortunate, modest, honest.

-und (Lat. -undus); moribund, jocund, rotund. Disguised: round, second.

-ulous (Lat. -ulus); querulous, sedulous.

-urn (Lat. -urnus); auburn (Low Lat. *alburnus*, whitish).

317. Verb Suffixes.

-ate (Lat. -atus, pass. part.); complicate, supplicate. Hybrid: assassinate.

-esce (Lat. -esco) denotes the beginning of an action; effervesce, coalesce.

-fy (Lat. -ficere, Fr. -fier. From facio); magnify, signify.

-ish (Fr. -issant, ending of present participle of verbs in -ir); nourish, finish, cherish, perish.

-ite, -ete, -t (Lat. -itus, -etus, -tus: pass. part.); connect, reflect, delete, expedite.

318. Greek Suffixes.

-ē (-η), *action*; strophe, catastrophe.

-y (-ια), *quality*; philosophy, monarchy.

-ad (-αδος), *Genitive ending*; Iliad, Troad, monad.

-ic, ics (-ικός), *belonging to*; politic, politics, ethics, logic, music, physic, physics, graphic, authentic, æsthetic.

-sis, -sy, -se (-σις), *action*; crisis, emphasis, genesis, palsy (paralysis), hyprocrisy, poesy, ellipse, phase, base.

-ma, -em, -me, -m (-μα), *the result of an action*; dogma, drama, diorama, system, diadem, theme, scheme.

-st (-στης), *agent*; baptist, sophist, botanist, iconoclast. Hybrids: educationist, educationalist, excursionist, protectionist, abolitionist, journalist, positivist, socialist, purist, specialist, royalist.

-te, -t (-της), *agent*; poet, comet, planet, apostate.

❧ -ter, tre (-τρον), *the instrument or means by which an action is performed*; metre, centre.

❧ -sm (-σμα), *result*; schism, cataclysm, spasm.

❧ -isk (-ισκος), *diminutive*; asterisk, obelisk.

❧ -ize (-ιζω), *verb-ending*; Philippize, baptize, Judaize. This termination is sometimes spelled -ise, but -ize is preferable in words derived directly from the Greek. It should not be confounded with the last syllable of circumcise (cædo). Minimize is a hybrid formation. Gorgonize (Tennyson).

319. OLD ENGLISH WORDS HAVING MODERN REPRESENTATIVES OR DERIVATIVES.

[*The more prolific roots are marked with an asterisk.*]

*Ác, oak: *acorn*, *Acton*, *Auckland*, *Auckworth*, *Axholme* (oak-island), *Ockley*, *Oakham*, *Uckfield*

acan, to *ache*

ácsian, to *ask*

ácumba, *oakum*; that which is *combed* out

adesa, an *adze*

ádl, disease; *addled*

*æcer, a field, *acre*; *God's acre*, *West-Acre*

*æfen, *even*; *eventide*

*áefre, always; *ever*, *every*

æfter, according to, *after*. 'Reward us not *after* our sins.'— *P. Book*

ægg, plu. ægru, *egg*. The plural in Middle English was eyren. Caxton writes, 'What sholde a man in theyse days now write —egges or *eyren*?' Eyry is not, as is sometimes stated, a corruption of *eggery*, but from Fr. *aire*, a nest of hawks

áeghwæther, *either*

ǽl, *awl*

ǽl, an *eel*; *eel-pout*

*ælc, *each*; *every* (= ever-each)

ælmysse, *alms* (G. eleemosyne).

æmtig, *empty*

æmyrie, *embers*

áenig, *any*

*áer, *ere*; *erst*, *early*. 'Come it *ear*', come it *late*, in May comes the cow-quake.'—*Old Proverb*

ærend, *errand*

ærian, to *plough*; to *ear*.—Deut. xxi. 4

*æsc (still pronounced *esh* in Lincolnshire), *ash*; *Ascot*, *Ashdon*, *Ashcombe*, *Escombe*, *Eskgill*, *Ashby*, *Ashbourne*, *Ashwell*

æsce, *ashes*

æspen, *aspen*

æstspornan, to kick; *spurn*

*æthele, noble; *ætheling*, prince; Edgar *Atheling*, *Ethelbert*

ætwitan, to *twit*

ágan, past ahte, to possess; *own*, *ought*

*áht, *aught*, *naught*

án, *one*; *only*, *alone*

ancleow, *ankle*

andlang, *along*

andswerian, to *answer*. Lit. to swear in opposition to. From *and-* = against, and *swerian*, to swear

angel, hook; *angle*

appel, *appl.*

árewe, *arrow*; the river *Arrow*

arm, *arm*; *armlet*

assa, *ass.* Cp. Ger. *Esel*, Lat.
asinus

áta, *oat*

áth, *oath*

bá, *both*

*bacan, to *bake*; *batch*, *baker*,
Baxter (a female baker)

*bæc, *back*; *backbiter*, *backwards*,
aback, *to back*, Saddle-*back*

*bælg, *bag*; *belly*, *bulge*, *bellows*
bær, *bier*, from *béran*

*bær, *bare*; *barefoot*, *barefaced*,
barely

bæst, inner bark; *bast*

bæth, *bath*; *Bath*. Cp. *Baden*

*báld, *bold*; *Baldwin* (bold in
battle; *win* = contest), *Ethel-
bald*

bán, *bone*

*bana, *bane*, slayer; *ratsbane*,
baneful, *henbane*, *fleabane*

banc, *bench*

bár, *boar*

*bát, *boat*; *boatswain*

beacen, *beacon*; *beckon*

beæftan, behind; *abaft*

bealu, *bale*; *baleful*

*beám; 1. a tree; 2. anything in
a straight line; *beam*, *horn-
beam*, *bog-beam*, *sun-beam*,
Bampton (Beam dún = tree-
hill), *Beamfleet*, *Bamfleet*,
Banfleet. Comp. Ger. *Baum*,
Dutch *boom*

bean, a *bean*

bearn, a child; *bairn*, from
béran, to bear

*beátan, past beót, to *beat*;
batter, *beetle*, a wooden hammer (O.E. bytl)

becuman, to happen; *become*

bed, *bed*; *bedridden* (O.E. *bed-
rída*. From *rída*, a rider).
The word was originally used
in a sarcastic sense

béd, a prayer; *bedesman*, *bead*
(from *biddan*, to pray). *Beads*
were little balls on a string,
used for helping the memory
in sayíng a number of prayers.

'To bid one's beads' was to
say one's prayers

beginnan, to *begin*

begytan, to *beget*

behofian, to require; *behove*

belle, *bell*; bellan, to *bellow*.
N.B.: Belfry is not from this
source, but from N.F. beffroi,
a watch-tower

bén, prayer. 'What is good for
a bootless *bene* ?'—*Wordsworth*

bendan, to *bend*. From *band*

beo, a *bee*

beódan, to command, *bid*;
beadle (O.E. bydel)

beofer, *beaver*

beón, to *be*; *become, albeit*

*beorgan, to save, shelter; *bur-
row* (Prov., shelter from the
wind, as in 'the burrow side
of the hedge'), *bury*, *burg-
lar* (a townrobber); *burgh*,
borough, *harbour* (O.E. *here* =
army), *harbinger*, one sent on
before to secure shelter; *borrow*, to obtain money on se-
curity

beorma, *barm*

bera, a *bear*

*béran, to *bear*; *burden*, *bier*, *bairn*,
birth, *berth*, *brood*, *burden*,
bird (the young of any animal)

bere, *barley*; *barn* (from *bere*,
barley, and *ern*, a place. Cp.
bæcces-ern, a baking place),
barton (a court-yard)

bereafian, to rob; *bereave*. Comp.
reever = (robber), *rive*, *rob*

berstan, past bærst, to *burst*;
outburst

besma, a *besom*

besprecan, to *bespeak*

*bétan, to make good; *better*,
best, *boot* (verb), *bootless*

betweonan, *between*. Cp. *two*,
twin

betweox, *betwixt*

biddan, to pray. See Béd

*bígan, or beogan, to bend; *bow,*
rainbow, elbow (the bending
of the arm. Cp. *ell,* the length
of the fore-arm, Lat. *ulna,*
the fore-arm), *bough, boughts*
(the coils of a rope), *bout*
('In notes with many a winding bout.'—*L'Allegro*), *bight*
as in the *Bight* of Benin,
buxom (O.E.bocsum = flexible,
tractable, obedient)

bill, falchion; *bill*-hook, brown-
bills (Lear)

bin, manger; *bin*

*bindan, past band, to *bind;*
bundle, band, bond, bondage,
hop-*bine,* wood-*bine, bandog*

birce, *birch*

bisgian, to *busy; business*

*bítan, to *bite; bit, beetle* (O.E.
bitel. Dim., the little *biter*),
bait, bitter

blác, pale; *bleach, bleak*

blæc, *black*

blæd, *blade.* From *blow,* to bloom

blæddre, *bladder*

bláwan, past bleów, to *blow;*
blast, blaze?

blendan, to mix; *blend*

bleo, colour; *blue*

bletsian, to *bless; blithe, bliss*

blind, *blind; blend*

blód, *blood; bleed*

*blówian, to blossom; *blow* (of
flowers), *blood, blade, blossom,*
bloom

bóc, *book; boc*-land (land held
by a charter or writing)

bodian, to announce; *forebode*

bodig, the chest; *body, bod-*
dice

bóld, *bold; bawd, bawdy*

bolla, a *bowl*

bolster, *bolster.* From *bolla*

bonda, a householder; hus-
band

bord, *board,* table, 'bed and
board,' 'The Lord's Board'

borgian, to *borrow.* See Beorgan

bósm, *bosom*

bót, remedy; *boot*-less, to *boot,* vb.

brád, broad; Bradfield, breadth,
Bredon (*denu,* valley)

brægen, *brain*

bræs, *brass; brazen, brazier*

bræth, *breath; breathe, breath-*
less

bræw, *brow; eye-brow*

*brand (from byrnan, to *burn*);
brand, fire-*brand, brand*-new

bréc, plu. of bróc, *breeches;*
brogues

*brecan, past bræc, to *break;*
breakers, brake, bracken,
breach, brick, break-fast,
break-water

bremel, *bramble*

breóst, *breast.* Cog. *brisket*

*breówan, to *brew; brewis, broth,*
brose, barley-*bree*

brér, *briar*

bricg, *bridge*

*brid, the young of any animal;
bird. From *béran*

bridan, to *braid*

bridel, *bridle.* From *bredan,* to
braid

bringan, past brohte, to *bring*

bróc, *brook; brooklet*

bróc, a badger; *Brocden, Brox-*
bourne (= badgers' stream),
Brocthorp

bróm, *broom; Brompton, Brom-*
ley (Broom-meadow). Cog.
bramble

bróther, *brother.* Gebrothru,
brethren, brotherhood

brýd, a *bride; bride*-groom
(*guma,* a man), *bridal*
(= bride-ale, a marriage feast)

*búan, to cultivate; *boor, boorish,*
neigh*bour, bower.* Cp. Du.
boer

buc, pitcher; *bucket*

búr, chamber; *bower*

*burh, *burgh* (see Beorgan);
Edin*burgh,* Borstal (*stal* =
seat), Canter*bury,* *burgher,*
boro*ugh.* Cog. *harness*

bylig, *bellows; bag, belly, bilge*

byrgan, to *bury, burial* (O.E. *birgels*, a sepulchre)

byrnan, to *burn* (past barn); *brim*stone, *brown* (burnt colour), *brunt, brand, brandy* (Ger. brannt-wein, distilled wine), *brindle.* Cog. *Bruin*

byrst, *bristle* (dim.)

cæg, *key*

cœrse, *cress.* 'Not worth a *curse*'=not worth a *cœrse.* Cp. 'Wisdom and witte now is nought worth a *carse.*' (Piers Plowman.) See Skeat

*cáld, ceald, *cold; chill, cool, Cald*well, *Cole*brook, *Col*burn

calu, bald; *callow.* Lat. *calvus*

camb, *comb.* See Cemban

cárian, to *care; careful, chary*

catt, *cat, cathin, kitten, kitling, cater*pillar (*pilosus*=hairy), *cater*waul

ceáca, *cheek*

ceafu, *chaff*

cealf, *calf, calve, Calver*ley, *Kelve*don (Calf's-hill)

*ceápian, to *buy*, ceáp, *bargain; cheap,chap*man (=merchant), *chaffer, Chep*stow, *Cheap*side, horse-*coper, chop.* Cp. Ger. *kaufen*, to sell, and *Kaufmann*, merchant. Also *Copen*hagen

ceaster, *city* (L. castra), Glou-*cester*

cemban, to *comb; kempster*, un-*kempt*

céne, *keen.* Cog. *ken, can*

*cennan, to *bring forth, kindle, kin, kind, kindred, kindly*

ceol, small ship; *keel, Chel*sea, *keel*son. Cog. Du. *keel*-haul

ceorfan, to *carve*

ceorl, a *churl, Charles*' wain (=the churl's wagon). Cp. O.N. *carl*, a man. Sc. *carle, carlin*

ceósan, to *choose*

ceówan, to *chew*

cépan, to *keep*

cese, *cheese*; from L. *caseus*

cetel, *kettle; kettle*-drum

cicen, pl. cicenu, *chicken; chick*-weed

cídan, to *chide*

cild, plu. cildre and cildrs, *child, Childermas* (Innocent's Day), *childhood, childing*

cin, *chin*

circe, *church.* Dan. *kirke*

cirps, *crisp.* Cp. Lat. *crispus*

clæg, *clay.* Cog. *clog*

cléne, *clean; cleanse*

clam, anything that is clammy or holds fast, *clam; clamp, clump, clams*

cláth, *cloth; clothe, clothier*

clawu, *claw*

cleófan, to *cleave; clearer*

cleopian, to *call; yclept*, to *clepe* (Macbeth)

clucgge, bell; *clock*

*clúfan, to *cleave*; clifan, to *cleave* to; *cliff, cleft, cloven*

clyppan, to *embrace; clip*

cnápa, *boy; knave, knavery*

cnáwan, to *know; knowledge*

cnedan, to *knead*

cnców, *knee*; knock-*kneed,kneel.* Cp. Lat. *genu*

cniht, youth; *knight*

cnoll, *knoll*

cnucl, *knuckle*

cnyll, *knell*

cnyttan, to *knit; knot*

cóc, *cock; chicken* (cicen), *chick*-weed, *chicken*-pox, *chicken*-hearted. Not chick-pea

cod, bag; pease-*cod*

cofa, *cove*

comb, *valley*; Bos*comb*, Chil-*comb*, Compton, *Comb*-Basset. W. *cwm*, pron. *coom*

corn, seed; *corn*, pepper-*corn, kernel.* Not acorn

coss, *kiss.* Ger. Kuss

crabbe, *crab*

cræft, art, *craft; crafty*, handi-*craft* (note the -i. The O.E. form is hand-gecræft)

cræt, *cart; carter, cartage*
crafian, to *crave; craven*
crán, *crane; Cranborne*
cranc, weak; *cranky*
cráwan, to *crow; crow, crow*-bar
('having a strong beak like a crow'—Skeat)
creópan, to *creep*
*cric, *crutch; crook, crooked, crotchet, crocket* (cp. Fr. *crochet*), *cricket* (cricket bats were formerly crooked)
cú, *cow;* pl. cý. Sc. kye
*cuc, cwic, alive, *quick; quicken, quick*-set, to cut to the *quick, couch* or *quitch* grass, *quick*-lime, *quick*-sand, *quick*-silver
cuman, to *come; comely*
*cunnan, to know, to be able; *can, con, cunning, canny, ken, uncouth,* ale-*conner* (inspector of ales)
cwéarn, a mill; *quern*
cwellan, to *kill; quell*
cwén, *queen, quean*
cwencan, to *quench*
cwethan, past cwæth, to *say; quoth, bequeath*
cyning, *king; Kingston, Kineton, Kingsbury.* Cp. Ger. König
cyrran, to turn; *jar,* on the *jar,* i.e. turn, *char*woman, one who does an occasional *turn* of work
cýte, *cot; cottage, sheep-cot, Cotswold*
dæg, *day; dawn, daisy*
*dǽlan, to divide; *deal* (verb), *dole, deal* (fir-wood), *dale, dell*
deaf, *deaf; deafen*
deág, *dye*
dearran, past durste, to *dare;* Sc. *dour*
deáth, *death,* Icel. *deyja,* to *die*
deaw, *dew; dew*-lap
delfan, to dig; *delve*
*déman, to judge; *deem, doom, dempster, Doomsday*
*denu, a valley; *den,* names of

places ending in -den, as Tenter*den,* Taunton *Dean,* Cob*den,* Rotting-*dean*
deofan, to *dive; di-dapper = dive*-dapper
deóp, *deep; depth, Dept*ford
*deór, beast; *deer* (originally generic. Thus Shakspere makes Mad Tom say in *King Lear:* 'But mice and rats and such small *deer* Have been Tom's food for seven long year'), *Durham, Der*by. Comp. Ger. Thier, a *beast*
deór, *dear; dearth, darling,* en*dear*
deorc, *dark; darken*
dic, *dyke; ditch*
dihtan, to dispose; *dight*
dóhtor, *daughter.* Comp. Gk. *thugatēr*
dol, foolish; *dull, dolt*
dón, past *dyde,* to *do; deed*
drǽdan, to *dread*
*dragan, to *drag; draw, draught, dray, draggle, dredge*
drencan, to *drench*
dreógan, to *drudge*
dreór, gore; *dreary*
*drífan, to *drive; drift, drove*
*drig, *dry; drought* (Sc. *drouth*), *drug* (= dried plant?)
drincan, to *drink; drunk, drunkard*
*dripan, to *drop; drip, dribble, driblet, drivel, droop*
dugan, to be good for (valere); to *do* as in 'How do you *do?* 'He will *do* well'
dumb, *dumb; dummy*
*dún, mountain; *down, adown* (= of dune, from the hill. Cp. Fr. *à mont* = to the hill, *à val* = to the valley), *Downs,* Snow*don,* Hunting-*don;* Down*ham*
duru, *door.* Cp. Gk. *thura*
dust, *dust: dusty*
dynan, to *dine: dinner*
dynt, stroke; *dint*

dyppan, to *dip*

dysig, foolish; *dizzy*

dwinan, to pine; *dwindle*

eác, also; *eke*, *nick*-name (an *eke*-name)

*eáge, *eye* ; *Egbert* (= bright eye), *eye*-bright (euphrasy), *eye*-brow, dais*y*. Cog. -*ow* in window (O.N. vind*auga*, wind-eye, an opening to admit air). Cp. Ger. *Auge*, Lat. *oculus*

eahta, *eight*. Ger. *acht*, Goth. *ahtau*, Lat. *octo*

' eald,*old*; *alder*man,*Ald*borough, *Alton*, Alford, Auburn, Authorpe, *elder*

eall, *all* ; *al*ready, with*al*

*ealu, *ale* ; brid*al* (= bride ale), Whitsun-*ales*. O.N. öl

eáre, *ear*; *ear*-wig (an insect supposed to lodge itself in the ear. *Wiega* or *wigga* = an insect), *ear*-ring. In O.E. the little finger was called by the disagreeable name of *eár*-*scrypel* = ear-scraper

earm, *arm*

earn, eagle; *Arnesby*, *Earnley*

earnian, to reap; *earn*, *earnings*

east, *east* ; *Essex*, *S*terling (= Easterling), *Easter* (from the goddess, Eostre, whose name is from the same source as *East*)

ebbe, *ebb*; *Ebbs*fleet, *ebb*, adj. = low. 'Cross the stream where it is *ebbest*.'—*Lancashire Proverb*. Same root as *even*

*ece, *ache*

ecg, *edge*; *Edge*hill, Strathdon-*edge*, Swirrell*edge*; to *egg*

*efer, a wild boar; *Everton*, *Everleigh*, *Ever*shot, *Evers*holt, *Evershaw*

efese, *eaves* of a house, a brim, brink,edge of a hill; *Eresham*, Habersham-*Eaves*,   eaves-dropper

*eft, again ; *after*, *afterwards*, *eftsoons*, *abaft*

ége, *awe*; *awful*

elles, *else*. El- in composition = other. Cp. Lat. *alius*

*embe, about, *Ember*. See *ryne*, course. Ember = going round. *Ymb-ren-wuce* = Ember-week

eorl, *earl* ; *earl*dom

eorthe, *earth* ; *earth*en, *earth*-quake

erian, to plough; *ear*. Cp. L. *aro*

etan, to *eat*. Cp. Ger. *essen*, Lat. *edere*. Also *fret* = for-eat

fæger, *fair* ; *fair*ly, *fair*ness

fægnian, to rejoice; *fain*. Cog. *fawn*, vb.

*fæst, *fast*; stead*fast*, sooth*fast*, shame*fast* (corrupted into shame-*faced*), *fasten*, *fastness*, *fast*, sb., *fast*-day. Cog. *fast* (Icel.) in '*fast* asleep'

fæt, vessel; *fat*, *vat*

fæther, *father*. Sanscr. *pitri*, Lat. *pater*, Ger. *Vater*

fæthm, *fathom*; the space between the two arms extended

fætt, *fat*

*faran, to go, *fare*, wel*fare*, thorough*fare*, way*faring*, sea*faring*, *ferry*, *fern* (' Probably named from the reputed use of the seed in magical incantations, being supposed to confer the power of *going* invisible.'— *Wedgwood*)

feallan, to *fall*; *fell* (= to cause to fall)

*fealu, *yellow* ; *fallow*-deer, *field*-*fare* (O.E. feala-for)

fearh, a little pig; *farrow*

feax, hair; Fair*fax*

feccan, to *fetch*. Cog. with *foot*

*fédan, to *feed*; *food*, *fodder*, *foster* (i.e. foodster), *forage* (= fodderage), *foray* or *forray*

fel, skin ; *fell*, *fell*-monger

feld, a *field*. Probably cog. with *fell*, a hill, a down

fen, *fen*

*fengan, to catch; *fang, finger,* new-*fangled* (snatching at new things)

feoh, cattle; *fee.* Comp. the connection of Lat. *pecunia* with pecus, cattle

feohtan, to *fight*

feól, a rasp; *file*

feónd, enemy; *fiend*

feorm, *farm*

feówer, *four; farthing, firkin,* Sc. *firlot* (fourth part of a boll of meal), *fourteen, forty*

ferran, *afar*

fersc, *fresh; freshen, freshet, freshman.* Cog. *frisky, fresco.* Comp. O.E. *cerse = cress*

fether, *feather*

fíf, *five* (an *n* has dropped out of fíf); *fifty.* Cp. Ger. *fünf,* Gk. *pente,* Lat. *quinque,* W. *pump*

*fillan, to *fill; full, fulfil*

*findan, to *find; foundling*

finol, *fennel.* L. feniculum

fisc, *fish. Fishguard* (fish-enclosure). Goth. *fisks.* Gr. *ichthys,* Lat. *piscis,* W. *pysg*

flǽsc, *flesh; flesher*

flaxe, *flask.* (Low Lat. *flasca*)

fleax, *flax*

*fleógan, to *flee; flight, fly, flea, flea*-wort, *fledged* (= ready to fly) *flit, flitter*mouse

floc, *flock.* Probably cog. with *folk*

flór, *floor*

*flótan, to *float; fleet, float,* ice-*floe, afloat,* North*fleet,* South*fleet.* Cog. *flotsam.* Lat. *fluctus*

flówan, to *flow; flood*

flýs, *fleece*

fola, *foal; filly.* W. filawg

folc, *folk; Norfolk, folk-lore*

folgian, to *follow*

fordón, to ruin, destroy; *foredo* (Lear)

fore, *before; further*

forleósan, to lose, perf. part. forloren, *forlorn*

forma, first; *former*

forsacan, to *forsake*

forswǽran, to perjure; *forswear, forsworn*

*fót, *foot,* pl. *fét; fetter, fet*lock. Cog. Gk. pous, podos, Lat. pes, pedis

fox, *fox;* fem. *vixen, fox*-glove

fram, *from, fro; fro*ward

freó, *free; freedom*

freónd, *friend*

freósan, to *freeze,* perf. part. *fróren; frore, frost*

fretan, to eat. From *for-etan,* intens.; *fret,* canker-*fret,* pock-*fretten.* Cp. Ger. fressen

frosc, *frog*

fugl, *fowl; fowler.* Ger. Vogel

fúl, *foul; fulsome, filthy, defile, foul*mart (a pole-cat, from the foul smell of the animal)

full, *full*

furh, *furrow; furlong,* the length of a *furrow*

fús, ready; *fuss, fussy*

fýr, *fire.* Ger. *feuer;* Gk. *pyr*

fyrst, *first.* Superlative of *fore.* Comp. Lat. *primus,* first, with *præ,* before

fýst, *fist; fist*ock

gád, *goad; gadfly*

gaderian, to *gather; together*

*gaers, *grass; grass* - hopper *Gearsley, Grasmere, Garston, Garstang* (grass-pool), *Garsby, Grasgarth* (grass-enclosure), *Gargrave* (grass-grove), *grazier*

gafol, tribute; *gavel*-kind

gál, merry; galan, to sing; nightin*gale.* Cog. *yell*

*gamenian, to *game; gamble, gamester*

*gangan, to *go; gang-way, gait, gate, ago, gang*

gár, spear: *gore,* a triangular piece let into a garment, *garlick* (leac = leek), *gar*fish *gást, breath; *ghost, aghast, ghast-ly*

gát, *goat*; *Gat*ford, *Gat*combe (=goat valley), *Gat*acre (=goat's field), *Gat*ton (=goat's town)

geac, a cuckoo, a simpleton; *gawky*

gealga, *gallows*

geáp, wide; *gape, gap*

gear, *year*

geara, formerly; of *yore*

geard (from gyrdan, to enclose), *yard*; *garden*, vine*yard*, hop*yard*. Cp. *garth*=enclosure

gearo, ready; *yarely* (Tempest)

geát, *gate*

*gehǽp, fit; *hap, happy*, mis*hap, happen, hap*-hazard

genoh, *enough*

geoc, *yoke*

geogoth, *youth*

geolo, *yellow*

geong, *young*; *youth*

geótan, to pour; *gutter*, in*got*, a mass of metal poured into a mould, *nugget* (=an ingot). Cp. Fr. lingot=l'ingot

geréfa, *reeve*; land-*reeve, sheriff* (scír-geréfa)

gese, *yes*

get, *yet*

gewiss, certainly; *i-wis*, often wrongly printed *I wis*

gicel, a small piece of ice; *icicle* (isgicel)

gifan, to *give*; *gift, gew-gaw*

girnan, to *yearn*

gitan, to *get*

glǽd, *glad*; *gladsome, gladden*

glæs, *glass*; *glaze, glazier*

glisnian, to *glisten*. Cog. *glitter, glint*

gliw, *glee*

gnæt, *gnat*

gnagan, to *gnaw*; *nag*

*God, *God, gossip* (=related in God), *god*head, *good*-bye

*gód, *good*; *goodwife, goody, gospel*

gold, *gold*; *gild, gilt*, mari-*gold*

góma, *gum*

gós, *goose*; *gosling, goshawk, Gosport, Gosford*. An *n* has been dropped out of *goose*. Cp. Ger. *gans*, Lat. *anser*, Gr. *chën*, Eng. *gander* and *gannet* (O.E. ganota)

græg, *gray, grey*; *grayling*, Cp. Fr. *gris*

*grafan, to dig; *grave* (vb. and subst.), *engrave, groove, grub*

*grápian, to handle; *grab, grapple, grapnel, grope*. See Gripan

grédig, *greedy*

*grén, *green*

greót, sand, gravel; *grit, grits, groats, grout*

grétan, to *greet*

grim, horrible; *grim*

gríndan, to *grind*; *grindstone, grist* (corn brought to a mill to be ground)

gripan, to *grip*, part. *gráp*; *gripes*, hand-*grip*

grówan, p. greow, to *grow*; *growth, green*

grund, *ground*; *grunsel* (=groundsill), *groundsel* (the ground-swallower. From swelgan, to swallow)

grút, meal; *groats, grouts*. See Greót

guma, man; bride*groom*

gyf, *if*

gyldan, to *yield*, pay; *guilt* (originally a *payment*, recompense)

gýlian, to *yell*

gyrd, *yard*. First applied to a rod or switch; then, perhaps, to fences made of interlaced rods; then to an enclosure

*gyrdan, to enclose; *girdle, gird, girth*. See gyrd.

gyrstan-dæg, *yesterday*

gyst, *guest*

gyt, *yet*

*habban, to *have*; *behave, haft* (what a thing is held by) hád, 1, person; 2, state; man-*hood*, wife*hood*, &c.

*hælan, to *heal*, hál, *hale*; *health*, *hail*, *whole*, *wholesome*, *wassail* (= wǽs hál, be whole)

hælfter, *halter*, from *healdan*, to hold

hæpse, *hasp*

hǽr, *hair*

hærfæst, *harvest*

hæringc, *herring*. Ger. *häring*, Fr. *hareng*. Said to be from O.E. *here*, an army

hǽst, *hot*; *hasty*, *hasten*

hǽte, *heat*; *hot*. Ger. *heiss*, hot

hæth, *heath*; hæthen, *heathen*, a dweller on a heath. Cp. *pagan*. Lat. *paganus*, one who lived in a village (pagus)

hafoc, *hawk*, *havoc*

*haga, *haw*, *hedge*; *Hagley*, *Haydon*, *Hay*, *Hayes*, *haw-haw*, a sunk fence; *haw*-thorn

hagol, *hail*

*hálig, *holy* (Ger. *heilig*), *halibut* (= holy fish. For -*but*, cp. turbot), *holly*-hock, *hallow*, All-*Hallows* (= All Saints), *halidom*

*hals, neck; *hauberk* (O.E. healsbeorg, from *beorgan*, to protect), *haubergeon*

*hám, *home*; *hamlet*, *Buckingham*

hamor, *hammer*

hán, *hone*

*hand, *hand*; *handiwork* (hand-geweorc), *handy*, *handi*cap (a name probably given to the drawing of lots from a cap), *hand*some (meant originally *handy*), *handle*, *hand*sel (earnest paid into the hand)

*hang, to *hang*; *hinge*, Stonehenge, *hank*, *hanker*

hár, *hoar*; *hoary*, *hore*-hound (O.E. hara-hunig)

hara, *hare*; *hare*bell, *harrier*

hás, *hoarse*

hát, *hot*; *heat*

hátan, to command; be*hest*

bátan, to call, past *hátte*, *hight*

hátian, to *hate*; *hatred*

*heáfod, *head*. Cp. Ger. *haupt*, Lat. *caput*

heáh, *high*; *height*

*healdan, to *hold*; *holding*, *behold*, *beholden*, *hilt* (cp. haft from *have*), *upholsterer*

healf, *side*; *half*, *behalf* (= by side)

heall, *hall*

healm, *haulm*. Cp. Lat. *culmus* stalk

heap, *heap*

*heard, *hard*; *harden*

hearm, *harm*

hearpe, *harp*

heáwan, to *hew*; *hoe*

*hebban, to *heave*; *heaven*, *heave*-offering, *head* (O.E. heafod), *heavy*. Ger. *heben*

hefig, *heavy*

hege, *hedge*. See Haga

hél, *heel*

hell, *hell*; *hélan*, to *cover*

helm, *helmet*

help, *help*; gehelpan, to *help*; past geheolp, holp, *help*-mate ('A coinage due to a mistaken notion of the phrase "an help *meet* for him."' Gen. ii. 18. Skeat)

hende, near; *handy*

heofon, *heaven* (that which is *heaved*)

heolster, a den, hiding-place; *holster*

heonon, *hence*

heord, *herd*; shep*herd*, neat*herd*, *hoard*

heort, *hart*; *Hartle*pool, *Hert*ford, *harts*horn

*heorte, *heart*. Ger. *herz*, Gk. *kardia*, Lat. *cor*

heorth, *hearth*

*here, *army*; *Hereford*, *harbour*, *heriot* (originally a tribute of war-apparatus), *herring* (the shoal-fish); bergian, to *harry*, *harrow*. Cp. ' the Harrowing of Hell '

hig, *hay* = cut-grass. Cog. *hew*.

hína, a servant; *hind*

hind, a *hind* (female deer)

hiw, *hue*

*hláf, *loaf*, *Lammas* (Aug. 1). It was customary to offer the first fruits of harvest on this day), *lord* (hláford), *lady* (hlæfdige)

hládan, to *lade* ; *ladle*

hlanc, *lank*

hleahtor, *laughter*

hleápan, to *leap*; *lap*-wing

hlehhan, to *laugh*

hleótan, to cast *lots*; al*lot*, *lot*tery

hlidan, to cover; *lid*

hlinian, to *lean*. Cp. Gk. *klinein*, to make to lean

hlúd, noisy ; *loud*

hlystan, *listen*

hnecca, the *neck*

hnesc, tender ; *nesh*

hnoll, crown of the head ; *knoll*

hnut, *nut* ; wal*nut* (= a foreign nut)

hóf, *hoof*

hóf, house ; *hovel*

hoh, heel ; *hough*, *hoch*

holen, *holly* ; *holm*-oak

hólian, to *hollow* ; *hole*

holm, a river-island ; Flat *Holm*

holt, a wood. Ger. *Holz.* Cog. *hole*, *holster*

horn, *horn*; *horn*-beam, *hornet*. Lat. *cornu*

hors, *horse*; wal*rus* (= hors-hwæl or whale-horse)

hraca, throat ; hræcan, to *retch*

*hradian, to hasten ; *ready*, *rathe*, *rather*

hrǽcan, to *reach*

hrǽdels, a *riddle*

hrægel, clothing ; *rag*, night-*rail*

hræn, *rein-deer*

hreac, *reek*, *reeky*. Cp. Ger. *rauchen*, to smoke

hrefn, *raven*

hreód, reed

*hreoh, *rough* ; *rugged*, *raw*

hreósan, to *rush*

hreówan, to *rue*

*hricg, back, *ridge*; Loughrigg Fells, Ask *Rigg*

hriddel, a sieve ; *riddle*

hrif, bowels ; mid*riff*

hrím, hoar-frost ; *rime*

hrinde, *rind*

hring, *ring*; *ringlet*

hróf, *roof*; *Rochester* (Hroveceaster)

hú, *how*

hund, *hound*, *hunt*. Ger. *hund*, Gk. *kyōn*, Lat. *canis*

hund, *hundred*

*hunig, *honey* ; *honey*suckle, hore*hound* (hara-hunig)

*hús, *house* ; *hus*band, *house*wife (*hussy*), *hus*ting

húsel, *housel*. Cp. ' unhouseled ' (*Hamlet*), Goth. *hunsl*, sacrifice

*hwá, *who* ; *where*, *what*, *why*, *whence*, *whither*

hwæl, *whale*; *walrus*

hwæt, sharp ; to *whet*, *whittle*, a knife

hwǽte, *wheat*, *Wheat*hampstead

hwearf, a place of exchange ; *wharf*

hweól, *wheel*

hwílon, *whilom*

hwistle, *whistle*

*hwit, *white*, *Whit*sunday (erroneously derived by some writers from Ger. Pfingsten = Pentecost. The earliest instance of the use of the word is found in the A.S. Chronicle under the year A.D. 1067. Here it is spelled Hwitan Sunnan dæg). *Whitchurch*, *whittle* (a large blanket; cp. blanket, from blanc)

hýde, *hide*

hýg, *hay*

hyldan, to incline ; *heel* (a ship)

hyngrian (impersonal), to *hunger*; *hungry*
hýr, *hire*; *hire*ling
hýran, to obey; *hear, hearken,
hear*say
hýth, shore; Rother*hithe*
ic, *I*
igland, *island*, from *ig* = island.
The *s* has no proper place in
this word. It has been inserted through following the
analogy of *isle*, in which it is
correctly used (Lat. *insula*)
*-ing, descendant of. Names of
persons in *-ing*, e.g. Hart*ing*.
Names ending in *-ingham*
(= inga hám, the home of the
sons of), e.g. Buck*ingham*.
Bill*ingham*, Boss*ington*, Wals-
ingham, Brent*ingley*, Brant-
ingham, Ard*ington*, Bann*ington*, Bletch*ingley*
*íren, *iron*. Older form *ísen*
iugian, to *yoke*. Cp. Lat. jungo
iúl or geól, the merry feast,
Christmas; *yule, yule*-log
kyrtel, *kirtle*
la, *lo*
léce, *leech* (doctor); *leech*-craft;
lácnian, to cure. The leech
(Lat. hirudo) is so called,
because of its use in healing
*lædan, to *lead*; *load*-star (the
north star), *load*-stone
lædder, *ladder*
læfan, to *leave*
læn, *lean*
lænan, to *lend*; *loan*
læran, to teach; *lore*
læs, *lest*. The *t* in *lest* is from
the union of *the* with læs.
The O.E. phrase thý *læs the*
= for this less that. Cp.
never the *less*
læsu, pasture; *læsow*; *léah*, meadow; *lea*, Bromley, Had*leigh*
læsung, lying; *leasing* (*Psalms*)
*læt, *late*; *latter, last, belated,
latter*-math (a second crop of
hay)

lætan, to *let*
lagu, *law* (what is laid or fixed)
lah, *low*
lám, *loam*
lám, *lame*
lamb, *lamb*
land, *land*
*lang, *long*; *along, length*, Lang-
don
lawerc, *laverock* (Sc.), *lark*
leac, *leek*; garlic, house-*leek*,
charlock, har*lock*, hem-*lock*
leaf, *leaf*
leas, false; *leasing* (Psalms)
Cp. *loose*
leas, *loose*, suffix *-less*
*lecgan, to *lay*; *lair, layer, law,
belay, outlay, lawyer*
lendenu, *loins*
lengcten, spring; *Lent*
leod, people; *léwed*, ignorant,
lewd
*leóf, dear; *lief, alderliefest*
(= dearest of all) Shakspere.
leman (= dearman) was orig.
of the com. gen. Ger. *lieb*
leofian, to *live*; *life, livelong,
livelihood*, a corruption of O.E.
liflode, from *lád*, a leading,
way, means of maintaining
life (no connexion with
-hood)
leógan, to *lie* (deceive); *liar*
leoht, *light*; *lighten, lightning*
leoht, easy; *light, lighten*
leornian, to *learn*
leósan (perf. part. *loren*), to
lose; *forlorn*
líc, corpse; *lich*-gate, *Lichfield*
liegan, to *lie*. See Lecgan
*lif, *life*; *live, livelihood* (O.E.
liflade, from *lád*, a leading,
way)
lifer, *liver*
lim, *limb*
lim, glue; *lime, birdlime*
lind, the *linden* or lime-tree;
*Lind*hurst, *Lind*field
li[...] Lat. [...]
lit, *[...]*

líthe, *lithe*; *lithe*some, *lissom*

loca, a *lock*; *locker*, *lock*-jaw, *lock*et

locc, *lock* (of hair)

lócian, to *look*

loma, household utensils; *loom*, (?) *lumber*. For the insertion of the *b*, cp. *slumber* from O.E. slumerian; *number* from Lat. numerus; *humble* from Lat. humilis. Archbishop Trench derives *lumber* from *Lombard*. He says, 'As the Lombards were the bankers, so also they were the pawnbrokers of the middle ages. . . . The "lumber" room was originally the Lombard room, or room where the Lombard banker and broker stowed away his pledges.'—Select Glossary.

lopystre, *lobster*. Probably a corruption of Lat. *locusta*, which meant: 1. a shell-fish; 2. a locust

losian, to *lose*; *loss*. See Leósan

lufian, to *love*; *beloved*. Cp. *lief*

lús, *louse*; pl. lýs; wood-*louse*

lyfan, *believe*. Ger. *glauben*

lyft, air; *loft*, *lift*, *aloft*

lysan, to *loose*; *loosen*

lystan, to please; *lust*, *list* (vb.), *listless* (= *lust*less, indifferent)

macian, to *make*

mæd, what is mowed; *mead*, *meadow*

mǽden, *maiden*. A derivative of mǽge, fem. of mǽg, a son

mægen, power; *main* (might and *main*). From *magan*

mǽl, time; piece-*meal*, inch-*meal*. Ger. *mal*

mǽnan, to *moan*; *bemoan*

mængan, to *mingle*; *among*, *mongre*

mænig, *many*; *manifold*

maga, stomach; *maw*. Cp. *haw* from *haga*

*mágan, past mihte, to be able, *may*, *might*, *mighty*

mál, spot; *mole*

malt, *malt*

malu, *mallow*

*mangian, to traffic; *monger*, coster*monger* (= costard-monger, apple-seller)

mann, *man*; connected with *mind*. *Man* is preeminently the *thinker*; *manikin*, *manhood*. Cognate forms are masculine, *male*, *mal*lard

mathu, *moth*

max, masc, *mesh*

mearc, a *mark*; boundary, *march*

méd, reward; *meed*

meledeaw, honey-dew; *mildew*. Cp. Lat. *mel*, honey. Gk. *meli*

meltan, to *melt*. Cp. *smelt* and *mellow*

melu, *meal*. From a root meaning to *grind*. Cp. *mill*

menigu, a multitude. Cp. a great *many*

meolc, *milk*; *milch*, *milk*-sop

*mere, a lake, *mere*, Butter*mere*, Winder*mere*, *Mer*ton. Cp. Welsh *mor*, sea, Ger. *meer*, Latin *mare*, *mersc*, *marsh*, i.e. mere-ish (full of pools)

metan, to measure, *mete*; *mete*-yard. Cog. Lat. *metior*, to measure; Gk. *metron*, a measure

*métan, to *meet*; *moot*-hall, to *moot*, *moot*-point, Witenage-*mote*

mete, *food*, *meat*; greenmeat, sweetmeat, meat-offering

metsian, to *feed*; *mess*, *mess*-mate. Cp. O.F. *mes*, a dish

*mid, *middle*; *amid*, *amidst*, *middling*, *middle*-man, *mid*-riff, *mid*-rib, *mid*-summer, *mid*-day

mihtig, *mighty*, *almighty*

milde, *mild*; *Mildred*

missian, to *miss*

mist, *mist*; *mizzle* (= mist-le). The *t* has similarly disappeared in the pronunciation of glisten, whistle

mixen, dunghill, *mixen*. O.E. *mix*, *meox*, dung. From *miscan*, to mix. Cp. Lat. *misceo*

mód, *mood*; *moody*. Mood, the grammatical term, is from Lat. modus, manner

molde, *mould*; *mole* or *mould-warp* (from O.E. *weorpan*, to cast) so called from casting up little heaps of mould; *moulder*, *mouldy*

*móna, *moon*; *month*, *moon*-light, *moon*-shine. Cp. Skt. *mâsa*, a month; *mâ*, to measure

mór, *moor*; Westmoreland, *mire*, *morass*, *moss* as in Chat *Moss*; *moor*-hen

morgen, *morning*, *morn*

morth, *death*; morther, *deadly sin*; *murder*

mús, pl. mýs, *mouse*. *Tit-mouse* is from *tit*, little, and *mâsc*, a tit-mouse

múth, *mouth*

mycel, great; *much*, *mickle*

mycg, *midge*; *mug*-wort (i.e. midge-wort, a herb used to ward off the attacks of insects)

mylen, *mill* (from Lat. *mola*, a mill, *molere*, to grind), *miller*, *Milner* (prop. name), *mill*-race

mynd, *mind*

mynet, *money*; *mint*. Lat. *moneta*

myrteth, *mirth*; from merg, *merry*

nacod, *naked*

næddre, a snake; *adder*. Cp. *apron* from *napron*, *umpire* from *numpire*

nædl, *needle*

nægel, *nail*

nafu, the *nare* of a wheel; *navel* (dim.)

*nama, *name*; *namesake* (= name's

sake). Cp. Lat. *nomen*. Gk. *onoma*

ncah, *nigh* (comp. near, sup nehst); *near*, *next*, *neigh*bour

nearo, *narrow*

neát, ox; *neat*, *neat-herd* 'Neat' is said to mean unintelligent, from O.E. *nitan* for *ne witan*, not to know

neb, face, beak; *nib*, *nibble*, *snipe*, *snap*, *snub*

*neód, *need*; *needs* (= Gen. of necessity), *needy*, *needless*

nest, *nest*; *nestling*, *nescock* (a fondling, from nest-cock) Cp. Lat. *nidus*

nett, *net*; *netting*, *network*

niesan, to *sneeze*

*niht, *night*; *night*ingale (Ger nachtigall) from O.N. gala, to sing, *night*mare (Icel. mara, an incubus, ogress), *night*shade *benighted*. Cp. Ger. *nacht*, Lat. *nox*, *ctis*, Welsh, *nos*

nither, down; *nether*, *nether-most*, *beneath*

niw, *new*; *news*, *renew*, *new*-fangled

north, *north*; *Norman*, *Norse*

*nosu, also nasu, a *nose*; nose, a *nose* of land; nos-thirl, *nostril* (literally *nose-hole*, from *thirlian*, to make a hole), *nozzle*, *nose*-gay, The *Naze*, *Sheerness*, *Totness*. Cp. Lat. *nasus*, Ger. *nase*

nu, *now*, *nowadays*. Cp. *new*

nygon, *nine*

ófer, shore; Andover, Wendover

óm, rust; óma, an ulcer; *gossomer* (Qy. gærs-oma, grass-rust. In the 'Promptorium Parvulorum' we find 'Gossomer, corrupcyon (gossumyr, or corrupcion, H. P.), *Filandrya*, *lanugo*.' The Scotch form of the word is *gar-summer*, which seems to point to the real origin of

the word. Wedgwood says
that the proper form of the
word is *God summer*, and
connects it with the legend
that 'the gossomer is the
remnant of our Lady's winding sheet, which fell away in
fragments when she was
taken up to heaven.'

ontýnan, to open; *untie*

open, *open*

ordǽl, *ordeal*. From *or* = free
from, and *dæl* = part. Hence
a trial in which no favour is
shown

other, second; *other*, every
other day, *another*

otor, *otter*

oxa, *ox*; *ox*-lip

pabol, *pebble*

pæth, *path*

pening, *penny*. Cp. Ger. *pfennig*

pic, *pitch*

*pic, point; *peak, pickets* (stakes
driven into the ground to tie
horses to), *pike, pike*-fish;
pickerel, peck (vb.), wood-
pecker, pick, pick-lock, The
Peak

pinewincle, *periwinkle* = pin-
winkle, so called because a
pin is used in getting the
winkle out of the shell.
Wincle is probably connected
with wilk (O.E. weolc)

píp, *pipe*; *pip*kin

plega, *play*; *playmate, playful*

pliht, condition; *plight*

púnd, *pound*. From Lat. *pondus*,
weight

pýle, *pillow*

pyt, *pit*; *armpit, cock-pit, pitfall*

*rǽdan, to *read; rede* (advice),
riddle (O.E. *rædels*). Ethel-
red the *Unready* was so
called, not because he was
unready, but because he was
'without *rede* or counsel.'
(Freeman.)   Mild*red* = mild
in counsel

rǽge (a small kind of deer), *roe*

ram, *ram*; *ram*-rod

rúp, *rope*; *stirrup*. See Stigan

rárian, to *roar*

*read, *red; ruddock* (red-breast),
ruddy, raddle

*reáfian, to *rob*; from *reáf*, clothing, spoil; *bereave, reever,
robber*

réc, vapour, *reek*; Auld *Reekie*
(Edinburgh)

recnan, *reckon*

reód, *reed*; *Reed*ham, *Rid*ley

rest, *rest*; *restful, unrest*

rícan, to *heed*; *reck, reckless*

rice, kingdom; *bishopric*. From
recan, to rule. Cp. Lat. *rego*

*rídan, to *ride; road, road-
stead*

rím, number; *rime* (erroneously
written *rhyme*)

rínan, to *rain*; *rainbow*

rípe, *ripe*; *reap* (to gather what
is ripe)

rísan, to *rise*; *arise*

risce, a *rush*; *Rush*-holme,
*Rush*ley, *Rush*mere, *Rush*-
worth, *Ris*borough

ród, cross; *rood, roodloft, Holy-
rood*

rówan, to *row*. Cp. Du. *roede*,
an oar

rúm, *room*. Ger. *Raum*

rún, alphabetic character; *rune,
runic*

ryge, *rye*

ryne, a course. (See Ember.)
From *yrnan*, to run

sǽ, *sea*

sǽd, *seed*; *seedling*. From *sawan*,
to sow

*sǽlig, blessed, *silly*. Cp. the
twofold meaning of *innocent*
and *simpleton*. Trench says:
'A deep conviction that he
who departs from evil will
make himself a prey, that
none will be a match for the
world's evil who is not himself evil, has brought to pass

the fact that a number of words, signifying at first goodness, signify next well-meaning simplicity; the notions of goodness and foolishness, with a strong predominance of the last, for a while interpenetrating one another in them; till at length the latter quite expels the former, and remains as the sole possessor of the word.' He traces ' silly ' through the following meanings : 1. blessed; 2. innocent; 3. harmless; 4. foolish. See ' Select Glossary '

salowig, *sallow*

sám, *half*; *sand*-blind (M. of Venice)

sand, *sand*; *Sand*wich

*sár, *sore*; *sorry*; sárian, to *sorrow*

sawel, *soul*. Ger. *seele*

scádan, to divide; *shed*, water-*shed*

scádu, *shadow*; *shade*

scáfan, to *shave*; *shavings*

*scapan, to *shape*; *shapely*, land-*scape*, friend*ship*

*sceacan (past sceoc), to *shake*; *shock*

sceacga, *shaggy*

sceaft, *shaft*. From scapan or scafan

sceal(past sceolde), *shall*; *should*

*sceamu, *shame*; *shame-fast*, wrongly written *shame-faced*

sceanca, *shank*; *Long-shanks*

sceáp, *sheep*; *shepherd*. *Shepton*, *Shipton*, *Shipley*, *Shipham*

scéarn, dung; *sharn* (prov. = dung). 'It is in this sense that " the shard-born beetle " is to be understood in Macbeth; dung-born, and not borne aloft on shards or scales.' — Wedgwood. See Scéran

scearp, *sharp*

sceat, a piece of money, price, *scot-free*, *scot* (tavern score), *scot* and lot

sceath, *sheath*

sceathan, to injure; *scathe*, *scatheless*

sceáwian, to *show*

*scel, *shell*; *shale*, *scale*, *scales*, *scalled* (in scalled head)

sceó, *shoe*; *shod*

sceoh, perverse; *askew*

sceorf, *scurf*; *scarf-skin*

sceorp, clothing; *scarf*

*sceótan, to *shoot*; *shot*, *shut* (to shoot the bolt), *shutter*, *shuttle*, *scud*

*scéran, to *shear*, *share*, *shire*, *shard* (the sharded beetle), *sheriff* (*scir*-geréfa, shire-reeve), plough*share*, *scar*, pot*sherd*, *shears*, *shred*, *sheer*, *score* (to notch), *shore*, *short*, *skirt*,*shirt* (the short garment)

scínan, to *shine*; *sheen*

scip, *ship*. Probably connected with scapan

scólu, a *shoal*; *school* of whales

scrincan, to *shrink*; *shrinkage*

scrob, a bush; *shrub*, *scrubby*, *Shrews*bury (Scrobbes burh), Wormwood *Scrubbs*

scrúd, clothing; *shroud*, en-*shroud*

scufan, to *shore*; *scuffle*, *sheaf*, *shovel*, *shuffle*. Cp. *scoop*

sculder, *shoulder*

scúnian, to *shun*; *shunt*

scúr, *shower*; *scour*

scyld, *shield*

seám, a *seam*; *seamstress*

secg, *sedge*; *Sedgemoor*

secgan, to *say*; *saw* (' wise saws'). Ger. *sagen*

segel, *sail*. Ger. *segel*

seld, rare; *seldom*. Ger. *selten*

sencan, to *sink*

sendan, to *send*; *Godsend*

seóc, *sick*; *sickness*, *home-sick*

seofon, *seven*

seolfor, *silver*. Ger. *Silber*

seón (part. geseah), to *see*; *sight*

seóthan, to *seethe*; *sodden*

*settan, to cause *to sit*, sittan, *to sit, to set*; *seat, settle, settler, saddle, saddler*. *-sæta*, as a termination, means *settler*; e.g. Somer*set*, Dor*set*

sib, related; *gossip*, related in God; 'As much *sibbed* as sieve and ridder, that grow in the wood together.' (Old Proverb.) In Suffolk the banns of marriage are called *sibberidge*

síde, *side*; *sidle, beside, aside*

singan (past. sang), to *sing*; *song, songster*

siththan, after; *sith, since*

síwian, to *sew*. Lat. *suo*

*slagan, to strike, *slay*; *slaughter, sledge* (in sledge-hammer)

sláp, *sleep*; *sleepy, sleepless*

sláw, *slow*; *sloth, slow*-worm

sleac, *slack*; *slacken*

slincan, to *slink*

slipan, to *slip*; *slop* (an over-garment, easily slipped on), *slipper, slippery, sleeve* (what one *slips* the arm into)

slítan, to *slit*

sluma, *slumber* (*b* excrescent. Cp. thum*b* and thim*b*le, from O.E. thúma)

smǽl, *small*

*smitan, to *smite*, *smith, smithy* (O. E. smiththe), Gold*smith*.

> Whence cometh Smith, albe he knight or squire,
> But from the smith, that smiteth at the fire?

smyrian, to *smear*

snáw, *snow*

*snican, to *sneak*; *snake, snail*

soft, *soft* (adj.); softe, *soft* (adv.)

sóna, *soon*; eft*soons*

*sóth, true, *sooth*; in *sooth*, for*sooth, soothsayer*

spáca, *spoke*; *spokeshave*

spád, *spade*

spætan, to *spit*; *spittle*

sparian, to *spare*

spearwa, *sparrow*; *sparrow-hawk*

spedan, to *speed*; *speedy*

*spell, history, message; *gospel* (good-tidings), *spell, spellbound*

spere, *spear*; *spar*

spinnan, to *spin*; *spinster, spindle, spindle*-side (=female side, of a family), *spindle* shanks, *spindle* tree

spiwan, to *spew*

springan, to *spring*; the *spring*

sprytan, to *sprout*

stæf, a *staff*; *flag-staff*

stæger, a *stair*; *stair*-case

stælcan, to *stalk*; *stalking-horse*

stæmn, a *stem*

stæp, a *step*; *footstep*

stær, a wall eye; *stark*-blind

stær, a *stare*; *starling*

*stálian, to *steal*; *stealth, stalworth*((O. E. stæl-weorth)= worth stealing, *stealthy*

stán, *stone*; *Stanley, Stanton, Staines, Stanhope*

stándan, to *stand*; *staddle*, with*stand*

stárian, to *stare*

steal, a *stall*, a place; Tun*stall*, Bor*stal*

steáp, *steep*; *steeple*

stearc, hard; *stark, starch*

*stede, place; *stead*, home-*stead*, steady, in*stead*, be*stead*, stead-fast, *Stead*combe, Hamp*stead*

stém, vapour, smoke; *steam*

stenc, *stench, stink*

*steopan, to bereave; *step*-mother, *step*-child

steor, a young beast; a *steer*, *stirk*

steóran, to *steer*; *starboard*, the right side of a vessel. 'The rudder consisted of an oar on the right side of the ship, where the steersman stood.'—

Wedgwood. *Steerage, steers-*
man

steorra, *star* ; *starfish, starwort*

steppan, to *step* ; *stepping-stone*

sticce, a piece; *steak* ; M. E.
stick-meal = piece-meal

*stician, to *stick* ; *stitch, stake,*
stickle, stickler, stock, stockade,
stockfish (fish dried for stock),
stock-still

stif, *stiff* ; *stiffen*

*stigan, to ascend ; *stile, stirrup*
(*stég*-ráp = mounting rope),
stair

stille, *still* ; *stillness, still-born,*
still-life

stingan, to *sting*

stirian, to *stir*

stiriga, a *sturgeon*

stirman, to *storm* ; storm, *storm*

*stoc, a place ; *Stoke,* Wood*stock,*
*Stoke-*Pogis

stód, a *stud* of breeding steeds

*stow, a place ; be*stow, stowage,*
stowaway, Chepstow (= trad-
ing-place), God*stow,* Felix-
stow, Bristol

strácian, to *stroke* ; *strike, streak,*
stricken

stréet, Lat. *strata, street* ; *Strat-*
ford, *Stretton, Stratton*

stráng, *strong* ; *strength*

streccan, to *stretch* ; *stretcher*

streow, *straw*

streowian, to *strew* ; *bestrew*

stunian, to *stun* ; *stunted*

stýl, *steel* ; *steelyard*

styrne, *stern* ; *astern*

súgu, *sow*

sum, a certain ; *some*

sumer, *summer*

suna, *soon* ; *eftsoons*

sund, a narrow sea ; *sound*

súnd, healthy ; *sound*

sundrian, to *sunder* ; *asunder,*
sundry

sunne, *sun* ; *Sunday*

sunu, *son*

súr, *sour* ; *sorrel.* Ger. *sauer*

súth, *south* ; *Sussex, Suffolk*

swá, *so*, al*so*

swan, *swan* ; *swanherd*

swán, *swain* ; *boatswain*

swapan, to *sweep* ; *swoop*

swát, *sweat*

*sweart, black ; *swart*-star,
swarthy. Ger. *schwarz*

*swelgan, to *swallow* ; *groundsel*
(grundswelige, the earth-
devourer), *swill*

swellan, to *swell*

sweltan, to die ; *swelter, sultry*
(= sweltry)

sweóster, *sister*

sweord, *sword*

swerian, to *swear* ; *forswear,*
an*swer* (O. E. andswarian,
from *and,* in opposition to)

swift, *swift* ; swifan, to move
quickly

swilc, *such* = swá-líc

swincan, to toil ; *swink* (Milton)

swingan, to scourge ; *swinge*

swymman, to *swim*

swýn, *swine* ; *Swin - burn* (=
swine-stream), Swin-hope

syl, post, log ; *sill* (as in window-
sill), *grunsel* (Milton)

synn, *sin* ; *sinner, sinful*

tá, *toe*

tácn, *token* ; *betoken*

táde, a *toad* ; *tadpole*

tæcan (past tæhte), to *teach*

tægel, *tail*

tæppan, to *tap* ; *tapster*

tæsan, to pluck, pull ; to *tease,*
teasel

tám, *tame.* Ger. *zahm,* Lat.
domare, Gk. *damaô*

taper, a *taper*

téar, a *tear.* Comp. Ger. *Zähre*

*tellan, to *tell*, reckon ; *tale, tell*
off, fore*tell*

téman, to *teem*

temian, to *tame,* yoke together ;
team

teón (past teah, pl. tugon), to
draw ; *tow, tug,* to educate,
wanton ill-brought up. Cp.
'wel-itogone'= well-bred

teor, *tar*
téran, to *tear*
thæc, *thatch ; theccan,* to cover
(Sc. theek). Comp. Ger. *Dach,*
a roof, *decken,* to cover ; Lat.
tegere ; Gk. *stegein,* to cover
thancian, to *thank*
thanon, *thence*
thawan, to *thaw*
theah, *though*
theáw, custom ; *thew*
thegen, servant ; *thane*
thencan, to *think.* Not to be
confounded with *thincan*
theóf, *thief.* Cp. Ger. *Dieb*
theoh, the *thigh*
therscan, to *thresh ; threshold*
(O.E. therscwald, from *wald*
= wood)
thic, *thick ; thicket*
thincan, to *seem ; methinks*
thing, *thing*
thing, a meeting, council (Danish); *husting* = house-council
thistel, a *thistle.* Cp. Ger. *Distel*
thrǽl, slave ; *thrall, enthrall,
thral*dom
thred, *thread*
threó, *three*
thringan, to *throng*
throte, *throat*
throwian, to suffer ; *throe*
thúma, *thumb ; thimble*
thuner, *thunder*
thurh, *through ; thoroughfare*
thurstig, *thirsty*
thus, *thus*
thúsend, *thousand*
thwang, *thong*
thweor, diagonal ; *thwart, a-
thwart*
*thyrel, a hole ; *drill,* no*stril* =
nose-hole, *thrill*
thyrn, a *thorn ; Thorney* (=
thorn-island)
thyrscel, a *threshold.* Wrongly
written sometimes thresh-
hold. See Therscan
thyrstan, to *thirst.* Cp. *thyr,*
dry

tíd, time ; *tide,* Whits*untide,*
be*tide* (to happen in time)
tígan, to *tie ; untie*
tigel (Lat. tegula), *tile*
tilian, to *till ; tilth*
tíma, *time ; betimes*
timber, *timber ;* timbrian, to
build. Cp. Ger. *Zimmer,* a
room
tin, *tin*
tírian, to vex, *tarre* (Shakspere)
tobrecan, to break in pieces, *to-
break* (Judges ix. 53)
to-dæg, *to-day (to* has the force
of a demonstrative in this
compound)
toh, *tough ; toughen*
tól, *tool*
tól, a *toll ; toll-bar, toll-booth*
top, a ball, a tuft at the *top* of
anything ; *topple ; topsy-*turvy
(= top-side t' other way)
tóth, *tooth ;* pl. Nom. and Acc.
*téth ; tooth*some
*tredan, to *tread ; treddle, trade*
(a *trodden* path, hence way of
life), *tradesman, trade-*wind (a
wind that blows in a constant
direction).

> Or I'll be buried in the king's
> highway,
> Some way of common *trade*, where
> subjects' feet
> May hourly trample on their
> sovereign's head ;
> For on my heart they *tread* now
> whilst I live.'
> *Rich. II.* iii. 3.

trendle, a circle ; *trundle, trin-
dle* (a coil of wax-taper),
trend (to turn or bend in
direction)
treów, a *tree.* Cp. Gk. *drys,* oak
treppe, a *trap ; entrap*
trog, tub ; *trough, trow*
*truwa, faith ; *true, truth, troth,*
be*troth, truism*
tumbere, a dancer, *tumbler.*
O. E. *tumbian,* to dance
tún, an enclosure, *town:* O. E.
tynan, to enclose

tunga, *tongue.* Ger. *Zunge*

turf, *turf*

tux, *tusk*

*twá, twí, *two*; *Twiford, twain, twin, between, twelve, twenty*

twiccian, to *twitch*

twig, *twig.* Ger. *Zweig*

twin, *twine*; *entwine*

tyman, to *teem* (bring forth); *teeming* (=replete)

tynder, *tinder*; tendan, to *tind*, set on fire

upan, *above*; *up*braid (O.E. up-gebreden)

út, *out*

wác, *weak*; O. E. *wican*, to be weak; *weaken, weakling*

*wácian, to *watch*; *wake*, church-*wake* (celebrated on the vigil of the patron-saint), *wakeful, awake*

*wúd, *wood*; *woodbine, woodruff, woodward*

wádan, to *wade*

wæcg, *wedge.* From O. E. *wacan*, to move

wæd, a garment; *weeds* (widow's)

wægen, *wagon, wain*

wæpen, *weapon*

*wǽr, *wary*; *beware, aware.* See Weard

wær, an enclosure; *weir, War*ham

wæring, a wall; *Warwick*

wæscan, to *wash*

wæter, *water*; wæt, *wet, Wed*more

wágian, to *wag*; *waggle, wag*tail

wáláwá, *welladay*

wald, *wood*; *Wealden*, names of places ending in -*wold*

wamb, *womb*

*wana, a deficiency; *want, wanton* (see Téon), *wan, wane*

wand-wurp, a mole; *want, oont* (Welsh Border)

wandrian, to *wander*

warnian, to beware; *warn*

*wealdan, to *wield*; *Bretwalda*;

names of persons ending in -*weald*

weall, a *wall* (from Lat. *vallum*, a rampart)

wealla, foreigner; *Welsh*man, *wal*nut, Cornwall, Wales

wealwian, to roll; *wallow*

weaps, a *wasp.* Lat. vespa

*weard, *ward* (a person under guardianship); the *ward* of a lock, *warden, warden*-pie, hay-*ward*, wood-*ward*; names of persons in -*ward*, as Ed*ward*, Ethel*ward*, Warburton (*bush*, town), *weir* (O.E. wær, an enclosure, a fishpond)

wearm, *warm*; *warmth*

weax, *wax*

weaxan (part. weox), to *wax*

wed, a pledge; *wed, wedlock, wedding*

weder, *weather*

*wéfan, to *weave*: *weaver, web*, cob*web* (attercop = spider), *Webster, woof, weft*

wég, *way*; *away, way*ward

wegan, to bear; *weigh*, to *weigh* anchor

wel, *well, well-nigh*

*wela, *weal*; *wealth, common-weal, wealthy*

wenan, to think; *ween*, over-*weening*

wendan, to go; *went*, to *wend*

weorc, *work*

weorpan, to throw, cast; *warp*, mould*warp* (Ger. *Maulwurf*)

weorthan, to become; *worth*, as in 'woe *worth* the day'

weorthe, *worthy*; stal*wart* = steel-worthy

weosnian, to dry up; *wizened*

wépan, to *weep*

werig, *weary*; *aweary*

wesan, to be; *was*

wesle, *weasel*

wéstan, to lay *waste.* Cp. Lat. *vastare*

wether, *wether*

wic, a dwelling; *Norwich, Wick*

wicca, a wizard ; *witch, witch-craft, wicked*

wid, *ride ; width*

widewe, *widow ; widower*

wif, *wife, woman ; hussy* = house-wife. Cp. Ger. *Weib*

wiht, thing, creature ; *wight, whit, aught*

wild, *wild ; wilderness, bewilder*

willa, *will ; wilful*

win, war ; God*win*, Bald*win*

win, *wine ; winebibber, wine-press*. Cp. Lat. *vinum*, Ger. *Wein*

win, joy ; *winsome*

wincle, a wilk ; *pinewincle*

wind, *wind ; windward, wind-hover, window* (= wind - eye. See *cage*), *windrow*

windan (part. wand) to *wind ; willow* (O.E. *windel*-treów)

winnan, to *win*

winter, *winter*

*witan (1st per. ic wat, past wiste), to know ; *wit, wisdom, wot, wist, wistful, witness, Witenagemote ; wise*, y-wis (wrongly written *I wis*)

with, against ; *withstand, with-hold*

wlæc, warm ; *luke*-warm

wód, mad ; *wood, Wodin*, the god who inspired men with martial fury, *Wednesday, Wansborough*

wolcen, cloud ; *welkin*

wóp, *whoop*

word, *word ; byword*

worth, farm ; *Worth*ing, Bos-*worth*

woruld, *world*

wós, juice ; *ooze*

wræcca, an exile; *wretch*

wræstan, to twist ; *wrest, wrestle*

wræth, *wrath*

wrécan, to avenge ; *wreak, wretch, wretched*

wregan, to accuse ; *bewray*

wrétha, a band ; *wreath, writhe*

wrihan or wrigan, to cover, to *rig*

wrincle, a *wrinkle*

wringan, to *wring*

writan (past wrát), to *write, writ*

wuce, *week*. Ger. *Woche*

*wudu, *wood*, *Wood*stock, *Odi*-ham (Hants)

wúl, *wool ; woollen*

wulf, *wolf*

wúna, *wont* ; from wunian, to dwell

wúnd, *wound ; woundwort*

wundrian, to *wonder ; wondrous,* '*woundy*' (prov.)

*wurthian, to honour ; *worship, worshipful*

wyl or well, a *well* ; from *weal-lan*, to spring up, boil

*wyrcan (past. worhte), to *work ; wrought*, *Wright* (proper name), wheel*wright*, ship-*wright*

wyrd, fate ; *weird*

wyrian, to curse ; *worry*

wyrm, a *worm* ; blind-*worm*, *worm-wood* (properly worm-wort)

wyrs, *worse*

*wyrt, a herb ; *wort*, *orchard* (= wort-yard), *wart*, called by analogy from growing on the skin

ýcan, to *eke*

ýdel, vain, empty ; *idle ; love-in-idleness* (properly love-in-idle, i.e. love in vain)

yfel, *evil*. Cog. *ill*

yrman, to *harm*

yrnan (past arn), to *run*

320. LATIN ROOTS.

[The more prolific roots are marked with an asterisk.]

absum, fui, esse, *to be away*; absent, absence, absentee

*acer, acris, acre, *sharp*; acrid, acerbity, acrimony, exacerbate, eager ('eager droppings into milk,' *Hamlet*), vinegar (vinaigre = sharp wine)

acidus, *sour*; acid

acuo, to *sharpen*; acute

adultus, *grown up*; adult

*ædes, *house*; edify (*facio*, to make), edifice, edification

*æquus, *equal*; equable, equation, equity, iniquity, equipoise, equinox

æstimo, *to value*; esteem, estimable, aim

æstus, *tide*; estuary

æternus, *eternal*; eternity

ævum, an *age*; coeval, medieval, primeval

*ager, *field*; agrarian, agriculture, peregrination

agger, *heap*; exaggerate

agito (frequentative from ago), to agitate

*ago, egi, actum, *to do, drive*; agent, act, action, exigence, actor, actuate, actual, cogent (from cogo = co-ago), counteract, exact, exigency, react, transact

ala, a *wing*; aisle

alacer, alacris, alacre, *brisk*; alacrity

alius, *another*; alias (= otherwise), alien, alibi (= otherwhere)

allaudo, to *praise* (Fr. allouer), allow

*alo, to *nourish*; aliment, alimony, coalesce, element?

*alter, *the other of two*; alternate, alternative, altercation, subaltern

*altus, *high*; altitude, exalt, altar, Fr. *haut*, haughty, It. *alto*

ambiguus, *doubtful*; ambiguity

ambio (eo, I go), *to go round about, to canvass for public office*; ambition, circumambient

ambulo, to *walk*; ambulatory, perambulator

*amo, to *love*, amicus, a *friend*; amorous, amiable, amateur, amity, inimical, enemy

amœnus, *pleasant*; amenity

amplus, *wide*; ample, amplitude

ango, xi, ctum and xum, to *throttle*; anxious, anguish

angulus, a *corner*; angle, triangle

*anima, *breath*; animate, animal, inanimate, reanimate

*animus, *mind*; magnanimous (large-minded), equanimity, animosity, animadvert, unanimity

annulus, *ring*; annular

*annus, *year*; annual, biennial, annals, anniversary, superannuated

antiquus, *ancient*; antique, antic, antiquity

anus, *old woman*; anile

*aperio, ui, tum, to *open*; aperient, aperture, April (the opening month)

apis, *bee*; apiary

*appello, to *call*; appellation, appeal, appellant, *peal* (of bells)

aptus, *fit*; apt, adapt, aptitude, attitude

*aqua, *water*; aquatic, aquarium, aqueous, aqueduct

aquila, *eagle*; Fr. aigle, aquiline

aurer, a *pr... of... d.* to;

O...... ary

*arbor, a *tree*; arbour, arboriculture

arca, *chest*; ark, arcanum (a secret, something kept in a chest)

*arcus, *bow*; arch, arc, arcade

*ardeo, to *burn*; ardent, ardour, arson

arduus, *steep, difficult*; arduous

area, *a vacant piece of ground*; area

arena, *sand*; arena

argentum, *silver*; argent, argentiferous

argilla, *clay*; argillaceous

arguo, *to prove*; argue, argument

aridus, *dry*; arid, aridity

*arma, pl. *arms*; arm, arms, alarm (It. all'arme = to arms), armistice (a staying of fighting)

aro, to *plough*; arable. Cp. O.E. earan

*ars, tis, *art*; artifice, artist, inert (Lat. iners = void of art)

*artus, *joint*, articulus, *a little joint*; article, articulate

asinus, *ass*; asinine

asper, *rough*; exasperate, asperity

atrox, *cruel*; atrocious, atrocity

audax, *bold*; audacious, audacity

*audio, *to hear*; audience, auditor, audible, 'Oyez,' obey, obedience, obeisance

*augeo, xi, ctum, *to increase*; augment, author (= one who increases),auctumnus,autumn

auris, *ear*; auricle (dim.), auricular

*aurum,*gold*; auriferous (=gold-bearing), Fr. *or*, ormolu

auspex (from *avis*, bird, and *specio*, to behold), *a bird-seer*, one who predicts from observing birds; auspicious

auxilium, *help* (from *augeo*); auxiliary

avarus, *greedy*; avaricious

avidus, *eager*; avidity

*avis, *bird*; aviary, ostrich (Fr. *autruche*, from Lat. *avis*, Gk. *strouthos*)

*barba, *beard*; barb, barber, barbel (the bearded-fish)

beatus, *blessed*; beatify, beatitude

*bellum, *war*; bellicose, belligerent, rebel

*bene, *well*; benefit, benefice, benediction

benignus, *kind*; benign, benignity

bestia, *beast*; bestial

bibo, to *drink*; imbibe, Fr. *boire*, beverage, beaver (part of a helmet)

bini, *two a-piece*; binocular, binary

*bis, *twice*; bisect, bissextile, balance (Lat. *bilanx*, from *lanx*, the dish of a weighing scale), biscuit (*bis* and *coctus*, baked; the bread or biscuit of the Roman soldiers being twice prepared in the oven)

blandus, *smooth*; bland, blandish, blandishment

bonus, *good*; boon, bounty

*brevis, *short*; brevity, breve, abbreviate, breviary, abridge (abbreviare, Fr. *abréger*. Cp. deluge, from *diluvium*)

bulla, *a little round ornament*, worn about the necks of Roman children; *a seal*; bull (papal decree), bulletin

byrsa, *leather*; bursar, purser, Bourse

caballus, *horse*; cavalry, Fr. cheval, chevalier, chivalry

cadäver, *corpse*; cadaverous

*cado, cecidi, casum, to *fall*; case, casual, cadent, cadence, incident, accident, coincide, decide, occasion

*cædo, cecidi, cæsum, to *cut, kill*; suicide, homicide, regicide, vulpecide, precise, incision, cement (cœdimentum = small stones, as cut from the quarry, used for walls)

calamitas, *disaster*; calamity

calcitro, to *kick*; recalcitrant (fr. *calx*, the heel, whence inculcate)

*calculus, *pebble*; calculate (pebbles being used for computation), calculus (fr. *calx*, a small stone, whence chalk, calcine)

calidus, *warm*; caudle (Fr. chaud)

callum, *hardened skin*; callous, callosity

camera, a *room*; chamber, comrade (It. camerata)

*campus, *plain*; camp, Fr. champ, champaign (country)

cancelli, *cross-bars, lattice work*; chancel, chancellor, cancel (to cross out), chancery

*candeo, to *shine*; candidus, *white*; candid, candour, candle, incandescent, candelabrum, incense, incentive, incendiary, chandelier, censer, candidate (persons who canvassed for public offices among the Romans went about in *white* robes, emblematical of purity)

canis, *dog*; canine, kennel

canna, *reed*; cane, canal, channel, canister (canista, a wicker-basket)

cannabis, *hemp*; canvas

*cano, cantum, to *sing* (also canto); cant, canticle, enchant, chanticleer, chant, incantation, recant, descant, accent

capillus, *hair*; capillary. Fr. cheveux; dishevelled (with the hair out of order)

caper, a *goat*; caprice, capriole

*capio, cepi, captum, *to take*; captive, capable, captious, cap-

ture, capacity, receive, deceive, accept, except, recipient, receipt, precept, conceit, caitiff (It. cattivo)

capsa, a *chest*; case, capsule, casement, chapel, chaplain, cash (money kept in the chest), cashier

*caput, *head*; capital, decapitate, Fr. *chef*, chief, kerchief, precipice, precipitate, precipitous, captain, chapter, chaplet

*carbo, *a live coal*; carbon, carbuncle (dim.), carbonado (to broil on the coal; hence to cut and score for broiling)

carcer, *prison*; incarcerate

cardo, *hinge*; cardinal

carina, *keel*; careen (to repair the keel)

carmen, *song*; charm

cāro, to *card*; carduus (a teasel used in dressing cloth)

*caro, carnis, *flesh*; carnal, carnage, carnivorous, charnelhouse, carnation (flesh-coloured), carnival (carnis levamen = solace of the flesh), carrion (Fr. charogne)

carpentum, *a car*; carpenter (wheel-wright)

carpo, to *pluck*; carp, vb.

carrum, *car*; chariot, carriage, char à bancs

*carus, *dear*; Fr. *cher*, charity, cherish, caress

caseus, *cheese*; caseine

castānea, *chestnut*

*castigo (from castus), to *correct*; castigate, chastise, chasten

castus, *chaste*; chastity

casus, *chance* (from cado); casual, casuist (one who studies cases of conscience)

catena, *chain*; concatenate

cauda, *tail*; cue, queue

caulis, *cole* or *cabbage*; cauliflower

*causa, a *cause*; causative, excuse, accuse

caveo, cavi, cautum, *to take care*; cautious, caution

*cavus, *hollow*; cave, excavate, cavity, cavern

*cedo, cessi, cessum, *to go, yield*; cede, proceed, procession, cease, accede, concede, exceed, ancestor, decease

celeber, bris, bre, *celebrated*; celebration

celer, eris, e, *swift*; accelerate, celerity

celo, to *hide*; conceal

clavis, *key* (Fr. clef); conclave (a room under lock and key), clef

*censeo, to *judge*; censure, censor

*centrum (fr. Gk. kentron, a point), centre; centrifugal, centralize

*centum, *hundred*; cent, century, centurion

Ceres, *Ceres*, the goddess of agriculture; cereal

*cerno, crevi, cretum, to *distinguish*; discern, discreet, secret, concern, secretary

certus, *sure*; certain, ascertain, certify, certificate. See Facio

cervix, *neck*; cervical

cesso, to *cease from*; cease, cessation

*charta, *paper*; chart, charter, cartel, cartoon, card

*cingo, nxi, nctum, to *gird*; cincture, encincture, precinct, succinct

circum, *round*; circumstance

circus, a *circle*; circus, circulate

cista (Gk. kistē), a *box*; chest, cist

*cito, to *rouse* (Fr. cieo, to move); cite, incite, excite, recite, resuscitate, citation

*civis, *citizen*, civitas, *state*; civic, civil, civilian, civilize, city, citizen

*clamo, to *shout*; claim, clamour, exclaim, disclaim, proclaim, reclaim, proclamation, exclamation

*clarus, *clear*; clarify, clarion, clarionet, claret ('Having a reddish tint, but not the full red of ordinary red wine.'—*Wedgwood*)

classis, a *class* or order of citizens; classicus, belonging to the highest class of Roman citizens; classic, classical

*claudo, si, sum, to *shut*; include, exclude, preclude, seclude, cloister, close, closet, enclose, clause

clavus, *nail*; clove (from its resemblance to a nail)

clemens, *mild*; clemency, inclement

cliens, tis, *dependant*; client

clino, to *bend*; incline, recline

*clivus, a *slope*; acclivity, proclivity, declivity

cœlebs, *bachelor*; celibacy, celibate

cœlum, *sky*; celestial, ceiling (originally the canopy of a bed)

cœpi, to *begin*; inception

cogito, to *think* (from co-agito); cogitate, excogitate

*cognosco, to *know*; recognize, cognition, cognizant, reconnoitre

cogo (from co-ago), to *compel*; cogent, coagulate

collum, *neck*; collar, colporteur

*colo, ui, tum, to *till*; colony, culture, cultivate, agriculture, horticulture

color, *colour*

columna, *column*; colonel, the officer at the head of a column (also spelled coronel, whence the pronunciation), colonnade

*comes, itis, *companion* (from cum and eo, to go); comity,

count, county, constable
(= comes stabuli, count of
the stable)

commodus, *convenient*; commodity, accommodate

communis, *common*; communi-
cate, community

conjux, gis, *husband* or *wife*;
conjugal. From jungo, I join

constare (Fr. coûter), *to stand
me in*; to cost

constipare, to *cram*; constipated, costive

contra, *against*; contradict,
counter, counterfeit

conviva, a *guest*; convivial

copia, *plenty*; copious

copulo, to *join together*; copulative, couple

*coquo, xi, ctum, to *boil*; cook,
decoct, decoction, kitchen

*cor, dis, *heart* (Fr. cœur);
cordial, courage, discourage,
encourage, core, concord, dis-
cord, record

*corium, *hide* (Fr. cuir, leather);
excoriate, currier, cuirass,
cuirassier, curry (vb.)

cornu, *horn*; cornet, cornucopia
(= horn of abundance)

*corona, *crown*; coronet, coronel,
coronation, coroner, older spelling crowner (crown-officer),
corolla (little crown), cornice

*corpus, oris, *body*; corpse, in-
corporate, corporal, corporeal,
corps, corset, corslet, (Sp.)
cuerpo, corpulent

cortex, icis, *bark*; cork, cortical,
decorticate

costa, *rib*; intercostal, accost,
cutlet (Fr. côtelette)

cras, *to-morrow*; procrastinate

crassus, *thick*; crass, Fr. gros,
grocer, gross, engross

*credo, to *believe*; creed, credible, credit, credulous, creditor, cred r'l als, a s i
miscreant (= misbeliever), recreant (= apostate). The two

latter terms originated during the period of the Crusades

*creo, avi, atum, to *create*;
creation, creature

*cresco, crevi, cretum, to *grow*;
(Fr. croître, to grow), cres-
cent, increase, increment,
accrue

creta, *chalk*; cretaceous, crayon

crimen, *crime*; criminal, in-
criminate, discriminate (all
from cerno)

crispus, *curled*, crisp. O.E. cirps
= crisp, curled

crudelis, *cruel*

crudus, *raw*; crude, recrudes-
cent

crusta, *crust*; custard (originally
written crustade)

*crux, cis, *cross*; (Fr. croix),
crucify, cruciform, crusade,
cruise (to cross the sea),
excruciate, crosier

*cubo, ui, itum, to *lie down*, in-
cubate, cubical, cubit, in-
cumbent, recumbent; Fr. cou-
rée, covey

cucullus, *cowl*

culmen, *top*; culminate

*culpa, *fault*; culpable, culprit,
inculpate, exculpate

culter, *knife*; coulter, cutlass,
cutler, curtleaxe (a corruption
of It. coltellaccio)

cumulus, a *heap*; accumulate,
encumber (to overload)

cupio, to *desire*; Cupid, cupidity,
concupiscence

*cura, *care*, curo, *to pay attention
to, to cure*; cure (of souls),
curate, sinecure, curator, secure, incurable, accurate,
procure

*curro, cursum, to *run*; current,
incur, recur, occur, incursion,
excursion, succour, course,
discourse, cursive, cursory,
...   r

*curves ... . Fr.
cou ph t is ri cure c   vet

A A

custos, odis, *keeper*; custody

cutis, *skin*; cuticle

cygnus, *swan*; cygnet

*damno, to *condemn*; damn, condemnation, damage, indemnify

*debeo, debitum, to *owe*; debt, debtor, indebted, Fr. devoir, perf. part. dû; due, duty, endeavour

debilis, *weak*; debility, debilitate

*decem, *ten*; decimal, December (the tenth month of the Roman year), decimate; decanal, dean (a chief of ten)

decens, *fit*, decent; decus, oris, *honour*; decorate

deliciæ, *treat*; delicious, delicacy

deliro, to *quit the furrow* (lira) *in ploughing*; delirium

*dens, dentis, *tooth*; dent, dentist, trident, indent (to notch a margin so as to make it like a row of teeth. Indentures are duplicate documents that are indented together, so that the notches correspond to each other), dandelion.

densus, *thick*; dense, condense

desero, ui, rtum, to *desert*; desert (subst.)

desidero, to *wish for*; desire

*Deus, *God*; deity, deify, deist, deodand (something to be given to God), O dear! divine, divination

dexter, *right-hand*; dexterous, dexterity

*dico, dictum, to *say*; dictionary, diction, benediction, benison, malediction, malison, dictate, predict, verdict, indict, indite, ditto

*dies, *day*, diurnus, *daily*; dial (for showing the time of day), diary, diurnal, (Fr. *jour*, a day), journal, journey, journeyman, sojourn, adjourn, meridian

digitus, *finger*; digit

*dignus, *worthy*; dignor, *to deem worthy*; dignity, dignify, condign, deign, indignity, indignation

diligo, lexi, lectum, to *love*; diligent, delight, dilettante (It.)

dirus, *fearful*; dire, direful

disco, to *learn*; disciple, discipline

discrimino, to *divide*; discriminate. See cerno

divido, i, sum, to *divide*; division, divisible

divinus (from same root as deus), *divine*; divinity

*do, datum, to *give* ; data (things given), dative, date, antedate, postdate, add, render, to give back (Fr. rendre), surrender, edit, tradition, treason

*doceo, ui, ctum, to *teach*; doctor, docile, doctrine

*doleo, to *grieve*; condole, doleful, dolorous

*dominus, *lord*; domina, *lady*; duenna, donna, dominate, domineer, dominion, domain, don (Spanish), damsel, dame, madame, mademoiselle

domo, to *tame*; indomitable. Cp. *tame*

*domus, *house*; domicile, domestic, dome, majordomo (master of the house)

*dono, to give, *donum*, a gift; donation, donative, condone, pardon

*dormio, ivi, itum; to *sleep*; dormitory, dormouse, dormant

dorsum, *back*; dorsal, endorse

dos, tis, *dowry*; dowager, endow

dubius (from *duo*, two, and *eo*, to go, to move alternately in two directions), *dubious*, *doubtful*; dubito, *to doubt*; indubitable

*duco, xi, ctum, to *lead*; duke,

doge, conduce, conduct, educate, induce, traduce, seduce, conduit, ducat, duchy

*duo, *two*; dual, duplex, double, duple, duet, doubloon (a double pistole), doublet

duodecim, *twelve*; duodecimals; Fr. douzaine, dozen

durus, *hard*, duro, to *harden*; durable, endure, indurate, during, duresse

ebrius, *drunk*; inebriate, sober

ebur, *ivory*. (Fr. ivŏire)

edo, ēdi, ēsum, to *eat*; esca, *food*; edible, esculent

edo, didi, ditum, *to give out*; edit, editor

ego, *I*; egotist, egoist

*emo, emi, emptum, to *buy*; redeem, redemption, exempt

*eo, ivi, itum, to *go*; exit, adit (approach), initial, perish, ambition (a going about), sedition, a going apart, issue (exire, Fr. issir)

equus, *horse*; equestrian, equerry, equine

*erro, to *wander*; err, error, erratic, aberration

examino, *weigh* (from *examen*, the tongue of a balance, and that from *agmen*), examine, examination

exemplum, *example*; sample, sampler, exemplary

exerceo, to *exercise*. See Arceo

expedio, to *set free* (from pes, dis, foot); expedite, expedient, expedition, impede

experior, tus, to *try*; expert, experiment, experience

exsul, *exile*. From *solum*, soil

extra, *outside*; extraneous

*facies, *a face*; facial, superficies, façade

facilis (from facio), *easy*; facile, facility, difficulty

*facio, to *make*; faber, a ... ... ; fabric, forge (Lat. fabrica), counterfeit, profit, confec-

tionery, office, comfit (= confect), faction, fashion, feat, feasible, feature (the make of the face), suffice, sufficient, efficient, affect, effect, infect; fabula, a *story*, fable, fabulous; facetus, *clever*; facetious, facetiæ

fallo, to *deceive*; fallible; false, falsify, fail

falx, a *scythe*, *hook*, falchion; falco, falcon (the hooked bird)

fama (fari, to speak), *report*; famous, infamy

fames, *hunger*; famine

fans, tis, *speaking*; infant, Infanta, fate, fatal

fanum, *temple*; fane, profane (outside the temple, not dedicated, common), fanatic

farcio, to *stuff*, farce (a play stuffed with fun), *forced*-meat (= farced meat)

farina, *flour*; farinaceous

fastidio, to *loathe*; fastidious

*fateor, fassus, to *confess*; profess, confession

fatigo, to *weary*; fatigue

fatuus, *foolish*; infatuate, fatuous

faveo, fāvi, fautum, to *favour*; fautor (supporter)

febris, *fever*; febrile, febrifuge

fecundus, *fertile*; fecund, fecundity

feles, *cat* (the fruitful, from same root as fœtus, *offspring* fecundity, Gk. phuein, *to beget*. Comp. O.E. beón, *to be*); feline

felix, *happy*; felicity, felicitate

femina, *woman*; feminine, effeminate

feriæ, *festival*; ferial

*fero, tuli, latum, to *bear*; infer, confer, refer, differ, differ... ... ... , defer, ... late, ... correlative

A A 2

ferox, *fierce*; ferocious, ferocity

*ferrum, iron; ferruginous, far-
rier (a worker in iron, a shoer
of horses), ferrule, an iron
ring

*ferveo, to *boil*; fervesco, to
begin to boil; fervent, fervid,
fervor, effervesce, ferment

festum, a *holiday*; feast, festival, fête, festoon

fibra, *fibre*; fibrous, fringe (Lat.
fimbria)

*fides, faith (Fr. foi); fidelity,
infidel; fido, to *trust*, confide,
diffident, perfidy, perfidious,
affidavit, defiance, affiance

*figo, xi, fixum, to *fix*; fixture,
crucifix, transfix

filius, *son*; filial, affiliate, Fitz

*filum, *thread*; file (of soldiers),
bill-file, defile (to march in
a line), filigree (ornaments
made of gold or silver wire),
fillet (a little thread: a
fillet of veal is bound together
by a thread), profile

findo, fissum, to *cleave*; fissure,
fissile

fingo, nxi, fictum, to *form*; fiction, figment, fictile, feign,
effigies (an image made),
feint, faint

*finis, *end*; finish, finite, infinite,
confine, define, fine, in fine,
finical, finance, final, finality,
affinity, finish

*firmus, *firm*; confirm, affirm,
affirmative, firmament, infirm,
infirmary, infirmity, farm.
'The inconvenience of payment in kind early made universal the substitution of a
money payment, which was
called *firma alba* or *blanche
ferme*, from being paid in
silver or with money instead
of victuals.' (Wedgwood.)

fiscus, *treasury*; confiscate,
fiscal

fiaccus, *flabby*; flaccid

flagellum, *whip*; flagellate,
Flagellants, flail

flagitium, *disgrace*; flagitious

flagro, to *burn*; flagrant, con-
flagration

flamma, *flame*; inflame, in-
flammable, flamingo (the
flame-bird), flambeau, fla-
men?

*flecto, xi, xum, to *bend*; inflect,
flexible, inflexion

fligo, flictum, to *dash*; afflict,
inflict, affliction

flo, flatum, to *blow*; inflate,
flatulent

*flos, floris, *flower*; flour, floral,
floriculture, florist, flourish

*fluo, fluxum, to *flow*; fluid, influence, influential, affluent,
influenza, flux, superfluous;
fluctus, a *wave*; fluctuate

focus, *hearth*; focus, focal

fodio, fossum, to *dig*; fossil,
fosse

foedus, eris, a *covenant*; federal,
confederate

*folium, *leaf*; foil, the gold or
silver leaf used to throw up
the colour of a gem, foliage,
folio, trefoil, cinquefoil,
portfolio

fons, tis, a *fountain*; font, fount

fores, *doors*; foras, *out of doors*;
foreign, (g, as in sovereign,
excrescent)

*forma, a *form*; formal, forma-
lity, inform, reform, formation, uniform, conform, Non-
conformist, perform, per-
formance, deformity, formula
(dim.)

formido, *fear*; formidable

fornax, *furnace*

fors, tis, *chance*; fortuitous;
fortuna, *fortune*; misfortune

*fortis, *strong*; fortitude, fortify,
fortress, comfort, force, en-
force, reinforce, effort, fort

forum, *market-place*; Fr. foire,
fair, forensic

*frango, fractum, to *break*;
fracture, fraction, fragment,
refractory, irrefragable, fragile, infringe, frail

*frater, *brother*; fraternal, (Fr.
frère) friar, fraternity

*fraus, fraudis, *deceit*; fraud,
fraudulent

frequens, *frequent*; frequentative

frico, xi, ctum, to *rub*; friction

frigus, *cold*; frigid, refrigerate

frivolus, *silly*; frivolous, frivo-
lity, fribble (a trifling fellow)

frons, dis, *leaf*; frond

*frons, tis, *forehead*; front,
frontispiece (properly fronti-
spice), frontal, affront, con-
front, frontier, frounce,
flounce, effrontery

fruor, fructus, to *enjoy*; fruit,
fruition, fruitage, fruiterer,
frugal, frugality, fructify

frustra, *in vain*; frustrate

frustum, a *piece*; frustum (of
a cone)

*fugio, to *flee*; fugitive, refuge,
febrifuge, refugee, subterfuge,
fugue, centrifugal

fulgeo, to *shine*; effulgent, re-
fulgent; fulmen, *thunderbolt*;
fulminate; fumus, *smoke*;
fume, fumigate, perfume, fumitory (Fr. fume-terre, earth-
smoke)

*fundo, fudi, fusum, to *pour*;
found, foundry, font, confound, confuse, infuse, refuse,
fuse, fusible, transfusion,
diffusion, foison,

*fundus, *bottom*; fund, founda-
tion, fundament, profound,
founder (to go to the bottom)

fungor, ctus, to *discharge*;
function, defunct

funus, eris, *funeral*; funereal

fur, *thief*; furtive

furor, *madness*; fury, infuriate,
furious

futilis, *that easily pours out*,

that cannot contain (from
fundo); futile, futility

garrio, to *chatter*; garrulous

gelu, *frost*; gelid, congeal, gela-
tine, jelly

gemma, *gem*; a *bud*, gem; gem-
mate

*gens, tis, *people*; gigno, genui,
genitum, *to beget*; gentile, gen-
teel, gentle, generation, genus, degenerate, gentry,
genuine, progenitor, con-
genital, ingenuous, ingenious,
congenial, genius, engine

genu, *knee*; genuflect

germen, *sprig*; germinate, ger-
mane, cousin german (of the
same stock)

*gero, gestum, to *bear*; belligerent, vicegerent, gesture,
suggest, digest, gesticulate,
congestion, indigestion

glacies, *ice*; glacial, glacier

gladius, *sword*; gladiator, glaive

glans, dis, *kernel*; gland, glan-
dular, glanders (a disease in
the glands of horses)

gleba, *clod*; glebe

globus, *ball*; globe, globule

glomero, to *make into a ball*;
conglomerate

gloria, *glory*; glorify, glorious

*gradus, *step* (Fr. gré); grade,
degrade, graduate, gradation,
degree; gradior, gredi, gressus,
to walk; progress, congress,
aggression, ingredient, gra-
dient

grandis, *great*; grand, grandee,
grandfather, aggrandize,
grandiloquent, gaffer, gammer

granum, *seed*; grain, pomegranate (so called from its
numerous seeds), granary, in-
grain. ('Scarlet grain or ker-
mes is an insect found on
certain kinds of oak, from
which the (?) were
dyed. The term grain is a

translation of Gk. κόκκος, given to the insect, from its resemblance to a seed or kernel.'—*Wedgwood*), garnet (so called from its similarity in colour to the seed of the pomegranate), granite (grain-stone), grenade, grenadier, grange, granule, granular, granulate, filigree

·gratia, *favour*, pl. *thanks*; grace, gracious, ingratiate, gratis, gratuitous

gratulor, to *wish joy*; congratulate

*gratus, *pleasing*, thankful; grateful, gratitude, gratis, Fr. gré, maugre (malgré), agree (à gré=to one's will)

*gravis, *heavy*; grave, gravity, aggravate, gravamen, grieve, aggrieve

*grex, gis, *flock*; egregious (standing out of the flock), aggregate, gregarious, congregate

guberno, to *steer*; govern

gula, *throat*; gullet, jole, gully

gurges, *whirlpool*; gorge, gorget, gurgle, gargle, regurgitate, gorgeous. (See Skeat)

gutta, *drop*; gout, 'gouts of blood' (Macbeth), gutter

guttur, *throat*; guttural

*habeo, habitum, to *have*; habit, habitual, prohibit, inhibit, exhibit, inhibition, able, rehabilitate, ability, habiliment, dishabille

habito, to *dwell*; habitation, inhabit, cohabit

*hæreo, si, sum, to *stick*; cohere, adhere, cohesion; hæsito, to *hesitate*

*hæres, dis, *heir*; inherit, hereditary, hereditament, heirloom (O.E. loma, a piece of domestic furniture)

halo, to *breathe*; inhale, exhale

haurio, haustum, to *draw*; exhaust

herba, *herb*; herbarium, herbage, herbalist

hibernus, adj. (from hiems, winter), *winter*; hibernate

hilum, *a little thing* (nihilum = ne hilum = ne filum = *not a thread*); nil, annihilate

hio, to *gape*; hiatus

histrio, *actor*; histrionic

*homo, *man*; humanus, *human*; homicide, humane, homage

honor, *honour*; honestus, *honourable*; honorary

*horreo, to *bristle*, *shudder*; horror, horrible, horrify, horrid

hortor, atum, to *exhort*; exhortation, hortatory

hortus, *garden*; horticulture, cohort (originally an enclosure), court

*hospes, itis, *guest*; hospitable, hospice, hospital, hotel, hostel, hostler, spital

hostia, *sacrifice*; the host

hostis, *enemy*; hostile, hostility

humeo, to *be moist*; humour, humid, humorous

humus, *ground*; exhume, humble (humilis, lowly)

idem, the *same*; identify, identity, identical

ignis, *fire*; igneous, ignite

ignoro, to *be ignorant*; ignoramus, ignore

mago, imaginis, *likeness* (from imitor; comp. vertigo, from verto); image, imagination

imbecillis, *weak*; imbecile, imbecility, embezzle (see Skeat)

imbuo, to *imbue*

imitor, atus, to *copy*; imitate

impedio, to *hinder*; impede, impediment, Fr. empêcher, impeach

impero, to *command*; imperative, imperious, empire, emperor. See Paro index, *forefinger;* indico, to *point out;* index, indicate, indication, indicative

industria, *industry* (root, struo)

inferus, *low;* inferior (comparative), infernal

*insula, *island;* insular, peninsula, insulate, isle, islet (not *island*)

integer, *whole;* integrity, integral, entire (Fr. entière)

intelligo, lexi, lectum, to *understand;* intelligent, intellect

intra, *within;* interior (comp.), *inner;* interior, internal

intro, to *enter;* entrance

invenio, to *find;* invent, invention, inventory

invideo, to *envy;* invidious

invito, to *invite;* invitation

ira, *wrath;* ire, irate; irascor, *to be angry,* irascible

irrito, *to provoke;* irritate

irrigo, *to water;* irrigate

item, *likewise;* item

*iter, itineris (from eo, itum, to go), *a journey;* itinerary, itinerant, eyre (justices in)

iterum, *again;* reiterate

jaceo, ui, itum, to *lie;* adjacent

*jacio, jeci, jactum, *to throw;* adjective, eject, object, reject, subject, conjecture, interjection, subjection; jaculum, a *dart,* ejaculate; Fr. jeter, jet (of water)

jejunus, *fasting;* jejune

jocus, *joke;* jocular, juggler, (joculator)

*judex, icis, *judge;* judicial, justice, justiciary, judgment, adjudicate

*jugum, *yoke;* conjugate, conjugal, subjugate; jugulum, *collar-bone;* jugular

juncus, *rush;* junket (It. giuncata, fresh cheese brought to market in rushes)

*jungo, nxi, ctum, to *join:* jointure, juncture, junction, conjunction, subjunctive, conjoin'; It. junto; joust, jostle

juniperus, *juniper;* gin (Fr. genièvre)

Jupiter, Jovis; *Jove,* jovial (born under the influence of Jupiter. Comp. mercurial, martial, saturnine)

*juro, avi, atum, to *swear;* juror, jury, perjury, conjure; jus, juris, *law;* justus, *just;* jurist, jurisprudence, jurisdiction, justify, injury.

jus, *gravy;* juice

juvenis, *young;* junior (comp.), *younger,* juvenile

juvo, to *assist;* adjutant, aid

juxta, *near* (from *jungo*), juxtaposition

labor, *toil;* labour, laborious, laboratory, elaborate

labor, lapsus sum, to *glide;* lapse, elapse, collapse

lac, lactis, *milk;* lacteal, lactation, lettuce (lactuca, so called from its milky juice)

lacero, avi, atum, to *tear;* lacerate

lacertus, *lizard;* alligator (el lagarto, the name given by the Spaniards to the American crocodile)

lacrima, *tear* (old form dacrima, cp. Gk. *dakru,* Eng. *tear*); lachrymose, lachrymatory

lacus, a *lake;* lacustrine, lagoon

*lædo, læsum, to *injure;* collide, collision, lesion, elide

lætor, to *rejoice;* Letitia

lambo, to *lick;* lambent, lamprey (Lat. lampetra = O.E. suck-stone), so called from sucking the rocks

lamentor, to *bewail; lament,* lamentation

langueo, to *be faint;* languid, languish

lanx, *the scale of a balance;* balance

*lapis, lapidis, *stone:* lapidary,

dilapidated (=falling away stone from stone)

lardum, *fat of bacon*; lard, larder (the place where the bacon was kept. Cp. pantry, the bread-place. Fr. pain= bread), to lard (to stuff in lard), interlard

largus, *abundant*; large, largesse, enlarge

lassus, *weary*; lassitude

lateo, to *lie hid*; latent

laterna, a *lantern*, corrupted into lanthorn, under the wrong notion that the second syllable was connected with the *horn* panes

latus, *broad*; latitude

latus, lateris, *side*; lateral, equilateral

laurus, *laurel*; laureate

*laus, laudis, *praise*; laud, laudatory, laudation, laudable, allow (allaudare, Fr. allouer)

*lavo, avi, lautum; *lave*, lavatory, laundry, lavender, lavish

laxo, to *unloose*; lax, relax

*lēgo, ēgi, ctum; to *choose, read*; elect, collect, lecture, select, legible, legend, lectern, prelection, lection, lesson, legion, élite (chosen), recollect

lēgo, avi, atum, to *send as ambassador*; legate, legacy, relegate, college, allege

legumen, *pulse*; leguminous

lenis, *soft*; lenio, to *soften*; lenient, lenitive

lentus, *slow*; lento, relent

leuca, Mid. Lat. a *measure*; *league* (measure)

leo, *lion*; lioness, leonine

lepus, oris, *hare* (Fr. lièvre), leveret

*lēvis, *light*; levo, to *lighten*; levity, alleviate, lever, elevate, relieve, relief, leaven, levy, levée, ledger-line (a light line above the staff. It. *leggier*)

*lex, legis (Fr. loi), *law*; legal, legislate, legislator, legitimate, allegiance, privilege, lawyer, loyal (cp. royal from regalis)

*liber, *free*; liberal, liberate, deliver, libertine, livery

*liber, *book*; library, libretto (It.), libel (Dim.)

libo, to *pour out in honour of a deity*; libation

*libra, a *pound*; libro, to *weigh out*; libration, deliberate, livre, level (Lat. libella, dim. a plummet), equilibrium

licet, *it is allowed*; license, licentious, illicit, leisure

lignum, *wood*; ligneous; lignaloes, lignite (coal showing traces of its woody origin)

*ligo, avi, atum, to *bind*; ligament, ligature, religion, league, oblige, obligation, allegiance, liege, liable, lien, rally, ally

lilium, *lily*

limen, *threshold*; eliminate, preliminary

*limes, limitis, *cross-path*; limit, limitation, lintel

linea, a *linen thread, line*; linear, lineal, delineate, lineament, lineage. See Linum

lingua, *tongue*, Fr. langue; lingual, language, linguist

*linquo, lictum, to *leave*; relinquish, delinquent, relict, relic, reliquary

linum, *flax, linen*; linseed, linnet, linsey-woolsey (made of linen and wool), lint, lining

*liqueo, to *be fluid*; liquid, liquor, liquefy

lis, litis, *strife*; litigate, litigious

litera, *letter*, pl. *literature*; literal, literary; Belles Lettres, literate, obliterate (not from lino, to smear)

litus, oris, *shore*; litoral

lividus, *pale* ; livid

*locus, *place* ; local, locate, allocate, locomotive, collocation, dislocate, Fr. lieu, in lieu, lieutenant, Fr. loge, lodge

longus, *long* ; longitude, prolong, elongate

*loquor, locutus, to *speak* ; loquacious, allocution, eloquent, colloquy

luceo, to *shine* ; lucid, elucidate, luminary, lunes, lunatic, lustre

lucrum, *gain* ; lucre, lucrative

luctor, to *wrestle* ; reluctant

lucubro, to *work by lamp-light* ; lucubration. See Luceo

*ludo, lusum, to *play* ; elude, delude, illusion, allude, interlude, prelude, ludicrous

lugeo, to *grieve* ; lugubrious

lumbus, *loin* ; lumbago, lumbar

*lumen, *light* ; illuminate, illumination, luminous, luminary, limn

*luna (from luceo), *moon* ; lunar, lunatic (moon-struck)

*luo, lutum, to *wash* ; ablution, dilute, alluvial, diluvial (diluvium = deluge)

*lustro, avi, atum, to *make light* ; lustre, illustrate, lustrous, lute-string (a shining silk)

lustro, to *purify* ; lustration

*lux, cis (from luceo), *light* ; lucid, elucidate, pellucid

luxus, *luxury* ; luxurious, luxuriant

māchīna (Gk. mēchanē), a *contrivance* ; machine, machinate

macies, *leanness* ; emaciate, meagre. Cp. *acer* and *eager*

macula, *spot* ; immaculate, mackerel (from the dark blotches on it), mail

*magister (connected with *magnus*), *master* ; magistrate, mister

*magnus, *great* ; magnitude,

magnate, magnify ; *major, greater* ; majority, mayor ; *maximus,* greatest ; maximum, maxim

malleus, *hammer* ; mallet, mall, the mall (from the game of pall-mall which somewhat resembled croquet. It. palla = ball). See Skeat

*malus, *bad, male,* badly ; malign, malevolent, malediction, malady, malison, malice, maltreat, malaria, maugre (= mal gré, not agreeable, in spite of)

mamma, *breast* ; mammalia

*mando, to *put into one's hand* ; mandate, commend, demand, remand, mandamus, mandate, Maundy Thursday (dies mandati)

*maneo, mansum, to *remain* ; mansion, manse, manor ; menial, permanent, remnant, mastiff, menagerie

*manus, *hand* ; manual, emancipate, manufacture, manacle, manifest, manuscript, manufacture, amanuensis, Fr. main, maintain, maintenance, manage, manure, manœuvre, mortmain (dead hand), manner, legerdemain (= light of hand)

*mare, *sea* ; maritime, marine, mariner, ultramarine, submarine, mermaid, rosemary

margo, *edge,* margin

Mars, *the god of war* ; martial, March (the month)

mas, a *male* ; masculine, maritus, *a husband* ; marital, marry, marriage

massa, a *lump* ; mass, massive

*mater, *mother* ; maternal, maternity, matriculate, matrimonium, matricide, matron, matrix

materies, ... ther-
studii material

*maturus, *ripe*; mature, maturity, immaturity, premature

matutinus, *belonging to the morning*; matins or mattins, matutinal

*medeor, to *heal*; medical, medicine, medicament, remedy, remedial

*medius, *middle*; medium, mediocre, mediate, mediator, meridian (medius dies), Fr. moyen, mean, moiety, mezzotint

mel, *honey*; mellifluous, Philomel, marmalade (originally made of quinces. Lat. melimelum, literally a honey-apple, a quince. See Skeat), molasses = honey-like

melior, *better*; ameliorate

*membrum, *limb*; member, dismember, membrane

*memini, *I remember*; memor, *mindful*; memory, commemorate, memoir, remember, memorandum, memento

mendax, *lying*; mendacious, mendacity

mendicus, *beggar*; mendicant, mendicity

mendum, *fault*; amend, amends, emend, emendation

*mens, mentis, *mind*; mental, vehement. Cp. mind

*mereo, meritum, to *earn*; merit, meritorious; *meretrix*, a harlot; meretricious

*mergo, mersum, to *dip*; merge, emerge, submerge, immerse, emergency

merus, *pure*; mere

*merx, cis, *goods, wares*; merchandise; mercor, to *trade*; commerce, merchant, mercer, mercenary, mercy, market, mart, Mercury, the god of commerce

*metior, mensus sum, to *measure*; immense (=immeasurable), mensuration, measure

*migro, to *remove*; migrate, emigrant, immigrant

*miles, militis, *soldier*; military, militia, militant, militate

*mille, *thousand*; mile, millenary, millennium, million

minæ, *threats*; minatory, menace, commination

minio, to *paint red*; miniature

minister (connected with *minus*. Cp. magister and *magis*), a *servant*; ministration, ministerial

minor, *smaller*; minority

minuo, to *lessen*; diminutive, diminish, minute, minim, minimum, mite, minuet

*miror, to *admire*; admire, admirable, miracle, marvel, mirage

*misceo, mixtum, to *mix*; miscellany, promiscuous, mixture

miser, *wretched*; miser, miserable; miseror, to *pity*; commiserate

mitigo, to *make mild* (mitis); mitigate, mitigation

*mitto, missum, to *send*; missionary, commit, admit, message, messenger, permit, mission, missile, promise, premise

modo, *lately*; modern

*modus, *measure*; mode, mood (grammatical term; not mood, state of mind, which comes from O.E. mód, mind), modify, modulate, model, modern, modish, accommodate, commodious, commodity

mola, *mill*; molar, immolate (sacred meal being sprinkled on the heads of sacrificial victims)

moles, a *heap*; mole, molecule

molestus, *troublesome*; molest

molior, to *exert oneself*; emolumentum (=profit acquired through labour), emolument mollis, *soft*; mollify, mollusc

*moneo, ui, itum, to *warn*; monition, monument, admonish, monitor, premonitory, admonition

*mons, montis, *mount*; mountain, promontory, amount, surmount, dismount, paramount, remount

*monstro, avi, atum, to *show*; demonstrate, monstrance, monster, muster

*morbus, *disease*; cholera morbus, morbid, morbific

mordeo, morsum, to *bite*; morsel, remorse, mordant, mortise, morsel (a bit)

moror, to *delay*; demur

*mors, mortis, *death*; mortal, mortuary; morior, to *die*; moribund, mortmain, mortgage, murrain

mos, moris, *custom*; moral, moralist, Fr. mœurs, demure

*moveo, motum, to *move*; mobile, momentum, moment, promote, motion, motor, emotion, mob (mobile vulgus, the fickle crowd)

mula, *mule*; mulatto

*multus, *many*; multitude, multiform, multiply

mundus, *world*; mundane

*munio, to *fortify*; munition, ammunition, muniment

*munus, muneris, *gift, public office*; remunerate, munificent, municipal

murus, *wall*; mural, immure, intramural

musa (Gk. *mousa*), *muse*; amuse, mosaic (musaicum opus)

musca, a *fly*; mosquito, musket. Many instruments of war have been called after living creatures. *Culverin* is said to be from Lat. coluber, a snake. So among the Romans testudo, &c.

mutilo, to *maim*; mutilate

*muto, avi, atum, to *change*; mutable, immutable, commute, transmute, mew (of hawks), moult

*narro, avi, atum, to *narrate*; narrative, narration, narrator

*nascor, natus sum, *to be born*; nascent, nature, natural, natal, Noël (Christmas Day), nativity, innate, cognate, nation, Fr. naïf, naïve

nasus, *nose*; nasal, nasturtium (= nose-wring. From *torqueo*, to twist), Fr. *nez*, pince-nez

nausea, *sickness*; nauseous, nauseate

nauta (Gk. naus, a ship), *sailor*; nautical, nautilus

*navis, *ship*; navy, naval, navigate, navigable, nave (from the likeness of the vaulted roof to a ship). Gk. *naus*, a ship

necesse, *necessary*; necessity, necessitate. From *cedo*, to give way

*necto, nexum, to *tie*; connect, connexion, annex

nefas (from *fari*, to speak), *wickedness*; nefarious

negligo, to *neglect*; negligence

*nego, avi, atum, to *refuse*; deny, negation, negative, renegade (runagate, Psalms)

negotium (from nec = not, and otium, idleness); negotiate, negotiable

nepos, otis, *grandson*; nepotism, nephew

nervus, *string*; nerve, enervate

neuter, *neither*; neutral

niger, *black*; nigritude, negro

nihil, *nothing*; annihilate. See Hilum

*noceo, to *injure*; noxious, innocent, obnoxious, innocuous, Fr. nuire, nuisance, annoy, noisome

non, *not*; nonage, nonentity, nondescript

norma, *rule*; normal, enormous

*nosco, nòvi, notum, to *know*; noto, to *mark*; note, notion, notice, notify, notification; nomen, a *name*; nominal, denominate, cognomen, noble, nobility, ignominy, notary, cognizance, recognize

noster, *our*; nostrum, a specific peculiar to ourselves

novem, *nine*; November (the ninth of the Latin months), nones (the ninth day before the ides), noon (originally the ninth hour of the day, whence the ecclesiastical word *nones*. When *nones* came to be said at mid-day, the term was still retained)

*novus, *new*; novel, renovate, novice, innovate, novitiate, novelty

*nox, noctis, *night*; equinox, nocturn, nocturnal

*nubo, nuptum, to *marry*; nuptial, connubial

*nudus, *naked*; nude, denude, denudation

nugæ, *trifles*; nugatory

nullus, *none*; nullify, annul, nullity

*numerus, *number*; numeration, enumerate, innumerable, supernumerary

*nuntio, to *announce*; nuncio, pronounce, annunciation, renounce

*nutrio, to *nourish*; nurse, nutrition, nutriment, nurture, nourishment

nympha, *nymph*. Gk. nymphē, a bride

obedio, to *obey* (from *audio*, I hear); obedience, Fr. obéir, obeisance

obire (from eo, to go), *to die*; post-obit, obituary

obliquus, *oblique*; obliquity

oblivisco⋅, to *forget*; oblivion, oblivious

obscenus, *impure*; obscene, obscenity

obscurus, *dark*; obscurity, chiaro oscuro

occulo, occultum, to *hide*; occult, occultation

occupo (from capio), to *seize*; occupy, occupation

*octo, *eight*; October (the eighth of the Roman months), octavo, octave

*oculus (Fr. œil), *eye*; oculist, ogle, binocular, inoculate, œillade (Lear)

odium, *hatred*; odious

*odor, *smell*; odour, odoriferous, olfactory, redolent

officium, *duty*; office, officious

omen, *prognostic*; ominous, abominate, abominable

omnis, *all*; omniscient, omnibus (for all), omnipotent

*onus, oneris, *burden*; onerous, exonerate

opacus, *shady*; opaque, opacity

operio (Fr. ouvrir), to *open*; overt, kerchief, curfew

opes, *wealth*; opulent, opulence. Cp. c-opious

opinor, to *think*; opine, opinion, opinionated

oppidum, a *town*; oppidan

opportunus (from portus) *opportune*; inopportune. Comp. importunate

optimus, *best*; optimist

*opto, atum, to *wish*; option, adopt, cooptative

*opus, operis (Fr. œuvre), *work*; operate, co-operate, opera, manœuvre, chef d'œuvre, manure

orbis, *circle*; orb, orbit, exorbitant

*ordo, ordinis, *order*; ordain, ordinance, ordinary, co-ordinate. From *orior*?

*orior, ortus sum, to *rise*; orient, origin, aborigines

orno, to *adorn*; ornament, ornate

oro, atum, to *pray*; orator, oracle, oracular, inexorable, peroration, Fr. *oraison*, orison, oratory, oratorio. From *os, oris*

os, oris, *mouth*; oral, orifice

*os, ossis, *bone*; ossify, ossifrage (the bone-breaker), osprey

osculor, to *kiss*; oscillate

ostendo, to *show*; ostentation, ostensible

ostium, *door* (ostiarius, door-keeper); usher

ovum, *egg*; oval, oviparous

*paciscor, pactus sum, to *make an agreement*; pact, compact

pagina, *page*; pagination

pagus, *village*; pagan, peasant (Fr. paysan), paynim

palatium, *palace*; palatial

palatum, the *palate*; palatal

palleo, to *be pale*; pallor, pallid, appal

pallium, *cloak*; pall, palliate

palma, *palm of the hand*; palmary, palmistry, palmate

palma, the *palm*; palmer (pilgrim)—

> The faded palm-branch in his hand
> Showed pilgrim from the Holy Land.
> *Scott.*

palmer-worm (said to be so called from its wandering about, but more probably from *palm*, the provincial name of the willow)

palpo, to *stroke* (palpito, freq.); palpable, palpitate

palus, *stake*; pale, impale, palisade

pando, pansum and passum, to *spread*; expand, expanse, pace (the distance covered in walking between raising the foot and setting it down again)

pango, pactum, to *fasten*; compact, impinge. See Paciscor

panis, *bread* (Fr. pain), pantry,

companion (=messmate), pannier, pantler (Shakspere)

*par, *equal*; parity, peer, nonpareil, on a *par*, umpire (O.F. nompair = not even, odd; an odd man chosen to arbitrate. Cp. apron from napron, adder from nadder)

parco, parsum, to *spare*; parsimony

pareo, ui, itum, to *come forth*; appear, apparent

pario, peperi, partum, *to bring forth*; parent, viviparous, oviparous, puerperal

*paro, avi, atum, to *get ready*; pare, prepare, repair, compare, comparison, separate, sever, apparatus, empire

*pars, partis, *part*; partior, to *divide*; particle (dim.), particular, impart, tripartite, partisan, partner, parse, participle, participate, parboil, parcel, portion

parum, *little*; paraffine (from *affinis*, akin. Paraffine is so called from having little affinity for an alkali)

*pasco, pastum, to *feed*; pasture, pastor, repast

passus, *pace*; trespass (Fr. trépas)

pateo, to *lie open*; patent. Cp. pando

*pater, *father*; paternal, paternity, patristic, patrician, patrimony, papa, pope, patron, padrone

*patior, passus sum, *to suffer*; patient, passive, passion, compatible, compassion

patria, *fatherland*; patriot, expatriate

*pauper (Fr. pauvre), *poor*; pauper, poverty, poor, impoverish

pario, to ... paya, navi..... of lime, small stones, ... m-

med down with a hammer),
pavement

pavo, *peacock*

*pax, pacis, *peace*; pacify, pacification, pacific; paco, to *appease*; pay

*pecco, avi, atum, to *sin*; peccable, peccant, peccadillo (dim.)

pectus, pectoris, *breast*; pectoral, expectorate

peculium, *private purse*; peculiar, peculation. Cp. pecunia

*pecunia (from *pecus*, cattle), *money*; pecuniary, impecunious. Cp. connexion between O.E. feoh, *cattle*, and fee

pellis, *skin*; peltry, pelice, pellicle, surplice, pilch (originally, a fur garment)

*pello, pulsum, to *drive*; expel, repel, expulsion, repulse, pulse, pulsate

*pendeo, pensum, to *hang*; pendant, pending, impend, propensity, pendulum, perpendicular, appendix, pent-house (a sloping shed, formerly written appentis); pendo, to *weigh out*, to *pay*; expend, expense, stipend, recompense, compensation

pene, *almost*; peninsula, penultimate

penetro, to *pierce*; penetrate, penetralia

penna, a *wing, feather*; pen, pinnacle, pinion, pennon

penuria, *want*; penury, penurious

perdo, to *lose*; perdition

perdrix, *partridge*

peregrinus, *foreign*; pilgrim. Cp. *pellucid* from *perlucidus*.

persona, *mask* used by actors. Hence a part, a *person*; personate, parson (the person who represented the Church in a pa..sh)

pertica, *a measuring-staff*; perch

*pes, pedis, *foot*; pedal, impede, pedestrian, expedite, biped, pedestal. Cp. Gk. pous, podos

pestis, *plague*; pest, pestilent, pestiferous

*peto, petitum, to *seek*; petition, repeat, compete, appetite, impetuous, petulant, impetus

petra, *stone*; petrify, petrifaction, saltpetre, petroleum, lamprey = rock-licker

pica, a *pie*; magpie, pied, piebald (bald = streaked. From W. *bal*, having a white streak on the forehead. See Skeat)

pila, *column*; pile, pilaster

pila, *ball*; pill, pellet

pilo, to *steal*; compile, compilation, pillage

pilus, *hair*; pile as in three-*piled*, depilatory, caterpillar, plush (Fr. peluche) peruke (cp. Spanish peluca, a wig), periwig, wig

*pingo, pictum (Fr. peindre), to *paint*; pigment, depict, picture, orpiment (auripigmentum, yellow-sulphuret of arsenic)

pinso, to *pound*; pistillum, a *pestle*, pistil

piscis, *fish*; piscatory, piscine

*pius, *pious*; piety, expiate, pity, piteous, pitiable

*placeo, to *please*; pleasant, complacent, placid, plea (Low Lat. *placitum*, a decision)

placo, to *appease*; placable, implacable

plaga, *blow*; plague

plagiarius, *one who stole children*; plagiarist

plango, to *bewail*; plaint, complain, plaintiff, plaintive

planta, *plant*; plantation, implant

*planus, *level* (It. piano); plain, explain, plane, plan

platea, a *broad street*; place, piazza

*plaudo, to *clap the hands*; applaud, applause, plaudit, plausible, explode (to drive off the stage)

plebs, *common people*; plebeian

*plecto, plexus, to *weave*; complex, perplex, pleat, plait

*pleo, evi, etum, to *fill*; replete, implement, complete, replenish, plenitude, supply, plenary, supplement, complement

*plico, avi, atum, to *fold*; ply, pliers, apply, reply, supplicate, suppliant, simple (one-fold, cp. O.E. an-feald), multiple, duplex (two-fold), duplicity, triplet, supple, display, employ, explicit, implicit, accomplice, deploy, employ

ploro, to *weep over*; deplore, implore

pluma, *plume*; plumage

*plumbum, *lead*; plumber, plummet, plumb-line, plumbago. Cp. *lumbago* from *lumbus*, loin

plus, pluris, *more*; plural, surplus, nonplus

*pœna, *punishment*; penalty, pain; punio, to *punish*; pœnitet, *it repents*; penitence, repentance, penance

polio, to *polish*; polite

pomum, *apple*; pomatum (originally made from apples), pomander, pommel, pomegranate

*pondus, ponderis, *weight*; pound, ponderous, preponderate, poise, avoir-du-pois, ponder

*pono, posui, positum, *to place*; pose, position, deponent, component, proposition, compound, impose, impostor, post, postage

*pons, *brida·· pontiff· ···· ··· — bridge maker·, pontoon

populus, *people*; public, publish, republic, popular; populor, *to lay waste*, depopulate

porcus, *pig*; pork, porcupine (the spiny pig), porcelain (so called from the resemblance of its glazed surface to the shell called in Italian *porcellana*, which was itself called from its resemblance to a little pig, It. *porcella*), · porpoise (the pig-fish, from piscis)

porrum, *leek*; porridge, porringer

*porta, *gate*; porter, portico, porch, portcullisse (Fr. couler, to slide), the Porte

*porto, avi, atum, *to carry*; import, export, portable, porthole, porter (porter's beer), port-folio, port-manteau

portus, a *harbour*; port, Portsmouth, Newport

*possum, posse (from potis, *able*, · and sum, *I am*), *to be able*; possible, potent, podesta, puissant

*post, *after*; posterior (comp.), postpone, posterity, preposterous (having the last first), postern (a back gate), posthumus (the last. The *h* is excrescent), position, post-obit

postulo, avi, atum, *to demand*; postulate, expostulate

poto, to *drink*; potation, potable, potion, poison. Cp. *reason* from *ratio*, *oraison* from *oratio*

prœda, *prey*; predatory, depredation

*prœbeo, to *furnish*; prebend, provender (the ration furnished to a soldier; afterwards applied to the allowances for monks and canons), prebendary

···· ·· ·· ··; · pice, ···· ·ato

præmium, *reward*; premium

pravus, *crooked*; deprave, depravity

*precor, atum, *to pray*; imprecate, deprecate, precarious (granted only on entreaty)

*prehendo, prehensum (Fr. prendre, perf. part. pris), *to take*, prehensile, comprehend, prize, prison, apprehend, apprise, comprise, misprision, reprisals; Fr. apprendre, *to learn*, apprentice

*premo, pressum, to *press*; oppress, repression, compress, print (O.F. *empreindre*, to print)

pretium, *price*; appreciate, appraise (to set a price on), praise, prize, precious

*primus, *first*; prime, primeval, primrose, primitive, primate, prince, principal, primogeniture, principle

prior, *former*; prior, priority

pristinus, *former*; pristine

*privo, to *separate*; deprive, private, privacy, privilege (a law for a private person), privy, privateer

*probo, avi, atum, to *try*; probe, probable (capable of being proved, likely), approbation, probate, probity; (Fr. prouver), prove, approve, improve, proof, waterproof

probrum, a *shameful act*; opprobrium, opprobrious

probus, *honest*; probity. From *probo*

prodigus, *lavish*; prodigal

proles, *offspring*; prolific

promptus, *ready*; prompt, promptitude. From promo, to *bring forth*

pronus, *leaning forwards*; prone

propago, a *slip, shoot*; propagate, propagandist

*prope, *near*; proximus, *nearest*; propinquity, proximate, approximate; propitius, *favourable*, propitious

*proprius, *one's own*; proper, propriety, property, appropriate

prora, *prow*; prore (Scott)

prurio, to *itch*; prurient

pudor, *shame*; pudet, *it shames*; impudent

puer, *boy*; puerile, puerility, puerperal

pugil, *boxer*; pugilist

pugna, *fight*; pugnus, *fist*; pugno, to *fight*; pugnacious, impugn, repugnant, poniard

pullus, *chicken*; pullet (Fr. poulet), poultry, poulterer

pulmo, *lungs*; pulmonary

pulpa, *pith of wood*; pulp

pulpitum, a *scaffold*; pulpit

puls, *pottage*; poultice. Gk. *poltos*

pulvis, veris, *dust*; pulverize, powder (cp. absoudre from absolvere)

pumex, *pumice*; pounce. Probably from *spuma*, foam

*pungo, punctum, *to prick*; pungent, expunge, puncture, punctual, point, appoint, punctilio, poignant, pounce

puppis, *stern*; poop

*pupus, a *boy*; pupillus (dim.), pupil, pupillage, puppet. The pupil of the eye is probably so called from the baby images seen in it

purgo, *to cleanse*; purge, purgation (from purus, clean)

purpura, *purple*. Gk. porphyra = the purple fish

purus, *pure*; purify, purification, impurity

pus, *matter*; suppurate, purulent

pusillus, *very little*; pusillanimous

*puto, avi, atum, *to cut, to think*; amputate, impute, repute, putative, reputation, dispute, compute, count, account putris, *rotten*; putrid, putrefy, putrescence

quadraginta, *forty*; quarantine, Quadragesima Sunday

*quæro, quæsitum, to *seek*; query, inquire, inquest, quest, question, exquisite, inquisition, perquisite

qualis, *of what kind*; quality, qualify

quantus, *how great*; quantity, quantitative

*quatio, quassum, to *shake*; concussion, percussion

*quatuor, *four*, quadra, a *square*; quart, the fourth part of a gallon, quarry (a place where stones are squared), square, squadron, quadratic, quadrant, quadrature, quadrille, quadroon, quadrilateral, quadrangle, quartan, quartet, quarto, quatrain, quaternion

queror, to *complain*; querulous

*quies, quietis, *rest*; quiet, quietus (Hamlet), requiem, quit (to silence a creditor), requite, quiescent, acquiesce, quite

quinque, *five*; quintessence, quintuple, quincunx, quintain, quinquennial

quot, *how many*; quota, quotient

rabies, *madness*; rabid, rage

racemus, *a bunch of grapes*, raisin

*radius, a *straight rod*; ray, eradiate, radiant, irradiate

*radix, radicis, *root*; radish, eradicate, radical

rado, rasum, to *scrape*; raze, erase, razor

ramus, *branch*; ramify

rancidus, *stinking*; rancid, rancour

*rapio, raptum, to *snatch*; rapt, surreptitious, rapid, rapture, rapine, rapacious (Fr. ravir), ravish, ravenous, ravage. Raven is from a Teutonic source

rarus, *thin*; rare, rarefy

*ratio, rationis (Fr. raison), *reason*; ratio, ration, rational, ratiocination. From *reor*

recupero, to *recover*; recuperation

*rego, rectum, to *rule*; correct, incorrigible, regulate, regimen, regent, region, regiment, rector, direct, rectitude, rectify, dress, adroit (Fr. *droit*), maladroit

reminiscor, to *remember*; reminiscence

ren, renis, the *kidneys*; reins, renal

reor, ratus, to *think*; rate, ratify

reperio, rtum, to *find*; repertory

repo, to *creep*; reptile, surreptitious (creeping under)

*res, *thing*; real, reality, republic, rebus (a riddle in which the meaning is indicated by *things*)

rete, *net*; reticule (dim.), retina, riddle (= sieve)

*rex, regis, *king*; regal, regicide: regnum, *kingdom*, regnant, reign, interregnum, realm; Fr. roi, *king*, royal (cp. *loyal*, from legalis)

*rideo, risum, to *laugh*; ridicule, deride, derision, risible

rigeo, to *stiffen*; rigid, rigour

rigo, to *water*; irrigate, irriguous

ripa, *a river bank*; riparian, arrive (to come to the bank. Fr. rive)

ritus, *ceremony*; rite, ritual, ritualist

*rivus, a *brook*; river, rivulet; rival (using the same stream, or dwelling on opposite sides of the same stream)

robur, oris, *strength*; robust, corroborate

*rodo, rosum, to *gnaw*; corrode, corrosion, erosion, rodent

*rogo, avi, atum, to *ask*; rogation, interrogate, arrogate, derogate, prorogue, prorogation

ros, roris, *dew*; rosemary (Lat. ros marinus)

rostrum, *bill of a bird, beak of a ship*, rostrum

*rota, *wheel* (Fr. roue); rota, rotate, rotary, roué, route, routine, to learn by *rote*, rowel (of a spur)

rotundus, *round*; rotundity, roundelay

ruber, *red*; rubric (printed in red letters), ruby (red stone), rubicund, rouge

rudis, *rude*; erudite, rudiment

ruga, *wrinkle*; corrugated

ruminare, to *chew the cud*; ruminate, ruminant

rumor, *hearsay*; rumour

*rumpo, ruptum, to *break*; rupture, corrupt, disruption, bankrupt, eruption, irruption

ruo, to *rush*; ruin

*rus, ruris, *country*; rural, rustic, rusticate

ruta, *rue*

saccus, *bag*; sack, satchel

*sacer, *sacred*; sacrament, sacrifice, sacristan, sexton, consecrate, desecrate, sacrilege, sacrifice

sacerdos, a priest; sacerdotal

*sagax, cis, *wise*; sage, presage, sagacious

*sal, *salt*; saline, salary (soldier's pay; an allowance of salt), salad, salt-cellar (salière), sausage (Fr. saucisse, from being cured with salt), saucer

*salio, to *leap*; salient, sally, assault, insult, result, saltatory, assail, salmon (the *leaper*), desultory

*salus, salutis, *health*; salutary, salute; saluber, *healthy*; salubrious; salvus, *safe*; salve, salvation, salver, Saviour

salvia, the herb sage; sage

sancio, sanctum, to *ordain*; sanction

*sanctus, *holy*; sanctify, saint, sonties (M. of Venice), sanctuary, sanctimonious; Samphire (herb of Saint Peter). In proper names the *t* of the Saint is often stuck on to the name of the Saint. Cp. Tawdry from St. Awdry, Tooley from St. Olave, Tanton from St. Anthony, &c.

*sanguis, sanguinis, *blood*; sanguine, sanguinary; consanguineus, *of the same blood*; cousin

*sano, atum, to cure; sanatory (relating to healing), sanatorium

*sanus, *healthy*; sanitas, *health*; sane, sanitary (relating to health), sanity

*sapio, to *taste*, to *be wise*; sapor, *flavour*; sapid, insipid, savour, sapient

sapo, *soap*; saponaceous

satelles, itis; *satellite*

satis, *enough*; satisfy, satiate; satur, *full of*; saturate

Saturnus, *Saturn*; saturnine, Saturnalia (a feast in honour of Saturn in which great license was allowed)

saxum, *stone*; saxifrage (the stone-breaker), sassafras

*scando, scansum, to *climb*; scala, a ladder; scan, ascend, scale, descent, ascension, escalade, transcend

*scindo, scissum, to *split*; rescind, scissors

scintilla, *spark*; scintilla, tinsel (Fr. étincelle)

*scio, scitum, to *know*; science, sciolist, conscious, conscience, omniscient, prescient

*scribo, scriptum, to *write*; scribe, script, scripture, describe, conscript, postscript, escritoire scrinium, a *chest*; shrine, en-shrine, screen

scrupulus, a *pebble*; scruple, scrupulous, scrupulosity

*scrutor, atum, to *examine carefully*; scrutiny, scrutineer, inscrutable

*seco, sectum, to *cut*; sect, bisect, insect, dissect, segment

*seculum, an *age*; secular (belonging to this age)

*sedeo, sessum, to *sit*; sedes, a *seat*; sido, to *set*; sedo, to *settle*; see, sedentary, sedulous, sedate, reside, subside, residence, sediment, assess, possess (from root of potis and sedeo), siege, assize, insidious

semen, *seed* (from sero, to sow); seminal, seminary, disseminate

semi, *half*; semicircle

*senex, *old man*; *senior*, elder; senate, senile, sir, signior, monsieur

*sentio, to *feel*; sentient, assent, consent, sentiment, sensual, sensuous, sentence, scent

separo, to *divide* (from se and pars); separate, sever (Fr. sevrer)

sepelio, sepultum, to *bury*; sepulture, sepulchre

*septem, *seven*; septennial, September (the seventh of the Roman months); septuagesimus, *seventieth*; Septuagesima

sequester, *one who holds a deposit*; sequestrate

*sequor, secutus, to *follow* (Fr. suivre); sequent, sequel, obsequies, execute, persecute, consecutive, sequence, consequence, sue, pursue, suit, suitor, second (the following one)

serenus, *calm*, *clear* serene, serenade

*sero, sevi, satum, to *sow*; sero, ui, sertum, *to put in a row*; sermo, a *discourse*; insert, dissertation, series, assert, desert

serus, late; sere

*servio, to *serve*; servo, *to preserve*; servus, *slave*; servant, servitude, servitor, preserve, serf, service, sergeant, reserve, reservoir

seta, a *hair*; seton (a running sore, produced by passing a twist of hair or silk under the skin of the neck)

severus, *stern*; severe, severity

sex, *six*; sextant; sexagenarius, *a man of sixty*, sexagenarian

sidus, cris, *star*; sidereal

*signum, *mark*; sign, signify, design, designate, signal, assign, seal (sigillum, dim.), consign, resign, ensign, insignia

sileo, to *be silent*; silence

silva, *wood*; sylvan, savage, (wild, forest-like)

*similis, *like*; simile, similar, dissimilar, assimilate, similitude, Fr. sembler; resemble, dissemble

simplex (semel, *once*, plica, *fold*), *simple*; simpleton, simplify

simul, *at the same time*; simultaneous

simulo, to *feign*; simulate, dissemble

sincerus (sine, *without*, cera, *wax*); sincere (originally applied to honey that was free from wax. Others say the word was applied to pottery free from flaws. The Roman potters used to rub wax into the flaws of unsound vessels)

singuli, *one by one*; single, singular

sinister, *on the left hand*, *unlucky*; sinister

sinus, *bosom, bay*; sinuous, insinuate (to get into the bosom)

*sisto, to *stop*; insist, desist, resistance, consistency, persistent

sobrius, *sober*; sobriety

*socius, *companion*; social, society, associate

sol, *sun*; solar, solstice

solea, *shoe*; sole

solemnis, *solemn, appointed*; solemn, solemnize

solicito, to *rouse*; solicitor; solicitus, *anxious*; solicitude

solidus, *solid*; consolidate, solder (to make solid). The French word *solde* = pay is said to be from *solidus*. Hence soldier

*solor, to *console*; consolation, desolate, solace

solum, *ground*; soil, exile

*solus, *alone*; sole, solitary, solitude, solo

*solvo, solutum, to *loosen*; solve, solvent, insolvent, resolve, absolution, resolute, dissolute, soluble, solution

*somnus, *sleep*; somnolent, somniferous, insomnia

sonus, *sound*; sonorous, unison, consonant, dissonance

sopor, *sleep* soporiferous, soporific

sordes, *filth*; sordid

spargo, sparsum, to *spread*; sparse, disperse, aspersion

spatium, space, spacious; *spatior*, to take a walk; expatiate. (The *s* of the root is lost in the *x* of the prefix.)

*specio, spectum, to *look*; specimen, aspect, respect, specious (showy); specto (freq.), *to look at*; respectable, spectator, speculum, special, specify, species (kinds), spice, specie, (in kind), specific, spectre, perspective, conspicuous, suspicion, despise, spy, despite

*spero, atum, to *hope* (**Fr.** espérer); despair, desperate, esperance (Shakspere)

spina, *thorn*; spiny, spinach (the prickly plant)

*spiro, atum, to *breathe*; spirit, sprite, respire, inspiration, spiracle, conspiracy

splendeo, to *shine*; splendid, splendour

spolium, *spoil*; spolio, *to rob*; despoil, spoliation

*spondeo, sponsum, to *promise*; respond, response, sponsor, despond; sponsus, *betrothed*; espouse, spouse, espousals

sponte, *of one's own accord*; spontaneous

spurius, *bastard*; spurious

*stagnus, *standing*; stagnum, a *pond*; stagnate, stagnant, Fr. étang (a pool), tank

*statuo, to *set up*; statue, statute, stature, constitute, destitute, institute, substitute

stella, *star*; constellation, stellated, stellar

sterilis, *barren*; sterile, sterility

*sterno, stratum, to *spread out*, to *stretch out*; prostrate, consternation, street (strata)

stilia, *drop*; distil, instil (to pour in drop by drop), still

stilus, *a pointed instrument used in writing on waxen tablets*; style

stimulus, *goad*; stimulus, stimulate

stinguo, ctum, to *quench*; extinct, extinguish, distinct

stipendium, pay (from stips, a *gift*, and pendo, to *weigh*); stipend

stipo, to *press together*; constipated, costive

stirps, a *stock, root*; extirpate. (The *s* of the root is lost in the *x* of the prefix. Cp. *expatiate* from spatium) *sto, statum, to *stand*; station, stamina, state, estate, statistics, stable, stature, extant, distant, substance, substantial, solstice, armistice, superstition, restive

strenuus, *vigorous*; strenuous

strangulo, to *throttle*; strangle, strangulation

*stringo, strictum, to *bind*; string, stringent, astringent, strict, strain, constrain, strait, distraint, district

*struo, structum, to *build*; construe, construct, instruct, destroy, destruction

*studium, *desire*; studeo, *to be eager about*; student, study, studio

stultus, *foolish*; stultify (to make a fool of)

*stupeo, to *be struck senseless*; stupid, stupefy, stupefaction

*suadeo, suasum, to *advise*; persuade, dissuade, suasion

suavis, *sweet*; suave, suavity, assuage

subitus, *sudden*

*sublimis (from levo, to *raise*) *uplifted*; sublime, sublimate, sublimity

subtilis (from texo, to weave), *thin-spun, fine*; subtle

sudo, atum, to *sweat*; exude, (cp. the disappearance of the *s* in *extirpate, expatiate*), exudation, sudatorium

suffragium, *vote*; suffrage

sui, sibi, se, reflexive pronouns of the third person; suicide

sum, esse, to *be*; ens, tis, *being*; futurus, *about to be*; absent, present, presence, interest, entity, nonentity, future, futurity, essence, essential

sumo, sumptum, to *take*; assume, consume, presumption, assumption

*super, *above*; superus, *high*; superior (comp.), supremus

or summus (sup.); supreme; supernal, soprano, sovran, sovereign, summit, consummate

supinus, *on the back*; supine

surdus, *deaf*; surd, absurd (like a reply from one deaf)

surgo, surrectum, to *rise*; surge, insurgent, resurrection, insurrection

taberna, a *booth, shop*; tavern, tabernacle. Cog. tabula

tabula, a *board*; table, tablet, tabulate, tabulation

taceo, to *be silent*; reticent, tacit, taciturn

*tango, tactum, to *touch*; tangent, tangible, tact, tactile, contingent, contiguous, contact, contagion, attain

tardus, *slow*; tardy, retard

taxo, to *tax*; taxation

*tego, tectum, to *cover*; detect, tectile, tile (tegula), integument. Cp. Eng. *deck* and *thatch*, Ger. dach, roof

temere, *rashly*; temerity

temno, to *despise*; contemn, contempt

*tempero, to *mix, moderate*; temper, verb (as to temper mortar); subst. (mixture of elements in the constitution), temperament, temperature

tempestas, *storm*, from *tempus*, time; tempest

templum, *temple*

*tempus, temporis, *time*; temporal, tense, temporary, contemporaneous, extempore

tempus, pl. tempora, *the temples of the head*; temporal

*tendo, tensum, to *stretch*; distend, extend, tense, intense, tendon (the sinew which attaches the muscles to the bones), tent, tenter hooks (for stretching cloth)

*teneo, tentum, to *hold*; tenure, tenant, tenement, tenacious, tenor, retain, sustain, maintain, contain, content, tenon, continuous, pertinent, sustenance, countenance, retentive, retinue

tener, *tender*; tendril (the tender shoot of a plant)

tento, to *try*; tempt, temptation, tentative, attempt

tenuis, *thin*; attenuate, extenuate (to make thin), tenuity

tepeo, to *be warm*; tepid, tepidarium

ter, *thrice*; ternary; tertius, *third*; tertiary

tergum, *back*; tergiversation

*terminus, *end*; term, terminal, terminate, determine, exterminate

*tero, tritum, to *rub*; trite (worn), contrite (broken down), contrition, detriment, triturate (to reduce to dust by rubbing); tribulo, to *thrash*, to *afflict*, tribulation

*terra, *earth*; terrace, terrier, tureen (Fr. *terrine*, an earthen vessel), terrene, terrestrial, territory, inter, disinter, subterranean, terra cotta

terreo, to *frighten*; terrible, terror, terrify, deter

*testis, *witness*; testify, attest, detest, testament, testator, protest, contest

*texo, textum, to *weave*; textile, text, texture, pretext, context, tissue

thesaurus (Gk. *thesauros*), *treasure*; treasury

timeo, to *fear*; timid, timidity

tinguo, to *dye* (Fr. teindre); tinge, tint, tincture

tolero, atum, to *endure*; tolerate

tollo, to *raise*; extol

torpeo, to *be numb*; torpor, torpid, torpedo

*torqueo, tortum, to *twist*; to torture, torment, contortion, distort, torsion, retort (a vessel with a mouth bent downwards), tortoise

*torreo, tostum, to *roast*; torrid, toast, torrent

totus, *all, the whole*; total

trado, to *give up*; tradition, treason

*traho, tractum, to *draw*; traction, subtract, subtrahend, attract, contract, traitor, betray (hybrid); tracto, to *handle*; (Fr. traiter), tractable, treat, tract, treatise, trail; Fr. trainer, to draw; train

tranquillus, *quiet*; tranquil, tranquillize

transire, to *go across* (from eo, to go); transit, trance

*tremo, to *tremble*; tremor, tremulous, tremble, tremendous; trepido, to *tremble*; trepidation, intrepid

tres, tria, *three*; trefoil, trident, trinity, tribe, trivet (Fr. trépied), a support on three feet

*tribuo, to *give*; tribute, attribute, contribute, distribute

*tribus, one of the *three* bodies into which the Romans were originally divided; tribune

triumphus, *triumph*; triumphal

trivia, *a place where three ways meet*; trivial (like the gossip about a crossing)

*trudo, trusum, to *thrust*; obtrude, intrude, intrusion

truncus, *trunk*; truncated

tuba, *a trumpet*; tube

tuber, *a swelling, a fungus*; tubercle, tubercular, truffle

tueor, itus, to *behold*; tutor, intuition, tuition

*tumeo, to *swell*; tumid, tumour, tumult, contumely, tuber

*tundo, tusum, to *pound*; contusion, obtuse

turba, *crowd*; turbulent; turbo, to *disturb*; turbid, trouble

turpis, *base*; turpitude

turtur, *turtle* (compare marmor, *marble*)

uber, *udder*; exuberant. Uber and udder are cognate

ubique, *everywhere*; ubiquity

ulcus, ulceris, *sore*; ulcer, ulcerate

*ultra, *beyond*; ulterior, *further*; ultimus, *last*; ultimate, penultimate, ultimatum

umbra, *shade*; umbrage, umbrageous, umbrella, adumbrate, penumbra

uncia, *twelfth part*; ounce, inch

unda, *wave*; undulate, abound, abundance, redound, inundation

*unguo, unctum, to *anoint*; unguent, unction, ointment

*unus, *one*; unit, unison, uniform, universe, unite, union, unity, unique, triune, onion (Fr. oignon)

urbs, *city*; urbane, suburb, urban

urgeo, to *press on*; urge, urgent

urna, *urn*; inurn

uro, ustum, to *burn*; combustion, adust (Bacon)

utor, usus, to *use*; utensil, abuse, peruse, usage, usual, usury (money paid for the *use* of money), usance (M. of Venice), usurp (from *usu rapere*, to seize for one's own use)

uxor, *wife*; uxorious

*vacca, *cow*; vaccine, vaccinate, bachelor (Low Lat. *baccalarius*, a cowherd. From bacca, a Low Latin form of vacca)

vacillo, to *waver*; vacillate

*vaco, to *be idle*; vacant, vacate, vacation, vacuum, evacuate

vado, vasum, to *go*; evade, invade, invasion

vagor, to *wander*; vagabond, extravagant, vagrant, vague, vagary

*valeo, to *be strong*; value, valour, valiant, valid, prevail, avail,

prevalent, convalescent; vale, *farewell*; valedictory

vallis, *vale*; valley, avalanche

vallus, *stake*; vallum, *rampart*; wall, circumvallation

valvæ, *folding doors*; valve

*vanus, *empty*; vain, vanity, vanish, evanescent

varius, *different*; various, variegate, variety

vapor, *steam*; evaporate

vappa, *flat wine*; vapid

varix, a *dilated vein*; varicose

vas, vasis, a *vessel*; vascular, vase, vesicle, vessel

vastus, *waste*; vast, devastate

vegeo, to *grow*; vegetable, vegetate, vigour

*veho, vectum, to *convey*; vehicle, conveyance, convex, inveigh

*vello, vulsum, to *pluck*; convulse, revulsion

velum, *veil*; reveal, envelope, develop

vena, *vein*; venous

*vendo, to *give* (do) *for sale* (venum = sale); veneo, to *go* (eo) *for sale*, venal, venality, vend, vendible, vendor

venenum, *poison*; venom, venomous, envenom

veneror, to *worship*; vereor, to *stand in awe of*; venerate, venerable, reverend (deserving to be honoured), reverent (showing honour)

venia, *pardon*; venial

*venio, ventum, to *come*; convene, convent, conventicle, advent, intervene, supervene, contravene, circumvent, revenue, covenant, covin (a fraudulent agreement) inventory

venter, *belly*; ventricle, ventriloquist

ver..., ...; venti..., to *fan*; venti...

ver, *spring*; vernal

*verbum, *word*; verb, adverb, proverb, verbal. Cognate with *word*; cp. *barba* and *beard*

vergo, to *lie towards*; verge, converge, diverge

*vermis, *worm*; vermiculate, vermicelli (little worms), vermilion (the berries of the *coccus*, from which scarlet dye was formerly obtained, are full of little worms), vermin

verna, *household slave*; vernacular

vertex, '*the crown of the head* where the hair turns round like a whirlpool, and thence the top of anything' (*Wedgwood*); vertical, *directly over the vertex*

*verto, versum, to *turn*; versatile, verse, pervert, vertebra, invert, reverse, conversion, divorce, vortex, advertise, universe, perverse, revert

*verus, *true*; verax, *truthful*; very (Fr. vrai), veracious, verify, verity, veritable, verdict

vesica, *bladder*; vesicle. See Vas

vestigium, *foot-print*; vestige, investigate

vestis, *garment*; vest, invest, vestment, vesture, vestry, divest, travesty (to disguise by changing the dress)

vetus, veteris, *old*; veteran, inveterate

vexo, to *molest* (freq. of veho); vex, vexation

*via, *way*; deviate, devious, obviate, pervious, viaticum = journey-money, trivial, voyage (Fr. voie)

vibro, atum, to *vibrate*

*vicis, *change, turn*; vice-roy, vicar, vicissitude, vicarious

vicus, *a village*; vicinus, *neighbouring*; vicinity

*video, visum, to *see*; visit, visor, visual, vision, visible, provi-dence, provide, provision, view, prudence, prudent, prude, survey, invidious, envy (to cast an eye on)

vigil, *wakeful*; vigil, vigilant

vilis, *cheap*; vile, vilify

villa, *a country house*; village, villain (= rustic), villatic (Milton)

*vinco, victum, to *conquer*; victor, victory, convict, victim (a beast killed in honour of victory), vanquish

*vindex, icis, *judge*; vindicate, Fr. venger, venge, vengeance, avenge, vindictive

vinea, a *vineyard, vine*; vignette

*vinum, *wine*; vinous, vintage, vinegar (Fr. vinaigre = sharp wine. See Acer)

viola, *violet*

vipera, *viper* (from *vivus*, living, and *pario*, to bring forth)

vir, *man*; virile, virtue, vertu, virtuoso, virago, triumvir

virgo, *virgin*; virginals, virginity

viridis, *green*; verdigris, verdant, verdure, verderer (a forester who had charge of the underwood)

virus, *poison*; virulent

vis, *force*; violate, violent

viscus, *birdlime*; viscid, viscous

vita, *life*; vital, eau-de-*vie* (water of life)

*vitium, *fault*; vitupero, to *blame*; vice, vicious, vitiate, vituperation

vitrum, *glass*; vitreous, vitrify, vitriol

vitulus, *calf*; veal, vellum (calf-skin)

*vivo, victum, to *live*; revive, vivid, vivacious, victuals, viands

*voco, atum, to *call*; convoke, revocation, voice, vocal, vowel, vocable, vocabulary. Vox, cis, *voice*; vociferate, vouch

(to answer to the call),
vouchsafe (to warrant safe
when called upon at law to
answer for something in dispute, to assure, deign, conde-
scend.— Wedgwood)

volo, to *fly*; volatile, volley

*volo, to *will*; volition. Vo-
luntas, *will*; voluntary, inveigle (It. invogliare)

voluptas, *pleasure*; voluptuous

*volvo, volutum, to *roll*; revolve,
involve, involution, voluble,
volume (a roll of writing),
convolvulus

voro, to *devour*; voracious

*voveo, votum, to *wish for, vow*;
vote, devote, votary, devo-
tion, Fr. vœu, vow, avow,
avowal

Vulcanus, *the god of fire*; volcano, vulcanite

*vulgus, *people*; vulgar, divulge,
Vulgate (the Latin version of
the Scriptures commonly
used)

vulnus, eris, *wound*; invulner-
able

vulpes, *fox*; vulpine, vulpecide

vultur, *vulture*

321. GREEK ROOTS.

abax, gen. abakos (ἄβαξ), *a cal-
culating board*; abacus

adamas (ἀδάμας, -αντος), *uncon-
querable* (a = *not*, damao = *to
conquer*); adamant, diamond
(so called on account of its
hardness)

*aër (ἀήρ), *air*; aerolite (sky-
stone), aeronaut (air-sailor),
aerostatics

aggelos (ἄγγελος), *messenger*;
angel, archangel, evangelist

agkura (ἄγκυρα) *anchor*. From
agkos, a *bend*

ago (ἄγω), *to lead*; synagogue

*agōn (ἀγών), *a contest*; agony,
agonize, antagonist, Samson
Agonistes

ainigma (αἴνιγμα), *a riddle*;
enigma

aisthanomai (αἰσθάνομαι), *to feel*;
aesthetic, anaesthetic

aithēr (αἰθήρ), *the upper air*;
ether, ethereal

Akadēmeia ('Ακαδήμεια), a gymnasium in the suburbs of
Athens where Plato taught;
academy

akē (ἀκή), *point*; acme (highest
point), acanthus (thorn)

akolouthos (ἀκόλουθος) *follower*;
acolyte *or* acolyth

akouō (ἀκούω), *to hear*; acous-
tics

*akros (ἄκρος), *at the top*; acro-
bat (rope-dancer), acrogenous
(growing from the end), acro-
polis (the upper city), acrostic
(a poem in which the first
letters of the lines make up
a word. See Stichos = line)

aktis (ἀκτίς), *ray*; actinism,
actinometer

alabastros (ἀλάβαστρος), *alabaster*; first applied to an alabaster vessel without handles.
From a = *not*, labē = *handle*

allēlōn (ἀλλήλων), *of one another*;
parallel, parallelogram

*allos (ἄλλος), *another*; allegory
(agoreuō = *to speak*), allopathy
(pathos = *suffering*)

alpha (ἄλφα), the first letter of
the Greek alphabet; bēta
(βῆτα), the second; alphabet

amarantos (ἀμάραντος), *unfad-
ing*; from marainō, to *fade*;
amaranth

amethystos (ἀμέθυστος), a gem
supposed to keep off drunkenness. From methu (μέθυ),
wine

*ampli (ἀμφί), *on both sides*.

around; amphitheatre (thea-omai, to *see*), amphibious(bios, *life*), amphibology, ambiguous speech (logos, a *discourse*), amphora, a pitcher with two handles (phero, to *bear*)

anachōreō (ἀναχωρέω), to *retire*; anchorite

*anemos (ἄνεμος), *wind*; anemometer (wind-measurer), anemone (wind-flower)

*anthos (ἄνθος), *flower*; anthology, polyanthus

anthrax (ἄνθραξ), *coal*; anthracite

*anthrōpos (ἄνθρωπος), *man*; anthropology, misanthrope (man-hater), philanthropist (lover of men), anthropomorphism (the attributing to God man's form; morphē, *shape*), anthropophagi (men-eaters; phagein, to *eat*)

aō (ἄω), to *blow*; asthma

apsinthos (ἀψίνθος), *wormwood*; absinthe

apsis, gen. apsidos (ἀψίς, ῖδος), *hoop of a wheel*; apse, apsidal

*archaios (ἀρχαῖος), *old*; archaic, archaism, archæology

*archē (ἀρχή), a *beginning*; archetype; archos, *chief*; archipelago

argillos (ἄργιλλος), *clay*; argillaceous

aristos (ἄριστος), *best*; aristocracy (rule by the best; kratos, *rule*)

*arithmos (ἀριθμός), *number*; arithmetic, logarithm

arktos (ἄρκτος), *bear*; arctic, Arcturus (the bear-watcher; ouros, *a guard*)

arōma (ἄρωμα), *spice*; aroma

arsēn (ἄρσην), *male*; arsenic (so called from its strength)

artēria (ἀρτηρία), *artery*; from aēr, *air*

askeō (ἀσκέω), to *exercise*; ascetic

*astēr (ἀστήρ), *star*; aster, asterisk (dim.), asteroid (a small planet), astrolabe (an instrument used in taking the position of the stars; lambanō, to *take*), astrology, astronomy

athlon (ἄθλον), *contest*; athlete, athletic, pentathlon

*atmos (ἀτμός), *vapour*; atmosphere (sphaira, *sphere*)

*autos (αὐτός), *self*; autobiography, autocrat, autograph, automaton (maō, to *move*), autonomy (nomos, *law*), autopsy (ocular examination: opsis, *sight*), autotype (self-printing; typos, *a model*), authentic

axinē (ἀξίνη), *axe*

axioō (ἀξιόω), to *lay down*; axiom (a self-evident truth)

*bainō (βαίνω), to *go*; basis, diabetes

*ballo (βάλλω), to *throw*; hyperbole, symbol, parabola, parable (a comparison), emblem (orig. inlaid-work)

*baptō (βάπτω), to *dip*; baptize, baptism, baptist

barbaros (βάρβαρος), *foreign* (apparently mimetic in formation); barbarous, barbaric, barbarism

*baros (βάρος), *weight*; barometer, baritone

*basileus (βασιλεύς), *king*; basilica, basilisk (a serpent which was said to have a *crown*-shaped spot on its head)

bathos (βάθος), *depth*; bathos

*biblion (βιβλίον), a *scroll*; dim. of biblos, *a book*; Bible, bibliography, bibliomania (mania, *madness*), bibliopole (pōleō, to *sell*)

*bios (βίος), *life*; biology, biography, amphibious

*blaptō (βλάπτω), to *injure*; blasphemy (phēmē, *fame*),

blame (Fr. blâmer, O.F. blasmer)

bombyx (βόμβυξ), silkworm, silk; bombast. When cotton was introduced into Europe it was confounded with silk, and called in Mid. Lat. bambacium, M.E. bombase. As cotton was used for padding clothes, bombast came to signify inflated language

boskō (βόσκω), to feed; botanē, pasture; botany

*bous (βοῦς), ox; Bosporus (oxford; pŏrŏs, ford), bucolic, buffalo (βούβαλος), bugloss (= ox-tongue)

*brogchos (βρόγχος), windpipe; bronchia, bronchitis, bronchotomy (temnō, to cut)

byssos (βυσσός), the depth of the sea; abyss (bottomless pit)

chainō (χαίνω), to gape; chasm

chalyps, bos (χάλυψ, βos), steel; chalybeate

chaos (χάος), empty space; chaos

charassō (χαράσσω), to engrave; character

charis (χάρις), thanks; Eucharist

chartēs (χάρτης), leaf of paper; charter, card, chart

*cheir (χείρ), hand; surgeon (originally chirurgeon, one who worked with his hand), chiromancy (manteia, prophecy), chiropodist (pous, foot), chiragra (gout in the hand; agra, seizure)

*chilioi (χίλιοι), a thousand; chiliarch, chiliast

chimaira (χίμαιρα), a fabulous monster; chimera, chimerical

chlōros (χλωρός), green; chlorine

*cholē (χολή), bile; choler, melancholy, cholera

chordē (χορδή), a string; chord

choros (χορός), chorus; choir, choragus

*chriō (χρίω), to anoint; Christ, chrism, chrisom, Christmas, Christology

*chrōma (χρῶμα), colour; chromatrope (tropos, turning), achromatic

*chronos (χρόνος), time; chronicle, chronograph, chronology

*chrysos (χρυσός), gold; chrysalis, chrysanthemum (anthos, flower), chrysolite (lithos, stone), chrysoprasus (prason, leek)

chylos (χυλός), juice; chyle

chymos (χυμός), juice; chyme

*daimōn (δαίμων), a divinity, an evil spirit; demon, demoniac, demonology

*daktylos (δάκτυλος), finger; dactyl (a poetical foot, composed of one long and two short syllables), pterodactyl (pteron, a wing)

deiknumi (δείκνυμι), to show; deigma, a specimen; paradigm

*deka (δέκα), ten; decade decagon (gōnia, angle), decagram, decahedron (hedra, base), decalogue, Decameron (hēmera, day), decasyllable

delta (δέλτα), the Greek letter (Δ) corresponding to D; delta, deltoid (eidos, shape)

dēmos (δῆμος), people; demagogue (ago, to lead), democrat, endemic, epidemic

dendron (δένδρον), tree; rhododendron (rhodon, rose), dendrite (a stone in which treelike figures are to be seen)

derma (δέρμα), skin; dermis, epidermis, dermatology

despotēs (δεσπότης), an absolute sovereign; despot

*deuteros (δεύτερος), second; Deuteronomy (the repetition of the Law)

diaita (δίαιτα), way of living; diet, dietetic

didaskŏ (διδάσκω), to *teach* ; didactic

dioikeŏ (διοικέω), to *manage* ; diocese, diocesan

diploŏ (διπλόω), to *double* ; diploma (a document of which a duplicate is kept)

dipsa (δίψα), *thirst* ; dipsomania (mania, *madness*)

*dokeŏ (δοκέω), to *think, seem* ; dogma, *opinion* ; dogma, dogmatic, dogmatize ; doxa (δόξα), *opinion* ; orthodox (orthos, *right*), heterodox (heteros, *the other*)

*draŏ (δράω), to *do* ; drama, drastic (quick in producing results)

dromas (δρόμας), running ; hippodrome (hippos, *horse*), dromedary (the runner)

*dynamis (δύναμις), *strength* ; dynamic, dynamite, dynamometer

echo (ἔχω), to *hold* ; epochē, *epoch* (a fixed point in time)

*ēchō (ἠχώ), *a sound* ; echo, catechize, catechist

eidōlon (εἴδωλον), *shape* ; idol, idolatry (latreia, *worship*)

*eidos (εἶδος), *form* ; cycloid (kyklos, *circle*), kaleidoscope (kalos, *beautiful*, and skopeŏ, to *see*), eidograph

*eikōn (εἰκών), *figure* ; iconoclast (klaŏ, to break), Icon Basilikē (the picture of the king : basileus, *king*)

eirēnē (εἰρήνη), *peace* ; Eirenicon (relating to peace)

eirōn (εἴρων), *a dissembler* ; irony, ironical

elaunŏ (ἐλαύνω), to *drive, beat out* ; elastic, elasticity

*ēlectron (ἤλεκτρον), *amber* ; electric, electrode (hodos, *way*), electrolyze (luo, to *loosen*), electrometer, electrotype (typos, *type*)

*eleëmosynē (ἐλεημοσύνη), *alms* ; eleeŏ, to have pity on ; alms O.E. ælmesse), eleemosynary, Kyrie Eleison (Lord, have mercy on us)

endon (ἔνδον), *within* ; endogamous (marrying within the same caste), endogenous

*enteron (ἔντερον), *intestine* ; enteric, enteritis (inflammation of the intestines), dysentery

ĕrēmos (ἔρημος), *desert* ; eremite, hermit

*ergon (ἔργον), *work* ; energy, energetic, metallurgy

ethnos (ἔθνος), *a nation* ; ethnic, ethnography, ethnology, ethnarch

ēthos (ἦθος), *custom, habit* ; ethics

ĕtymos (ἔτυμος), *true* ; etymology

*eu (εὖ), *well*, takes the form of *ev* in some compounds ; eucharist (charis, *thanks*), eulogize (logeŏ) to speak well of, eulogium, eulogy, euphemism (phēmē, *saying*), euphony (phōnē, *sound*), euphrasy (*eyebright*, from phrēn, the *mind*, eyebright being supposed to have a healthy influence on the mind), euthanasia (*easy death*, thanatos, *death*), evangelist

*exŏ (ἔξω), *without, on the outside* ; exoteric (applied to the public outside a teacher's inner class, his *esoteric* disciples) ; exotic (foreign)

gagglion (γάγγλιον), *tumour* ; ganglion

gaggraina (γάγγραινα), *a canker* ; gangrene

gala, gen. galaktos (γάλα, γάλακτος), *milk* ; galaxy (Milky Way). Cp. Lat. lac

*gamos (γάμος) ; bigamy, monogamy, gamopetalous (petalon, *a flower-leaf*), misogamy (misos, *hate*), misogamist

*gastĕr (γαστήρ), belly; gastric, gastronomy, gastropod (pous, podos, foot)

*gē (γῆ), the earth; geocentric (having the earth for centre), geology, geodesy (daiō, to divide), geography, geometry, apogee, perigee

*gennaō (γεννάω), to beget; gignomai (γίγνομαι), to be born; genos (γένος), race; genesis, parthenogenesis (parthenos, a virgin), genealogy, hydrogen, oxygen, nitrogen

gigas, gigantos (γίγας, γίγαντος), giant; gigantic

*gignōskō (γιγνώσκω), to know; gnōmōn (γνώμων), 1, one that knows; 2, the index of a dial; 3, a carpenter's square; gnomon, gnostic, physiognomy (physis, outward shape, look), diagnose, prognosis, prognostic, prognosticate

glōssa (γλῶσσα), tongue; gloss, glossary, bugloss (ox-tongue; bous, ox)

glōttis (γλωττίς), the mouth of the windpipe; glottis, epiglottis

*glykys (γλυκύς), sweet; glucose, liquorice (see Rhiza), glycerine

*glyphō (γλύφω), to carve; hieroglyph (hieros, sacred), glyptic, triglyph

*graphō (γράφω), to write; graphic, digraph, graphite, monograph, geography, biography, paragraph, telegraph (tele, distant), physiography (physis, nature), bibliography. Gramma, a letter; gram (the French unit of weight, viz. 1/₁th part of an ounce), grammar, epigram, diagram, monogram

*gymnazo (γυμνάζω), to train naked (gymnos); gymnasium, gymnast, gymnastics, gymnosophist

*gynĕ, gen. gynaikos (γυνή, γυναικός), woman; gynecocracy, misogynous (woman-hating; misos, hate)

*hagios (ἅγιος), holy; hagiology, hagioscope, trisagion

haima (αἷμα), blood; hæmoptysis (blood-spitting; ptuō, to spit), hæmorrhage (rhēgnumi, to break), hæmorrhoid, corrupted into emerod (piles; rheō, to flow), hæmatite (red iron-ore), hæmatine (the colouring matter of blood)

*haireo (αἱρέω), to take; aphæresis; haireomai, to take for oneself; heresy, heretic, heresiarch

harmozō ((ἁρμόζω), to join; harmony

hebdomas (ἑβδομάς), the space of seven days; hebdomadal

hĕdra (ἕδρα), seat; cathedral

hēgeomai (ἡγέομαι), to guide; exegeomai, to interpret; exegesis, exegetical

*hekaton (ἑκατόν), a hundred; hecatomb, hectogramme, hectolitre, hectometre

*helios (ἥλιος), sun; heliacal, heliocentric, helioscene (sunshade for the outside of windows; skēnĕ, cover), helioscope (skopeō, to see), heliotrope (tropos, turning. Cp. tournesole and girasole), heliotype

hēmera (ἡμέρα), day; ephemeral (lasting for a day)

*hēmi- (ἡμι-), half; hemisphere (sphaira, ball), hemistich (stichos, a line of verse)

hēpar (ἧπαρ), liver; hepatic

hērōs (ἥρως), a demi-god; hero, heroic

*hieros (ἱερός), sacred; hierarch (archos, ruler), hieroglyphic (glyphō, to hollow out), hierophant (phainō, to manifest) hilaros (ἱλαρός), *cheerful*; hilarity

hippos (ἵππος), *horse*: hippodrome (dromos, *a course*), hippogriff (gryps, a *griffin*), hippophagist (phagein, to *eat*), hippopotamus (potamos, *river*)

historia (ἱστορία), *narrative*; history, story, historiographer

hodos (ὁδός), a *way*; exodus, period, cathode, anode

holos (ὅλος), the *whole*; catholic, holocaust (kaiō, to *burn*)

*hŏmos (ὁμός), *one and the same*; homoios (ὅμοιος), *like*; homogeneous (genos, *kind*), homologous (logos, *saying*), homœopath (pathos, *suffering*), homoousion (the *same* substance); homoiousion (*like* substance)

hoplon (ὅπλον), *armour*; panoply

hōra (ὥρα), *hour*; horologe, horoscope

hŏrizō (ὁρίζω), to *divide*; horizon

*hydōr (ὕδωρ), *water*; hydrant, hydra (*water-serpent*), hydrangea (aggeion, ἀγγεῖον, *vessel*), hydrate, hydrocephalous (kephalē, *head*), hydraulics (aulos, *tube*), hydrodynamics (dynamis, *power*), hydrogen (the water-producer; gennaō, to *produce*), hydrometer, hydrophobia (phobos, *fear*) dropsy (contracted from hydropsy), hydrostatics

hygiēs (ὑγιής), *sound*; hygiene

hygros (ὑγρός), *wet*; hygrometer

hymnos (ὕμνος), *song*; hymn, hymnology

hystera (ὑστέρα), *womb*; hysteria

*ichthys (ἰχθύς), *fish*; ichthyology, ichthyolite (fossil-fish; lithos, *stone*), ichthyosaurus (sauros, *lizard*)

*idea (ἰδέα), *notion, the look of a thing*; idea, ideal

*idios (ἴδιος), *peculiar to oneself*; idiom, idiosyncrasy (a peculiarity of mind or temper; krasis, *mixing*), idiot (originally a private person; then unskilled, ignorant, an idiot)

*isos (ἴσος), *equal*; isobars (lines of equal barometric pressure, baros, *weight*), isochronous (chronos, *time*), isosceles (skelos, *leg*), isotherm (thermē, *heat*)

isthmos (ἰσθμός), *neck*; isthmus

*kainos (καινός), *new*; cainozoic (zōē, life)

*kaiō (καίω), to *burn*; kaustikos, *burning*; caustic, cauterize, encaustic

kakos (κακός), *bad*; cacodæmon (daimōn, *spirit*), cacoëthes (ethos, *custom*), cacography, cacophony (phōnē, *sound*)

*kaleō (καλέω), to *call*; ecclesiastic, kalends (the first days of the Roman months, so named from the priest's announcing to the people the new moon)

*kalos (καλός), *beautiful*; caligraphy, calotype (typos, *type*), calisthenics (sthĕnos, *strength*), kaleidoscope (eidos, *form*; scopeō, *to see*)

*kalyptō (καλύπτω), to *hide*; calyx, apocalypse

kanōn (κανών), *rule*; canon, canonize, canonical

*katharos (καθαρός), *pure*; Katharine, cathartic

kenos (κενός), *empty*; cenotaph (a tomb in memory of some one buried elsewhere)

*kentron (κέντρον), *point*; centre, concentric, eccentric

*kephalē (κεφαλή), *head*; cephalic, hydrocephalic (hydor, *water*), acephalous

keramos (κέραμος), *potter's earth*; ceramic

kerannumi (κεράννυμι), *to mix*; krasis, *a mixing*; crasis (blending of two vowels), crater (originally a mixing bowl)

klēros (κλῆρος), *lot*; clerk, clergy

*klinē (κλίνη), *bed*; clinical (at the bedside, as clinical baptism, clinical lectures)

*klinō (κλίνω), to *make to slope*; klima, *slope*; klimax, *ladder*; climate, clime, acclimatize, climax, anticlimax, incline, decline, enclitic

klyzō (κλύζω), to *dash against*; cataclysm

*kogchē (κόγχη), *mussel or cockle*; conch, conchology; kochlos, *a bivalve, shell-fish*; cockle, cochleate

koimaō (κοιμάω), to *sleep*; cemetery (a sleeping-place)

koinos (κοινός), *common*; coenobite (bios, *life*), epicene

kōma (κῶμα), *sleep*; coma, comatose, cemetery

komētēs (κομήτης), *long-haired*; comet

kōnōps (κώνωψ), *gnat*; canopy (originally a mosquito-net)

kōnos (κῶνος), *fir-cone*; cone, conical, conics

kopros (κόπρος), *dung*; coprolite (petrified dung; lithos, *stone*)

*kosmos (κόσμος), *order*; kosmeō, to *adorn*; cosmos, cosmical, cosmogony (gonē, *birth*), cosmography, cosmorama (horaō, to *see*), cosmopolite (politēs, *citizen*), cosmetic (used to beautify the complexion)

kranion (κράνιον), *skull*; cranium, craniology

*krinō (κρίνω), to *judge*; crisis,

criterion, critic, hypercritical, hypocrisy

*kryptō (κρύπτω), to *hide*; crypt, cryptogamous (gamos, *marriage*), cryptography (secret-writing), cryptology, Apocrypha

*krystallos (κρύσταλλος), *clear-ice*; crystal (it was formerly believed that crystal 'was ice or snow which had undergone such a process of induration as wholly and for ever to have lost its fluidity.'— *Trench*), crystalline

kubos (κύβος), a *cube*; cubical. NOT cubicle, which comes from Lat. cubo

*kyklos (κύκλος), *circle*; cyclamen (a plant with round leaves), cycle, encyclical, cycloid (eidos, *form*), cyclone, cyclopædia (paideia, *instruction*), cyclops (ōps, *eye*)

kylindros (κύλινδρος), *roller*; cylinder, cylindrical

kymbos (κύμβος), *hollow*; cymbal

*kyōn, gen. kynos (κύων, κυνός), *dog*; cynic (dog-like), cynocephalous (dog-headed; kephalē, head), cynosure (north pole-star; oura, *tail*), quinsy (Gk. kynagchē, κυνάγχη = a dog-throttling)

*kyrios (κύριος), *lord*; kyriakos, belonging to a lord; church (the Lord's house), Kyrie

lambanō (λαμβάνω), to *take*; syllable, epilepsy, catalepsy, lemma, dilemma

lampas (λαμπάς), *lamp*

*laos (λαός), *the people*; lay, laic, laity

*legō (λέγω), to *say*, to *choose*; eclectic, elegy, elegiac, eulogy, eclogue; lexis, *speech*; lexicon, lexicographer leipō (λείπω), to *leave*; ellipse, eclipse, ecliptic

leitos (λεῖτος), *of* or *for the people*; liturgy, liturgiology

lepis (λεπίς), *scale*; leper, leprosy

*lithos (λίθος), stone; lithic, lithocarp (karpos, *fruit*), lithograph, lithophyte (phuŏ, to *bring forth*), lithotomy (tomē, *cutting*), coprolite (kopros, *dung*), aerolite (aēr, *air*) monolith

*logos (λόγος), *speech, reason, ratio*; logic, logarithm (arithmos, *number*), logomachy (*word-fight*; machē, *battle*), zoology, dialogue, syllogism

*luŏ (λύω), to *loosen*; analyse, paralysis (contracted into *palsy*)

lyra (λύρα), *lyre*; lyrist, lyrical

magos (μάγος), *a magus, sorcerer*; magic, magician

*makros (μακρός), *long*; macrocosm (kosmos, *world*)

*manthanō (μανθάνω), to *learn*; mathematics

martys (μάρτυς), *witness*; martyr, martyrdom (hybrid compound), martyrology, protomartyr

*mēchanē (μηχᾰνή), *contrivance*; Lat. machina, machine, mechanic, mechanics, mechanist, mechanician

*megas (μέγας), *great*; megalosaurus (sauros, *lizard*), megatherium (thērion, *wild beast*)

*melas, melaina, melan (μέλας, μέλαινα, μέλαν), *black*; melancholy (cholē, *bile*), Melanesia (nēsos, *island*)

melos (μέλος), *song*, music; melody, melodrama

*metallon (μέταλλον), *mine*; metal, metallurgy (ergon, *work*) mettle, mettlesome, high-mettled. (' The allusion

is to the temper of the metal of a sword-blade,' Skeat.)

*mētēr (μήτηρ), *mother*; metropolis

*metron (μέτρον), *measure*; metre, meter, metric, hypermetrical, hexameter, micrometer (mikros, *small*), thermometer, barometer, electrometer, hydrometer, metronome

miainŏ (μιαίνω), to *pollute*; miasma

*mikros (μικρός), *small*; microscope (skopeŏ, to *see*), microcosm (kosmos, *world*), micrometer

*mimos or mimētēs (μῖμος or μιμητής), an *imitator*; mimic, mimetic, pantomime

*misos (μῖσος), *hate*; misanthrope (anthrōpos, *man*), misogamist (gamos, *marriage*), misogynist (gynē, *woman*)

mnaomai (μνάομαι), to *remember*; amnesty

mnēmē (μνήμη) *memory*; mnemonics

*monos (μόνος), *alone*; monk, monachism, monastery, minster, monarch, monad, monandria (plants having but a single stamen; anēr, andros, *man*), monocarpous (karpos, *fruit*), monody, monochord, monogamy (gamos, *marriage*), monogram (gramma, *letter*), monograph (a treatise on a single topic), monolith (lithos, *stone*), monologue, monomania, monophysite (a person who believes that Christ had only one nature; physis, nature), monopoly (pōleŏ, to *sell*), monosyllable, monotheist (theos, *god*), monothelite (a person who believes that Christ had only one will; thelŏ, to *will*), monotone

*morphē (μορφή), *shape*; amorphous, Morpheus (the sleeper, the god of dreams), morphia

muō (μύω), to *be shut*; mystēs, *one initiated*; mysterion (μυστήριον), *a secret rite*; mystic, mystery

narkoō (ναρκόω), to *benumb*; narcotic

*naus (ναῦς), *ship*; nautical, nausea (sea-sickness); naumachy (machē, *fight*)

*nekros (νεκρός), *dead body*; necropolis (polis, *city*), necromancy (mantis, *prophet*), corrupted into nigromantia under the wrong impression that it was derived from Lat. niger, *black*. Magic was hence often spoken of as ' the black art '

nektar (νέκταρ), the *drink of the gods*; nectar, nectarine

*neos (νέος), *new*; neology, neophyte (a novice ; phuō, to *make grow*)

*nēsos (νῆσος), *island*; Polynesia (polys, *many*), Melanesia

*neuron (νεῦρον), *string* ; neuralgia (algos, *pain*), Lat. nervus

nomas, gen. -ados (νομάς, -άδος), *wandering*; nomad, nomadic

nomisma (νόμισμα) *current coin*; numismatics, Lat. *nummus*

*nomos (νόμος), *law*; astronomy, gastronomy (gastēr, *belly*), anomalous

nosos (νόσος), *disease*; nosology

nostos (νόστος), *a return home* ; nostalgia (home-sickness ; algos, *pain*)

nymphē (νύμφη), 1. bride; 2. *a goddess presiding over springs, &c.*; nymph ; nymphios, *husband*; paranymph, the bridegroom's friend

obelos (ὀβελός), a *spit*; ὀβελίσκος (Dim.), a little spit; obelisk

odē (ᾠδή), a *song*; m1., *c.* ; *i*

*odous, gen. odontus (ὀδούς,

óντος), *tooth*; odonto, mastodon (so called from the resemblance of its molar teeth to the breast, μαστός, of a woman)

*oikeō (οἰκέω), to *dwell*; oikoumenē, pres. part. *the habitable world*; ecumenical

oikos (οἶκος) *house*; economy, economize, economist, parish

*oktō (ὀκτώ), *eight* ; octagon (gōnia, *angle*), octopus (pous, *vot*)

oligos (ὀλίγος), *few*; oligarchy

ōn, ontos (ὤν, ὄντος), *being*; ontology

*onoma (ὄνομα), *name*; onomatopoeia (poieō, to *make*), synonym, patronymic (patēr, *father*), anonymous

ōon (ᾠόν), *egg*; oolite (lithos, *stone*)

*ophis (ὄφις), *serpent*; ophicleid (a serpent-shaped brass musical instrument; kleis, -dos, *key*) ; ophidian

*ophthalmos (ὀφθαλμός), *eye*; ophthalmia, ophthalmic

*optomai (ὄπτομαι, obsolete), to *see*; used to eke out the tenses of oraō (ὁράω), to *see*; optics, optician, synoptic, panorama, panopticon

orchēstra (ὀρχῆστρα), *place of the chorus*; orchestra

organon (ὄργανον), *instrument*; organ, organic

*ornis, gen. ornithos (ὄρνις, ἴθος), *bird*· ornithology ; ornithorhynchus (rhygchos, ῥύγχος, *a snout*)

orphanos (ὀρφανός), *bereft* ; orphan

osteon (ὀστέον), *bone*; osteology

*oxys (ὀξύς), *sharp*; oxygen (gennaō, to *produce*), oxymoron (a witty absurdity: mōros, *foolish*), paroxysm, oxytone

[...] hy- [...]

*pais, gen. paidos (παῖς, παιδός),
  boy; pedagogue (agōgos,
  guide), pædo-baptism, pai-
  deutics (the science of education), cyclopædia (kyklos,
  circle)
*palaios (παλαιός), *old*; palæo-
  crystic (krystallos, *clear ice*),
  palæography, palæontology,
  palæozoic (zōon, an *animal*)
*pan (πᾶν), *all*; panacea (akos,
  cure), pandect (an entire
  treatise; dektos, *received*);
  pandemonium, Pandora (dōra,
  gifts), panegyric (agora, *assembly*), panorama (oraō, to
  see), pantechnicon (technē,
  art), pantheist, panoply, pan-
  theon (theos, *god*), pantomime
  (mimos, *actor*), diapason
'Pan (Πάν), a rural god; panic
  (from the fear said to be
  occasioned by the sudden
  appearance of the god)
pateō (πατέω), to *walk*; peri-
  patetic
*pathos (πάθος), *suffering*; pathos,
  pathetic, sympathy, patho-
  logy (logos, *discourse*), allopathy (allos, *other*), homœo-
  pathy (homoios, *like*)
pauo (παύω), to *stop*; pause
*pente (πέντε), *fire*; pentagon,
  pentahedron (hedra, *seat*);
  pentameter; pentateuch (teu-
  chos, *book*); pentēkostos,
  fiftieth; Pentecost
peptō (πέπτω), to *soften, digest*;
  dyspeptic, pepsine
petalon (πέταλον), *flower-leaf*;
  petal. From petannumi, to
  expand
*petra (πέτρα), *rock*; petrify,
  Peter, petrel (dim. of Peter)
*phagō (φάγω), to *eat*; sarco-
  phagus (a coffin, made of a
  species of limestone, which
  rapidly destroyed the *flesh*;
  Gk. sarx, gen. sarkos, *flesh*)
*phainomai (φαίνομαι), to *appear*;

phantasy, fancy, phantasm,
  fantastic, phantom, phantas-
  magoria (agora, *assembly*),
  phenomenon, phase
phalagx (φάλαγξ), a *body of soldiers*; phalanx
*pharmakon (φάρμακον), *drug*;
  pharmacy,   pharmacopœia
  (poiein, to *make*)
phemi (φημί), to *say*; euphemism, emphasis, prophet
*phero (φέρω), to *bear*; periphery, phosphorus (light-
  bearer), Anaphora, the part
  of the Communion Service
  beginning ' Lift up your
  hearts '
*philos (φίλος), *loving*; philan-
  thropy, philharmonic, Philip
  (horse-lover),   Philadelphia
  (adelphos, brother), philology,
  philomel (nightingale; melos, *song*), philosophy (sophia,
  wisdom); philter (love-potion)
*phōnē (φωνή), *voice*; phonic,
  phonetic, phonograph, sym-
  phony, euphonious, cacopho-
  nous
*phōs, -tos (φῶς, -τός), *light*; phosphorus (pherō, to *bear*), pho-
  tograph, photophone, photo-
  zincography (a hybrid compound)
phrassō (φράσσω), to *fence*; dia-
  phragm
*phrazō (φράζω), to *tell*; phrase,
  paraphrase,   periphrasis,
  phraseology
phrēn (φρήν), *mind*; phrenzy,
  phrenetic (frantic), phreno-
  logy
phtheggomai (φθέγγομαι), to
  speak; apophthegm
phthino (φθίνω), to *waste away*;
  phthisis (consumption)
phthoggos (φθόγγος), *sound*;
  diphthong
*phuō (φύω), to *bring forth*;
  physis, *nature*; physics, phy-
  siology, physiognomy, phy-

siography, zoophyte (zōon, *animal*)

phylassō (φυλάσσω), to *keep guard*; phylactery

piptō (πίπτω), to *fall*; ptōma, *a fall*; symptom

planētēs (πλανήτης), *planet*; from planaomai, to *wander*; planetoid

*plassō (πλάσσω), to *mould*; plastic, plaster

pleiōn (πλείων), *more*; pleistos (πλεῖστος), *most*; pleiocene, pleistocene (kainos, *new*)

pleonazō (πλεονάζω), to *go too far*; pleonasm; plēthō, to *be full*; plethora

plēssō (πλήσσω), to *strike*; plēgē, *a stroke*; (Lat. plaga) plague

*pleura (πλευρά), *rib*; pleurisy, pleuro-pneumonia (pneumōn, *lung*)

ploutos(πλοῦτος),*riches*; Plutus, plutocracy

pneō (πνέω), to *breathe*; pneumatics, pneumonia

*poieō (ποιέω), to *make*; poet, poem, poesy, onomatopœia (onoma, *name*), pharmacopœia (pharmakon, *drug*)

polemos (πόλεμος),*war*; polemic

pōleō (πωλέω), to *sell*; monopoly

*polis (πόλις), *city*; metropolis, Constantinople; polites, *citizen*; police, polity, policy, polite, politics

*polys (πολύς),*many*; polyanthus (anthos, *flower*); polychrome (chrōma, *colour*), polygamy (gamos, *marriage*), polyarchy (archē, *rule*), polyglot (glōtta, *tongue*); polygon, polyhedron, Polynesia (nēsos, *island*), polyp, polypus (pous, *foot*), polytechnic (technē, *art*), polytheist

pompē (πομπή), *a solemn procession*; pomp

poros (πόρος), *passage*; pore, Bosporus

*pous, gen. podos (πούς, ποδός), *foot*; tripod, podagra (gout; agra, *seizure*)

*prassō (πράσσω), to *do*; pragma (πρᾶγμα), *that which is done*; pragmatical, practise, praxis

presbys (πρέσβυς), *an old man*; presbyter, priest

priō (πρίω), to *saw*; prism, prismatic

*prōtos (πρῶτος), *first*; protocol (kollaō, to *glue*), a rough draft; protomartyr, protoplasm (plassō, to *shape*), prototype

psallō (ψάλλω), to *sing to a harp*; psalm, psaltery

*pseudēs (ψευδής), *false*; pseudonym (onoma, *name*), pseudoprophet, pseudomartyr

*psychē (ψυχή), *soul*; psychic, Psyche, psychology

*pteron (πτερόν), *wing*; apteryx, pterodactyle (daktylos, *finger*)

pygmē (πυγμή), *length from elbow to knuckles*; pygmy

pyle (πύλη), *gate*; pylorus (ouros, *warder*)

*pyr (πῦρ), *fire*; pyrotechnics (technē, *art*), pyrites (a stone from which sparks may be struck), pyre, pyrometer, pyroligneous (a hybrid word, applied to acid obtained by the distillation of wood. Lat. lignum = wood), pyroxyline (gun-cotton; xylon, *wood*)

rhachis (ῥάχις), *spine*; rickets (*rhachitis*, a disease of the spine)

*rheō (ῥέω), to *flow*; rhetoric, rheometer, rheum, rheumatics, hæmorrhage (haima, *blood*), hæmorrhoid, rhythm, ... rb, diarrhœa

rhis ... rhino ... (.. *nose*),

nose; rhinoceros, (kĕras, *horn*)

rhiza (ῥίζα), root; liquorice (gly-cyrrhiza = sweet-root, from glykys [γλυκύς], sweet)

rhodon (ῥόδον), rose; rhododen-dron (dendron, *tree*), Rhodes, famous for its roses

sardonion (σαρδάνιον), a Sardi-nian plant which was said to distort the face of the eater; sardonic

sarx (σάρξ, σαρκός), flesh; sarco-phagus (see Phagō), sarcasm (a jest which, as it were, cuts into the flesh; sarkazō, *to tear the flesh*)

sauros (σαῦρος), lizard; ichthyo-saurus (ichthys, *fish*), plesio-saurus (plĕsios, *near to*. The plesiosaurus had a very long neck and a very short body)

sbennumi (σβέννυμι), to *quench*; asbestos (indestructible by fire)

schizō (σχίζω), to split; schism, schist, schismatic

scholē (σχολή), leisure; school, scholar, scholium, scholiast

seiō (σείω), *to move to and fro*; seismograph (an apparatus for registering the shocks and motions of earthquakes)

sēpia (σηπία), *cuttle fish*; sepia (formerly supposed to be made from the dark liquid ejected by the cuttle fish)

sēpō (σήπω), *to be rotten*; septic, antiseptic

siphōn (σίφων), *reed*; siphon

sitos (σῖτος), *food*: parasite (one who receives his food at another's table. Hence a flatterer)

skalēnos (σκαληνός), *uneven*; scalene

skandalon (σκάνδαλον), snare; scandal, slander

skellō (σκέλλω), *to be withered*; skeleton.

skēnē (σκηνή), *tent, stage*; scene, proscenium, scenic

skeptomai (σκέπτομαι), to doubt; sceptic

skēptron (σκῆπτρον), *staff*; scep-tre

sklēros (σκληρός), *hard*; scle-rotic

skopeō (σκοπέω), to see; tele-scope, microscope, bishop (episcopos = overseer), epis-copal, scope, laryngoscope (larynx, *the upper part of the windpipe*), stethoscope (stē-thos, *breast*), spectroscope (spectrum = image)

sophos (σοφός), wise; sophist, sophism, sophistic; sophia, *wisdom*, philosophy

spaō (σπάω), to draw; spasm, spasmodic

speira (σπεῖρα), *coil*; spiral

speirō (σπείρω), *to sow seed*; spore, Sporades

sperma (σπέρμα), *seed*; sperm, spermaceti (kētos, *whale*)

sphaira (σφαῖρα), *ball*; sphere spheroid (eidos, *form*)

sphyzo (σφύζω), to *beat* (of the pulse); asphyxia

splēn (σπλήν), *milt, spleen*; spleen, splenetic

stalazō (σταλάζω), to *fall in drops*; stalactite, stalagmite

stasis (στάσις), *standing* (from histēmi, to *stand*); statics, hydrostatics (hydor, *water*)

stear (στέαρ, ατος), *hard fat*; stearine

stellō (στέλλω), to send; apostle, epistle, stole, systole, dia-stole

stenos (στενός), *narrow*; steno-graphy

stereos (στερεός), solid; stereo-scope (skopeō, to *see*), stereo-type

stichos (στίχος), *line*; acrostic (akros, *at the end*), distich, hemistich stizō (στίζω), to *brand*; stigma, stigmatize

stoma (στόμα), *mouth*; stomach

*stratos (στρατός), army; strategy, stratagem

*strephō (στρέφω), to *turn*; strophe, antistrophe, catastrophe, apostrophe

strychnos (στρύχνος), *nightshade*; strychnine

stylos (στῦλος), *a post, a stilus*; style, Stylites, peristyle

stypho (στύφω), to *contract*; styptic

sykon (σῦκον), *fig*; sycamore (moron, *a mulberry tree*), sycophant (fig-shower, a person who informed concerning the forbidden exportation of figs from Athens. Hence a mean flatt erer; phainō, to *show*)

syrigx (σῦριγξ, gen. σύριγγος), *a pipe*; syringe

tapēs (τάπης, gen. τάπητος), *carpet*; tapestry

taphos (τάφος), *grave*; epitaph

tauto (ταὐτό), *the same thing*; tautology, tautophony

taxis (τάξις), *arrangement*; syntax, taxidermy (derma, *skin of animals*)

technē (τέχνη), *art*; technical, polytechnic

*teinō (τείνω), to *stretch*; tetanus (lock-jaw), tone, tonic, monotony, hypotenuse

*tēle (τῆλε), *distant*; telegraph, telephone, telescope

temnō (τέμνω), to *cut*; tome, epitome, anatomy, entomology

*tetra (τέτρα), *four*; tetrachord (chordē, a *string*), tetragon, tetrarch

thalamos (θάλαμος), *bride-chamber*; epithalamium

thauma (θαῦμα), *wonder*; thaumatrope (tropos, *turning*)

*theaomai (θεάομαι), to *behold*; theatre, amphitheatre; thaumaturgy (ergon, *a work*),

theodolite (dolichos, *long*) theory, theorem

*theos (θεός), *God*; theobroma (broma, *food*), theocracy, theogony (gonos, *descent*), theology, theism, enthusiasm (entheos, *full of a god*), theophany (phainomai, *to appear*), theosophy (sophia, *wisdom*)

thērion (θηρίον), *wild beast*; thēriakē (an antidote, made of the viper's flesh, against the poison of the viper); treacle (a name given at first to this antidote, then to any confection)

*thermē (θέρμη), *heat*; thermal, isotherm (isos, *equal*), thermometer (heat-measurer), thermopile (piloō, to press close), thermoscope (scopeō, to *see*)

*thēsis (θέσις), *placing*; thema *a subject laid down*; tithēmi, to *place*; thesis, synthesis, theme, apothecary, hypothecate (hypothēkē, *mortgage*)

thymos (θυμός), *mind*; enthymeme

*tithēmi (τίθημι), to *place*; thesis, apothecary, treasure (thēsauros, *anything stored up*), anathema, anathematize, synthesis, hypothesis

*topos (τόπος), *place*; topic, topography

*toxon (τόξον). *bow*; toxikon, *poison in which arrows were dipped*; toxicology, toxophilite

*tracheia (τραχεῖα), *windpipe*; trachea, tracheotomy (see Temnō)

tragos (τράγος), *he-goat*; tragedy (ᾠδή, *song*), a goat-song, so called either because a goat was the prize, or because the actors performed in goatskins

*treis (τρεῖς), *three*; tripod, trigonometry, triclinium (klinē, *couch*), trichord (chordē, *a string*),trilobite(lobos, *a lobe*), trilogy, trinity, triptych (ptyssō, to *fold*), an altarpiece in three compartments, trireme, trisagion (hagios, *holy*)

trephō (τρέφω), to *nourish*; atrophy

*trepō (τρέπω), to *turn*; trophy (a monument erected at the place where the enemy *turned*), tropics

trōglē (τρώγλη), *care*; troglodyte (duō, to *enter*)

tympanon (τύμπανον), *drum*; tympanum

*typtō (τύπτω), to *strike*; typos, a *blow*, the impress of a seal, type, stereotype, typography

tyrannos (τύραννος), *an absolute sovereign*; tyrant

zēlos (ζῆλος), *emulation* (from zeō, *to be hot*); zeal, zealot

zeō (ζέω), to *boil*; eczema (a skin-eruption)

*zeugnumi (ζεύγνυμι), to *join*; zeugma (a joining together of two incompatible grammatical constructions)

zōnē (ζώνη), *girdle*; zone

*zōon (ζῶον), *animal*, zodion (dim.), *a little animal*; zoetrope (tropos, *turning*),zoolite (lithos, *stone*), zoology, zoophyte (phyton, *plant*), zodiac (so called because the signs of the zodiac are represented chiefly by animals)

Greek Alphabet.

A, α = ā́	H, η = ĕ	N, ν = n	T, τ = t
B, β = b	Θ, θ = th	Ξ, ξ = x	Υ, υ = ŭ
Γ, γ = g *hard*	I, ι = ī	O, o = ŏ	Φ, φ = ph
Δ, δ = d	K, κ = k	Π, π = p	X, χ = ch
E, ε = ĕ	Λ, λ = l	P, ρ = r	Ψ, ψ = ps
Z, ζ = z	M, μ = m	Σ, σ, s = s	Ω, ω = ō

NOTE.—*G* (γ) before *g*, *k*, *ch*, or *x* is pronounced *ng*, e.g. *aggelos* is pronounced *angelos*.

APPENDIX.

FIGURES OF SPEECH.

A Figure of Speech is a departure from our ordinary modes of expression, for the purpose of heightening the effect upon the mind of the hearer. It may consist in some new meaning attached to a word, in some pleasing association of ideas, or in some deviation from the usual construction of sentences, e.g. 'The *torrent* of his eloquence;' 'Our little life is *rounded with a sleep*;' 'He never *deviates* into common sense;' 'What time he can spare from *the neglect of his duty*, he devotes to the adornment of his person.' The chief figures of speech may be classified as follows:—

I. Figures turning more or less on *Associations of Resemblance or of Difference*, e.g. Simile, Metaphor, Allegory, Fable, Parable, Abstract for Concrete, Personification, Antithesis, Irony, Epigram.

II. Figures turning on *Associations of Contiguity*, e.g. Metonomy and Synecdoche.

Other figures of speech not so easily admitting of classification are Hyperbole, Litotes, Climax, Anti-climax, Exclamation, and Apostrophe.

A Simile (Lat. *similis*, like) is a comparison formally expressed between objects of different kinds, and is generally introduced by some such word as *like, so, as, thus,* &c.

> Thy soul was *like a star* and dwelt apart,
> Thou hadst a voice, whose sound was *like the sea*.
> > *Wordsworth.*

> Eternal smiles his emptiness betray,
> *As shallow streams run dimpling all the way.—Pope.*

A simile may be used to elucidate our meaning or merely to awaken pleasing or other emotions. If we wish to elucidate our meaning the comparison should be sufficiently familiar to be at once intelligible ; if we wish to arouse any particular emotions, we must bear in mind what the emotion is which we have in view.   Otherwise we may aim at the sublime and reach the ridiculous.   We may raise a common-place theme by a lofty simile, or degrade a noble theme by some ignoble comparison.   Strained and over-ingenious similes should be avoided in serious composition, because they suggest effort, a result which always interferes with the effect of perfect art.   Donne, writing a poem to his wife from abroad, compares himself and her to the two legs of a pair of compasses.   He is the wandering leg ; she the fixed. The farther he wanders the more she leans towards him. The nearer home he approaches, the more erect she grows, until at last he ends his wanderings where they began. Such a simile as this is not in keeping with the subject.   Even Lord Byron's famous simile on the untimely death of Kirke White is pursued into too much detail.

> 'Twas thine own genius gave the final blow,
> And helped to plant the wound that laid thee low ﹒
> So the struck eagle, stretched upon the plain,
> No more through rolling clouds to soar again,
> Viewed his own feather on the fatal dart,
> And wing'd the shaft that quivered in his heart ;
> Keen were his pangs, but keener far to feel,
> He nursed the pinion which impelled the steel ;
> While the same plumage that had warmed his nest
> Drank the last life-drop of his bleeding breast.

The mere length of the simile gives us time to feel the unreality of the comparison between the powers of reflection possessed by the poet and those possessed by the eagle.

A **Metaphor** (Gk. *meta*, change, and *phero*, to bear) is a comparison that is implied but not formally stated, the thing compared being spoken of as though it were the thing with which it is compared, e.g. 'He was *the pillar* of the State ;' 'The *iron entered into his soul* ;' '*Footprints on the sands of Time.*'

> We watched her breathing through the night,
>   Her breathing soft and slow,
> As in her breast *the wave of life*
>   Kept heaving to and fro.—*Hood.*

> Wisdom is ofttimes *nearer when we stoop*
> Than when we soar.—*Wordsworth.*

A **Mixed Metaphor** is one in which several comparisons are blended, so as to involve the simultaneous presentation to the mind of incongruous images, e.g. "I am now about to *embark* into the *feature* on which this question *hinges.*' Here we have three images—a ship, a human face, and a door—and the language that is applicable to one is inapplicable to the others. We cannot embark upon a face. A door does not turn upon a feature. Cp.

> I *bridle* in my struggling Muse with pain
> That longs to *launch* into a bolder *strain.—Addison.*

A mixture of metaphorical language and language intended to be understood literally often produces a ludicrous effect, e.g. 'He threw his *soul* into the cause and his *body* into the saddle.' 'He had an active *mind* with *legs* to correspond;' 'Boyle was the *father* of philosophy and *brother-in-law* of the Earl of Cork;' 'She went off *in a flood* of tears and a *sedan chair*;' 'She was a faithful *wife* and affectionate *mother* and *painted in water-colours*;' 'Armed with rustic *weapons* and irresistible *fury*.'

An Allegory (Gk. *allos*, other, and *agoreuo*, to speak) is a description of one thing under the image of another; it is, therefore, a continuous metaphor, e.g. 'Thou hast brought a vine out of Egypt; Thou hast cast out the heathen, and planted it. Thou preparedst room before it, and didst cause it to take deep root, and it filled the land. The hills were covered with the shadow of it, and the boughs thereof were like the goodly cedars. She sent out her boughs unto the sea, and her branches unto the river.'—Psalm lxxx. 8-11.

Not infrequently an allegory is expanded into the proportions of a story, e.g. 'The Faerie Queen;' 'Pilgrim's Progress;' 'The Tale of a Tub;' 'The Rocky Island.' Such allegories are generally intended to convey some moral or other instruction.

A **Fable** (Lat. *fari*, to speak) is a short allegory, generally drawn from the animal world, and intended to convey some moral, e.g. 'The Hare and the Tortoise.'

A **Parable** (Gk. *para*, beside, and *ballo*, to cast) is an allegory drawn from the incidents of human life and intended to convey some moral or spiritual truth, e.g. 'The Prodigal Son,'

Abstract for Concrete is the name given to the employment of a general or abstract term in a concrete sense, e.g.—

> Let not *Ambition* mock their useful toil,
> Their homely joys and destiny obscure;
> Nor *Grandeur* hear with a disdainful smile
> The short but simple annals of the poor.—*Gray*.

Here 'Ambition' = the ambitious, and 'Grandeur' = the great.

A Personification is an ascription of thoughts, feelings, and actions peculiar to man to an abstract idea or to something that is inanimate, e.g.—

> Wisdom, *in sable garb arrayed,*
> *Immersed in rapturous thought profound,*
> And Melancholy, *silent maid*
> *With leaden eye, that loves the ground,*
> *Still on thy solemn steps attend :*
> Warm Charity, *the sincere friend,*
> With Justice, *to herself severe,*
> And Pity, *dropping soft the sadly pleasing tear.—Gray.*

This figure should be distinguished from the last mentioned. In the example given, *Wisdom, Melancholy, Charity, Justice,* and *Pity* do not stand for the wise, the melancholy, the charitable, the just, and the pitiful, but are represented as actual persons.

An Antithesis (Gk. *anti*, against, and *tithēmi*, to set) is a figure in which there is some striking contrast between the ideas presented.   Thus, Pope addresses man as

> Chaos of *thought and passion,* all confused;
> Still by himself *abused* or *disabused*;
> Created *half to rise and half to fall*;
> Great *lord* of all things, yet a *prey* to all;
> Sole *judge of truth, in endless error hurled*;
> The *glory, jest, and riddle* of the world.

Irony (Gk. *eirōneia*, dissimulation) is intended to convey a meaning opposite to that which the words literally express, as when we call a *stupid* person a *Solomon.* Cp. 'Cry aloud : for he is a god ; either he is talking, or he is pursuing, or he is in a journey, or peradventure he sleepeth, and must be awaked.'—1 Kings xviii. 27. 'We are none of us infallible—*not even the junior Fellow.*'

An Epigram (Gk. *epi*, upon, and *grapho*, to write) is a short utterance, setting forth some single thought with exceptional terseness and force. It is often paradoxical in form, e.g. 'Summer has set in with its usual severity,' 'He hadn't a single redeeming vice.'

> Come, gentle Sleep, and hear thy votary's prayer;
> And though Death's image to my couch repair;
> How sweet, though lifeless, yet with life to lie,
> And, without dying, O, how sweet to die !—*Warton.*

A Metonomy (Gk. *meta*, change, and *onoma*, name) is a figure in which a thing is represented by something closely associated with it. Thus we speak of the *bench*, when we mean the bench of bishops ; of the *crown*, when we mean the sovereign. Cp. the *buskin*, the *sock*, the *toga*, the *cloth*, the *pen*, *grey hairs*, the *Vatican*. The object of a Metonomy is usually to call up a picture of the object by referring to some symbol or feature that is characteristic of it, e.g. 'I feel that the aged instructor is protecting life, insuring property, fencing the *altar*, guarding the *throne*.' 'The *pen* is mightier than the *sword*.' 'The *wine cup* has drowned more than the ocean.' 'Then shall ye bring down my *gray hairs* with sorrow to the grave.'—Gen. xlii. 38. 'Ye devour widows' *houses*.'—Luke xx. 47.

A Synecdoche (Gk. *syn*, with, *ek*, out, and *dechomai*, to receive) is a figure in which a part stands for the whole, or the whole for the part, or the material for the object made of it, or a passion for its object. Thus we speak of a ship as 'a *sail*,' and a workman as a '*hand*.'

> I have ventured,
> Like little wanton boys that swim on bladders,
> These many *summers* in a sea of glory.—*Shakspere.*

An Hypérbŏle (Gk. *hyper*, above, and *ballo*, to throw) is an exaggeration in which there is no intention to deceive, e.g. '*rivers* of blood and *mountains* of slain.'

> Now pile your dust upon the quick and dead
> *Till of this flat a mountain you have made*
> *To o'ertop old Pelion, or the skyish head*
> *Of blue Olympus.—Shakspere.*

> Will all *great Neptune's ocean* wash this blood
> Clean from my hand ? No, this my hand will rather
> *The multitudinous seas incarnadine,*
> *Making the green—one red.—Id.*

A **Lĭtŏtēs** (Gk. *litos*, slender) is the assertion of something by denying its contrary, e.g. ' A citizen *of no mean city*,' i.e. of a highly important city.

An **Apostrophe** (Gr. *apo*, from, and *strepho*, to turn) is a turning from the main current of discourse to address something or somebody that is absent, e.g.—

> Judge, O you gods, how dearly Cæsar loved him.—*Shakspere.*

An **Aposiopēsis** (Gk. *apo*, from, and *siopao*, to be silent) is a sudden breaking off under the influence of some great emotion or with a view to implying more than could be expressed, e.g.—

> I will have such revenges on you both
> *That all the world shall*—I will do such things—
> What they are, yet I know not; but they shall be
> The terrors of the earth.—*Shakspere.*

A **Prolepsis** (Gk. *pro*, before, and *lambano*, to receive) is a figure in which some anticipated result is spoken of as if it had actually happened, e.g.—

> So the two brothers and their *murdered man*
> Rode towards Florence.—*Keats.*

The man was not yet murdered, but the poet anticipates the murder.

An **Oxymoron** (Gk. *oxus*, sharp, and *mōros*, foolish) is a witty absurdity, an expression which produces a powerful effect but will not admit of rigid analysis, e.g. ' A *cruel kindness*,' ' The *wisest fool* in Christendom,' ' *Hasten slowly*,' ' *Take time* that we *may make an end the sooner*,' ' *The half* is more than *the whole*.'

> And Pity, dropping soft the *sadly pleasing tear*.—*Gray.*

A **Paronomasia** (Gk. *para*, beside, and *onoma*, name) is a play upon words for some rhetorical effect, e.g.—

> Old *Gaunt*, indeed ; and *gaunt* in being old ;
> Within me grief hath kept a tedious fast ;
> And who abstains from meat that is not *gaunt* ?—*Shakspere.*

An **Euphemism** (Gk. *eu*, well, and *phemi*, to speak) is a mild expression used to denote some painful or repulsive idea, e.g.—

> Rachel mourning for her children, and will not be comforted because they *are not*.—*Bible.*

A Climax (Gk. *klimax*, a ladder) is a period so constructed that the effect goes on increasing with each successive particular, e.g.—

It is an outrage to *bind* a Roman citizen; to *scourge* him is an atrocious crime; to *put him to death* is almost a parricide; but to *crucify* him—what shall I call it?—*Cicero against Verres.*

An Anti-climax is a period which begins pretentiously and produces less and less effect as it proceeds, e.g.—

> And thou Dalhousie, *the great god* of war,
> *Lieutenant-General* to the Earl of Mar.

The Anti-climax is often used for burlesque effect, as when Byron wrote of a certain traveller, whose name he found in a guide-book—

> He went to Athens and—*he wrote his name.*

Dr. Wolcott, writing of Johnson's style, says—

> Alike in every theme his pompous art
> Heaven's *awful thunder* or a *rumbling cart.*

Exercises.

Classify the following figures of speech and, if occasion require, criticise them :—

a. They melted from the field, as snow,
When streams are swollen, and south winds blow,
Dissolves in silent dew.—*Scott.*

b. The voice of thy brother's blood crieth unto Me from the ground.—*Gen.* iv. 10.

c. Yet all experience is an arch wherethrough
Gleams that untravelled world, whose margin fades
For ever and for ever when I move.—*Tennyson.*

d.   In Vienna's fatal walls
God's finger touched him and he slept.—*Id.*

e. Life's but a walking shadow; a poor player
That struts and frets his hour upon the stage,
And then is heard no more; it is a tale
Told by an idiot, full of sound and fury,
Signifying nothing.—*Shakspere.*

f. Can Honour's voice provoke the silent dust,
Or Flattery soothe the dull cold ear of Death?—*Gray.*

g.   Earth felt the wound ; and Nature, from her seat,
Sighing through all her works, gave signs of woe,
That all was lost.—*Milton.*

h.   Philosophy will clip an angel's wings.—*Keats.*

i.   Then felt I like some watcher of the skies
When a new planet swims into his ken.—*Id.*

k.   Most wretched men
Are cradled into poetry by wrong.—*Shelley.*

l.   Life, like a dome of many-coloured glass,
Stains the white radiance of eternity.—*Id.*

m.   I am escaped with the skin of my teeth.—*Book of Job.*

n.   There is a reaper whose name is Death,
     And with his sickle keen
He reaps the bearded grain at a breath
     And the flowers that grow between.—*Longfellow.*

o.   None but himself can be his parallel.—*Theobald.*

p.   Adam, the goodliest man of men since born
His sons, the fairest of her daughters Eve.—*Milton.*

q.   At whose sight all the stars
Hide their diminished heads.—*Id.*

r.   A man of pleasure is a man of pains.—*Young.*

s.   To love her was a liberal education.—*Steele.*

t.   Lowliness is young Ambition's ladder.—*Shakspere.*

u. The Puritans hated bear-baiting not because it gave pain to
the bear, but because it gave pleasure to the spectators.—*Macaulay.*

v.   Those honourable men whose daggers have killed Cæsar.
                              Shakspere.

w. I was sailing in a vast ocean without other help than the
pole-star of the ancients, and the rules of the French stage among
the moderns.—*Dryden.*

x.   The labour we delight in physics pain.—*Shakspere.*

y.   Some mute inglorious Milton here may rest,
Some Cromwell guiltless of his country's blood.—*Gray.*

z.   It flows through old hushed Egypt and its sands
    Like some grave mighty thought threading a dream.
             Leigh Hunt's Sonnet, 'The Nile.'

HINTS ON PARSING.

It cannot be too strongly impressed on the young student that the parsing of a word depends not on its origin, or on its form, but wholly and solely on its *function* in the particular construction in which it occurs. A word may have been a noun once, but if it is used as a verb in the passage in which it occurs, it should be parsed as a verb. No reliance should be placed on the *form* of a word in a language like ours, that is so destitute of distinctive terminations. The termination *-ing* may belong to a common noun, a verbal noun, a participle, or an adjective, e.g. The *writing* was bad (Common Noun). In *writing* we should be careful to make our meaning clear (Verbal Noun). A man, *writing* a dozen books a year, will be sure to write some bad books (Participle). A *writing* lesson differs from a drawing lesson (Adj.). The termination *-ly* may belong to an adjective as well as to an adverb, e.g. It was a *womanly* action (Adj.). He sang *sweetly* (Adv.)

Most of the difficulties that occur in parsing arise from disregarding the *function* of the word with which we have to deal, or from our inability to determine precisely what the function is. The student will be assisted in doubtful cases by mentally analysing the sentence in which the word occurs, by substituting some other word or a phrase for the word in question, or, if he know a foreign language, by considering how he would translate the word. As language is highly elliptical, it frequently happens that a sentence cannot be properly parsed until the ellipse has been filled in, but the student should be quite sure that the words supplied have been really dropped out, and are not introduced merely to get over a difficulty. In old English certain adjectives governed cases without any intervening preposition, and instances of this usage still survive, e.g. He is *like* his *uncle*. It is *worth sixpence*. In such constructions we are not justified in supplying prepositions to account for the case of *uncle* and *sixpence*. The adjective governs the case, as in Latin and many other languages. The antecedent of the relative pronoun is often omitted. In such a construction we may legitimately supply the omitted word, e.g. I know ∧ *who* did it = I know [the person]

who did it. This is what I want = This is [that] what I
want. Take *that* thine is = Take [that] that is thine.
What and *that* are sometimes treated as compound relative pronouns when they are equivalent to *that which*, but it
is better to restrict the term 'compound relative' to such
real compounds as *whoever, whatever, whichever,* &c. If the
dropped antecedent be not supplied, the words *what* and
that are best treated as simple relative pronouns standing
in a double syntactical relation. (See p. 57.)

The student is strongly recommended to observe a fixed
method in parsing. The most logical method is to state:—

1. The class and sub-class to which the word parsed
belongs;

2. The inflexions of the word as it occurs, if it have
any;

3. The syntactical relations in which the word stands to
other words.

As parsing is a practical application of our knowledge
of the logical classification of words and of the relations
subsisting between them, it is indispensable that the student
should possess a thorough knowledge,

1. Of the definitions of the parts of speech, and

2. Of the definitions of the terms which designate the
various syntactical relations, e.g. Agreement, Government,
Qualification, Limitation, &c. (See pp. 159–61.)

The attention of the student is specially directed to the
following classes of difficulties, in dealing with which
beginners are liable to go astray:—

NOUNS.

1. The **Nominative Absolute** is often confounded with
a subject qualified by a participle.

> Cæsar, having defeated the enemy, retired.
> Cæsar having defeated the enemy, his troops withdrew.

In the former sentence 'Cæsar' is Nominative to 'retired;'
in the latter it is used absolutely, the subject to the principal verb being 'troops.' (See p. 164.)

2. The **Nominative Case** is used after many copulative verbs besides the verb 'to be,' e.g. *become, turn out, prove,* &c. See pp. 162–3, and compare the following sentences :—

> His coat *became* (Transitive Verb) him.
> He *became* (Copulative Verb) a soldier.

3. The **Direct or Indirect Object after the Passive Voice** is often a source of difficulty, e.g.—

> He was taught *music* (Dir. Obj.).
> Music was taught *him* (Ind. Obj.).

Dr. Abbott recommends that these Objects should be parsed as 'the Retained Object after a Passive Verb,' or simply as 'the Retained Object.' (See 'How to Parse,' p. 91.)

4. In **Factitive Constructions** containing a passive verb, the noun following the verb should be parsed as the 'Retained Factitive Object' of the verb, e.g.—

> He was made *king*.

Dr. Abbott would call 'king' here the 'Subjective Supplement,' because it is identical with the Subject, 'He.' In

> We made him *king*

he would call 'king' the 'Objective Supplement,' because here it is identical with the Object.

In Latin the Nominative Case is used after a verb of making in the Passive Voice, e.g.—

> Numa Pompilius *rex* creatus est.
> Numa Pompilius was made *king*.

5. In dealing with **Adverbial Objects** it is not necessary to supply a preposition, e.g.—

> He swam three *miles*.
> It weighed six *pounds*.

It is a mistake to suppose that we cannot have an objective case without a transitive verb or preposition to govern it. The mere sense of the passage may determine the case. (See pp. 172–3.)

6. In dealing with the **Cognate Object**, say that the Object is governed by the intransitive verb used transitively, e.g.—

> She dreamt a *dream*.

D D

ADJECTIVES.

1. Adjectives used after certain verbs are liable to be confounded with adverbs, e.g.—

He looked *cold*.
It smelled *sweet*.

It will be observed that 'cold' and 'sweet' relate to the Subject and not to the verb. Cp. 'He looked *coldly* on the scheme.' 'She sang *sweetly*.' (See p. 63.)

2. Certain Pronominal Adjectives are identical in form with pronouns, e.g. *his, each, either, neither, many, much, all, few, some, several,* &c. When these words are followed by a noun, they are to be parsed as adjectives, when used alone they should be parsed as pronouns, e.g.—

This is *his* (Pro.).
His book is here (Adj).

3. Certain Adjectives govern cases, e.g. *like, near, worth.* Do not supply a preposition to account for the case. (See p. 161.)

4. The with comparatives should be parsed as the old Ablative Case of the Demonstrative adjective 'the,' e.g.—

The more *the* merrier.

The first 'the' = *by how much*; the second = *by so much*.

PRONOUNS

1. Both the **Relative Pronoun** and its **Antecedent** are frequently omitted. They should both be supplied in parsing, e.g.—

Here is the book ∧ you were seeking (Relative omitted).
I know ∧ who is there (Antecedent omitted).

2. The **Emphatic** and the **Reflexive Pronoun** are alike in form, but should be carefully distinguished, e.g.—

I *myself* did it (Emphatic).
I hurt *myself* (Reflexive).

3. The treatment of what and that has been already pointed at. (See p. 384.)

4. Whoever and other compounds of the Relative Pronoun seem to belong to both the Principal Sentence and the Adjective Clause. Supply the antecedent, e.g.—

> *Whoever* trespasses in this field [he] will be punished.
> Take [that] whatever you like.

5 Interrogative Pronouns sometimes occur in sentences that are not directly interrogative. They should be parsed as 'Interrogative Pronouns in the Oblique Construction,' e.g.—

> He asked me *who* did it.

Dr. Abbott would parse the interrogative pronoun here as a Conjunctive Pronoun ; but this is not a happy name, for all Relative Pronouns are Conjunctive, i.e. they attach the Adjective Clause to the Principal Sentence.

6. Somewhat, something, and **nothing** are sometimes used adverbially, e.g.—

> He was *somewhat* shy.
> He was *nothing* ashamed.

7. What is used adverbially in such constructions as the following : ' *What* with the heat and *what* with the length of the journey I was worn out.'

VERBS.

1. An Intransitive Verb cannot be used in the Passive Voice unless it be compounded with a preposition, and in that case the verb and preposition should be parsed together as a Compound Transitive Verb. We cannot say, 'I am laughed,' but we can say, 'I am laughed at.' The true verb here is not 'laugh,' but '*laugh at.*' Cp. 'He was *coughed down*,' ' We were *preached at.*'

2. Compound Verbal Forms such as—

> a. He *may go.*
> b. You *might have gone.*
> c. She *would have been pleased.*

should be broken up into the auxiliary and the infinitive governed by it, e.g.—

> a. *May,* mood auxiliary, indicative, pres., third per. sing., agreeing with its nom. 'he.'
>
> *go,* verb intrans., impf. infinitive, governed by 'may.'

b. might, mood auxiliary, indicative, past, second per. sing., agreeing with its nom. ' you.'

have gone, verb intran., perf. infin., governed by ' might.'

c. would, mood auxiliary, indicative, third per. sing., agreeing with its nom. ' she.'

have been pleased, verb trans., passive, perfect infinitive, governed by ' would.'

3. The Periphrastic Imperative of the first person plural and of the third person singular and plural should be broken up, e.g.—

Let us go.

Let, verb transitive,[1] imperative, active, present, second per. sing., agreeing with ' thou ' understood.

us, pro. personal, first per. plu., dir. obj., governed by ' let.'

go, verb intrans., imperf. infinitive, governed by ' let.'

In Latin or French we should express ' Let us go ' by a single word, e.g. Fr. *allons*, Lat. *eamus*.

4. Words compounded of Participles and Prefixes should be parsed as adjectives, e.g. *un-forgiving, un-determined.* We have no such verbs as un-forgive, un-determine.

5. Verbal Nouns may govern a Case, e.g.—

In *reading* good books we enter into good society.

Here ' reading ' is governed by ' in,' and itself governs ' books.'

6. The Imperfect Participle is often used predicatively after the object of a verb of perception, e.g.—

I saw him *walking.*
I heard him *talking.*

(See p. 202, § 218.)

7. The Present Perfect Tense of verbs of *going* and *coming, rising* and *falling, escaping, arriving,* &c., should not be confounded with the *Passive Voice.* Cp.

He *is gone* (Active Present Perfect).
He *is loved* (Passive Pres. Imperfect).

Such verbs have two perfects, e.g. He *is gone*, He *has*

---

[1] The transitive force of this verb is restricted in this construction to the governing power of ' let.' When ' let '=allow, permit, ' Let us go ' has a different meaning.

gone. The former is used when the predominant reference is to the state of the person or thing represented by the subject; the latter when the predominant reference is to the completeness of the action or state.

8. Many verbs are used both **Transitively** *and* **Intransitively**, e.g. *return, move, continue, enter.* Cp.

> He will not *return* (Intrans.).
> *Return* this book (Trans.).

9. Infinitives and Participles are Perfect or Imperfect, i.e. they denote a complete or incomplete state or action, but they have no number or person. Some grammarians speak of *present* and *past* participles and infinitives, but it is better to use as distinguishing epithets *imperfect* and *perfect.*

ADVERBS.

1. Some Adverbs are identical in Form with Adjectives, e.g. *fast, quick, ill.* In O.E. the Adverb was often formed by adding *-e* to the adjective. Hence, when, in process of time, the *-e* was dropped, the adverbial and adjectival forms became identical.

2. Interrogative Adverbs are often used in oblique or indirect constructions, e.g.—

> Tell me *where* is Fancy bred.

In such cases they should be parsed as Interrogative Adverbs used in an oblique construction. See the treatment of Interrogative Pronouns, p. 387. Dr. Abbott calls the adverb in such constructions as these a *conjunctive adverb.* The same objection lies against this name as against *conjunctive pronoun.* Other adverbs are conjunctive, e.g. *where, wherein, whereby,* &c.

> This is the house *where* he was born.

3. Certain words are used both as **Adverbs and Prepositions,** e.g. *on, in, up, down, below, beneath,* &c. When these words denote position or direction without governing a case, they are adverbs of direction; when they carry the mind on to some expressed object, they are prepositions. Cp.

> Go *on* (Adv.).
> He went *on* deck (Prep.).

4. Adverbial Phrases may be parsed like single words, e.g. *at once, at random.*

5. Adverbs in -ly should be distinguished from *adjectives in -ly.*

> A *masterly* hand (Adj.).
> They wrote *rapidly* (Adv.).

PREPOSITIONS.

1. Prepositions are often **separated** from the words which they govern, e.g.—

> This is the book *that* you were speaking *of.*
> *Whom* were you talking *to*?

2. Prepositions often enter into **Adverbial Phrases,** and in such cases govern some nouns understood, e.g. *in* short [speech]; *in* brief [terms]. Where the noun cannot be easily supplied, the phrase should be parsed as a whole.

3. Some prepositions are now **incorporated in other Parts of Speech.** In parsing such forms as *a-dying, a-fishing,* it is necessary to separate the prefix, and to state that it is a contracted form of *in* or *on.* In adverbs like *aboard, abed,* &c., the prepositional force of the prefix need not be recognised.

CONJUNCTIONS.

1. Conjunctions should be carefully distinguished from prepositions and adverbs having the same form, e.g. *since, for, so.* Cp.

> I have not seen him *since* Tuesday (Prep.).
> *Since* you are here, you may as well stop (Conj.).
> This is *for* you (Prep.).
> He cannot have gone, *for* I hear his voice (Conj.).
> She sang *so* sweetly that we were obliged to listen (Adv.).
> It was in vain to argue; *so* I gave up the attempt (Conj.).

2. Compound Conjunctions may be parsed as single words, e.g. *inasmuch as, in as far as.*

3. Adverbial Conjunctions discharge a double function, which s̈ould be pointed out.

WORDS OF EXCEPTIONAL DIFFICULTY.

As—(1) It fell *as* the snow-flakes fall.
 (2) He acted *as* clerk.
 (3) *As* is the priest, so is the people.
 (4) I have *as* (*a*) much *as* (*b*) I want.
 (5) *As* you are dissatisfied I will resign.
 (6) Such articles *as* we needed were not to be had.
 (7) He trembled *as* he spoke.
 (8) Summer with us, *as* usual, is very wet.
 (9) This is *as* (*a*) good *as* (*b*) that.
 (10) He was so kind *as* to invite me.
 (11) It is *as* if the mouth should tear the hand.
 (12) *As* regards his ability there can be no question.

The primary function of *as* is that of an adverbial conjunction of comparison, and all the other uses of it grow out of elliptical constructions.

(1) *As*, adverbial conjunction of comparison, limiting ' fell,' and connecting the adverbial clause 'the snow-flakes fell' with the principal sentence ' It fell.'

(2) *As*, adverbial conjunction of comparison, limiting ' acted,' and connecting ' He acted ' with the elliptical adverbial clause ' [a] clerk [acts].'

(3) *As*, demonstrative adverb of comparison, limiting ' is ' and correlative with ' so.' Cp. '*ut* populus *sic* sacerdos.'

(4) *As* (*a*), demonstrative adverb of degree, limiting ' much.' [' As much ' may be taken together as an adjective phrase of quantity. Cp. Lat. *tantus*, Fr. *tant*.]

(*As*) (*b*), relative pronoun, third per. sing., objective case, governed by ' want.' Cp. the use of the relative pronoun after demonstratives in Latin, idem . . . . qui ; tantus . . . . quantus, &c.

(5) *As*, causal conjunction connecting ' I will resign ' with ' you are dissatisfied.'

(6) *As*, relative pronoun, third per. plural, objective case governed by ' needed.' If the ellipse be filled up we must supply after ' as,' ' those articles which,' in which case ' as ' would be an adverbial conjunction of comparison.

(7) *As*, adverb of time, limiting ' trembled.'

(8) *As*, adverbial conjunction connecting ' Summer with us is very wet ' with ' [it is] usual.'

(9) *As* (*a*), demonstrative adverb of degree limiting ' good.' (See (4).)

As (*b*), adverbial conjunction connecting 'This is as good' with ' that [is].'

(10) *As*, adverbial conjunction connecting 'He was so kind' with 'to invite me.' Correlative to 'so.' This construction seems to be confounded with the use of the infinitive after the adverb 'enough.' Cp. 'He was kind enough to invite me.'

(11) *As*, adverbial conjunction connecting 'It is' with 'if the mouth should tear the hand.' This construction is highly elliptical. The full form would seem to be 'It is as [it would be] if the mouth,' &c.

(12) *As*, adverbial conjunction limiting 'can be no question' and connecting the adverbial clause with the principal sentence. 'There can be no question as [so far as the matter] regards his ability.'

But—(1) He came *but* did not stop.
  (2) He did *but* speak.
  (3) There was no one there *but* him.
  (4) There was no one *but* pitied him.
  (5) He would have been first *but* for his idleness.
  (6) She was all *but* perfect.

The primary meaning of *but* is *besides, except, without*, from *be* = by and *útan* = without.

(1) *But*, adversative conjunction coupling the two co-ordinate sentences 'He came' and '[he] did not stop.'

(2) *But*, an adverb of degree limiting 'did speak.' The sentence is equivalent to 'He spoke *only*.'

(3) *But*, preposition (= except) governing 'him.' Many writers, losing sight of the prepositional use of 'but,' use the Nominative Case after it. If we say, 'There was no one there but *he*,' we must assume an ellipse, 'but he [was there].'

(4) *But* [= who . . . . not], relative pronoun, third per. sing., nom. to 'pitied.' This use of 'but' arises out of the desire of brevity. The full form would seem to be, 'There was no one but [those who] pitied him.' In this complete construction 'but' has its usual force of 'except.'

(5) *But*, conditional conjunction connecting 'He would have been first' with 'for his idleness.' 'But' = if it had not been.

(6) *But*, preposition governing '[being] perfect.' 'She was all [you could wish] except [being absolutely] perfect.'

Since—(1) He has been ill *since* Wednesday.
  (2) He has been ill *since* he went to London.
  (3) *Since* you are here, you may as well dine with us.

(1) *Since*, preposition governing 'Wednesday.'

(2) *Since*, adverbial conjunction of time limiting 'He has been ill' and connecting it with 'he went to London.'

(3) *Since*, causal conjunction connecting 'you may as well dine with us' with 'you are here.'

Even—(1) *Even* I could do that.
(2) He could read *even* Chinese.
(3) She talked *even* in her sleep.

(1) *Even*, adverb of emphasis limiting some such elliptical sentence as [such an incapable or weak person as] 'I' [am].

(2) *Even*, adverb of emphasis limiting 'Chinese.'

(3) *Even*, adverb of emphasis limiting 'in her sleep.'

All—(1) We were *all* greatly pleased.
(2) *All* of us were there.
(3) He was *all* the better for his bath.
(4) *All* the boys sing.

(1) *All*, indefinite numeral pronoun, nom. in apposition with 'we' and limiting 'we.'

(2) *All*, indefinite numeral pronoun, third person plural, nominative case, subject to 'were.'

(3) *All*, adverb of degree limiting 'better.' 'All ' = here 'wholly.'

(4) *All*, indefinite numeral adjective limiting 'boys.'

Many—(1) *Many* are called.
(2) There were *many* persons there.
(3) *Many* a man has failed in that.

(1) *Many*, indefinite numeral pronoun, third per. plural, subject to 'are called.'

(2) *Many*, indefinite numeral adjective, limiting 'persons.'

(3) *Many*, numeral adverb limiting 'a.' The old English expression is 'many-one.' Cp. German, 'Manch' ein Mann.'

What—(1) *What* do you want
(2) *What* man is that?
(3) I have *what* I want.
(4) *What* a man he was!
(5) *What* with one thing and *what* with another, I was quite distracted.

(1) *What*, interrogative pronoun, objective case, governed by 'want.'

(2) *What*, interrogative adjective limiting 'man.'

(3) *What*, pronoun relative, objective case, governed by 'have' and 'want.' If we supply the word 'that' before 'what,' the latter will be governed by 'want' only.

(4) *What*, exclamatory pronominal adjective limiting 'man.'

(5) *What*, distributive adverb limiting 'was distracted.'   'What = here 'partly.'

> **More**—(1) I have *more* than you.
> (2) We had *more* falls than apples.
> (3) I was *more* annoyed than angry.
> (4) I said no *more*.
> (5) This he said and nothing *more*.

(1) *More*, indefinite numeral pronoun, comparative degree, objective case, governed by 'have.'

(2) *More*, indefinite numeral adjective, comparative degree, limiting 'falls.'

(3) *More*, adverb of degree, comparative degree, limiting 'annoyed.'

(4) *More*, indefinite pronoun of quantity, comparative degree, objective case, governed by 'said.' It would be better perhaps to take 'no more' together as a compound indefinite pronoun.

(5) *More*, adverb of quantity (= in addition) limiting 'said.'

> **No**—(1) Are you going? *No.*
> (2) *No* man saw him.
> (3) He was *no* taller.

(1) *No*, adverb of negation limiting 'go.'

(2) *No*, numeral adjective limiting 'man.'

(3) *No*, adverb of degree limiting 'taller.' Cp. 'He was somewhat taller,' 'He was much taller,' 'He was slightly taller.' 'He was not taller' is not precisely equivalent to 'He was no taller.'

Methinks (= it seems to me).

me, personal pronoun, first per. sing., indirect object, governed by 'seems.'

thinks, verb intransitive, indicative, pres., third per. sing., used without an expressed subject.   (See p. 103.)

A-dying, as in 'She lay a-dying.'

a (= on), preposition governing the verbal noun 'dying.'

QUESTIONS SET AT PUPIL TEACHERS' EXAMINATIONS.

(FIRST YEAR).

1. *Bounded* the *fiery steed* in air,
 The rider *sat erect* and fair ;
 Then like a bolt from steel cross-bow
 Forth launched, along the plain they go.

Analyse this passage, and parse the words in italics.

2. What is case ?   How do you know the nominative, possessive, and objective cases ?

3. Point out the affixes, with their meaning, in the following words :—'scholar,' 'goodness,' 'friendship,' 'maiden,' 'speaker,' 'lambkin.'

4. State any English terminations which mean belonging to, likeness, direction, and negation, and give instances of words in which they occur.

5. What is meant by regular, irregular, auxiliary, defective, transitive, and intransitive verbs ?   Give examples.

6. What are the different meanings of the English termination 'en,' when added to a noun, an adjective, and a verb ?   Give instances.

7. How would you parse fully a noun ?   Explain each term you use.

8. *Returning* then the bolt he *drew*,
 And the *lock's* murmurs growled *anew*.
 Roused at the sound, from *lowly* bed
 A captive *feebly raised his* head.

Analyse this passage, and parse the words in italics.

9. What is the meaning of the following English terminations :—'less,' 'hood,' 'ling,' 'ly' ?   Give words in which they occur.

10. What is an adjective ?   State, with examples, the different kinds of adjectives.

11. Give examples of adverbs of manner, time, and place.

12. Distinguish between personal and demonstrative pronouns. Name the personal pronouns.

13. Explain the force of the terminations in the following words:—'oaken,' 'sapling,' 'ringlet,' 'noisome,' 'mighty,' and give instances of words with similar endings.

14. What does the voice of a verb show? Give examples of verbs in the different voices.

15. In what three ways is the distinction of sex of living things marked in the nouns that stand for them? Give examples.

(Second Year.)

1. Far up the *lengthening* lake were spied
   Four *darkening* specks upon the tide,
   That, slow enlarging on the view,
   Four manned and masted *barges grew*,
   And bearing *downwards*, from Glengyle
   Steered full upon the opening isle.

Turn this passage into prose.

2. Analyse the above passage, and parse the words in italics.

3. What is the meaning of 'ad,' 'ex,' and 'ob'? Give words in which they occur. How and when are they sometimes changed in composition?

4. State the various kinds of subordinate sentences. Why are they so called? and how are they distinguished?

5. State with examples some of the Latin terminations in English abstract nouns.

6. *There are* who have at *midnight* hour
   In slumber *scaled* a dizzy tower,
   And on the *verge that beetled o'er*
   The ocean *tide's incessant* roar,
   Dreamed calmly out their dangerous dream
   Till wakened by the morning beam.

Turn this passage into prose.

7. Analyse the above passage, and parse the words in italics.

8. What are some of the principal terminations of nouns formed from the Latin? Give words in which they occur.

9. What are subordinate conjunctions? Give examples.

10. Is there any exception to the rule that conjunctions do not require an objective case after them? If there is, give an example.

11. Explain clearly the words 'subject,' 'predicate,' 'object,' 'extension of predicate,' and 'enlargement of subject.' Give examples of each,

(THIRD YEAR.)

1. His *thoughts* I scan not, but I *ween*
    That, could their import *have been seen,*
    The *meanest* groom in *all* the hall
    That e'er tied courser to a stall
    Would scarce have wished to be *their prey,*
    For Lutterward and Fontenaye.

Turn this passage into prose.

2. Analyse the above passage, and parse the words in italics.

3. What is the force of these prefixes :—'be,' 'for,' 'mis,' 'un,' 'amphi,' 'anti,' 'cata,' 'hemi'? Give words in which they occur, with their meaning.

4. What are the means of readily distinguishing between words of English and Latin origin?

5. *On through* the hamlet *as* they paced,
    Before a porch, *whose* front was graced
    With bush and flagon trimly *placed,*
    Lord Marmion *drew* his rein :
    The *village* inn seemed large, *though rude* ;
    Its cheerful fire and *hearty* food
    Might well relieve his train.

Turn this passage into prose.

6. Analyse the first four lines of this passage, and parse the words in italics.

7. Servant, steward, bondage, magistrate, freedom, temperance, friendship, fortitude, arithmetic. Point out the English words in this list. How do you distinguish them?

8. Give examples of the various ways in which the subject of a sentence may be expanded.

9. Give instances to show how the spelling of the Latin prepositions sometimes changes in composition.

10. Give examples to show how the infinitive mood may form (*a*) the subject, (*b*) the object, of a sentence.

11. Give three words compounded with each of the following Latin prepositions : 'ob,' 'præ' (pre), 'trans' (tres).

12. 'What' is said to be a compound relative. Explain this, and give four or five examples of sentences in which the word occurs, and in which its case would require to be specially made plain to a class of learners.

13. Show what is the precise meaning of the prefix in each of the following words. Say from what language it is derived, and give in each case another word similarly formed : -'improper,' 'impose,' 'amphibious,' 'unclean,' 'recover,' 'reform,' 'conceal,' 'contradict,' 'behave,' 'antedate,' 'antithesis.'

(Fourth Year.)

1. *'Twas now* a *place* of punishment,
   Whence if *so* loud a shriek *were sent*
   As reached the upper air,
   The hearers blessed *themselves,* and said
   The *spirits* of the sinful *dead*
   Bemoaned *their* torments there.

Analyse this passage, and parse the words in italics.

2. From what Latin roots are the following words derived :—
'library,' 'locomotion,' 'eloquence,' 'elucidate,' 'legitimate,' 'lunatic,'
'extravagant.'

3. When did the following writers live, and what are their
principal works: Spenser, Pope, Milton, Locke, Chaucer ?

4. Which kinds of words are derived from the Anglo-Saxon
language? State any difference in inflection between the English
and Anglo-Saxon languages.

5. State the various ways by which words of Latin origin have
been introduced into our language.

6. *Thus, while* I *ape* the measure *wild*
   Of tales *that* charmed me *as a child,*
   Rude *though they be, still* with the chime
   Return the *thoughts* of early time ;
   And feelings *roused* in *life's first* day
   Glow in the line and prompt the *lay.*

Analyse this passage, and parse the words in italics.

7. What English words are derived from the Latin verbs ' verto,'
I turn; ' video,' I see; ' venio,' I come ; ' scribo,' I write ; ' rego,'
I rule ?

8. ' Modern English is only a somewhat altered form of the
language which was brought into England by the Saxons and
Angles.' Show that this was the case from what you know of the
history of the language.

9. What are the proper prepositions to use after ' difference,'
' agree,' ' averse,' ' compared ' ?

10. Show in what respects our language affords evidence of the
different races which have inhabited this country.

11. What are the Latin words from which the following names
of places are derived :—Chester, Stratford, Fossbury? Give the
meaning of each Latin word, and mention any other names of places
that may occur to you which are derived from the same.

CANDIDATES FOR ADMISSION INTO TRAINING COLLEGES. 1886.

MALE AND FEMALE CANDIDATES.

TWO-AND-A-HALF *hours allowed for this Paper.*

(No abbreviation of less than three letters to be used in parsing or analysis.)

All candidates must do the composition, parsing, and analysis.

COMPOSITION.

(*a*) Write a letter descriptive of the town or village in which you live, or of any famous building in or near it;

OR,

(*b*) Write a short essay on one of these topics :—

    (i) Truthfulness, in act and in word.
    (ii) Poetry.
    (iii) The Queen rules over an Empire on which the sun never sets.

GRAMMAR.

1. Analyse fully the first five lines of this stanza, and parse the words printed in *italics* :—

> Milton ! thou shouldst be living at this hour :
> England *hath need* of thee ; she is a fen
> Of stagnant waters ; altar, sword, and pen
> Fireside, the heroic wealth of hall and bower,
> Have forfeited their ancient English dower
> Of inward happiness. *We are* selfish *men* ;
> Oh ! raise us up ; return to us again ;
> And give us manners, virtue, freedom, power.
> Thy soul was *like a star*, and dwelt apart ;
> Thou hadst a voice *whose sound* was like the sea ;
> Pure as the naked heavens, majestic, free,
> So *didst thou travel* on life's common way,
> In cheerful godliness ; and yet thy heart
> The lowliest *duties* on herself *did lay.*

2. Paraphrase the foregoing extract ; and select from it any example of words or phrases which are not used literally, but as 'figures of speech.'

3. Name six of the most famous English writers. Say when each of them lived, and what books he wrote.

4. Take each of the following words, and add to it a prefix or a suffix. Explain, in each case, what change in the meaning of the word has been effected by the additional syllable:—

| Just. | Admire. | Faith. | Pure. | Brother. |
| Friend. | Sincere. | Wise. | Hard. | Speak. |

5. Explain each of the following grammatical terms, and give an example illustrating its use :—

Infinitive. Relative. Apposition. Government. Predicate. Dative. Subjunctive. Transitive. Inflection.

6. Show by examples the different uses which may be made in English of the words 'what' and 'that.' Parse the sentence :

'What seemed his head,
The likeness of a kingly crown had on.'

7. If you think there is anything wrong in any of the following sentences, correct it, and give your reasons :—

(*a*) I should have liked to have seen so fine a sight.

(*b*) I do not think him a reliable person.

(*c*) There let him lay.

(*d*) Preferring to know the worst, than to dream the best.

(*e*) The courage of the soldier and of the citizen are essentially different.

(*f*) Each thought of others rather than themselves.

(*g*) The orator spoke of the notion that the national debt might be repudiated with absolute contempt.

8. How do you account for the presence in English of so many words of Latin origin? Say by what token—either as regards spelling or construction—you can recognise that an English word is derived from Latin ; and give some examples.

1885.

COMPOSITION.

Write a letter, or an essay, on *one* of the following subjects :—

(1) Your favourite flowers, and the way to cultivate them.

(2) The moral lessons of the microscope and the telescope.

(3) The advantages and disadvantages of town life as compared with life in the country.

(4) Examinations.

GRAMMAR.

1. Parse the words in italics in the following passage, not omitting to give and explain their *syntax*:—

> Breathes *there* a man with soul *so* dead
> Who never to himself *hath said*,
> This is my own, my native *land!*
> *Whose* heart hath ne'er within him burned
> As home his footsteps he hath turned
> From *wandering* in a foreign land?
> If such there *breathe*, *go*, mark him well;
> For him no minstrel raptures swell!
> High *though* his titles, proud his name,
> Boundless his *wealth*, *as* wish can claim,
> *Despite* those titles, power, and *pelf*,
> The wretch, concentred *all* in self,
> Living, shall forfeit fair renown,
> And, doubly dying, shall *go* down
> To the vile dust from *whence* he *sprung*
> Unwept, unhonoured, and *unsung*.

2. Analyse either the first or the last half of the passage into its component sentences, and show in separate columns:—

(a) The nature of the sentence.

(b) (If dependent) its relation to the principal sentence.

(c) Subject.

(d) Its enlargements (if any).

(e) Predicate.

(f) Its extensions (if any).

(g) Object (if any).

(h) Its enlargements (if any).

3. Explain by a paraphrase, or otherwise, the portion of the passage which you take for analysis.

4. Examine and illustrate the etymology of any five of the following words from the above:—

Own, native, whose, heart, foreign, minstrel, raptures, titles, boundless, claim, wretch, concentred, forfeit, renown.

5. Distinguish common, proper, and abstract Nouns, cardinal and ordinal Numbers, intransitive and neuter Verbs, continuative and disjunctive Conjunctions, personal, possessive, reflexive, and relative Pronouns.

6. It is often said that English is less of an *inflected* language in its later than in its earlier stages. Explain what is meant by this, and give a few instances of inflection in English as now spoken.

E E

7. Show by examples how analysis helps us to parse correctly.

8. At which periods, and in connection with what events, in the history of this island did the most important changes take place in the language of the inhabitants? Illustrate your answer.

CAMBRIDGE SENIOR LOCAL EXAMINATION.

A.

1. Into what classes may Pronouns be divided? Give one example of each class.

2. Give in outline the history of the Auxiliary Verbs. Discuss the following constructions: (1) I did come. (2) I have come. (3) I ought to come. (4) I ought to have come.

3. State what changes in mode of expression are made when a speech is reported in the indirect form. Deduce from the following report the words used by the original speaker :—' He urged them to tell him of a single enterprise in which they had succeeded, and, if they could not, to give him some better reason than their own word to believe that they were blameless. He would inquire into the facts and judge for himself.'

4. Analyse :—

As thro' the land at eve we went
And pluck'd the ripen'd ears,
We fell out, my wife and I,
And kiss'd again with tears.
And blessings on the falling out
That all the more endears
When we fall out with those we love
And kiss again with tears !

5. Parse fully the words in italics :—
Read *me that.*—Read you *what?*—You know *what,* the *Queen* of *Prussia's* letter.
You are *too* fond of *doing what* is mischievous.

B.

1. Give the etymology of *six only* of the following words: fowl, gazette, tinsel, blame, court, lord, loyal, archbishop, sheriff.

2. Point out anything that is incorrect in the following sentences :—

(1) Directly we fight we will be beaten, without you support us.

(2) The town consists of three distinct quarters of which the western one is by far the larger.

3. Write an essay (*to occupy not more than half an hour*) on one of the following subjects : (1) The influence of fiction. (2) Common sense. (3) John Bull. (4) The British Constitution. (5) A country walk. (6) The uses of Athletics.

QUESTIONS SELECTED FROM PAPERS SET FOR CANDIDATES FOR CERTIFICATES OF MERIT.

(FIRST YEAR.)

1. Give examples of words derived from the stems—'love,' 'wise,' 'strong,' 'right ;' and give the meaning of the suffixes you employ.

2. Explain the meaning of the Greek prefixes 'apo,' 'peri,' and of the Latin 'pro ' and 'præ,' with examples.

3. Give the older forms of 'when,' 'where,' 'king,' 'book,' 'thane,' 'alderman,' 'church ;' and give the derivations of ' Lancaster,' 'Suffolk,' ' Exminster,' ' Cheapside,' and ' Holborn.'

4. Write out definitions of a complex sentence, cardinal numerals, interjections, and reciprocal pronouns ; and explain the grammatical terms cardinal, mood, and predicate.

5. ' Kingdom,' ' pitiable,' ' worship,' ' strengthen,' ' kindness,' 'perilous.' Give the force of the suffix in each of these words, and of other words derived from the same stem.

6. Assign the prefixes of the following words to the language from which they are derived, and give their meanings :—'acceptable,' 'mismanage,' ' perplex,' ' analysis,' ' enthrone,' ' anarchy,' ' interview,' ' sustain,' ' antichrist,' ' distorted.'

7. Explain the grammatical terms—reflexive pronoun, disjunctive conjunction, relative adverb, neuter verb, nominative of address, adverb of degree, making short sentences to illustrate your explanation.

8. Prepare the outline of a first lesson on subordinate sentences to Standard VI.

9. What is meant by syntax ? Give, with examples, three of the more important syntactical rules, and explain why there are fewer such rules in English than in some other languages.

10. Give examples of the same word used in one sentence as an adverb and in another as a preposition. Explain, as to a class of children, how you distinguish between these two uses.

11. If you think any of the following sentences faulty, correct them, and give reasons for your correction : ' There have been

three famous orators in our day, either of whom would illustrate my meaning.' 'He finished the work like he had been ordered to do.' 'The officer was replaced by one more skilful than himself.' 'My friend and myself took a walk together.' 'I should have liked much to have seen the sight.'

MATRICULATION QUESTIONS, LONDON UNIVERSITY, 1886.

[Questions 1, 7, and 15 must be attempted by everyone; and of the rest not more than *Seven*.]

1. Write out and punctuate the passage read by the examiner.

2. What do you know of the origin of our alphabet? Illustrate its imperfections.

3. Classify the consonants. What is meant by a spirant? Which are the oldest vowels?

4. Discuss the pronunciation of 'chivalry,' 'project,' 'humble,' 'Deuteronomy,' 'dynamiter,' 'either.' How do there come to be such different pronunciations of the vowel 'a' as are heard in such words as 'master'?

5. Classify our words. Show that to some extent the form of a word indicates its class. Why only 'to some extent'? To what class or classes belong 'that,' 'ink,' 'after,' 'stand,' 'parallel,' 'good'?

6. State the force or forces of the suffixes—'ster,' 'ism,' 'let,' 'some,' 'ard,' 'ish.' Mention three prefixes of Teutonic origin and three of Romanic.

7. Describe our two conjugations. Which is the living one? Does any verb belong to both? What traces are there of reduplication?

8. What is the origin of the *d* in the preterite of 'love'? What of the *d* in its past participle? Explain the forms 'had,' 'made,' 'left,' 'built,' 'clad,' 'methinks.'

9. When is 'dare' inflected in the 3rd sing. pres. ind.? Can you cast any light on the forms 'durst' 'wist,' 'wrought,' 'sold,' 'sought,' 'ago'?

10. Mention some cognates of 'better,' 'nether,' 'among,' 'noun,' 'rather,' 'toward.'

11. What is the difference in meaning between 'monitory' and 'monetary,' 'definite' and 'definitive,' 'credible' and 'creditable,' 'confident' and 'confidant,' 'virtuous' and 'virtual,' 'expedient' and 'expedi⁓⁓ is'?

12. Point out what is idiomatic in these phrases: 'There came a letter.' 'Let them fight it out.' 'We spoke to each other.' 'Many a man would flee.' 'What an angel of a girl!' 'What with this, and what with that, I could not get on.'

13. What error has crept into the phrases 'ever so many,' 'to do no more than one can help,' 'these sort of things'? Suggest some explanation of 'mine' in such phrases as 'a friend of *mine*.'

14. What is the use of the 'analysis of sentences'? What shapes may the subject of a sentence assume? And in what ways may it be extended?

15. Analyse: 'I saw them run.' 'He can make it go.' 'Let her depart.' 'Who is it?' 'He was crowned king.' 'He was hanged—a well-deserved punishment.'

16. Write a sentence containing three extensions of the predicate, one of them a clause, and let this clause contain a subject with two extensions.

LONDON UNIVERSITY, 1887.

[N.B.—Not more than *Ten* questions are to be attempted; and in the ten must be included Nos. 1, 10, 14.]

1. Write out and punctuate the passage read by the examiner.

2. Both from its grammar and its vocabulary, as they now are, show that English is a Teutonic language.

3. Mention as many words as you can that have been adopted into our language during the last half century.

4. Give examples of all the various sounds of *a* in our language; also of those of *ough* and of *ch*.

5. Write down the plural form of 'wharf,' 'colloquy,' 'potato,' 'Mary,' 'Knight Templar,' 'canto,' and state and discuss the rule you go by in each case. Mention some words in which the *s* of the stem has been mistaken for the plural flexion.

6. What are our commonest Adjective formatives? Illustrate our habit of using nouns both with and without change of form, and also of using adverbs as adjectives.

7. What indefinite article do you use before the words 'history,' 'historical,' 'European,' 'usual,' 'humble,' 'ewer'? Give your reasons for your answers. Can you mention any instances of the transference of the *n* of the indefinite article to the beginning of the following noun?

8. Is there any difference in usage between 'each' and 'every'? Why should you not say, 'Neither of the ten suited me'? What alternative form of expression is there to 'That is mine and nobody else's'? Which do you think is to be preferred?

9. Repeat and criticise the current definition of a verb. Which seems to you the least unsatisfactory, and why?

10. What are the characteristic marks of the strong conjugation? Make a list of some half-dozen weak verbs that have vowel-change in the past tense; also of half-a-dozen that have no change there; also of half-a-dozen that do change, but not in the way of addition.

11. Classify conjunctions with reference to (a) their use; (b) their origin.

12. Parse the italicised words and phrases:—

(a) *Down* with it!

(b) His *having been beaten* once only made him *the* more determined to succeed.

(c) *Seeing* is *believing*.

(d) The *hearing* ear and the *seeing* eye the Lord hath made *even* both of them.

(e)   *Whatever* sceptic could inquire for,
For every *why* he had a *wherefore*.

(f) *Let* knowledge *grow* from *more* to more.

13. Distinguish between 'farther' and 'further,' 'gladder' and 'gladlier,' 'nearest' and 'next,' 'latest' and 'last,' 'peas' and 'pease,' 'genii' and 'geniuses.'

14. Give some general directions for the analysis of sentences; and apply them to a sentence of your own composing.

15. Analyse:—

(a)   O what a tangled web we weave,
When first we practise to deceive!

(b)   She sat like Patience on a monument,
Smiling at grief.

(c)   And statesmen at her Council met
    Who knew the seasons, when to take
    Occasion by the hand, and make
The bounds of freedom wider yet.

HINTS FOR ANSWERING QUESTIONS [1]

Set at the Matriculation Examinations of London University.

1. Account for the letters in italics in—nam*e*, thes*e*, thos*e*, pas*s*enger, sovere*i*gn, wet*t*est, ci*t*ies, potato*e*s, sceptre, sceptic, handi*w*ork, righ*t*eous, tom*b*, cou*l*d, our.   (1879.)

name. O.E. nama. The final *a* in Early Middle English was reduced to *e*. (See p. 281.)

these. O.E. thâs. The final *e* keeps the previous vowel long. *These* is only a dialectical form of *those*.

those. O.E. thás, the old plural of thas=this. Used at a later period as the plural of *that*. The final *e* is not a sign of inflection here, but merely keeps the previous vowel long.

passenger. (See p. 290, *d*.) The original form of the word was *possager*. The *n* was inserted to facilitate pronunciation. Cp. messenger (messager), porringer (porridger).

sovereign. Ignorantly conformed in spelling to *reign*, with which it has no philological connection. O.F. *soverain*. Lat. *super*.

wettest. The *t* is doubled to indicate that the previous vowel is short.

cities. The *t* belongs to the root, Lat. *civitas*. In the English of two centuries ago the singular ended in *ie*. Hence the plural in 'ies' was quite regular.

potatoes. Spelled with an *e* in conformity with *toes*, the plural of *toe*. As a rule foreign words in *-o* form their plural in *-s*. *Echoes* and *heroes* are exceptions.

sceptre. Gk. skeptron. (See Greek Roots.)

sceptic. Gk. skeptomai. (See Greek Roots.)

handiwork. O.E. hand-geweorce. The *i* represents *ge*. In *handicraft* the *i* has been wrongly inserted in imitation of *handiwork*, the O.E. form being *handcraft*.

---

[1] These hints are supplied with the intention of enabling the student to bring scattered information to bear on particular points and of furnishing additional illustrations of principles dealt with more or less fully in other parts of the book. They are not intended to enable him to dispense with the systematic study of the English language. It is impossible to thoroughly understand isolated bits of organised knowledge. Particular instances must be referred to general principles, and general principles must be elucidated by particular instances; one truth must be accepted in the light of some other complementary truth, and, in dealing with difficulties, a large body of related facts and general principles must be simultaneously present to the mind.

righteous. O.E. *rightwis,* wise as to what is right. Cp. weather-wise. Not from right-ways, as wrongly stated p. 307.

tomb. Lat. *tumba.* Gk. *tumbos.*

could. The *l* is wrongly inserted in imitation of *would,* where it rightly appears as part of the root. (See p. 107.)

our. O.E. *úre.* Poss. plu. of *we.* Stands for *ús-ere.*

2. What cases had nouns formerly in English ? Which of them still exist ? Of how many of them can the force still be expressed by the simple form of the word without a preposition ? Give full examples. (1879.) (See pp. 22-29.)

3. What was the ancient form of the Feminine Gender ? What traces remain of it ? How has it been supplanted ? Discuss the meaning and origin of the termination *-ster.* (1879.) (See pp. 11-15.)

4. Classify Adjectives irregularly compared. Give the positive and superlative of *more, farther, former, utter, hinder, less, rather, further, latter, nearer*; and tell what you know of the history of each. (See pp. 40-44.)

5. Explain the construction of *self.* What part of speech is it ? Trace its history. (1879.)

self was originally an adjective meaning *same,* and is used in this sense in Richard II., 'in that *self* mould.' In O.E. *self* agreed with the pronouns to which it was attached; at a later period the nominative of *self* was used with the *dative* of the personal pronouns. In the thirteenth century the *possessive* was substituted for the *dative.* As a separate word *self* is a *noun* and forms its plural in *-ves.* In *myself* the possessive pronoun survives, in *himself* the *dative* pronoun survives. (See p. 50.)

6. What are *weak verbs* ? Classify *bring, sing, take, seek, treat, set, brew, eat,* as weak or strong verbs. Give reasons in each case, and call attention to peculiarities. (1879.) (See pp. 88-9.)

7. What part is taken by the verb *have* in conjugating English verbs ? Explain the means by which *have* came to be used, and discuss the following :—

'I *have* a letter,' 'I *have* written a letter,' 'I *have* come to post it,' 'The post *is* gone.' (1879.)

The primary meaning of *have* is to *possess,* as in 'I have a letter.'

'I *have* written a letter' originally meant *I have a letter written*. In O.E. the perfect participle agreed with the noun which it now governs. (See p. 73, § 70.),

'I *have* come' conforms to the analogy of 'I have written;' though the verb 'come' is intransitive. It differs from the other perfect tense 'I *am* come' in this respect, that the former refers mainly to the completion of the action, while the latter refers mainly to the state of the subject. (See footnote, p. 75.)

8. What are the different uses of the verb *to be*? From how many verbs are the parts of this verb formed? (1879.) (See pp. 97–8.)

9. Classify adverbs (*a*) as to the ideas they express ; (*b*) as to their origin. (1879.) (See pp. 110–115.)

10. What are *verbal* prepositions? Give six examples, and show how they came to be used prepositionally. (1879.) (See p. 118, § 105, *d*.)

11. Correct or justify the following expressions :—

(*a*) I am verily a man who am a Jew [is].

(*b*) Too great a variety of studies distract the mind [distracts].

(*c*) Who do you speak to? [whom].

(*d*) The river has overflown its banks [overflowed].

(*e*) Man never is but always to be blest [Insert 'blest' after 'is.']

(*f*) Neither our virtues or our vices are all our own [nor].

(*g*) That's him [he].

(*h*) Many a day [Correct].

(*i*) I expected to have found him better [to find].

(*k*) I am to blame [Correct].   (1879.)

In (*a*) the antecedent to 'who' is 'man;' the verb, therefore, should be of the third person. 'Am' was probably used by the writer owing to the *attraction* of the pronoun and verb in the principal sentence. In (*b*) the subject 'variety' is singular. In (*c*) the interrogative pronoun is governed by 'to.' In (*d*) 'fly' is confounded with 'flow;' the perfect participle 'flown' is from 'fly,' not from 'flow.' In (*e*) the full construction is 'Man never is blest, but he is always to be blest,' i.e. Man is never actually happy, but is carried on by the hope of future happiness. In (*f*) the correlative of 'neither' is 'nor;' 'or' is the correlative of 'either.' In (*g*) the pronoun after the verb 'to be' must agree with the nominative which precedes it. In (*h*) 'many' is used adverbially. In (*i*) the perfect gerundial infinitive is used instead of the imperfect. 'I expected to find him,' not 'to have found him.' 'Expected' carries us back to a past condition of mind, and has nothing to do with any subsequent experience. The confusion arises from trying to convey in one expression a past and present experience. In (*k*) the active gerundial infinitive is used with a passive signification. The idiom is very common. Cp. 'A house *to let*,' 'Maison *à louer.*'

12. To what family of languages does English belong? Give any facts showing its relation to some other language of Europe. (1879.) (See pp. 237–40.)

13. English '*three*' is Latin '*tres*,' in German '*drei*. State and explain by examples the law to which a change of this kind is attributed. (1879.) (See pp. 294–5.)

An aspirate in the Classical languages is represented by a corresponding *soft* sound in the Low German language, and by a *hard* sound in the High German. Cp. Gr. *Thugater*; Low Ger. *daughter*; O.H.G. *tohtar*; Modern Ger. *tochter*.

14. How many sounds might possibly be represented by the English alphabet? Classify the actual letters of the alphabet according to their sound. (1879.) (See pp. 285–90.)

15. Name and define each of the parts of speech. (1879.)

16. Show how we came by the possessive case in 's and by the plural in *s*. Tell what you know about nouns forming their plurals in *en*. (1879.) (See p. 24, pp. 16, 17.)

17. Explain what is meant by the *infinitive mood* of a verb. Explain as fully as you can the infinitive form in the phrase, 'This house to let.' (1879.) (See answer to (11); also pp. 69–70 and 197–200.)

18. Discuss the following past tenses of verbs:—*Loved, taught, ate, sang*. Tell what you know of the forms *ought* and *must*. (1879.) (See pp. 88–91, p. 100, and pp. 108–9.)

19. Classify the pronouns. (1879.)

20. Write two sentences showing the same word used in one as a preposition, in the other as a conjunction; also two sentences showing the same word used as a preposition and as an adverb. (1879.) (See pp. 389, 390.)

21. Distinguish between the Classical and Teutonic elements in English. Point out the several ways in which words of Latin origin have been introduced into the language. (1880.) (See pp. 242–4, 268–9 for Teutonic elements; pp. 253–268 for Classical elements. Also Greek Roots.)

22. Define the words *vowel, diphthong, consonant.* What letters are called mutes, and how are they subdivided? Tell the substance of Grimm's Law. (1880.) (See pp. 286–9 ; also p. 294.)

23. Describe the several ways of indicating gender in English nouns, including explanation of the words *woman, lady, vixen, seamstress, mistress, bridegroom, widower, drake.* (1880.) (See pp. 11–15.)

24. What arguments might be used for and against the recognition of the article as a distinct part of speech? Tell what you know of the history of *an* and *the.* (1880.) (See pp. 35–36.)

Note that *a* is a contraction of *an.* It is a mistake to say that *n* is added to *a* before a vowel. The *n* is dropped before words not beginning with a vowel. The original meaning was *one.*

25. Trace as fully as you can the history of the inflexions of *thou,* and of *he, she, it,* in singular and plural   (1880.) (See pp. 47–9.)

26. Account for the separate forms *two* and *twain,* and for the words *ten, eleven, twelve, hundred, thousand, first, second, dozen, score, fortnight.* (1880.) (See pp. 35–6. For *first,* see p. 43.)

Dozen, from Fr. douzaine ; Lat. duodecim. *Fortnight,* from fourteen-night. Cp. se'nnight.

27. Discuss the inflexions of *may, can, shall, have, will, do.* (1880.) (See pp. 97–108.)

28. Account for the use of *to* in the infinitive present, and for its occasional omission in an infinitive after a verb, as '*I dare say.*' (1880.) (See pp. 101–2, 197–201.)

To before the infinitive originally denoted *purpose* (moral direction). Cp. I am going *to* town ; I am going *to* swim. The *infinitive* in O.E. was treated as a noun, and the dative form in *-anne* or *-enne* after *to* denoted purpose. By degrees *to* came to be used to express other relations, and finally was added to the infinitive, even when the latter was used as the subject or direct object of a sentence. In '*I dare thee to say*' the prepositional sign of the dative is retained.

29. Distinguish between Syntax and Prosody. Define a *perfect rhyme.* (1880.) (See pp. 159, 221–2.)

30. Make a table showing the relationship of English to the other languages of the Indo-European family. (1880.) (See p. 239.)

31. Classify the nouns, the pronouns, the verbs. (1880.)

32. Discuss, with reference to their history, the words *ye* and *you, her, its, this, that, which.* (1880.) (See pp. 47–9.)

33. Explain what is meant by *tense* and *mood* of verbs. Add a few notes upon past and present forms of the future tense and of the subjunctive mood in English verbs, and on the use of the subjunctive. (1880.) (See chapter on 'Verbs,' pp. 77–8, and pp. 195–7 ; also pp. 77–8.)

In O.E. there were no *personal* distinctions in the forms of the present and past subjunctive.

34. Explain the following terms applied to the structure of words :—*Root, stem, primary derivative, secondary derivative, compound word.* Apply your explanation to the words *song, bait, batch, suds, thicket, spider, farthing, landscape, knowledge, wedlock, hemlock, eyry, along, gossip, waylay, walking-stick.* (1880.)

A *root* is a word or a part of a word which cannot be referred to any earlier form. Thus *duke, doge, conduct,* &c., can all be carried back to an Aryan form, *du,* but we cannot go farther. Hence we speak of *du* as a *root.*

A *stem* is that form which the root assumes before undergoing inflexional modifications—e.g. *lov-* is the stem of *lovable, loving, lovely,* &c.

Stems are formed from roots by the addition of a demonstrative root, by a change of the radical vowel, by reduplication, and by combination with other stems. (See Morris's ' Historical Outlines,' p. 211.)

A Primary Derivative is formed directly from the root—e.g. *droop* fra *drop,* O.E. *dropa.*

A Secondary Derivative is one formed from a primary derivative—e.g. *dribble* from *drip*, a primary derivative from *drop*.

song. Primary Derivative from root *sing*. Stem *sing*.

bait. Primary Derivative from root *bhid*, to draw.

batch. Primary Derivative from root *bhag*. Stem *ba*. For termination, cp. match, latch, witch, wretch, ratch.

suds. Secondary Derivative from O.E. root *seothan*, to boil, p.p. *soden*. The noun is derived from the participle, and means 'things sodden.'

thicket. Primary Derivative from O.E. root *thicce*. Stem *thick*.

spider. Secondary Derivative from root *spa*, to draw out. Original form *spinther*. Stem *spin*.

farthing. Secondary Derivative from root O.E. *feówer*. Cf. Lat. *quatuor*; Gk. *tettares*; Skt. *chatvar*. Stem *four*; *-th*, adjectival suffix; *-ing*, diminutive suffix. Not a compound of *thing*.

landscape. A Primary Derivative from O.E. *land*. The suffix *-scape* corresponds to *-ship* in *friendship*.

knowledge. A Primary Derivative from O.E. *cnáwan*. The suffix *-ledge* is the O.E. *-lác*. Cp. wedlock. Stem *cnáw*.

hemlock. A compound word. The first part is of unknown origin; the second is a weak form of O.E. *leác*, lock, plant. Cp. gar*lic*, char*lock*.

eyry. Primary Derivative from Fr. *aire*, a nest of hawks. No connection with the M.E. *ey*, an egg.

along. Primary Derivative from O.E. *lang*, long. Root *laugh*, to spring. The prefix *and-* is O.E. = over against.

gossip. Compound of O.E. *god* = God and *sib* = related.

way-lay. Compound of *way* and *lay*. *Lay* is a Primary Derivative from *lie*.

walking-stick. Compound of *walking* and *stick*.

35. At what different periods has a Latin element been introduced into our language ? Give examples of Latin words introduced in the several periods mentioned. (1881.) (See pp. 253–9.)

36. What is meant by English *roots* ? What letter-changes from the English roots have occurred in the following words :—*Each, thunder, speak, crumb*? (1881.) See Q. 34.

The O.E. form of *each* is ælc = *á-ge-lic*. The word has undergone *syncope*. (See p. 290.) The O.E. form of *thunder* is *thunor*. The *d* is intrusive. This change is called *epenthesis*. (See p. 291.) Cp. kindred, from *cyn-raeden*; spindle, from *spinl*. The O.E. form of *speak* is *sprecan*. The change is called *syncope*. The O.E. form of *crumb* is *cruma*. The *b* is intrusive. The change is called *epithesis*. (See p. 291.) Cp. thum*b* (O.E. thuma), lim*b* (O.E. lim).

37. Define the grammatical term *gender*. What is the original force of the suffix in *hunter, maltster*? Account for the gender of *sun* and *moon* in modern English. (1881.) (See pp. 11–12 ; also p. 304–5, for suffixes *-er* and *-ster*.)

38. Mention any English nouns which form their plurals by processes generally obsolete. Which of the following are genuine plurals, and how do you account for the forms which are not such :—*Alms, summons, banns, sessions, costs, eaves, weeds, riches, dice ?* (1881.) (See p. 17.)

Banns is the plural of *ban*, a proclamation. Cp. the *ban* of the Empire. The plural refers to the different askings. The plural *sessions* refers to the sittings day by day. The plural *costs* refers to the separate items charged. The plural *weeds* refers to the different articles of a widow's mourning. The plural *dice* refer to the separate dies. *Alms, summons, eaves*, and *riches* are singular forms. (See p. 20, § 19.)

39. What is the origin and what is the meaning in English grammar of the term *case*? Of what lost case-endings are the traces still discernible in our language? (1881.) (See pp. 22–9.)

40. Enumerate and explain the origins of the various kinds of suffixes employed in the formation of English ordinals. Give the etymology of *foremost*. (1881.)

For *first* see p. 43. *Second* is from the Latin *secundus*. The suffix *-d* in *third*, and *-th* in *fourth, fifth*, &c., is said to have been originally a superlative termination. For *foremost* see p. 41, § 40.

41. What do you know concerning the origin and history of English Possessive Pronouns? Account for the form *ours*. (1881.) (See pp. 48–51.)

Ours is a secondary possessive form from *our*. '*Of ours*' in 'He is a friend *of ours*,' is a triple possessive. The *-s* and the redundant *of* have been doubtless added in conformity to the analogy of the posssesive forms of nouns.

42. Which are the English auxiliary verbs properly so

called? Explain the forms of the preterites of the verbs *have, make, can*. (1881.)   (See pp. 103–108.)

43. Discuss the words italicised in the following:—
Long *ago* we were *wont* to let plain *living* accompany high *thinking*.'

'*Methinks* you *might* have spoken, but you *durst* not.' (1881.)

Ago is a corruption of the old perfect participle of the verb *agon* = to pass or go by.   *Wont*, perfect participle of *won*, to dwell.   First used as an adjective, then as a noun. Cp. 'Use and wont.'   In wont-*ed*, we have a double participial ending.   *Living* and *thinking* are verbal nouns corresponding to the older forms in -*ung*.   [N.B.—Do not confound the verbal noun with the imperfect participle. (See p. 73)].   For *methinks*, see p. 103 ; for *might*, p. 106. *May* itself is an old past.   The second per. sing. is *miht*. Cp. *wilt, shalt*.   In O.E. past was *mihte*.   For *durst*, see pp. 101–2.

44. Distinguish between co-ordinating and subordinating conjunctions.   What are the various uses of *but* in English? (1881.)   (See pp. 121, 392.)

45. Give instances of the use of *proper* nouns as *common* nouns in English.   What are the derivations of *dunce, copper, tramway, gipsy*? (1881.)   (See pp. 271–278.)
Tramway is erroneously derived from *Outram*.   The original meaning of *tram* was a *beam*, a *log* of wood.   The *tramway* was probably at first a road laid on logs or sleepers. (See Skeat.)

46. State clearly the rules of English syntax with regard to the use of *shall* and *will*. (1881.)   (See pp. 77, 104–105.)

47. Give examples of grammatical Pleonasm and Ellipse in English.   (1881.)
Pleonasm (Gk. *pleon*, neuter comparative = more) means an expression in which some word or phrase is superfluous, e.g. 'They *returned* the book *back* to the *same* shop from which they had obtained it.'   'It was *universally* believed by *everybody*.'   Ellipse (Gk. *ek*, out, and *leipo*, to leave) is an expression in which some word is left out, e.g. 'I heard ∧ what he said.'

48. What are the two main sources from which the English vocabulary is derived ?   From which of them comes our grammar ? Illustrate your answer by examples. (1885.) (See p. 241.)

49. Distinguish between the terms *cognate* and *derived*, as applied to words.   Mention some words cognate with *bear* (the verb) and some derived from it.   (1885.)

Cognate words are words of the same family but not necessarily derived one from another. *Bear* is cognate with the Latin *fero*, Gk. *phero*, Skt. *bhri*. All these are evidently descended from some common stock, but it would be incorrect to speak of one as derived from another. Teutonic, Latin, Greek, and Sanskrit are related as cousins might be, not as parent and child.   Derivatives from *bear* are *bairn*, *barrow, berth, bier, bird, burden, forbear, overbearing*.

50. Discuss the forms *brethren, seamstress, indices fisherman, cherry, kine, swine, cherubim, riches, uttermost.* (1885.)

51. To which conjugation do the following verbs severally belong :—*See, saw, say, sow, sew, sue, sit, seethe, salt ?* Write down the past tense and the past participle of each one, noticing any irregularities.   (1885.)

52. What three origins has our substantive verb? Explain *worth* in ' Woe *worth* the day ! '   Mention some usages in which *am*, as an auxiliary, has been ousted by *have*.   (1885.)   (See pp. 97-9, 102.)

53. Parse *after* in each of the following sentences :— ' His *after* life shows him to great advantage,' ' *After* him then and bring him back,' '*After* he came all went wrong,' ' You go first and I will come *after*,' '*After* that I will say no more;' and *out* in ' *Out*, brief candle! ' 'He was quite *out* of it,' '*Out* upon it!' ' He was beaten *out* and *out*,' 'He proved an *out* and *out* deceiver.' (1885.)   (See 'Parsing of Difficult Words.')

54. Point out and correct anything wrong or dubious in the following sentences :—

(*a*) I had hoped never to have seen the statues again. [Never to see.]

(*b*) Luckily the monks have recently given away a couple of dogs, which were returned to them, or the breed would have been lost. [Luckily, a couple of dogs, which the monks recently gave away, were returned, &c.]

(*c*) It was the most amicable, although the least dignified, of all the party squabbles by which it had been preceded. [It was more amicable, although less dignified, than any of, &c. It is absurd to say of a squabble that it was the most amicable of *preceding* squabbles.]

(*d*) Having perceived the weakness of his poems, they now reappear to us under new titles. [He republished them under.]

(*e*) Neither you nor I am right. [Not absolutely wrong. 'Neither are you right, nor am I,' is preferable.] (See p. 193, § 200.)

(*f*) I am one of those who cannot describe what I feel. [What they feel.]

(*g*) Whom they were I cannot specify. [Who.]

(*h*) Whom do you say I am? [Who.]

(*i*) His is a poem—one of the completest works that exists in any language. [His poem is one of the completest works that exist.]

(*k*) He was shot at by a secretary, under notice to quit, with whom he was finding fault—very fortunately without effect. [Insert the parenthetical clause, 'very fortunately,' &c., after 'shot at.'] (1885.) (See Syntax.)

55. Make a list of all the flexions the English verb has now left it. How is it there are so few, and how do we manage to get on with them? (1886.)

Voice Auxiliaries, Tense Auxiliaries, and Mood Auxiliaries take, to a large extent, the place of inflexions. (See p. 103.)

56. Can you explain the italicised letters in the following words:—Chil*d*ren, woul*d*, coul*d*, agains*t*, gen*d*er, vic*t*uals, frontispiec*e*, crayfis*h*, mice. (1886.)

*chil*d*ren.* (See p. 17.)

*woul*d* and *coul*d*. (See pp. 105–6.)

*agains*t*. The *s* is the adverbial suffix -*es*. The final *t* is excrescent. Cp. amongs*t*, behes*t*, mids*t*, whils*t*, earnes*t*.

*gen*d*er. The *d* is intrusive. Fr. *genre*, Lat. *genus*. (See p. 290 § 303, *d*.)

*vic*t*uals. The *c* is a pedantic return to the Latin spelling *victualia* = provisions. M E. *vitaille*.

*frontispiec*e. (See p. 284.) No connection with *piece*.

F F

crayfish. (See p. 283.) No connection with *fish*.

mice. 'The A.S. plural was originally *músis*, which passed into the form *mysis*, and was then shortened to *mÿs*.' (Skeat's 'Principle, of English Etymology,' p. 153.) Cp., for change of vowel sounds *louse, lice ; cow*, Tudor English and provincial English, *kye*.

57. Mention some nouns (i.) with two plural forms, (ii.) with no plural form, (iii.) with only a plural form, (iv.) of plural form which are treated as singulars, (v.) of singular forms which are treated as plurals. (1886.) (See pp. 18–9.)

58. Parse each of the four words, 'But me no buts.' What other parts of speech may *but* be ? Would you say 'They all ran away but me,' or 'They all ran away but I ?' (1886.)

But, transitive verb, imperative, agreeing with 'thou' or 'ye' understood.

Me, personal pronoun, first per. sing., indirect object. (Ethical Dative, see § 157.) *No*, the zero of cardinal numerals, limiting *buts*. *Buts*, common noun, third per. plu., objective case, dir. obj. governed by 'but.'

For the construction compare '*Grace* me no *grace*, and *uncle* me no *uncle*'—Rich. II. '*Thank* me no *thanks*, and *proud* me no *prouds*.'—Rom. and Jul. '*Diamond* me no *diamonds*, and *prize* me no *prizes*.'—Tennyson.

(See 'Parsing of Difficult Words' for other uses of 'but.')

59. Point out what is idiomatic in these phrases :— 'There came a letter,' 'Let them fight it out,' 'We spoke to each other,' 'Many a man would flee,' 'What an angel of a girl!' 'What with this and what with that, I could not get on.' (1886.)

60. Mention as many words as you can that have been adopted into our language during the last half-century.' (1887.) (See pp. 270–1.)

61. Write down the plural form of *wharf, colloquy, potato, may, knight templar, canto*, and state and discuss the rule you go by in each case. Mention some words in which the *s* of the stem has been mistaken for the plural flexion. (1887.) (See pp. 16–21.)

62. What are our commonest Adjective formations ? Illustrate our habit of using nouns both with and without change of form, and also of using adverbs as adjectives. (1887.)

63. What indefinite article do you use before the words *history, historical, European, usual, humble, ewer*? Give your reasons for your answers. Can you mention any instances of the transference of the *n* of the indefinite article to the beginning of the following noun? (1887.)

We use *a* before an aspirate but not in the case of polysyllabic words accented on the second syllable, e.g. '*A* history; *an* historical novel.' Initial *u*, *eu*, and *ew* have a *y* sound, and usually take *a*, not *an*, before them.

Newt, nickname, and *niggot* (Mod. E. nugget) all contain an initial *n* derived from the indefinite article *an*. *An ewt* became *a newt*; *an eke-name* became a *nickname*, and so on. Cp. *nuncle* and *naunt* from *mine uncle* and *mine aunt* In another class of cases the initial *n* of the noun has been dropped, e.g. *adder* from *nadder*; *apron* from *napron*; *once* from *nonce*; *umpire* from *numpire*. *A nadder* became *an adder*, and so on. In *nonce* the *n* comes from the dative form of the definite article. *For the nonce = for then ones*, where *then = thám*.

64. Is there any difference in usage between *each* and *every*? Why should you not say 'Neither of the ten suited me?' What alternative form of expression is there to 'That is mine and nobody else's?' Which do you think is to be preferred? (1887.)

Each directs attention to the fact that the separate individuals referred to are all included; *every* to the fact that not one of them is excluded. *Neither* is strictly applicable to only *two* objects. *Nobody else's* is an ugly phrase. The sign of the Possessive should be attached to the pronoun 'nobody' and not to the adverb 'else.' Still more elegant would be 'That belongs to me and to nobody else.'

65. Classify Conjunctions with reference to (*a*) their use, (*b*) their origin. (1877.) (See pp. 121–2.)

66. Distinguish between *farther* and *further*, *gladder* and *gladlier*, *nearest* and *next*, *latest* and *last*, *peas* and *pease*, *genii* and *geniuses*. (1877.) (See pp. 19. 42 13.)

Gladder is an adjective; *gladlier* an adverb.

Nearest refers to space; *next* to time as well as space.

Latest relates to time; *last* to order in a series.

Farther is an adjective formed from far, the *th* having been inserted in imitation of the adverb *further*, which is the comparative of *forth*.

67. Explain the terms *voice, mood, infinitive.* Show how frequently in English transitive verbs are used intransitively and *vice versâ.* Mention some Causative verbs. (1887.) (See pp. 62–3.)

68. Parse *must* in ' He says he *must* go' and 'He said he *must* go,' and mention some other verbs that are similarly unchanged. What do you know of the verbs *quoth, wot, thinks* in *methinks* ? (1887.) (See pp. 102, 108.)

In the first sentence *must* is a present auxiliary ; in the second a past. Cp. *ought.* ' He *ought* to leave to-day,' 'He *ought* to have left yesterday.' ' *Could*' and '*would*' are properly past tenses, but are also used in the present tense.

69. Describe fully, with examples, English Verbs of Incomplete Predication. (1888.)

A Verb of Incomplete Predication is one which does not suffice in itself to make an assertion, e.g. copulative verbs like *be, become, seem, appear,* and transitive verbs, as *love, praise,* &c. ' I walk' is a complete sentence, but 'I shoot' is not. ' Walk' makes complete sense in itself, but 'shoot' carries on our mind to some object shot at.

70. Correct or justify—

(*a*) They drowned the black and white kittens.

(*b*) Thinking of them, my pen tarries as I write.

(*c*) The then ministry.

(*d*) It is me.

(*e*) I intended to have written to him.   (1888.)

Of these sentences (*a*) is ambiguous. The writer may have meant the black kittens and the white kittens; or the kittens that were both black and white ; or the black kitten and the white kitten.

(*b*) Implies that the pen was thinking. Write, ' As I write and think of them my pen tarries.'

(*c*) The *then* ministry is not strictly correct, *then* being an adverb, and not an adjective ; but this use derives some support from such expressions as 'his *after*-life.' It would be safer to say, 'The ministry then in office.' We should never think of saying, 'The *now* ministry.'

(*d*) 'It is me' should be 'It is I,' but there is a reluctance observable in English, as in other languages, to use the nominative case as a disjunctive pronoun. Cp. 'C'est *moi*.' There is not the same reluctance to use the nominative form of pronouns of the second and third person.

(*e*) 'I intended to have written to him' should be, 'I intended to write,' &c., unless the speaker contemplated some other future action before which the writing was to have been completed.

71. State some differences as regards verbal forms, case-endings, and suffixes, between the English of the fourteenth century and that of the present day. (1888.) (See p. 281.)

72. Distinguish between Rhyme, Alliteration, and Metre, and show how each has affected poetical expression in England. (1888.) (See pp. 221–4.)

73. Give the derivation of the following words :—*Alive, dead, many, alert, entail, result, heresy, ideal, knife, key, bury, rather, king, lady.* (1888.) (See pp. 297–374.)

Alive = on life (see English Prefixes) ; *dead* = O.E. deád, Gothic, *dau-th-s*, a participial form from *dau*, the past tense of *diwau*, to die. *Die* has come to us through a Scandinavian medium, there being no such verb in O.E. ; *many* = O.E. manig ; *alert* (see p. 266) ; *entail* (Fr. *tailler*, to cut) ; *result* (Lat. *salio*, to leap; *results* is a frequentative from *salio*) ; *heresy* (Gk. *haireomai*, to take for oneself; see Greek Roots) ; *ideal* (Gk. *idea*, the look of a thing, hence a notion) ; *knife* (O.E. *cnif*, originally an instrument for nipping off. Cp. Fr. *canif*) ; *key* (O.E. *cæg*) ; *rather* (see p. 43) ; *king* (O.E. *cyning*, the son of the tribe ; see p. 13) ; *lady* (see p. 13).

74. Explain the suffixes of the following words :— *Kingdom, every, seemly, business, farthing, hardship, piece-meal, nostril, gospel, orchard, namesake.* (1888.)

See English Suffixes for -dom, -ly, -ness, -ing, -ship, -meal. For *every, nostril, gospel, orchard, namesake*, see O.E. Roots under *alc, nosu, spell, ort, nama*.

APPENDIX.

A TABLE OF ENGLISH LITERATURE

WRITERS BEFORE THE CONQUEST.

Unknown Author (before 600)	Beowulf, an epic
Cædmon (670) . . .	Paraphrase of Old and New Testament, in verse
Bede (673–735) . .	Translation of St. John's Gospel
King Alfred (849–901) .	Translation of the History of Orosius and Boethius' Consolations of Philosophy

FROM THE CONQUEST TO THE DEATH OF CHAUCER.

Layamon (1205) . .	Brut, a poem based on French versions of old Welsh legends
Ormin (1215) . . .	Ormulum, a sacred poem on the services of the Church's year
Sir John Mandeville (1300–1356)	Travels
William Langland (1362)	Vision concerning Piers the Ploughman, a poem on the morality and religion of the day
John Wiclif (1324–1384) .	Translation of the Bible
John Gower (1325–1408) .	Confessio Amantis, a dialogue on Love
Geoffrey Chaucer (1340–1400)	House of Fame; Legend of Good Women; Canterbury Tales

FROM CHAUCER TO ACCESSION OF ELIZABETH.

John Lydgate (1374–1460)	Falls of Princes; Story of Thebes; Troy Book
Sir Thomas Malory (1485)	Translation of Morte d'Arthur
John Skelton (1460–1529)	Satires
Sir Thomas More (1480–1535)	History of Richard III.
William Tyndale (1477–1536)	Translation of the New Testament
Tyndale, Rogers, Coverdale (1540)	Cranmer's Bible
Cranmer and others (1549)	First English Prayer Book
Latimer (1470–1555) .	Sermons
Roger Ascham (1515–1561)	Toxophilus, a treatise on Archery; The Schoolmaster
Sir Thomas Wyatt (1503–1541)	Poems
Earl of Surrey (1516–1547)	Poems

ELIZABETHAN WRITERS.

Sackville, Lord Buckhurst (1536–1608)	The Induction to The Mirror for Magistrates (*i.e.* rulers)
John Lyley (1554–1600) .	Euphues, a prose story
Sir Philip Sidney (1554–1586)	Arcadia, a prose romance
Richard Hooker (1553–1600)	The Laws of Ecclesiastical Polity
Lord Bacon (1561–1626) .	Essays; The Advancement of Learning; History of Henry VII.
Edmund Spenser (1552–1599)	The Shepherd's Calendar; The Faërie Queen
Michael Drayton (1563–1631)	The Civil Wars of Edward II. and the Barons; Polyolbion, a description of Britain
Christopher Marlowe (1562–1593)	The Jew of Malta; Edward II.; Dr. Faustus
William Shakespeare (1564–1616)	Sonnets; Venus and Adonis; Plays

Ben Jonson (1574–1637) .   The Fox ; The Alchemist ; The
                            Silent Woman

FROM ELIZABETH'S DEATH TO THE RESTORATION.

John Webster (died 1638)	Dramatist
Thomas Dekker (died 1638)	Dramatist
George Chapman (1577–1624)	Dramatist and translator of Homer
James Shirley (1594–1666)	Dramatist
J. Donne (1573–1631)	Poet
George Herbert (1593–1632)	Poet. The Temple
Jeremy Taylor (1613–1667)	Divine. The Liberty of Prophesying ; Holy Living and Holy Dying
Robert Herrick (1591–1674)	Poet. The Hesperides
Thomas Hobbes (1588–1679)	Philosophical writer. The Leviathan
Thomas Fuller (1608–1661)	Church History
John Milton (1608–1674)	L'Allegro ; Il Penseroso ; Comus ; Lycidas ; Sonnets ; Paradise Lost ; Paradise Regained ; Samson Agonistes ; numerous prose works

FROM THE RESTORATION TO THE END OF QUEEN ANNE'S REIGN.

Samuel Butler (1612–1680)	Poet. Hudibras
John Bunyan (1628–1688)	Pilgrim's Progress ; Holy War
John Dryden (1631–1700)	Poet. Absalom and Ahithophel ; The Hind and the Panther ; Fables (i.e. Stories) ; Plays ; Translation of Virgil
William Wycherley (1640–1715)	Dramatist

William Congreve (1672–1728)	Dramatist
George Farquhar (1666–1726)	Dramatist
Sir John Vanbrugh (1678–1707)	Dramatist
John Locke (1632–1704)	Essay on the Human Understanding
Alexander Pope (1688–1744)	Poet. Essay on Criticism; Essay on Man; Rape of the Lock; Dunciad; Translation of Homer
Jonathan Swift (1667–1745)	Tale of a Tub; Gulliver's Travels; Battle of the Books
Daniel Defoe (1661–1731)	Robinson Crusoe; Memoirs of a Cavalier
Sir Richard Steele (1671–1729)	Essayist and dramatist. Papers in 'Tatler' and 'Spectator'
Joseph Addison (1672–1719)	Essayist and poet. Cato; papers in 'Tatler' and 'Spectator'
Bishop Berkeley (1684–1753)	Metaphysician. Minute Philosopher
Joseph Butler (1692–1752)	Divine. Analogy of Religion, Natural and Revealed, to the Constitution and Course of Nature

FROM THE DEATH OF QUEEN ANNE (1704) TO 1800.

James Thompson (1700–1748)	Poet. The Seasons; Castle of Indolence
Thomas Gray (1716–1771)	Poet. Elegy in a Country Churchyard; Odes
William Collins (1720–1756)	Poet. Ode on the Passions; Ode to Evening
Edward Young (1681–1765)	Night Thoughts
Samuel Johnson (1709–1784)	Essayist. Lives of the Poets; English Dictionary; Rasselas; London; The Vanity of Human Wishes

Oliver Goldsmith (1728–1774)	Poet, essayist, novelist, and dramatist. The Traveller; The Deserted Village; She Stoops to Conquer; The Vicar of Wakefield
Samuel Richardson (1689–1761)	Novelist. Clarissa Harlowe; Sir Charles Grandison
Henry Fielding (1707–1754)	Novelist. Joseph Andrews; Tom Jones
Tobias Smollett (1721–1771)	Novelist. Roderick Random
Lawrence Sterne (1713–1768)	Novelist. Tristram Shandy; Sentimental Journey
David Hume (1711–1776)	History of England; Essays
Edward Gibbon (1737–1794)	Decline and Fall of the Roman Empire
Adam Smith (1723–1790)	Wealth of Nations; Moral Sentiments
Edmund Burke (1730–1797)	Political and philosophical writer. On the Sublime and Beautiful; Reflections on the French Revolution

FROM 1800 TO THE ACCESSION OF QUEEN VICTORIA.

Robert Burns (1759–1796)	Poems
William Cowper (1731–1800)	Poet. The Task; Translation of Homer
George Crabbe (1754–1832)	Poet. The Village; The Register; Tales of the Hall
Robert Southey (1774–1843)	Poet and prose writer. Thalaba; Roderick; The Curse of Kehama; Life of Nelson
William Wordsworth (1770–1850)	Poet. Lyrical Ballads; Prelude; Excursion
Sir Walter Scott (1771–1832)	Poet and novelist. Lay of the Last Minstrel; Marmion; Lady of the Lake; Novels
Samuel Taylor Coleridge (1772–1834)	Poet and philosopher. Ancient Mariner; Christabel
Charles Lamb (1775–1834)	Essayist. Essays of Elia

Thomas De Quincey (1785–1859)	Essayist. Confessions of an English Opium-eater
Thomas Campbell (1777–1844)	Poet. Pleasures of Hope; Gertrude of Wyoming
Samuel Rogers (1762–1855)	Poet. Pleasures of Memory; Italy
Thomas Moore (1799–1852)	Poet. Irish Melodies; Lalla Rookh
Lord Byron (1788–1824) .	Poet. Childe Harold; Giaour; Bride of Abydos; Corsair; Lara; Plays
Thomas Hood (1798–1845)	Poet and Humourist
Percy Bysshe Shelley (1792–1822)	Poet. Odes; Queen Mab; Alastor; The Revolt of Islam; Prometheus Unbound; Cenci, a play
John Keats (1796–1820)	Poet. Endymion; Hyperion; Eve of St. Agnes

FROM THE ACCESSION OF QUEEN VICTORIA (1837).

Lord Macaulay (1800–1859)	Historian and essayist
Lord Lytton (1805–1873)	Novelist
Robert Browning (born 1809)	Poet. The Ring and the Book; Dramatic Sketches
Lord Tennyson (born 1810)	Poet. Idylls of the King; Maud; In Memoriam; Plays
W. Makepeace Thackeray (1811–1863)	Novelist
Charles Dickens (1812–1870)	Novelist
Charlotte Brontë (1815–1855)	Novelist
Charles Kingsley (1819–1875)	Novelist and essayist
J. Ruskin (born 1819)	Modern Painters; Stones of Venice
Thomas Carlyle (1795–1881)	Historian. French Revolution; Oliver Cromwell; Frederick the Great
Mary A. ``vans (George Eliot) (1820–1880)	Novelist. Adam Bede; Romola; Middlemarch; Daniel Deronda

INDEX.

☞ *This Index contains the references to Parts I.—IV. The Index to the History and Derivation of the English Language is given separately.*

[The figures refer to the Paragraphs.]

INDEX

TO

THE HISTORY AND DERIVATION OF THE ENGLISH LANGUAGE.

———◆◇◆———

[The figures refer to the Paragraphs.]

INDEX

TO

DERIVATION OF WORDS.

NOTE.—*The numbers refer to Pages.*

CAV	CHO	COU
cavalcade, 266	chocolate, 264	companion, 266, 349
ceiling, 336	choir, 363	Compton, 316
celandine, 283	cholera, 363	comrade, 266, 335
celerity, 336	chop, 316	concatenate, 335
celibacy, 336	chord, 363	conceal, 336
cement, 335	Christ, 363	concert, 266
cemetery, 367	chromatrope, 363	conchology, 367
cenotaph, 366	chronology, 363	conclave, 336
centre, 366	chrysanthemum, 363	conduct, 339
censure, 336	chrysolite, 363	cone, 367
ceramic, 367	chyle, 363	confess, 339
cereal, 336	chyme, 363	conflagration, 340
certify, 336	cicerone, 271	conglomerate, 341
cervical, 336	cigar, 264	congratulate, 342
chafe, 260	circumference, 301	conjugal, 343
chain, 284, 260	citadel, 266	connect, 347
chalcedony, 276	citizen, 336	constable, 283, 337
chalice, 254	civic, 336	constellation, 356
chalybeate, 363	claim, 336	contemn, 357
chamber, 262	clamp, 316	contraband, 301
champaign, 335	claret, 336	contralto, 266
chance, 308	clemency, 336	control, 301
chancel, 309	clergy, 367	conversazione, 266
chancellor, 309	clerk, 367	convex, 359
chance-medley, 283	click-clack, 279	convulse, 359
chanticleer, 335	client, 336	cook, 337
chaos, 363	climate, 367	Copenhagen, 316
chapel, 335	clinical, 367	copious, 337
Chapman, 316	clog, 316	copper, 276
chapter, 262	cloister, 336	coprolite, 367
character, 363	clout, 249	cordwainer, 276
charlatan, 266	clove, 283	cork, 264
charm, 335	cobalt, 269	cornet, 337
chart, 336	coble, 249	cornice, 266
charwoman, 317	cobra, 265	coroner, 337
chary, 316	cobweb, 292	corpse, 337
chasm, 363	cochineal, 264	corridor, 266
chaste, 335	cock, 249	corrugated, 354
chauvinism, 271	cocoa-nut, 265	cortical, 337
cheap, 316	coeval, 333	cosmopolite, 367
cheat, 283	cogent, 333	cost, 301
Chelsea, 316	cogitate, 336	costermonger, 283, 324
cherry, 276	cohort, 342	costive, 356
chest, 292	collar, 336	cottage, 317
Chester, 253	college, 344	couch, 261
chevalier, 261	colonel, 336	could, 292
chief, 262	colonnade, 266	coulter, 261
chiliast, 363	Colt, 271	count, 259
chimera, 271, 363	combustion, 359	counterpane, 283
china, 276	comely, 317	couple, 261
chine, 249	comet, 367	courage, 337
chiropodist, 363	comfit, 339	court, 342
chivalry, 292	commodore, 265	cousin, 354
chlorine, 363	compact, 349	cousin german, 341

DOC

dock, 249
doff, 298
Doge, 266
dogma, 364
dole, 317
dollar, 276
Dolomites, 272
dolt, 317
domestic, 338
domineer, 338
domino, 266
don, 298
Doomsday, 317
dormouse, 338
double, 260, 339
doubloon, 339
dowager, 338
dower, 338
down, 317
Doyley, 272
dozen, 339
draconian, 272
dragon, 292
drastic, 364
draught, 317
dreary, 317
dredge, 317
drench, 317
dress, 260
dribble, 307, 317
drill, 330
dromedary, 364
droop, 317
dropsy, 283
drought, 317
drug, 317
drunkard, 304
ducat, 339
duenna, 264
Dungeness, 252
dull, 317
Dumbarton, 248
dummy, 317
dunce, 272
duodecimal, 339
duty, 338
dwindle, 318
dynamite, 364
dysentery, 303

each, 313
eager, 333
ear, 318
early, 313

EAR

Earnley, 318
earth, 318
earwig, 318
easel, 283
Easter, 318
eavesdropper, 318
eccentric, 366
economy, 369
eczema, 374
edible, 339
edify, 333
editor, 339
educate, 339
effervescence, 340
effigy, 340
eft, 290
eftsoon, 318
Egbert, 318
egotist, 339
egregious, 342
eight, 318
Eirenicon, 364
ejaculate, 343
elapse, 343
elastic, 364
elbow, 293
elder, 318
El Dorado, 261
elecampane, 284
electric, 364
element, 333
ellipse, 368
elysian, 276
embargo, 264
embarrass, 264
ember, 284
emigrant, 346
emolument, 346
emperor, 342
empiric, 303
employ, 260
encumber, 337
endogamous, 364
endorse, 338
energy, 364
engineer, 309
enigma, 361
enough, 290
enteritis, 364
enthusiasm, 373
enthymeme, 373
entomology, 373
envy, 360
epaulette, 263

FAB

ephemeral, 365
epicure, 272
epilepsy, 367
epitaph, 373
epithalamium, 373
epoch, 364
equestrian, 339
equinox, 339, 348
ermine, 276
eremite, 364
erratic, 339
esculent, 339
Essex, 318
estuary, 333
Ethel, 313
ethereal, 361
ethnarch, 364
etymology, 364
Eucharistic, 363, 354
eulogy, 367
euphemism, 370
euphrasy, 364
euphuistic, 272
euthanasia, 364
evade, 359
evangelist, 361, 364
ever, 313
Everton, 318
every, 313
exaggerate, 333
examine, 339
exasperate, 334
excite, 336
execute, 355
exempt, 339
Exeter, 253
exhaust, 342
exile, 339
exodus, 366
exorbitant, 348
exotic, 364
expatiate, 356
expedite, 350
extenuate, 358
extirpate, 356
extol, 358
extravagant, 359
extravaganza, 267
exuberant, 359
eye, 318
eyre, 313

fable, 339
fair, 339

MAN

mandrake, 284
manhood, 311
manifesto, 267
mankind, 304
manœuvre, 345
manor, 345
Mantua, 277
marble, 292
march, 273
margin, 345
margrave, 269
mariner, 345
mariolatry, 273
marmalade, 265
marriage, 345
marsh, 324
martello, 267
martial, 273
martin, 273
martinet, 273
martyrdom, 368
masquerade, 267
mass, 254
massive, 345
master, 345
matador, 264
material, 345
mathematics, 368
matriculate, 345
matrimony, 310, 345
mattock, 250
mature, 346
maudlin, 273
maugre, 345
Maundy Thursday, 345
mausoleum, 273
maw, 324
may, 273
mayor, 345
meadow, 324
meagre, 345
meander, 277
meat, 324
medicine, 346
meed, 324
meerschaum, 269
megatherium, 368
melancholy, 368
melody, 368
membrane, 346
menace, 346
mendacious, 346
mensuration, 346
mental, 346

MEN

mentor, 273
mercer, 346
mercurial, 273
mere, 346
meretricious, 346
meridian, 346
Merry Andrew, 273
mesh, 250
mesmerism, 273
messenger, 291
messmate, 324
metal, 368
metaphor, 304
mete, 324
methylene, 304
metropolis, 368
mew (to moult), 347
mezzotinto, 267
miasma, 368
mickle, 325
micrometer, 368
midriff, 324
might, 324
mildew, 324
Mildred, 324
militia, 346
mill, 324, 325, 346
milliner, 277
milner, 325
mimic, 368
miniature, 346
minister, 346
mint, 325
miracle, 346
misanthrope, 368
mischief, 302
miscreant, 337
mislead, 302
misogamist, 368
misogynist, 368
missile, 346
mite, 346
mitigate, 346
mixen, 325
mixture, 345
mizzle, 324
mnemonics, 368
mob, 347
moidore, 265
molasses, 346
mole, 325
molecule, 346
molest, 346
mollusk, 347

NEA

monandria, 368
mongrel, 324
monk, 254, 368
monocarpous, 368
monogram, 368
monopoly, 368
monster, 347
month, 325
monument, 347
mood, 346
moot, 324
mop, 250
moral, 347
morass, 325
morbid, 347
morel, 277
morganatic, 269
morocco, 277
Morpheus, 369
morris, 273, 277
morsel, 347
mortmain, 347
mosaic, 347
mosquito, 265
moss, 325
motett, 267
motto, 267
moult, 347
moustache, 267
muggy, 250
mugwort, 325
mulatto, 265
mundane, 347
municipal, 347
mural, 347
murder, 325
musket, 347
muslin, 277
mutilate, 347
mystery, 368

nankeen, 277
narcotic, 369
nascent, 347
nasturtium, 347
natal, 347
naught, 60
nausea, 347
nauseous, 347
nautical, 369
nave, 347
navel, 325
neatherd, 325

H H

UPH	VER	WIT
upholsterer, 321	vertical, 360	wake, 331
upper, 300	vertu, 268	wall, 250
urban, 359	very, 360	walnut, 331
urgent, 359	vessel, 309	walrus, 285
usher, 349	vestige, 360	wander, 307, 331
usurp, 359	vesture, 360	wane, 331
usury, 359	veteran, 360	want, 250
utensil, 359	viand, 260	wanton, 300, 329, 831
Utopian, 278	vicarious, 360	warp, 331
uxorious, 359	vice, 260	wart, 332
	viceroy, 303	Warwick, 331
	vicinity, 360	was, 331
	victim, 360	wasp, 291, 331
vacant, 359	victuals, 360	wassail, 285
vaccinate, 359	view, 260	wastrel, 305
vacillate, 359	vigilant, 360	water, 306
vagrant, 359	vignette, 360	watershed, 327
vague, 359	vigour, 359	wear, 268
valedictory, 359	vilify, 360	Webster, 331
valentine, 275	villain, 360	wed, 250
valid, 359	vindicate, 360	wedding, 331
valve, 359	vinegar, 360	wedlock, 305, 331
van, 261	violent, 312	Wednesday, 297
vanilla, 265	virago, 360	weeds, 331
vanish, 359	virtuoso, 268	ween, 331
vapid, 359	virulent, 360	weir, 331
varicose, 359	viscid, 360	weird, 332
variety, 359	visible, 360	welfare, 318
vascular, 359	vista, 268	welkin, 332
vassal, 250	vital, 360	Wellingtons, 275
vast, 359	vitiate, 360	welsh, 331
vat, 318	vitriol, 360	welt, 250
vaunt-courier, 261	vixen, 304	wend, 331
veal, 260, 309	vocabulary, 360	Wendover, 325
vedette, 268	volatile, 361	wharf, 322
vegetable, 359	volcano, 275, 268	wheelwright, 332
vein, 260, 359	volley, 361	where, 307
vellum, 360	voltaic, 275	whit, 332
vendor, 359	volume, 361	Whitby, 251
venerable, 359	vortex, 360	whither, 300
venial, 359	votary, 361	Whitsunday, 322
venom, 359	vouchsafe, 361	whittle, 322
ventilate, 359	vowel, 360	wick, 252
ventriloquist, 359	voyage, 360	wicked, 332
verbal, 360	vulcanite, 275	wicket, 250
verbose, 312	Vulgate, 361	wight, 332
verderer, 360	vulpecide, 361	windlass, 285
verdict, 360		window, 332
verdigris, 285		wisdom, 332
verge, 360		witch, 332
vermicelli, 268	waddle, 307	witchcraft, 332
vermilion, 268	wafer, 292	Witenagemote, 332
vernal, 359	wain, 250	withdraw, 300
vernicle, 275	wainwright, 306	withstand, 300

PRINTED BY
SPOTTISWOODE AND CO., NEW-STREET SQUARE
LONDON

U

CPSIA information can be obtained
at www.ICGtesting.com
Printed in the USA
BVOW06*1544141117
500281BV00034B/364/P